CRIMINAL JUSTICE

Anthea Hucklesby
Senior Lecturer in Criminal Justice,
School of Law, University of Leeds

Azrini Wahidin
Reader in Criminology and Criminal Justice,
School of Sociology, Social Policy and Social Work,
Queen's University, Belfast

OXFORD
UNIVERSITY PRESS

OXFORD
UNIVERSITY PRESS

Great Clarendon Street, Oxford OX2 6DP

Oxford University Press is a department of the University of Oxford.
It furthers the University's objective of excellence in research, scholarship,
and education by publishing worldwide in

Oxford New York

Auckland Cape Town Dar es Salaam Hong Kong Karachi
Kuala Lumpur Madrid Melbourne Mexico City Nairobi
New Delhi Shanghai Taipei Toronto

With offices in

Argentina Austria Brazil Chile Czech Republic France Greece
Guatemala Hungary Italy Japan Poland Portugal Singapore
South Korea Switzerland Thailand Turkey Ukraine Vietnam

Oxford is a registered trade mark of Oxford University Press
in the UK and in certain other countries

Published in the United States
by Oxford University Press Inc., New York

British Library Cataloguing in Publication Data

Data available

Library of Congress Cataloging in Publication Data

Data available

Typeset by Newgen Imaging Systems (P) Ltd., Chennai, India
Printed in Great Britain
on acid-free paper by
Ashford Colour Press Ltd, Gosport, Hants

ISBN 978–0–19–921554–6

10 9 8 7 6 5 4 3 2 1

CRIMINAL JUSTICE

This book is dedicated to our grandmothers:
Edith May Humby (1907–2005)
Mah-Wan-Kechik binti Che-Din (1926–2008)

Foreword

A common-sense view might be that what guides the criminal justice system is simply a desire to catch criminals, take them to court, judge them and, if they are found guilty, punish them. But this is overly simplistic. This collection of essays takes to heart the very real difference between popular representations of the criminal justice system and how it operates in practice. It also tries to capture something of the ongoing changes in regard to criminal justice. So often authors take snapshots of the criminal justice system and the text is out of date almost before the ink is dry. Thus the key focus of this book is on the critical questions of what shapes and 'drives' the criminal justice system and what kinds of values and debates inform its operation in a context of social change.

Social transformations since the 1950s in particular have led to what David Garland (2001) describes as the 'culture of control' (*The Culture of Control: Crime and Social Order in Contemporary Society*). The decline of manufacturing and the rise of the service industry, the emergence of a technologically driven society, increased mobility and changes in the structure of the family and functioning of community all feature here. Sociological analyses of late modernity also include consideration of changes in the source of 'trust' and the growth of 'ontological insecurity' which reflects the erosion of localised trust. The rise of individualism too, with its associated hedonism, consumerism and emphasis on 'individual rights' has contributed to the crystallisation of social anxieties and exposed lines of division in terms of notions of competence, and the trustworthiness and legitimacy of the authorities.

And who are the authorities? The several hundred new offences and masses of new legislation that have been created since Labour came to power in 1997 point us in the direction of political authority. The editors and authors of this book carefully and critically argue that we need to take into account legal, spatial, historical, cultural and social and economic factors as well in order to reveal just how powerful the criminal justice system is. The criminal justice system is embedded in social life; it serves as a touchstone for social as well as criminal justice and also provides a basis for feelings of security and safety.

Between them, the contributors focus on every stage of the criminal justice system—from crime prevention and the police through to prosecution, sentencing and punishment in the community and in prisons. They also look at particular groups of offenders and victims to show how age, gender and ethnicity might mediate experiences of criminal justice. More than this, there is important discussion of the systems in both Scotland and Northern Ireland and forward looking reflections on how the current crises of resources and legitimacy might be solved or indeed exacerbated in the future.

This is an accessible and thought-provoking book designed for a contemporary readership. The authors encourage readers to reflect deeply and critically, and to look backwards, forwards, and around in attempts to understand the shape and current direction of criminal justice in the UK. There has been a proliferation of edited volumes on crime and criminal justice in recent years, as well as textbooks on criminology and criminal justice, but none directly address the challenges of the 21st century in quite the same way. It is for the breadth and depth and rich detail of each chapter, as well as for the overarching analytical themes, that this book should command both close reading and wide readership. It is a twenty-first century book for twenty-first century students.

Loraine Gelsthorpe
Reader in Criminology and Criminal Justice
Institute of Criminology
University of Cambridge

OUTLINE CONTENTS

DETAILED CONTENTS

LIST OF FIGURES

LIST OF TABLES

LIST OF CONTRIBUTORS

Michael Cavadino *Professor of Law, University of Central Lancashire*

James Dignan *formerly Professor of Comparative Criminology and Criminal Justice, University of Leeds*

Gavin Dingwall *Reader in Law, De Montfort University*

Graham Ellison *Senior Lecturer in Criminology, Queen's University, Belfast*

Daniel Gilling *Senior Lecturer in Criminal Justice Studies, University of Plymouth*

Barry Goldson *Professor of Criminology and Social Policy, University of Liverpool*

Anthony Goodman *Professor of Criminal and Community Justice Studies, Middlesex University*

Matthew Hall *Lecturer in Criminology and Law, University of Sheffield*

Anthea Hucklesby *Senior Lecturer in Criminal Justice, University of Leeds*

Helen Johnston *Lecturer in Criminology, University of Hull*

Gerry Johnstone *Professor of Law, University of Hull*

Stuart Lister *Lecturer in Criminal Justice, University of Leeds*

George Mair *Professor of Criminal Justice, Liverpool John Moores University*

Aogán Mulcahy *Senior Lecturer in Sociology, University College Dublin*

John Muncie *Professor of Criminology, The Open University*

Mike Nellis *Professor of Criminal and Community Justice, University of Strathclyde*

David Scott *Senior Lecturer in Criminology, University of Central Lancashire*

Basia Spalek *Senior Lecturer in Criminal Justice Studies, University of Birmingham*

Azrini Wahidin *Reader in Criminology and Criminal Justice, Queen's University, Belfast*

Sandra Walklate *Eleanor Rathbone Chair of Sociology, Head of School of Sociology and Social Policy, University of Liverpool*

The late Brian Williams, *formerly Professor of Community Justice and Victimology, De Montfort University*

Anne Wilson *Senior Teaching Fellow University of Abertay, Dundee*

Guide to the Online Resource Centre

Criminal Justice is accompanied by an interactive Online Resource Centre, which you can access at www.oxfordtextbooks.co.uk/orc/hucklesby/. The Online Resource Centre is closely integrated with the book, and provides students with ready-to-use teaching and learning resources. These resources are available free of charge, designed to complement the textbook, and offer additional materials which are suited to electronic delivery. All the resources can be downloaded and (with the exception of the flashcard glossary) are fully customisable, allowing them to be incorporated into a Virtual Learning Environment.

Lecturer resources

These resources are password-protected to ensure that only adopting lecturers can gain access. These free resources are an ideal complement to lecturers' own teaching materials. Registering is easy: go to 'Lecturer Resources' on the Online Resource Centre, complete a simple registration form, and access will be granted within three working days (subject to verification). Each registration is personally checked to ensure the security of the site.

Test bank

The test bank is a fully customizable resource containing ready-made assessments with which to test students. It offers versatile testing tailored to the contents of each particular chapter and there are questions in several different formats: multiple choice; multiple response; matching; fill in the blanks; true/false; and short answer. The test bank is downloadable into Questionmark Perception, Blackboard, WebCT, and most other virtual learning environments. The test bank questions are also downloadable in formats suitable for printing directly by the lecturer.

Lecture notes

These complement each chapter of the book and are a useful resource for preparing lectures and handouts. They allow lecturers to guide their students through the key concepts, ideas and theories and can be fully customised to meet the needs of the course, enabling lecturers to focus on the areas most relevant to their students.

Student resources

These are accessible to all students, with no registration or password access required, enabling students to get the most out of their textbook.

Web links

A selection of annotated web links, chosen by the chapter authors, allows you to easily research those topics that are of particular interest. These links are checked and updated regularly to ensure they remain relevant and up to date.

Glossary

A useful one-stop reference point for all the keywords used in the textbook. In addition to a standard, alphabetical glossary, you will also find key term 'flashcards' which can be downloaded to your own computer or an ipod and used to test your knowledge.

Introduction

Anthea Hucklesby and Azrini Wahidin

Symbolically, the criminal justice system is often portrayed as a woman holding the scales of justice in one hand and the sword of truth in the other. She is also blindfolded to signify the impartiality of law and justice, meaning that it is equally applied to all, irrespective of: place; *gender*; sexual preference; age; disability; ethnicity; 'race'; religious belief; wealth; or status. The popular representation of the criminal justice system fostered by fiction writers, films, and the media also portrays a system which convicts the guilty and acquits the innocent through a system which involves professionals going about their work ethically and efficiently. In both representations, justice is done and, most importantly, seen to be done. Victims and the public at large are portrayed as having confidence in the criminal justice process and are content with the process by which offenders are brought to justice. The reality, however, is rather different, as the heated debate surrounding the criminal justice system and the numerous examples of miscarriages of justice demonstrate (Walker and Starmer, 1999). The gap between the theory and popular representations of the criminal justice system and how it operates in practice is the central focus of this book.

The criminal justice system is a key institution of society and is embedded in a particular legal, spatial, cultural, historical, political, economic, and social context. It has a key role to play in assessments of social justice, feelings of security and safety, as well as being a barometer of a country's democratic credentials. It impinges directly and indirectly upon a large number of individuals including victims, suspects, defendants, and offenders, and their families and friends. The criminal justice system, therefore, raises important questions including what is it for? How does it operate? Who does it deal with? How does it treat victims, suspects, defendants, and offenders? Does it work?

This book explores the key issues relating to the criminal justice system at the beginning of the twenty-first century. It aims to provide undergraduate students with a critical introduction to institutions and agencies of the criminal justice system and the issues that arise with the process by which individuals are convicted and punished for transgressing the criminal law. Figure 0.1 shows the basic process through which suspects travel in order to be convicted of an offence. The first ten chapters of the book guide the reader through this process, whilst the following chapters explore issues thematically and in relation to particular groups' experiences of the criminal justice system and the smaller jurisdictions within the United Kingdom. Before doing this, we provide an introduction to the issues and debates which follow.

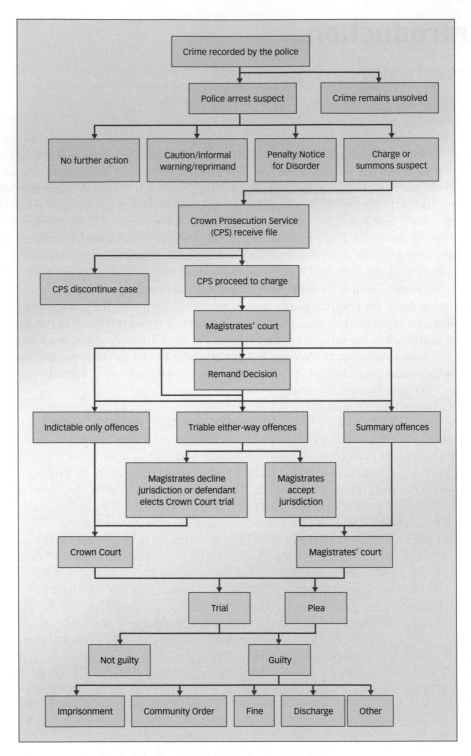

Figure 0.1 The Criminal Justice Process in England and Wales

Source: adapted from Home Office (1999: 28, 40)

What is the criminal justice 'system'?

There are three distinctive criminal justice systems within the United Kingdom: England and Wales; Scotland; and Northern Ireland. Each of these operates with different laws, procedures, and, in some cases, institutions and agencies. They also come under the auspices of different Ministries (Home Office/Ministry of Justice in England and Wales; the Justice Department in Scotland; and the Northern Ireland Office). Most of this book refers to the criminal justice system in England and Wales. Despite differences between the jurisdictions, there are common themes between them.

The criminal justice system is the term used to describe the institutions and agencies which respond officially to the commission of offences, including the police, the Crown Prosecution Service (CPS), the courts (magistrates' courts and the Crown Court), prison and probation services, and the Youth Offending Service in England and Wales. Many voluntary sector organisations and some private sector companies as well as criminal defence solicitors are also involved in delivering services in the criminal justice system. Officially, the purpose of the criminal justice system is to:

> ...deliver justice for all, by convicting and punishing the guilty and helping them to stop offending, while protecting the innocent. It is responsible for detecting crime and bringing it to justice; and carrying out the orders of court, such as collecting fines, and supervising community and custodial punishment. (Criminal Justice Online (2008) at <http://www.cjsonline.org/the_cjs/aims_and_objectives/>)

Yet even simple, 'common sense' descriptions of what the criminal justice system does and who is involved in its operation masks a variety of tensions and problems.

Although the criminal justice institutions and agencies are by and large described separately in this volume they are not isolated and are all part of the broader criminal justice process. In this way, they are interdependent and closely related, and what one institution or agency does has consequences for other agencies in the process. For instance, the CPS depends almost entirely on the police for the information on which it bases its decisions about whether to proceed with cases. They in turn affect the caseload of the courts. Court decisions impact upon the workloads of the prison and probation services, and so on. For this reason, the criminal justice process is often referred to as a 'system'. While this is helpful in some respects because it highlights the interconnectedness of the criminal justice agencies, it does not describe reality. The term 'system' suggests that the process runs systematically and is coordinated, with each agency consulting with others in the process. But the reality is rather different. All of the agencies in the criminal justice process have different and, sometimes, competing objectives, which means that different goals may be simultaneously pursued by different organisations. These aims are not easily reconciled, either in the system as a whole or within specific agencies. For this reason the criminal justice process cannot be perceived to be coordinated or systematic in spite of the increasing number of examples of agencies working together. One specific initiative, which aims to increase coordination between agencies and policies, was the introduction of Local Criminal Justice Boards. They consist of all the Chief Officers of criminal justice agencies who coordinate activity and share responsibility for criminal justice policy in their area. They are supported by a National Criminal Justice Board, which comprises of high-ranking officials from all the government and criminal justice agencies. The term criminal justice process recognises the lack of a coordinated and systematic approach to criminal justice. However, because all stages of the process are governed by a set of discrete rules, are interrelated, and impact upon outcomes (see Uglow, 1995) this book generally utilises the term criminal justice system.

The criminal justice system in context

Criminal Justice is a moving target because the pace of change is rapid and relentless. Since 1997 a total of 40 Acts of Parliament have been passed which deal with crime, police, or other aspects of the criminal justice process. This makes studying the criminal justice process both exciting and frustrating. On the one hand, there are always new laws and policies to examine, but on the other hand it appears that nothing stays still and students and everyone employed in the criminal justice process have to continually learn about (and implement) new initiatives. The constant changes to the criminal law and criminal justice policies and process arise largely from the position of law and order at the forefront of the battleground between political parties. Criminal justice has been at or near the top of the political agenda since the election of the Thatcher government in 1979 who claimed to be the party of law and order. Since then the major parties vie for the honour of being seen as the party of law and order because they view this as a means of gaining electoral success. As a consequence, initiative after initiative is introduced, often without allowing them to bed in or become fully operational before they are superseded by the next big idea.

The media is constantly covering criminal justice related stories both at a local and national level. Indeed, the impact of exceptional cases on the criminal law and criminal justice policy has been immense. Cases such as Gary Newlove, who was murdered by a group of young men whilst trying to curb anti-social behaviour outside his home, and Damien Hanson, Elliott White, and Anthony Rice who were convicted of murders committed whilst on licence (HMIP, 2006a; 2006b) have a disproportionate impact on criminal justice policy. The most notable example of this was the murder of James Bulger by two 10-year-old boys in 1993. This resulted in a reversal in the direction of penal policy (Newburn, 2003). Such cases are used to argue for amendments to the law and/or policy without any recognition that they are the exception rather than the rule. The legal changes that result are often ill-thought-out, knee-jerk reactions in order to satisfy media concerns and public anxieties.

Most media coverage and political debate is couched in terms of criminal justice outcomes being too lenient and/or the criminal justice system failing to take appropriate action. Therefore, it usually calls for criminal justice policy to be toughened up and for punishment to become harsher. This has contributed to the ratcheting up of sentences and the toughening up of enforcement policies and so on. Politicians (and others) who fail to concur with calls for greater harshness risk being labelled as 'soft on crime', which is viewed as political suicide. Despite this, research suggests that the public are not as punitive as is often suggested (Hough and Roberts, 1999).

The rise of discourses relating to risk provides an important lens through which to view the criminal justice process in the early twenty-first century. The criminal justice process is being used increasingly to manage risk (Feeley and Simon, 1992; Kemshall, 2003). This has resulted in the introduction of a range of techniques and tools for measuring risk. However, the measurement of risk is not an exact science and prediction tools are more often wrong than right (Kemshall, 2003). Consequently, some individuals are wrongly assessed, leading to false positives (those detained unnecessarily) and false negatives (those released erroneously). Despite problems of measurement, criminal justice legislation and initiatives are often targeted at high-risk populations, for example, persistent offenders, sex offenders, and dangerous offenders. Criminal justice decision-makers are also becoming more risk averse partly because they fear the consequences, which they perceive would emanate from decisions that turn out to be wrong in retrospect.

A dramatic increase in the prison population has been one of the most visible consequences of the more punitive climate, which has been termed 'populist punitivism' (Cavadino and Dignan, 2007). In 1992, the prison population stood at 45,800 and had risen to 64,700 by 1999 (Home Office, 2003). But the rise in the prison population has been most dramatic during the early years of the twenty-first century when it rose to 74,490 in 2004, 80,804 by 2007, and continues to rise at the time of writing (Home Office, 2004; HM Prison Service, 2008). This has resulted in a significant increase in the imprisonment rate from 92.1 per 100,000 population in 1992 to 148 per 100,000 population in 2007 (Walmsley, 2007). This is one of the highest rates of imprisonment in the old European Union, but it is still far behind the rate of the United States (Walmsley, 2007). The Ministry of Justice projects that the prison population will continue to rise, reaching up to 95,800 by 2015 (Ministry of Justice, 2008b). The rapidly rising prison population has had far reaching effects in terms of overcrowding, the standard of regimes, and the conditions in which prisoners are accommodated (see Chapter 7). It has been argued that the prison system is in crisis as a result (Cavadino and Dignan, 2007).

The criminal justice system is often portrayed as a balancing exercise. On the one hand are the rights of suspects, defendants, and offenders, and on the other are the rights of victims. Generally, this is viewed as a zero sum game meaning that improving the rights of one group necessarily results in the diminishing of the rights of the other group. However, the reality is more complex partly because the groups overlap as many offenders are also victims (Fattah, 1994). Victims have historically been viewed as the forgotten people in the criminal justice process (Williams and Hall, this volume, Chapter 14). This has begun to be addressed through a range of initiatives. However, improving the experiences of victims has been used as a tool to justify calls by criminal justice agencies, the media, and politicians for legal and policy changes which often seek to erode the rights of suspects, defendants, and offenders. Consequently, victims' interests have been a significant driver for changes in the criminal justice system, but this does not always coincide with the interests of victims or the knowledge of the groups that represent them such as Victim Support. Meanwhile there has been significant erosion of the due process rights of suspects and defendants in the final decade of the twentieth century into the twenty-first century (see Chapter 3).

The criminal justice system processes a large number of individuals. In England and Wales in 2006/07 955,100 people were stopped and searched and just under one and a half million people were arrested for notifiable offences (Ministry of Justice, 2008c). In 2006, 1.779 million people were proceeded against in magistrates' courts. A total of 128,990 defendants/offenders were received into prison in 2006 including 83,750 remand prisoners (Ministry of Justice, 2007a). At the time of writing (October 2008) the prison population stood at 83,383 (HM Prison Service, 2008). In 2006, a further 155,610 commenced court orders supervised by the Probation Service (Ministry of Justice, 2007a). The Probation Service had a caseload of 146,530 offenders on court orders and 90,740 subject to pre- and post-release supervision in December 2006. Around a third of males in England and Wales have been convicted of a criminal offence at some time (Home Office, 2004).

The processing of this number of individuals is costly. Responsibility for the criminal justice process in England and Wales falls largely within the remit of the Ministry of Justice which was separated from the Home Office in 2007. However, some criminal justice agencies and functions, most notably the police, still come under the auspices of the Home Office, which also has responsibilities for non-criminal justice areas such as immigration. Consequently working out the expenditure on criminal justice alone is not a simple exercise. However, in 2006/07 the Ministry of Justice budget was nearly £9.5 billion whilst the Home Office budget was £9.2 billion (Ministry of Justice, 2007b). Soloman *et al.* (2007) estimate that the UK spent 2.5 per cent of its Gross Domestic Product on law and order in 2006 with a total of £22.7 billon being spent in 2007/08.

Assessing the effectiveness of the criminal justice system

A quick scan of the newspapers would suggest that concerns exist about how the criminal justice system operates and its effectiveness. It would also lead to the conclusion that there is a general perception, if not a concrete acknowledgement, that public confidence in this important state institution is low. So, how can we assess whether the criminal justice system 'works'? Attempting to answer this seemingly straightforward question is complex and in order to do so there must be agreement about the purpose of the criminal justice system. Most people would agree that the primary goal of the criminal justice system is to reduce crime, but it also has the function of punishing offenders for wrongdoing (see Chapter 4). If the latter function is deemed the most important, it raises questions about the effectiveness of the criminal justice process because most offences remain unsolved. It is estimated that only about 3 per cent of the crimes that are committed result in a conviction (Ashworth, 2005). Consequently, changes in sentencing policy have a very limited impact on crime rates.

Most commonly the effectiveness of the criminal justice system is measured in terms of its impact on offending. One way of assessing this would be to study crime rates and assess whether changes in criminal justice policies have had an impact. However, there are a wide-range of factors which may intervene so even if an effect can be detected it does not necessarily mean that one caused the other. Furthermore, there is no way of knowing the direction of causation. For example, if a new initiative is introduced to channel offenders into drugs treatment and the crime rate falls for the period after its implementation this may have resulted from the initiative. Equally, however, it may have resulted from many other factors such as a rise in the use of imprisonment during the same period or demographic changes in the population. The second way to assess the impact of the criminal justice system on offending is reconviction rates. This is the usual approach but this too has its flaws (Lloyd *et al.*, 1994). First, re*conviction* rates only measure known offending, which is dealt with by the courts. They do not take account of offences for which offenders are not caught. Consequently, they do not measure reoffending. Second, reconviction rates usually do not take account of changes in frequency and severity of offending, although the Ministry of Justice has recently started to calculate these (Ministry of Justice, 2008d). This is important because it is often unrealistic to expect offenders to desist from offending totally in the short term. Desisting from crime is a process rather than an event, meaning that offenders are likely to have relapses in much the same way as people who are trying to give up smoking (Farrall and Calverley, 2006; Maruna, 2000) Thirdly, differences in reconviction rates may simply represent differences in police and prosecution practices. Fourthly, reconviction rates provide no explanation about why changes have occurred or differences exist. Despite these problems, reconviction rates are commonly used. They indicate that just over three-fifths of adult males and just over half of female adults are reconvicted after two years whilst around three-quarters of young males are reconvicted within two years (Home Office, 2004).

GUIDE TO THE BOOK

The book is designed to be a course text for modules that introduce the criminal justice system to students, or to be dipped into for less specialised modules examining all or part of the criminal justice process. The book is aimed primarily at first- and second-year undergraduates who have little or no prior knowledge of the criminal justice process. However, it also provides challenges to readers who have more knowledge of the process by introducing the main issues pertinent to each chapter which can then be explored in more depth by using the further reading sections. Review questions appear at the end of sections within chapters and discussion questions are provided at the end of chapters for use by both students and lecturers. A glossary of key terms is provided at the end of the book. A website accompanies the book which provides teaching resources, namely outline lecture notes and multiple choice questions.

The first ten chapters of the book work through the criminal justice process from the beginning to the end. In Chapter 1, Dan Gilling examines crime prevention. He provides an overview of crime prevention before exploring how and why crime prevention policy has developed. Chapter 2 focuses on policing. Stuart Lister provides an introduction to the role of the police in England and Wales. He highlights what the police do, how they do it, and from where they draw their authority. In so doing, he introduces some of the key debates and recurring themes related to the police and policing. In Chapter 3, Anthea Hucklesby examines some of the main theoretical and conceptual issues within the prosecution process as well as exploring a number of key trends in recent criminal justice law and policy. In Chapter 4, David Scott explores issues relating to theories of punishment providing an overview of the nature and justifications for punishment. He questions the role of punishment and the legitimacy of the prison in modern society. In Chapter 5, Gavin Dingwall provides an overview of sentencing policy and practice, focusing particularly on issues related to sentencing 'dangerous' offenders, and consistency in sentencing. In Chapter 6, Helen Johnston provides a critical introduction to the history of prisons and explanations for the birth of the prison. In Chapter 7, Azrini Wahidin highlights some of the key issues and challenges facing the prison system currently and critically appraises the extent to which prison can be considered to work. In Chapter 8, George Mair provides an overview of the history of community sentences focusing specifically on their role as alternatives to imprisonment. In Chapter 9, Gerry Johnstone explores the core ideas of restorative justice and looks at some of the ways in which they are being put into practice. In Chapter 10, Mike Nellis and Anthony Goodman outline the history and development of the Probation Service in England and Wales and examine how the Probation Service became subsumed into the National Offender Management Service (NOMS).

The remainder of the book takes a thematic approach. Chapters 11, 12, 13, and 14 explore particular groups' experiences of the criminal justice system. Sandra Walklate, Basia Spalek, Barry Goldson and John Muncie, and Brian Williams and Matthew Hall critically examine the criminal justice system's treatment of women, minority ethnic groups, young people, and victims respectively. In Chapters 15 and 16, Anne Wilson and Graham Ellison and Aogan Mulcahy examine the particular issues relating to the operation of the criminal justice system in Scotland and Northern Ireland respectively. In the final chapter, Michael Cavadino and James Dignan speculate about some different ways in which criminal justice might develop in the foreseeable future.

ACKNOWLEDGEMENTS

The process of completing this book has been long and at times tortuous. Our contributors have borne with us and we owe them a great debt. Most of them produced their chapters on time and they all happily acceded to our requests to make changes to their chapters. We thank you for your work and hope that you are pleased with the result.

We are grateful to Tom Young from Oxford University Press for his humour, enduring patience, advice, and support (and the Hudson's lunches) throughout this project.

Several others have contributed to the shaping of this book in various ways. Anthea acknowledges the enduring support of John Walter. Azrini would like to acknowledge, Che-Mah Wahidin and Wan-Nita Wahidin for their support, love and laughter and Dylan who waited patiently to be taken out for walks. We would both like to acknowledge our colleagues at the Centre for Criminal Justice Studies, at the University of Leeds and at the School of Sociology, Social Policy and Social Work at Queen's University.

REFERENCES

Ashworth, A. (2005) *Sentencing and Criminal Justice*. Cambridge: Cambridge University Press.

Cavadino, M. and Dignan, J. (2007) *The Penal System: an introduction* (4th ed). London: Sage.

Farrall, S. and Calverley, A. (2006) *Understanding desistance from crime*. Maidenhead: Open University Press.

Fattah, E. (1994) *The Interchangeable Roles of Victims and Victimizer*. Helsinki: European Institute of Crime Prevention and Control.

Feeley, M. and Simon, J. (1992) 'The New Penology: notes on the emerging strategy of corrections and its implications'. *Criminology* 30: 449–74.

Her Majesty's Inspectorate of Probation (HMIP) (2006a) *An Independent Review of a Serious Further Offence case: Damien Hanson and Elliot White*. London: Her Majesty's Inspectorate of Probation.

Her Majesty's Inspectorate of Probation (HMIP) (2006b) *An Independent Review of a Serious Further Offence case: Anthony Rice*. London: Her Majesty's Inspectorate of Probation.

HM Prison Service (2008) *Monthly Prison Brief* <http://www.hmprisonservice.gov.uk/resourcecentre/publicationsdocuments/index.asp?cat=85>.

Home Office (2001) *Criminal Justice: The Way Ahead* Cm. 5074 (Feb).

Home Office (2003) *Prison Statistics England and Wales 2002* Cm. 5996. London: Home Office.

Home Office (2004) *Statistics on Women in the Criminal Justice System*. London: Home Office.

Hough, M. and Roberts, J. (1999) *Attitudes to Punishment: findings from the British Crime Survey*. Home Office Research Study No. 179. London: Home Office.

Kemshall, H. (2003) *Understanding Risk in Criminal Justice*. Buckingham: Open University Press.

Lloyd, C., Mair, G., and Hough, M. (1994) *Explaining Reconviction Rates: a critical analysis*. Home Office RDS Research Findings 12. London: Home Office.

Maruna, S. (2000) *Making Good*. Washington: American Psychological Society.

Ministry of Justice (2007a) *Offender Management Caseload Statistics 2006*. London: Ministry of Justice at <http://www.justice.gov.uk/docs/omcs2006.pdf>.

Ministry of Justice (2007b) *Comprehensive Spending Review*. London: Ministry of Justice at <http://www.justice.gov.uk/news/newsrelease091007c.htm>.

Ministry of Justice (2008a) *Population in custody*. London: Ministry of Justice at <http://www.justice.gov.uk/publications/populationincustody.htm>.

Ministry of Justice (2008b) *Prison population projections 2008–2015*. Statistical Bulletin. London: Ministry of Justice at <http://www.justice.gov.uk/docs/stats-prison-pop-sep08.pdf>.

Ministry of Justice (2008c) *Arrests for Recorded Crime (Notifiable Offences) and the Operation of Certain Police Powers Under PACE* 2006/7. London: MoJ.

Ministry of Justice (2008d) *Reoffending of Adults: results from the 2006 cohort England and Wales*. London: Ministry of Justice at <http://www.justice.gov.uk/docs/re-offending-adults-2006.pdf>.

Newburn, T. (2003) *Crime and Criminal Justice Policy*. Harlow: Pearson Education.

Soloman, E., Garside, R., Eades, C., and Rutherford, M. (2007) *Ten Years of Criminal Justice Under Labour: an independent audit*. London: Centre for Crime and Justice Studies.

Uglow, S. (1995) *Criminal Justice*. Sweet and Maxwell: London.

Walker, C. and Starmer, K. (1999) *Miscarriages of Justice*. London: Blackstone.

Walmsley, R. (2007) *World Prison Population List*, London, International Centre for Prison Studies, King's College, available at <http://www.kcl.ac.uk/depsta/law/research/icps/downloads/world-prison pop-seventh.pdf>.

1

Crime prevention

Daniel Gilling

INTRODUCTION

This chapter examines an area of *crime control*—namely *crime prevention*—that takes place to a large extent outside of the criminal justice process. We begin with an overview of crime prevention, focusing particularly upon the difficulties of defining and demarcating crime prevention from other approaches, before moving on to look at how crime prevention policy has developed over only the last few decades to put it in its now central position in contemporary crime control strategies. Following this overview we turn our attention to an account of the rise of crime prevention: why has it risen from a position of relative obscurity to a position of such importance? The reasons are important because they draw attention to controversies and unresolved tensions that play themselves out in the policy and practice of crime prevention. This practice forms the focus of the larger part of this chapter, and we examine, in turn, situational and social crime prevention as the two main constituent elements of contemporary policy, paying particular attention to the criticisms that have been levelled at them. We then end with a conclusion that summarises the discussion and draws attention to the key themes raised in the chapter.

BACKGROUND

Crime prevention and the problem of definition

It would be reasonable to assume that a major reason for the existence of the criminal justice system is the prevention of *crime*. Such an assumption is given weight by the frequency with which the phrase 'the prevention of crime' appears in historical documents associated with the emergence of different parts of the system. Thus, for example, it appears in the instructions issued to the new Metropolitan Police, the first permanent professional police service set up in 1829 (Gilling, 1997), and it also appears in the title of an Act of Parliament from 1908, concerned specifically with the introduction of the Borstal system for young offenders (Muncie, 1999). However, crime prevention also exists outside of criminal justice, and it is this latter kind of crime prevention upon which this chapter focuses.

Attempts to define crime prevention generally recognise that it occurs within and outside of criminal justice, and that it takes distinct forms. Thus, for example, Tonry and Farrington (1995) establish a typology of four forms of prevention, namely law enforcement, developmental, communal, and situational, before moving on in their volume to concentrate on the latter three, which represent the forms of crime prevention less associated with traditional criminal justice responses. In a similar way, this time drawing upon the distinctions used in medical epidemiology, Brantingham and Faust (1976) differentiate between primary, secondary, and tertiary prevention. Primary prevention seeks to reduce opportunities for crime by protecting victims or targets. Secondary prevention seeks to change people who may be considered particularly *at risk* of offending. Tertiary prevention seeks to truncate the criminal careers of those who have already offended, and is therefore more within the domain of traditional reactive criminal justice. There is, incidentally, broad similarity between primary prevention and Tonry and Farrington's situational category; and between secondary prevention and their developmental and communal categories. Developmental prevention aims to prevent the emergence of criminality in (risky) individuals, while communal prevention aims to prevent the emergence of criminality within (risky) communities.

As noted above, the focus of this chapter is upon crime prevention beyond or outside criminal justice. For van Dijk, this *is* crime prevention: it is 'the total of all policies, measures and techniques outside the boundaries of the criminal justice system' (1990: 205). Yet we have just seen that crime prevention also exists within the system's boundaries. Attempts to specify exactly where the boundary lies are probably doomed to failure because the boundary is in any case a shifting one (Crawford, 1998). It is better to accept, therefore, that crime prevention is 'notoriously amorphous' (Hughes, 1998: 2), and to settle, as other authors have done, for trying to make distinctions between the objects of prevention, rather than its location. Van Dijk and de Waard (1991), for example, distinguish, as objects of prevention, offenders, victims, and situations; whilst Pease (2002) distinguishes between preventive interventions that target the structure (broader social and economic changes), the psyche (individual motivations and inclinations), and the circumstance (whether social or physical) where crime occurs. In this chapter, we shall use two broad categories that are commonly used within the literature. These are situational crime prevention, which focuses on preventing opportunities for crime (and is thus most similar to Brantingham and Faust's primary prevention), and social crime prevention, which focuses upon preventing criminal motivations, and can be sub-divided into developmental and community crime prevention, following Tonry and Farrington (1995). Some criminologists object to this distinction, because, like Pease's (2002) circumstance, situations can have both social and physical aspects, but the virtue of this simple distinction, as Crawford (1998: 18) observes, is that it 'explicitly recognises and embodies different assumptions about *what causes crime*' (original emphasis).

The development of crime prevention policy

An important point to recognise at the outset is that crime prevention has become an area of policy and practice that has grown significantly in recent decades. The early origins of a distinctive crime prevention policy can be traced back to the 1950s and 1960s, when the *Home Office* came under particular pressure from the insurance industry to develop publicity campaigns and corporate approaches to property crime prevention (see Gilling, 1997), in large part because of the growing costs of insured property losses that accompanied the post-war rise in crime (O'Malley and Hutchinson, 2007). Two key points can be made about early policy developments. Firstly, the main orientation was that of situational crime prevention (although the term was not coined until the late-1970s), focusing especially on the reduction of opportunities for property crime by relatively simple means: the publicity slogans of the time, such as 'lock it or lose it' and 'watch out, there's a thief about', very much capture the spirit of the time. Secondly, in recognition of the fact that the means to prevent crime lay beyond the direct control or action of government, the idea of a *partnership* between citizens and the state was integral.

The great leap forward in policy came in the 1980s. Following research and development work on the situational approach (Mayhew *et al.*, 1976), the Home Office established a *Crime Prevention Unit* to promote the spread of crime prevention practice, and issued two circulars, in 1984 and again in 1990, that put public agencies under pressure to establish non-statutory local crime prevention partnerships—with each other, with businesses, and with the public—as the main vehicles for delivery. It also funded two initiatives, the Five Towns Initiative (from 1985) and the much larger Safer Cities Programme (Gilling, 1997). The Safer Cities Programme, which operated in two phases from 1988 through to the mid-1990s, covered some 40 major urban centres across the country, using Home Office funding to employ a crime prevention coordinator, to establish local partnerships and to fund a variety of locally-tailored crime prevention initiatives (see Sutton, 1996; and Knox *et al.*, 2000). The partnership model also lay at the heart of provisions in New Labour's Crime and Disorder Act 1998, that this time required the establishment of statutory partnerships, with a responsibility to prevent crime, in each of the 376 lower-tier local authority areas of England and Wales.

As crime prevention policy has evolved, it has encountered certain difficulties, two of which stand out. Firstly, the strong emphasis placed upon situational crime prevention was not welcomed by everyone, and despite the Home Office's preferences, local practitioners often steered more of a social crime prevention direction in practice. This was seen particularly in the Safer Cities Programme (Sutton, 1996), but it was also evidenced by the emergence of a 'replacement discourse' (van Swaaningen, 2002). That is to say that, particularly in politically left leaning urban local authorities, practitioners started talking not of crime prevention, but of *community safety*, conceived as a more progressive approach that combined social and situational approaches, addressed the fear of crime as well as crime itself, and placed crime within the context of other harms, such as environmental pollution, that impacted negatively on the community's collective safety and quality of life. The idea of community safety received some official endorsement when the Morgan report (Home Office, 1991) suggested that its use, rather than that of the term crime prevention, might encourage participation from a broader range of agencies than had hitherto been prepared to jump on the crime prevention bandwagon. The emergence of community safety illustrates the politics of crime prevention: people have very different ideas about how best to prevent crime, and about how to conceive of and contextualise the problem of crime.

Secondly, as Pease (2002) observes, at the heart of the preventive enterprise is a non-event. Crime prevention seeks to stop crimes from happening, but it is difficult to know whether it has been successful in such terms. If crimes do not occur, is it because the crime prevention is effective, or is it because the crimes were not going to occur anyway? When crime prevention involves the use of scarce resources, as indeed it does, there is understandably some concern to ensure that those resources are used to best effect. Consequently, policy-makers and others concerned with the question of 'what works' began talking in the 1990s not of crime prevention, but of *crime reduction*. Especially since the landmark Crime and Disorder Act 1998, crime reduction has become the preferred term in official discourse. Thus the statutory partnerships established in all local authority areas of England from April 1999 were called crime reduction partnerships; and from that same time the government launched its new *Crime Reduction Strategy*.

The significance of the term crime reduction lies in the fact that it can be achieved in other ways besides crime prevention. It is possible to reduce local crime problems, for example, by catching prolific offenders and taking them out of circulation, and into custody; or by high profile policing strategies that have some deterrent effect, albeit usually only temporary. Referring back to our earlier distinction between crime prevention inside and outside the criminal justice system, what crime reduction in effect does is to open the door of crime prevention to the criminal justice system. This is no less political than the challenge offered by community safety. It allows criminal justice agencies to reclaim an expertise in the control of crime that the emergence of crime prevention as a distinct policy area had done much to challenge, as we shall see in the next section.

In this introductory overview, then, we have established that crime prevention is difficult to define clearly, but that most simply it is seen as being constituted by situational and social approaches that operate with different understandings of the causes of crime, and that therefore target different things, respectively opportunities and motivations. As an area of policy and practice beyond the familiar repertoire of the traditional criminal justice system, crime prevention has grown markedly over recent decades. In so doing, it has undergone certain mutations, as community safety and crime reduction. While such mutations appear pragmatic responses to, respectively, the alleged limitations of situational crime prevention and the problem of establishing what works in crime prevention, they also reflect and contribute to a politics of crime prevention that cannot be ignored. In the next section we shall explore the reasons for the emergence of crime prevention as a significant policy area in its own right, before moving on, in the following sections, to explore situational and social crime prevention in more detail.

REVIEW QUESTIONS

1 The idea of partnership has always been integral to the development of crime prevention. Why is this so, and how has government sought to foster it?

2 The idea of crime prevention has been challenged by two alternative 'imaginings' of the same basic concept. What are they, and how do they differ from crime prevention?

Accounting for the rise of crime prevention

There are a number of reasons why crime prevention has moved from a position of relative obscurity to centre stage in crime control strategies. Firstly, from the 1950s onwards, as officially recorded rates of crime began their inexorable post-war rise (see Figure 1.1), a growing sense emerged that the criminal justice system did not work well. If it was there

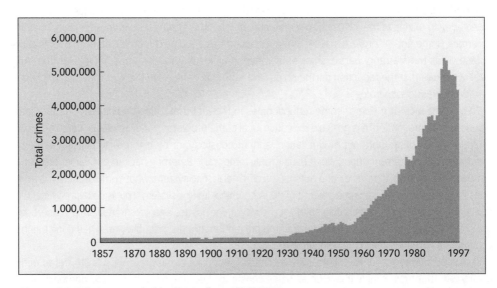

Figure 1.1 Crimes recorded by the police, 1857–1997

Source: From Barclay and Tavares (1999) Digest 4: Information on the Criminal Justice System in England and Wales. London: Home Office Research Development and Statistics.

to prevent crime, why was crime continuing to rise so alarmingly? Officially sponsored research studies into the effectiveness of different aspects of criminal justice started to come back with the depressing conclusion that 'nothing works' (Brody, 1976; Clarke and Hough, 1980).

Secondly, alongside studies of the (in)effectiveness of criminal justice, other criminological research, most notably crime and *victimisation surveys*, began to shed light on the dark figure of unreported and unrecorded crime. The 'revelation' that police crime statistics undercounted crime was less important than the implication that such surveys had for our understanding of the reach of the criminal justice system. *British Crime Surveys* from 1982 onwards have shown that a relatively small proportion of crime comes to the police's attention, and of this small proportion an even smaller proportion results in a caution or conviction. In other words, the British Crime Survey has allowed researchers to calculate the *attrition rate* for crime; and in 1997, for example, it was revealed that only 3 per cent of all crimes result in either a caution or a conviction, and only 0.3 per cent of all crimes result in a custodial sentence (Barclay and Tavares, 1999—see Figure 1.2). What this means is that the criminal justice system, which is commonly regarded as being at the vanguard of our formal response to crime, only ever gets to touch the tip of the iceberg of all crime. Thus, the idea that the solution to the crime problem lies in additional investment in criminal justice is seriously flawed, and the answer to the question of how to prevent crime lies largely outside of, rather than within, the criminal justice system.

Thirdly, the landscape of late-modern Britain has undergone a political transformation, initially following the unprecedented political success of a resurgent Conservative

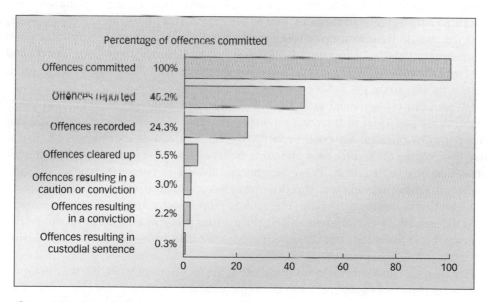

Figure 1.2 Crime attrition

Source: From Barclay and Tavares (1999) Digest 4: Information on the Criminal Justice System in England and Wales. London: Home Office Research Development and Statistics.

Party under the leadership of Margaret Thatcher. One strong element of the Conservative's political project was neo-liberalism, which promoted the idea of 'rolling back the frontiers of the state', in order to create less dependency upon state institutions, and more space for individual initiative and responsibility. There was a close resonance between this idea and the realisation of the limited reach of the criminal justice system. The implication was that if crime was to be prevented, there needed to be less dependence upon the criminal justice system, and greater *responsibilisation* of others, such as private citizens and private businesses. This does not mean that the government simply gave up on criminal justice, but it did do much to spread the crime prevention message beyond the confines of the criminal justice system, and this is why many of the key policy developments in crime prevention date from around this time.

Fourthly, crime prevention has fed off a number of changes—economic, political, social, and cultural—that have coalesced around the notion of *globalisation*. Globalisation for various reasons has been accompanied by a growing sense of insecurity and anxiety which is easily projected onto a problem such as crime. The fear of crime, therefore, has been something of a criminological 'discovery' of the 1980s. Accompanying the fear of crime is a corresponding quest for security, and there is an elective affinity between this and the spread of crime prevention beyond the boundaries of the criminal justice system. The quest for security encourages the *commodification of security*, and if the state cannot provide it through criminal justice then this opens up space for private sector providers. Hence we have seen an expanded and flourishing market for security in residential areas (e.g. private security patrols, gated communities), and leisure and commercial areas (e.g. security guards in shopping malls, CCTV systems). As a valued commodity, security becomes an important consideration for states and cities, as much as for private enterprise, since each is seeking to attract inward investment within the global marketplace. For those with a choice, who would want to live or work in a high crime neighbourhood, and who would want to shop or seek their cultural entertainment in a run-down and dangerous city centre? A number of crime prevention measures, then, both feed off and feed into the commodification of security that follows on the heels of late-modern social insecurity and anxiety.

Fifthly, criminology itself has not been immune to these changes, with Garland (2001) discerning a particular shift away from orthodox 'criminologies of the other' that dominated the discipline for most of the twentieth century; to newer 'criminologies of everyday life'. Where the former took offending behaviour to be essentially pathological or abnormal, the latter accepts crime as a normal feature of contemporary society, and isolates the thing to be explained as the criminogenic situation: what is it about a person or target that makes it particularly vulnerable to crime? Such criminologies have particularly influenced the development of situational crime prevention, though we should not assume that criminologies of the other have lost all their influence or have no bearing on crime prevention practice.

Having established the reasons for the rise of crime prevention, we are now in a position to explore its two main approaches in more detail.

REVIEW QUESTIONS

1 Explain how the findings of victimisation surveys and studies into the effectiveness of criminal justice have served to strengthen the case for crime prevention beyond the criminal justice system.

2 How have political changes, and the general phenomenon of globalisation, helped to further the cause of crime prevention?

Situational crime prevention

A brief description

Situational crime prevention is classically defined as involving the 'management, design or manipulation of the immediate environment' (Hough *et al.*, 1980: 1). It is the product of a way of thinking and acting about the problem of crime that differs from traditional criminal justice responses. Its focus is upon the offence, not the offender; and it is premised upon the idea that opportunities for committing offences are embedded within the immediate *situation* in which such offences occur—hence the name of the approach. As we discussed above, situational crime prevention takes theoretical inspiration from the rise to prominence of criminologies of everyday life, which take it as axiomatic that crime is a normal, routine feature of everyday life. The thing to be explained, therefore, is not the offender. Routine activity theory, for example, simply assumes that motivated offenders exist (Felson, 1994), while for rational choice theory, as its name suggests, offending is the rational choice of largely 'normal' people presented with situations where the perceived benefits of committing crime outweigh the perceived costs (Clarke, 1980).

This way of thinking about crime betrays a pessimism that, given continued year-on-year rises in crime, little can be done to correct criminal behaviour at source. Thus advocates of situational crime prevention frequently argue, with some justification, that it is much easier to change situations than it is to change behaviour. They take inspiration from studies that seek to explain crime in terms of characteristics of the environment, rather than of the offender. One particularly influential study was that produced by Oscar Newman (1973), who conducted a statistical analysis of the crime rates and design features of different housing estates in the USA. His analysis suggested that there was a correlation between certain design features, most notably high-rise buildings and the number of entrance and exit points in buildings and the estates themselves. In other words, crimes were more likely to occur in environments that had such features, and this led Newman to propose, within his notion of *defensible space*, a set of design principles that in his view would make crime less likely. Amongst these principles was the injunction to privatise public space, for example by enclosing open land around buildings with fences or walls that would encourage a sense of territoriality; and by designing buildings in such a way that maximised their natural surveillance potential, so that, for example, one building overlooked another, and windows were sited to overlook potentially vulnerable spaces.

The implications of Newman's work were that crime could be 'designed out'. This could be done by making modifications to the existing built environment or, more efficiently, by incorporating defensible space principles into the planning of new developments. Newman's ideas are certainly not without their critics (see Gilling, 1997), but nevertheless they have had a major practical impact. In the USA, his ideas, and those of others (e.g. Jeffery, 1971), contributed to a multi-million dollar federal programme called *Crime Prevention Through Environmental Design* (CPTED), whilst in the UK they have been used to justify substantial modifications to high-crime public housing estates, including the removal of many high-rise buildings under the *Priority Estates Programme*. They also underpin the *Secured By Design* standard for new buildings and developments, and inform the advice proffered by specialist police *Architectural Liaison Officers* to those planning new developments across the UK.

It was within the UK Home Office that the ideas of Newman and others began to coalesce into a model of situational crime prevention that researchers were keen to test out in practice (Gladstone, 1980). This highly rationalistic model, reproduced in Figure 1.3, suggested that crime could be prevented by analysing the situation in which the offence occurred, and then intervening in such a way that made the situation less vulnerable, by taking away the criminal opportunity. In large part, this meant either target hardening, through measures such as locks, bolts, and other security devices; or increasing surveillance, for example by applying defensible space designs, or by deploying CCTV cameras or personnel, such as security guards, park keepers, or bus conductors, who could perform a surveillance role.

In its original formulation, situational crime prevention was relatively straightforward, and much of its attractiveness lay in its simplicity, and its capacity to target established problems—crime *hotspots*—that the spatial analysis of crime statistics was able to isolate. In such hotspots, the characteristics of offenders generally remained unknown, because most were not apprehended, whereas their situations were known, and thus

---

A systematic approach to decision making about crime prevention

1. A thorough analysis of the situation in which the offence occurs in order to establish the conditions (opportunities, motivation, legislation) that need to be met for the offence to be committed;

2. The identification of measures which would make it more difficult or impossible to fulfil each of these conditions;

3. An assessment of the practicability, likely effectiveness and costs of each of these measures, and

4. Selection of the most promising measures

Figure 1.3 The situational crime prevention process

Source: Gladstone (1980:10)

open to analysis. Notwithstanding the debate about whether hotspots are generators or receptors of crime (see Crawford, 1998), situational crime prevention had considerable pragmatic appeal and it is easy to see how it quickly grew to become a major constituent element of crime control strategies (O'Malley, 1992), not least because it was something that could be performed not only by state agencies, but also by others within the private sector.

The theory and practice of situational crime prevention

For many people, situational crime prevention—making crime harder to commit—is little more than common sense, but it would be wrong to suggest that it lacks a theoretical base. Rather, the emergence of situational crime prevention has stimulated the development and refinement of the criminologies of everyday life, notably rational choice theory and routine activity theory. In turn, these very practical theories have then fed back into practice, helping to make situational crime prevention a more complex and sophisticated approach to crime control. Routine activity theory, for example, has contributed to an understanding of crime as a triangular interaction of targets, offenders, and places, each of which may be controlled, respectively, by 'guardians', 'handlers', and 'managers'. Practically, this has informed the development of the *Problem Analysis Triangle* (see Figure 1.4), which is now widely used by crime prevention practitioners (see Clarke and Eck, 2003).

Rational choice theory, meanwhile, has helped to focus attention upon how certain *crime facilitators*, such as the presence of glass bottles in pubs, can influence the choice structuring properties of situations, making criminal event choices more likely. The upshot of this synergy between theory and practice is the development of a quite

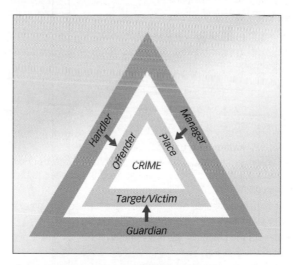

Figure 1.4 The Problem Analysis Triangle

Source: Clarke and Eck (2003) Become a Problem-Solving Crime Analyst in 55 Small Steps. London: Jill Dando Institute of Crime Science. <http://www.ucl.ac.uk/jdi/publications/other_publications/55steps.php>.

sophisticated typology of 25 techniques of situational crime prevention which is reproduced in Figure 1.5.

This typology shows that situational crime prevention has moved beyond the general reliance upon target hardening (increasing the effort) and surveillance (increasing
the risk) that characterised its early days (Hughes, 1998). In addition to these two broad

Increase the effort

1. Harden targets
2. Control access to facilities
3. Screen exits
4. Deflect offenders
5. Control tools/weapons

Increase the risk

6. Extend guardianship
7. Assist natural surveillance
8. Reduce anonymity
9. Utilise place managers
10. Strengthen formal surveillance

Reduce the rewards

11. Conceal targets
12. Remove targets
13. Identify property
14. Disrupt markets
15. Deny benefits

Reduce provocations

16. Reduce frustrations and stress
17. Avoid disputes
18. Reduce emotional arousal
19. Neutralise peer pressure
20. Discourage imitation

Remove excuses

21. Set rules
22. Post instructions
23. Alert conscience
24. Assist compliance
25. Control drugs and alcohol

Figure 1.5 25 Techniques of situational crime
prevention

Source: Clarke and Eck (2003: 32)

categories we have a range of measures intended variously to reduce the rewards, reduce provocations, and remove excuses. The last two of these categories show that situational crime prevention must now be regarded as much more than just a 'technological fix' to the problem of crime, even though technological fixes, such as CCTV, often predominate. Indeed, to some extent, through these additional categories situational crime prevention has been 'socialised', in the sense that it appears to be paying equal attention to offender motivations. Thus, for example, the setting of rules serves to stimulate the conscience of potential offenders, whilst neutralising peer pressure is very much about taking people out of social situations where they may be influenced by anti-social peers. Such measures would not be out of place in social crime prevention strategies (see below), and their presence in the more recent typology of situational crime prevention shows not only the difficulty of holding a clear distinction between the situational and the social, but also the response of advocates of situational crime prevention to criticisms of its asocial character (Shaftoe, 2004).

CCTV—an example of situational crime prevention

A good example of a situational crime prevention measure is CCTV. It is one of the most high-profile crime prevention measures. In the UK there are estimated to be in excess of four million cameras: this means that the UK possesses nearly one-fifth of all of the world's supply of cameras—that is one camera for every 15 citizens (McSmith, 2008). Since the mid-1990s central government has invested millions of pounds in local schemes run by local authorities and crime prevention partnerships, and CCTV is also used widely in shopping centres, schools and colleges, hospitals, and other public spaces. Given such widespread usage, one might reasonably conclude that CCTV is a very effective crime prevention measure.

Advocates argue that CCTV acts as a deterrent, whilst its capacity to store images and to track perpetrators of crime in real-time means that it also assists in crime detection, and in gathering evidence for court cases. They also argue that in an age of insecurity it has an important reassurance function, allowing members of the public to feel sufficiently safe in their everyday lives. Indeed, so important is this function that CCTV is increasingly being regarded as a 'must have' for proprietors of retail, leisure, and other public facilities, and CCTV schemes also increasingly penetrate residential space.

Evidence of CCTV's apparent successes is not hard to find. Crime-related CCTV footage, and the resultant 'catch', makes up a significant proportion of the 'infotainment' diet that currently occupies television programming schedules, whilst news broadcasts have illustrated vividly the virtues of CCTV in piecing together the movements of suspects in high profile cases such as the 7 July London bombings. There are also research studies which have shown, for example, spectacular reductions in crime following the introduction of CCTV schemes in particular areas (see Welsh and Farrington, 2002).

However, other research studies suggest more caution. Gill and Spriggs's (2005) Home Office-funded study of 14 CCTV schemes found a discernible crime reductive effect in only one of them, a scheme centred around a car park. This finding echoes the conclusions of Welsh and Farrington's (2002) systematic review of several CCTV scheme evaluations, which indicated that whilst CCTV schemes had a small reductive impact upon crime, this impact was most noticeable in schemes focused on car parks, and least noticeable upon schemes focused on town centres, public housing estates, or public transport facilities. They note that CCTV can have a significant reductive effect upon vehicle crime, but a minimal effect upon violent crime, suggesting that CCTV is at its most deterrent for opportunist crimes involving rational decision making, and least deterrent for impulsive or emotional crimes, where consideration of the presence of cameras is unlikely to figure prominently in the offender's mind.

The capacity of CCTV schemes to detect crimes depends upon a number of factors. Cameras are not always pointed in the right direction, given an unobstructed view, loaded with film, switched on, working properly, or capable of generating high-quality images. They can be put out of action by potential offenders, and their effectiveness undermined by relatively simple counter-measures, such as the wearing of helmets, balaclavas, or 'hoodies'. The cameras, moreover, are only as good as their operatives, not all of whom are necessarily well trained or supervised, as some studies have found (Norris and Armstrong, 1999).

In terms of reassurance, while survey evidence suggests that many are indeed reassured by the cameras' presence, others are less happy. Some civil libertarians have in mind an Orwellian, nightmare vision of 'big brother' watching us. Others express concern at the potential invasion of privacy, particularly from concealed cameras; from cameras that can hear as well as see; and from incompetent or unscrupulous operators who may lose or misuse video data—there are some notorious cases. Still others are worried at the kind of society that saturation CCTV coverage ushers in: for them it is a society founded on mistrust and suspicion, where the cold face of technology is used to extend surveillance into social space, in order to identify and exclude risky 'others', such as young people, who then become increasingly marginalised from mainstream society. This negative assessment, however, must contend with more progressive uses of CCTV, for example in police custody centres, where cameras can offer some protection to, rather than marginalisation of, the suspect.

Criticisms of situational crime prevention

Situational crime prevention has considerable intuitive appeal. In place of the pessimism that is generated by the realisation that most offenders are not caught or, even if they are, are rarely reformed or deterred from future criminal choices, there is an optimism that something relatively simple can be done to prevent or reduce crime. Yet it also has its critics, perhaps especially because it has broken with criminological and criminal justice orthodoxies.

Firstly, it stands accused of being limited in its scope. It has been suggested that situational crime prevention is more applicable, and in practice has been far more extensively applied, to street crimes than to other crime such as *domestic violence*, corporate crime, or state crimes (Hughes, 1998). In particular, the approach and its rationalistic underpinnings fit much better with acquisitive crimes than emotive, spur-of-the-moment offences. Especially since it is more reliant on efforts made beyond the boundaries of the criminal justice system and the state, it is also argued that situational crime prevention is limited to those best able to pay for it: it protects the relatively well off, and in so far as it deflects the risk of victimisation on to others, it may therefore increase the immiseration of the relatively poor.

Secondly, it is argued by some that situational crime prevention is not effective (Gilling, 1997). The main issue here is that of crime displacement: situational crime prevention does not directly address criminal motivations, and thus while crime opportunities may be blocked by situational methods, motivated offenders will simply find other opportunities. There are a number of different displacement possibilities:

- spatial displacement: the same offence in a different location;
- temporal displacement: the same offence at a different time;
- tactical displacement: the same offence committed in a different way;
- target displacement: same type of offence, different type of target;
- crime-type displacement: same offender, different type of crime from that originally intended;
- perpetrator displacement: new offenders always available to fill space vacated by existing perpetrators.

It is also argued that the effects of situational measures can be blunted over time (Crawford, 1998). Measures that may at first appear formidable obstacles, such as CCTV, can lose a lot of their deterrent effect as they become a normal part of the physical landscape, and as impressions about their fallibility take root. Alternatively, as some of the forms of displacement indicate, offenders can adapt to these measures and find ways round them, thereby making situational crime prevention practice akin to an 'arms race' between potential offenders and crime preventers (Crawford, 1998).

Thirdly, it is argued that too great an emphasis upon situational crime prevention can produce a number of unwelcome side effects. While the security that crime prevention seeks to provide is a valued social end, it can conflict with other social ends. Practically, for example, it can hinder fire safety, by placing too much security gadgetry in the way. This gadgetry can also contribute to the creation of a *fortress society* that is not only aesthetically but also socially undesirable, communicating a sense of mistrust that tends to manifest itself in division and exclusion. Crime prevention, particularly in its surveillant forms, thus becomes a matter of protecting 'us' from 'them', with 'them' being defined in risk-based terms that often have strong discriminatory or intolerant overtones (e.g. the banning of youths with 'hoodies' from some shopping centres). Perversely, moreover, whilst crime prevention measures are intended to generate security, their proliferation can end up generating its very opposite, because their obtrusiveness can communicate insecurity and fear: the presence of crime prevention can communicate the message that there is, to coin a phrase, a clear and present danger.

REVIEW QUESTIONS

1 According to the notion of defensible space, how can space be better defended to make it less vulnerable to criminal attack?

2 Summarise the main criticisms of situational crime prevention.

Social crime prevention

Social crime prevention is a label covering an array of ideas and interventions oriented towards the prevention of criminality. It is 'social' in the sense that its focus is upon people (not situations), and the factors that motivate or dispose some individuals and groups to engage in criminal activity. Whilst crime prevention as a distinct policy domain outside of the criminal justice system has moved more to the fore, it would be fair to say that compared to the situational approach the social approach has played much more of a back-seat role. Nevertheless, many social crime prevention interventions have been in existence for some time, either as elements of social policy, rather than criminal justice policy, or because they have resonated with criminological orthodoxies that have moved in and out of political fashion. Amongst those who have promoted community safety, and under New Labour's much-vaunted progressive third way, however, social crime prevention has undergone a minor renaissance (Gilling, 2007).

Accounts of social crime prevention tend to divide it into two broad types, namely developmental and community. The former aims to prevent the development of criminality in individuals by addressing its social and social-psychological causes. Now clearly criminal justice has an interest in preventing the further development of criminality in those who have already offended, particularly young people, but this tends to be pursued through the punitive and rehabilitative practices of the criminal justice system, as tertiary prevention, and these practices are therefore explored elsewhere in this volume.

 CASE STUDY: SURE START

Sure Start is a New Labour programme that has social crime prevention as one of its purposes, and that is based upon similar models operating in the USA, namely the High/Scope Perry Pre-School Programme, which ran in the 1960s, and Head Start, which started in the 1960s and continues in the present. Both of these models were developmental in their crime prevention orientation, targeting pre-school education at children from deprived backgrounds, along with home visits and support for their parents. The Perry Pre-School Programme was well researched via a longitudinal study, and by the time child beneficiaries of the programme had reached the age of 40, researchers calculated that for every dollar spent on the programme, thirteen dollars were saved in the longer run, because the children made less demands on such things as welfare services and payments, and, importantly, criminal justice expenditure. In other words, amongst other benefits, children subjected to the programme committed less crime than those in a matched control group: by the time they had reached 19, for example, the arrest rate of these children was 40 per cent less than that of their control group peers.

The USA models were quickly identified in the UK as examples of 'What Works' in crime prevention (Graham, 1998), and in the form of Sure Start, New Labour introduced its own version. This was explicitly identified by Tony Blair as an anti-crime measure, thereby demonstrating, in contrast to the previous Conservative regime, New Labour's commitment to longer term social crime prevention measures. Sure Start was announced in July 1998 and became operational in 1999. Initially it involved 250 separate programmes targeted at deprived areas. Although there was no national blueprint for the programmes (Clarke, 2007), their design generally entails the establishment of a local children's centre which acts as a joined-up 'one-stop-shop' where pre-school education and childcare are integrated together with parenting advice, child and family health services, and employment advice for parents. The programmes were increased to 500 by 2004, and thereafter the Sure Start idea was 'mainstreamed' (Pugh, 2007) and rolled out across the country, so that by 2010 there will be a national network of more than 3,000 children's centres. It is through these centres, then, that the developmental crime prevention is delivered, particularly through the pre-school education and parenting advice and support, which it is thought will do much to improve the life chances of its beneficiaries.

It is too early to tell for sure what impact Sure Start will have upon the future offending behaviour of its beneficiaries, although a national evaluation programme is in place to track this. However, there is a potential problem. While one general aim of Sure Start is to improve the life chances of the most deprived and excluded children, who are also those most at risk of committing crime in later life, there is evidence to suggest that Sure Start is not reaching such a group (Gilling, 2007; National Audit Office, 2006). Rather, since the children's centres are open to all, it appears to be the case that most use of their services is being made by better-off parents and their children—those at less risk of future criminal behaviour. This problem is likely to be exacerbated by the mainstreaming of Sure Start after 2004. This demonstrates a common problem with social crime prevention schemes, where crime prevention is only one of a number of possible aims. In the case of Sure Start, government targets show that there are many other aims, such as improving children's education potential, improving family health, and reducing the number of unemployed households (National Audit Office, 2006), and it may be that such aims are better met by universalising and mainstreaming Sure Start. But, in the meantime, it may be the crime prevention aim that suffers and is overlooked. Even were Sure Start to reach the most deprived children, as its USA counterparts did, there are those who argue that a more effective approach to preventing crime in such a group is not by addressing their alleged parenting deficits, but rather by addressing the material inequalities that so obviously disadvantage them in the first place (Clarke, 2007).

Young people form the main focus of developmental prevention (see the Case Study on the Sure Start Programme), and much of the discourse surrounding developmental prevention involves the concept of risk. Since evidence shows young people to be disproportionately involved in offending behaviour (mostly minor, and mostly street crimes), and because youth, as a point of transition to full adulthood, is regarded as a point of particular vulnerability, young people in general are regarded as being at risk of offending. More specifically, longitudinal research has demonstrated that certain young people are more at risk of offending than others, because of their association with certain risk factors, which are predictive of future offending (see Farrington and Coid, 2002). Initial offending behaviour is predictive of future offending behaviour, but what concerns us more in this chapter are those risk factors embedded within the social circumstances in which young people find themselves. These include, in a far from exhaustive list: social deprivation; elements of schooling, such as poor discipline; bullying experienced as either victim or perpetrator; low educational attainment; truancy and exclusion; family circumstances, including inadequate or inconsistent parenting, offending parents and siblings; and association with delinquent peers. For each risk factor there is an associated preventive intervention. Social deprivation, for example, might be tackled through income redistribution, housing improvements, and better education and training opportunities; whilst association with delinquent peers may be tackled through the provision of better leisure facilities that provide opportunities to engage in pro-social activities with appropriate role models.

Community crime prevention, meanwhile, picks up on the long-standing association between high rates of crime and certain places, particularly inner-city areas or multiply deprived neighbourhoods, notably some large social housing estates. This association persists, as evidenced in spatial analyses of police crime statistics and the British Crime Survey (see Trickett *et al.*, 1995). The implication that flows from this association is that something in the community, geographically imagined, causes the crime, and that the community is therefore the appropriate site of preventive intervention. Exactly what it is about the community that causes the crime, and how it might be tackled, is the subject of considerable contention.

Many commentators assume high-crime communities to be pathological, possessing some defect that renders them incapable of being 'normal' or 'healthy'. Such a view is underpinned by various 'criminologies of the other', such as the Chicago perspective, from the original work of Shaw and McKay (1942), which argues that high-crime communities are socially disorganised: they possess a culture that fails adequately to exercise control over its members, and that lacks pro-social norms and values. The solution that flows from the Chicago perspective is to develop and organise communities where no such organisation exists: something attempted by the long-lasting *Chicago Area Project*. In the UK, policy has ploughed a not dissimilar furrow via a number of different urban regeneration schemes since the 1960s, most recently under the mantle of New Labour's *New Deal for Communities* (Gilling, 2007).

The Chicago perspective on the causes of urban crime is conservative but sympathetic, regarding it as a consequence of rapid population turnover and waves of in- and out-migration from the inner city. An equally conservative but less sympathetic (and more moralistic) reading of the same phenomenon locates the problem in an indigenous culture of poverty characterised by inadequate parenting, a lack of responsibility, dependency on welfare 'handouts', and a penchant for immediate gratification expressed through 'lifestyle choices' such as sexual promiscuity, substance misuse, and violent *masculinity*. Some commentators have coined, or perhaps resurrected, a distinctive term—the *underclass*—to describe such a phenomenon (Murray, 1990). For such people, community crime prevention is less of a solution than neo-conservative strategies of containment, control, and *punishment*. However, in so far as some are interested in the organisation of communities as a solution to the problem of crime, they see such organisation coming through the defensive actions of the decent or 'respectable majority' against disrespectable or anti-social others. Defence against crime and anti-social behaviour is thus thought to be the glue that will stick these disorganised communities back together.

A more progressive take on the problems of high-crime communities recognises that the problem is not their level of organisation *per se*, but rather their relationship to broader structural forces that result in the material deprivation of people living within their boundaries, and the cultural knock-on effects that result ultimately in high rates of crime. For example, those living in deprived circumstances, with high levels of social stress, may find it much harder to provide protective factors such as effective parenting, support for education, and pro-social leisure opportunities that can help to insulate children from criminality. Marginalised from the mainstream, they may find it hard to retain a stake in conformity, and may seek out their own delinquent solutions, according to their own particular market positions (Taylor, 1999), as their pathways to 'success' and self-esteem. Here, social crime prevention might involve a combination of redistributive social policies to reduce income inequality and increase *social justice*; improved welfare services that provide access to decent housing, education, and health services; and reforms that enhance the engagement and participation of such people in the democratic processes that govern their lives. It involves a shift, broadly, from exclusion to inclusion; entailing, in Hope's (1995) terms, the strengthening of both the horizontal and vertical dimensions of community linkages.

Criticisms of social crime prevention

Social crime prevention probably has less intuitive appeal than situational crime prevention as a putative solution to crime, because the causes it seeks to address are more distant than the immediate situation, and because the preventive strategies are often uncertain, diffuse, and seemingly only of benefit in the medium- to long-term. It is more likely to find favour amongst those on the political left who support progressive social reforms to counteract the negative criminogenic consequences of market societies. For our purposes, we can summarise in what follows the various criticisms that have been levelled at the approach.

Firstly, there are a range of questions revolving around the issue of effectiveness. Critics (Clarke and Cornish, 1983) have pointed out that what could be regarded as a mass exercise in social crime prevention, namely the establishment of the welfare state from the late-1940s through to the 1970s, coincided not with a period in which national crime rates fell, but rather with a period in which we witnessed a substantial rise, contrary to what many had anticipated. Others (Crawford, 1998) question the logic of such thinking, pointing out that crime rates actually rose faster from the end of the 1970s through to the 1990s—a period marked by the dismantling of parts of the welfare state, and substantially widening income inequalities. The point remains, nevertheless, that the kinds of changes required by social crime prevention, to living standards, quality of life issues, education, parenting, a developing sense of community and so forth, are all essentially long-term changes that are manifestly harder to achieve than the relatively quick and easy manipulations of the physical environment required by the situational approach (Pease, 2002).

On a related point, some might see social crime prevention projects as fundamentally aspirational and utopian, rather than achievable. They are so because they face substantial implementation problems (Hope and Foster, 1992). The general view of risk factors, for example, is that they are most predictive of criminality when they work in combination, and this means that different risk factors have to be addressed at the same time. Yet this requires coordinated action, and a joining-up of different public services that experience of partnership working tells us is, at the very least, problematic (Gilling, 2005). This is particularly the case where, for example, health- or welfare-oriented agencies may be required to prioritise potential offenders as recipients of services such as drug treatment, when such agencies have scarce resources that they would rather devote to client groups they may regard as more deserving. Media stories abound of drug treatment 'queue-jumping' by offenders, or of anti-social youngsters being 'rewarded' with adventure holidays while better behaved children go without.

The difficulties of engaging and building communities are no less challenging than those of partnership working. Moreover, it may be equally hard to foster the support of political decision-makers for social crime prevention schemes that promise only longer-term changes rather than the immediate results that electoral politics demand; that are often very costly (partly because of the inaccuracy of interventions—see below); and that may be perceived by a sceptical and punitive-minded electorate to be helping groups that are essentially undeserving of such help. It is unsurprising, in view of this, that social crime prevention is rarely 'mainstreamed', and often takes the form only of relatively small-scale, time-limited projects and schemes (Crawford, 1998).

A second set of criticisms revolves around the issue of the accuracy of social crime prevention interventions, and the question of whether they hit the right targets, or are themselves the right interventions. The main underlying problem here is that the primary targets of social crime prevention are potential offenders; that is, people who have not yet been processed through the criminal justice system, and who are therefore not officially known. In the absence of 'hard knowledge' of those who are likely to offend, practitioners have to rely upon 'soft knowledge', in the form of social scientific prediction, which as we have seen is based upon the possession of risk factors, or the high-crime location in which a person lives. Yet these predictions are fraught with problems: people may possess certain risk factors and yet not go on to offend, and most people who live in high-crime areas do not in fact turn to crime. This means that interventions may end up being targeted at people who do not really need them for purposes of crime prevention. On the one hand, in the context of scarce resources, this might be seen as a potential waste; though on the other hand, because there are reasons, other than crime prevention, for addressing social deprivation, inadequate parenting, and other risk factors, this might be regarded as a perfectly acceptable opportunity cost, or even a spin-off, of any intervention.

From a perspective of economic rationality, the aspiration to target resources at those who most need them—in this case, those who are most likely to offend—has intuitive appeal, but we should be mindful that in the real world there are other considerations to take into account. One of the problems with highly targeted interventions, even were it possible to be that accurate, is that they can end up being stigmatising. Providing parenting classes just to those whose 'inadequate parenting' has been identified as a risk factor in their children's potential delinquency may do little more than to consolidate those parents' self-images as bad parents. Residents of areas 'benefiting' from crime prevention spending, meanwhile, might not see the benefit when their job applications are turned down by local employers who may be inclined to write those areas off as notorious 'criminal badlands'. Again, criminology—especially the labelling perspective—has had much to say about the dangers of this kind of stigmatisation.

With particular regard to community crime prevention, there is an argument that both target and solution are wrongly conceived. The dominant discourse, as we have seen, is that of the disorganised community; and such discourse is fed by a range of normative assumptions. Community in its idealised form—'the good community'—is imagined as a consensual, cooperative, and essentially crime-free environment. The logic runs that high-crime neighbourhoods must lack this idealised form of community, and thus community is the solution, to be implanted from outside. Notwithstanding the formidable obstacles confronted by those seeking to implant community where it does not appear to exist, the normative ideal itself perhaps does not exist either. Thus, relatively low-crime middle class neighbourhoods, which are thought to be the bastions of the good community, are often no such thing (Crawford, 1998), and the putative solution of an homogeneous, close-knit territorial community is increasingly anachronistic as the nature of community life is changing. Many of us, for example, are more likely to be familiar with the *Neighbours* of Ramsay Street, than with those actually living next door.

Moreover, just as 'the good community' is not necessarily the solution to high-crime neighbourhoods, so the disorganised community is not necessarily the problem. There are some very well-organised communities whose very organisation—think of mafias or youth gangs—is a major source of the crime problem. The problem to be tackled, then, may be more about organisation, and particularly *differential* organisation and the conflict it can create, than about disorganisation. This issue applies also more generally: community crime prevention tends to hold within its sights the organised or disorganised street crimes of the relatively marginalised working and non-working classes, and thereby loses sight of the often more highly organised corporate and state crimes that can inflict much more harm on society.

With regard to targeting, risk factors work in combination, in complex ways. Some risks may be manifestations of other risks, and so addressing the former makes little sense without addressing the latter. For example, it may be that inadequate parenting has a lot to do with living in conditions of social deprivation. Consequently, establishing parenting classes to improve the quality of parenting is likely to have a limited impact if the social deprivation is not also tackled. As a further example, in recent years considerable faith has been placed in cognitive-behavioural programmes as a means of preventing crime. Such programmes aim, in effect, to improve the quality of an individual's thinking and decision making. Individuals who are highly impulsive, for example, and who might resort too quickly to violence, may be taught to curb their impulsiveness, and thus their violence. Impulsiveness in this instance is the risk factor that a cognitive-behavioural programme would aim to address. Yet it may be that this impulsiveness is born of other risk factors, such as social deprivation, which is well known, criminologically-speaking, for creating a strain, or a sense of frustration and powerlessness. This may be at the root of the problem of impulsiveness, and therefore if the deprivation is not addressed the likely effectiveness of cognitive-behavioural programmes may be quite limited. In support of such a point, Newburn (2007), cites the results of a Home Office study which shows that whilst young people on a cognitive-behavioural programme offended less than a matched group of young offenders in the first year after the programme, in the second year there was no discernible difference—the effects of the programme appeared to have worn off.

The third general criticism that can be directed at social crime prevention is that, like situational crime prevention, it can produce unwanted side-effects. Risk-based thinking has its own dynamic which can end up widening the net of *social control*, and a good example of this is the way that developmental crime prevention has extended its reach to the foetal stage: we can now identify children at risk of criminality before they have been born, by targeting their risky mothers, and 'helping' them with parenting skills and other forms of social support. When such help is offered on a voluntary basis this may be just about acceptable, but where compulsion or coercion is involved, there are major ethical concerns.

Another potential side-effect is that of *up-tariffing*. What this means is that if someone commits a crime despite all the preventive support that they have been provided with, they may end up being treated more harshly than they would have been had the support not been provided in the first place. Their offending effectively means that they stand accused not only of committing a crime, but also of failing to respond positively to the 'help' that was on offer. Faced with such offenders, sentencers may feel obliged to offer fewer 'last chances', and to move quickly from similar forms of help to tougher sentences, culminating in relatively premature recourse to custody.

Finally, social crime prevention increases the risk of the *criminalisation of social policy*. This means that social policy measures come to be defined increasingly in terms of the specific aim of crime prevention: crime prevention becomes their principal rationale. Two problems accrue from this. Firstly, we lose sight of other rationales for social policy measures, such as the pursuit of social justice. We might try to lift people out of deprivation, for example, in order to create a more equal and just society, not simply because it may be a way of stopping them from committing crime. Secondly, if social policy measures fail to work as tools for crime prevention—and we have discussed many problems that can make their failure highly probable—then a rationale for their continued use becomes harder to find. The criminalisation of social policy therefore threatens to chip away at the edges of a welfare state and its associated social rights that were hard won in the 1940s, only to become increasingly vulnerable in more recent times.

REVIEW QUESTIONS

1 Set out the distinguishing features of developmental crime prevention and community crime prevention.

2 Summarise the main criticisms levelled at social crime prevention.

CONCLUSION

In this chapter we have reviewed crime prevention as a distinctive area of policy and practice that takes place beyond the boundaries of the criminal justice system. Its emergence over the last few decades was attributed to a number of factors. These include criminological changes in which explanatory attention has shifted from 'the other' to those features of 'everyday life', embedded in physical situations, that make them vulnerable to motivated offenders. They also include a growing understanding of the limited reach of the criminal justice system, and a growing concern about the ineffectiveness of criminal justice responses. As one might expect, however, the criminal justice system has not simply taken this lying down, and since the pessimistic low-water mark of the 'nothing works' era, various attempts have been made to improve the effectiveness of criminal justice, or at least to assert it through a rhetorical appeal to 'what works', which spans, for example, cognitive-behavioural programmes for offenders, but also high-profile measures such as zero-tolerance and intelligence-led policing.

The rise of crime prevention also was attributed to the complex changes comprising globalisation, which have made governments keener to search for non-state solutions to problems such as crime, in order to minimise the fiscal burden, and to keep the economies of nation states competitive in the global marketplace. Crime prevention is attractive here because it opens up spaces for *privatisation*, and for increasing the responsibility of private citizens for their own safety and security. A significant problem, however, is that this neo-liberal agenda must contend with another side-effect of globalisation, to which it has itself contributed, namely the growth of insecurity. This means that at exactly the same time as governments seek to spread the responsibility for crime prevention beyond the state, growing insecurity results in growing demands for protection. The well-off may be able to protect themselves through the purchase of various preventive technologies and services, but others demand not so much crime prevention as more traditional articles of faith, such as 'more bobbies on the beat', and certain punishment for offenders. This lands governments with a 'sovereignty predicament' (Garland, 2001), and helps to explain why, at the same time as we have witnessed the growth of crime prevention, we have seen a significant expansion in policing—particularly through 'the *extended policing family*' (Crawford and Lister, 2004)—as well as a marked increase in the use of punitive sanctions and the size of prison populations. It is important, then, that we analyse crime prevention within its wider context, in order to understand the pressures to which it is subject.

We have seen that crime prevention ultimately boils down to approaches that rest upon different understandings of the causes of crime, namely situational crime prevention and social crime prevention. Situational crime prevention now boasts an array of often highly creative techniques oriented towards the manipulation of opportunities that makes crime harder to commit. Social crime prevention incorporates developmental measures that seek in effect to neutralise the risk factors that threaten to propel risky individuals—particularly young people—into crime, and community measures that seek variously to bring organisation to disorganised communities, or to strengthen communities by addressing the structural disadvantages that have resulted, ultimately, in their social exclusion.

Each approach has its attractions, but also its flaws, though these are often specific to particular measures, deployed in particular contexts, rather than to the approach as a whole (not all situational crime prevention results in displacement, for example, whilst not all social crime prevention hits the wrong targets). The existence of situational and social crime prevention attests not only to different understandings of the causes of crime, but also to contested understandings. That is to say that the choice of how best to prevent crime is not just a technical one, although it is often dressed up in this way by rationalistic problem-oriented processes, devices such as the Problem Analysis Triangle, and preventive technologies themselves, such as CCTV, that have an intuitive, common-sense appeal.

Deciding how best to prevent crime is also a political issue that involves, for example, implicit or explicit consideration about where the moral responsibility for the causes of crime lie; the limits of state action; and the proper role of the private market, and of civil society, in the provision of security. Within the policy domain criminologists and practitioners sometimes take up entrenched positions: they may be for situational crime prevention and against social crime prevention, or vice versa. Others see the merits of combining approaches, perhaps using one approach to overcome the deficiencies of the other, and there is some virtue in this, though it must be recognised that such outcomes are as much political as they are pragmatic.

Attention should be focused, too, on where decisions about crime prevention are taken. The dilemma for governments here is that successful crime prevention often depends upon those beyond the state—private citizens and businesses—taking more responsibility for their security, and yet governments lack much in the way of leverage to encourage such responsibility. They do, however, have leverage over local state agencies, and, as we have seen, pressure has been exerted upon them to work in partnership with themselves and with non-state actors in developing local strategies to prevent or reduce local crime problems. Consequently, a lot of the political baggage surrounding crime prevention—particularly social crime prevention, which remains a largely state-led activity—is loaded on to these partnerships: it is here that decisions are taken about which problems should be prioritised, how they should be tackled, and so forth. It is here, then, that the 'big' political issues noted above are worked through, though they are also overlain with a host of other political issues relating, for example, to relations between central and local government, and between different local agencies. These are the most obvious and researchable sites of crime prevention politics, although we need to consider also the role of increasingly important non-state actors, whether it be the owners of shopping malls who ban 'street people' from their premises, or the actions of private householders, whose insecurity may gain expression through an exclusionary and often racialised 'othering' of those such as young people hanging around on street corners, whom they perceive to pose a threat to their security. Crime prevention, it turns out, is about so much more than 'what works'.

QUESTIONS FOR DISCUSSION AND EXERCISES

1 We often do not recognise the widespread adoption of situational crime prevention techniques because they have become so absorbed into our daily routines that we take them for granted. One way of recognising their pervasiveness is to deliberately look for them. Using Clarke and Eck's (2003) list of 25 situational techniques as a checklist, see how many different techniques you can find. This is something that is good to do in groups, and digital photographs can be used, appropriately, to evidence what you have found.

2 As noted in the chapter, Oscar Newman's idea of defensible space has been incorporated into a set of *Secured By Design* principles used and promoted by the police. These principles are accessible as a downloadable design guide from the *Secured By Design* website <http://www.securedbydesign.com>. Download a copy of the SBD principles, and use them to assess different parts of the physical environment within which you live. Again, if this is done in groups different groups can go to different specified areas and compare their findings, using digital photography as evidence.

3 CCTV cameras have their advocates and their detractors. Around locations in which they are used (e.g. town centres, nightspots, shopping centres, bus or railway stations, university campuses, etc.) you could conduct a short survey that sought to determine, for example, whether respondents were aware of the cameras' presence; whether they made them feel safer; whether they thought they were effective as a deterrent or an aid to detection; whether they thought they were an intrusion into their privacy, and so on. It is worth collecting basic details about, for example, respondents' age, *gender*, and ethnicity, so that results can be broken down accordingly—although bear in mind the sampling limitations of these kinds of street surveys, and consider the need to gain the permission of landowners when conducting the surveys.

4 It was mentioned in the conclusion that the politics of crime prevention were often played out in the local *Crime and Disorder Reduction Partnerships* (CDRPs) that were established following the Crime and Disorder Act 1998. These CDRPs produce reviewable strategies that set out what they intend to do locally to reduce crime; and they are normally published on local authority or dedicated CDRP websites. Download a CDRP strategy and read its contents. Try to get a sense of the balance the strategy seeks to strike between social and situational measures, for example. In view of the discussion in this chapter (about crime prevention being about measures occurring beyond the criminal justice system, but crime reduction being about measures that more closely involve criminal justice agencies), you might also see to what extent the strategy is dominated by the actions of criminal justice agencies. If this exercise is done in groups, different groups could look at different CDRP strategies: urban CDRPs could be compared with rural ones; high-crime areas could be compared with low-crime ones; or traditionally Labour-controlled areas could be compared with traditionally Conservative-controlled ones. If there is uniformity across different kinds of areas consideration might be given to how far the contents of strategies are influenced by Home Office priorities 'from above'.

5 Utilising some of the contents of this chapter and further reading, hold a debate on the following question: which is best, situational crime prevention or social crime prevention? The debate will require two 'sides', and students should be encouraged to suspend their own personal views, if necessary, in order to argue the case for the particular side on which they have been placed.

GUIDE TO FURTHER READING

In the last decade or so an increasing number of books have appeared on the subject of crime prevention. Although it is now a little dated, Crawford's *Crime Prevention and Community Safety* (1998) provides a good, well-informed, and comprehensive introduction to the subject area. The collection edited by Hughes, McLaughlin, and Muncie, entitled *Crime Prevention and Community Safety: New Directions* (2002) offers a more detailed and advanced conceptual engagement with the subject matter, whilst also having a number of chapters on policy issues in the UK, and comparative developments elsewhere. Gilling's *Crime Reduction and Community Safety* (2007) provides a specific more recent account of the direction in which crime prevention has been pulled under successive New Labour governments. Clarke's *Situational Crime Prevention: Successful Case Studies* (1997) usefully showcases a range of situational measures, whilst Clarke and Eck's *Become a Problem-Solving Crime Analyst in 55 Small Steps* (2003) provides a valuable insight into the technical, if not the equally important political, aspects of crime prevention practice.

WEB LINKS

The internet has become an important source of information about crime prevention, and it has been used to establish an international marketplace for the exchange of ideas and initiatives. Most internet resources reflect the practical concerns of their host agencies and are oriented towards practitioners: thus, they are there to inform about good practice, to identify what works, and to promote the cause of crime prevention more generally. This does not mean that they are necessarily entirely uncritical, but we should not expect to find a lot of critical social scientific knowledge and understanding in their content. They are, nevertheless, useful sources of information for the development of such knowledge and understanding. Here are five web links that merit further exploration:

http://www.securedbydesign.com

This is a link to the police-led Secured by Design (SBD) scheme, which promotes the idea of designing out crime, particularly at the planning stage. Intellectually indebted to the work of Oscar Newman, the website contains a lot of practical information on the SBD scheme, and it offers an insight into the work of practitioners in this area of crime prevention.

http://www.crimeprevention.gov.au

This is a link to the Australian Government's national community crime prevention programme, a federally-funded initiative. From this website there are links to reports and evaluations of projects funded by the national programme, and there is also practical advice and guidance, targeted both at practitioners and at members of the public.

http://www.crimereduction.homeoffice.gov.uk

This is a link to the UK Government's crime reduction activities, hosted by the Home Office. It is a veritable mine of information that is generally well organised. Through the website one can access a number of important policy documents that seek to shape local practice. There is also a lot of good practice advice and guidance targeted at practitioners, as well as links to research reports, the conclusions of which have helped to shape such advice and guidance.

http://www.crime-prevention-intl.org/

This is a link to the International Centre for the Prevention of Crime (ICPC), established in the mid-1990s. ICPC comprises a network of policy makers, practitioners, and academics, brought together by a common commitment to the United Nations' guidelines for the prevention of crime. There is a strong interest in the promotion of best practice, and the website is a good place from which to access a range of publications, many involving elements of comparative analysis. The website also hosts the proceedings of annual conferences, and there is a newsletter, the International Observer, which is a good source of information on contemporary developments.

http://www.urbansecurity.org

This is a link to the European Forum for Urban Safety (EFUS). EFUS comprises a network of over 300 European urban local authorities, all with a shared interest in what they call urban safety, which is broadly the same thing as community safety. The members are particularly interested in promoting the role of local authorities in the delivery of urban safety. Through the website one can access relevant policy documents of different European countries, some comparative studies, and advice and guidance themed by specific crime-related problems, such as youth crime, or the fear of crime.

REFERENCES

Barclay, G. and Tavares, C. (1999) *Digest 4: Information on the Criminal Justice System in England and Wales.* London: Home Office Research Development and Statistics.

Brantingham, P. and Faust, F. (1976) 'A conceptual model of crime prevention'. *Crime and Delinquency* 22: 284–96.

Brody, S. (1976) *The Effectiveness of Sentencing.* Research Study Number 35. London: Home Office.

Clarke, K. (2007) 'Prevention and early intervention with young children: the Sure Start programme'. *Criminal Justice Matters* 69: 6–7.

Clarke, R. (1980) Situational crime prevention: theory and practice. *British Journal of Criminology* 20: 136–47.

Clarke, R. (ed) (1997) *Situational Crime Prevention: Successful Case Studies* (2nd edn). New York: Harrow and Heston.

Clarke, R. and Cornish, D. (eds) (1983) *Crime Control in Britain: a Review of Policy Research.* Albany: State University of New York Press.

Clarke, R. and Eck, J. (2003) *Become a Problem-Solving Crime Analyst in 55 Small Steps.* London: Jill Dando Institute of Crime Science. Downloadable in sections from <http://www.ucl.ac.uk/jdi/publications/other_publications/55steps.php>.

Clarke, R. and Hough, M. (eds) (1980) *The Effectiveness of Policing.* Farnborough: Gower.

Crawford, A. (1998) *Crime Prevention and Community Safety*. Harlow: Addison Wesley Longman.

Crawford, A. and Lister, S. (2004) *The Extended Policing Family: Visible Patrols in Residential Areas*. York: Joseph Rowntree Foundation.

van Dijk, J. (1990) 'Crime prevention policy: current state and future prospects' in G. Kaiser and H. Albrecht (eds) *Crime and Criminal Policy in Europe*. Freiburg: Max Planck Institute.

van Dijk, J. and de Waard, J. (1991) 'A two-dimensional typology of crime prevention projects'. *Criminal Justice Abstracts* 23: 483–503.

Farrington, D. and Coid, J. (eds) (2002) *Early Prevention of Adult Anti-Social Behaviour*. Cambridge: Cambridge University Press.

Felson, M. (1994) *Crime and Everyday Life*. Thousand Oaks: Pine Forge Press.

Garland, D. (2001) *The Culture of Control*. Oxford: Oxford University Press.

Gill, M. and Spriggs, A. (2005) *Assessing the Impact of CCTV*. Home Office Research Study 292. London: Home Office.

Gilling, D. (1997) *Crime Prevention: Theory, Policy and Politics*. London: UCL Press.

Gilling, D. (2005) 'Crime prevention partnerships' in N. Tilley (ed) *Handbook of Crime Prevention and Community Safety*. Cullompton: Willan.

Gilling, D. (2007) *Crime Reduction and Community Safety: Labour and the Politics of Local Crime Control*. Cullompton: Willan.

Gladstone, F. (1980) *Co-ordinating Crime Prevention Efforts*. London: HMSO.

Graham, J. (1998) 'Promoting a less criminal society. What works in preventing criminality' in P. Goldblatt and C. Lewis (eds) *Reducing Offending: An Assessment of Research Evidence on Ways of Dealing with Offending Behaviour*. Home Office Research Study 187. London: Home Office.

Home Office (1991) *Safer Communities: The Local Delivery of Crime Prevention Through the Partnership Approach*. London: Home Office.

Hope, T. (1995) 'Community crime prevention' in M. Tonry and D. Farrington (eds) *Building a Safer Society*. Chicago: Chicago University Press.

Hope, T. and Foster, J. (1992) 'Conflicting forces: changing the dynamics of crime and community on a 'problem' estate'. *British Journal of Criminology* 32(4): 488–504.

Hough, M., Clarke, R., and Mayhew, P. (1980) 'Introduction' in R. Clarke and P. Mayhew (eds) *Designing Out Crime*. London: HMSO.

Hughes, G. (1998) *Understanding Crime Prevention*. Buckingham: Open University Press.

Hughes, G., McLaughlin, E., and Muncie, J. (eds) (2002) *Crime Prevention and Community Safety: New Directions*. London: Sage.

Jeffery, C. (1971) *Crime Prevention Through Environmental Design*. Englewood Cliffs: Prentice Hall.

Knox, J., Pemberton, A., and Wiles, P. (2000) *Partnerships in Community Safety: An Evaluation of Phase 2 of the Safer Cities Programme*. London: DETR.

Mayhew, P., Clarke, R., Sturman, A., and Hough, J.M. (1976) *Crime as Opportunity*. Research Study Number 34. London: Home Office.

McSmith, A. (2008) 'The big question: are CCTV cameras a waste of money in the fight against crime?' *The Independent*, 7 May 2008.

Muncie, J. (1999) *Youth and Crime. A Critical Introduction*. London: Sage.

Murray, C. (1990) *The Emerging British Underclass*. London: Institute for Economic Affairs.

National Audit Office (2006) *Sure Start Children's Centres*. London: The Stationery Office.

Newburn, T. (2007) *Criminology*. Cullompton: Willan.

Newman, O. (1973) *Defensible Space*. London: Architectural Press.

Norris, C. and Armstrong, G. (1999) 'CCTV and the social structuring of surveillance' in K. Painter and N. Tilley (eds) *Surveillance of Public Space: CCTV, Street Lighting and Crime Prevention*. Monsey: Criminal Justice Press.

O'Malley, P. (1992) 'Risk, power and crime prevention.' *Economy and Society* 21: 252–75.

O'Malley, P. and Hutchinson, S. (2007) 'Reinventing prevention: why did 'crime prevention' develop so late?' *British Journal of Criminology* 47(3): 373–89.

Pease, K. (2002) 'Crime reduction' in M. Maguire, R. Morgan, and R. Reiner (eds) *The Oxford Handbook of Criminology* (3rd edn). Oxford: Oxford University Press.

Pugh, G. (2007) 'Policies in the UK to promote the well-being of children and young people' in A. France and R. Homel (eds) *Pathways and Crime Prevention: Theory, Policy and Practice*. Cullompton: Willan.

Shaftoe, H. (2004) *Crime Prevention: Facts, Fallacies and the Future*. Basingstoke: Palgrave Macmillan.

Shaw, C. and McKay, H. (1942) *Juvenile Delinquency and Urban Areas*. Chicago: University of Chicago Press.

Sutton, M. (1996) *Implementing Crime Prevention Schemes in a Multi-agency Setting: Aspects of Process in the Safer Cities Programme*. Research Study Number 160. London: Home Office.

van Swaaningen, R. (2002) 'Towards a replacement discourse on community safety: lessons from the Netherlands' in G. Hughes, E. McLaughlin, and J. Muncie (eds) *Crime Prevention and Community Safety: New Directions*. London: Sage.

Taylor, I. (1999) *Crime in Context*. Cambridge: Polity Press.

Tonry, M. and Farrington, D. (1995) 'Strategic approaches to crime prevention' in M. Tonry and D. Farrington (eds) *Building a Safer Society*. Chicago: Chicago University Press.

Trickett, A., Ellingworth, D., Hope, T., and Pease, K. (1995). 'Crime victimization in the eighties—changes in area and regional inequality.' *British Journal of Criminology* 35(3): 343–59.

Welsh, B. and Farrington, D. (2002) *Crime Prevention Effects of Closed Circuit Television: a Systematic Review*. Home Office Research Study 252. London: Home Office.

2

Police and policing

Stuart Lister

INTRODUCTION

This chapter provides an introduction to the role of the police in England and Wales. It highlights what the police do, how they do it, and from where they draw their authority. In so doing, it introduces students to some of the key debates and recurring themes related to the police and policing. Studying the police in the broader context of 'criminal justice' is important, not least because it helps to explain the focus of the 'criminal justice system' on specific types of offences and certain groups of offenders. More broadly, the chapter aims to highlight the interconnections between 'policing' and 'justice'. The main sections of the chapter are structured as follows. First, the role of the police is introduced; second, the way the police are organised to deliver policing services is described; third, the main legal powers used within 'street policing' are explored; fourth, the role of *discretion* and culture in police work is explained; finally, issues concerning the accountability, governance, and control of the police are outlined.

BACKGROUND

Accounting for 61 per cent of the £22.7 billion of government expenditure on the criminal justice system (Solomon *et al.*, 2007), the police are the largest and most visible agency involved in the criminal justice process. Indeed, the very sight of a patrolling police officer serves as a tangible reminder of the authority of the state to intervene directly in the lives of its citizens. This authority is bestowed in the police by an array of coercive and far-reaching legal powers which they have been granted over time to pursue their broad mandate of providing security, maintaining order, and controlling *crime*. It is these powers, for example, to stop and search, to arrest and to detain, which give the police a central role within the modern criminal justice system. Importantly, as police officers represent the sovereign embodiment of the state and the rule of law, then the values and ethics they enact on the streets can have a broader impact on the legitimacy of the criminal justice system and more generally on perceptions of government. It is therefore important that those delivering policing—whether public or private agents—are rendered accountable to ensure that they use their power justly, humanely, and proportionately.

Since being established by the Metropolitan Police Act of 1829, the police have become a hugely powerful institution of the modern British state. As its main law enforcement agency, they are widely perceived to be *the* professional experts on matters of crime and security, a status that affords them an enormously influential voice within the politics of law and order and, by implication, criminal justice policy. Here it is important to recognise that the values of the police derive from the 'crime fighting' aspects of the role. In order to secure this objective, the police may demand evermore extensive legal powers which potentially erode the basic freedoms of citizenship (e.g. to record the DNA of a person who is arrested but not charged with any offence). Further, they may perceive legal safeguards designed to protect the rights of suspects (e.g. the right to silence) as restricting their effectiveness to control crime. As a consequence, the values of the police sometimes bring them into conflict with other criminal justice agencies, whose overriding concern may be less about ensuring security and repressing crime and more about protecting the innocent and ensuring fairness in the criminal justice process. Equally, it may bring them into conflict with civil liberties groups who desire a society free from intrusive policing and state oppression (Choongh, 1997). Unsurprisingly, the police are a hugely controversial institution.

Procedurally, the police are mostly involved in the front-end of the criminal justice process and have responsibility for detecting crime, apprehending suspects, and collecting evidence used in the *prosecution* of suspects and defendants. They therefore have ownership over proceedings from the initial engagement with an unlawful incident up to the point at which a suspect is 'charged' with an offence. For this reason, the police are often referred to as the 'gatekeepers of the criminal justice system'. This metaphor is helpful in at least three respects. First, it implies the autonomy of the police to determine which individuals are administered in to the criminal justice process. As such, the police act as primary definers of deviance in public places, where patrol takes place. Second, it indicates that the types of offences and offenders prioritised by the police become the main focus of the work of the other criminal justice agencies. Third, it denotes that any errors made by the police over procedural or evidential matters can have a pervasive and amplified impact on the entire justice system, particularly when they lead to *miscarriages of justice* (Walker, 1999).

Despite the potential for police intrusions to impinge on civil liberties, it was not until the 1960s that the police attracted sustained research attention. A series of seminal studies (e.g. Goldstein, 1960; Bittner, 1967; Skolnick, 1966) began to explore the role of the police, the socialisation of police officers, and the way they dispensed authority. These small-scale observational studies took place during an era within criminology when '*labelling theory*' was in the ascendancy (Becker, 1963). Prior to the emergence of this 'interactionist' perspective, criminological enquiry had focused mainly on developing explanatory theories of 'crime' and 'criminals'. Labelling theory developed new and critical ways of thinking about the processes by which people became defined as 'deviant'. Crucially, it led researchers to consider whether those attracting disproportionate levels of adversarial policing were merely a reflection of the stereotypes and biases of those in positions of authority, such as politicians who made the rules and police officers who enforced them. Following this, the discretionary use of authority by police and its links to discriminatory practices in relation to age, *gender*, class, and ethnicity, has been a recurring theme of research on the police (e.g. Smith and Gray, 1983; Young, 1991). Other important studies have considered the extent to which the post-arrest practices of the police subvert the procedural safeguards of suspects (e.g. McConville *et al.*, 1991; see Sanders and Young, 2007). Since the 1970s onwards, a growing number of studies have focused on forms of 'policing beyond government' (e.g. South, 1988; Jones and Newburn, 1998). These studies reflect academic interest in the private security industry, as well as municipal forms of policing (i.e. *the extended policing family*), the role of which is largely focused on the provision of public safety rather than the pursuit or administration of criminal justice (Crawford *et al.*, 2005).

Clearly it is important to distinguish between police and policing, as the two concepts are not synonymous. Policing is a specific aspect of *social control*, which Reiner (2000: 3) defines as 'a set of activities aimed at securing a particular social order, through the creation of systems of surveillance coupled with the threat of sanctions for discovered deviance'. Policing can therefore be undertaken by variety of institutional actors (e.g. public police officers or privately paid nightclub bouncers), but it always serves specific interests and is underpinned by recourse to coercive power. A key issue for criminologists is the source and *legitimacy* of power within policing. The police, whose moral and legal authority is drawn from the state, are defined by Innes (2003: 64) as a 'specific, modern organisation, endowed with the state's legal authority to use physical coercion or the threat of it, to enforce the law in pursuance of the maintenance of social order'. This definition takes its lead from the American sociologist, Egon Bittner, who suggested that, given the breadth of the role, the police ought to be defined in terms of their institutional authority (i.e. how they do it, rather than what they do). For Bittner (1974), the distinguishing feature of the police is the authority to wield legitimate force over the citizenry. Given this text is concerned with criminal justice, the discussion to follow focuses mostly on the police. As suggested above, non-police forms of policing, and particularly so private security, often deal with 'offenders' without recourse to the state's criminal justice system, preferring instead to dispense other, more immediate, forms of 'punishment' such as exclusion from specific territory (e.g. a nightclub or shopping centre) (Crawford et al., 2005).

The role of the police

This section explores the role of the police, which historically has been primarily concerned with the provision of security and the preservation of public tranquillity. Over time the police role has become increasingly complex and diverse in scope, encompassing several overlapping functions. These include order maintenance, crime detection, crime *prevention*, public reassurance, emergency assistance, and traffic management (Morgan and Newburn, 1997; Bowling and Foster, 2002). It is important to recognise that the breadth of the police role gives rise to tensions, in particular, between the law enforcement aspects of police work and more service-orientated tasks.

'Force' versus 'service'?

The *crime control* function of the police emphasises the coercive edge of the role, in which policing takes place *of* communities; service type and assistance-based activities speak to more consensual forms of policing, suggesting it takes place *for* communities. This dichotomy has given rise to a debate about whether the police should be described as a *force* or *a service*. This is important because if the police are to be successful in controlling crime and maintaining order, they require the cooperation and support of the public which is most effectively achieved through consensual rather than coercive methods of policing.

Public narratives of the police role tend to depict it in narrow terms, emphasising its 'crime fighting' responsibilities in which the police enforce the law, detain suspects, investigate crimes, and disrupt criminal activities. Research shows, however, that much of what the police do is unrelated to matters of 'crime'; rather officers spend a greater proportion of their time providing members of the public with general assistance in a variety of emergency and non-emergency situations (Hough, 1985; Skogan, 1990; PA Consulting, 2001). As the police provide a 24-hour emergency response service, they are summoned to deal with a wide range of incidents. Hough's study (1985), for example, found that of 1,944 incidents attended by police patrols about one-third involved a crime incident, with 14 per cent related to accidents, 19 per cent to public order, and 31 per cent to social service. Because this service function is not widely recognised and often concerns 'people plight' (e.g. missing people, lost property, collapsed drunks, persistent beggars and vagrants, psychiatric emergencies, suicide attempts, discovered corpses, etc.), the police have been described as the 'secret social service' (Punch and Naylor, 1973). Yet much service-type work is routinely mundane and contrasts with images held by the public and police alike, of what 'real' police work involves. As a consequence, the implementation of more service-orientated modes of policing (e.g. 'community polic-ing') often face resistance from rank-and-file officers (Reiner, 2000).

Research, however, has queried the orthodoxy that most police work is service-orientated. Some researchers argue the proportion of police time spent dealing with crime-related tasks is likely to be contingent on whether an area is 'low crime' or 'high crime' (Jones *et al.*, 1986). Others have problematised the way incidents dealt with by police are classified as 'crime-related' or otherwise. Simply because an officer does not enforce the law in a given situation does not mean a criminal incident might not have developed had it been dealt with differently. For example, officers may be deployed to a pub where the presence of two groups of rival and rowdy football supporters is threaten-ing disorder. By sending one group of supporters on its way, trouble is averted, no law has been enforced, and no 'crime' occurs. It, therefore, may be more accurate to consider many incidents dealt with by police as 'potential crimes'—incidents that might lead to a crime being committed (Morgan and Newburn, 1997). Research adopting this approach has found that over half of calls to the police could be classified as 'potential crime', with 20 per cent relating to social disorder, 18 per cent to information and service provision, and 8 per cent to traffic issues (Shapland and Vagg, 1990).

Despite the breadth of the role, the police themselves clearly view 'crime fighting' to be their core business, as evidenced by its continued high status within the organisational and *occupational cultures* of the police (Foster, 2003). Government, too, has tended to overlook the breadth of the police role. The White Paper, *Police Reform: A Police Service for the Twenty-first Century*, stated that the '[T]he main job of the police is to catch criminals' (Home Office, 1993, para. 2.3). Over the last decade, this view resulted in performance assessments of the police being narrowly drafted in terms of their effectiveness at con-trolling crime. More recently, however, an important review of policing suggested that levels of public trust and confidence in the police ought to have primacy within police performance assessments (Flanagan, 2008). This proposal recognises that the role of the police is not merely that of a specialist crime-fighting agency, but extends into other aspects of social life, such as providing general assistance, promoting reassurance, and tackling low-level disorder.

Peacekeeping and order maintenance

Transcending the 'force' versus 'service' debate, there is widespread consensus among academics that the primary role of the police is 'peacekeeping' or 'order maintenance' (Morgan and Newburn, 1997). Early studies of the police found that officers seldom invoked their formal legal powers in situations of conflict, but instead typically relied on personal skills combined with the moral and legal authority of their office to negotiate peaceful and consensual outcomes 'in the shadow of the law' (Bittner, 1967; Skolnick, 1966). Officers recognised that enforcing the law potentially aggravates conflict and undermines the function of peacekeeping; consequently, it is only in serious incidents, or when police authority is challenged, that the law, as a last resort, is enforced. Lord Scarman, in his report into the Brixton riots of 1981, drew attention to this tension when he advocated that the overarching goal of the police ought to be preserving public tranquillity (Scarman, 1981). It is in this context that Reiner (2000) suggests that police work mostly involves emergency 'order maintenance', by which he means the settlement of low-level disputes without the need to enforce the law.

The 'order maintenance' function varies in size, scale, and complexity, but also in the level of coercion deployed. It leads police to be deployed to a myriad of situations where there is (at least potential for) social conflict. At one end of the spectrum, paramilitary methods of policing can be adopted to control crowds in 'public order' situations (e.g. political rallies, football matches, industrial disputes); at the other end, police patrols are routinely summoned to restore order to low-level conflicts (e.g. resolving disagreements between neighbours, moving on groups of rowdy children). Order maintenance tasks sharply expose the political edge of policing, for order is always maintained on behalf of vested interests and specifically those who are able to assert their definition of a situation over that of another's. Consider here the routine police task of 'moving on' a group of youths from a specific location whose mere presence may be perceived as threatening by older residents. Police literally act on behalf of one set of community interests against those of another, despite no offence having taken place. Unsurprisingly, therefore, the order maintenance function, and policing in general, can be socially divisive.

Ultimately, the breadth of the police role reflects the wide range of social situations which may require the potential for authoritative interventions based on the legal capacity to use force (Waddington, 1999a). This capacity for decisive action underpins much of what the police do, including the public reassurance and emergency assistance functions. For, as Bittner (1974: 30) suggests, demands on police arise whenever there is 'something that ought not to be happening and about which someone had better do something now!'

REVIEW QUESTIONS

1 Why do the police undertake such a wide range of tasks?

2 Why is there a potential tension between the functions of 'crime control' and 'order maintenance'?

3 What is the distinguishing feature of the police role?

The organisation of the police

This section describes the way police resources are organised to deliver local policing services. As the focus of the section is local policing, it does not discuss those policing bodies that operate at the national level, such as the British Transport Police, the *National Policing Improvement Agency,* and the *Serious and Organised Crime Agency.*

The police workforce

Increased investment in greater numbers of police has become a primary means by which the government attempts to appease public anxieties over law and order (Crawford *et al.*, 2005). As a result, over the last decade the number of police officers has increased to record levels, with almost 142,000 in England and Wales (Bullock, 2008). Almost a quarter of all police officers are female, but this proportion decreases dramatically as one ascends the rank structure (Bullock, 2008). Just over 4 per cent of all officers are from ethnic minority groups, and in the Metropolitan force, by far the most ethnically diverse police force, this figure increases slightly to just over 7 per cent (Bullock, 2008). All police officers enter the organisation as police constables and, on promotion, proceed through the rank structure (see Table 2.1), which means that all senior ranking officers have experience of frontline policing duties.

In addition to police officers, the police employ over 95,000 civilians in police staff roles (Bullock, 2008). Successive governments have promoted greater use of civilians within the police, largely as a means of gaining efficiency savings. As a result, civilians now undertake a wide variety of administrative tasks previously performed by police officers. With the introduction of '*police community support officers*', under the Police Reform Act 2002, they also have an increasing operational role. These civilian, uniformed officers have limited powers and are mostly dedicated to providing high visibility patrols and tackling anti-social behaviour. Since 2003 almost 16,000 police

Table 2.1 The rank structure of the British police

Organisational role	Provincial forces	Metropolitan Police
Strategic managers	Chief Constable	Commissioner
(ACPO ranks)	Deputy Chief Constable	Deputy Commissioner
	Assistant Chief	Assistant Commissioner
	Constable	Deputy Assistant
		Commissioner
		Commander
Middle managers	Chief Superintendent	Chief Superintendent
(Superintending ranks)	Superintendent	Superintendent
Managers	Chief Inspector	Chief Inspector
Supervisors	Inspector	Inspector
Practitioners	Sergeant	Sergeant
(Federated ranks)	Constable	Constable

Source: Adapted from Mawby and Wright (2008: 234)

community support officers have been recruited in England and Wales, reflecting the Government's determination to raise police visibility in local communities. There are also presently over 14,500 'special constables', who are unpaid volunteer police officers working at least four hours per week alongside police officers. They wear uniforms, have full powers of the constable and reflect the imagery of the 'citizen in uniform', which has been central to the construction of legitimacy within the British police (Reiner, 2000).

Police organisational structure

The police service in England and Wales has a devolved structure, which presently comprises 43 local police forces. Police forces are autonomous units which represent the way the police organise and manage resources to provide geographic coverage across the whole country. In Scotland there are eight police forces, and Northern Ireland has one police force. Of the police forces of England and Wales, 41 are provincial forces whose boundaries map on to one or more councils, and two cover London, the Metropolitan Police, and the City of London Police (the latter being a minute force covering the square mile of the city's financial district). There are eight so-called 'Metropolitan' forces (Greater Manchester; City of London; Merseyside; Metropolitan Police; Northumbria; South Yorkshire; West Midlands; and West Yorkshire) which police the main population centres and their outlying areas. These 'urban' forces have far greater resources than other (more rural) forces because the larger populations they police give rise to greater demands. For example, the eight Metropolitan forces, which experience relatively high crime rates, account for 47 per cent of all serving police officers. The largest force, the Metropolitan Police Service, employs over 31,000 police officers, which accounts for 22 per cent of all officers (Bullock, 2008). By contrast, smaller forces experiencing lower levels of crime, such as Bedfordshire and Warwickshire, have little more than 1,000 police officers (Bullock, 2008).

Overtime, police forces have been subject to amalgamation, resulting in fewer covering larger areas. This shift has brought various organisational benefits, including efficiency savings arising from economies of scale, greater standardisation of policy and practice, more functional specialisation of roles, and increased capacity to respond to unforeseen upswings in demand for service (Stallion and Wall, 1999). It has also facilitated greater centralised control of local police forces by the *Home Office*, which arguably has been detrimental to the British tradition of delivering policing which is community-focused and locally-accountable. Debates over the optimal size and number of police forces reflect on-going struggles between national and local stakeholders over the nature of the police service and the way it is governed and made accountable (Jones, 2003). Although a recent Home Office proposal to upscale local police forces into 'regional forces' was unsuccessful (see HMIC, 2005), the efficiency pressures which motivated it are unlikely to ease. Hence, the argument for larger police forces is likely to be recurring and, if historical trends continue with the same trajectory, ultimately successful.

For operational and management purposes police forces divide their territory into police divisions, which are commonly referred to as 'Basic Command Units' (BCUs). These are the units of organisation that actually deliver policing services to local communities.

To facilitate inter-agency working with *'Crime and Disorder Reduction Partnerships'*, the boundaries of BCUs are usually coterminous with local authority districts (hence the Metropolitan Police Service has 32 divisions, one for each London borough). BCUs are overseen by a divisional commander who receives strategic policy directives as well as specialist operational and organisational support from force headquarters, where the force's senior command team is located.

The division of labour in the police

The bulk of operational resources in police divisions are typically allocated between three types of police team, 'relief teams', 'neighbourhood teams', and 'detective teams'. Sometimes referred to as '24/7 responsive policing', relief teams work time-based shifts enabling a 'round the clock' response to calls for service. They have a wide range of generic duties including attending court, engaging in special activities (e.g. public order events, specialist operations, etc.), conducting routine enquiries, and patrolling on foot or, more usually, in marked vehicles (Smith and Gray, 1983). As relief teams are tasked to respond reactively to high priority calls from the public (e.g. emergency incidents, crimes in progress, etc.), their function has been described as 'fire-brigade policing'. The level of patrol they can provide, however, is often undermined by various factors including levels of sickness, training requirements, and the abstraction of officers to undertake other duties (PA Consulting, 2001). Moreover, a recent study found the paperwork demands of dealing with suspects and preparing prosecution files led relief officers to spend as much time in the police station as they do on the streets (Chatterton and Bingham, 2006).

Whereas relief teams tend to operate across the entire district of a BCU, 'neighbourhood policing teams' are dedicated to more localised sectors. Across the 43 police forces, there are now 3,600 such teams comprising 13,000 police officers and 16,000 police community support officers (Flanagan, 2008). Rolled-out nationally in 2005, *'neighbourhood policing'* reflects the Government's wish to improve public confidence in the police, reduce fear of crime, and tackle anti-social behaviour (see Home Office, 2004). Part of its ambition, therefore, is to provide a visible, accessible, and familiar style of policing. As neighbourhood officers, in effect, have organisational ownership over local areas, they are expected to adopt longer-term and problem-solving approaches to public safety concerns (Home Office, 2004). Recent research, however, suggests that neighbourhood officers are frequently pulled (back) into responsive policing duties, as the establishment of neighbourhood teams has eroded staffing levels among relief teams (Chatterton and Bingham, 2006). This paradoxical situation demonstrates that the 'emergency service' function always gains priority over other (less urgent) demands for service (e.g. reassurance patrols). Moreover, it reveals the tensions within operational policing which emerge due to the breadth of the police role and the multiple demands to which it gives rise.

The Criminal Investigation Department (CID) has responsibility for investigating crimes of a more serious nature (e.g. robbery and serious wounding). Accounting for some 15 per cent of police resources (Audit Commission, 1996), CID work is generally accorded high status by officers because of its 'crime fighting' focus. Its officers are plain-clothed detectives who work mostly reactively, conducting enquiries and collecting evidence by talking to victims, suspects, and witnesses (Bayley, 1994). Increasingly they also work proactively, gathering intelligence about persons suspected of criminal intent or involvement, for example, through covert surveillance and the use of informants (Maguire, 2008). Not all crimes brought to the attention of the CID are investigated, nor are all offences investigated with the same degree of rigour (see Macpherson, 1999). Bayley (1994) suggests two factors influence the decision to investigate; firstly, the likelihood of gaining evidence sufficient for a successful prosecution, which itself is strongly influenced by the identification of a suspect, and secondly, the seriousness of the offence. Critics have argued that investigative work is less concerned with 'searching for the truth' and more with building a case against a known suspect (McConville *et al.*, 1991). Other (persistent) concerns about the work of the CID include its ineffectiveness at catching criminals, unethical relationships with 'criminals' and informers, corruption and abuses of power, intrusive methods of investigation, and a lack of transparency and accountability (Newburn, 1999; Maguire, 2008).

REVIEW QUESTIONS

1 Why is it important for the police workforce to become more diverse?

2 What are the arguments for and against larger police forces?

3 What functional differences exist between different types of police team?

Police powers and street policing

This section describes the main legal powers that police use when patrolling. The main legal framework of police powers is the Police and Criminal Evidence Act 1984 (PACE) and accompanying Codes of Practice. Although, as mentioned earlier, police officers tend to dispense their authority without recourse to their formal coercive powers, it is the option to use them which underpins all consensual methods of policing (Sanders and Young, 2000). Formal police powers have an important role within the investigation of crime, for example, allowing a person suspected of an offence to be stopped and searched, then arrested and detained in police custody for questioning. They are controversial because, on the one hand, they offer a source of protection to communities, whereas on the other, they can have significant and detrimental implications for the rights of the individual. In order to balance this tension, the exercise of police powers is governed by legal rules which seek to place constraints upon the way in which they can be used. This means that anyone can challenge in court the legality of their use.

Debates over police powers and the regulation of police behaviour reflect tensions between different approaches to the criminal justice process (Sanders and Young, 2007). Those preferring a more laissez faire or 'crime control' approach argue that procedural safeguards for suspects (i.e. those who remain innocent until found guilty) hamper police efficiency by restricting what officers can legally do to investigate crime, but also 'tying them up' in bureaucratic (i.e. paperwork) obligations (e.g. Oxford, 1986). Preventing police abuses of power and miscarriages of justice, however, is important not simply for moral reasons but also for instrumental ones. Public cooperation is a vital component of effective policing, not least because most crimes are solved by information received from the public and not by sleuth-type processes of investigation (Bayley, 1994). The ensuing discussion is selective not comprehensive and focuses on three widely used powers that are available to police officers.

Stop and search

The legal authority to stop and search is a controversial and widely debated power. If used in an oppressive and discriminatory manner it can have severe implications for the rights of individuals to walk the streets free of police intrusion, but also for police–community relations (Bowling and Philips, 2002). Police are empowered to stop and search people under various pieces of legislation, including PACE 1984, the Criminal Justice and Public Order Act 1994, and the Terrorism Act 2000.

PACE 1984 introduced a national uniform power to stop and search. It contains various safeguards over how the power can be used. Officers can only stop and search people or vehicles where there is 'reasonable grounds for suspicion' that evidence of stolen goods, weapons, or other prohibited items will be found. 'Reasonable suspicion' must have an objective basis and cannot be supported by personal factors such as the age, race, appearance, and previous convictions. Further, suspects can only be detained for an amount of time that is reasonable to complete the search, more intimate searches must be undertaken out of public view, and details of the constable, as well as the grounds for the search and a record of it, must be made available to the person being searched.

A key concern about the powers is the extent to which legal safeguards inhibit police behaviour. Research shows use of the powers is commonly based on unsubstantiated suspicion (Quinton, et al., 2000). Since 1992 the proportion of all recorded stop and searches leading to an arrest has varied between 11 and 13 per cent (Sanders and Young, 2007). The vagueness and subjectivity of the concept of 'reasonable suspicion' gives much scope to officers to justify post hoc their use of the power in relation to the situational circumstances (Sanders and Young, 2008). Indeed, the relevant Code of Practice states reasonable suspicion can sometimes exist without specific information, for instance, where in certain contexts someone's behaviour is associated with criminality (Rowe, 2008). For this reason, Sanders and Young (2008) describe the powers of stop and search as an example of an 'enabling rule' that officers may invoke to legitimate their use of authority in a wide variety of situational contexts.

Concerns have also been raised over the effectiveness of monitoring procedures designed to regulate the use of the power. Dixon et al. (1989) found that only one-quarter of supervising officers checked the paperwork that officers are required to complete when they have used the powers. Nor do officers always comply with this requirement. Official police statistics show that during 1999 there were 825,000 recorded 'stop and searches' in England and Wales, yet the comparable figure estimated by the British Crime Survey was 1.1 million (Clancy et al., 2001). It is widely accepted, therefore, that officers have much discretion over how they use stop and search powers.

Arrest

Arrest is a pre-cursor to detention and charge, and has become the primary means by which the formal investigative process begins—and, indeed, PACE 1984 prohibits the interviewing of suspects prior to arrest. Prior to 2005, the presence of a legal distinction between 'arrestable' and 'non-arrestable' sought to ensure that the power of arrest was exercised proportionately to the circumstances, such that people were not arrested and detained for relatively trivial (i.e. 'non-arrestable') offences (e.g. common assault and careless driving). Subsequently, however, the power has been broadened such that the police can now arrest anyone in circumstances where they reasonably believe it necessary for the purpose of crime investigation (Sanders and Young, 2007). This power extends to anyone the police reasonably suspect is committing, is about to commit, or has already committed an offence. When making an arrest officers are entitled to use 'reasonable force', under the Criminal Law Act 1967. In 2006/07, almost 1.5 million people suspected of committing a recordable (notifiable) offence were arrested by police (Ministry of Justice, 2008).

As reasonable suspicion is a necessary ingredient of a lawful arrest, officers have much discretion to invoke the power. Furthermore, the vagueness of the criminal law broadens this discretion, particularly for trivial 'public order' offences (e.g. behaviour causing harassment, alarm, or distress), which, in effect, allow officers to determine when a 'crime' has taken place (Sanders and Young, 2007). Importantly, however, evidence gained under a wrongful arrest is inadmissible at court, which in itself may motivate officers to use the power cautiously and by the 'rulebook'. Nonetheless, the breadth of the power of arrest raises concerns over civil liberties because an arrest can be made in the absence of any evidence of guilt, which potentially gives rise to innocent people being stigmatised and deprived of their liberty merely to 'help police with their enquiries'. This concern is magnified because police investigations often proceed initially by 'rounding up the usual suspects' for the purpose of arrest and interrogation (Maguire, 2008).

Penalty Notices for Disorder

'Penalty Notices for Disorder' (PND) represent a discretionary way the police can deal with low level 'offenders', without the need to process them through the normal channels resulting in attendance at court. Since being introduced by the Criminal Justice Act 2001, the power to issue a PND has become an increasingly important tool within 'street policing', as well as a 'major feature of the criminal justice landscape' (Young, 2008: 166). PNDs are a type of 'fixed penalty' fine that police (and police community support officers) can issue, either in the street or (after arrest) at the police station, to anyone over 16 years of age who they have 'reason to believe' has committed one of 25 eligible offences. Such offences were initially restricted to a range of low-level, anti-social, and nuisance offending (e.g. throwing fireworks, being drunk and disorderly, wasting police time), but have subsequently been expanded to include the 'high volume' offences of theft (under £200 value) and criminal damage (under £500 value). 'Offenders' do not have to accept a PND, but can instead opt to have their case heard in court. Those that do accept the sanction have up to 21 days to pay the fine (of either £50 or £80 dependent on the offence committed), or they face court proceedings and an increase in the value of the fine. In this regard Lister *et al.*, (2008) suggest that issuing a fiscal punishment to individuals who routinely commit retail theft to support their drug use may have the unintended consequence of stimulating the very behaviour the penalty seeks to deter.

PNDs were designed to provide an expedient form of 'summary justice', lowering the administrative time burden on police and courts. In 2006, police issued 201,200 PNDs, equating to just over 14 per cent of all 'offences brought to justice' (i.e. where an offender has been cautioned, convicted, or had the offence taken into consideration) (Ministry of Justice, 2007). Of these, over 60 per cent were issued for the two offence categories of 'behaviour likely to cause harassment, alarm or distress' (82,200) and 'drunk and disorderly' (43,600). Although 52 per cent (104,500) of all PNDs issued in 2006 were paid without any court action (Ministry of Justice, 2007), Young (2008) disputes whether any efficiency savings have been gained from their introduction. He argues that the sanction has led to a form of *'net widening'* and 'mesh thinning' (Cohen, 1985) in which the type of behaviour that officers previously dealt with informally is now being dealt with formally via a PND, resulting in increasing numbers of people being 'swept up' by the powers. Young (2008) also queries the extent to which the use of PNDs enables officers to stay on patrol. Instead, he suggests, officers face a variety of pressures to issue the sanction at a police station (rather than on the 'street'), including the need to sober up potential recipients, to avoid escalating any potential disorder, to confirm the offender's identity, and to collect physical evidence (e.g. fingerprint and DNA) from them.

Perhaps the major concern with the use of PNDs is that, in effect, they allow police to be both 'judge' and 'jury' in the dispensation of punishment, as it is the officers' (legally unchallenged) interpretation of events that establishes someone's culpability (i.e. 'reason to believe'). PNDs therefore circumvent all the legal safeguards that are built in to the criminal justice process, such as judicial oversight and legal representation and advice. As a consequence, Young (2008) criticises the introduction of the PND for extending police discretion at the very margins of criminality (i.e. low-level, disorder-type offences), which, it is claimed, may extend not alleviate the over-representation of some social groups within police and, more broadly, criminal justice statistics.

REVIEW QUESTIONS

1 Why might the concept of 'reasonable suspicion' enable rather than constrain the use of stop and search powers by the police?

2 What concerns potentially arise from the breadth of the power of the arrest?

3 Why might the introduction of the Penalty Notice for Disorder lead more people to come into contact with criminal justice agencies?

Discretion and culture in police work

This section explores the nature and dynamics of police discretion. It also outlines the role of culture in policing, which many scholars argue helps to explain patterns in the use of discretion. Understanding the role of discretion in policing is important because it provides insights into how officers apply the law on the streets, therein turning 'black letter law' into 'blue letter law' (Reiner, 2000).

The role of discretion in policing

Discretion is a routine and inevitable aspect of policing (Newburn and Reiner, 2007). It enables a pragmatic approach to policing in which officers apply the law in a flexible way to fit the circumstances. Crucially, police officers use the law as a resource to secure various objectives, whether imposing order, asserting authority, or acquiring information (Bittner, 1967). In the hands of police officers the law, therefore, becomes a control device, which is not slavishly enforced in a mechanical or universal way. Indeed, research suggests that in some circumstances officers frequently 'turn a blind eye' to a wide range of low-level misdemeanours (Smith and Gray, 1983). In many respects, selective enforcement of the law reflects the need for officers to prioritise their activities, as demand for police time outstrips supply (Rowe, 2008). Moreover, if the law was enforced against every person suspected of an infringement, no matter how minor the offence, then the safety of officers would be jeopardised (i.e. 'discretion is the better part of valour'), police resources would become exhausted, public cooperation with the police would decline, and accusations of state oppressiveness would become vociferous (Reiner, 2000).

Discretion is enabled by certain characteristics of policing and its legal regulation. Although the criminal law provides the tools for policing, offence thresholds and criteria need interpretation in light of circumstances (e.g. when is someone deemed to be drunk and disorderly; what is threatening or insulting behaviour?). Similarly, as we have seen, the elasticity of the rules governing police powers (e.g. 'reasonable suspicion'; 'reasonable use of force') affords officers much latitude over when and how they exercise them (Reiner, 2000). Equally, the contextually-specific nature of police–public encounters means there is no formal 'rule-book' detailing how officers should behave in any given situation. Nor can they usually be instructed, as most routine policing is 'low visibility' work that takes place far beyond the supervisory gaze of the police command and control system (Goldstein, 1960). Importantly, therefore, discretion increases as one descends the police hierarchy, bringing much autonomy to the lower ranks to dispense their authority as they see fit (Wilson, 1968). But the 'problem' of police discretion is not that it exists, rather that it results in the non-uniform, selective, and discriminatory use of authority (Davis, 1975).

The pattern of police discretion

The pattern of police discretion is shaped by variables of class, race, gender, and age, which results in some segments of society receiving a different response from the police than others. Research into policing has consistently found that powerless and minority groups are 'over-policed' and 'under-protected' (Newburn and Reiner, 2007). Hence, police powers are disproportionately used against young, black, lower-class, men, whom patrolling officers come to view as legitimate objects for close scrutiny (i.e. 'police property'). Those who have an offence history or are friends, relatives, or associates of such individuals, become 'known to the police' and, consequently, a target for regular police surveillance and intervention (Lister et al., 2008). Such proactive policing inevitably alienates its recipients, producing and sustaining negative views of police (Fitzgerald *et al.*, 2002); it also has a self-fulfilling dimension, as when stopped these groups are more likely than others to challenge police authority which reinforces the police view that they merit attention (Waddington, 1999a). Moreover, Choongh (1997) argues that such discretionary use of police power is concerned less with investigating and controlling crime, and more with exerting state authority over marginalised individuals and communities. Here, policing becomes an expedient source of punishment, which veers markedly from the principle that punishment by the state ought to be restricted to those who have been found guilty of an offence via the criminal justice process.

Concern about the operation of police discretion has been most acute in regard to race. Allegations of police mistreatment of ethnic minority groups, and particularly the black community, have blighted the police service for over 30 years (Bowling and Philips, 2002). Recent statistics show that black people in England and Wales are about seven times more likely to be stopped and searched and three and a half times more likely to be arrested by the police than white people (Ministry of Justice, 2007). Research also suggests that the use of stop and search powers against black people is often speculative in nature (Norris *et al.*, 1992). Although social pressures and economic disadvantage may lead young black men to disproportionately engage in the types of offences which police perceive to be their core business (e.g. 'street robbery'), racial profiling based on negative stereotyping appears to be a strong contributing factor to this pattern of discretion (Bowling and Philips, 2002). In other words, the skewing of police powers towards groups deemed to be 'police property' is partly explained by such groups being disproportionately involved in some types of offences, but partly it reflects the influence of prejudicial attitudes shaping the use of police discretion (Reiner, 2000). The inverse of this prejudice also shapes the way police respond to female offenders, who are under-represented in police and criminal justice statistics (see Chapter 11). Except for a few offence categories (e.g. prostitution and shop-lifting), females do not fit the police stereotype of offenders; they are therefore less likely to attract police suspicion.

The discriminatory use of discretion against socially and economically marginalised groups also shows itself through inaction, notably when victims of crime receive a poor response from the police. This lack of protection occurs despite the greater risk of victimisation among such groups. It was exemplified by the incompetent police investigation into the unprovoked murder of the black teenager Stephen Lawrence in 1993 (see Macpherson, 1999), which led to the Metropolitan police being labelled 'institutionally racist' (see Case Study). Similarly, research shows that female victims of *domestic violence* have often received an inadequate response from police officers, who—viewing behaviour within a marriage as 'private business'—may opt not to arrest and initiate prosecution proceedings against (male) offenders (Hoyle, 1998).

 CASE STUDY: THE LAWRENCE INQUIRY AND 'INSTITUTIONAL RACISM'

The publication of the Lawrence Inquiry report (Macpherson, 1999) into the failed police investigation of the murder in 1993 of the black teenager Stephen Lawrence was a landmark event for debates about race and racism within policing. The inquiry, which was ordered by the *Home Secretary* after a prolonged campaign by the victim's family and support groups, dramatically re-emphasised the lack of trust and confidence among ethnic minority groups in the police.

The Macpherson report has to be read in the context of the Scarman report (1981) into the Brixton riots, which almost 20 years earlier had blamed the disturbances on the indiscriminate use of police powers by a few 'bad apples'. In contrast to Scarman's 'individualistic' analysis, Macpherson expounded a more collective and 'systemic' notion of discrimination. It identified the failings of the murder investigation as professional incompetence, poor leadership, and *institutional racism*. Crucially, the ethnicity of the victim and the sole witness to the murder, were deemed to be central in shaping the inadequacy of the police response. The report defined 'institutional racism' as:

> The collective failure of an organisation to provide an appropriate and professional service to people because of their colour, culture, or ethnic origin. It can be seen or detected in processes, attitudes and behaviour which amount to discrimination through unwitting prejudice, ignorance, thoughtlessness and racist stereotyping which disadvantage minority ethnic people. (para. 6.34)

The report led to an extensive programme of reform, incorporating over 70 recommendations, which included:

- greater performance monitoring of reporting and recording racist incidents;
- greater focus on recruitment, retention and progression of ethnic minority recruits;
- greater racism awareness and diversity training;
- a new definition of a 'racist incident' and changed practices of investigating and recording of racist incidents;
- introduction of a requirement to record stops as well as searches;
- application of race relations legislation to police;
- improved procedures for victim and witness liaison;
- introduction of revised disciplinary and complaints procedures.

At the forefront of the recommendations was the establishment of a ministerial priority for the police to 'increase trust and confidence in policing amongst minority ethnic communities'. The majority of the report's recommendations were accepted and a steering committee established to oversee their introduction. The label of 'institutional racism', however, has not been without controversy. Critics voiced concerns over its impact on police efficiency, suggesting that in the aftermath of the report officers became fearful that using stop and search powers against ethnic minority groups would lead to allegations of racism (Hague, 2000; cited in Rowe, 2008). Nonetheless, empirical research into the impact of the Lawrence Inquiry suggests it has been an important lever for change in the police service (Foster *et al.*, 2005). To varying degrees, these researchers identify improvements to the recording, monitoring, and response to '*hate crime*' and racist incidents, to the management of murder investigation and family liaison, and to consultation with local minority communities. They are, however, cautious over the extent to which police forces have been able to engage meaningfully with the concept of 'institutional racism', suggesting that 'certain groups in society continue to receive an inappropriate or inadequate service because of their culture or ethnic origin' (Foster *et al.*, 2005: ix).

The cultural explanation of police discretion

Many scholars have engaged with the concept of 'occupational culture' to explain the pattern of police discretion (see Westmarland, 2008). In this context, culture refers to a set of shared values, norms, beliefs, and attitudes that emerge in response to the pressures of the policing task (Reiner, 2000). To varying degrees, the occupational culture of the police is thought to provide a framework that helps officers make sense of, cope with, and respond to, the challenging social situations that routinely confront them. Arguably, therefore, it is central to the way policing is delivered and experienced on the streets (Reiner, 2000). Sub-cultural explanations of police discretion contrast with 'individualistic' accounts that suggest police recruits tend to be more authoritarian and prejudicial in outlook than a similar civilian sample (see Bowling and Philips, 2002).

Although police culture is not monolithic, broadly defined it has a fairly stable and enduring set of universal characteristics (Waddington, 1999b). Skolnick's (1966) pioneering study of the 'working personality' of police officers identified the key traits of 'suspicion', 'social isolation', and 'solidarity'. Suspicion arises from the personal dangers of the job and the organisational pressures officers face to 'get results'. As a consequence, officers are continually 'on the look out' for troublemakers, which requires them to make immediate assessments of people's moral character. In so doing, however, they may draw on negative stereotypes which arise from exclusively dealing with specific groups of people in highly selective and adversarial encounters. Internal solidarity arises from the need to support colleagues in often hostile and dangerous situations. It promotes in-group loyalty, but can also shield officers from investigations into malpractice. Social isolation is due partly to the demands of shift work, and partly to the social distance that recourse to legal authority places between officers and civilians. It promotes a mentality of 'them and us' which, Reiner (2000) suggests, reinforces a pessimistic and cynical outlook among officers, who come to view themselves as an isolated and beleaguered minority (i.e. 'the thin blue line').

Developing these themes, Reiner (2000) identifies the following (largely mutually reinforcing) key characteristics of 'cop culture': mission-action-cynicism-pessimism; suspicion; isolation-solidarity; conservatism; machismo; racial prejudice; and pragmatism. These characteristics, it is claimed, have various (largely malignant) implications for policing. These include engraining widespread 'rule-bending' among officers who may perceive the end to justify the means, promoting impulsive and short-term decision making over longer-term and more considered judgements, prioritising displays of authority and demands for deference within encounters with the public, encouraging resistance to 'politically-driven' management reforms, and sustaining intolerant and discriminatory attitudes towards those labelled as 'police property' (Reiner, 2000; Foster, 2003).

Debates about the value of cultural explanations of police discretion have often focused on the extent to which the traits of the culture translate into practice. Shearing and Ericson (1991), for example, suggest the cultural 'talk' of officers provides them with a guide to action rather than an instruction or rule book. Adopting a more 'appreciative' stance towards the policing task, Waddington (1999b) argues that the culture is less a driver for action, more a collective means of easing tension and sustaining occupational self-esteem. Reiner (2000), however, maintains that culture cannot be understood solely as prejudicial talk: to some degree it is acted out in differentiated enforcement patterns. Among these debates, however, there is some consensus that officers are active interpreters of the culture, rather than mere passive recipients who slavishly enact its characteristics (Newburn and Reiner, 2007).

Equally, it is important to recognise that the cultural adaptations of officers are linked to the broader structural role of the police. The police literally maintain the social and political order on behalf of dominant groups and against socially and economically less powerful groups. The policing function replicates the structural inequalities of race, gender, class, and age. For instance, police officers are deployed most intensively to areas where society's most marginalised groups reside (e.g. inner city areas)—lacking resources, these groups (e.g. homeless people, beggars, etc.) tend to spend more time in public space and so are more available for police-initiated, adversarial encounters. Therefore, the task of policing is firmly shaped by social inequalities, resulting in police activities being focused largely on the petty offences of powerless groups. Consequently, as Newburn and Reiner (2007) observe, the prejudices of the police culture may be more an effect than a cause of differential enforcement practices.

REVIEW QUESTIONS

1 To what extent is discretion a desirable feature of policing?

2 Why do police officers have much discretion in their use of the law?

3 To what extent does culture help explain the shape of police discretion?

Police accountability

This section describes the way in which police are held accountable for their actions. Given the wide discretion police have to deploy 'non-negotiable coercive force' (Bittner, 1978: 33), a crucial aspect of their legitimacy is that they are accountable and subject to a system of oversight and redress. Accountability operates at two distinct levels—we can talk about the *individual* accountability of police officers, but also the *institutional* accountability of police forces. Let us briefly consider each in turn.

Accountability of police officers

As policing involves the use of force against members of the public, often in volatile and hostile situations, it is unsurprising that allegations of misconduct arise against officers. In addition to internal organisational mechanisms of accountability (e.g. codes of conduct, professional standards, supervision procedures, etc,) there are three external layers of accountability by which a complainant can seek redress. Firstly, as 'citizens in uniform', officers are subject to the criminal law and can be tried for a criminal offence committed whilst on duty. Several factors, however, undermine the effectiveness of this mechanism. These include: juries tending to require a greater weight of evidence to convict a police officer than an ordinary citizen; the 'low visibility' of police work leading to a lack of independent witnesses to corroborate the testimony of the 'victim'; and the likelihood of officers being able to discredit the complainant (Smith, 2001).

Second, complainants can make a civil law claim against the police in which, if successful, they can be awarded a financial settlement (i.e. 'damages'). Over the last two decades civil claims have increased markedly. In 1979 there were seven cases against the Metropolitan police and less than £2,000 paid in damages; by 1996/7 the same force faced over 1,000 threatened actions and paid out more than £4 million to claimants (Bowling and Foster, 2002). Yet, as police forces are liable for the civil 'wrongs' of their officers, it is uncertain whether such actions serve as an effective deterrent to individual misconduct. Related, police forces seldom instigate disciplinary action against officers whose behaviour leads to an award for damages (Fielding, 2005).

Third, the *Independent Police Complaints Commission* (IPCC) oversees the system of complaints in England and Wales. This is the system by which complaints against police officers are recorded and investigated, potentially resulting in disciplinary or criminal proceedings. In 2007/08 there were over 45,000 complaints, 60 per cent of which related to allegations of neglect or failure of duty, incivility or intolerance, and assault (IPCC, 2008). Historically, the complaints system has been widely criticised for a lack of independence, in relation to both the processes of investigation and adjudication (Reiner, 2000). Despite the civilian forerunner to the IPCC, the Police Complaints Authority, gaining the powers to 'supervise' or 'direct' police investigations into serious complaints, questions remained over the validity of a system that allowed police officers to investigate complaint allegations against other police officers (Reiner, 2000). During the late 1990s, for example, the ratio of substantiated complaints to recorded allegations was consistently about 2 per cent. Moreover, even when a complaint allegation is substantiated only 25 per cent of the officers involved faced criminal or disciplinary proceedings (Smith, 2004). The resulting lack of public confidence in the old complaints system led to the establishment of the IPCC, under the Police Reform Act 2002.

As the appointed 'guardian of the complaints system', much credence has been placed by the government on the 'independence' of the IPCC. Its work is overseen by 17 commissioners, none of whom may have worked for the police. It also has greater powers than its predecessor to supervise, manage, and where necessary directly conduct (and re-conduct on appeal) investigations, for which purpose it employs a team of *civilian* investigators. Critics, however, have queried the extent to which the IPCC differs from its discredited predecessors, specifically in its level of 'independence'. Seneviratne (2004) laments the absence of any statutory requirement for the IPCC to conduct investigations, that the police retain systemic control of the complaints procedure, and that investigators appointed by the IPCC can be serving police officers. Furthermore, Smith (2006a) argues that the resource constraints of the IPCC, with a team of about 80 investigators, are likely to restrict the agency to fulfilling a primarily symbolic investigative function. Although the effectiveness of these new arrangements will become clearer over time, Smith (2006b) is not optimistic. He argues that owing to the power imbalances that characterise relations between police and the individual, the interests of the latter are continually marginalised during the process of reform, resulting, for example, insufficient powers and resources being granted to police 'watchdogs' such as the IPCC.

Accountability of police forces

The accountability of police forces concerns subjecting the discretionary policy decisions of Chief Constables (e.g. over resource deployment, strategic priorities, and operational styles) to external oversight. Central to debates over police institutional accountability has been the tension between ensuring the political impartiality of the police and connecting (and thus legitimating) police power to democratic structures. Policing, so the argument runs, ought to be free from the interference of politicians who have their own self-serving agendas. But at the same time it is too important merely to be left to the police. Therefore, the challenge of police governance concerns '*how* and to *whom* the police should be accountable' (Bowling and Foster, 2002: 1016).

The Police Act 1964 sought to address this constitutional dilemma by establishing the 'tripartite arrangement' in which Chief Constables, the Home Secretary, and local government (i.e. local police authorities) each gained some responsibility for local policing. Since the Act, the history of police governance can be read in terms of the shifts in the relative power balance between these three constituents in relation to who controls local policing. Over the last 30 years or so, there have been many examples of local police authorities, which symbolically represent the interests of the local community, legally challenging the policy decisions of their respective Chief Constables. Reflecting Lord Denning's famous words that the police 'should be accountable to the law and the law alone', the courts have confirmed the autonomy of Chief Constables, as enshrined in the 'doctrine of constabulary independence'. Over time, the local dimension of the 'tripartite arrangement' has been further weakened by successive pieces of legislation which have increased the power of the Home Secretary to intervene in, and set objectives for, local policing.

The shift towards greater central government control over local policing has also been enabled by changes in the landscape of policing. Jones (2003) identifies several salient features of this centralisation process including, the gradual reduction in the number of police forces; the growth of national training structures shaping the outlook of senior officers; the introduction of national policing bodies, for example the National Policing Improvement Agency and the Serious Organised Crime agency; and increased Home Office use of performance targets and inspection regimes to steer operational aspects of local policing. Reiner (2000) suggests the growth of national control over local forces leaves the tripartite structure of governance largely redundant, as political accountability is now almost entirely skewed towards central government. Interestingly, however, both main political parties in the United Kingdom have recently outlined proposals to re-orientate the local political accountability of the police by introducing locally-elected 'police commissioners'. Such plans are likely to be widely resisted by the Association of Chief Police Officers (ACPO) and the Association of Police Authorities, not least because they risk local policing becoming hijacked by partisan, and potentially extremist, political interests. It is unclear what such an outcome might do to public confidence in the police.

REVIEW QUESTIONS

1 Why is it difficult to use the criminal and civil law to deter misconduct among police officers?

2 Why is 'independence' an important feature of the complaints procedure?

3 To whom should police forces be accountable?

CONCLUSION

This chapter has presented an overview of some of the key issues and themes surrounding the police. It has described the role of the police—and the way the police are organised to fulfil that role in the delivery of policing services. The chapter has drawn particular attention to the way policing, whether undertaken by public or private agents, involves the use of coercive power and, accordingly, is intimately connected with notions of 'justice'. A key issue within policing, therefore, is that powers are used proportionately and delivered equitably. Despite the legal rules governing the use of police powers, patrolling officers retain much discretion over their use. This discretion skews law enforcement activities towards those groups located at the social and economic margins of society. As a consequence, such groups appear disproportionately in criminal justice statistics (see Chapters 3, 11, and 12). Finally, the discussion sought to emphasise the importance of accountability within policing. As Sir Ronnie Flanagan stated in his recent report to government 'policing is much too important and too impactive on all our lives to be left to the police alone . . .' (2008: 2). In which case should policing be undertaken to serve the interests of the state or ought it to be undertaken on behalf of the local community? It would be unwise to think that the interests of the two are always easily reconcilable.

QUESTIONS FOR DISCUSSION

1 In what ways is 'policing' linked to 'justice' in society?

2 What do the police do—and what should they do?

3 Should police officers be allowed to issue formal means of punishment in the street?

4 Why is understanding police discretion a crucial aspect of the study of policing?

5 Why is accountability such an important concept within policing?

GUIDE TO FURTHER READING

Newburn, T. and Reiner, R. (2007) 'Policing and the Police', in M. Maguire, R. Morgan, and R. Reiner, *The Oxford Handbook of Criminology* (4th edn). Oxford: Oxford University Press.

This chapter provides an excellent and accessible overview of the main themes in policing, co-written by two of the UK's leading policing scholars.

Newburn T. (ed) (2008) *The Handbook of Policing* (2nd edn). Cullompton: Willan.

This edited collection is the most comprehensive and up-to-date text available on policing. Written by leading scholars in the policing field and organised into four thematic sections, its 30 chapters cover all the major aspects of academic interest in policing.

Newburn, T. (ed) (2005) *Policing: key readings*. Cullompton: Willan.

This edited collection brings together 45 seminal articles on policing. It includes several 'early classic' studies which have inspired students of policing over the past 30 or so years, as well as more recent and important contributions to debates on policing. The collection is organised into six thematic parts, each of which has an accessible 'scene setting' introduction.

Reiner, R. (2000) *The Politics of the Police* (3rd edn). Oxford: Oxford University Press.

This book remains the most authoritative and engaging UK text on policing. It is divided into three parts, covering the history, sociology, and law and politics of policing. Containing a wealth of research and argument, it is an invaluable resource for students.

Rowe, M. (2008) *Introduction to Policing.* London: Sage.

This book provides an accessible introduction to the main themes relevant to the study of policing. Its content closely maps onto many undergraduate UK policing courses.

WEB LINKS

http://www.police.uk/forces.htm

This website provides access to the homepages of all the police forces in England, Wales, Scotland, and Northern Ireland, as well as those of non-geographic policing bodies.

http://police.homeoffice.gov.uk/

This Home Office website contains a breadth of information about policing policy and initiatives. It is therefore an excellent resource for keeping up to date with national policing developments.

http://inspectorates.homeoffice.gov.uk/hmic/

Her Majesty's Inspectorate of Constabulary (HMIC) aims to promote efficiency and effectiveness of policing in England, Wales, and Northern Ireland by driving up standards and improving operational performance. Its website is an excellent resource for students, giving access to a range of statistics, as well as HMIC inspection reports and thematic reviews.

http://www.polfed.org/

The Police Federation represents the interests of all police officers below the rank of superintendent. Its website is a useful learning resource, providing insights into the collective concerns of the lower ranks of the police service towards strategic and operational policing developments.

http://www.acpos.police.uk/

The Association of Chief Police Officers (ACPO) is a strategic body whose members are at least of the rank of Assistant Chief Constable. Its website outlines the views of ACPO towards thematic policy areas.

http://www.apa.police.uk/apa

The Association of Police Authorities represents the interests of the police authorities of England, Wales, and Northern Ireland. Its website carries a host of reports and information about various aspects of policing and its governance.

http://www.ipcc.gov.uk/
The Independent Police Complaints Commission oversees the system of police complaints in England and Wales. Its website outlines in depth the complaints procedure and gives access to its various research reports into the activities and performance of the IPCC.

REFERENCES

Audit Commission (1996) *Streetwise*. London: Audit Commission.

Bayley, D.H. (1994) *Police for the Future*. New York: Oxford University Press.

Becker, H. (1963) *The Outsiders*. New York: Macmillan.

Bittner, E. (1967) 'The Police on Skid Row: A Study in Peacekeeping'. *American Sociological Review*, 32(5): 699–715.

Bittner, E. (1974) 'Florence Nightingale in Pursuit of Willie Sutton: A Theory of the Police' in H. Jacob (ed) *The Potential for Reform of Criminal Justice*. Beverley Hills, CA: Sage.

Bittner, E. (1978) 'The function of the police in modern society', in P.K. Manning and J. van Maanen (eds) *Policing: A View from the Street*. Santa Monica, CA: Goodyear.

Bowling, B. and Foster, J. (2002) 'Policing and the Police' in M. Maguire, R. Morgan, and R. Reiner (eds), *The Oxford Handbook of Criminology* (3rd edn). Oxford: Oxford University Press.

Bowling, B. and Philips, C. (2002) *Racism, Crime and Justice*. Harlow:Pearson Education.

Bullock, S. (2008) *Police Service Strength: England and Wales, 31 March 2008*. Home Office Statistical Bulletin 08/08, London: Home Office.

Chatterton, M. and Bingham, E. (2006) *24/7 Response Policing in the Modern Police Organisation: Views from the Frontline*. Leatherhead: Police Federation.

Choongh, S. (1997) *Policing as Social Discipline*. Oxford: Clarendon Press.

Clancy, A., Hough, M., Aust, R., and Kershaw, C. (2001) *Crime, Policing and Justice: the Experience of Ethnic Minorities Findings from the 2000 British Crime Survey*. Home Office Research Study 223. London: Home Office.

Cohen, S. (1985) *Visions of Social Control*. Cambridge: Polity Press.

Crawford, A., Lister. S., Blackburn, S., and Burnett, J. (2005) *Plural Policing: the mixed economy of visible patrols in England and Wales*. Bristol: Policy Press.

Davis, K.C. (1975) *Police Discretion*. St. Paul, Minn.: West Publishing.

Dixon, D., Bottomley, A.K., Coleman, C., Gill, M., and Wall, D. (1989) 'Reality and Rules in the Construction and Regulation of Police Suspicion'. *International Journal of the Sociology of Law*, 17(2):185–206.

Fielding, N. (2005) *The police and social conflict* (2nd edn). London: Glasshouse Press.

Fitzgerald, M., Hough, M., Joseph, I., and Qureshi, T. (2002) *Policing for London*. Cullompton: Willan Publishing.

Flanagan, R. (2008) *The Review of Policing: Final Report*, London: Home Office.

Foster, J. (2003) 'Police Cultures' in T. Newburn (ed) *Handbook of Policing.* Cullompton: Willan Publishing.

Foster, J., Newburn, T., and Souhami, A. (2005) *Assessing the impact of the Stephen Lawrence Inquiry*, Home Office Research Study 294. London: Home Office.

Goldstein, J. (1960), 'Police discretion not to invoke the criminal process: Low-visibility decisions in the administration of justice'. *Yale Law Journal*, 69(4): 543–94.

Her Majesty's Inspectorate of Constabulary (HMIC) (2005) *Closing the gap: A review of the 'fitness for purpose' of the current structure of policing in England and Wales*. London: Her Majesty's Inspectorate of Constabulary.

Home Office (1993) *Police Reform: A Police Service for the Twenty-first Century*. London: Home Office.

Home Office (2001) *Policing a New Century: A blueprint for reform*. London: Home Office.

Home Office (2004) *Building Communities, Beating Crime*. London: Home Office.

Hough, M. (1985) 'Organisation and resource management in the uniformed police' in K. Heal, R. Tarling, and J. Burrows (eds) *Policing Today*. London: HMSO.

Hoyle, C. (1998) *Negotiating Domestic Violence: Police, Criminal Justice and Victims*. Oxford: Oxford University Press.

Independent Police Complaints Commission (IPCC) (2008) *Police Complaints: Statistics for England and Wales 2007/8*. IPCC Research and Statistics Series: Paper 12, London: Independent Police Complaints Commission.

Innes, M. (2003) *Understanding Social Control*. Maidenhead: Open University Press.

Jones, T. (2003) 'The Governance and Accountability of Policing' in T. Newburn (ed) (2003) *The Handbook of Policing*. Cullompton: Willan.

Jones, T., MacLean, B., and Young, J. (1986) *The Islington Crime Survey*. Aldershot: Gower.

Jones, T. and Newburn, T. (1998) *Private Security and Public Policing*. Oxford: Clarendon Press.

Lister, S., Seddon, T., Wincup, E., Barrett, S., and Traynor, P. (2008) *Street Policing of Problem Drug Users*. York: Joseph Rowntree Foundation.

McConville, M., Sanders, A., and Leng, R. (1991) *The Case for the Prosecution*. London: Routledge.

Macpherson, W. (1999) *The Stephen Lawrence Inquiry, Report of an Inquiry by Sir William Macpherson of Cluny*. Cmnd 4262-1. London: HMSO.

Maguire, M. (2008) 'Criminal investigation and crime control' in T. Newburn (ed) *The Handbook of Policing* (2nd edn). Cullompton: Willan Publishing.

Mawby, R.C. and Wright, A. (2008) 'The police organisation' in T. Newburn (ed) *The Handbook of Policing* (2nd edn). Cullompton: Willan Publishing.

Ministry of Justice (2007) *Statistics on Race and the Criminal Justice System—2006*. London: Ministry of Justice.

Ministry of Justice (2008) *Arrests for Recorded Crime (Notifiable Offences) and the Operation of Certain Police Powers under PACE—England and Wales 2006/07*. London: Ministry of Justice.

Morgan, R. and Newburn, T. (1997) *The Future of Policing*. Oxford: Clarendon Press.

Newburn, T. (1999) *Understanding and Preventing Police Corruption: Lessons from the literature*. London: Home Office.

Newburn, T. and Reiner, R. (2007) 'Policing and the Police' in M. Maguire, R. Morgan, and R. Reiner (eds) *The Oxford Handbook of Criminology* (4th edn). Oxford: Oxford University Press.

Norris, C., Fielding, N., Kemp, C., and Fielding, J. (1992) 'Black and Blue: An Analysis of the Influence of Race on Being Stopped by the Police'. *British Journal of Sociology* 43(2): 207–23.

Oxford, K. (1986) 'The Power to Police Effectively' in J. Benyon and C. Bourne (eds) *Police: Powers, Properties and Procedures*. Oxford: Pergamon Press.

PA Consulting Group (2001) *Diary of a Police Officer*. Police Research Paper 149. London: Home Office.

Punch, M. and Naylor, T. (1973) 'The Police: A Social Service'. *New Society*, 24: 358–61.

Quinton, P., Bland, N., and Miller, J. (2000) *Police Stops, Decision-making and Practice*. Police Research Series, London: Home Office.

Reiner, R. (2000) *The Politics of the Police* (3rd edn). Oxford: Oxford University Press.

Rowe, M. (2008) *Introduction to Policing*. London: Sage.

Sanders, A. and Young, R. (2007) *Criminal Justice* (3rd edn). Oxford: Oxford University Press.

Sanders, A. and Young, R. (2008) 'Police powers' in T. Newburn (ed) *The Handbook of Policing* (2nd edn). Cullompton: Willan Publishing.

Scarman, Lord (1981) *The Brixton Disorders*. Cmnd 8427. London: HMSO.

Seneviratne, M. (2004) 'Policing the Police in the United Kingdom', *Policing & Society* 14 (4): 329–47.

Shearing, C. and Ericson, R. (1991) 'Culture as Figurative Action'. *The British Journal of Sociology* 42(4): 481–506.

Skogan, W. (1990) *The Police and Public in England and Wales: A British Crime Survey Report*. Home Office Research Study No. 117. London: HMSO.

Skolnick, J.H. (1966) *Justice Without Trial. Law Enforcement in Democratic Society*. New York: Wiley.

Shapland, J. and Vagg, J. (1990) *Policing by the Public*. London: Routledge.

Smith, D. and Gray, J. (1983) *Police and People in London*. London: Policy Studies Institute

Smith, G. (2001), 'Police complaints and criminal prosecutions'. *Modern Law Review* 64(3): 372–92.

Smith, G. (2004) 'Rethinking police complaints'. *British Journal of Criminology* 44(1): 15–33.

Smith, G. (2006a) 'Police complaints in the reform era'. *Criminal Justice* 63, 26–27.

Smith, G. (2006b) 'A Most Enduring Problem: Police Complaints Reform in England And Wales'. *Journal of Social Policy* 35(1): 121–41.

Solomon, E., Eades, C., Garside, R., and Rutherford, M. (2007) *Ten years of criminal justice under Labour*. London: Centre for Crime and Justice Studies.

South, N. (1988) *Policing for Profit*. London: Sage.

Stallion, M. and Wall, D.S. (1999) *The British Police: Police Forces and Chief Officers 1829–2000*. Bramshill: The Police History Foundation.

Waddington, P.A.J. (1999a) *Policing citizens: authority and rights*. London: UCL Press.

Waddington, P.A.J. (1999b) 'Police (Canteen) Sub-Culture'. *British Journal of Criminology* 39(2): 287–309.

Walker, C. (1999) 'Introduction' in C. Walker and K. Starmer (eds) *Justice in Error*. London: Blackstone Press.

Westmarland, L. (2008) 'Police Cultures' in T. Newburn (ed) *The Handbook of Policing* (2nd edn). Cullompton: Willan Publishing.

Wilson, J.Q. (1968) *Varieties of Police Behaviour: The Management of Law and Order in Eight Communities*. Cambridge, MA: Harvard University Press.

Young, M. (1991) *An Inside Job*. Oxford: Oxford University Press.

Young, R. (2008) 'Street Policing after PACE: The Drift to Summary Justice' in E. Cape and R. Young (eds) *Regulating Policing: The Police and Criminal Evidence Act 1984 Past, Present and Future*. Oxford: Hart Publishing.

3

The prosecution process

Anthea Hucklesby

INTRODUCTION

This chapter explores issues relating to the *prosecution process*. This is the process by which suspects are convicted and become officially recognised as offenders. Studying the prosecution process enables us to understand how *crime* is investigated and suspects, defendants, and offenders are prosecuted and convicted. The process may start in several ways: through suspects being stopped and searched, arrested or summonsed. Once a person becomes a suspect there is a series of stages through which they have to go in order to be convicted. Space constraints precludes an in-depth analysis of the process (see Ashworth and Redmayne, 2005; Sanders and Young, 2007 for a more thorough examination). Instead this chapter will introduce some of the main theoretical and conceptual issues within the prosecution process, as well as exploring a number of key trends in recent criminal justice law and policy. It begins by outlining the main institutions and agencies involved in the prosecution process before examining some fundamental theoretical concepts and debates. Finally, it explores some key issues in the prosecution process.

BACKGROUND

The issues discussed in this chapter reflect the fundamental dilemma of the prosecution process, which attempts to reconcile the rights of suspects, defendants, and offenders on the one hand with the rights of the victims and the protection of the public on the other. The operation of the prosecution process in any society is one of the barometers by which 'democracy' is measured particularly with regard to *suspects' and defendants' rights* which give the process legitimacy. The prosecution process is also required to comply with Human Rights legislation including the Human Rights Act 1998 and the European Convention on Human Rights.

The rights of suspects and defendants are often portrayed as in opposition to the rights of victims and the public in general which are also laid down in domestic and international legislation. This has been illustrated recently by the Government's policy of 'rebalancing the criminal justice system in favour of the law-abiding majority' (Home Office, 2006). The concept of balance is unhelpful. It portrays an image of the 'law-abiding majority' on the one hand, and the suspects, defendants, and offenders on the other, and if one groups' rights increase, the other's must necessarily decrease. Reality is more complex. Firstly, the categories of suspect, defendants, and offenders and victims overlap (Fattah, 1994). Secondly, the rights of offenders and victims are not necessarily opposed. There is emerging evidence that treating individuals fairly and justly during their contact with the criminal justice process enhances legitimacy and improves short-term compliance with sentences and longer term compliance with the law (see for example Paternoster *et al.*, 1997).

The purpose of the prosecution process is to convict the guilty of the offences they have committed in a manner which conforms to legal rules and procedures. In so doing, it should sieve out the innocent so that they are not convicted. However, in the last quarter of the twentieth century a string of *miscarriages of justice* occurred including the Birmingham Six, the Guildford Four, the Maguire Seven, Judith Ward, Stefan Kiszko, the Taylor Sisters, the Bridgewater Three, and the Cardiff Three (see the Case Study for details of some of these cases). These cases involved innocent people who were wrongly convicted and imprisoned. The causes of the miscarriages of justice varied but there were several common features, namely the suppression of evidence by the police and prosecution agencies which was useful to the defence; false confessions secured by the police using psychological pressure, ploys, and lies; and the fabrication and manipulation of prosecution evidence (Walker and Starmer, 1999). These events resulted in genuine concern for suspects and defendants as well as the granting of key legal rights including the right to legal advice.

One of the first high-profile miscarriages of justice was that of three youths who were wrongly convicted of the murder of Maxwell Confait. This case resulted in the setting up of a Royal Commission on Criminal Procedure (Philips, 1981). The Philips Commission set out a blue print for a 'fair, workable and efficient' system. It proposed a radical overhaul of the criminal justice process in order to 'balance' the rights of suspects and the powers of the police as well as preventing further miscarriages of justice. The recommendations of the Philips Commission were largely enshrined in the Police and Criminal Evidence Act 1984 (PACE) which regulates police powers and the Prosecution of Offences Act 1985. These two crucial pieces of legislation will be discussed later in the chapter.

Throughout the 1980s, further miscarriages of justice came to light (Walker and Starmer, 1999). A second Royal Commission was established (Runciman, 1993) to examine the causes of the miscarriages of justice. The report was not well received, being viewed as a whitewash and a missed opportunity (McConville and Bridges, 1994). It recommended no major changes to the criminal justice process in order to prevent miscarriages of justice; rather it stated that there was no reason to believe that the majority of verdicts were not correct (Runciman, 1993). Many of its recommendations favoured the interests of the police and the prosecution rather than suspects' rights. To a large extent, the report was a product of its time as the general climate in which the criminal justice process was operating had changed dramatically. Concerns about suspects', defendants', and offenders' rights had been overtaken by concern for the rights of victims and public protection, demonstrated most significantly in the aftermath of the killing of Jamie Bulger, by two ten-year-olds in 1993 (Newburn, 2003). This marked a watershed in criminal justice policy, which continues to the present day, whereby the protection of the public and the rights of victims take precedence over the rights of suspects, defendants, and offenders. This has resulted in constant legal and policy changes aimed at curtailing suspects' and defendants' rights. This chapter will illustrate these trends and demonstrate how many of the protections afforded to suspects and defendants are largely presentational and are often undermined.

 CASE STUDY: MISCARRIAGES OF JUSTICE

Confidence in the criminal justice process was rocked by a succession of high-profile miscarriages of justice in the last quarter of the twentieth century. The section provides details on some of the cases. The cases have been selected carefully but they represent only a small proportion of the miscarriages of justice which have occurred. Further examples can be found in Walker and Starmer (1999) and Rosenburg (1992).

There are a number of important themes which arise from these examples. First, the role that fabrication of evidence by the police and unreliable forensic evidence played in the original convictions. Secondly, the fact that appeals were refused on a number of occasions before they were successful. Thirdly, often no one involved in the original investigation was prosecuted. Fourthly, that the real offenders are rarely convicted.

The Birmingham Six

The Birmingham Six (Hugh Callaghan, Patrick Hill, Gerry Hunter, Richard McIlkenny, Billy Power, John Walker) were convicted in 1975 of two pub bombings in Birmingham in 1974. The bombings were carried out by the *Irish Republican Army* (IRA) and 21 people were killed. The 'six' were convicted on three main grounds: confessions; forensic evidence; and circumstantial evidence (Walker and Starmer, 1999). The 'six' claimed that the confessions had been beaten out of them and that the forensic evidence which purported to show that they had been handling explosives was unreliable. They were refused leave to appeal in 1976 but in 1988 their case was referred back to the Court of Appeal, which turned it down. After this further evidence came to light including that the police had fabricated statements and that the forensic tests used were unreliable (the original tests had shown that two of the six men had handled explosives but this was later confirmed not to be explosives but from other sources, perhaps from cigarettes or playing cards). They were eventually released in 1991. No one has been prosecuted for their part in the miscarriage of justice and no one has been convicted of the pub bombings.

Judith Ward

Judith Ward was convicted in 1974 of supplying bombs which were used on a coach travelling along the M62 carrying army personnel, killing 12 people. The *Home Secretary* referred her case back to the Court of Appeal in 1991 and she was released in 1992. Her confessions had been shown to be unreliable. Additionally, scientific evidence provided by the same scientist involved in the Birmingham Six case was shown to be unreliable, and allegations were made about non-disclosure of evidence.

The Bridgewater Four

In 1978 a 13 year old newspaper boy called Carl Bridgewater was shot dead when he disturbed a burglary at Yew Tree Farm near Stourbridge in the West Midlands. Three men, Michael Hickey, Vincent Hickey, and James Robinson were convicted of the murder, and a fourth man, Patrick Malloy was convicted of manslaughter. Leave to appeal was denied in 1981 but the case was originally referred back to the Court of Appeal in 1987 but the convictions were upheld. In 1996 the case was again referred back to the Court of Appeal and the men were finally released in 1997, although Patrick Molloy had died in prison in 1981. The main evidence in the case was Patrick Molloy's confession, which he subsequently retracted. He had been denied access to a solicitor during police interviews and claimed that he had been tricked by the police into giving the false confession. Later tests on the original interview documents proved this to be the case.

The Tottenham Three

The Tottenham Three (Mark Braithwaite, Engin Raghip, and Winston Silcott) were convicted of murdering PC Blakelock during the Broadwater Farm riot in North London in 1985. They had been refused leave to appeal in 1988 but their cases were finally referred back to the Court of Appeal in

1991 and their convictions were quashed in December of that year. The appeal succeeded because scientific tests on the notes taken during original interviews showed that they had been altered subsequently to include confessions. Engin Raghip was also cleared on another ground. Originally, a prosecution and defence psychiatrist had found him to be of average intelligence and normal suggestability. However, subsequent tests found that he was of low intelligence and abnormal suggestibility in pressurised situations. Neither the psychiatrists nor police officers involved were prosecuted.

Stefan Kizsko

Stefan Kizsko was convicted of the sexual assault and murder of Lesley Molseed in 1975 in Rochdale. During police interviews he confessed to committing the offence but he did not have a solicitor present. His conviction was quashed by the Court of Appeal in 1992 on the grounds of flawed forensic evidence. His innocence was proven conclusively by medical evidence showing that Stefan Kizsko was infertile and, therefore, could not have committed the sexual assault. Two witnesses who were questioned by the police but not called during the trial were also found. They stated that Stefan had been in a shop at the time of the murder. None of the people involved in the original investigation have been prosecuted, although Stefan Kizsko received an apology and compensation, but died before he received the full amount. Ronald Castree was convicted of the murder of Lesley Molseed in 2007.

The Cardiff Three

The Cardiff Three (Yasuf Abdelaki, Tong Paris, and Steven Miller) were convicted of the murder of Lynette White in Cardiff in 1988. They were largely convicted on the basis of Miller's confessions. The convictions were quashed in 1992 after the Court of Appeal heard tapes of the police interviews with Miller which demonstrated that undue pressure had been put on him during the interviews by the use of hostile questioning and intimidation, despite the presence of a defence solicitor. The real murderer has since been found and convicted.

Institutions and agencies of the criminal justice process

This section introduces the main criminal justice agencies which are involved in the prosecution process. The police, prison, and *probation* services are not discussed as they are examined elsewhere in this volume. Although the criminal justice institutions and agencies have their own objectives and are described separately, they are not isolated and are all part of the broader criminal justice process. The policies and practices of agencies impact upon other agencies in the process. Nonetheless, there is a lack of coordination, cooperation, and communication between agencies, although this is improving. For this reason it is difficult to describe the criminal justice process as a 'system'.

The courts

There are two main types of courts in which *criminal trials* take place, magistrates' courts and the Crown Court. The personnel and cases dealt with in the two courts differ and are discussed below.

Magistrates' courts

Magistrates' courts are often described as the 'lower courts' partly because they deal with less serious cases. However, nearly all cases begin in magistrates' courts and they deal with around 95 per cent of criminal cases (Ashworth and Redmayne, 2005). For this reason they are often referred to as the 'workhorses' of the court system (Darbyshire, 2002). The sentencing powers of magistrates' courts are limited to six months' imprisonment for any one offence up to a maximum of 12 months imprisonment and/or a £5,000 fine. They also have the power to send cases to Crown Court for trial and/or sentencing if the offence is serious enough to warrant a longer sentence than they can impose. There are two types of decision makers in magistrates' courts, magistrates and District Judges (Magistrates' Courts) (formerly known as Stipendiary magistrates). Both magistrates and District Judges decide on the guilt of defendants/offenders and their sentence. They are, therefore, judges of both fact and law, which raises questions about whether decisions taken in magistrates' courts are impartial and fair (Ashworth and Redmayne, 2005).

Magistrates are lay members of the local community and have historically lived within a short distance of the court in which they sit (Parker *et al.*, 1989; Raine, 1989). However, magistrates are now able to sit in any magistrates' court. This illustrates the demise of the ideal of 'local justice' whereby justice was dispensed locally by local people (Raine, 1989). Magistrates are not legally qualified and are unpaid. There are about 30,000 magistrates in England and Wales (DCA, 2007a). Magistrates sit in court at least 26 times a year and usually in groups of three. They are assisted by legal advisors (sometimes referred to as court clerks) who are normally legally qualified and provide legal advice as well as managing the court (Darbyshire, 2002). Magistrates are often criticised for being amateurs, slow, inconsistent, and too ready to accept the police and prosecution version of events and convict defendants (Ashworth and Redmayne, 2005; Darbyshire, 2002). By contrast, magistrates are also praised because they ensure the involvement of local and lay people in the criminal justice process, help to demystify the legal process and make it comprehensible to all, and increase public confidence in the criminal justice process (Darbyshire, 2002). Magistrates are also significantly cheaper than their professional counterparts. One of the stated benefits of magistrates is that they can represent the local community, ensuring that they understand local issues and that defendants' are tried by their peers. However, magistrates are not representative of the local community and are particularly removed from the defendant/offender population (Darbyshire, 2002; Dignan and Whynne, 1997). Magistrates lack diversity and are predominantly white, middle class, and older (Dignan and Whynne, 1997). Particular attention has focussed on the lack of magistrates from minority ethnic groups (Darbyshire, 2002). Despite recent attempts to change the appointments process, it remains the major reason for the lack of diversity of magistrates and has been termed a 'self-perpetuating oligarchy' (Darbyshire, 2002).

District Judges (Magistrates' Courts) also sit in magistrates' courts. They are paid professionals who are legally qualified and who have been a solicitor or barrister for at least seven years. There are about 130 full-time District Judges in England and Wales and many more who sit part-time (DCA, 2007a). Lack of diversity is also an issue with District Judges (Darbyshire, 2002). There has been considerable debate about the relative qualities of District Judges and magistrates, which mirror wider debates about the merits of lay and professional involvement in public services (Morgan and Russell, 2000; Seago *et al.*, 2000). District Judges are perceived to be more professional, consistent, and faster, dealing with cases more quickly, thus helping to reduce delays in the court system (Morgan and Russell, 2000; Seago *et al.*, 2000). There is also some evidence that they deal with more serious cases than magistrates and that they are more effective case managers (Morgan and Russell, 2000). However, because District Judges sit alone, there is also scope for 'maverick' decision making and it raises questions about whether the power to convict and sentence defendants should be held by a single person.

The Crown Court

The Crown Court deals with cases involving more serious offences. There are three types of offences which are categorised according to seriousness. Indictable-only offences can only be tried at Crown Court and are more serious and include murder and manslaughter. Triable either-way offences make up the bulk of offences and may be tried in either the Crown Court or magistrates' courts. The venue for the case is decided in the magistrates' courts. Cases end up in the Crown Court either because District Judges or magistrates send the case there because it is too serious for them to deal with or because defendants elect jury trial. Finally, summary offences are less serious and are only tried in magistrates' courts.

Whatever the category of offences involved, most cases which are tried in the Crown Court begin in the magistrates' court. Cases heard in the Crown Court involve both a judge and jury. The basis of the jury system is trial by one's peers and nearly everyone is eligible for jury service. The role of the jury is to listen to the evidence and determine whether defendants are guilty. The role of the judge is to preside over the court, hear debates over legal technicalities, and decide upon sentence. Like, magistrates, judges have been criticised for being unrepresentative as they are predominantly male, white, middle class, and Oxbridge-educated (Sanders and Young, 2007).

Unlike magistrates' courts, the roles of convicting and sentencing defendants are split. This arguably produces a fairer process than in magistrates' courts where the roles are combined (Sanders and Young, 2007). Indeed, many defendants, especially those from minority ethnic groups, are more confident that they will receive fair and just treatment at the Crown Court rather than in magistrates' courts (Bowling and Phillips, 2002). Attempts have been made recently to curtail the right to jury trial by removing defendants' right to elect jury trial in some circumstances. These were motivated by the cost of Crown Court trials and the fact that many cases heard in Crown Court involve guilty pleas and/or sentences which are within the sentencing powers of magistrates' courts. However, the proposals failed to recognise that most cases heard in Crown Court are sent there by magistrates' courts rather than defendants' electing to go there. The proposals were unsuccessful largely because it is perceived to be a fundamental right in a democratic society that one can choose to be tried by one's peers. Despite this, certain types of trials, such as those involving terrorists in Northern Ireland and complex fraud cases in England and Wales, can be heard without a jury (Jackson, 2002).

Crown Prosecution Service

The Crown Prosecution Service (CPS) was created in 1985 by the Prosecution of Offences Act and became operational in 1986. It is an independent prosecution agency set up as a result of a recommendation of the Philips Commission (Philips, 1981). The Philips Commission made its recommendation on a number of grounds. First, the functions of investigation and prosecution of crime should be split as their aims conflicted. Both roles had been hitherto undertaken by the police but the Philips Commission believed that it resulted in weak cases, i.e. cases where there was not enough evidence to prosecute, proceeding to court. This happened because the police were unlikely to take an impartial view of cases once they had invested time and resources on investigations. Secondly, there were strong civil liberties arguments for an independent agency as suspects' rights were open to abuse under the existing system. Thirdly, variations in decisions between areas occurred which resulted in calls for more uniformity; and finally, there were too many weak cases being prosecuted which had resource implications as well as consequences for defendants.

The CPS is responsible for prosecuting most offences in England and Wales. Until recently, the CPS took over responsibility for cases from the police once suspects had been charged. However, the recent introduction of statutory charging means that the CPS is now also responsible for charging decisions in all but the most minor of cases (Brownlee, 2004). The CPS reviews cases to decide if there is enough evidence to charge and prosecute. In order to make these decisions, it relies on the police file, which contains information about the offence and the circumstances surrounding it, albeit from the police point of view (McConville *et al.*, 1991). Consequently, the information it relies upon is not objective but a particular version of events, which arguably limits their ability to make independent decisions (McConville *et al.*, 1991). The CPS has no investigatory powers and this will always limit its independence. The independence of the CPS has been perpetually questioned. Before statutory charging was introduced, it was argued that the CPS's role as reviewer of police decisions to prosecute compromised its independence particularly because the prosecution had gained its own momentum by the time it became involved (McConville *et al.*, 1991, Sanders and Young, 2007). More recently, the introduction of statutory charging has raised the issue again. On the one hand, the CPS should be more independent because it decides the appropriate charge but on the other hand, it is located in police stations where it may be subject to undue influence from the police (Brownlee, 2004).

The CPS has the power to discontinue cases. This was seen as one of its major roles and a way of preventing weak cases from getting to court. The test by which it decides whether to discontinue cases is 'is there a realistic prospect of conviction?' This is a two-stage test. First, cases must meet the evidential test, i.e. is there enough evidence to gain a conviction? If there is then the second test, whether it is in the public interest to prosecute, comes into play. This essentially means that factors such as defendants' age, health, and family circumstances are taken into consideration alongside factors relating to victims. This concept has been criticised for being too vague and open to numerous interpretations, resulting in the public and particularly victims being unclear about why cases are discontinued (Sanders and Young, 2007). Since its inception the CPS has been criticised for either discontinuing too many cases or not enough (Ashworth and Redmayne, 2005; Sanders and Young, 2007).

The CPS has also been criticised for downgrading too many charges. This means that offenders are convicted of lesser charges than they were originally charged with, which inevitably results in lighter sentences being imposed (Ashworth and Redmayne, 2005; Sanders and Young, 2007). An example would be when offenders who were originally charged with the more serious offence of robbery are convicted of theft. Certainly, the downgrading of offences often happens in cases, but the crucial question is why it occurs. There is some evidence, albeit largely anecdotal, that the police regularly over-charge defendants (Glidewell, 1998). Indeed, this is one of the reasons why the system of statutory charging has been introduced (Brownlee, 2004). Furthermore, the level of charges may change because cases are dynamic and the quantity and strength of the evidence against defendants changes over time, for example, the results of forensic tests become available or witnesses come forward or decline to testify, and this can alter the balance of the evidence against defendants. More controversially, *plea bargaining* may occur.

Since its creation the CPS has faced extensive criticisms from many quarters for being inefficient, disorganised, and ineffective. Some of these problems were related to the setting up of a new organisation where staff shortages were one of the main issues. As a consequence, the CPS has faced a constant stream of changes to its organisational structure (Ashworth and Redmayne, 2005; Glidewell, 1998). A further criticism of the CPS is that they do not take sufficient account of victims' wishes nor do they provide adequate information to them (Glidewell, 1998; Sanders and Young, 2007).

Defence solicitors

Defence solicitors are not a criminal justice agency in the strict sense but they play a crucial role in the prosecution process. Defence solicitors generally are partners in, or work for, private firms. Their work is either paid for by the state through legal aid or privately by individuals. The role in the criminal justice process is to represent their clients' interests both at the police station and in court. In so doing, they are expected to safeguard their rights and ensure that they are treated according to the law. For these reasons, defence solicitors are often perceived to be the friend of defendants and opposed to the police and the prosecution. However, what little research has been undertaken on defence solicitors suggests that this is not the reality (McConville *et al.*, 1994). The research suggested that defence solicitors often presume defendants to be guilty and fail to protect their clients' interests. It also found the quality of defence solicitors' work to be generally poor, with them preferring to ensure their credibility in the eyes of fellow criminal justice professionals rather than protecting the interests of their clients (McConville *et al.*, 1994). Since the research was conducted changes have been made to improve the quality of legal advice; most notably an accreditation scheme for anyone who represents defendants at police stations has been introduced.

REVIEW QUESTIONS

1 What are the main benefits and criticisms of magistrates and District Judges?

2 What are the main differences between magistrates' courts and the Crown Court?

3 What criticisms have been levelled at the CPS?

Making sense of the criminal justice process

This section introduces some of the key theoretical concepts, which are used to understand how the criminal justice process operates. They also help us to make sense of why the criminal justice process works in the way that it does.

The criminal justice process in the UK is based on adversarial legal principles. This requires the prosecution to prove the guilt of the accused. As the name suggests the prosecution and the defence are adversaries and are central to the process. They prepare and present their cases in court to judges who are neutral and act as umpires. Judges are not involved in the investigations of offences and have no prior knowledge of cases before they appear in court as they do under inquisitorial systems. The role of the judge is to listen to the evidence, ensure procedures are followed, and make final decisions.

Models of the criminal justice process

Models of the criminal justice process provide a theoretical framework to understand and analyse how the criminal justice process operates. Over time there has been considerable debate about which models provide the best fit with reality. Space constraints preclude a thorough analysis of these debates. Instead, this section provides an introduction to the models and readers are directed to sources in the further reading section for a more in-depth examination.

There is only a limited match between how the law is intended to operate (the law in books) and how it functions in practice (the law in action). The models help us to understand why this difference exists. It has been explained in two main ways: firstly, criminal justice personnel such as the police mould how they use and apply the law (Packer, 1969; King, 1981); and secondly, the way in which the law is drafted enables it to be applied differently to the way that it was originally intended (McBarnett, 1981). The most comprehensive explanation is provided where both the law and how it is applied are examined (McConville *et al.*, 1991).

The models which are most widely used are Packer's (1969) 'crime control' and *'due process'* models. The two models are extremes, being at either end of a continuum. Consequently, they are 'ideal types' which means that they do not describe reality (Packer, 1969). Instead, the models are explanatory tools. In practice, most criminal justice processes fall somewhere in between the two extremes and draw on elements of both. Packer (1969) also suggested that the models describe the typical values held by different criminal justice agencies. He, therefore, depicted the police as holding 'crime

control' values while defence solicitors have 'due process' values. While these representations may be viewed as stereotypical and exceptions always exist, they are useful for
describing different agencies' reactions to events and legal and policy changes.

Crime control

The *crime control* model characterises the criminal justice processes as an assembly line
with a conveyor belt, which moves people through the criminal justice process with
the minimum of difficulty towards the final outcome of conviction and sentence. The
primary objective of this model is to prevent crime and this is achieved through *punishment*. The importance of crime control results in a criminal process, which measures success in terms of a high rate of apprehension and conviction. The process, therefore, needs
to be efficient at apprehending, trying, convicting, and disposing of a high proportion
of offenders. Accordingly, the process is quick and efficient and requires informality
and uniformity. It condones extra-judicial practices or the 'disregard for legal controls'.
Consequently, laws, rules, and procedures to protect defendants have little value as they
are seen as obstacles to the repression of crime. Implicit in this model is that the innocent are screened out at an early stage and those who are guilty are dealt with quickly.
Therefore, a presumption of guilt exists because police and prosecutors are assumed to
screen out the innocent early on in the process. All decisions are final and no appeals
procedures exist.

Due process

A criminal process that runs according to due process principles is analogous to an obstacle course whereby each stage is a hurdle, which, if hit, results in the person leaving
the process. Under this model, the primary function of criminal process is as arbitrator
of conflicts between individual and state. The accused must be protected from arbitrary
power of the state and the onus is on the state to prove the case. Consequently, there is a
presumption of innocence. Under a due process model, informal methods of investigation are unacceptable because they may result in error. So, there are rules governing the
operation of the process, which means that cases must be heard publicly by impartial
tribunals where defendants have the opportunity to discredit the case against them.
But, because mistakes happen, the decision is never final and can be overturned if new
evidence comes to light.

   The difference between the due process and crime control model relates to reliability
and efficiency. Both models acknowledge that mistakes happen and that the innocent
can be convicted. The due process model focuses on the prevention and elimination of
mistakes, whilst the crime control model sees this as a price worth paying. The due process model rejects absolute efficiency because reliability is more important. Introducing
quality controls inevitably decreases the quantity and speed of cases going through the
process. The due process model accepts the need for controls as the power held by the
criminal process is open to abuse. Therefore, the accused are protected by rules and safeguards and if they are not adhered to, then they will be found not guilty. The process is
as much about protecting the factually innocent as convicting the guilty and operates
on the principle that it is better that ten guilty people go free than one innocent person
is convicted.

Additional models of the criminal justice process

Packer's original models have been supplemented and adapted in various ways (Ashworth and Redmayne, 2005; Bottoms and McClean, 1976; King, 1981; Sanders and Young, 2007). Debates have taken place about the original meaning and purpose of Packer's models (McConville *et al.*, 1997; Smith, 1997). These have culminated in an uneasy consensus that 'crime control' is an inappropriate term to describe the model (McConville *et al.*, 1997; Smith, 1997); that the overriding aim of the criminal justice process is the *prevention* of crime; and that the models do not describe the aims but the values of the criminal justice process (McConville *et al.*, 1997; Smith, 1997). The models have also been criticised in a number of respects (Ashworth and Redmayne, 2005; Sanders and Young, 2007). Most notably, Ashworth and Redmayne (2005) argue that the models fail to take account of the importance of managing resources and victims' interests. While these omissions are largely explainable by changing priorities over time, they do suggest that the models require updating. A number of attempts have been made to do this including Ashworth's 'Human Rights' model which suggests that the criminal justice process is not just about truth but also fairness and justice (Ashworth and Redmayne, 2005). He uses the European Convention on Human Rights to suggest 12 ethical principles, which should underlie the criminal justice process. Whilst acknowledging that they provide an important set of standards to which criminal justice processes should aspire, they have been criticised for being too vague (Sanders and Young, 2007). Sanders and Young (2007) also criticise Ashworth's model because it does not provide guidelines about which ethical principles take precedence when they conflict. To deal with this problem, Sanders and Young (2007) propose the 'Freedom model', which suggests that the goal of the criminal justice process is to protect and enhance freedom and personal autonomy. They argue that ensuring the greatest freedom should be the yardstick for deciding which principles/rights are prioritised whilst also recognising that justice and fairness are important (Sanders and Young, 2007). However, this concept is vague and difficult to put into practice.

Managerialism

Managerialism is not really a theory but a guiding principle by which the criminal justice process operates. It has greatly influenced the operation of the criminal justice process in the last three decades and has been one of the predominant drivers for change. Fundamentally, managerialism or New Public Management (Raine and Willson, 1993) involves the idea that the criminal justice process (and other public services) has to provide 'value for money'. It can be defined as:

> The implementation of a variety of techniques, generally borrowed from the private sector within a culture of cost efficiency and service effectiveness. (James and Raine, 1998: 31)

The principles behind managerialism are epitomised by the three 'E's': economy; efficiency; and effectiveness. Its key function is to cut costs. Beyond this, there is some debate about its core features (Newburn, 2003). Nevertheless, it is a very pragmatic response to the problems of the criminal justice process and lacks any philosophical or theoretical basis (McLaughlin, 2006).

Managerialism characterised the criminal justice process of the 1970s as 'spendthrift, idiosyncratic and unaccountable' (Raine and Willson, 1997). Managerialism aimed to tackle these inadequacies by introducing private sector practices and mechanisms. In short, it aimed to make the criminal justice process more business-like (Newburn, 2003). There were two waves of managerialism (McLaughlin, 2006; Raine and Willson, 1997), which relate broadly to the Conservatives' term of office in government between 1979 and 1997 and the New Labour government after 1997. The first wave aimed to create a cost-effective and efficient criminal justice system which worked towards agreed targets (McLaughlin, 2006). The second wave emphasised value for money and better quality services. It introduced performance management to improve productivity, and included the creation of strategic plans and the setting of targets (key performance targets, KPTs) and goals, which are published and scrutinised (McLaughlin, 2006; Raine and Willson, 1997). It also introduced the philosophies of '*What Works*' and 'evidence based practice', meaning that only measures which are shown to be effective through systematic evaluation are funded and resourced (Chapman and Hough, 1998; McGuire and Priestley, 1995). It continued to enhance multi-agency working with the development of 'multi-functional, multi-agency *partnerships*' involving all the main criminal justice agencies (McLaughlin, 2006).

The introduction of managerialist principles led to a range of policy developments, most notably the contracting out of many services in the criminal justice process, including prisons and court escort duties and the creation of a consumer culture. It has also contributed to shifts in the criminal justice policies, particularly in relation to reducing delay in the process. Criminal justice personnel have also been targeted because they were perceived to be a source of costly and bureaucratic practices. Most notably, the legal profession has come under increasing pressure as a major cause of delays and costs in the process (Carter, 2006).

Discretion

Discretion is very important to our understanding of the criminal justice process. All criminal justice personnel are afforded a considerable degree of discretion and it exists at every stage of the process. It arises because it is not possible for the law to prescribe what should happen in every potential situation. Consequently, criminal justice personnel have a considerable degree of autonomy to decide what to do in any given situation. At its extreme, discretion means an absence of constraint, but in practice, discretion is structured so that restrictions exist on what actions may be taken. Legal discretion is usually structured in one of two ways: by the use of criteria such as 'reasonable suspicion' for arrest, 'a realistic prospect of conviction' for prosecution, and 'proof beyond reasonable doubt' for conviction; or by restricting the level at which discretion is exercised. For example, police superintendent's rank or above are the only personnel who can decide to detain suspects for longer than the limits specified by the law.

There is a great deal of concern about the use of discretion in the criminal justice process. This arises because of its consequences, which are two-fold. Firstly, the use of discretion can result in unfair practices and particularly differential treatment of certain groups of people (Bowling and Phillips, 2002). Secondly, it has resulted in both law and policy being undermined so that the outcomes are not what were intended (Ashworth and Redmayne, 2005; McConville *et al.*, 2001; Sanders and Young, 2007).

REVIEW QUESTIONS

1 What are the main elements of:
  (i) The due process model
  (ii) The crime control model

2 What are the main components of managerialism?

3 What are the concerns about the level of discretion afforded to professionals in the criminal justice process?

Diminishing defendants' rights

In the introduction to this chapter, it was suggested that suspects' and defendants' rights have been diminished over the last two decades partly as a result of what the present government terms the 'rebalancing' agenda (Home Office, 2006). This section explores these issues in greater depth through a number of examples. It aims to demonstrate some of the mechanisms by which suspects' and defendants' rights have been eroded as well as providing knowledge about how the criminal justice process operates.

Reduction of suspects'/defendants' rights

This section will explore one area where defendants' rights have been curtailed, namely, the right to bail whilst awaiting trial. When courts adjourn cases so that they can reconvene at a later date, they usually make remand decisions. Courts, therefore, have to decide if defendants can be granted bail either unconditionally or with conditions thus releasing them into the community or remanded in custody resulting in imprisonment (Hucklesby, 2002). These decisions are crucial because the majority of defendants are unconvicted and legally innocent and should not have their freedom removed unnecessarily. Additionally, custodial remands have detrimental effects on later stages of the criminal justice process and defendants' lives (Hucklesby, 2002).

The law governing remand decisions is the Bail Act 1976 (as amended). This legislation was enacted as a result of concerns about the unnecessary and over use of custodial remands. The Bail Act 1976 provides a presumption in favour of bail in most circumstances. In other words, a right to bail exists, meaning that defendants must be released unless there are good reasons for not doing so. The law has always provided guidance on what the reasons for refusing bail might be which broadly relate to risks that defendants would abscond, commit offences, or interfere with witnesses.

The Bail Act 1976 has been amended significantly since it was introduced and this has restricted defendants' right to bail (Hucklesby, 2002). This has not impacted directly upon all defendants but has concentrated upon those charged with serious offences and/or offences committed on bail. This follows concerns about levels of offending on bail and a number of cases involving serious offences committed whilst on bail (see Hucklesby, 2002). The law has been amended so that in cases where it is alleged that defendants committed an offence whilst on bail, the presumption of bail is reversed in most cases. The presumption in favour of bail is also, in effect, reversed for defendants charged with serious offences including murder, manslaughter, and *rape* as courts are required to provide reasons *for* granting bail in such cases (Hucklesby, 2002). Taken together, these legal changes have removed some defendants' right to bail altogether or eroded it to such an extent that it does not exist in reality and made it much more likely that they will be remanded in custody while awaiting trial or sentence. Whether this is necessary to ensure that defendants do not abscond, commit further offences, or pose a risk to the public is debateable, particularly when a substantial minority will be acquitted or receive non-custodial sentences (Hucklesby, 2002).

Undermining suspects'/defendants' rights

Another mechanism through which defendants' rights have been undermined is through the actions of the criminal justice agencies whose role it is to ensure that their rights are enforced. Many legal measures, which protect the rights of defendants, require them or their representatives to ask or apply for their rights to be enforced. For example, in the previous section it was noted that defendants have a right to bail but the process still requires that they apply for bail if the prosecution objects to bail being granted. Similarly, the Police and Criminal Evidence Act 1984 brought in a right to free legal advice for suspects held at the police station. This followed a recommendation by the Philips Commission (Philips, 1981), which argued that legal advice was a vital and effective safeguard for suspects and assisted in militating some of the effects of detention. Previously access to legal advice had been left largely to the discretion of the police who generally did not recognise the right of suspects to consult solicitors. Consequently, access to legal advice for suspects detained at police stations was uncommon.

Historically, the police have been resistant to legal advice being available to suspects as they perceived it as impeding their investigations. Nevertheless, they are responsible for the process by which suspects' access legal advice (Ashworth and Redmayne, 2005; Sanders and Young, 2007). This provides the police with both the motivation and power to stop defendants accessing legal advice. Research suggests that this has indeed happened since free legal advice was made available for the first time by PACE (Sanders and Bridges, 1990). Research has consistently shown that suspects have not received the advice to which they have a right (Bucke and Brown, 1997; Sanders and Bridges, 1990). Successive changes to the Codes of Practice have tightened up procedures and improved the take up of legal advice (Sanders and Young, 2007). However, the majority of suspects still do not take up the offer of free legal advice whilst at the police station (Bucke and Brown, 1997). Sometimes this happens because defendants genuinely do not want legal advice. Nonetheless, the police sometimes break the law i.e. by not contacting solicitors, but more frequently they bend the law, for example, by not explaining suspects' rights comprehensively or by the use of 'ploys' or tactics (Sanders and Bridges, 1990). Consequently, it is often suggested that an opt-out rather than opt-in system is the only mechanism by which suspects will receive the legal advice they are entitled to (Sanders and Young, 2007).

By-passing suspects'/defendants' rights

Another way in which suspects' and defendants' rights have been diminished is by evading legal regulations which enforce them. The treatment of suspects at the police station is heavily regulated by PACE and its accompanying codes of practice. As well as providing defendants with the right to legal advice, they limit the amount of time suspects can be held in detention and provide standards for the conditions in which they may be held. They also enforce strict guidelines about how interviews should be conducted and require them to be tape-recorded. These regulations were brought in to limit the opportunities for police malpractice (Ashworth and Redmayne, 2005; Sanders and Young, 2007). Recently, these protections are being evaded by legislation and policies which are dealing with suspects and offenders before they arrive at the police station (Young, 2007). There are an increasing number of ways in which the public can become caught up in the criminal justice process or penalised for an offence, albeit a relatively minor offence, without setting foot in a police station. Examples include street bail which enables police officers to bail certain suspects without first taking them to the police station (Hucklesby, 2004); and penalty notices for disorder which allow the police and *community support officers* to issue fines without taking the offenders to the police station (Young, 2007). The trend is likely to continue with proposals to take fingerprints, DNA samples, and footwear impressions at the point of arrest, and the creation of 'short-term holding facilities' in shopping centres or town centres to process suspects as quickly as possible (Home Office, 2007). One of the official reasons for the introduction of such measures is to speed up justice and to save police and court time (Home Office, 2003; Office of Criminal Justice Reform, 2006). This fits neatly within the Government's agenda to cut bureaucracy and to bring in 'simply speedy summary justice' (DCA, 2007b). However, it also bypasses the regulatory framework of PACE, particularly the right to legal advice (Cape, 2007).

REVIEW QUESTIONS

1 In what ways have suspects' and defendants' rights been eroded?

2 How has the presumption in favour of bail been dismantled for certain groups of defendants?

3 In what ways are suspects' and defendants' rights evaded?

Differential treatment

This section explores the key concern of equality of treatment in the criminal justice process. Suspects, defendants, and offenders are treated differently in the criminal justice process. This occurs partly because of the discretion afforded to criminal justice professionals by the law. The three main areas where disparities in the treatment of suspects, defendants, and offenders have been identified are race, *gender*, and geography, and these will be discussed in turn.

Race

Minority ethnic groups are overrepresented at all stages of the criminal justice process (Ministry of Justice, 2008b). Nevertheless, there are also important differences between ethnic groups, which are sometimes greater than differences between the White and minority ethnic groups as a whole (Bowling and Phillips, 2002). Concerns about the treatment of minority ethnic groups have focused particularly on the police use of stop and search.

The police have wide discretion to stop and search anyone. Their discretion is structured by PACE which requires them to have 'reasonable grounds for suspicion' that evidence of relevant offences will be found. As Sanders and Young (2007) note, this is a very vague term, which enables the police to apply the law in a random and discriminatory way. The effectiveness of the power to stop and search as a crime detection tool is limited as only just over a tenth result in arrests (Ministry of Justice, 2008b). However, the use of stop and search also has intelligence-gathering and social disciplinary functions (Choogh, 1997). Historically stop and search has been a cause of friction between communities and the police and was a contributory factor in the Brixton Riots, as well as being discussed at length during the Stephen Lawrence inquiry (Scarman, 1981; Macpherson, 1999).

Large numbers of people are stopped and searched every year. In 2006/07, over 955,000 stops and searches were recorded by the police (Ministry of Justice, 2008b). The number has been rising steadily since PACE was enacted in 1986. Stop and search powers are also targeted at some groups more than others. The best predictors of being stopped are being black, male, and under 30 (Fitzgerald and Hough, 2002). According to the most recent *Ministry of Justice* figures, Black people are seven times more likely than White people to be stopped and searched, and Asians are twice as likely to be stopped and searched compared with White people (Ministry of Justice, 2008b). There have been extensive debates about whether this overrepresentation can be explained by 'objective' factors such as differences in offence patterns, socio-demographic characteristics, research methodology, and so on, none of which is conclusive or provides a satisfactory explanation (Bowling and Phillips, 2002; Millar *et al.*, 2000; Quinton, *et al.*, 2000; Waddington *et al.*, 2004). Consequently, there is general agreement that some minority ethnic groups, most notably Black people, but increasing individuals of Asian origin, are targeted by police through the use of stop and search powers.

Most research relating to minority ethnic groups has focused on police decision making. Consequently, there is only limited research on other areas of the criminal justice process. However, what there is suggests that minority ethnic groups are treated differently and often more harshly than White suspects/defendants in the criminal justice process. There is some limited evidence that bail decisions vary between different ethnic groups and the Black defendants are more likely to be remanded in custody (Brown and Hullin, 1991). There is also evidence of different decisions being made by the CPS in relation to defendants from minority ethnic groups compared with White defendants

(Barclay and Mhlanga, 2000; Mhlanga, 1999). These studies suggest that there were significant differences in the outcomes between the two largest ethnic groups and White defendants which included variations in CPS decisions to discontinue cases or downgrade charges and subsequent court decisions.

Gender

It is widely acknowledged that women are treated differently to men in the criminal justice process, yet there is no agreement about whether women are treated more leniently or harshly than men. In terms of criminal justice decision making, the picture often appears contradictory. Men are more likely to be stopped and searched, while women are less likely than men to be charged, have their cases dealt with in the Crown Court, or be remanded in custody (Ministry of Justice, 2008a). Women are more likely than men to have no further action taken against them, be cautioned, and receive community sentences (Ministry of Justice, 2008a). At first sight these findings suggest that women are generally treated more leniently than men in the criminal justice process as they are less likely to be prosecuted and case outcomes tend to be less punitive. However, this picture becomes more complex when consideration is given to the fact that women's offending is on a much more limited scale, both in terms of extent and seriousness than men's (Ministry of Justice, 2008a). This has been used to argue that women are treated more harshly than men in the criminal justice process because they are likely to be imprisoned for less serious offences than men and with far fewer, if any, previous convictions (see Hedderman and Gelsthorpe, 1997; Heidensohn 1996).

These two contradictory hypotheses are referred to by several different terms, but for our purposes we will call them the 'chivalry' and 'evil women theory' (Cavadino and Dignan, 2007; Heidensohn, 1986). The chivalry hypothesis suggests that women are treated more leniently because of the chivalrous nature of the police and courts, which are dominated by men. It is argued that men treat women favourably in all aspects of life and they continue to do so in the criminal justice process. Indeed, it is suggested that men do not want to impose hardship or punishment on women, particularly if it involves taking women away from their caring responsibilities. This relates to the practical reasons why women may be treated more leniently than men in that sentencers may not wish children to be taken into care (Carlen, 1985). By contrast, the evil women hypothesis suggests that women are treated more harshly because offending is perceived as 'unfeminine' and transgressing not only the criminal law but the norms of how women should behave (Carlen, 1985; Heidensohn, 1996; Morris, 1987). Consequently, women offenders are 'doubly-deviant'.

The research evidence suggests that some women are treated more leniently while others are treated more harshly (Hedderman and Gelsthorpe, 1997). This can be explained with reference to ideas of the 'respectable women' and conforms to the evil women hypothesis (Carlen, 1985; Morris, 1987). It relates to the stereotype of women as good wives and mothers. Women who are married and looking after their children and who therefore conform to this stereotype are treated leniently. By contrast, women who do not conform to it, for example, because they are sex workers or their children are in care, are perceived as 'bad' mothers and treated more harshly. Consequently, women's but not men's marital status and family circumstances are considered by criminal justice agencies when making decisions (Carlen, 1985; Morris, 1987).

Geography

Official statistics and research findings demonstrate that there are differences between geographic areas in decisions made by the police and the courts (Home Office, 2006; Hucklesby, 1997; Moxon and Hedderman, 1984). This has been termed '*justice by geography*' and basically means that to some extent what happens to suspects, defendants, and offenders partly depends on where they happen to be. This pattern can be seen across all stages of the criminal justice process. There are wide variations in the use of stop and search powers between police forces. These range from 596 per 100,000 in Essex to 5,017 per 100,000 by the Metropolitan Police (Ministry of Justice, 2008c). The average rate per 100,000 for England and Wales was 2,026 (Ministry of Justice, 2008c). Differences have also been uncovered in request and contact rates for legal advice at police stations (Bucke and Brown, 1997; Phillips and Brown, 1998), in police and court bail decisions (Bucke and Brown, 1997; Hucklesby, 1997; 2001), in the rates at which suspects confess in police custody (Phillips and Brown, 1998) and how cases are dealt with by the police including rates of charging and no further action. Phillips and Brown (1998) also found differences in CPS decision making by area. These findings suggest that 'local cultures' exist which affect the decision making of criminal justice professionals in particular areas (Parker *et al.*, 1989; Hucklesby, 1997). A pertinent question is whether it matters that there are local variations in decision making. Historically, the legal system in Britain has been based on local justice and many people would still champion the system of 'local' justice whereby local circumstances and priorities can be taken into consideration (Raine, 1989). Others see variations in the decisions being taken as unfair and unjust and a threat to the legitimacy of the criminal justice process.

REVIEW QUESTIONS

1 What evidence exists to support the argument that stop and search powers are used differently by the police for some groups?

2 What are the 'chivalry' and 'evil women' hypotheses?

3 What evidence exists to support the idea of 'justice by geography'?

CONCLUSION

This chapter has introduced the main institutions and agencies involved in the criminal justice process and highlighted some of the key issues and controversies relating to how the criminal justice process operates. It has demonstrated that the criminal justice process is complex and that it does not always operate in the way in which it is intended. It has been suggested that there is a gap between how the process is supposed to work, i.e. what the law and policy says should happen, and how it operates in practice. This disjuncture is partly explained by the ways in which law is operationalised and used by the criminal justice agencies, and partly by the way the laws and policies are drafted. A key feature of the criminal justice process is the wide discretion afforded to criminal justice agencies which empowers them to use the law in different ways.

The criminal justice process is supposed to be based on the principles of due process whereby the rights of suspects and defendants are protected from the power of the state. However, this chapter has suggested that key due process rights, such as the presumption of bail, the right to legal advice at the police station, and the safeguards provided by PACE, are increasingly being undermined by legal and policy changes. This has occurred as part of the Government's agenda to 'rebalance' the criminal justice process in favour of the 'law-abiding majority'. These measures have significantly reduced the rights of suspects and defendants and made the criminal justice process more crime-control orientated. The wisdom of these moves can be questioned as they are likely to undermine the legitimacy of the process and lead to miscarriages of justice.

QUESTIONS FOR DISCUSSION

1 What are the main agencies and institutions involved in the prosecution process and what are their roles?

2 Compare the advantages and disadvantages of the magistrates' and Crown Court.

3 Compare and contrast the due process and crime control models of the criminal justice process.

4 Does the prosecution process deal with all suspects and defendants equally and fairly?

5 What rights should suspects and defendants have?

GUIDE TO FURTHER READING

Ashworth, A. and Redmayne, M. (2005) *The Criminal Process*. Oxford: Oxford University Press.
This book provides a comprehensive exploration of the criminal justice process which is organised thematically.

McConville, M., Sanders, A., and Leng, R. (1991) *The Case for the Prosecution*. London: Routledge.
This is a seminal study of the use of police powers and the role of the Crown Prosecution Service.

McConville, M. and Wilson, G. (eds) (2002) *The Handbook of the Criminal Justice Process*. Oxford: Oxford University Press.
This book draws together chapters written by experts on every area of the criminal justice process.

Sanders, A. and Young, R. (2007) 'From suspect to trial' in M. Maguire, R. Morgan, and R. Reiner (eds) *The Oxford Handbook of Criminology*. Oxford: Oxford University Press.
This chapter is a comprehensive introduction to the themes and debates relating to the prosecution process and provides a shorter introduction to the issues explored in the authors' book *Criminal Justice*.

Sanders, A. and Young, R. (2007) *Criminal Justice*. Oxford: Oxford University Press.
This book is the most comprehensive and up-to-date examination of the criminal justice process and deals with each stage of the process in turn.

WEB LINKS

Most relevant material can be found on the Ministry of Justice website at <http://www.justice.gov.uk>. Material relating to the period before the creation of the Ministry of Justice can be found on the Home Office website at <http://www.homeoffice.gov.uk> or on the Department of Constitutional Affairs website at <http://www.dca.gov.uk>. Information on the Crown Prosecution Service is available at <http://www.cps.gov.uk>. Extensive information about the operation of the prosecution process is also available from <http://www.cjsonline.gov.uk>.

REFERENCES

Ashworth, A. and Redmayne, M. (2005) *The Criminal Process: An Evaluative Study* (3rd edn). Oxford: Oxford University Press.

Barclay, G. and Mhlanga, B. (2000) *Ethnic differences in decision on young defendants dealt with by the CPS*. Home Office Research Statistics Development Section 95 Findings 1. London: Home Office.

Bottoms, A.E. and McClean, J.D. (1976) *Defendants in the Criminal Process*. London: Routledge.

Bowling, B. and Phillips, C. (2002) *Racism, Crime and Justice*. Harlow: Longman.

Brown, D., Ellis, T., and Larcombe, K. (1992) *Changing the Code: police detention under the revised PACE Code of Practice*. Home Office Research Study No. 129. London: Home Office.

Brown, I. and Hullin, R. (1991) 'A Study of Sentencing in the Leeds Magistrates' Court'. *British Journal of Criminology* 32(1): 41–53.

Brownlee, I. (2004) 'The Statutory Charging Scheme in England and Wales: towards a unified prosecution system' *Criminal Law Review*: 896–907.

Bucke, T. and Brown, D. (1997) *In Police Custody: Police Powers and Suspects' Rights under the Revised PACE Codes of Practice*. Home Office Research Study No. 174. London: HMSO.

Cape, E. (2007) *Pace then and now: 21 years of rebalancing*, paper presented at the Policing and Defending in a post-PACE world. University of the West of England, 29 March.

Carlen, P. (1985) *Criminal Women*. Oxford: Polity Press.

Carter, Lord (2006) *Legal Aid: a market-based approach to reform*. London: The Stationery Office.

Cavadino, M. and Dignan. J. (2007) *The Penal System* (4th edn). London: Sage.

Chapman, T. and Hough, M. (1998) *Evidence Based Practice: A guide to effective practice*. London: HM Inspectorate of Probation.

Choogh, S. (1997) *Policing as Social Discipline*. Oxford: Clarendon Press.

Darbyshire, P. (2002) 'Magistrates' in M. McConville and G. Wilson (eds) *The Handbook of the Criminal Justice Process*. Oxford: Oxford University Press.

Department of Constitutional Affairs (DCA) (2007a) Magistrates, at <http://www.dca.gov.uk> accessed on 1 May 2007.

Department of Constitutional Affairs (DCA) (2007b) *Delivering Simple, Speedy, Summary Justice*. London: DCA.

Dignan, J. and Whynne, A. (1997) 'A Microcosm of the Local Community?' *British Journal of Criminology* 37: 184.

Fattah, E. (1994) *The Interchangeable Roles of Victims and Victimizer*. Helsinki: European Institute of Crime Prevention and Control.

Fitzgerald, M. and Hough, M. (2002) *Policing for London*. Cullompton: Willan Publishing.

Glidewell, L.J. (1998) The Review of the Crown Prosecution Service Cm. 3960. London: Home Office.

Hedderman, C. and Gelsthorpe, L. (1997) *Understanding the Sentencing of Women*. Home Office Research Study No. 170. London: HMSO.

Heidensohn, F. (1986) 'Models of Justice: Portia or Persephone?' *International Journal of the Sociology of Law* 14: 287–8.

Heidensohn, F. (1996) *Women and Crime*. Basingstoke: Macmillan.

Heidensohn, F. (2002) 'Gender and Crime' in M. Maguire, R. Morgan, and R. Reiner (eds) *The Oxford Handbook of Criminology*. Oxford: Oxford University Press.

Home Office (2003) *Criminal Justice Act 2003: Bail Elsewhere than at the Police Station*. Circular 61/2003, London: Home Office.

Home Office (2006) *Rebalancing the criminal justice system in favour of the law-abiding majority*. London: Home Office.

Home Office (2007) *Modernising Police Powers: review of PACE 1984*. London: Home Office.

Hucklesby, A. (1996) 'Bail or Jail? The practical operation of the Bail Act 1976'. *Journal of Law and Society* 23: 213.

Hucklesby, A. (1997) 'Court Culture: an explanation of variations in the use of bail in magistrates' courts'. *Howard Journal* 36(2): 129–45.

Hucklesby, A. (2001) 'Police bail and the use of conditions'. *Criminal Justice* 1(4): 441–464.

Hucklesby, A. (2002) 'Bail in Criminal Cases' in M. McConville and G. Wilson (eds) *The Handbook of the Criminal Justice Process*. Oxford: Oxford University Press.

Hucklesby, A. (2004) 'Not necessarily a trip to the police station: the introduction of street bail'. *Criminal Law Review*: 803–13.

Jackson, J. (2002) 'The Adversary Trial and Trial by Jury Alone' in M. McConville and R. Wilson (eds) *The Handbook of the Criminal Justice Process*. Oxford: Oxford University Press.

James. A. and Raine, J. (1998) *The New Politics of Criminal Justice*. London: Longman.

King, M. (1981) *The Framework of Criminal Justice*. London: Croom Helm.

MacPherson, W. (1999) *The Stephen Lawrence Inquiry, Report of an inquiry by Sir William Macpherson of Cluny*, Cmnd 4262-1. London: Home Office.

McBarnett, D.J. (1981) *Conviction: law, the state and the construction of justice*. London: Macmillan.

McConville, M. and Bridges, L. (1994) *Criminal Justice in Crisis*. Aldershot: Edward Elgar.

McConville, M., Hodgson, J., Bridges, L., and Pavlovic, A. (1994) *Standing Accused*. Oxford: Clarendon Press.

McConville, M., Sanders, A., and Leng, R. (1991) *The Case for the Prosecution*. London: Routledge.

McConville, M., Sanders, A., and Leng, R. (1997) 'Descriptive or Critical Sociology'. *British Journal of Criminology* 37: 347–58.

McGuire, J. and Priestley, P. (1995) 'Reviewing "What Works": Past, Present and Future' in J. McGuire (ed) *What Works: Reducing Reoffending*. Chichester: Wiley.

McLaughlin, E. (2006) 'Managerialism' in E. McLaughlin and J. Muncie, *The Sage Dictionary of Criminology* (2nd edn). London: Sage.

Mhlanga, B. (1999) *Race and the Crown Prosecution Service*. London: The Stationery Office.

Millar, J., Bland, N., and Quinton, P. (2000) *Upping the PACE? An Evaluation of the Recommendations of the Stephen Lawrence Inquiry on Stop and Search*. Police Research Series Paper 128. London: Home Office.

Ministry of Justice (2008a) *Statistics on Women and the Criminal Justice System 2005/6*. London: Ministry of Justice.

Ministry of Justice (2008b) *Statistics on Race and the Criminal Justice System 2006/7*. London: Ministry of Justice.

Ministry of Justice (2008c) *Arrests for Recorded Crime and the Operation of Certain Police Powers under PACE England and Wales 2006/7*. London: Ministry of Justice.

Morgan, R. and Russell, N. (2000) *The Judiciary in the Magistrates' Courts*. London: Home Office and Lord Chancellor's Department.

Morris A. (1987) *Women, Crime and Criminal Justice*. Oxford: Blackwell.

Moxon, D. and Hedderman, C (1994) 'Mode of Trial Decisions and Sentencing Between Courts'. *Howard Journal* 33: 97–108.

Newburn, T. (2003) *Crime and Criminal Justice Policy*. Harlow: Longman.

Office of Criminal Justice Reform (2006) *Penalty Notices for Disorder: review of practice across police forces*. London: OCJR.

Packer, H. (1969) *The Limits of the Criminal Sanction*. Stanford University Press, Stanford.

Parker, H., Sumner, M. and Jarvis, G. (1989) *Unmasking the Magistrates*. Milton Keynes: Open University Press.

Paternoster, R, Brame, R., Bachman, R., and Sherman, L. (1997) 'Do Fair Procedures Matter? The Effect of Procedural Justice on Spouse Assault'. *Law and Society Review* 31: 163–204.

Philips, Sir C. (1981) *The Report of the Royal Commission on Criminal Procedure* Cmnd 8092. London: HMSO.

Phillips, C and Brown, D. (1998) *Entry into the Criminal Justice System: a survey of police arrests and their outcomes* Home Office Research Study No. 185. London: Home Office.

Quinton, P., Bland, N., and Millar, J. (2000) *Police Stops, Decision Making and Practice*, Police Research Series Paper No. 130. London: Home Office.

Raine, J. (1989) *Local Justice*. London: T. and T. Clark.

Raine, J. and Willson, M. (1993) *Managing Criminal Justice*. Hemel Hempstead: Harvester Wheatsheaf.

Raine, J. and Willson, M. (1997) 'Beyond Managerialism in Criminal Justice'. *Howard Journal* 36(1): 80–95.

Rosenburg, J. (1992) 'Miscarriages of Justice' in E. Stockdale and S. Casale (eds) *Criminal Justice Under Stress*. London: Blackstone.

Runciman, Viscount (1993) *The Report of the Royal Commission on Criminal Justice*, Cm 2263. HMSO: London.

Sanders, A. and Bridges, L. (1990) 'Access to Legal Advice and Police Malpractice'. *Criminal Law Review*: 494.

Sanders, A. and Young, R. (2007) 'From Suspect to Trial' in M. Maguire, R. Morgan, and R. Reiner, *The Oxford Handbook of Criminology* (3rd edn). Oxford: Oxford University Press: 1034–75.

Sanders, A. and Young, R. (2007) *Criminal Justice* (3rd edn). Oxford: Oxford University Press.

Scarman, Lord (1981) *The Scarman Report* Cmnd 8427. London: Home Office.

Seago, P., Walker, C., and Wall, D. (2000) 'The Development of the Professional Magistracy in England and Wales' *Criminal Law Review*: 631–51.

Smith, D. (1997) 'Case Construction and the Goals of Criminal Process' *British Journal of Criminology* 37: 319–46.

Waddington, P.A.J., Stenson, K., and Don, D. (2004) 'In proportion: race and police stop and search' *British Journal of Criminology* 44(6): 899–914.

Walker, C. and Starmer, K. (1999) *Miscarriages of Justice*. London: Blackstone.

Young, R. (2007) *Street Policing After PACE: The drift toward summary justice*, paper presented at the Policing and Defending in a post-PACE world. University of the West of England, 29 March.

4

Punishment

David Scott

INTRODUCTION

It has often been said that the way we deal with wrongdoers is a reflection of our society. Punitive responses to wrongdoing by the *capitalist state* inevitably generate profound moral and political dilemmas, as punishments are invasive and harm-creating practices contradicting many of our most highly regarded moral values (Christie, 2004). Most notably, *punishment* is diametrically opposed to the belief that harming others is wrong. This chapter considers the three main ways of approaching the justifications of punishment: *consequentialist* philosophies that look to justify punishment in terms of preventing future offending; *retributive* philosophies that focus on responding proportionately to the actual offence; and *abolitionist* philosophies that maintain that punishment cannot be either morally or politically justified. The central aim of this chapter is to raise a question mark against the legitimacy of the penal apparatus of the capitalist state, and highlight possible alternatives to the *punitive rationale* as a means of dealing with problematic human conduct.

BACKGROUND

Punishment, in essence, is the deliberate infliction of pain and suffering. The definition of punishment has, however, been an area of considerable controversy. Primoratz (1989: 1–2), for example, has argued that punishment should be defined as an 'evil' and an unwanted imposition or burden, rather than be described as the infliction of pain and suffering. He argues that talk of pain and suffering tap into the imagery of harsh physical penalties of times past, rather than the more lenient forms of punishment dominant in Western 'civilised' nations today. His position, though, is tantamount to a 'denial of injury' (Cohen, 2001), contradicting overwhelming evidence that penal sanctions are harmful, degrading, and bring about psychological suffering (Scott and Codd, 2009). For present purposes then, a penal sanction can be understood as 'state punishment' if an authorised agent of the capitalist state with the aim of *intentionally* hurting a person who is believed to have committed a legally prohibited act, initiates a harm that causes an offender pain and suffering (Flew, 1954; Duff, 2001).

It is perhaps somewhat surprising that punishment is widely seen as the normal response to '*crime*'. It would be much more logical to assume that it is *not* automatically correct to hurt someone when they have done a wrong. Given that the delivery of the state's right or power to punish is out of kilter with many other human values, it necessarily requires legitimation. Criminologists have attempted to assess the legitimacy of state punishment on three different grounds: pragmatic, political, and moral.

Pragmatic evaluations consider whether punishment does what it claims in terms of reducing future harms and wrongdoing, and is closely associated with *consequentialism*. Political evaluations of punishment require a consideration of the rightfulness of the current distribution and application of the power to punish. This entails an examination of the delivery of penalties within current socio-economic and political contexts, and has led some criminologists to claim that the current punishment orgy is rooted in a punitive ideology aimed at disciplining and controlling certain identifiable subgroups within the population (Mathiesen, 2006). Political considerations have been very important when discussing the merits of *retributivism*.

The third approach to assessing the legitimacy of the state's repressive penal apparatus, concerns the moral rightfulness of governing authorities to deliberately hurt someone for breaching the law. Questions around moral legitimacy have been central to *abolitionism*, with some abolitionists arguing that the normal response to wrongdoing should be non-punitive sanctions that do not intend to harm the offender (Boonin, 2008). Braithwaite and Pettit (1990: 9) call this principle '*parsimony*'. This is a presumption of either non-intervention or the use of the most minimum restrictions possible in response to wrongdoing. A parsimonious approach dictates that the 'onus of proof' falls on those justifying state intrusion and control, rather than upon those arguing for the diminishing of state punishment. If there is reasonable doubt that punishment is not justifiable, then the presumption for less punishment should be accepted. This principle of parsimony underscores the evaluation of consequentialist, retributivist, and abolitionist perspectives in this chapter.

Consequentialism

Consequentialists identify which human goods provide the best overall welfare for society, and then calculate the most effective means that can be deployed to promote such ends. The chosen means must be efficient, do more good than harm, and provide the best available ways in which such ends can be maximised. There are a number of consequentialist approaches to punishment, including communitarianism (Lacey, 1988) and republicanism (Braithwaite and Pettit, 1990), but it is *utilitarianism* which is the most well known and developed approach, and as such is the central focus here. For utilitarians, morality is based upon the degree to which actions maximise pleasure and reduce or eliminate pain. This is known as the greatest happiness principle.

Utilitarians, such as Beccaria and Bentham, argue that punishment is an 'evil' that can only be morally permissible if it can be proved that its infliction will prevent greater harm and suffering in the future. The main purpose of punishment is conceived as 'nothing other than to dissuade the criminal from doing fresh harm to his compatriots and to keep other people from doing the same' (Beccaria, 1764: 23). Human beings are viewed as rational actors where 'pain and pleasure are the great springs of human action' (Bentham, 1830: 19). Through ensuring that the pains of punishment outweigh the pleasure of crime, future offending is prevented. It is this notion of general *prevention* which Bentham (1830: 20–21) finds the most important justification of punishment. In a widely quoted passage he stated:

> General prevention ought to be the chief end of punishment, as it is its real justification. If we could consider an offence which has been committed as an isolated fact, the likes of which would never recur, punishment would be useless. It would be only adding one evil to another. But when we consider that an unpunished crime leaves the path of crime open not only to the same delinquent, but also to all those who may have the same motives and opportunities for entering upon it, we perceive that the punishment inflicted on the individual becomes

a source of security to all. That punishment, which, considered in itself, appeared base and repugnant to all generous sentiments, is elevated to the first rank of benefits... [becoming] an indispensable sacrifice to the common safety.

This overall focus on the maximisation of human happiness does, however, leave the utilitarian approach vulnerable on a number of grounds. First, they put themselves under an obligation to prove empirically that punishment does actually have a utility, i.e. that punishment is effective in reducing future crimes. Second, by judging the effects of punishment purely upon its wider consequences, utilitarianism has no inbuilt logic to prevent the punishment of innocent people, if their intentional suffering would bring more overall human happiness than not doing so. Third, and for similar reasons, it incorporates no safeguards to ensure that the severity of the sentence is commensurate to the harm of the offence. Excessively harsh punishments can be invoked for relatively minor offences, if felt that making an example of a given offender would create a greater general preventive effect. A fourth concern is that offenders are used as 'a means subservient to the purposes of another' rather than being treated as ends in themselves, thus denying their inherent human dignity (Kant, 1887: 195).

Utilitarians are reluctant advocates of punishment, and where it would fail to serve the greater good they argue it should be abandoned. This principle, though, may again leave unchecked inequities and bias in who is punished. For Bentham (1830: 20) punishment can serve the greater good in three ways: by taking from the offender the physical powers of offending; by taking away the desire of offending; and by making the offender afraid of offending.

In other words utilitarian justifications are premised upon the notions of *incapacitation*, *rehabilitation*, and *deterrence* through the 'intimidation or terror of the law' (Bentham, 1830). Let us then consider each of these in turn.

Incapacitation

Incapacitation involves removing the capacity to commit future 'crimes' and includes forms of punishment such as physical maiming, the death penalty, banishment and imprisonment. Incapacitation appears very straightforward, and has a particular mechanical fit with the basic function of imprisonment—the denial of physical capacity to participate in the wider society (Zimring and Hawkins, 1995). It also would appear to have a foolproof logic in terms of meeting its aims (Bentham, 1830). There are two forms of incapacitation: collective incapacitation and selective incapacitation. Collective incapacitation involves sentences aiming to contain offenders of specific offences, such as burglary. There is no attempt to categorise offenders between those likely or unlikely to commit further wrongs in the future, and the denial of physical freedom is determined by the nature of the 'crime' committed. By contrast, selective incapacitation is directed at high-risk offenders who are predicted as being *at risk* of committing future harms. Offenders are identified individually based upon past behaviour and personality traits, and high-risk offenders are given disproportionately long sentences to prevent future offending. In other words, a sentence of imprisonment is deemed appropriate because of the offender's perceived future 'riskiness' or *dangerousness* rather than their past wrongs.

Incapacitation may, however, simply lead to the postponement of wrongdoings, with the offender having a greater propensity to offend on return to society, whilst imprisoned offenders may continue to control criminal activities on the outside. Imprisonment also has what Honderich (2006: 77) has called 'capacitating effects', in that it actually gives rise to opportunities and desires for new wrongs, such as male *rape*, or may degrade offenders to such an extent they undertake more dangerous or heinous acts in the future. On the outside the families and communities from which prisoners are drawn will also suffer the collateral consequences of the sentence, whilst the offenders themselves may be prevented from doing good deeds or repairing harms in the community.

Collective incapacitation is unlikely to have a long-term impact on the crime rate, as reported 'crimes' are cyclical and generational, and so for incapacitation to work we would have to constantly incarcerate large sections of each generation. The removal of [working class] persistent offenders only has an impact for a small number of years, as their place would eventually be taken by new, probably younger, people. The cost of locking up enough criminals to make a real difference is simply beyond the capitalist state's fiscal capacities. It is just too expensive to incapacitate enough offenders to have the required good consequences for society (Golash, 2005).

Selective incapacitation is grounded in *positivism* and risk assessments, and has major moral flaws. Not only does it contravene the basic principles of penal law that only the legally guilty should be punished, but also we do not actually have the ability to accurately predict who will commit serious offences in the future (Mathiesen, 2006). Braithwaite and Pettit (1990) claim that even the best prediction techniques are wrong at least twice as often as they are right, whilst Golash (2005) estimates that predictions are generally wrong eight times out of nine. A further problem is that, based upon these unreliable and inaccurate predictive scores, some offenders are given more severe sentences than they should, and so are undeservedly punished (von Hirsch, 1987).

REVIEW QUESTIONS

1 Why is the definition of punishment controversial?

2 What is the principle of parsimony and why is it important when thinking about punishment?

3 What are the strengths and weaknesses of utilitarianism?

Rehabilitation

The definition of rehabilitation is also an area of considerable debate. Raynor and Robinson (2005: 9–11) identify a number of competing definitions, arguing that rehabilitation has both been construed as an essential component of punishment, *and* seen as an 'antidote' or means of undoing the harmful disadvantages punishment has created. Rehabilitation can perhaps best be understood as an attempt to restore the individual to the person they were before the 'crime' was committed. It is assumed that the individual has in some way been changed by their wrongdoing, or that the 'crime' occurred because of their mental, physical, or moral degradation. Wrongdoing is conceived as an individual or social disease, and, if the problems can be correctly diagnosed, we can cure the offender. Rehabilitationists therefore focus on providing treatment for criminogenic symptoms and offender 'needs', epitomising the main principles of the medical model and positivist criminology. Punishment is a form of 'moral surgery' for it can be seen as being 'like surgery, a necessary evil to be undertaken in no spirit of revenge, but with the same wise economy as a surgeon handles his knife' (Whitby, 1910: 895).

Underscoring rehabilitative punishment are three fundamental beliefs: first, offenders are different from 'normal' people and that this difference is directly linked to their offending behaviour; second, we can positively alter or 'normalise' people through social engineering and that we have the right to do so; and third, that punishment generally, and imprisonment specifically, can act as a catalyst for this *restoration* or alteration of the offender.

A number of concerns have been raised against the rehabilitative justification. Many critics start by highlighting the obvious: 'crime' is not an 'illness' or 'disease' but a social construction and wrongdoers may not be that different from law-abiding people. By focusing on the offender instead of the 'crime', and upon perceived pathologies rooted in individual or social defects, rehabilitation is profoundly deterministic and denies human agency and moral choices. There is also the danger that, whilst appearing benevolent, many alleged 'cures' can create more harm than the 'crimes' they aim to treat. Rehabilitation can also be perceived as unfair and undermining procedural rights, as rehabilitative sentences can be indeterminate or disproportionately long, as the offender must complete the proposed transformation or cure before the treatment programme can end (Hudson, 1996).

Advocates of rehabilitation have sometimes been reluctant to admit that the cures that are attempted through coerced detention are a form of punishment at all (Wooton, 1965), thus wrapping highly painful practices within a humanitarian and caring language. On empirical grounds rehabilitation has historically proved to be largely ineffective in reducing future harms (Martinson, 1974), with the small number of successful cases being the exceptions that prove the rule. The deliberate infliction of pain is likely to be counter-productive, embedding a psychology promoting a rejection of rejecters, whilst it is widely acknowledged that prisons are 'school for scoundrels'. For one penal critic the conclusion that must be drawn from the last 200 years of rehabilitation in prison is crystal clear: 'Not only can we most certainly say that the prison does not rehabilitate. Most likely we can also say that it in fact *de*habilitates' (Mathiesen, 2006: 53).

In recent years a number of repackaged versions of rehabilitation have come to prominence, claiming to avoid many of the problems that shackled the old rehabilitative ideal. 'Neo-rehabilitation', promoted in theory by Rotman (1990), and in policy by Lord Justice Woolf (1991), no longer sees rehabilitation as a general justification, but rather portrays it as a 'right' (Rotman, 1990) or 'legitimate expectation' (Woolf, 1991) of offenders. The capitalist state is construed as being under an obligation to ensure that wrongdoers are given opportunities to make prudent choices that can help them learn how to behave responsibly and thus reduce their risk of re-offending. The focus upon risk and the protection of the public are also central to the equally influential '*What Works*' rehabilitative agenda (Maguire, 1995), which locates the causes of problematic behaviours in offender's cognitive defects and deficient thinking skills. Critics, however, maintain that contemporary rehabilitative programmes are just as flawed as their predecessors. Specifically, concerns are raised that they individualise, responsibilise, and 'other' law-breakers as cognitively different, whilst ignoring wider problematic social circumstances and structural divisions, such as poverty, sexism, and racism (Kendal, 2002).

Deterrence

Deterrence, the idea that people refrain from certain actions because they fear the consequences arising through such actions appears to have an almost self-evident common-sense rationale, and yet the deterrent effect has been remarkably difficult to prove. The empirical measurement of deterrence is largely impossible because we are attempting to assess events that do not actually occur. Rather than being able to provide scientific calculations, much of the believed effects of deterrence come down to guess work. A ploy by advocates of deterrence, such as Walker (1993), is to simply pass off common-sense assumptions as unproblematic. It remains crucial, however, that we investigate the very foundations of deterrence when assessing its legitimacy.

There are two types of deterrence—individual deterrence and general deterrence—and the manipulation of the rationality of the wrongdoer is central to both. Individual deterrence is directed at the actual wrongdoer and involves the use of an *individual fear calculus*, where the pain of the punishment outweighs the pleasure of the offence, resulting in a reduction of the offender's desire to do future wrong. In contrast, general deterrence is all about *social control*. Central to this approach is the *social fear calculus*, as individuals themselves are not subjected to pain but rather are witness to the pain of others.

Proponents of deterrence concede that the deterrent effect is contingent upon a number of different variables, such as the kinds of norm being violated, the level of seriousness of the wrongdoing, or the stage that the offence occurs in the offender's criminal career (Andeneas, 1974; Wright, 1994). Very significant also is the *certainty* of being caught and convicted. The lower the degree of perceived risk of apprehension by the offender, the less likely the penal law will intimidate them against perpetrating wrongful acts in the future (Andeneas, 1974).

There are a number of problems with deterrence. One of the most damning criticisms is that deterrence is irrelevant, because most people who refrain from problematic behaviours do so for reasons unconnected to the penal law. Moral conscience or family reputations may act as a barrier to prevent the wrongdoing in the first instance, whilst persistent offenders may grow out of 'crime' (Golash, 2005; Honderich, 2006). Put simply, deterrence is most likely to work for those who need it least. People with strong social ties, support networks, and access to emotional and material resources, are likely to be intimidated by penal law, because they have so much to lose. People who are already stigmatised, impoverished, and excluded are less likely to fear further stigmatisation. Indeed a criminal record may become a sign of status. Deterrence is also gendered, with its main audience being male offenders. There is relatively wide acknowledgement, even in official circles (Corston, 2007), that deterrent sentences are inappropriate for women because they refrain from 'crime' for other reasons. What is clear is that there is a lack of universality, for what deters one person may not deter another (Hudson, 1996; Mathiesen, 2006).

The very logic of deterrence has also been questioned. It is likely that most people do not rationalise and calculate costs and benefits about 'crimes' or ordinary daily activities. Impulse, opportunity, excitement, and strong emotions play important roles in determining actions, and these are not thought out in advance. Further, in some circumstances the most rational or moral action may be to break the law. Empirical evidence that individual deterrence works is also unpromising. In terms of imprisonment the recidivism rates are high for both young (75 per cent) and adult offenders (50 per cent), and even then we do not know who offends but is not caught (Scott and Codd, 2009).

Defenders of general deterrence argue that harsh and severe sentences are an effective means of intimidating potential future law breakers. Yet the only empirical findings to date that appear to support this are reductions in drink-driving. The problem here is that during the decline, the public were also presented with powerful and thought-provoking media campaigns highlighting the dreadful consequences of drink-driving. Falls could well be the result of changes in popular morality about the correctness of drinking and driving, as much as the fear of strong penal sanctions (Hudson, 1996).

General deterrence is an attempt to communicate a 'message from the state' (Mathiesen, 2006: 65) through the penal law, but the difficulty is that the message may be misinterpreted by its intended audience. It may be distorted, reinterpreted, or never received. In other words the 'signal is not effective, and the message not understood as the sender has meant it' (2006: 74). Punitive sentencing may be counterproductive and perceived as 'more oppression, more moralising and more rejection' (2006: 74). It is likely that it is much more effective to communicate moral disapproval through *moral education* than severe sentencing.

General deterrence is also based on the dubious principle of punishing one person so that it may deter another completely different person from committing a similar offence (Mathiesen, 2006). In advanced capitalist-patriarchal societies the penal law punishes the poorest people hardest, meaning that general deterrence is a way not of preventing the 'crimes' of all people, but rather a way of *sacrificing poor people* in order to keep other poor people on the straight and narrow (Mathiesen, 2006). If the final result is a reduction in future crimes by this sub-population, it does not matter if the person punished was guilty or innocent (Mathiesen, 2006). We can only ask is this a legitimate justification for the use of the penal law?

 CASE STUDY: MONSTERS IN OUR MIDST: DANGEROUS AND SEVERE PERSONALITY DISORDER

Recent policies concerning people labelled as having 'dangerous and severe personality disorder' [DSPD] illustrate the tensions between different consequentialist philosophical justifications. DSPD is conceived as a permanent and deeply entrenched problem, rooted within the personality, rather than a temporary illness that can be cured. These problematic personality traits are understood as having a direct causal relationship with violent behaviour. A person with DSPD is considered unempathetic and unemotional—a psychopath—yet their 'grossly abnormal "inner world"' does not mean they are 'suffering from mental illness' (Keith, 2006: 144). DSPD, it is maintained, is a condition that cannot be treated.

Debates on DSPD have oscillated between responses focused upon rehabilitation and incapacitation, reaching fever pitch in the last decade following the murders of Lin and Megan Russell by Michael Stone in 1996. The Michael Stone case highlighted concerns that the sentencing powers for perceived incurable 'dangerous offenders' were inadequate. It was argued that the criminal law failed to provide public protection, because people with DSPD were released at the end of their sentence still a danger to the public, whilst the belief that DSPD was incurable meant that the offender could not be sectioned to be treated in a mental hospital. In its initial response to these concerns in the late 1990s, the New Labour government followed the logic of incapacitation, making proposals for people with DSPD to be detained indeterminately under civil powers. Immense trust was to be placed in the predictive skills of risk assessors—skills which many critics believe are largely non-existent—and elements of this approach reached fruition with the indeterminate sentencing powers for dangerous offenders in the Criminal Justice Act (CJA) 2003.

After considerable controversy and criticism, the proposal for new laws to punish people for future crimes were greatly diluted, with government policy on DSPD following a dual strategy of incapacitation and rehabilitation. The major legal amendment that eventually arose from political concerns over DSPD was a change to the 'treatability' test in the Mental Health Act (MHA) 2007. Rather than wholesale reform, in the end the government opened four new DSPD units with 300 places in total—two high secure special hospital units (Broadmoor and Rampton) operating under the authority of the MHA 2007, and two prison units (Whitemoor and Frankland) operating under the powers of the CJA 2003.

There are major concerns regarding human rights and due process with the Government's consequentialist policies on DSPD, which are also clearly a modern form of 'monstering' offenders. Yet the problems go even deeper. Critics argue that the very notion of DSPD is fundamentally flawed, as the concept is a political invention rather than a medical or legal concept. There is no agreed consensus as to how to assess DSPD, with some commentators doubtful such a condition actually exists. DSPD is also a tautology (a circular argument) as people considered a high risk of causing serious harm are automatically defined as having DSPD, whilst those deemed to have a severely disordered personality are defined as inherently harmful. Considerable ambiguity and flexibility exists regarding who is actually labelled as having DSPD, leading to problems of accuracy and consistency. For example, Prison Service Order 1700 suggests that anyone in a prison segregation unit for more than three months should be considered as having a personality disorder, but it is common practice in many prisons for prisoners with mental illness to be placed in segregation units for long periods of time, because there is nowhere else for them to go (Seddon, 2008; Scott and Codd, 2009).

DSPD seems to be a very convenient diagnosis, individualising blame upon the prisoner when their very real needs have been neglected, and provides an important example of how philosophical debates on punishment go right to the heart of current penal policy.

REVIEW QUESTIONS

1 Should the effectiveness of penalties in reducing future offending be an important factor when considering the legitimacy of state punishment?

2 Should we focus on the 'crime' or the offender?

3 Is it ever defensible to harm one person for the benefit of others?

Retribution

Retributivists argue that we should punish because the guilty deserve to suffer. Though often labelled as merely a form of vengeance, advocates of *retribution* claim it is intimately tied up with justice, rather than an emotional, individualised, or disproportionate reaction to an event. For retributivists, wrongdoers should be treated as ends rather than means, and as a result the social consequences of punitive sanctions, positive or negative, are deemed irrelevant. Retributivism is grounded in the principle that through harming another human being in the past, wrongdoers *deserve* to be harmed. In so doing retributivists focus on an offender's guilt and equate the penalty with the wrong done. This is known as the principle of *proportionality*—lesser 'crimes' should be punished lesser and greater 'crimes' punished more harshly. This also provides a moral framework in which it is clear that innocent people should not be punished. One of the most influential proponents of retributivism was the German philosopher Immanuel Kant. In a famous passage from *The Philosophy of Law* he claimed:

> Even if a Civil Society resolved to dissolve itself with the consent of all its members—as might be supposed in the case of a People of an island resolving to separate and scatter themselves through the whole world—the last Murderer lying in the prison ought to be executed before the resolution was carried out. This ought to be done in order that every one may realise the desert of his [sic] deeds, and the bloodguiltiness may not remain upon the people; for otherwise they might all be regarded as participators in the murder as a public violation of justice. (Kant, 1887: 198)

For Kant (1887), then, we have both a moral right and *duty* to punish. For some penal commentators, however, the above statement indicates that even the well-trained mind of Kant is lost 'in atavistic emotional impulses' when applied to consideration of the penal law (von Hentig, 1937: 124). Retributivism is vulnerable to criticism on a number of grounds. One of the most significant limitations is that there is no space for forgiveness and *mercy* in its rationale of punishment. Kant's demand for the rigid enforcement of the penal law would also almost certainly create a highly punitive and totalitarian system of control, whilst the potentially serious future consequences of punishments, such as the alienation or embitterment of wrongdoers, are ignored. It is also questionable whether the demand for the infliction of pain and suffering against offenders is healthy, as the venom of punishment is poisonous for all it encounters. Retributivism also does not differentiate between good and bad laws, and so ultimately can provide a justification for the defence of the existing social and political order, whatever its moral basis.

Most significantly of all, though, retributivism struggles to explain *why* an offender should be punished, what form that punishment should take, or why the capitalist state should be given the power to undertake such harms. It indicates that there should be a response, and infers restoring balance, but does not explain why this should take the form of pain infliction. Pain cannot repair or redress the harm and hurt created by the misdemeanour. Wrongs cannot be undone simply by doing another wrong. Rather than prevent or 'annul' (Hegel, 1896) harmful acts, penalties only create new harms. Retributivism has taken many forms but three of the most well known are forfeiture of rights, reprobation, and *just deserts*. Let us now consider these in turn.

Forfeiture of rights

Some retributivists have attempted to justify pain infliction on the grounds that, as an offender violates the rights of the victim, they should as a result forfeit their own rights. The intention is to make the loss of rights equivalent to the harm done. Retributivists, though, are unclear about *which rights* should be lost and which retained, and *why*. The equivalence argument appears untenable when we consider deplorable acts that have debased human dignity, such as sexual violence. To remove rights in a like-for-like manner would be as equally inhumane as the offence, and so morally unjustifiable. Further, to claim that a total loss of rights should arise from the harmful act would be counter-intuitive, as it negates the assertion that we have any human rights at all. It would also be irrelevant *who* punished a person with no rights, providing tacit legitimation to vigilantism. Human rights are also distinguished between moral and legal rights. Claims that infringements of victims' legal rights should lead to the removal of equivalent offender legal rights threatens *due process* and the rule of law, whilst claims based on the infringements of moral rights only would lead to the punishment of the legally innocent. Overall, retributivists struggle to explain why a person should so easily lose their rights through the perpetration of an illegal act (Boonin, 2008).

Reprobation

Retributivists have also argued that punishments can be deployed as a means of morally denouncing wrongdoing. This way of attributing blame through pain is known as moral censure or reprobation. Duff (2001), a leading advocate of this approach, argues that punishment should communicate the censure offenders deserve for their past crime, but that this message should also aim to persuade wrongdoers to repent their actions and undergo personal reformation. The sentence would be proportionate, as the intensity of the pains inflicted conveys a message to the offender regarding the degree of wrongness of the criminal act. In short punishment is conceived as a 'species of secular penance' (Duff, 2001: xix), because the act of punishment can induce a realisation that the infringement of the social norm was indeed morally wrong, leading to desistance and reconciliation.

   The reprobative justification falls short, however, on a number of grounds. The connection between moral defects and criminal activity is questionable, as it fails to consider the structural fault lines of society when understanding the criminalisation process. It is also doubtful whether the capitalist state can achieve positive transformations of offenders through moral reform. Parental censure can be an effective means of reprobation if a strong attachment exists between parent and child. Indeed, condemnation is painful because it involves the negative judgement of such a significant other. Quite simply such a close relationship does not and cannot ever exist between the capitalist state and the wrongdoer, even in a communitarian society emphasising mutual respect, and a strong commitment to everyday norms and shared values (Golash, 2005).

   It is also unlikely that suffering really does expiate guilt or provide a good way of restoring relationships, and punishment is anyway not a very effective means of moral communication (Mathiesen, 2006). Finally, reprobation fails to establish *why* the state has the right to punish, especially when there are alternative non-punitive means of censure and moral education available (Hudson, 1996; Boonin, 2008).

Just deserts

Central to the desert rational is the principle of commensurability. For a sentence to be commensurate to a 'crime', the severity of the punishment must be proportionate to the gravity of the offence, and the blameworthiness of the wrongdoers' deeds. Hudson (1987: 138) points out that there are five essential propositions of just deserts:

> proportionality of punishment to crime; determinate sentences; an end to judicial and administrative discretion; an end to disparity in sentencing; [and] protection of rights through due process.

Offenders have taken an *unfair* advantage over law-abiding citizens through their offence, and so punishment is invoked as a means of rebalancing the distribution of benefits and burdens disturbed by the 'crime'. The classic statement of this position comes from von Hirsch (1976: 47).

> When someone infringes another's rights, he gains an unfair advantage over all others in society—since he has failed to constrain his own behaviour while benefiting from the other persons' forbearance from interfering with his rights. The punishment—by imposing a counterbalancing disadvantage on the violator—restores the equilibrium.

For critics, just deserts turns out to be nothing but an 'incoherent hodgepodge of contradictory justifications' (de Haan, 1990: 28) that flounders on two grounds: its claims to deliver justice, and its attempts to scientifically devise proportionate sentences. The Achilles heel of just deserts is that we live in an unjust society where people do not get what they deserve (Murphy, 1973). Even von Hirsch (1976: 149), a leading advocate of this model, admits this problem, stating that as 'long as a substantial segment of the population is denied adequate opportunities for a livelihood, any scheme for punishing must be morally flawed'. As such, the idea that punishments justly redress imbalances created through 'crime' is simply not plausible. As Ten (1987: 64) succinctly puts it, the 'problems of general social injustice cannot be solved by punishment'. Braithwaite and Pettit (1990: 182) argue persuasively that structural bias in society and in the application of the criminal justice system mean that 'where desert is greatest, punishment will be least'. It is the powerful who are often most deserving of sanctions, yet it is the powerless and marginalised who are punished by the penal law. Utilising the principle of parsimony, Braithwaite and Pettit (1990) maintain that to achieve complete equality in criminal justice, we could either punish, or grant mercy, to all people who are guilty. For moral and practical reasons granting mercy would be the fairest outcome.

> We are lucky to punish 10 per cent of the guilty, leaving 90 per cent of crimes unpunished. It follows that the more of the currently punished 10 per cent that can be extended mercy, the more equitable the criminal justice system will become. (Braithwaite and Pettit, 1990: 197)

Just deserts theorists have also encountered significant difficulties in attempts to translate a given offence into a specific sentence for the wrongdoer. Whilst there is some agreement about what the most and least *serious* criminal offences are, difficulties arise when trying to rank the large number of middle range offences (Hudson, 1996). Mathiesen (2006) reminds us that social or emotional distance between offender-victim perform as big a part as the harm perpetrated in shaping perceived seriousness. Indeed many of the most serious social harms never enter the realm of criminal justice (Hillyard *et al.*, 2005). There is also no inherent principle within just deserts to guide how much punitiveness is applicable to a given scale of offences. When thinking of translating the pains of victims into pains against offenders, the 'pains are so *different* that they cannot be compared' (Mathiesen, 2006: 135), thus blurring levels of just pain infliction. A further set of difficulties arises regarding notions of culpability and blameworthiness. Ezorsky (1973: xxvi) argues that we should take a 'whole life view', placing wrongdoing within the context of the sufferings experienced in the entire life of the offender. When the overall poverty of life of those criminalised by the capitalist state is taken into consideration, it becomes much more difficult to evaluate them as morally culpable for their 'crimes' (Mathiesen, 2006).

Proportionate penalties also fail to take into account that people have different levels of sensitivity to pain. The intensity of suffering and the ill effects a given penalty inflicts varies from offender to offender, depending upon age, *gender*, ability, and social status. Two people given exactly the same sentence will almost certainly *not* experience similar hardships, inconvenience, or ill-health (Scott and Codd, 2009). Sentencing will never be completely just as there exists what Walker (1993: 106) calls '*obiter punishment*': where the pains of punishment undeservedly spread to innocent people such as the families of offenders.

Perhaps the most significant failing of just deserts is that it cannot establish why a wrongdoer should be punished. Commensurate punishments are claimed to derive from the Jewish principle of the *lex talionis*, popularly referred to as 'an eye for an eye'. Remarkably, though, the *lex talionis* is really all about equivalence and reconciliation rather than retribution. Daube (1947: 104), in a detailed linguistic study of the meaning of *lex talionis* in Hebrew, states that in the books of Exodus and Leviticus, the term means 'in the place of'. The *lex talionis*, in practice, was invoked as a means of limiting responses to wrongdoing and providing equivalent compensation, and so must be understood as 'life in place of life, breach in the place of breach, eye in the place of eye, [and] tooth in the place of tooth' (1947: 114). The *lex talionis* is not about harm escalation or retribution, but restoration of balance (Zehr, 1985).

REVIEW QUESTIONS

1 In what ways is just deserts undermined though the social divisions of advanced capitalist-patriarchal societies?

2 Why is proportionality so difficult to achieve?

3 When we strive for equality in the criminal justice system would it be better to aim for more punishment or more mercy?

Abolitionism

Abolitionism is a broad movement informed by a number of different philosophical credos, including Anarchism, Christianity, Libertarianism, Marxism, Moral Rationalism, Phenomenology, Post-Structuralism, and Symbolic Interactionism. What unites abolitionists is their general opposition to the current deployment of the capitalist state's penal apparatus. 'Absolute abolitionists' (Duff, 2001) argue that the criminal justice system cannot be saved by minor reforms, as punishment itself is morally bankrupt. There is no hope that the moral inadequacies of either the consequentialist or retributivist justifications can be addressed. As a result, abolitionists argue that we need to completely rethink how we deal with wrongdoers, and use our sociological imagination to conceive of a more just society that can exist without punishment (de Haan, 1990, 1991).

Abolitionists have questioned whether defining harms and wrongs as 'crime' is actually useful. They argue that 'crime' does not exist as a stable phenomenon and has no ontological reality or core essential components that differentiate it from other problematic acts (Hulsman, 1986). Rather the concept of 'crime' is like a 'sponge' (Christie, 2004: ix) that can be used to absorb an endless supply of unwanted acts, providing a way of organising and structuring meanings that are highly suited to legitimating the expansion of the penal apparatus of the capitalist state. The troubling behaviours of others are more likely to be categorised as 'crimes', and the penal law applied, when the wrongdoer can be distanced from the victim. It appears that it may be harder to justify the infliction of pain against a close friend than against distant strangers, even if they have done the most deplorable of acts (Christie, 2004; Mathiesen, 2006).

Abolitionists acknowledge that there always will be moral conflicts and disputes, whatever the prevailing socio-economic contexts, but that the term 'crime' should be replaced with alternative terms such as 'problematic', 'wrongful', or 'troublesome' behaviours. Abolitionists argue that these problematic behaviours must be taken seriously, but the penal law has consistently failed to solve problems or protect the vulnerable, and as such should not be used to regulate human interactions. Indeed punishment is seen as a way of creating social problems rather than solving conflicts.

Abolitionists acknowledge that society is profoundly unequal with major deficiencies around *social justice*, and look to promote solutions that will provide more justice, inclusion, integration, safety, and security for all citizens. They argue that suffering, pain, and harm should be reduced wherever, and whenever, possible for all concerned. Christie (1977: 59–60) argues that current forms of *crime control* the capitalist state steals the victims' and offenders' conflicts, with state agents, primarily lawyers, taking possession and becoming empowered with the responsibility to resolve problems. For Christie, this results in not only the loss of an important ritual encounter, but also of important skills in conflict resolution and the opportunity for the public to participate in 'norm clarification' and shaping the law. Alternatives to the penal law have ranged from concrete projects that look to work with offenders, to radical socialist political transformations challenging the dominant forms of governmental sovereignty and political economy. For abolitionism, legitimate responses to problems, wrongs, and troubles must be aimed at resolving, rather than escalating, conflict, repairing damage rather than ignoring the harms of the victim, and restoring relationships rather than creating greater forms of distance.

Abolitionism has been criticised on a number of grounds. First, for those dismissive of abolitionism, the approach is simply the 'spirit of political nihilism and intellectual anarchism' (Wright, 1994: 5), too pessimistic in its assessments of the utility of punishment (Lippke, 2007). Second, abolitionists have struggled to convince critics that their proposed alternatives effectively respond to the most serious offences. As such, it has been claimed that life would be 'nasty, brutish and short' without punishment (von Hirsch, 1987: 48). Third, there are also concerns that by refusing to allocate blame or censure against wrongdoers', abolitionist solutions are morally unacceptable. A fourth claimed limitation is that abolitionists are not actually calling for *'alternatives to punishment* but rather *alternative punishments'* which have more reparative aims (Duff, 2001: 34). Abolitionists have responded to these concerns, promoting a number of rational responses to wrongdoing, two of which are outlined below.

Redress

Abolitionists argue we rely on punishment because we are unsure of what else to do. De Haan (1990) argues that the last line of defence of punishment is that there are no alternative ways of responding to 'crime', and therefore, the continued application of the power to punish is inevitable. For de Haan, a 'moral rationalist' (1990: 104), abolitionists must advocate a 'politics of bad conscience' (1990: 81), making it as difficult as possible to justify punishment and to do so by offering plausible and rational non-punitive reactions to socially problematic behaviours. De Haan offers the concept of redress in place of 'crime' and punishment. Redress is a concept with ancient origins and involves the consideration of historical and anthropological forms of dispute settlement and conflict resolution. Redress means:

> To put right or in good order again, to remedy or remove trouble of any kind, to set right, to repair, rectify something suffered or complained of like a wrong, to correct, amend, reform or do away with a bad or faulty state of things, to repair an action or misdeed or offence, to save or deliver from misery, to restore or bring back a person to a proper state, to happiness or prosperity, to the right course, to set a person right by obtaining or (more rarely) giving satisfaction or compensation for the wrong or loss sustained, teaching, instructing and redressing the erroneous by reason. (Concise Oxford Dictionary, 1976, cited in de Haan, 1990: 158)

Redress requires a mandatory response to the undesirable act. Actions against the wrongdoer must follow a particular process, but it allows flexibility in determining what the proper response should be. For abolitionists moral conflicts may well be unavoidable, but the application of the penal law is not.

Restorative justice

Similar principles to redress are implied in the other R's of community justice: *reparation*, restitution, repayment, reconciliation, and reintegration. Importantly, all of these visions are inclusionary rather than exclusionary modes of social control rooted in social integration (Cohen, 1985). *Restorative justice* places the victim and offender at the centre of the response to 'crime', and has been understood in terms of processes, outcomes, and values (Johnstone, 2003). It is a *process* in that the conflict is addressed through direct mediation between the victim and offender, who play a key role in determining a resolution. Restorative justice also aims to achieve certain *outcomes*, including the reparation of damages and the repairing of harms, repentance, and reintegration. Finally it has also been understood as a set of *values*, such as healing, care, love, and support (Johnstone, 2003).

A number of concerns have been raised against the use of restorative justice. For some critics restorative justice is punishment under a different name. Whatever the definition or benevolent intentions of practitioners, the application of pain infliction continues, but disturbingly now its reality is disguised (Daly, 2001). On a practical level the concern is that the capitalist state is still given penal power, but that legal rights, safeguards, and protections of wrongdoers are in effect removed, resulting in potentially heavier pain infliction than through the penal law (Hudson, 1996; Ashworth, 2002). To be sure, any morally defensible use of restorative justice needs to ensure that wrongdoers have the same legal guarantees as other offenders processed by the criminal law (Hudson, 1998).

On a philosophical level it has been claimed that restorative justice is either a variant of rehabilitation (Raynor and Robinson, 2005) or retribution (Duff, 2001, 2002). Duff (2002: 382) argues that in practice what is really occurring is 'restorative retribution', though Boonin (2008) challenges this critique, arguing that there exists both punitive and non-punitive forms of restorative justice; that this distinction is important; and that abolitionists promote the non-punitive kind. For Hudson (1998), a number of problems arise when applying restorative justice to deplorable acts, such as those of racial and sexual violence. There may be a perception that 'victims' are receiving second-rate justice, and that in displacing the role of the capitalist state, the power imbalance between the parties in the mediation process may be reproduced and reinforced, rather than providing a means of redress for the victim or challenging problematic behaviours.

For restorative justice to be credible it must be seen to take all harms seriously, but for some restorative justice can never entirely displace the criminal law (Ashworth, 2002; Johnstone, 2003; Christie, 2004). The problem with a dual system is that the delivery of penalties in the community can become a new way of expanding the penal 'net' for those at the bottom end of the system. Alternatives may not be used as alternatives, but become ways of making social controls better. Informal means of control could be used to further extend the power to punish and legitimate new modes of discipline, surveillance, and regulation. In other words restorative justice could blur legal boundaries and bring into the criminal justice system more petty offenders (Cohen, 1985).

REVIEW QUESTIONS

1 Has restorative justice been co-opted by the capitalist state?

2 Is restorative justice a form of punishment or an alternative to punishment?

3 Does penal abolitionism remain plausible in a time of penal expansion?

CONCLUSION

The magicians trick

Punishment has constantly re-invented itself when one of its justifications has become implausible. It seems to have a 'chameleon-like' (Harding and Ireland, 1989: 125) nature which allows it to perform many different functions. This has been perhaps its greatest strength and one of the reasons why we seem to think that punishment, as a last resort, is necessary. For its advocates, punishment appears to be somehow bestowed with magical powers. Judges need to simply dip into their box of sentencing tricks and deploy their power to punish. Miraculously, an impressive number of different ends are achieved—with just one shake of the sentencer's wand reassuring messages are sent to society, people are trans-formed, society is protected, remorseful and penitent offenders produced, and justice delivered. Yet when examining its purported claims closely we discover that such ends are in fact nothing more than a magician's illusion, providing only a new cloak of legitimacy to profoundly immoral actions. Punishment, whether assessed on pragmatic, political, or moral criteria, fails to deliver cast-iron justifications for its continued existence. The discussion above highlights that state punishment is shackled by the over-whelming negative consequences of punitive sanctions, and cannot explain why we should harm people rather than look to provide means of redress.

The deployment of punishment is not just harmful for offenders, but, as we have seen, it has a dir-ect impact upon their families and their communities. Yet the harms of punishment are even greater than this—they have a direct impact on society as a whole. The more brutal we are to those who do wrong, the greater the acceptance of cruelty, the weaker the sensitivity to pain. The more we dehu-manise offenders, the more our society itself is desensitised and dehumanised. Punitive societies are callous and morally indifferent to the suffering of others. We must be very conscious of just how reliant our society is becoming upon the deliberate infliction of pain to deal with those people who we see as strangers, and the consequences this may have on eroding compassion and other moral values. Our reli-ance upon punishment must be problematised, and its targeting of the poor exposed. Following Hudson (1996: 151), we must accept that:

> punishment cannot be a synonym for 'justice' ... Rather than imposing penalties with self-righteous confidence, we should always punish with a bad conscience.

When looking to successfully deal with wrongdoing we are much more likely to succeed through social policies aimed at social integration and facilitating informal networks of social attachment. When we talk of justice it must be understood as *social* justice (Hudson, 1996), and include the need for a radical transformation not only in the way in which we deal with wrongdoers, but also in the socio-economic and political order of society as whole (de Haan 1990; Mathiesen, 2006; Scott and Codd, 2009). What is certain is that whilst restorative approaches cannot wave a magic wand and solve all moral conflicts and troubled acts, they are a move in the right direction towards a more parsimonious response to wrongdoing. Unfortunately, without fundamental socialist transformations of our capitalist-patriarchal society, non-punitive approaches to harm cannot really be expected to fair much better in delivering just outcomes than those rooted in punishment itself.

QUESTIONS FOR DISCUSSION

1 Is social policy more important that penal policy in preventing social harms and troublesome behaviours?

2 Is blame through the delivery of pain necessary for a morally acceptable response to harmful acts?

3 Is there a suitable amount of 'crime' in our society? How might this be related to the needs of crime control?

4 Why has the deliberate infliction of pain continued to be seen as the normal response to wrongdoing when it appears to be in opposition to most of our moral values?

5 What problems might arise if punishments are abolished by name but the capitalist state continues to allow coerced treatments or harsh community reparations?

GUIDE TO FURTHER READING

Hudson, B.A. (2009) *Understanding Justice* (3rd edn). Buckingham: Open University Press.

An excellent introduction and probably the best place for students new to the topic to start. As well as providing a very good review of consequentialist and retributivist theories the text covers 'hybrid' theories and human rights approaches as well as making key connections with the sociology of punishment.

Mathiesen, T. (2006) *Prison on Trial* (3rd edn). Winchester: Waterside Press.

One of the most impressive overviews ever written, this text is essential reading. Placing imprisonment itself in the dock, the book provides a damning critique of the philosophical justifications of the prison.

Boonin, D. (2008) *The Problem of Punishment*. New York: Cambridge University Press.

This text covers all the themes discussed in this chapter, but also considers less prominent justifications of punishment such as self-defence. Boonin also reviews a number of important texts from the USA that are sometimes overlooked in European assessments of the legitimacy of punishment.

Golash, D. (2005) *The Case Against Punishment*. London: New York University Press.

An outstanding analysis of recent debates in the philosophy of punishment. Written from an abolitionist standpoint this book also provides a comprehensive overview of the different attempts to justify the punitive rationale.

Walker, N. (1993) *Why Punish? Theories of punishment reassessed* (revised edn). Oxford: Oxford University Press.

A wide-ranging and detailed discussion of the main theories and philosophies of punishment. The text is written in straightforward language, and is one of the few recent commentaries to provide a concerted defence of the Utilitarian approach at the expense of retributivism.

WEB LINKS

Utilitarian resources

http://www.utilitarianism.com

A large number of sources on utilitarian thinkers and thought past and present.

Howard League of Penal Reform

http://www.howardleague.org

A leading penal reform group that provides details and critical reviews of latest policy developments.

Kant on the web

http://www.hkbu.edu.hk/~ppp/Kant.html

A website with links to the major writings of retributivist thinker Immanuel Kant.

Hegel resource site

http://www.gwfhegel.org

A website with links to the major works of retributivist thinker G.W.F. Hegel.

No More Prison

http://www.alternatives2prison.ik.com

UK abolitionist website that provides some very good resources, alongside details on penal activism in the UK and links to other anti-prison groups.

ICOPA

http://www.youtube.com/watch?v=VtZY159f0p0

A fascinating 63-minute documentary on the 11th International Conference on Penal Abolition held in Tasmania in 2006.

Critical Resistance

http://www.criticalresistance.org

US abolitionist website with many important resources on penal abolitionism.

Restorative Justice Online

http://www.restorativejustice.org

Provides a useful definition and a very comprehensive listing of literature on restorative justice.

REFERENCES

Andeneas, J. (1974) *Punishment and Deterrence*. Michigan: The University of Michigan Press.

Ashworth, A. (2002) 'Responsibilities, rights and restorative justice' in G. Johnstone (ed) (2003) *A Restorative Justice Reader*. Cullompton: Willan Publishing, 426–37.

Bean, P. (1981) *Punishment: A Philosophical and Criminological Inquiry*. Oxford: Martin Robertson.

Beccaria, C. (1764/1986) *On Crimes and Punishment* (trans. D. Young). London: Hackett Publishing Company.

Bentham, J. (1830/2004) *The Rationale of Punishment*. Honolulu: University Press of the Pacific.

Boonin, D. (2008) *The Problem of Punishment*. New York: Cambridge University Press.

Braithwaite, J. and Pettit, P. (1990) *Not Just Deserts: A Republican Theory of Criminal Justice*. Oxford: Clarendon Press.

Christie, N. (1977) 'Conflicts as property' in G. Johnstone (ed) (2003) *A Restorative Justice Reader*. Cullompton: Willan Publishing, 57–68.

Christie, N. (2004) *A Suitable Amount of Crime*. London: Routledge.

Cohen, S. (1985) *Visions of Social Control*. Cambridge: Polity Press.

Cohen, S. (2001) *States of Denial*. Cambridge: Polity Press.

Corston, J. (2007) *The Corston Report*. London: Home Office.

Daube, D. (1947/1969) *Studies in Biblical Law*. New York: KTAV Publishing House.

Daly, K. (2001) 'Restorative justice: the real story' in G. Johnstone (ed) (2003) *A Restorative Justice Reader.* Cullompton: Willan Publishing, 363–81.

de Haan, W. (1990) *The Politics of Redress: Crime, Punishment and Penal Abolition.* London: Sage.

de Haan, W. (1991) 'Abolitionism and crime control: a contradiction in terms?' in K. Stenson and D. Cowell (eds) (1991) *The Politics of Crime Control.* London: Sage.

Duff, R.A. (2001) *Punishment, Communication, and Community.* Oxford: Oxford University Press.

Duff, R.A. (2002) 'Restorative punishment and punitive restoration' in G. Johnstone (ed) (2003) *A Restorative Justice Reader.* Cullompton: Willan Publishing, 382–97.

Ezorsky, G. (1972) 'The ethics of punishment' in G. Ezorsky (ed) (1972) *Philosophical Perspectives on Punishment.* New York: State University of New York Press, xi–xxvii.

Flew, A. (1954) 'The justification of punishment' in H.B. Acton (ed) (1969) *The Philosophy of Punishment.* London: Macmillan.

Golash, D. (2005) *The Case Against Punishment.* London: New York University Press.

Harding, C. and Ireland, R. (1989) *Punishment: Rhetoric, Rule and Practice.* London: Routledge.

Hart, H.L.A. (1968) *Punishment and Responsibility.* Oxford: Clarendon Press.

Hegel, G.W.F. (1896/2005) *Philosophy of Right.* New York: Dover Publications.

Hillyard, P., Gordon, D., Pantazis, C., and Tombs, S. (eds) (2005) *Beyond Criminology.* London: Pluto Press.

Honderich, T. (2006) *Punishment: The Supposed Justifications Revisited.* London: Pluto Press.

Hudson, B.A. (1987) *Justice Through Punishment.* London: Macmillan.

Hudson, B.A. (1996) *Understanding Justice.* Milton Keynes: Open University Press.

Hudson, B.A. (1998) 'Restorative justice: the challenge of sexual and racial violence' in G. Johnstone (ed) (2003) *A Restorative Justice Reader,* Cullompton: Willan Publishing, 438–50.

Hulsman, L. (1986) 'Critical criminology and the concept of crime' in *Contemporary Crises: law, crime and social policy* 10: 63–80.

Johnstone, G. (2003) 'Restorative approaches to criminal justice' in G. Johnstone (ed) (2003) *A Restorative Justice Reader.* Cullompton: Willan Publishing, 1–18.

Kant, I. (1887/1974) *The Philosophy of Law.* Clifton: Augustus M Kelley Publishers.

Keith, Justice (2006) *The Zahid Mubarek Inquiry (Volume 1).* London: HMSO.

Kendal, K. (2002) 'Time to think again about cognitive behavioural programmes' in P. Carlen (ed) (2002) *Women and punishment: the struggle for justice.* Cullompton: Willan Publishing, 182–98.

Lacey, N. (1988) *State Punishment.* London: Routledge.

Lippke, R.L. (2007) *Rethinking Imprisonment.* Oxford: Oxford University Press.

Maguire, J. (ed) (1995) *What Works: Reducing Reoffending.* Chichester: John Wiley & Sons.

Martinson, R. (1974) 'What works?—Questions and Answers about Prison Reform' in R. Matthews (ed) (1999) *Imprisonment.* Aldershot: Dartmouth Publishers, 143–76.

Mathiesen, T. (2006) *Prison on Trial (3rd edn).* Winchester: Waterside Press.

Murphy, J.G. (1973) 'Marxism and Retribution' in R.A. Duff and D. Garland (eds) (1994) *A Reader on Punishment.* Oxford: Oxford University Press, 47–70.

Primoratz, I. (1989) *Justifying Legal Punishment.* New Jersey: Humanities Press.

Raynor, P. and Robinson, G. (2005) *Rehabilitation, Crime and Justice.* London: Macmillan.

Rotman, E. (1990) *Beyond Punishment: A New View of the Rehabilitation of Offenders.* Westport: Greenwood Press.

Scott, D.G. and Codd, H. (2009) *Controversial Issues in Prisons.* Buckinghamshire: Open University Press.

Seddon, T. (2008) 'Dangerous liaisons: personality disorder and the politics of risk'. *Punishment and Society* 10(3): 301–18.

Ten, C.L. (1987) *Crime, Guilt and Punishment.* Oxford: Clarendon Press.

von Hentig, H. (1937) *Punishment: Its Origin, Purpose and Psychology.* London: William Hodge and Co. Ltd.

von Hirsch, A. (1976) *Doing Justice.* Boston: Northeastern University Press.

von Hirsch, A. (1987) *Past or Future Crimes: Deservedness and Dangerousness in the Sentencing of Criminals.* London: Rutgers University Press.

Walker, N. (1993) *Why Punish? Theories of punishment reassessed*. Oxford: Oxford University Press.

Whitby, C.J. (1910) 'Is punishment a crime?'. *Hibbert Journal* 8: 850–61.

Woolf, L.J. (1991) *Prison Disturbances April 1990: Report of an Inquiry (Part I)*. London: Stationery Office.

Wooton, B. (1965) *Crime and the Criminal Law*. London: Stevens and Sons.

Wright, R.A. (1994) *In Defence of Prisons*. London: Greenwood Press.

Zehr, H. (1985) 'Retributive justice, restorative justice' in G. Johnstone (ed) (2003) *A Restorative Justice Reader*. Cullompton: Willan Publishing, 69–82.

Zimring, F.E. and Hawkins, G. (1995) *Incapacitation: Penal Confinement and the Restraint of Crime*. Oxford: Oxford University Press.

5 Sentencing

Gavin Dingwall

INTRODUCTION

Few areas of criminal justice attract the level of media scrutiny, popular concern, and legislative frenzy as the sentencing of offenders. It is strange then that criminologists have less to say on the subject than, say, on policing, which has developed into what is in effect a sub-discipline with specialist journals and even specialist degree courses. This neglect, though, is comparative and not absolute. There is still a vast literature and choices have had to be made as to what to include and, as importantly, what to exclude from this chapter.

This process of selection was not as difficult as might be expected as certain key issues and debates stood out for inclusion. These included the recent development of sentencing policy; consistency in sentencing; ways of responding to disparity; and, finally, issues of ethnicity and *gender* in sentencing. Sentencing, as both a practice and an area of study, benefits from an awareness of the legal principles underpinning it. The relevant law is found both in a surprising number of Acts of Parliament and in a host of reported cases. This chapter is written primarily with criminal justice students in mind. Although an overview of the sentencing process is provided, only brief mention will be made of the most important statutory provisions and no mention will be made of case law in the chapter itself. The recommended sources at the end of this chapter include two legal texts (Ashworth, 2005; Easton and Piper, 2008) which will provide this detail if required.

BACKGROUND

Sentencing relates to the process of imposing a *punishment* on an offender in a *criminal court*. Those who break rules in other contexts, say university disciplinary rules or breaches of professional rules of conduct, may also be subjected to a formal process which determines the consequences of their breach. Perhaps criminologists should be more interested in these alternative processes, not least as the consequences can be severe. This chapter, though, is concerned with the sentencing of adult offenders by the courts in England and Wales. This is a large-scale enterprise: 1,176,400 adults were sentenced in 2006 (Ministry of Justice, 2007a, para. 5.7).

It is often said that sentencing has become a highly political issue, but it has been for some time. A recent Sentencing Commission Consultation Paper listed 56 Acts of Parliament between 1993 and 2007 which have had a significant effect on sentencing (Sentencing Commission Working Group, 2008, Annex K). Both the Conservative Party (who were in government between 1979 and 1997) and the Labour Party (who have been in government since 1997) have tried to convince the electorate of their 'law and order' credentials. The way in which they attempt to do this is crude and often involves little more than raising the punitive bar a notch higher than their opponents. This worryingly simplistic approach stems from a belief that the public do not think that the sentences imposed by the courts are sufficiently severe (see further Roberts and Hough, 2002; Smith, 2007).

Criminologists are interested in a number of aspects of sentencing. Studies have shown that judges can impose very different sentences for similar offences (Ministry of Justice, 2007a: Table 2.13) and some have tried to explain why this might be the case and to explore ways in which such disparity might be reduced (e.g. Dingwall, 2006/07). Another concern has been that female offenders and those from minority ethnic backgrounds appear to receive sentences that differ from White male offenders (e.g. Dowds and Hedderman, 1997; Hood, 1992). These are just examples of the kind of questions that interest criminologists. Lawyers also research sentencing, but their focus is usually different. Often it will involve the close study of relevant Acts of Parliament and cases in order to build up an understanding of how the law operates (e.g. Hungerford-Welch, 2004: chap. 14). Some legal scholars (e.g. Ashworth, 2005; 2007; Easton and Piper, 2008; Koffman, 2006) analyse sentencing in a broader social context. This is often referred to as *socio-legal research*.

This chapter will not be concerned about community penalties or custody once a decision has been taken to impose such a sentence. There are chapters on both in this volume. One cannot, however, totally divorce discussions about community penalties and custody from sentencing. If, for example, sentencers perceive community penalties to be too 'soft' that might explain in part why they appear so keen to use imprisonment instead. Similarly, 'justifications' for punishment, such as *deterrence* and *rehabilitation*, are addressed elsewhere in this volume. When a sentence is designed with a particular objective in mind—for example public protection—consideration will not be given in this chapter to whether or not the literature suggests that punishment can achieve that particular aim. It would, however, be misleading to claim that sentencing reform is always evidence-based. Whilst the government does periodically undertake research on the relative 'success' rates of different sentences (e.g. Lart *et al.*, 2008), changes are more often based on political expediency than careful evaluation. Or, to put it another way, '[focus] groups, tabloid front pages and political advisors have had more influence on government proposals and policies than have criminal justice professionals, systematic evidence or subject-matter experts' (Tonry, 2004: 3).

An overview of the sentencing process

This section provides a brief outline of the sentencing process. Those wanting more detailed accounts are recommended to consult either Ashworth's chapter in the *Oxford Handbook of Criminology* (2007: chap. 29) or his book *Sentencing and Criminal Justice* (2005). Alternatively, Easton and Piper (2008) provide an excellent explanation.

The first important consideration is the court which hears the case. This depends primarily on the seriousness of the offence charged (see Chapter 3). If defendants are convicted, or more commonly plead guilty, they will usually, though not always, be sentenced by the same court. Although guilt or innocence is decided by a jury in the Crown Court, if the jury convict the defendant they have no say whatsoever about the subsequent sentence.

Ashworth (2007: 1004) identifies five sources of information that assist sentencers: the police *antecedents* statement; the defence plea in *mitigation*; a medical report; and the offender's own appearance in court. Details about previous convictions or cautions are taken from the Police National Computer (PNC) so that sentencers are aware of the offender's past offending behaviour. In certain situations (see Ward and Davies,

2004: 170) a pre-sentence report is obtained. In England and Wales the prosecutor does not advocate any particular penalty (see further Ashworth, 2005: 347–8) although there is a duty to highlight any *aggravating* or *mitigating* factors associated with the case, which make it either more or less serious than normal. The defence, however, will try to influence sentencers with a plea in mitigation, the purpose of which is to try to persuade sentencers to be lenient by drawing attention to anything about the offender or the offence which could be looked upon favourably. Examples would include the fact that the offender had never been in trouble before or that the *crime* was not premeditated or planned. One of the most controversial mitigating factors is the guilty plea.

Roughly two-thirds of defendants plead guilty in both the magistrates' court and in the Crown Court (Ministry of Justice, 2007b: paras 1.19–1.20). A guilty plea ordinarily results in a reduction of between a third and a tenth of the sentence depending on the stage where defendants indicated that they would plead guilty (SGC, 2007b: para. 4.2). In some situations it can make the difference in the type of punishment imposed. Rewarding a guilty plea in this way is controversial for two reasons. The first is a matter of principle. If an offender is rewarded for admitting guilt, it follows that a defendant who pleads not guilty and is subsequently convicted will receive a harsher sentence. Yet defendants are merely exercising their legal right: it is (usually) for the prosecution to prove the defendant's guilt beyond reasonable doubt. The allied problem is that an individual may feel under enormous pressure to plead guilty knowing that the consequences of a conviction after trial would be worse. There is the possibility that such an individual may be factually innocent or may have a valid legal defence. A study by Baldwin and McConville (1977) went further and suggested that defence lawyers may put their clients under pressure to plead guilty even if professional codes of conduct stipulate that lawyers should inform clients not to plead guilty unless they have committed the offence.

Are there any arguments which could be used to support a discount for a guilty plea? The traditional justification is that an admittance of guilt demonstrates remorse for the offence. This assumes both that the reason behind the plea is remorse (many offenders quite simply have no realistic defence) and that, even if the offender is genuinely remorseful, this should be treated favourably when determining sentence. A more pragmatic (and the official) rationale might be that it expedites the process by reducing the number of contested trials, reduces costs, and also spares victims and witnesses the ordeal of having to testify (SGC, 2007b: para. 2.2).

The main penalties that can be imposed by the court are: imprisonment; a community sentence; a fine; a conditional discharge; an absolute discharge; and a compensation order. These penalties effectively form a scale, often referred to as the *tariff*, depending on their relative seriousness. The idea is that the court should impose a punishment that is proportionate to the seriousness of the offence. Just as it would be inappropriate to imprison someone who committed a minor offence, it would be unjust to fine someone who committed a serious offence. The term 'tariff' can have another meaning in sentencing, as will be discussed later, but it is usually obvious in which sense it is being used.

Sentences from magistrates' courts can be appealed to the Crown Court (Magistrates' Court Act 1980, s. 108) whilst those from the Crown Court can be appealed to the Court of Appeal, provided the Court of Appeal gives leave (Criminal Appeal Act 1968, s. 9). The Court of Appeal, though, seldom gives leave and is reluctant to allow an appeal

(Hungerford-Welch, 2004: 512–15). If an appeal from either court is successful the original sentence may be quashed and replaced with one that is more appropriate (Supreme Court Act 1981, s. 48(2); Criminal Appeal Act 1968, s. 11(3)). Relatively recently, the *Attorney-General* (the chief legal advisor to the Crown in England and Wales) was given the controversial right to challenge unduly lenient Crown Court sentences (Criminal Justice Act 1988, ss. 35 and 36). All indictable offences can be challenged on this ground, as can a limited number of triable either-way offences, but the case law shows that the Court of Appeal seldom increase sentences, partly due to a desire to maintain judicial *discretion* (see later) and partly because it is seen as undesirable as a matter of principle to increase sentences, save in the most extreme cases.

Sentencing policy: a recent history

The Criminal Justice Act 1991 provides a very obvious starting point for any analysis of recent sentencing policy (for slightly lengthier analyses see Easton and Piper, 2008: 72–80; Koffman, 2006). According to the Act, sentences were primarily to be calculated with regard to the gravity of the offence (there were exceptional provisions relating to 'dangerous' violent and sexual offenders). The Act gave sentencers little guidance on how to calculate seriousness, but it was clear that the harm caused by the offence was key. Characteristics of the offender could be taken into account, but only in so far as they mitigated or aggravated the seriousness of the offence. Having come to a conclusion about the seriousness of the offence, sentencers were then meant to impose a proportionate punishment. The predominant justification for punishment in the 1991 Act was very clearly *retribution*: the punishment had to be a proportionate response to the offence in question.

Commentators generally welcomed the Act. Koffman comments (2006: 285) that retributivism had almost become a 'new orthodoxy' by the late 1980s as penologists recognised 'the failure (and potential injustice) of deterrent sentencing, the discriminatory nature and arbitrariness of rehabilitative and indeterminate sentencing, and the problems of prediction and lack of proportionality inherent in incapacitative sentencing'. There was a belief that focusing on the offence would lead to greater consistency and that a proportionality requirement would reduce the use of imprisonment for more minor offences. Overcrowding in prisons, which had led to rioting in some institutions, meant that there were both philosophical and pragmatic reasons for introducing the legislation (see Woolf and Tumim, 1991).

One reason for the overcrowding was that sentencers had become more willing to take an offender's previous record into account. This meant that someone convicted of a relatively minor offence, say theft, could nonetheless receive a custodial sentence if they had committed other offences, even minor ones, in the past. The Act attempted to end this practice by stating that an offence was not to be regarded as more serious 'by reason of any previous conviction of the offender or any failure of his [sic] to respond to previous sentences' (s. 29(1)). In effect, the court had to assume that a defendant was not a habitual criminal (Jones, 2002: 183); on occasions this would obviously entail a considerable suspension of judicial belief.

What is remarkable is not that the Act was subjected to criticism but the rapidity with which the government responded to it by amending key provisions of the Act. The first reaction was inevitable. Sentencers complained, albeit perhaps more publicly than could have been anticipated, about the restrictions placed on their previous discretion. One of their main complaints was that they could no longer decide whether previous convictions had any relevance. Sustained pressure led to the Criminal Justice Act 1993 amending the 1991 Act so that sentencers could once again take into account any of the offender's previous convictions.

The 1993 Act also repealed a new system for calculating fines which the 1991 Act had introduced which was based on offenders' ability to pay. If it was felt appropriate to fine an offender, the amount was calculated on the basis of a number of units, the value of which would depend upon the offender's disposable income. In itself there is nothing unusual or objectionable to a unit-based approach. Many other jurisdictions have used variants of the system and a fine has to take account of an offender's ability to pay if it is to affect everyone equally—fining a uniform amount could result in a fine which would be regarded as no more than an irritation by a millionaire but which could severely affect a poorer offender. However, in a jurisdiction unfamiliar with such a system, the media latched on to the perceived injustice of cases where wealthy offenders were fined more than poorer individuals who had committed more serious offences. No defence of the approach was offered.

Accounting for these rapid and significant policy reversals demonstrates the impact that politics has on criminal justice. The Labour Party, who by this time had been in opposition for more than a decade, believed that their approach to criminal justice was perceived by voters as too lenient and that, in order to get elected, would have to be revised. By now Tony Blair was the shadow Home Secretary and he sought to convince the electorate that the opposition would be 'tough on crime, tough on the causes of crime' if elected. The Labour Party started to challenge the Conservative Party's traditional claim to be the party of 'Law and Order'. Whereas previous governments could introduce criminal justice legislation with little political opposition, from now on both the Conservative government and the subsequent Labour government were extremely cautious of introducing any sentencing measure that could be portrayed as unduly lenient by the press or by the other party.

The next significant Act, the Crime (Sentences) Act 1997, returned to the theme of persistent offenders. It provided *mandatory sentences* for repeat Class A drug dealers, domestic burglars, and those who committed specified serious violent or sexual offences unless it was 'unjust to do so in all the circumstances'. This development was treated with dismay. It was, and is, widely accepted that mandatory sentences 'always produce unwanted side-effects of arbitrariness, injustice in individual cases, hypocritical efforts at circumvention and extreme sentencing disparities' (Tonry, 2004: 17). The sentencing statistics for burglary certainly support the claim that sentencers will often avoid using mandatory sentences. Despite the Act introducing a mandatory sentence of three years' imprisonment for an offender convicted of a third domestic burglary, only 229 out of the 22,675 burglars sentenced in 2006 were sentenced under this provision (Ministry of Justice, 2007a: Table 2.6). Clearly in many cases where the mandatory sentence should have applied sentencers believed that it would have been unjust to have imposed it. In practice then the provisions may have little more than a symbolic effect, not least as many of the offenders in question would have received similar sentences in any event.

The most radical and far-reaching changes came in the Criminal Justice Act 2003 (see Ashworth and Player, 2005; Koffman, 2006). In order to understand the reforms it is necessary to consider the report of the Halliday Committee (Home Office, 2001) which reviewed the existing sentencing framework and whose recommendations heavily influenced the subsequent Act. Two of the most compelling problems that the Committee identified were the 'unclear and unpredictable' approach to persistent offenders and the 'gradual erosion' of the approach set out in the Criminal Justice Act 1991, which had led to 'muddle, complexity, and lack of clear purpose or philosophy' (Home Office, 2002: para. 0.2). Other problems were identified but, as this section provides an overview of dominant policy concerns, attention will be devoted to the Committee's recommendations regarding persistent offenders and determining which factors should influence sentencing.

To some extent the Committee believed that the issues were linked. Proportionality should be 'retained' but 'revised' so that account is taken of previous convictions (Home Office, 2002: para. 0.6). The Committee justified this approach on a number of grounds: the existing approach to dealing with repeat offenders led to unpredictability (Home Office, 2002: para. 1.11); a clearer system was needed given the disproportionate number of crimes committed by such offenders (Home Office, 2002: para. 1.14); a continued pattern of offending despite previous attempts by the state to correct it justified an increased punishment (Home Office, 2002: para. 2.7); longer sentences would allow more time for providing treatment for repeat offenders (Home Office, 2002: para. 1.76); and the proposal reflected popular opinion about the effect that previous convictions should have on sentences. According to research that was cited in the report, 86 per cent of those questioned said that persistence of offending should have 'a great deal of influence' on the appropriate sentence (Home Office, 2002: Annex 5, para. 14).

Although the Committee favoured the retention of proportionality, it was argued that relying solely on retribution was unsatisfactory as 'it provides a less than complete guide to the selection of the most suitable sentence in an individual case' (Home Office, 2002: para. 1.19). This, in effect, is a call for more judicial discretion. Why was this necessary? Two justifications, one legitimate and one seemingly pragmatic, were offered. The valid objection to the existing approach was that no account could be taken of *crime reduction* or *reparation* (Home Office, 2002: para. 1.10). The other exposes the schism between official policy and judicial practice. Sentencers frankly admitted that they were not inhibited from using their discretion to take account of factors other than proportionality (Home Office, 2002: para. 1.10). This gap between the legal framework approved by Parliament and the approach taken by judges was 'worrying' but, at the same time, was seen as a factor which legitimated restoring greater discretion. One of the key recommendations of the Halliday Committee was that the rationales for sentencing needed to include crime reduction and reparation as well as punishment (Home Office, 2002: para. 1.70).

Drawing largely on these recommendations, the Act stated that a sentence should take account of a number of factors: namely the punishment of offenders; the reduction of crime (including its reduction by deterrence); the reform and rehabilitation of offenders; the protection of the public; and the making of reparation by offenders to persons affected by their offences (s. 142(1)). The thrust of the policy is clear. In terms of penal theory, there has been a move away from retribution to an inclusive approach which encompasses several utilitarian justifications for punishment including deterrence and *incapacitation*. The Act also contained a new presumption that previous convictions made an offence more serious if the court considered that it was reasonable for the conviction(s) to have this effect (s. 143(2); see further Ashworth, 2005: 191–201).

It is not unreasonable for a government to be concerned with, and to periodically review, the aims of punishment. Why though have the government been so concerned with persistent offenders? Tonry (2004) offers two hypotheses. The first is that the Labour administration was 'unusually authoritarian' and regarded a continuing pattern of offending as deviant and deserving of punishment in its own right (Tonry, 2004: 35). If this is the case, the logic is unconvincing. Recidivism cannot automatically be equated with deviance as individuals re-offend for a variety of reasons, such as their economic situation or sheer opportunism. What von Hirsch (2002: 202) neatly describes as the 'how dare you' theory is also objectionable at a more fundamental level. In a supposedly free society, defiance of authority in itself should not result in punishment. Tonry's second argument (Tonry, 2004: 36) is that 'the pre-occupation with persistent offenders may have little if anything to do with persistent offenders and everything to do with image-positioning'. Certainly few feel sympathy for persistent offenders—they do after all adversely affect people's quality of life. It would take a brave politician to try to convince the electorate that most offenders in this category face significant social problems which would be better addressed outside a prison. Instead Tony Blair claimed that the 100,000 most persistent offenders were responsible for half of all crime: a statement that was 'totally hypothetical, yet very politically convenient' (Young, 2003: 40).

Any short overview of sentencing policy is misleading, yet a comparison of the Criminal Justice Acts of 1991 and 2003 demonstrates two very different approaches. An Act which stated that (ordinarily) individuals had to be sentenced on the basis of the seriousness of the offence has been replaced by an Act which requires sentencers to attempt to balance a number of competing justifications. Save in situations where it would be 'unfair', 'seriousness' now includes not only a requirement that the offender's previous conviction(s) are considered but that the sentence should be increased on that basis. Some fundamental principles from the 1991 Act do remain (see further Dingwall, 2008). The tests for imposing a custodial sentence, a community sentence, or a fine remain dependent on the seriousness of the offence, albeit with the proviso that persistence is now part of the calculation. One trend which is beyond dispute is that governments of whatever political hue have become far more willing to legislate on sentencing matters, often for short-term political gain and without regard to the overall coherence of sentencing policy.

REVIEW QUESTIONS

1 Why was the seriousness of the offence central to the Criminal Justice Act 1991?

2 What factors should sentencers consider according to the Criminal Justice Act 2003?

3 Why has the government become so preoccupied with persistent offenders?

Sentencing the 'dangerous'

Most offenders do not pose a danger to the public. A minority do, however, present a genuine risk and special sentences have long been available to try to minimise the risk of future harm occurring. Before turning to the current provisions, it is necessary to say something about the difficulties inherent in assessing and responding to '*dangerousness*'. An initial problem is what is meant by 'dangerousness'? Although it is usual to talk about 'danger', what is actually being assessed is 'risk'—namely 'the probability that a harmful event or behaviour will occur' (Ward and Davies, 2004: 207). Research has shown that it is incredibly difficult to predict risk with any great degree of accuracy (Ashworth, 2005: 215–16). This means that certain individuals who pose no future risk will mistakenly be judged to be 'dangerous' whilst some individuals who pose a significant risk will not be detected (called false positives). No system can therefore guarantee that the public will be protected from those that they need protecting from.

Public protection would appear to necessitate imposing sentences considerably in excess of those ordinarily imposed for the offence committed. To what extent is it acceptable to ignore the seriousness of the offence on the basis of a predicted risk? Usually the offender will have committed a serious violent or sexual offence which would have attracted a lengthy custodial sentence in any event. What, though, if the offence is more minor but it is believed that it may be a precursor to more serious offending? As predictions may be wrong and because a prediction of risk will usually result in a significant enhancement to the sentence, it has to be recognised that this is a very contentious area of sentencing policy. Often people seem to believe that 'dangerous' offenders are, by definition, mentally disordered. Some are, though many individuals who are seen to pose a risk are not. This section will not consider the special sentencing powers relating to mentally disordered offenders (see instead Ashworth, 2005: 370–9; Easton and Piper, 2008: 229–35) but will review the current provisions for sentencing 'dangerous' offenders.

The Criminal Justice Act 2003 contains three sentences specifically designed for 'dangerous offenders': imprisonment for life; imprisonment for public protection; and an extended sentence of imprisonment (see further Easton and Piper, 2008: 155–61). If an individual is convicted of one of a number of serious offences listed in the Act which is punishable with life imprisonment, and the court is of the opinion that there is a 'significant risk' to members of the public of 'serious harm' being committed by the offender or further offences specified in the Act, then the court must impose a life sentence. If all of the other criteria are met but the offence is not punishable with life imprisonment but by a term of ten years or more, or where the court considers that the offence is not sufficiently serious on its own merits to justify life imprisonment, a sentence of imprisonment for public protection must be imposed. This, like life imprisonment, is an *indeterminate sentence*. This means that the offender does not serve a fixed term, as is usual, but becomes eligible to be considered for release by the Parole Board after a period known as the *tariff* has expired. The tariff is determined by the judge when the offender is sentenced. Offenders are only released when the Parole Board deems the risk to be minimal or manageable. In extreme cases offenders may never become eligible for *parole*. Extended sentences apply in situations where offenders have committed an offence specified in the Act which has a maximum penalty of less than ten years imprisonment and the court considers that they pose a significant risk of serious harm to members of the public. These sentences comprise of the appropriate custodial sentence term and a further period on licence. The term of the licence is determined by the court who decide on the length which they believe is necessary to protect members of the public from serious harm. Offenders who are on licence can be recalled to prison by the authorities at any time and may have to abide by certain conditions.

What is of central importance to all of these sentences is how the courts assess 'whether there is a significant risk to members of the public of serious harm occasioned by the commission by him or her of further such offences'. The Act stipulates that there is a significant risk of serious harm unless it would be unreasonable to draw such a conclusion. Ashworth (2005: 387) recognises that this 'so-called test' is 'broad, unspecific and skewed by a presumption of dangerousness'. It is worrying that this presumption exists in light of the difficulties of calculating risk and the fact that the Act lists no fewer than 153 offences to which these provisions apply. The ease with which an offender is judged to be 'dangerous' is illustrated by the fact that the specified offences include assault occasioning actual bodily harm and keeping a brothel, which are not very serious offences. These provisions are also designed in a way which does not give the courts power to extend sentences where there is evidence to suggest future risk but, crucially, gives them the right to determine that the offender does not pose a risk. In practice, much depends on how often sentencers are prepared to depart from the presumption on the grounds that it is unreasonable to conclude that there is a significant risk of serious harm occurring in the future. The net has been cast wide and the onus falls on the court to justify why a particular individual should not be caught within it. Certainly this stance is not based on a criminological understanding of risk. Instead the explanation lies in the perceived need to respond to tragic, atypical cases which are the subject of intense media coverage; examples would include the murders of James Bulger or Sarah Payne. It would be too simplistic to trace every legal development to one particular case. Old newspapers and law reports show that similar cases occurred in the past. The real question is why did this government respond in this way at this time? It is suggested that the changes stemmed from a political conviction that public opinion demanded action be taken, allied to the knowledge that the proposals were unlikely to be met with serious opposition and the political nature of sentencing.

REVIEW QUESTIONS

1 What are the problems associated with imposing sentences for public protection?

2 When must imprisonment for life, imprisonment for public protection, and an extended sentence be imposed?

3 What criticisms can be made about the provisions for sentencing 'dangerous' offenders in the Criminal Justice Act 2003?

CASE STUDY: THE MANDATORY SENTENCE FOR MURDER

When the Law Commission (2006, para. 1.61) were recently asked to review the law of murder, they were forbidden from considering the mandatory sentence of life imprisonment (Murder (Abolition of Death Penalty) Act 1969).

Why then should murder carry a mandatory life sentence? The first argument, and the one which probably plays most on the minds of politicians, is the symbolism of having such a sentence. Murder, as the most serious offence in English law, must attract the most serious penalty. This is essentially a retributive argument: the seriousness of the offence means that the only proportionate punishment is life imprisonment. Another argument, often advanced by politicians and often challenged by penologists, is that having such a penalty serves as a deterrent to potential killers. Finally there is a public protection argument. Some of these offenders (though it is difficult to know how many) are clearly dangerous. A life sentence means that they can be monitored for a lengthy period of time before any decision is taken about releasing them.

Each of these arguments has been challenged by those who oppose the mandatory penalty. First, the retributive argument is somewhat simplistic. If the proportionate penalty is always the same there is an implicit acceptance that the offence is always equally serious. Yet are all murders equally serious? Is the Harold Shipman case, where hundreds were killed, no more serious than a case with one victim? To some extent the law recognises that not all murders are the same. When a murderer is sentenced, the judge will set the tariff saying when, if ever, he is eligible to be considered for parole. This certainly does not mean, as is sometimes supposed, that the offender will automatically be freed at that point but it does state when such a decision could be taken. The law then does distinguish between different types of murder in some contexts.

It is also unclear whether having a mandatory life sentence acts as a deterrent. Such a claim is easy to make but in fact very difficult to prove, or for that matter disprove. The deterrent effect of the death penalty in other jurisdictions has been exhaustively researched and the consensus opinion is that it has no effect on the homicide rate (Donohue and Wolfers, 2005). This conclusion, of course, may not apply to life imprisonment, but certain aspects of the death penalty research are valuable. The research clearly challenges the view that offenders who commit murder are always acting rationally, carefully weighing up the advantages and disadvantages of committing the offence. If the possibility of the death penalty does not act as a sufficient deterrent, it is difficult to see how a mandatory life sentence would. What the research shows is that it should not be presumed that a mandatory sentence has a significant, or even any, deterrent effect.

Finally, and perhaps surprisingly, the notion that a mandatory sentence is necessary to protect the public is debatable. Implicit to this argument is the notion that murderers will re-offend if at liberty. Releasing some murderers back into the community may lead to catastrophic results. Some offenders, though, pose no risk. Many released murderers live law-abiding lives, and murderers have the lowest reconviction rates. The difficulty, if there is to be any system of parole, is to calculate which offenders pose a risk and which do not. It should also not be forgotten that a lengthy discretionary sentence of imprisonment offers public protection. The question is whether a mandatory sentence is necessary to achieve this aim.

It is telling that the Law Commission were told that the mandatory sentence for murder was not to be reviewed, but it is hardly surprising. Any government brave enough to amend the law would be subjected to a barrage of hostile media comment. It is far easier to maintain the status quo rather than reform such a symbolic sentence.

Consistency in sentencing

A perennial question is whether individuals who commit similar offences receive similar sentences. This deceptively simple question raises a fundamental concern: if offenders who commit like offences receive radically different sentences there would appear to be obvious injustice. All offences have a maximum punishment that can be imposed but these are often extremely high and are seldom used. According to the *Daily Telegraph* (2006), only 2½ per cent of those sentenced in the Crown Court and 2 per cent of those sentenced in the magistrates' court received the maximum penalty. Very few offences carry a mandatory penalty (see above for some notable exceptions). What factors may a sentencer take into account when determining an appropriate sentence?

Section 142(1) of the Criminal Justice Act 2003 requires sentencers to have regard to the following considerations: the punishment of offenders; the reduction of crime (including its reduction by deterrence); the reform and rehabilitation of offenders; the protection of the public; and the making of reparation by offenders to persons affected by their offences. This is a lengthy list and one that would appear to give sentencers considerable scope (see Ashworth and Player, 2005). Although two sentencers could both 'have regard' to the list, there would appear to be nothing stopping one of them prioritising public protection and the other rehabilitation. The *Home Office* stated that:

> Sentencers will be required to consider these purposes when sentencing and how the sentence they impose will provide the right balance between the purposes set out above, given the circumstances of the offence and the offender. (Home Office, 2002, para. 5.9)

Despite this reassurance, Ashworth's comment that the approach is a 'recipe for inconsistency' (2004: 529) seems apposite. In order to test the consistency of decision-making, the next section will consider the use of custodial sentences.

Consistency and the custodial threshold

One of the most important decisions that sentencers make is whether an offender should receive a custodial sentence. There are a number of external pressures that may influence sentencers making such a decision, such as popular perceptions of different types of punishment and the problem of prison overcrowding (see Millie *et al.*, 2007), but the legal test is found in s. 152(2) of the Criminal Justice Act 2003:

> The court must not pass a custodial sentence unless it is of the opinion that the offence, or the combination of the offence and one or more offences associated with it, was so serious that neither a fine alone nor a community sentence can be justified for the offence.

What evidence is there that sentencers are interpreting the section consistently? National statistics suggest that there is considerable variety in the use of custody, suggesting that there is at least a degree of '*justice by geography*'. The rate for all offenders sentenced in magistrates' courts for indictable offences in 2006 ranged from 7 per cent in Northumbria to 19 per cent in Cheshire (Ministry of Justice, 2007a, para 5.13) whilst the custody rate for those sentenced in the Crown Court varied from 46 per cent in Durham to 69 per cent in Northamptonshire (Ministry of Justice, 2007a, para. 5.14). There may be legitimate reasons why the use of particular punishments would vary between areas— for example to reflect a difference in the seriousness of the offences being sentenced. There is, though, the possibility that the differences are the result of arbitrary and inconsistent decision making.

Many offences, of course, pose sentencers with few problems; they are either so trivial that no one could sensibly argue that the test has been met or so serious that the test is easily satisfied. It is instructive, though, to consider the sentencing patterns for a comparatively common offence which does cause more difficulties. Is burglary an offence which is so serious that 'neither a fine alone nor a community sentence can be justified'? The official statistics show that 41 per cent of those sentenced for the offence received a sentence of immediate custody (Ministry of Justice, 2007a, Table 2.13) whilst a further 8 per cent were given a *Suspended Sentence Order* (Ministry of Justice, 2007a, Table 2.22). These figures demonstrate just how borderline the offence is: in just under half of cases the offence was judged to be so serious that only custody could be justified. Although this position may lack certainty, sentencers would maintain that they need a range of sentences in order to reflect the relative severity of each case as not all burglaries are identical. For example, some burglaries are of domestic dwellings which are occupied at the time, whilst others involve commercial premises. Similarly a sentencer would argue that each offender is different and that account should be taken of any particularly relevant characteristics of the offender, such as old age or drug addiction (for the views of a lawyer, see Cooper, 2008). A difficult balance has to be struck between allowing the discretion that is needed to arrive at a just sentence in any given case and the need to ensure that sentences for the same offence are broadly similar.

REVIEW QUESTIONS

1 What factors should sentencers consider when determining sentence?

2 What evidence is there to suggest that there is inconsistency in sentencing?

3 Why might the use of custody vary geographically?

Providing guidance to sentencers: from 'guideline' judgments to the Sentencing Guidelines Council

Traditionally the Court of Appeal issued 'guideline' judgments on sentencing some offences (see Ashworth, 2001; Dingwall, 1997). This approach was not wholly successful as the guidance tended to concentrate on serious offences and not on those more common offences which could be classified as moderately serious, such as burglary. This could partly be explained by the fact that the Court of Appeal hears sentencing appeals from the Crown Court, but this merely demonstrates an inherent limitation with using Court of Appeal judgments as the primary source of guidance.

Another vital source of reference was the *Magistrates' Court Sentencing Guidelines* (2004; see further Ashworth, 2005: 64–65). These provided magistrates with the maximum available sentence for each offence, along with a guideline penalty, some factors that may mean that the guideline should be departed from, and the impact that any other relevant factors should have. In practice these were very important given the proportion of offenders sentenced in magistrates' courts, even though the guidelines had no legal authority and were purely advisory. The Crime and Disorder Act 1998 created a new body, the *Sentencing Advisory Panel*, to assist the Court of Appeal. The Panel's task was to provide the Court with useful information and suggestions, all of which is available online at <http://www.sentencing-guidelines.gov.uk>.

By far the most radical step to date has been the establishment of a *Sentencing Guidelines Council* charged with drafting 'definitive' guidance on the sentencing of particular offences or on particular sentencing concerns. Membership of the Council includes the Lord Chief Justice, a Circuit judge, a District judge (Magistrates' Courts), and a magistrate, as well as individuals with experience of policing, criminal *prosecution*, criminal defence, and victim support (s. 167). Every court has to 'have regard to' these definitive guidelines (s. 172(1)).

Evaluating the Sentencing Guidelines Council

If the only criterion by which the Sentencing Guidelines Council was to be judged was the need to achieve greater consistency in sentencing, it would appear easy to assess how successful it had been. All that would be required would be a statistical analysis of sentencing trends for a particular offence prior to and after the Council's guidance became operative. However, their remit is broader which makes evaluation more problematic. Dingwall (2006/07: 14–15) has argued that '[sentencing] guidance has...not only to *provide* guidance, in the hope of obtaining consistency, but has to *account for* the guidance in the hope of achieving justice'. Three forms of potential injustice were identified: a failure to achieve like sentences for like offences; a failure to differentiate between individuals who commit the same offence but with different degrees of culpability; and a failure to reflect differences in seriousness between different offences (Dingwall, 2006/07: 15).

The first concern—consistency—can be measured statistically, although this would not be easy (Wasik, 2000, 259–60), and the results in themselves may be of little value. If the guidelines are simplistic, then the 'correct' sentence may be easy to determine. However, the cruder the advice the less likely it is to be suitable for all cases and the greater the risk that sentencers will depart from it. Conversely, more nuanced guidance may result in what appears to be a higher degree of inconsistency but in fact increases the likelihood of an appropriate and/or a judicially acceptable sentence being imposed.

The second concern that was identified was the need for guidance to differentiate fairly between individuals who commit the 'same' offence but with different degrees of culpability. Guidance which fails to do this is ultimately unjust in that offenders who commit the same offence in legal terms often do so in very different circumstances. Robbery is used as an example to consider how successfully the guidelines achieve this aim. The Council differentiate the offence into five types (SGC, 2006: section C): street robbery; robberies of small businesses; less sophisticated commercial robberies; violent personal robberies in the home; and professionally planned commercial robberies. The first three categories are judged to be equally serious and are further subdivided into

Table 5.1 Guidelines for the offence of Robbery

Type/nature of activity	Starting point	Sentencing range
The offence includes the threat or use of minimal force and removal of property.	12 months' custody	Up to 3 years' custody
A weapon is produced and used to threaten, and/or force is used which results in injury to the victim.	4 years' custody	2–7 years' custody
The victim is caused serious physical injury by the use of significant force and/or use of a weapon.	8 years' custody	7–12 years' custody

Source: Sentencing Guidelines Council (2006: 11)

three levels of severity depending on the gravity of the threat and/or the degree of force used (SGC, 2006: section D). A grid is then provided which indicates the appropriate starting point and range (SGC, 2006: section G—violent personal robberies in the home and professionally planned commercial robberies were not included in the grid).

The third concern, that guidelines have to reflect differences between offences, matters for two reasons. First of all, the Criminal Justice Act 2003 stated that 'seriousness' remained relevant to sentencing (Dingwall, 2008). Secondly, there is a risk that individual guidelines would lose sight of the bigger picture: it is not enough to determine how one robbery should be sentenced with reference to other robberies, it is also necessary to assess how robbery should be sentenced in comparison to other offences.

It is to the Council's credit that they recognised the importance of providing guidance on seriousness. The guidelines state that '[harm] must always be judged in the light of culpability' (SGC, 2004: para. 1.17) but recognise that '[assessing] seriousness is a difficult task, particularly where there is an imbalance between culpability and harm' (SGC, 2004: para. 1.14). No one doubts this, but to what extent do the guidelines offer genuine assistance? It is worth returning to the crucial question of whether an offence is so serious 'that neither a fine alone nor a community sentence can be justified for the offence' (Criminal Justice Act 2003, s. 152(2)). The Council claimed that '[it] would not be feasible to provide a form of words or to devise any formula that would provide a general solution' and that '[it] is the task of *guidelines for individual offences* to provide more detailed guidance on what features within that offence point to a custodial sentence' (SGC, 2004: para. 1.37, original emphasis). What this means is that the general guidance on seriousness becomes dependent upon the guidance for particular offences. As a consequence, no overall consideration is given to the relative severity of different offences. The danger of this approach is shown by comparing the guidance for robbery (SGC, 2006) with the guidance issued for sexual offences (SGC, 2007a). Combining the two, a level three street robbery merits an identical sentence to a sustained *rape* or a rape involving more than one offender. Surely this demands an explanation? The Council (2008) have published definitive guidelines on sentencing in magistrates' courts. This is an important development as it gives legal authority to what are largely the pre-existing *Magistrates'*

Court Sentencing Guidelines. Yet this compounds the problem by providing guidance for a large number of offences—from assault occasioning actual bodily harm to zebra crossing contravention—without considering their relative severity.

Recognising some of these concerns, the Sentencing Advisory Panel (2008) have recently issued a Consultation Paper entitled *Overarching Principles of Sentencing.* Amongst other matters, the Paper contained proposals on offence-severity (SAP, 2008: paras 27–41), the effect of previous convictions (SAP, 2008: paras 42–60), and aggravating and mitigating factors (SAP, 2008: paras 61–76). Crucially the Panel proposes that there should be a presumption of a custodial sentence where serious physical, psychological, financial, or social harm was intended, whether or not the harm was actually inflicted; or where death or serious physical or social harm was caused by an offender who acted with a callous disregard as to whether such harm was likely to be occasioned or not; or where public policy demands a custodial sentence. This is a welcome development in that it does provide a general test and not one dependent on the guidance for particular offences.

REVIEW QUESTIONS

1 Why is it difficult to evaluate sentencing guidelines?

2 Why is it necessary to determine the relative severity of different offences?

3 When, according to the Sentencing Advisory Panel, should there be a presumption that an offender will receive a custodial sentence?

Ethnicity and sentencing

This section considers the evidence on whether offenders from ethnic minority backgrounds are discriminated against at the sentencing stage. Official data show that a higher proportion of Black offenders receive a custodial sentence than their White or Asian counterparts (see Ministry of Justice, 2008a, chap. 6). The question is whether this difference can be explained in whole or in part on the grounds of ethnicity. Earlier studies were inconclusive (Hudson, 1993: 6–8). Researchers identified a number of factors which could be relevant such as: discrimination earlier in the criminal justice process; other social-personal factors such as relative rates of unemployment; the higher proportion of Black defendants who elect trial by jury, thereby increasing their possible sentences after conviction; and the smaller proportion of Black defendants who plead guilty (Hudson, 1993: 7). One of the main reasons why the early research was often inconclusive was because the small samples only allowed tentative conclusions to be drawn (Dholakia and Sumner, 1993: 36).

The most detailed study was undertaken by Hood (1992). The author attempted to predict the sentencing outcome in Crown Court cases in the West Midlands by considering characteristics of the offence and the offender. The offender's ethnicity was excluded from the calculation. Hood concluded that ethnicity could not be totally disregarded when the predicted rates were compared to the actual rates of imprisonment. Taking account of other factors, there was still a 5 per cent greater probability that a Black offender would receive a custodial sentence (Hood, 1992: 78). Asian offenders generally appeared to be sentenced in the same way as White offenders (Hood, 1992: 183). Hood himself claimed that the results needed to be treated with some caution (Hood, 1992: 130), but the implications are profound. It is clear that the issues raised need to be carefully monitored even if the study is over 15 years old and sentencers have had more training in the interim.

Very few sentencers come from ethnic minority backgrounds. In the Crown Court, only 3 per cent of High Court judges, 3 per cent of Circuit judges, and 5 per cent of Recorders come from ethnic minority backgrounds (<http://www.judiciary.gov.uk/keyfacts/statistics/ethnic.htm>) and, in magistrates' courts, 2 per cent of District judges (Magistrates' Court) and 7 per cent of magistrates (Ministry of Justice, 2008a: 113) come from ethnic minority backgrounds.

Gender and sentencing

In common with ethnicity, there are considerable difficulties in researching the relevance of gender in sentencing. At first glance the 2006 sentencing statistics would suggest that females are sentenced very favourably. Twenty-nine per cent of men aged over 21 who were sentenced for an indictable offence received an immediate custodial sentence compared to 17 per cent of females (Ministry of Justice, 2007b, Table 1.8). At the lower end of the spectrum, female offenders were more likely to get an absolute or a conditional discharge (Ministry of Justice 2007b: Table 1.8; 23 per cent as opposed to 13 per cent) whereas men were more likely to be fined (Ministry of Justice, 2007b: Table 1.8: 20 per cent as opposed to 15 per cent). These figures, though, do not provide the full picture. No account is taken of offence type or a range of other factors which may influence sentence. However, the data relating to sex and offence group (Ministry of Justice, 2007b: Table 2.13) show that a higher proportion of men were sentenced to immediate custody for all 10 groups of indictable offences and both categories of summary offence. And, if the offender received a custodial sentence, in all categories except two (sexual offences and criminal damage), the average sentence length was longer for men (Ministry of Justice, 2007b: Table 2.14).

The most detailed research into the sentencing of women was undertaken by Dowds and Hedderman (1997). Three types of offence were analysed. With regards to shoplifting, regardless of whether the offender had previous convictions, the authors found that 'women were generally more likely than men to be discharged or given a probation order, less likely to be fined and less likely to be given a custodial sentence' (Dowds and Hedderman, 1997: 11). These findings are consistent with the overall sentencing statistics for 2006 (see above). Turning to violent offences, the trend appears similar with a disproportionate number of females being put on *probation* or discharged (Dowds and Hedderman, 1997: 18). An important caveat is that female offenders generally have fewer previous convictions than men (which would affect the sentencing of repeat offenders) and that female offenders are usually involved in less serious cases (which would affect the sentencing of both first time and repeat offenders) (Dowds and Hedderman, 1997: 19). These factors clearly make comparisons difficult.

This pattern proved different for drug offences where gender was not significantly associated with the use of custody (Dowds and Hedderman, 1997: 19). The authors comment that female drug offenders appeared to be especially 'deviant': first time offenders were older than their male counterparts; they were more likely to be charged with a serious offence; they were more likely to be sentenced in the Crown Court; and repeat offenders tended to be older and have a history of fraud offences. When account was taken of other variables, it was found that first time female drug offenders were less likely to receive a prison sentence than male offenders whereas repeat offenders were just as likely to be imprisoned. Two important questions are raised by this study. Despite there being a tendency to imprison fewer female offenders, why is there a marked difference in the use of custodial sentences for some offences but not for others? Secondly, as men are more likely to be fined whereas women are more likely to be discharged or to receive probation, are some women who would have been fined being treated more leniently whilst others are being treated more severely than men?

It will probably come as no surprise that there are no simple explanations for these findings. Some sentencers certainly appear to stereotype female offenders. One magistrate in Gelsthorpe and Loucks' (1997: 26) study commented that you '[think] of them as greedy, needy or dotty'. Gelsthorpe and Loucks concluded that the relative inexperience of female offenders and their corresponding 'nervousness' in court may make them appear more genuinely remorseful than male offenders who are often more experienced both in terms of offending and appearing in court (Gelsthorpe and Loucks, 1997: 43–4). There also appeared to be a more marked distinction drawn between 'troubled' and 'troublesome' female offenders. Magistrates believed that a higher proportion of female offenders would benefit from a Probation Order (Gelsthorpe and Loucks, 1997: 44). As has been said, this probably cuts both ways as some female offenders given probation would in all probability have been fined if they were male, whilst others probably avoided a custodial sentence.

The proportion of female sentencers decreases with seniority. As of April 2008, 50 per cent of magistrates, 23 per cent of District judges, 15 per cent of Recorders, 13 per cent of Circuit judges, and 10 per cent of High Court judges were female (<http://www.judiciary.gov.uk/keyfacts/statistics/women.htm>).

REVIEW QUESTIONS

1 Why is it difficult to assess the impact of ethnicity or gender on sentencing?

2 How might a female offender's lifestyle influence sentencing?

3 What effects may the Criminal Justice Act 2003 have on the sentencing of female offenders?

CONCLUSION

This chapter started with the claim that few areas of criminal justice attract the same degree of public disquiet and, at times, disbelief as sentencing. Politicians and the media appear to interpret this anxiety as a belief that sentencing is too lenient (Roberts and Hough, 2002). Yet research by Smith (2007: 12–13) found that only 4 per cent of his sample thought about lenient sentencing when deciding how confident they were about the criminal justice system; ten factors weighed more heavily on their minds. Despite this, when the sample were asked what measures would improve their confidence in the system, 44 per cent cited tougher sentencing (Smith, 2007: 16). This suggests that there is political capital in promising tougher sentences. Different people will naturally have different opinions about whether sentences are too lenient. Nonetheless, it is worth noting that, in comparison to most other Western countries, England and Wales appears to be relatively punitive (Pakes, 2004: 121–6), that sentences have recently become more severe for many offences, and that the public routinely underestimate the sentences that the courts actually impose (Roberts and Hough, 2002).

One surprise from Smith's study (2007: 12–13) is that the most common factor considered (by 33 per cent of the sample) when deciding about confidence in the criminal justice system was consistency in sentencing. There certainly is evidence of inconsistency (e.g. Ministry of Justice, 2007a: para. 5.13) but what is remarkable is the impact that this had on judgments about confidence in the system. Certainly the wide geographical differences in the custodial rate does raise concerns about injustice, as does the evidence relating to the differential sentencing of offenders from ethnic minority backgrounds (Hood, 1992). In fairness, these concerns have been recognised by the government and it has to be hoped that the work of the Sentencing Guidelines Council helps rectify the most blatant discrepancies.

It is perhaps appropriate to end with a note of caution. As long as some dangerous individuals are released only to reoffend, as long as depressing numbers of property offenders are re-incarcerated, and as long as ever-escalating penalties fail to deter, the public will remain dissatisfied. It is worth asking to what extent complaints about sentencing are really complaints about the limitations of punishment.

QUESTIONS FOR DISCUSSION

1   Should someone who pleads guilty be rewarded with a lesser sentence?

2   Section 142(1) of the Criminal Justice Act 2003 requires sentencers to have regard to the following: the punishment of offenders; the reduction of crime (including its reduction by deterrence); the reform and rehabilitation of offenders; the protection of the public; and the making of reparation by offenders to persons affected by their offences. How would you prioritise these aims? Explain your reasons.

3   Do you think that burglary is an offence which is always, sometimes, or never 'so serious that neither a fine alone nor a community sentence can be justified for the offence'?

4   A and B both drink and drive. A is stopped and charged with driving when under the influence of drink or drugs. B hits someone and kills him. B is charged with causing death by careless driving when under the influence of drink or drugs. Are they equally blameworthy? Do they deserve the same sentence?

GUIDE TO FURTHER READING

Ashworth, A. (2005) *Sentencing and Criminal Justice* (4th edn). Cambridge: Cambridge University Press.

This book by one of the leading sentencing experts provides a comprehensive account of sentencing law and practice. Professor Ashworth is the current Chair of the Sentencing Advisory Panel.

Ashworth, A. and Player, E. (2005) 'Criminal Justice Act 2003: the Sentencing Provisions' *Modern Law Review* 68:822.

This article discusses the most important recent Act of Parliament on sentencing.

Easton, S. and Piper, C. (2008) *Sentencing and Punishment: the quest for justice* (2nd edition). Oxford: Oxford University Press.

Another book aimed at undergraduate students which supplies an accessible but detailed account of sentencing law and practice. It also has useful material on the justifications for punishment which are explored in another chapter of this book.

Hood, R. (1992) *Race and Sentencing*. Oxford: Oxford University Press.

This is still the most important study on whether those from ethnic minority backgrounds are discriminated against in the sentencing process. The sections on methodology will be daunting for undergraduate students, but are necessary in order to explain how the author provided for a number of other variables which could have explained apparent discrepancies.

Ministry of Justice (2007a) *Sentencing Statistics 2006*. London: Ministry of Justice.

The official statistics tell you everything you want to know about sentencing different offences and the use of different types of punishment.

WEB LINKS

http://www.sentencing-guidelines.gov.uk

This site contains copies of all final guidance from the Sentencing Guidelines Council along with advice from the Sentencing Advisory Panel.

http://www.justice.gov.uk

The Ministry of Justice site gives details of Statistical Bulletins, Statistical Findings, Research Studies, Occasional Papers and Research Findings. Although some of them are short and summarise recent findings, some are very detailed and run to several hundred pages. Information from before May 2006 can be found on the Home Office site <http://www.homeoffice.gov.uk>.

http://www.magistrates-association.org.uk

The vast majority of offenders are sentenced by magistrates. This user-friendly site explains what they do, what powers they have, and, if you are interested, how you can become a magistrate yourself.

www.judiciary.gov.uk/learning_resources/quiz_british_justice_survey/ quiz_britishjusticesurvey.htm

Although this site contains a clear account of the roles of different members of the judiciary, I have given the direct link to a short quiz on sentencing. It is a shame that its primary purpose appears to be to show how tough sentences really are, especially by pointing out that burglary can include reaching through a window and stealing a milk bottle.

http://www.cjsonline.gov.uk

There are two reasons why this site is particularly useful: it gives information on all aspects of the criminal justice system, including sentencing; and it provides an excellent list of hyperlinks to other criminal justice sites.

REFERENCES

Ashworth, A. (2001) 'The Decline of English Sentencing and Other Stories' in M. Tonry and R.S. Frase (eds) *Sentencing and Sanctions in Western Countries*. New York: Oxford University Press.

Ashworth, A. (2004) 'Criminal Justice Act 2003 (2): Criminal Justice Reform: Principles, Human Rights and Public Protection'. *Criminal Law Review:* 516.

Ashworth, A. (2005) *Sentencing and Criminal Justice* (4th edn). Cambridge: Cambridge University Press.

Ashworth, A. (2007) 'Sentencing' in M. Maguire, R. Morgan, and R. Reiner (eds) *The Oxford Handbook of Criminology* (4th edn). Oxford: Oxford University Press.

Ashworth, A. and Player, E. (2005) 'Criminal Justice Act 2003: the Sentencing Provisions'. *Modern Law Review* 68: 822.

Baldwin, J. and McConville, M. (1977) *Negotiated Justice*. Oxford: Martin Robertson.

Cooper, J. (2008) 'The Sentencing Guidelines Council—A Practical Perspective'. *Criminal Law Review:* 277.

The Daily Telegraph (2006) 'Maximum Sentence for Only One in 40 Criminals' 11 December 2006.

Dholakia, N. and Sumner, M. (1993) 'Research, Policy and Racial Justice' in D. Cook and B. Hudson (eds) *Racism & Criminology*. London: Sage Publications.

Dingwall, G. (1997) 'The Court of Appeal and "Guideline" Judgments'. *Northern Ireland Legal Quarterly* 48(2): 143.

Dingwall, G. (2006/07) 'From Principle to Practice: reconsidering sentencing guidance'. *Contemporary Issues in Law* 8(4): 7.

Dingwall, G. (2008) 'Deserting Desert? Locating the Present Role of Retributivism in the Sentencing of Adult Offenders'. *Howard Journal of Criminal Justice* 47(4): 400.

Donohue, J.J. and Wolfers, J. (2005) 'Uses and Abuses of Empirical Evidence in the Death Penalty Debate'. *Stanford Law Review* 58: 791.

Dowds, L. and Hedderman, C. (1997) 'The Sentencing of Men and Women' in C. Hedderman and L. Gelsthorpe (eds) *Understanding the Sentencing of Women*. Home Office Research Study No. 170. London: Home Office.

Easton, S. and Piper, C. (2008) *Sentencing and Punishment: the quest for justice* (2nd edn). Oxford: Oxford University Press.

Gelsthorpe, L. and Loucks, N. (1997) 'Magistrates' Explanations of Sentencing Decisions' in C. Hedderman and L. Gelsthorpe (eds) *Understanding the Sentencing of Women*. Home Office Research Study No. 170. London: Home Office.

Home Office (2001) *Making Punishments Work: report of a review of the sentencing framework for England and Wales*. London: Home Office.

Home Office (2002) *Justice for All* Cm 5563. London: HMSO.

Hood, R. (1992) *Race and Sentencing*. Oxford: Oxford University Press.

Hudson, B. (1993) 'Racism and Criminology: concepts and controversies' in D. Cook and B. Hudson (eds) *Racism & Criminology*. London: Sage Publications.

Hungerford-Welch, P. (2004) *Criminal Litigation and Sentencing* (6th edn). London: Cavendish Publishing.

Jones, P. (2002) 'The Halliday Report and Persistent Offenders' in S. Rex and M. Tonry (eds) *Reform and Punishment: the future of sentencing*. Cullompton: Willan Publishing.

Koffman, L. [2006] 'The Rise and Fall of Proportionality: the failure of the Criminal Justice Act 1991'. *Criminal Law Review:* 281.

Lart, R., Pantazis, C., Pemberton, S., Turner, W., and Almeida, C. (2008) *Interventions aimed at reducing re-offending in female offenders: a rapid evidence assessment*. Ministry of Justice Research Series 8/08. London: Ministry of Justice.

Law Commission (2006) *Murder, Manslaughter and Infanticide*. Law Commission No. 304. London: The Stationery Office.

Millie, A., Tombs, J., and Hough, M. (2007) 'Borderline Sentencing: a comparison of sentencers' decision making in England and Wales, and Scotland'. *Criminology & Criminal Justice* 7(3): 243.

Ministry of Justice (2007a) *Sentencing Statistics 2006*. London: Ministry of Justice.

Ministry of Justice (2007b) *Criminal Statistics 2006*. London: Ministry of Justice.

Ministry of Justice (2008a) *Statistics on Race and the Criminal Justice System 2006/7*. London: Ministry of Justice.

Ministry of Justice (2008b) *Statistics on Women and the Criminal Justice System 2005/6*. London: Ministry of Justice.

Pakes, F. (2004) *Comparative Criminal Justice*. Cullompton: Willan Publishing.

Roberts, J.V. and Hough, M. (2002) *Changing Attitudes to Punishment: public opinion, crime and punishment*. Cullompton: Willan Publishing.

Sentencing Advisory Panel (SAP) (2008) *Consultation Paper on Overarching Principles of Sentencing*. London: SAP.

Sentencing Commission Working Group (SGC) (2008) *A Structured Sentencing Framework and Sentencing Commission*. London: Ministry of Justice.

Sentencing Guidelines Council (SGC) (2004) *Overarching Principles: Seriousness*. London: SGC.

Sentencing Guidelines Council (SGC) (2006) *Definitive Sentencing Guidelines on Robbery*. London: SGC.

Sentencing Guidelines Council (SGC) (2007a) *Definitive Sentencing Guideline—Sexual Offences Act 2003*. London: SGC.

Sentencing Guidelines Council (SGC) (2007b) *Reduction in Sentence for a Guilty Plea: definitive guidelines*. London: SGC.

Sentencing Guidelines Council (SGC) (2008) *Magistrates' Court Sentencing Guidelines*. London: SGC.

Smith, D. (2007) *Confidence in the Criminal Justice System: what lies beneath?* Ministry of Justice Research Series 7/07. London: Ministry of Justice.

Tonry, M. (2004) *Punishment and Politics: Evidence and emulation in the making of English crime control policy*. Cullompton: Willan Publishing.

Von Hirsch, A. (2002) 'Record-Enhanced Sentencing in England and Wales: Reflections on the Halliday Report's proposed treatment of prior convictions' in S. Rex and M. Tonry (eds) *Reform and Punishment: the future of sentencing*. Cullompton: Willan Publishing.

Ward, R. and Davies, O.M. (2004) *The Criminal Justice Act 2003: a practitioner's guide*. Bristol: Jordans.

Wasik, M. (2008) 'Sentencing Guidelines in England and Wales—State of the Art?' *Criminal Law Review:* 253.

Woolf, H. and Tumim, S. (1991) *Prison Disturbances April 1990*. The Woolf Report Cm 1456. London: HMSO.

Young, J. (2003) 'Winning the Fight Against Crime? New Labour, populism and lost opportunities' in R. Matthews and J. Young (eds) *The New Politics of Crime and Punishment*. Cullompton: Willan Publishing.

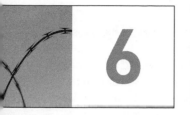

6 Transforming the prison: histories of prison and imprisonment, 1770–1952

Helen Johnston

INTRODUCTION

This chapter considers the emergence of imprisonment as the predominant form of *punishment* for the majority offences from the mid-nineteenth century onwards in Britain. It examines imprisonment before and during the eighteenth century through to the Victorian period. During this time, the use and purpose of prisons changed from places of detention to institutions for transforming the character and behaviour of offenders. In addressing the change or transformation in the purpose of the prison, this chapter provides an overview of the key changes and developments that shaped the use of imprisonment and prison regimes between the late eighteenth and the mid-twentieth centuries. In particular, it addresses the period of prison 'reform' in the late eighteenth century, noting the influence of key figures such as John Howard and Elizabeth Fry, and outlines how the change in the purpose of prison has been interpreted by criminologists and historians.

When examining developments from the beginning of the nineteenth century, the chapter considers the *separate* and *silent systems* of imprisonment, and the reformative potential that these systems were thought to offer. From the mid-nineteenth century, prison regimes became more severe and focused on long hours of hard labour and harsh living conditions with the purpose of deterring prisoners from future offending. Following this, *convict prisons* were established to hold long-term prisoners, and *local prisons* came under government control in 1878. The final section of this chapter examines the changes in prison policy and practice, from the Gladstone Committee report in 1895, through the first half of the twentieth century until the Prison Act 1952. Throughout the chapter reference is made to other changes in punishment which affected the use and nature of imprisonment, particularly the decline in the use of execution and the transportation of offenders to America and later to Australasia.

In examining prison history, it is important to remember that there is not just one 'history' of prisons and imprisonment, but rather there are different histories, accounts, and perspectives. These distinct interpretations are offered by prisoners, prison officials, 'reformers', chaplains, and social commentators who were writing at the time, and, latterly, by criminologists and historians, who look back at events and attempt to understand the histories and experiences of prison and imprisonment. Finally, although this chapter is concerned with the transformation of imprisonment between the end of the eighteenth and the mid-twentieth centuries, many of the issues raised are relevant when examining prisons and imprisonment in the twenty-first century.

BACKGROUND

The use of imprisonment has a long history. The term 'prison' comes from the Latin word meaning to 'seize', the place being defined as a building to which people are legally committed to await trial or punishment. In the eighteenth century, prisons existed in two forms: *gaols* or *jails*; and *houses of correction* or *bridewells*. During this time, prisons were used predominantly to hold offenders for short periods before trial or sentence, until transportation abroad, or until they were executed. However, by the 1770s and 1780s the idea that prisons could offer more than just detention developed.

Before the late eighteenth century, gaols were purely places of detention. They held individuals awaiting trial or sentenced or detained until debts were paid. Houses of correction or bridewells (named after Bridewell Palace which was a building set aside to hold petty offenders in England in 1555) emerged in the sixteenth century in Britain. They also developed during the sixteenth and seventeenth centuries across Europe, for example, rasphouses in the Netherlands and spinhouses in Germany. Houses of correction or prison workhouses (Spierenburg, 1991; 2005) were the first attempt to alter the behaviour of offenders. They used hard labour in an attempt to instil habits of domestic or workplace industry and discipline on petty offenders including those committed for vagrancy, drunkenness, petty delinquencies, being 'idle and disorderly', and other offences associated with the poor (Innes, 1987; Melossi and Pavarini, 1981). By the eighteenth century, the distinction between gaols and *house of corrections* or bridewells was not always clear. In some locations, they were on the same site, or in the same building, distinguished by using different rooms. In 1865, the Prison Act renamed gaols and houses of correction or bridewells with the collective phrase 'local prison', a term still used today.

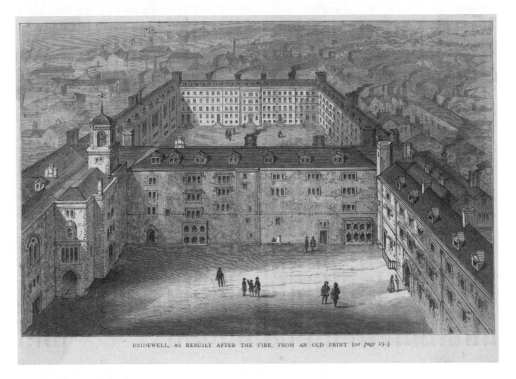

BRIDEWELL, AS REBUILT AFTER THE FIRE, FROM AN OLD PRINT (*see page* 191.)

Figure 6.1 Bridewell

Source: © Mary Evans Picture Library

The eighteenth-century prison and the 'reform' movement

During the eighteenth century the living conditions in prisons were very different from those which exist today. Prisons were more closely linked with the local community. They were not the closed off and secretive institutions of the Victorian period. Local people and tradesmen visited prisons to sell their wares, visit those confined, or perhaps lived in the prison. Debtors' families often lived with them and they were free to leave during the day. A fictional example from the nineteenth century is found in Charles Dickens' *Little Dorrit*, where the main character lives in Marshalsea Debtors Prison, London with her father.

Conditions in eighteenth-century prisons varied and were often dependent on prisoners' ability to pay. Prisons were run for profit, fees were charged for entry, discharge, lodgings, bedding, the prison 'tap' (alcohol) and food, and the gaoler took his income from such fees. Prisons were organised by customary practices and the day was unregulated; some prisoners worked for their own profit, others begged, and the 'usual complaint...was that occupants passed their time in game, gambling and drunkenness' (McGowen, 1998: 75). Frequently, prisons in this period were characterised by disease, squalor, and disorder and were termed, *squalor carceris*—the squalor of prison. As we will see in the Case Study this drew the attention of reformers who questioned the nature and purpose of imprisonment.

As prisons were often only used to detain prisoners until trial or until the sentence was carried out, the main options open to courts when sentencing offenders for felonies were to execute them, or through *mitigation*, transport them to the colonies. Petty offenders were subject to public punishments such as flogging and the pillory, and offenders were also fined or could be required to join the military (McGowen, 1998).

The use and practice of public execution changed significantly throughout the eighteenth and nineteenth centuries. This was the time of the 'Bloody Code', so called because of the large number of capital offences which existed numbering about 250 in total. However, it was perhaps not as 'bloody' as the phrase first suggests; many offences were minutely defined by individual statute and in some cases this led to defendants' acquittal (Emsley, 2005). The criminal justice system and the law, whilst appearing universal, were deeply class orientated, and it was frequently the poor and the propertyless who found themselves at the end of the noose (Hay, 1975; Gatrell, 1994). During the eighteenth century concerns grew about the message being conveyed to the masses by executions. Executions were public and thousands of people would congregate to observe the 'spectacle of suffering'. In London, for example, offenders were paraded through the streets from Newgate Prison to Tyburn in an open cart. The public lined the streets, cheering, jeering, and plying prisoners with drink, although the crowds' reaction depended on the offence and public sentiment towards offenders. Once at the scaffold, offenders delivered a dying speech, and then were strangled to death in an exhibition of the power of the law. This gruesome spectacle concerned many who felt that it brutalised observers and had little deterrent effect (McGowen, 1994). It was frequently claimed that *crime* was rife during an execution as pickpockets and swindlers took advantage of the crowded streets. Although many people were sentenced to death, they could not all be executed. Instead many were reprieved which added to concerns about the arbitrary and unjust system (Gatrell, 1994).

From the mid-eighteenth century, many of the customs related to executions began to be withdrawn. The procession from Newgate to Tyburn ended in 1783. Instead executions took place outside Newgate prison, where the crowd could be controlled more easily. Offenders appeared to the crowd at the last moment and the event lasted minutes rather than hours. The use of the drop (a trap door in the floor of the gallows) meant that the worst strangulations were avoided. However a miscalculation by the executioner could still lead to strangulation or decapitation (Taylor, 1998). The number of executions fell also. Between 1770 and 1830 over 7,000 people were executed, but between 1837 and 1868 this had reduced to 347 (Gatrell, 1994). The criminal law was consolidated in the early years of the nineteenth century, and the number of capital offences reduced to four. By the late 1830s, people were rarely executed for offences other than murder (Emsley, 2005). In 1868 executions were removed from public view. Subsequently, they were carried out inside prisons, away from the gaze of the public, reflecting how sensibilities towards such punishments had changed (Pratt, 2002).

Many offenders who were sentenced to execution had sentences mitigated to transportation. The Transportation Act 1718 allowed the courts to transport offenders to America. Before 1776, it is estimated that 30,000 offenders were transported from England to America (McConville, 1998b). The practice came to an abrupt halt with the outbreak of the American War of Independence in 1776. After this date, offenders were still being sentenced to transportation by the courts but there was nowhere to send them so they had to be held in this country. To deal with these prisoners, hulks (prison ships) were established on the Thames (and later on the south coast). Usually, these were decommissioned warships which housed prisoners in appalling conditions of squalor and deprivation. In the first 20 months of use, one in four prisoners sent to the hulks died (Evans, 1982). The hulks were intended to be temporary but they remained for over 80 years and were only fully abandoned in the 1850s (Beattie, 1986).

The changes in punishment also influenced the development of the prison. At the end of the eighteenth and beginning of the nineteenth century a shift in punishment can be observed. This is referred to as the 'great transformation' of punishment whereby public bodily punishments began to give way to imprisonment which was used to change or alter the mind or the soul of offenders. Consequently the focus of punishment moved away from the body to the soul. This shift reflected the ideas of the Enlightenment whereby progressive thinkers such as Cesare Beccaria maintained that the existing punishments were barbaric. They argued, instead, that punishment should be rational and certain, fit the crime, and act as a deterrent to future offending (Emsley, 2005).

After the end of transportation to America, a different solution was required to deal with offenders. Plans were drawn up to hold offenders in a large prison. It was agreed by way of the Penitentiary Act 1779 that two penitentiaries should be built. This signalled a significant change in the purpose of punishment. The term 'penitentiary' (a place where offenders do penitence) suggested its purpose was for prisoners to repent their sins and seek forgiveness. The building of the penitentiaries was put out to tender. Jeremy Bentham submitted his plans for the *Panopticon*, a prison design influenced by Enlightenment thought. Bentham's plan for the Panopticon was based on inspection and labour. The six-storey circular construction with a central observation tower would allow the guards to observe all cells, whilst remaining unseen. 'The prisoner would be perpetually on display, the guard perpetually obscured', the prisoner would never know 'if they were *actually* being observed, the prisoners would internalize the surveillant gaze of the guard and modify their behaviour accordingly' (Fiddler, 2008: 196). However, the Panopticon was never built and neither were the two penitentiaries. Instead the problem of what to do with criminals sentenced to transportation was partially solved by the discovery of Australia. From 1787, until the mid-nineteenth century, criminals under such sentence would be sent to the other side of the world. It is estimated that 168,000 people were sent to the Antipodes in this way (Godfrey and Cox, 2008).

Whilst the discovery of Australia alleviated some of the concerns about what to do with those prisoners sentenced to transportation, it still remained the case that prisoners had to be detained until ships were available. In 1816, the first government-run prison Millbank Penitentiary opened in London. It was constructed to hold 1,000 prisoners awaiting transportation. Prisoners were held in seclusion for the first half of the sentence and then worked in association. In the following years, the regime became more severe, focusing on solitude and isolation. The detrimental effects of this quickly became evident as growing numbers of prisoners were pronounced insane, and periods of association had to be introduced. At one point, the penitentiary had to be abandoned due to a scurvy epidemic which was caused by a reduction in diet as the administrators bowed to claims that the diet was too full. The epidemic resulted in the deaths of at least 30 prisoners (McConville, 1981).

  CASE STUDY: Prison 'Reform': John Howard and Elizabeth Fry

Prison reform has a long history and started with individuals such as John Howard and Elizabeth Fry. The tradition continues today with organisations such as the Howard League for Penal Reform (see <http://www.howardleague.org/>) and the Prison Reform Trust (see <http://www.prisonreformtrust.org.uk/>).

Whilst the changes in transportation and public execution were occurring, John Howard began investigating the conditions in gaols and houses of correction across the country and later across Europe. He was appalled at what he found. Howard had been appointed Sheriff of Bedford in 1773, and in 1777 published *The State of the Prisons in England and Wales*. Howard was concerned with the poor management of prisons, which often left prisoners with little food and water, open to diseases like gaol fever, and confined in damp and poorly ventilated buildings with little work. Prisoners, he discovered, were left to idleness and debauchery for much of the time and women, men, young, old, petty offenders, and hardened criminals mingled together in poor sanitary conditions and a corrupting moral and physical environment (Howard, 1777/1929). This discovery led Howard to raise questions about the purpose of imprisonment. Howard also found that some prisoners were unable to obtain release as they were unable to pay the required discharge fee. Gaolers derived their income from fees paid by prisoners: instead Howard advocated that gaolers should be paid a proper salary to prevent this exploitative relationship. Due to his recommendations fees were abolished in the Gaols Fees Abolition Act of 1815.

Similarly, **Elizabeth Fry**, a Quaker, was drawn to prisons through her religious persuasion and began visiting female prisoners in Newgate prison, London in 1813. Fry was part of a group of evangelically minded Quakers concerned with social issues, who believed that through voluntary efforts, personal contact could induce religious consciousness and produce reform (McGowen, 1998). Fry was particularly concerned that female prisoners should be superintended by a matron and male officers should not have access to them. Fry promoted *Ladies Committees* for visiting prisoners and outlined her views in *Observations on the Visiting, Superintendence and Government of Female Prisoners* (1827).

The Gaols Act 1823 did incorporate some of Howard's and Fry's recommendations. The Act introduced a new system, known as classified association, where prisoners were confined in different parts of the prison according to their *gender* and to the type of crime they had committed. It also ordered all prisons to appoint a chaplain and a surgeon, and alcohol was prohibited.

REVIEW QUESTIONS

1 What purpose did prison serve before and during the eighteenth century?

2 How would you explain the increasing use of imprisonment after the 1770s?

3 What policies and changes to imprisonment did reformers advocate?

Reforming the prison: policies, practices, and experiences, 1820–1865

From the early nineteenth century, the prison sentence became a period during which prisoners could be fundamentally changed rather than just detained. Two different disciplinary regimes emerged in prisons, the separate and the silent system. Both systems were thought to offer the potential to transform offenders into law abiding citizens. They operated on the belief that communication between prisoners should be limited to prevent moral contamination; for example, young or first time offenders should be protected from the corrupting influences of hardened offenders. Both systems originated in America; the *separate system* operated at Walnut Street and at the Eastern Penitentiary at Cherry Hill, both in the state of Philadelphia. The silent system was used in the state of New York, at Auburn and Sing Sing Prisons (Henriques, 1972).

Under the separate system, prisoners were completely isolated from each other. They would spend all of their time in their cells where they would work, sleep, and eat. Through isolation and religious instruction from the prison chaplain, prisoners were provided with time to reflect on their behaviour and alter their future conduct. Prisoners left their cells only to attend exercise or to go to the prison chapel. Even during exercise or chapel, separation was maintained as prisoners were placed in individual stalls in chapels, or were required to wear a mask over their face to prevent recognition (Forsythe, 1987). The silent system also sought to prevent moral contamination through the use of silence. Prisoners laboured in association in workrooms during the day, but they had to be silent at all times. They were closely observed by staff to prevent even the smallest of gestures between prisoners (McGowen, 1998). Silence, it was thought, allowed prisoners to contemplate their behaviour in order to begin the process of reform. The silent system operated through a system of incentives and punishments. Badges, financial rewards, and better occupations could be obtained by well-behaved prisoners, whilst those who defied the regime were punished with increasing severity the longer defiance lasted (Forsythe, 1987). The separate system was more expensive to operate than the silent system because buildings had to be altered to accommodate separate cells. However, the silent system required more staff to constantly watch over prisoners.

Whilst the government was interested in these new ideas of prison discipline, they were newcomers to prison administration. Many reforms were initiated in local prisons (gaols and houses of correction/bridewells) which were controlled by the local authorities and were effectively run by the local magistrates. Consequently, the implementation of the regimes in prisons across the country was reliant on local individuals. Practice and impetus varied into the nineteenth century because of the 'reform' programme's reliance on individual magistrates, governors, or chaplains who had to convince their colleagues of the benefits of such regimes. In many areas, even where some of the strongest advocates of the separate or the silent systems were located, changes to prisons were slow, and authorities were often reluctant to commit the finances required for these new prison regimes (DeLacy, 1981).

After the construction of Millbank, the next step on the road to government control of all prisons was the establishment of government inspectors of prisons. Two of the first inspectors, William Crawford and Reverend Whitworth Russell, were influential advocates of the separate system. This became the preferred system and was legislated for by the Prison Act 1839 which required it to be implemented in all prisons. The government kept an eye on developments by stating that all separate cells had to be certified by one of the inspectors. This signalled the beginning of the growing influence of central government. As the nineteenth century progressed, this government influence grew and attempted to regulate local authorities by linking financial assistance to the condition and administration of local prisons.

The influence of the use of classification and then separation of prisoners within prisons during this period had also led to the idea that young offenders should be kept separate from a corrupting adult environment. In 1838, Parkhurst prison opened as the first separate state-run establishment for juvenile offenders. Parkhurst combined *deterrence* and employment in order to provide young offenders with a trade for life in the colonies. Prisoners' performance whilst under sentence determined the nature of their transportation (McConville, 1981).

After the demise of Millbank penitentiary, the government's attention turned to the development of a new adult 'model' prison, Pentonville. Opened in 1842, the operation of the separate system had been written into the very fabric of the building, which was to hold 520 prisoners. Yet, even before Pentonville opened, critics voiced concerns about the severity of the separate system. *The Times* stated the separate system was 'unnecessarily cruel, impolitic, and injudicious' for the prisoners. 'Death can only relieve them; and if the system be carried too far, madness will seize those whom death has for the present spared' (20 May 1841, cited in Johnston, 2006: 107). On entering Pentonville, prisoners'

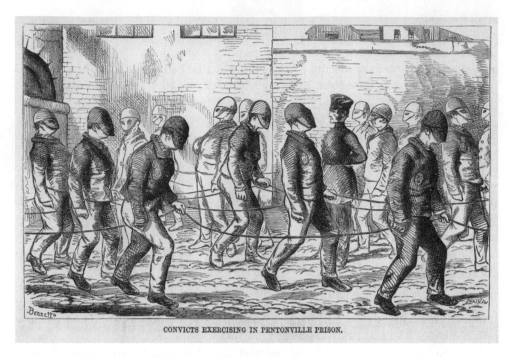

CONVICTS EXERCISING IN PENTONVILLE PRISON.

Figure 6.2 Convicts exercising in Pentonville prison

Source: © Mary Evans Picture Library

names were replaced with numbers, their heads were shaved, and they were placed in identical uniforms in identical cells, initially to endure separation for 18 months. The silence was only broken by the screams of those whose minds were severely affected and who were unable to cope in the loneliness and isolation (Ignatieff, 1978). After a short time, the regime was altered. The period of separation was reduced to 12 and then to nine months. In the end, Pentonville's demise was relatively swift, and by the mid 1850s it became a convict depot like Millbank.

As we have seen, Pentonville 'model' prison had already been subject to criticism even before it was opened. Yet in the years that followed, criticism of the separate system increased. But critical voices swayed between two positions. On the one hand, there was concern over the rates of insanity and damaging psychological effects of the regime on prisoners. Yet by the late 1840s and early 1850s, criticism changed direction and became focused upon the lavishness of prison regimes and calls for a greater degree of severity and deterrence in prison. It was also clear that some magistrates exceeded their powers and misused the separate system. Two investigations of local prisons, both in 1854, revealed the severity of such regimes. A 15-year-old offender, Edward Andrews, died at Birmingham Gaol and the subsequent investigation revealed a number of suicides and severe practices in the prison. At Leicester Gaol, an investigation uncovered that prisoners' meals had been withdrawn when they had failed to meet the daily target on the crank (a pointless device where prisoners turned a handle which was set to a certain level of resistance) of 14,400 revolutions per day.

However, the calls for greater severity in prison were influenced by wider concerns about crime and the criminal justice system, particularly the identification of a supposed 'criminal class' and a moral panic about 'garotting' during the 1850s and early 1860s. In terms of the existence of a criminal class, the public became increasingly aware of their existence from the 1850s. It was thought that this group were a hardcore of criminals, who lived solely by crime, and were repeatedly returning to prison (Emsley, 2005). Whilst there is some contention about whether the 'criminal class' actually existed, it is clear that the Victorian public believed that they did. They were frequently confronted by newspapers and periodicals documenting their existence (McGowen, 1990). These concerns coincided with a 'moral panic' about garotting (where the Adam's apple is pressed until the victim is unconscious but later applied by the media to various forms of street violence) which began after an attack on a Member of Parliament, Pilkington, on 17 July 1862 as he was returning home. Attacked by two men, Pilkington was grabbed around the throat, held until unconscious, and then robbed. Those responsible for the attack were thought to be convict prisoners who had been released early from prison, on a 'ticket of leave' (form of *early release* for good behaviour) and who had learnt this technique on convict ships (Davis, 1980; Sindall, 1990). The existence of a 'criminal class' and concerns about violent street crime caused a great deal of anxiety about crime which was frequently linked to the idea that prisons were not working properly. It was thought that criminals needed to be punished more severely in order to deter them. This anxiety about crime and offenders was also fuelled by the virtual end of transportation of convicts to Australia. The public, once safe in the knowledge that offenders were shipped to the other side of the world, were confronted with the uncomfortable reality that long-term offenders would have to be imprisoned and later released in this country.

By the 1850s and 1860s only a small number of convicts were being transported, the rest were imprisoned in England. To provide for this, the government established the *convict prison* system in which convicts served sentences of penal servitude. Through two Penal Servitude Acts in 1853 and 1857, the convict system was set up. Dartmoor, Portsmouth, Portland, Chatham, and Borstal were built or adapted for use in the new system. Under the Acts, prisoners served sentences of penal servitude. Four to six years penal servitude was equivalent to seven to ten years transportation, and six to eight years penal servitude represented ten to fourteen years transportation. The Director of Convict Prisons, Joshua Jebb, suggested that the minimum sentence should be four years including one year in separate confinement and three years on public works (for example, building or labouring in naval dockyards) (Tomlinson, 1981). Prisoners would experience a regime of progressive stages. Three stages would need to be passed through in order to obtain release. The 1857 Act reduced the minimum sentence to three years (Tomlinson, 1981). By 1864, reflecting the shift towards a more deterrent system, the minimum sentence of penal servitude was increased to five years for the first conviction, and seven years for repeat offenders. Photography was also introduced to identify repeat offenders (Tomlinson, 1981).

Initially, those offenders sentenced to 14 years transportation or for life were still shipped abroad, but this was abolished by the second Act in 1857. A small number of offenders were still transported to Western Australia, but the last fleet left in 1868 (Godfrey and Cox, 2008).

'Hard labour, hard board, hard fare' to 'a good and useful life': 1865–1952

Throughout this chapter, we have examined a constant jostling between the perceived aims of imprisonment—to *detain*, to *reform*, to *deter*—and the type of regime used within prisons to achieve these often conflicting aims. On the one hand, the politicians and public were opposed to the cruelties and abuse that resulted from penal experiments. However, they wanted to ensure the regime was severe enough to deter prisoners from future criminality, and perhaps alter prisoners' behaviour, transforming them, through religion, moral instruction, and hard labour into law-abiding citizens. The problem of *'less eligibility'* was also recurrent, as it was argued that under this principle, conditions in prison should be worse than living conditions of poor honest people outside prison. The principle underlying this concept is also reflected in contemporary debates about prison. One example of this is the argument that prisoners should not have in-cell televisions or games consoles, as disadvantaged people outside prisons may not have access to them (Johnston, 2008a).

Deterrence triumphed as the aim of imprisonment after the collapse of 'reform' in the 1850s, as a result of concerns about 'garotting' and the criminal classes, and the end of transportation. As a result the prison regime became more severe, characterised by the term *'hard labour, hard board, hard fare'*. The regime used harsh living conditions, poor diet, and long hours of hard labour, at the crank or on the treadwheel, to instil the necessary deterrence in prisoners. The separate system remained in the sense that prisoners were still kept separate, but any ideas of its reformative influence were gone. This regime operated through long sentences of penal servitude in the convict system (see above), and in local prisons was embodied in the Prison Act 1865 (following the recommendations of the Carnarvon Committee in 1863). It was this focus on severity, discipline, uniformity, and deterrence that lasted at least until the end of the century.

By the 1870s the two systems of imprisonment, the government-run convict system for long-sentenced prisoners and local prisons (for shorter sentences, administered by the boroughs and counties) were operating a deterrent penal philosophy. Yet there remained some concerns. It was not always the case that the administrators of local prisons implemented government policy and for a number of decades the government (through the prison inspectors) had been concerned that prison practice was not uniform across the country. Finally, the Prison Act 1877 enabled the government to take control of local prisons, bringing both systems under the control of the Prison Commission, chaired by Edmund Du Cane.

Centralisation resulted in the closure of some local prisons bringing the number to 112 by 1877. It also ushered in a more bureaucratic and uniform system and closed off prisons from the outside world. Offenders serving long periods for the most serious offences were held in convict prisons, and those offenders serving up to two years were held in local prisons. The majority of offenders were held in local prisons. Prison sentences were often short, averaging around ten days. Turnover was high in local prisons. In 1877, there was an average of around 20,000 prisoners in local prisons at any one time, but around 187,000 committals during the year (McConville, 1998a).

By the early 1890s, the prison system was coming under considerable criticism for the severity of the prison regime and the bureaucratic control and lack of accountability under Du Cane. These criticisms came from various sources. One example is a series of articles, appearing in the Daily Chronicle in 1894 entitled '*Our Dark Places*', thought to have been written by Reverend W.D. Morrison, the chaplain at Wandsworth Prison. In the first article, Du Cane's autocratic control and management of the system was highly criticised, as was the military organisation of the system. The local prison system, the critic wrote, 'is costly, yet it is starved; it is cruel, and it is ineffective; it is mechanical, and it does not work' (Anon, 1894: 5). Prisoners' memoirs from the preceding decades were also influential on the calls for the amelioration of the grinding prison regime (Anderson and Pratt, 2009). Growing discontent and concern led to the establishment of a Departmental Committee to inquire into prisons; this Committee, chaired by Herbert Gladstone, reported in 1895 (Gladstone Committee, 1895).

The Gladstone Committee (1895) advocated a balance between deterrence and reform. It recommended the abolition of unproductive labour, that prisoners should work in association, and that education should be an important part of their overall *rehabilitation*. It also recommended that remission was extended to local prisons, and prisoners were to be given more support on release which was enacted in the Prisons Act 1898. However, even before these changes occurred, the public's attention was once again drawn to prisons, when in 1896, the poet and writer Oscar Wilde was imprisoned for two years' hard labour for offences against homosexuality laws. After being transferred to Reading Gaol, due to ill-health, he wrote *The Ballad of Reading Gaol*. This was originally published under the pseudonym 'C.3.3', Wilde's cell number. Wilde launched a scathing attack on the cruelties and brutalities of the system, as this example shows:

> Each narrow cell in which we dwell
> Is a foul and dark latrine
> And the fetid breath of living Death
> Chokes up each grated screen,
> And all, but lust, is turned to dust
> In Humanity's machine (Wilde, 1898/2002, 136).

The period after the Gladstone report until the First World War (1895–1914) has been heralded by some criminologists as the key period in which the modern 'penal-welfare complex' was established (Garland, 1985). From 1895, following the Gladstone Committee, a number of groups were removed from the prison (juveniles, the mentally ill, inebriates) and new policies and practices were developed for different types of offenders, such as preventive detention and *probation*. The focus was on individual prisoners (reflecting positivist criminological thought at the time), and centred on the idea that crime was caused by offenders' environment and family background rather than their morality (Garland, 1985). Other authors are cautious of identifying these changes as a different phase in the development of prisons (Forsythe, 1990; Bailey, 1997). Instead they suggest that continuity rather than change characterised this period, particularly the use of deterrent and severe practices inside prisons and other institutions. They also point out that whilst the Gladstone Committee recommended changes, frequently these applied only to long-term prisoners (Forsythe, 1990). Those serving sentences in local prisons remained in conditions dominated by separation and silence, at least until the 1920s and 1930s (Forsythe, 1990; Johnston, 2008b). Hobhouse and Brockway's *English Prison To-Day*, published in 1922, an unofficial enquiry into the prison system, revealed the continuities in the machine-like operation and the rigid and regimented silent regimes of this period.

There were some important changes in the penal system in the first half of the twentieth century, notably the establishment of the Probation Service in 1907 and development of a separate juvenile justice system. Borstal training emerged as a new method for tackling young offenders (up to 21 years), combining military training with the organisation of public schools (cellblocks were called houses, each had a housemaster, staff did not wear uniforms) and aimed to encourage responsibility (McConville, 1998b).

Alexander Paterson became a prison commissioner in 1922; although he was never the Chairman, his influence over this period often marks it as the 'golden age of prison reform'. Paterson is most famous for his assertion that prisons were to be used '*as* punishment, not *for* punishment' (Ruck, 1951: 23), underlining the main principle of the liberal perspective on imprisonment. The first open prison was established in 1936 at New Hall, Wakefield. It was also realised that prisons could and should operate at different security levels (McConville, 1998b).

In the inter-war years, a number of prisons were closed and the crime rate was declining. Yet even before the Second World War was over this began to change. From 1945 the crime rate and the prison population grew, and a large prison-building programme developed. Seventeen new open, medium-security, and Borstal establishments were built, and Victorian cells once used for one person accommodated three prisoners (Soothill, 2007). The prison rules in operation today are rooted in the Prison Act 1952, particularly Prison Rule No. 1, that prison should encourage convicted prisoners to 'lead a good and useful life' reflecting the earlier principles of the Gladstone Committee.

REVIEW QUESTIONS

1 What factors influenced the increasing severity of prison regimes from 1865 onwards?

2 Why was the prison system 'in crisis' in the 1890s and what changes were recommended by the Gladstone Committee in 1895?

3 How did the end of transportation of offenders affect the prison system?

Theoretical perspectives: interpreting and understanding prison histories

What is evident from the discussion is that there was a transformation in the use and the purpose of imprisonment, between the late eighteenth and the early to mid-nineteenth century. The prison moves from operating as a place of detention to a place of punishment, where prisoners serve a sentence under a regime designed to change or alter their behaviour, or, less optimistically, to deter them from future offending. In addition, the philosophies of punishment used inside prisons were written into the architectural fabric and design of the nineteenth-century prison (Jewkes and Johnston, 2007). This section examines how this change has been interpreted by criminologists and historians. There are a number of different perspectives and positions taken by commentators and these are explored through three broad perspectives for clarity and convenience.

Whig or orthodox accounts

Whig or orthodox accounts see the rise in the use of imprisonment as a progressive move, taking society away from barbaric punishments like public execution, reflecting the development of a more civilised society. Whig accounts tend to focus on the individual achievements of reformers or magistrates, and how their humanitarianism or benevolent views triumphed over the squalor in prison and brutal punishments of a bygone era. This approach provides for a linear view. Put simply, in the past prisons were poor, after reform, prisons were better and this was largely thanks to the philanthropy and enlightened benevolence of well intentioned individuals. Examples of Whig accounts include Webb (1963), Stockdale (1977), and Radzinowicz and Hood (1990).

Revisionist accounts

The revisionist accounts of the 1970s and 1980s ask more critical questions about the changes in punishment and the birth of the prison. They remind us to question the motives of the reformers and asked questions such as whether there was more than straightforward benevolence and philanthropy behind the impetus for change. They also explore other questions such as whether the new prisons were 'better', what the consequences of these new regimes were for those who experienced them, and so on. All revisionist accounts see the prison as emerging in society alongside other types of institutions including schools, hospitals, asylums and factories. These institutions share similar disciplinary techniques to control and regulate the population. We shall briefly examine three revisionist positions starting with Michel Foucault.

Foucault (1977), in *Discipline and Punish*, begins by contrasting the horrific public torture, mutilation, and execution of regicide Damiens in 1757, with the minutely regulated and ordered timetable for young offenders at Mettray reformatory in 1838. For Foucault, two developments occurred between these two events: first, the decline in use and public displays of torturous punishment; and second, the emergence of the prison. During this time, the target of punishment changes from bodily punishment to the mind or the 'soul' of the offender. The objective of punishment moves to altering offenders rather than avenging the crime. Foucault demonstrates how experts (psychiatrists, criminologists, social workers) were introduced into the criminal justice system to gain knowledge about offenders' characters and backgrounds and ultimately to try to reform individuals through understanding the roots of their criminality. But Foucault does not necessarily see this change as bringing about a reduction in the severity of punishment as Whig accounts do. Instead he argues that this change allowed reformers 'not to punish less, but to punish better...to insert the power to punish deeply into the social body' (1977: 82).

Foucault suggests that the disciplinary techniques used in the prison were also used by other institutions (schools, the army, hospitals, and asylums) in order to train individuals and to produce 'docile and obedient bodies'. Foucault locates this range of institutions on a 'carceral continuum', as the boundaries between these institutions were often blurred. The design, which for Foucault provided the most efficient system of regulation and surveillance, was Jeremy Bentham's Panopticon (see above).

Marxist interpretations link the birth of the prison with the rise of capitalist mode of production. In *The Prison and the Factory* (1981), Melossi and Pavarini trace the early origins of compulsory labour to instil discipline and obedience in prisoners, to the houses of correction in sixteenth-century Europe (see above). Recognising these historical origins, Melossi and Pavarini (1981: 144) argue the relationship between labour and the prison is most clearly seen in the 'prison as a machine' from the early nineteenth century. They suggest that in periods of high unemployment, prison conditions are made more severe in order to deter offenders. However, when unemployment is low and wages are rising, the prison puts prisoners to useful labour in order to recycle them back into the free market. Thus, the prison operates 'like a factory, producing proletarians' (1981: 145). So, for Melossi and Pavarini, the prison is inextricably linked to the capitalist mode of production. Similarly to Foucault's position, prisons are linked to other social institutions (schools, workhouses, and factories) in disciplining the workforce for the benefit of capitalist production.

There are also three important accounts examining the motives of prison reformers and the consequences of prison reform, provided by David Rothman, Anthony Platt, and Michael Ignatieff. In *The Discovery of the Asylum*, Rothman argues we need to be cautious when examining what appears to be progressive change and that the notion of 'humanitarianism' in reform was rhetoric more than reality. Instead he suggests that reforms may have unintended consequences and even though they were 'designed with the best of motives may have disastrous results' (1971: 295). Similarly, Platt argues that reforms in the juvenile reformatories in the US resulted in longer sentences and militaristic discipline, demonstrating that the 'child savers' should in 'no sense be considered libertarians or humanists' (1969: 176). Ignatieff's *A Just Measure of Pain* (1978) also sees a more complicated relationship between the reformers and class interests in the ideological origins of the penitentiary. He argues that reformers had genuine religious and philanthropic views, and this reform succeeded as it was not just a response to crime, but to social crises at the time and a way to re-establish order (1978: 210).

Post-revisionism

This section draws together different accounts which can be collectively termed 'post-revisionism'. These authors have challenged the views of the revisionists and offered different approaches to understanding changes in punishment in the eighteenth and nineteenth centuries.

In *Punishment and Welfare* (1985), Garland challenges the revisionist accounts by suggesting that the modern 'penal-welfare' complex developed at the end of the nineteenth century, rather than the late eighteenth and early nineteenth centuries. In the period 1895 to 1914, Garland argues a more rehabilitative or welfare approach emerged, strongly influenced by positivist criminological thought. During this period, a number of different categories of offenders are removed from the prison (juveniles, mentally ill, recidivists and inebriates). Special policies are also created to deal with offenders who are seen as needing treatment to 'cure' their behaviour or who need to be dealt with differently, for instance, the establishment of a separate juvenile justice system and alternatives to custody such as probation and aftercare services. Pieter Spierenburg also challenges the timing of the changes in punishment in the late eighteenth to mid-nineteenth century. He argues that changes in punishment and imprisonment evolved over a much longer period of time, beginning in the seventeenth century and lasting until the 1870s (1984, 1991, also Spierenburg, 2005).

Despite the critical perspectives of the revisionist accounts of the 1970s and 1980s, they were often gender-blind and contained little, if any, analysis of the ways in which imprisonment, and punishment more broadly, were experienced according to the gender of offenders. Feminist writers such as Rafter (1985) and Zedner (1991) have demonstrated the gendered nature of prison regimes for women in the nineteenth and twentieth centuries. Female prisoners were seen as different from men, requiring different treatment in regimes which operated to feminise women and return them to 'normal' womanhood (Zedner, 1991). Foucauldian accounts, such as Dobash et al., (1986) and Sim (1990), emphasise the power of experts in legitimising these regimes, particularly from the 1850s onwards. Psychiatrists, psychologists, medical officers, believed that women's criminality was linked to their physiology and that individualised treatment could resurrect their natural maternal and feminine feelings. At the end of the nineteenth century a range of semi-penal institutions emerged for women and girls. Reformatories, refuges, and homes were established for wayward, immoral, deviant, and guilty women, combining disciplinary techniques from the prison and the domestic sphere in order to return women to an acceptable standard of feminine behaviour (Wiener, 1990; Barton, 2005). Inebriate reformatories, for example, were not unlike local prisons, and despite lower rates of drunkenness, over 80 per cent of the commitments to them were women. This reflected the conceptualisation of habitual drunkenness as a gendered problem principally associated with women (Morrison, 2009).

A body of research on local imprisonment has also challenged revisionists by questioning the extent to which the reforms were actually carried out in prisons across the country. They have criticised the revisionists for focusing on national penitentiaries, like Pentonville, run by the government, and argued that these prisons were not representative of most prisons and were experienced by a comparatively small number of prisoners. They have also questioned the extent to which the separate system or other disciplinary techniques were used in local prisons and tried to make sense of the diversity in prison practice (DeLacy, 1981; Johnston, 2004; Ireland, 2007).

REVIEW QUESTIONS

1 What regimes were used to 'reform' the prisoners?

2 What are the main differences between the Whig and revisionist accounts of the 'birth of the prison'?

3 What do you understand by the 'penal-welfare' complex (Garland, 1985)?

CONCLUSION

What we have seen over the period examined here is a fundamental change in the nature and use of imprisonment, from a place of detention to a place of punishment. Overall, we have observed that by the mid-nineteenth century a number of key shifts have taken place; a movement towards a central state-organised system; the increasing use of categorisation and classification of prisoners (by age, gender, offence, for example); and the increasing use of experts within the penal system to provide specialised intervention with offenders. We could examine these changes in terms of phases: the movement to reform (1770–1840s); the movement to more repressive practices based on deterrence (1850s–1895); and the movement towards rehabilitation or welfare-orientated approaches from 1895 onwards. This is a useful framework in which to understand these developments and shows how prison legislation and policy developed. However, throughout the centuries there remained contradictions and uneven practice.

Government control of prisons allowed secrecy to prevail as the prison was severed from the outside world, at least until the early sociological accounts of the 1950s and 1960s (Sykes, 1958; Mathiesen, 1965). The Victorian prison is not, however, consigned to the history books, but remains a central feature of our current system, housing thousands of prisoners everyday. Many Victorian prisons remain in central locations in towns and cities across the country (Hull, Leeds, Leicester, Shrewsbury, for example), and their long austere wings and small windows remain central to popular ideas about what prisons are like (Jewkes and Johnston, 2007). As McConville observes, 'progress' is often used in self-congratulation rather than in warning, and as we continue to invent and adapt new methods, policies, and practices for use in prison, 'neither reformers nor administrators consider it worth while seriously to ponder the experience of earlier generations' (1998b: 139).

QUESTIONS FOR DISCUSSION

1 What do you understand by the 'great transformation' of punishment?
2 Identify phases in the objectives of imprisonment and what factors influenced these.

GUIDE TO FURTHER READING

Readers are encouraged to examine Morris and Rothman's (1998) (eds) *The Oxford History of the Prison*, a collection of essays which examine prisons and imprisonment in the Western world over a long historical period from the medieval to the contemporary.

John Pratt's (2002) *Punishment and Civilisation* also provides a long view of changes in punishment from the nineteenth to the late twentieth century, examining changing penal sensibilities and practices in Western societies.

Research by William Forsythe, *The Reform of Prisoners* (1987) and *Penal Discipline, Reformatory Projects and the Prison Commission, 1895–1939* (1990) are excellent studies of prison reform and reformatory projects in the nineteenth and early twentieth centuries.

Extracts from Foucault (1977); DeLacy (1981); Zedner (1991) and others are collected together in the first part of Y. Jewkes and H. Johnston (eds) (2006) *Prison Readings: A Critical Introduction to Prisons and Imprisonment* (Cullompton: Willan), providing an introduction to this topic.

WEB LINKS

http://www.oldbaileyonline.org

Old Bailey Proceedings Online allows the searching of a database of all published accounts of trials held at the Old Bailey, London, between 1674 and 1913.

http://www.learningcurve.gov.uk/candp/default.htm

Through the National Archives at Kew, London (where all government papers and many other collections are held), the Learning Curve website provides a basic introduction to the criminal justice system and its development; you will also be able to examine historical documents digitised for use on this site.

http://www.learnhistory.org.uk/cpp

Similarly the Learn History website, although aimed at schools, provides a good introduction to crime and punishment in the historical perspective.

For more information on prison reformers see:

John Howard <http://www.howardleague.org/index.php?id=johnhoward>

Elizabeth Fry <http://www.howardleague.org/index.php?id=elizabethfry>

REFERENCES

Anderson, S. and Pratt, J. (2009) 'Prisoner memoirs and their role in prison history' in H. Johnston (ed) *Punishment and Control in Historical Perspective*. Basingstoke: Palgrave Macmillan.

Anon (1894) 'Our Dark Places'. *The Daily Chronicle* 23 January.

Bailey, V. (1997) 'English Prisons, Penal Culture and the Abatement of Imprisonment, 1895–1922'. *Journal of British Studies* 36: 285–324.

Barton, A. (2005) *Fragile Moralities and Dangerous Sexualities: Two Centuries of Semi-Penal Institutionalisation for Women*. Aldershot: Ashgate.

Beattie, J.M. (1986) *Crime and the Courts in England, 1660–1800*. Oxford: Oxford University Press.

Davis, J. (1980) 'The London Garotting Panic of 1862: A Moral Panic and the Creation of a Criminal Class in Mid-Victorian England' in V.A.C. Gatrell, B. Lenman, and G. Parker (eds) *Crime and the Law: The Social History of Crime in Western Europe*. London: Europa Publications.

DeLacy, M. (1981) '"Grinding Men Good?" Lancashire's Prisons at Mid-Century' in V. Bailey (ed) *Policing and Punishment in the Nineteenth Century*. London: Croom Helm.

Dobash, R.P., Dobash, R.E., and Gutteridge, S. (1986) *The Imprisonment of Women*. Oxford: Basil Blackwell.

Emsley, C. (2005) *Crime and Society in England, 1750–1900* (3rd edn). Harlow: Longman.

Evans, R. (1982) *The Fabrication of Virtue: English Prison Architecture, 1750–1840*. Cambridge: Cambridge University Press.

Fiddler, M. (2008) 'Panopticon' in Y. Jewkes and J. Bennett (eds) *Dictionary of Prisons and Punishment*. Cullompton: Willan Publishing.

Forsythe, W.J. (1987) *The Reform of Prisoners 1830–1900*. London: Croom Helm.

Forsythe, W.J. (1990) *Penal Discipline, Reformatory Projects and the English Prison Commission, 1895–1939*. Exeter: Exeter University Press.

Foucault, M. (1977) *Discipline and Punish: the Birth of the Prison*, trans. A. Sheridan. Harmondsworth: Penguin.

Fry, E. (1827) *Observations on the Visiting, Superintendence and Government of Female Prisoners* (2nd edn). London: J. and A. Arch.

Garland, D. (1985) *Punishment and Welfare: A History of Penal Strategies*. Aldershot: Gower.

Gatrell, V.A.C. (1994) *The Hanging Tree—Execution and the English People 1770–1868*. Oxford: Oxford University Press.

Gladstone Committee (1895) *Report from the Departmental Committee on Prisons* (C.7702) Vol. LVI. London: Home Office.

Godfrey, B. and Cox, D. (2008) 'The "Last Fleet": Crime, Reformation and Punishment in Western Australia'. *Australian and New Zealand Journal of Criminology* 41(2): 236–58.

Hay, D. (1975) 'Property, authority and the criminal law' in D. Hay, P. Linebaugh, J. G. Rule, E.P. Thompson and C. Winslow (eds) *Albion's Fatal Tree: Crime and Society in Eighteenth Century England*. London: Allen Lane.

Henriques, U.R.Q. (1972) 'The Rise and Decline of the Separate System of Prison Discipline'. *Past and Present* 54: 61–93.

Hobhouse, S. and Brockway, A.F. (1922) *English Prisons To-day*. London: Longmans, Green & Co.

Howard, J. (1777/1929) *The State of the Prisons*. London: Dent & Son.

Ignatieff, M. (1978) *A Just Measure of Pain—The Penitentiary in the Industrial Revolution*. London: Macmillan.

Innes, J. (1987) 'Prisons for the poor: English bridewells, 1555–1800' in F. Snyder and D. Hay (eds) *Labour, Law and Crime: An Historical Perspective*. London: Tavistock.

Ireland, R.W. (2007) *A Want of Order and Good Discipline: Rules, Discretion and the Victorian Prison*. Cardiff: University of Wales Press.

Jewkes, Y. and Johnston, H. (2007) 'The Evolution of Prison Architecture' in Y. Jewkes (ed) *Handbook on Prisons*. Cullompton: Willan Publishing.

Johnston, H. (2004) *Transformations of imprisonment in a local context: A case study of Shrewsbury in the nineteenth century*. Unpublished Ph.D. thesis. Keele University.

Johnston, H. (2006) ' "Buried Alive": Representations of the Separate System in Victorian England' in P. Mason (ed) *Captured by the Media: Prison discourse in popular culture*. Cullompton: Willan Publishing.

Johnston, H. (2008a) 'Less Eligibility' in Y. Jewkes and J. Bennett (eds) *Dictionary of Prisons and Punishment*. Cullompton: Willan Publishing.

Johnston, H. (2008b) ' "Reclaiming the Criminal": The role and training of prison officers in England, 1877–1914'. *Howard Journal of Criminal Justice* 47(3): 297–312.

Mathiesen, T. (1965) *The Defences of the Weak: A Sociological Study of a Norwegian Correctional Institution*. London: Tavistock.

McConville, S. (1981) *A History of English Prison Administration Vol. 1 1750–1877*. London: Routledge.

McConville, S. (1998a) 'Local Justice: the Jail' in N. Morris and D.J. Rothman (eds) *The Oxford History of the Prison—The Practice of Punishment in Western Society*. New York: Oxford University Press.

McConville, S. (1998b) 'The Victorian Prison, 1865–1965' in N. Morris and D.J. Rothman (eds) *The Oxford History of the Prison—The Practice of Punishment in Western Society*. New York: Oxford University Press.

McGowen, R. (1990) 'Getting to know the criminal class in nineteenth-century England'. *Nineteenth-Century Contexts* 14: 33–54.

McGowen, R. (1994) 'Civilising Punishment: The End of Public Execution in England'. *Journal of British Studies* Vol. 33: 257–82.

McGowen, R. (1998) 'The Well-Ordered Prison, England, 1780–1865' in N. Morris and D.J. Rothman (eds) *The Oxford History of the Prison—The Practice of Punishment in Western Society*. New York: Oxford University Press.

Melossi, D. and Pavarini, M. (1981) *The Prison and the Factory*. London: Macmillan.

Morrison, B. (2009) 'Controlling the 'hopeless': re-visioning the history of female inebriate institutions c.1870–1920' in H. Johnston (ed) *Punishment and Control in Historical Perspective*. Basingstoke: Palgrave Macmillan.

Platt, A.M. (1969) *The Child Savers: The Invention of Delinquency*. Chicago: University of Chicago Press.

Pratt, J. (2002) *Punishment and Civilisation—Penal Tolerance and Intolerance in Modern Society*. London: Sage.

Radzinowicz, L. and Hood, R. (1990) *A History of English Criminal Law and its Administration from 1750, Volume 5: The Emergence of Penal Policy*. Oxford: Clarendon Press.

Rafter, N.H. (1985) *Partial Justice: Women in State Prisons 1800–1935*. Boston: Northeastern University Press.

Rothman, D.J. (1971) *The Discovery of the Asylum*. Boston: Little, Brown and Co.

Ruck, S.K. (ed) (1951) *Paterson on Prisons*. London: Frederick Muller.

Sim, J. (1990) *Medical Power in Prisons: The Prison Medical Service in England, 1774–1989*. Milton Keynes: Open University Press.

Sindall, R. (1990) *Street Violence in the Nineteenth-century: Media panic or real danger?* Leicester: Leicester University Press.

Soothill, K. (2007) 'Prison histories and competing audiences, 1776–1966' in Y. Jewkes (ed) *Handbook on Prisons*. Cullompton: Willan Publishing.

Spierenburg, P. (1984) *The Spectacle of Suffering*. Cambridge: Cambridge University Press.

Spierenburg, P. (1991) *The Prison Experience: Disciplinary institutions and their inmates in early modern Europe*. New Brunswick: Rutgers University Press.

Spierenburg, P. (2005) 'The Origins of the Prison' in C. Emsley (ed) *The Persistent Prison: Problems, Images, Alternatives*. London: Francis Boutle.

Stockdale, E. (1977) *A Study of Bedford Prison, 1660–1877*. Chichester: Phillimore.

Sykes, G.M. (1958) *The Society of Captives*. Princeton, NJ: Princeton University Press.

Taylor, D. (1998) *Crime, Policing and Punishment in England, 1750–1914*. Macmillan: London.

Tomlinson, H.M. (1981) 'Penal Servitude 1846–1865: A System in Evolution' in V. Bailey (ed) *Policing and Punishment in Nineteenth Century Britain*. London: Croom Helm.

Webb, S. (1963) *English Prisons under Local Government*. London: Frank Cass.

Weiner, M.J. (1990) *Reconstructing the Criminal: Culture, Law and Policy in England, 1830–1914*. Cambridge: Cambridge University Press.

Wilde, O. (1898/2002) *De Profundis, The Ballad of Reading Gaol and Other Writings*. Ware: Wordsworth Classics.

Zedner, L. (1991) *Women, Crime and Custody in Victorian England*. Oxford: Clarendon.

7

Prisons in context

Azrini Wahidin

INTRODUCTION

> The ultimate expression of law is not order—it's prison. We have hundreds upon hundreds of prisons, and thousands of laws, yet there is no social order, no social peace. (Jackson, 1972: 52)

The prison has been viewed in different ways over time and has been perceived as performing different functions within the penal system. Prisons moved from merely being a repository for those awaiting trial, sentence, or death in the sixteenth and seventeenth centuries to a site where *punishment* was inflicted on a wide range of offenders during the course of the eighteenth and nineteenth centuries. By the twentieth century prisons stood at the centre of the criminal justice system both practically and symbolically. Hardly thought of as a dominant form of punishment for the serious offender in 1800, by 1900 the prison was firmly established in both the popular consciousness and the practice of the courts as the most potent means by which offenders might be punished (see Helen Johnston's and David Scott's chapters 6 and 4 respectively in this volume).

In order to explore prisons today this chapter will focus on the prison system of England and Wales and offers an overview of the key variables and challenges that the prison system is facing. In the final part of this chapter we shall spend a little time considering the growing debate around the abolition of prisons. The first section will provide a brief overview of the key moments in prison policy before turning to prisons in context today.

BACKGROUND

Important moments in prison policy

On 1 April 1990 prisoners at HMP Strangeways in Manchester began the longest and most devastating riot in British penal history. It began on 1 April and continued until 25 April. At the time Strangeways was the largest prison in England and Wales and, indeed, one of the largest in Europe. It was extremely overcrowded holding 1,647 prisoners when its *certified normal accommodation* was 970 (prison overcrowding at the time was defined by the Prison Service as a prison containing more prisoners than the establishment's certified normal accommodation (CNA). Almost three-fifths of the prisoners held there were on remand. During the 25 days of the siege at HMP Strangeways serious riots broke out in five other prisons, and various forms of disruption occurred in more than 30 establishments across England and Wales. As a result of the events at Strangeways one prisoner lost his life and 147 prison officers and 47 prisoners were injured. In response an inquiry was launched which became known as the Woolf report (Woolf and Tumim, 1991). The 600-page report of the Inquiry was published only nine months after the riots. It was heralded as a blueprint for the future of the prison system. In it Woolf argued that the disturbances were caused by an imbalance between *security*, *control*, and *justice*. *Security* relates to the measures used to prevent prisoners escaping. *Control* relates to measures to deal with disruptive prisoners and prevent riots and other disturbances in prisons. Woolf's concept of *justice* relates both to conditions and regimes within the prison and to the decisions made about prisoners and the procedures used to do this. The report suggests that the disturbances occurred because the Prison Service placed too much emphasis on security, used inappropriate methods of control, and there was a lack of justice in prisons. Woolf suggested that sufficient attention must be paid to: *security*, *control*, and *justice*, and that the three must be kept in balance (para. 9.19). Justice should not be seen as some sort of privilege or award for good behaviour; rather, it should be a basic requirement that prisoners would receive humane treatment, be subject to fair procedures, and be provided with reasoned explanations for decisions made that affected their situation. These initial ideas formed what become known as the *Decency Agenda*.

Woolf's recommendations covered greater co-ordination in the criminal justice system, more visible leadership of the Prison Service, the setting of standards for prison conditions, and a variety of changes to the nature of regimes, including grievance procedures. In Part 1, Woolf concentrates on the circumstances of the riots, their management by the Prison Service, and on proposing a number of technical and managerial strategies to improve security and control. In Part II, he collaborates with Judge Stephen Tumim, Her Majesty's Chief Inspector of Prisons, to provide a wide-ranging review of prison conditions. Woolf explains that the 12 key recommendations of his report represent signposts, and that the 204 accompanying proposals are, 'the steps which, over a period of time, the Prison Service should take in order to reach these destinations (Woolf and Tumim, 1991: para. 1.15). There was, as Woolf concluded, 'no single cause of the riots and any simple solution or action which will prevent the rioting' (1991: para. 9.23). Nor was there any basis on which prisoners could be categorised for 'control' as opposed to 'security' purposes (para. 9.48). Woolf suggested that more attention needed to be paid to the quality of relationships between prisoners and staff, to the nature of regimes, to procedural justice, and to day-to-day fairness (section 9).

The Government's response to the Woolf report was published as the White Paper, *Custody, Care and Justice* (Home Office, 1991). In the aftermath of Strangeways and the Woolf inquiry there were a number of incidents which once again drew attention to the issues of security and control. First was an attempted escape from Whitemoor prison in 1994 which led to the Woodcock report, and subsequently an escape from Parkhurst on the Isle of Wight. In response, two inquiries were established—the Woodcock Inquiry into the Whitemoor case and the Learmont inquiry into the Parkhurst escape (Home Office, 1994; 1995). In contrast to the Woolf report, the Learmont report makes no reference to justice and sees 'care' and 'custody' as conflicting elements. Its emphasis was on security. The Learmont Inquiry recommended the building of an American-style 'supermax' prison to house all prisoners deemed to be high-risk (King and McDermott, 1995). However, rather than the introduction of a British supermax, in 1998 the Prison Service introduced what are known as Close Supervision Centres (CSCs) (Clare and Bottomley, 2001) which removed the most seriously disruptive prisoners from mainstream dispersal and training prison holding them instead in small, closely-supervised units.

The riots at the beginning of the 1990s and the escapes of two groups of high security prisoners in the middle of that decade shook the prison establishment to the core. Unlike Woolf, Woodcock and Learmont were not at all interested in Woolf's insistence on the need for a balance between considerations of security, control, and justice. They were much more concerned with allocating blame for what had happened than with understanding why it had happened. In the years following the Woodcock and

Learmont reports, the Prison Service concentrated its attention and resources on security issues. The political climate during the period of the late 1990s to early 2000s was marked by an increased use of imprisonment in England and Wales. Rather than being regarded as a place of the last resort, prison became an important tool in the Government's 'war on crime' agenda.

Prisons today

Out of the 142 prisons in the UK, no two prisons are the same. The prison buildings vary considerably in terms of size, date of construction, design, level of physical security, and status—i.e. whether they hold remand prisoners, women prisoners, young offenders, etc. The Prison Service in England and Wales employs almost 50,000 people, covering a wide range of grades and specialisms. In a typical year the Prison Service recruits around 6,000 staff (McHugh, Heavens, and Baxter, 2008).

During the 1960s one of the periodic, yet very significant, crises that grips the prison system from time to time occurred. On this occasion it was a 'security crisis' (Rutherford, 1986) or what became known as a 'crisis of containment' (Cavadino and Dignan, 2007), and the official response has had a profound impact upon the prison system ever since. Prior to the 1960s, security (preventing prisoners escaping) was not a priority for the Prison Service. However, during the 1960s several high-profile prisoners escaped, thus catapulting security to the top of the Prison Service agenda. Two inquiries took place into the circumstances of the escapes which resulted in two policy changes which are still in place today (Mountbatten Report, 1966; Home Office, 1995). The first of these was the introduction of the security classification for prisoners and prisons. All prisoners are security classified A, B, C, or D. Category A prisoners, are those 'whose escape would constitute a danger to the public, the police or the security of the state'. Category B and C prisoners are those required to be held in closed conditions providing more or less security. Remand prisoners, with the exception of a few provisionally categorised as A, are all assumed to be Category B. Category D prisoners are those suitable for open conditions, that is, those who could reasonably be entrusted not to abscond and serve their sentence in open conditions. Prisons are also categorised according to these security categories and prisoners can only be held in prisons which have the same or a higher security classification.

The second policy change was the introduction of a dispersal policy to deal with category A prisoners who are deemed to be a high security risk. As part of this policy, category A prisoners are 'dispersed' around the prison system in specially adapted prisons. These dispersal prisons also hold other categories of prisoners who are by default held in high security conditions which is unnecessary and expensive. The alternative policy, of concentrating all high security prisoners in one prison, was rejected on the grounds that it posed significant risks in terms of the potential for control problems to arise. This highlights a significant feature of prison policy in that it often assumes that the prisoners who pose security risks are the same prisoners who pose control risks. This is demonstrated most markedly in the so called 'toxic mix' of prisoners who have been historically blamed for many of the problems within the prison system (Cavadino and Dignan, 2007).

As well as differences in security categorisation, prisons have different functions. There are two main types of institutions. First, the *local prisons* and remand centres; their

Table 7.1 Types of institution

Local Prisons: These hold those awaiting trial on remand and sentence prisoners for short periods.

Open Prisons: For those prisoners held to pose no real risk to the public.

Young Offender Institutions: For offenders under 21.

Dispersal Prisons: For convicted criminals whose escape would be deemed highly dangerous.

Women's Prisons: Open and Closed.

Remand Centres: For untried prisoners, usually part of a Young Offender Institution or a local prison.

Training Prisons: Open and Closed.

Private Prisons: For remand and convicted prisoners.

Note: Some prisons perform more than one function and classification is subject to change.

primary task is to house short-term and remand prisoners and also prisoners who have just been sentenced before they are allocated to other prisons where they will serve the majority of their sentence. Secondly, there are Young Offender Institutions (YOIs) and the adult training prisons. The latter are further sub-divided into closed and open institutions and reflect security classifications. Table 7.1 provides more details of the types of institutions which make up the prison estate.

A new type of prison has entered the penal policy debate: *Titan prisons*. In December 2007 the government accepted Lord Carter of Cole's proposals to develop three large (Titan) prisons which will provide up to 2,500 places. The Government's aim is to have the first Titan built and open by 2012 at a cost of £350 million.

Private prisons

Although private sector involvement in prisons may be traced back a century or more (see Johnston in this volume; Ryan, 1983; Ryan and Ward, 1989), there has been a major revival of interest and activity in this area since the late 1980s. *Privatisation* involves 'the systematic transfer of government functions and programmes into the private sector' (Adam Smith Institute, n.d.: 17–18). Thus, in broad terms, privatisation refers to the process whereby public services, which have traditionally been carried out by the state, are administered by private agencies. The description 'prison privatisation' is normally used to describe one of two models of prison management. The first is where the entire operation of a prison is contracted to a commercial company or a not-for-profit organisation. In this case the state builds and continues to own the prison buildings and enters into a contract with the company about the way in which the prison is to be managed. Thereafter the state takes no part in the daily management, other than to ensure that contractual commitments are being met. The second model involves a commercial company taking control of a prison's design, its construction, its financing, and its management. It is the second of these models which is the most prevalent in England and Wales.

The modern notion of prison privatisation in the United Kingdom was first advocated by the Adam Smith Institute in 1984. It proposed that the government should privatise the building and management of prisons on the grounds that 'it would overcome both the spiralling costs of the prison system and the shortage of places by using innovative managerial and technological methods and by concentrating resources on capital investment rather than increased labour costs' (Omega Report on Justice Policy, 1984: 5). At the time, this idea was not taken seriously either by the *Home Office* or the House of Commons. The *Home Secretary*, Douglas Hurd on 16 July 1987, stated to the House of Commons that: 'I do not think there is a case, and I do not believe that the House would accept a case, for auctioning or privatising the prisons or handing over the business of keeping prisoners safe to anyone other than government servants' (HC Deb vol. 119, col. 1299, 16 July 1987). However, by March 1989 Douglas Hurd announced to the Commons that the private sector would in future be authorised to both build and/or manage remand prisons, and by 1992 legislation was in place giving the Home Secretary powers to introduce private prisons into the rest of the prison system (See Ryan and Ward, 1989: 9).

In a remarkably short space of time, prison privatisation in England and Wales has progressed from being a proposal to a competitive multi-million pound enterprise. How, then, was such a *volte-face* possible in such a short space of time? A number of diverse influences can be identified. First, a House Affairs Select Committee report in 1987 (Prison Officers' Association, 1987) called for private firms to be allowed to tender for the construction and management of custodial institutions, especially the remand system as overcrowding was concentrated there. Secondly, political pressure was growing, mainly from some Conservatives (members of the House of Commons Select Committee on Home Affairs), who had visited private prisons in the United States and believed it was feasible to introduce them in Britain. Thirdly, several high-level public servants (ex-prison officers, civil servants, and the prison inspectorate) were recruited and employed by the private sector. Fourthly, and arguably most importantly, there was a growing pressure on the prison system because of the rising prison population. It is probably no surprise that the countries with the highest prison populations also have the most developed policy of prison privatisation (Lilly, 1993). Fifthly, the Adam Smith Institute (Omega Report on Justice Policy, 1984) advocated privatisation partly as a means of breaking the 'monopolistic provision' of imprisonment by the state and also to counter trade union influence on prison policy. Sixthly, there was also a growing feeling that the Prison Service was failing to innovate and change.

The Criminal Justice Act 1991 contained a provision which allowed the management of any prisons, not just remand centres, to be contracted out to any agency that the Home Secretary considered appropriate. HMP Wolds was the first contracted-out prison in the UK. HMP Wolds was an experiment to test the feasibility of private sector involvement in prison management. Secondly, this experiment was also aimed at seeing if improvements could be made to the conditions in which prisoners remanded in custody were held. Thirdly, there was a renewed commitment throughout the Prison Service, in the wake of the 1990 prison disturbances and the vision offered by the Woolf report, to address the fundamental issues of ensuring the effective provision of custody, care, and justice in British prisons, and particularly for remand prisoners. This, then, was the political and policy context in which the Wolds Remand prison opened on 6 April 1992. When it opened, Wolds was a category B prison with Certified Normal Accommodation (CNA) for 320 adult male prisoners and was the first prison in the UK to hold only adult remand prisoners.

Table 7.2 Examples of privately run prisons in England and Wales

Prison	Managed by
HMP Altcourse	GSL
HMP Ashfield	Serco
HMP Bronzefield	United Kingdom Detention Services (UKDS)
HMP and YOI Doncaster	Serco
HMP Dovegate	Serco
HMP/YOI Forest Bank	United Kingdom Detention Services (UKDS)
HMP Lowdham Grange	Serco
HMP/YOI Parc	G4S Justice Services
HMP Peterborough	United Kingdom Detention Services (UKDS)
HMP Rye Hill	GSL
HMP Wolds	GSL

Source: HM Prison Service (2008) at <http://www.hmprisonservice.gov.uk/>.

Although HMP Wolds was seen as an 'experiment', a foray into the private sector, the government did not wait for the results of this before deciding whether to increase private sector involvement in the penal system. In the same year, the Private Finance Initiative was launched, which encouraged all departments to explore increasing the private financing of public services. It was feared that the transfer of the Prison Service to agency status was part of a process of wholesale privatisation, although this was denied by the Home Office. Nevertheless, the private sector was playing an increasing role in providing services within prisons generally, together with what appeared to be plans to extend significantly the private management of prisons. In 2007, England and Wales already has the most privatised prison system in Europe (Shefer and Liebling, 2008). At the time of writing there are 11 private prisons contractually managed by private companies such as Serco and G4S Justice Services (see Table 7.2). Private prisons now account for 10 per cent of the prison population holding around 8,243 prisoners.

Ultimately, privatisation has blurred the boundaries between the private and public sector and in turn has invited a re-examination of the adequacy of state-centred approaches to the management of *crime control*. The privatisation of prisons is unlikely to provide the answer to the malaise affecting the public prison system and could easily become an instrumental part of the problem.

The privatisation of prisons has been described as the 'penal experiment of the century', and as 'one of the most important [recent] developments in penal administration' (Harding, 1997: 269).

REVIEW QUESTIONS

1 Should remand prisoners be treated in the same way as prisoners who have been convicted of an offence?

2 Explain the differences between the Woolf, Woodcock, and Learmont reports.

3 What are the advantages and disadvantages of creating prisons that can hold over 2,000 prisoners at each individual prison?

Facts: who are the prisoners?

The prison population is socially and economically disadvantaged relative to the population generally. A survey of prisoners conducted in 1991 on behalf of the Home Office (Walmsley 2003) shows that prisoners were disproportionately working class (83 per cent of male prisoners were from manual, partly skilled, or unskilled groups, compared to 55 per cent of the population generally) and exhibited telling indicators of social stress. A high proportion, 23 per cent, reported having been in local authority care before the age of 16 (this may have more to do with prisoners' contact with social services when children) compared to 2 per cent of the population generally. For prisoners under 21 the figure is 38 per cent (Social Exclusion Unit, 2002).

In terms of education, 43 per cent said that they left school before the age of 16 (compared to 11 per cent of the population generally), and of the remainder very few continued education beyond 16 (NACRO, 2000); 43 per cent had no educational qualifications whatsoever (many of these prisoners are functionally illiterate), and only 8 per cent had qualifications beyond GCSE. They have low levels of literacy and educational attainment (Walmsley, 2003).

Short-term prisoners constitute the majority of those sentenced to imprisonment each year: in 2003, 64 per cent of all adult males sent to prison were sentenced to less than 12 months. In 2002, 95,000 people in total were sentenced to prison and of those, 53,000 were sentenced to six months or less. Short-term prisoners have higher reconviction rates than other offenders (Halliday Report, 2000; Prison Reform Trust, 2008). Most offenders are released from prison without a job to go to, remain unemployed for a long time (NACRO, 1993; Hagell *et al.*, 1994), and many are placed in temporary accommodation. And not surprisingly, offenders with multiple social problems of this nature are more likely to be reconvicted (King and McDermott, 1995). Furthermore, 13,440 people held in custody are on remand awaiting trial (Ministry of Justice, 2008b). However, owing to prison overcrowding many remand prisoners have been held in police cells. They will all be subject to random drug testing and, unlike convicted prisoners, those on remand are not assessed for security category, unless they are perceived as being very high risk. One in five (19 per cent) of men and 18 per cent of women were held on remand before trial in 2005 and were acquitted (RDS NOMS, 2005). Only half of all remanded prisoners go on to receive a prison sentence and two-thirds of people received into prison on remand awaiting trial are accused of non-violent offences. In 2005, 53 per cent of men and 41 per cent of women on remand received an immediate custodial sentence (RDS NOMS, 2005). At the end of October 2007 there were 957 women on remand, which equals one in five of the female prison population (Ministry of Justice, 2007).

Table 7.3 Social characteristics of prisoners

Characteristics	General population	Prison Population
Run away from home as a child	11%	47% of male and 50% of female sentenced prisoners
Taken into care as a child	2%	27%
Regularly truanted from school	3%	30%
Excluded from school	2%	49% of male and 33% of female sentenced prisoners
No qualifications	15%	52% of men and 71% of women
Numeracy at or below Level 1 (level expected 11 year olds)	23%	65%
Reading ability at or below Level 1	21–23%	48%
Unemployed before imprisonment	5%	67%
Homeless	0.9%	32%
Suffer from two or more mental disorders	5% men and 2% women	72% of male and 70% of female sentenced prisoners
Psychotic disorder	0.5% men and 0.6% women	72% of male and 70% of female sentenced prisoners
Drug use in the previous year	13% men and 8% women	66% of male and 55% of female sentenced prisoners
Hazardous drinking	38% men and 15% women	63% of male and 39% of female sentenced prisoners

Source: Adapted from Social Exclusion Unit (2002)

Women in prison

The prison population in England and Wales reached 83,190 and 4,510 were female on 30 June 2008 (Ministry of Justice, 2008c). From June 2007 to June 2008 the sentenced population increased by 4 per cent or 3,460. Over the same period, the male population climbed by 4 per cent to 78,690 and the female population by 5 per cent to 4,510. There are 15 prisons for women and they are categorised as either: closed, where sentenced women will be held; semi-open prisons; open; local, who take prisoners directly from court, and may also hold sentenced women (see Howard League for Penal Reform, 2006). Many of the prisons used to accommodate women were formerly used for men or are prisons within a male prison, and thus the facilities are not always appropriate.

The female prison population consists of fewer recidivists (repeat offenders) and relatively more foreign nationals and minority ethnic individuals than the male population. At the

Table 7.4 Gender breakdown of prison staff

	Men Number	%	Women Number	%
Prison Officers	19,455	81	4,470	19
Governor Grades	1,044	81	248	19
Other Grades	1,528	52	10,502	48
Total	22,027	68	15,220	32

Source: Ministry of Justice 2008b

end of December 2007, there were 974 foreign national women in prison, 22 per cent of the female population (Ministry of Justice, 2008a; Carlen and Worrall, 2004). Almost two-thirds of women are held on remand (Prison Reform Trust, 2008). Usually, they are repeat offenders, imprisoned for petty, non-violent *crimes*, and, increasingly, for drug-related offences. Sixty-six per cent of women in prison have dependent children under the age of 18, and of those, 34 per cent had children under the age of five and at least one-third are single mothers (Ministry of Justice, 2008a). There are eight mother-and-baby units in women's prisons. These generally accommodate women with children up to the age of 18 months, after which children have to be separated from their mothers (Hansard, 2008). However, there are no mother-and-baby units in Wales, and Welsh mothers and babies serve their sentences within prisons in England (Hansard, 2007a). A high priority for many women prisoners is to be able to see their children and other family members. Because there are relatively few prisons for women they tend to be held at least 58 miles from their home (Hansard, 2007b).

Studies estimate that up to 60 per cent of all women in prison have suffered sexual or physical violence from a member of their family or from a stranger, with the figure rising to 80 per cent once all physical violence is included (Carlen, 1988). Finally, female prisoners generally have a low level of formal education, and, at best, sporadic employment histories (Corston Report, 2007, HMCIP, 1997). Such is the constitution of the female estate. Each of these elements has been documented in Prison Service surveys and annual reports, in a way which forms an image of a 'typical' female prisoner.

At the end of 2006, HM Prison Service in England and Wales employed 48,425 staff of which 32 per cent were female (and who were mostly confined to the lower ranks of the Prison Service). Although some progress has been made in making the staff group more diverse, prison work and the culture continues to be a largely white, male occupation (see Bennett, Crewe, and Wahidin, 2007). Because most prison officers are men (see Table 7.4), it is not surprising that male officers are present in female prisons, which may make the prisoners feel uncomfortable.

The rising prison population

By the summer of 2006 the prison system of England and Wales had reached a critical level of overcrowding. This was a situation that had been building up over several years, despite a prison-building scheme and more places being created. As the prison population

Table 7.5 The ten most overcrowded prisons in England and Wales, January 2008

Prison	In Use Certified Normal Accommodation	Operational Capacity	Population	% Overcrowded
Shrewsbury	175	328	322	184%
Kennet	171	338	311	182%
Lancaster	96	177	175	182%
Swansea	240	422	423	176%
Preston	429	750	728	170%
Usk	150	250	250	167%
Altcourse	794	288	1,295	163%
Leicester	210	392	341	162%
Durham	591	981	923	156%
Lincoln	436	738	675	155%

Source: NOMS (2008) Monthly Bulletin: London Prison Service

rose after the Second World War, and even outstripped the increased capacity provided by the largest ever prison-building programme, so the frequency and violence of prison disturbances increased. The prison population in England and Wales dropped from a high of over 30,000 in 1877—when the Prison Act was passed—to a low point of a little over 9,000 at the end of the First World War. Thereafter, the population rose slightly, but generally hovered between 10,000 and 12,000 in the years up to the Second World War. In 1946 there were about 40 prisons, approximately 15,000 prisoners, and around 2,000 staff: a prisoner to staff ratio of 7.5:1. During the period 1945 to 1985 the prison system in England and Wales suffered escalating overcrowding. There was virtually no overcrowding in the 1950s, but by 1988–9 the prison population peaked at around 50,000 and then declined to around 45,000 in the period 1990–93. There then began the largest prison-building programme since the middle of the nineteenth century, and the story since has been one of expansion. The trend has not been unilinear, and there are important lessons to be learnt from the falls as well as the rises. Nevertheless, it is the growth in the prison population, indeed, what has been referred to elsewhere as the 'crisis in prison numbers' (Cavadino and Dignan, 2007), that has set the tone for much that has happened in criminal justice policy making since 1945. It is no surprise to experts within the field, or to over-stretched, under-resourced prison officers, that our prison system has reached its critical mass (see Bennett, Crewe, and Wahidin, 2007).

The statistics speak for themselves of how stretched the Prison Service now is.

- In 2008 England and Wales had the highest prison population in Western Europe: 147 per 100,000 of the national population (Prison Reform Trust, 2008).

- The number of prisoners in England and Wales has increased by 25,000 in the 10 years from 1996 to 2006. When Labour came into government in May 1997, the prison population was 60,131. Previously it took nearly four decades (1958–1995) for the prison population to rise by 25,000.

- England and Wales had the highest number of life sentenced prisoners in Europe. It has more than Germany, Italy, the Russian Federation, and Turkey combined (Council of Europe Annual Penal Statistics, 2007).

The overcrowding crisis is leading to a breakdown in the ideals of the Decency Agenda that the Prison Service has been attempting to inculcate and maintain over the years. The Prison Service's own statement of purpose articulates that: 'Our duty is to look after them with humanity and to help them lead law abiding and useful lives in custody and after release' (HMP Prison Service: <http://www.hmprisonservice.gov.uk/abouttheservice/statementofpurpose>). It is much more likely that situations of unrest will occur in conditions that are very overcrowded (Woolf and Tumim, 1991). Moreover, in a state of severe overcrowding there is much less opportunity for *rehabilitation*, which in turn calls into question the statement of purpose. Since the Enlightenment period it has been recognised that to enable rehabilitation time and resources must be invested in the reform of prisoners. In today's terms this means constructive regimes, education, and skills training. It should also entail positive environments where suicide, self harm, and bullying are minimised.

> Any realistic attempt to improve prison conditions must take account of two pivotal aspects of the prison system, namely population and capacity. Indeed, the inter-connections of this penal trinity of population: capacity and condition forms the heart of the reform quagmire. (Rutherford cited in Whitfield 1991: 4)

The Prison Service in its own statement of purpose sets out three objectives which are vital to the protection of the public:

- holding prisoners securely;
- reducing the risk of prisoners re-offending;
- providing safe and well-ordered establishments in which we treat prisoners humanely, decently, and lawfully (Her Majesty's Prison Service. <http://www.hmprisonservice.gov.uk/abouttheservice/statementofpurpose>)

It can be argued most strongly that these objectives are difficult to achieve in the everyday running of a modern prison. However, with the current level of overcrowding, the task is made near impossible. Although the media recognises that the Prison Service is in crisis, this never diminishes the public's desire, fuelled by sometimes unhelpful and biased reporting, to see criminals 'behind bars' rather than accepting the need for greater use of community penalties. The standard media reaction to any politician promoting the use of alternative sentencing ideas is usually to suggest that anything less than a prison sentence is not within the ideals of punishment.

Over recent years, legislation has been enacted that has given tougher, longer penalties for more crimes, and has led to the current state of crisis in our prison system. However, in reality prison is not providing an effective protection from crime, either in the short term or the long term. The high recidivism rate illustrates that in terms of reducing offending, prison is a failure. For example, male offenders in 2008 were more likely to be reconvicted than females: 64.7 per cent of males released from prison were reconvicted within two years (Ministry of Justice, 2008c). The latest available data for juvenile offenders discharged from custody in the first quarter of 2005 shows a 76.2 per cent rate of re-offending (Hansard, 2007b). Yet if we compare the rates of re-offending rates for all community sentences, they fell from 53.2 per cent in 2000 to 50.5 per cent in 2004 (Ministry of Justice, 2008a).

The overcrowding situation is not unfamiliar to professionals, government ministers, and most members of the public. The details of the effects of this situation need greater exploration by most people if they are to gain a better understanding of the whole system. Most members of the public can only imagine the horrors of the realities of an overcrowded, under-resourced prison, with all the surrounding issues of violence, bullying, suicides, drug abuse, and self harm. As Stern says 'Prison must be one of the least known aspects of British life' (Stern, 1987: 2).

CASE STUDY: SUICIDE IN PRISON

Sarah died at the hands of the State in 2003, aged 18, while in the 'care' of HMP Styal. She arrived at the jail on a Friday night, and was dead 24 hours later. As a little girl she was sexually abused over a period of several years. At the age of 15, she was *raped*, became clinically depressed, and started taking drugs. By the age of 17, she was a self-harming heroin addict.

At aged 18, she and another woman approached a man and asked for money. There was no violence. The man collapsed with a heart attack, and died. Both women were charged with manslaughter. Sarah was jailed for three years and was sent to Styal prison, near Wilmslow, Cheshire on 17 January 2003. She was placed in the segregation unit, where she died the following day after swallowing 120 Dothiepin tablets. When the paramedics arrived, they were stopped at the gates for eight minutes before being allowed through. Sarah at the time lost consciousness, and whilst in hospital never regained consciousness. Less than 24 hours after arriving at Styal, she was dead. She became the third and the youngest of six women to die at the Cheshire jail in a 12-month period between August 2002 and 2003.

In 2005, the inquest jury did not return a suicide verdict, because it was clear that Sarah had not intended to die. The jury did say the 'failure to maintain the duty of care' contributed to her death. In 2006, the Home Office accepted full liability of her death, and admitted her human rights had been violated under the European Convention of Human Rights.

If the prison system is to develop, let alone maintain the objectives within its own statement of purpose, overcrowding must be brought under control. There is little point in trying to maintain constructive regimes and employ imaginative methods for rehabilitation and recidivism reduction, if the day-to-day running of a prison is reduced to crowd control and achieving the basic minimum of care with over-stretched, under-resourced, and de-motivated staff. In times of overcrowding many ideals fall by the wayside, and we have seen that violence, self harm, and drug abuse are likely to increase (see Edgar, O'Donnell, and Martin, 2002). This is not acceptable in a modern day institution. What makes it unacceptable is the simple fact that it fails to reduce recidivism and crime continues. In such circumstances, prisons revert to the simple warehouses for prisoners that were familiar 200 years ago.

From nothing works to something works

Since its emergence in the late eighteenth century, the modern prison has been intended to fulfil a number of roles such as *incapacitation*, punishment, *deterrence*, reform, and rehabilitation. These goals have often sat uneasily together, and, depending on the political pressures of the day, one or more of these goals has taken precedence over the others. For example, the 1950s and 1960s were characterised by the belief in rehabilitation. By the 1980s the Thatcher government 'extolled' the prison as a place to punish. However, at the same time, ministers recognised that for less serious offenders, using prisons was 'expensive and ineffective' (Crow, 2001: 104).

Prisons are complex institutions and the rate of imprisonment is a consequence of overlapping pressures. Some of these pressures are caused by overcrowding, prisoner protests, or staff culture. Some are due to law and order campaigns, and tougher sentencing policies. Research has shown that levels of use of imprisonment owe more to public attitudes and political decisions than to rates of crime (Hough and Mayhew, 1985). The increased use of prison has recently been picked up by politicians as a way of responding to modern fears about public safety and the desire to be protected from crime.

On 6 October 1993 at the Conservative Party conference Michael Howard, the sixth Conservative Home Secretary in 14 years, reasserted the view that prison was the institution for preventing crime through a penal policy based on the punitive combination of: discipline, *retribution*, deterrence, and incapacitation. He outlined in his 27-point plan how to get tough on criminals, in which he set a clear political agenda by declaring 'Let us be clear. Prison Works', by announcing the building of six new prisons, and by promising a new era of austerity in prison regimes. Michael Howard in his now notorious speech averred that:

> Prison works . . . It makes many who are tempted to commit crime think twice . . . this may mean that more people will go to prison. I do not flinch from that. We shall no longer judge the success of our system of justice by a fall in the prison population. (Crow, 2001: 6)

In this pursuit of harsher law and order policies, Howard repealed many of the precepts that had underpinned the Criminal Justice Act 1991 by means of the Criminal Justice Act 1993. In particular, the ethos of the Criminal Justice Act 1991 was to reduce the use of custody so that a larger proportion of offenders would be punished in the community. The Criminal Justice Act 1993 signalled the end to this, and public protection became the primary rationale for sentencing, making incapacitation the principal justification for punishment. In April 2005, in the run up to the general election, one of Howard's main themes in his electoral campaign was to 'build out crime' by bringing back capital punishment and to build more prisons. Like the prisons of the early nineteenth century, under Howard's lens, the late twentieth century descendent was to subject prisoners to regimes based on disciplined austerity (Sparks, 1996).

Table 7.6 Does prison work?

Prison is a brutalising and damaging experience:

- During 2007, 181 people killed themselves in Prison Service care. This included 27 people on remand and eight women (http://inquest.gn.apc.org/stats_prison.html).

- In 2007, 12 young people aged 21 and under died either in prison or in a Secure Training Centre.

Prison is expensive:

- It costs on average of £40,992 to keep a person in prison in England and Wales (Hansard, 2008).

- The actual cost per prisoner placed in Northern Ireland in 2006-2007 was £90,298 (Northern Ireland Prison Service, 2007).

- To build a new prison costs the equivalent of two district hospitals or 60 primary schools. (PRT, 2008).

Some could argue that in reflection of the previous passages, progress to improve the prison system has been extremely slow. This results not from a lack of desire for change by the professionals within the system, but rather from the rate of increase in the prison population, coupled with a lack of resources, funding, and long-term policy initiatives. Indeed, some commentators have pointed out that our prisons are the slowest reforming body within our modern society.

> There can be little doubt that John Howard, rising from his grave, would find much more that is familiar to him within the prison than across society as a whole. (Whitfield 1991: 2)

It must be recognised that our prison system is extremely slow to respond to change, and that a serious result of overcrowding and understaffing has led to an increase in deaths in custody, prison disturbances, and self harming to name a few indicators that the prison system is failing those in their 'care' (see Case Study). The total figure for deaths in custody from 1993 to 2007 was 2,315 which includes men and women, Black Minority Ethnic (BME) prisoners, and those on remand (and therefore unconvicted). For the same period 129 women to date have died in prison (see <http://inquest.gn.apc.org/data_deaths_in_prison.html>). In comparison with other social changes, one can see how lethargic prison reform has been:

> The most striking aspect of prison reform over the last two centuries is how little of it there has been...even the more substantial changes pale against the broad sweep of political, social and economic progress over this period. (Rutherford cited in Whitfield 1991: 2)

All historical and comparative studies concur to demonstrate that the level of incarceration of a given society bears no relation to its crime rate: it is at bottom an expression of cultural and political choices (Christie, 1981). Churchill once noted that 'the mood and temper of the public in regard to the treatment of crime and criminals is one of the most unfailing tests of the civilisation of any country'. The overdevelopment of the penal sector over the past three decades is indeed a reflection of the shrivelling of the welfare state, and the criminalisation of the poor. Just as in other societies, the discourses that seek to connect crime and punishment on both sides of the Atlantic 'have no value other than ideological' (Wacquant, 2005: 7). This chapter in its concluding section will therefore argue that it is only by exploring alternative possibilities to prisons that we can begin to move beyond our over-reliance on imprisonment.

At one level it can be argued that it is only through well funded alternatives to custody, changes in sentencing, and a concerted effort to divert offenders from custody, that this can be achieved. The reason for caution is that research has shown that programmes that have been introduced into the women's prison have been appropriated by the prison system. Hannah-Moffat (2002) used the concept of *encroachment* to describe how pre-existing organisational norms frequently encroached upon and undermined the rationale of these programmes. Secondly, the reliance on alternatives to custody fails to critically address social divisions such as class, age, *gender*, and ethnicity.

By turning our attention to the abolitionist debate we can see how this perspective can take the penal policy debate beyond alternatives to custody by creating an alternative vision of justice. The term *'abolitionism'* stands for a social movement, a theoretical perspective, and a political strategy. As a social movement, it is committed to the abolition of the prison or even the entire penal system. Abolitionism originated in campaigns for prisoners' rights and penal reform and, as Sim has pointed out:

> [the abolitionist debate is] increasingly connected with the emerging discourses and debates around human rights and social justice which they see as mechanisms for developing negative reforms, thereby promoting a response to social harm that is very different from the destructive prison and punishment systems that currently exist. (Sim 1994: 52)

Subsequently, it developed into a critical theory and praxis concerning crime, punishment, and penal reform (see Sim, 2005). As a theoretical perspective, abolitionism takes on the twofold task of providing a radical critique of the criminal justice system while showing that there are other, more rational ways of dealing with crime. Abolitionism emerged as an anti-prison movement when, at the end of the 1960s, a distinctive impulse took hold of thinking about the *social control* of deviance and crime among other areas (Cohen, 1985; Zimring, and Hawkins, 1991). In Western Europe, anti-prison groups aiming at prison abolition were founded in Sweden and Denmark (1967), Finland and Norway (1968), Great Britain (1970), France (1970), and the Netherlands (1971). This movement demanded change in general thinking concerning punishment, humanisation of the various forms of imprisonment in the short run, and in the long run, the replacement of the prison system. Abolitionists argue that punishment cannot be justified at all: they challenge the conventional assumption that punishment is a necessary feature of any modern society and that we should aim not simply to refer or limit our penal practices and institutions, but to abolish them (Mathiesen, 1974, 1986; Christie, 1981; Bianchi and van Swanningen, 1986; de Haan, 1991; Duff and Garland, 1994). From the abolitionist point of view, the criminal justice system's claim to protect people from being victimised by preventing and controlling crime seems grossly exaggerated. In the words of the Dutch abolitionist, William de Haan, the prison 'is counter productive, difficult to control and [is] itself a major social problem' (de Haan, 1991: 206–07). Punishment is seen as a self-reproducing form of violence. The penal practice of blaming people for their supposed intentions (for being bad and then punishing and degrading them accordingly) is dangerous because the social conditions for recidivism are thus reproduced. Morally degrading and segregating people is especially risky when the logic of exclusion is reinforced along the lines of difference in sex, race, age, class, culture, and religion. As Mathiesen, an abolitionist, has maintained, the prison has to be understood both as a material place of confinement and as an ideological signifier. Not only does the institution reinforce powerlessness and stigmatisation, but it also establishes 'a structure which places members of one class in such a situation that the attention we might pay to the members of another is diverted' (Mathiesen, 1990: 138).

As Mathiesen (2004) points out, a theoretically refined abolitionism can offer a new way of thinking about the world and a vision of the future which contrasts sharply with traditional methods of penality based on incapacitation, deterrence, punishment, and rehabilitation. It directly confronts the 'cynicism and anomie' of postmodernism, it reaffirms the argument that prisons don't work 'either as punishment or as a means of ensuring the safety and stability of the commonwealth', and it recognises that predatory behaviour needs to be responded to and dealt with within the structural and interpersonal contexts of power and politics (Thomas and Boehlefeld, 1991: 246–49). This vision can be compared with the present situation here and elsewhere, which is evoked in the quote that the chapter begins with. In thinking about abolition we should examine how important it is to abandon the very concept of crime as wrongdoing to which the community should respond with condemnation.

CONCLUSION

We know that prison does not reduce the crime rate. Instead it causes a *revolving door syndrome* and it exacerbates the problems that offenders have to encounter once released. It is only by thinking about alternatives to imprisonment that we can begin an imaginative re-thinking of the whole penal policy debate. The questions that you the reader need to ask when thinking about prisons and prisoners as prison numbers spiral out of control are these and this is not an exhaustive list. First, how do penal policies intersect with other spheres of culture, politics, or economic structures of the social formations which they arise (see Sparks, 2003: 105). Secondly, can we develop informal modes of justice procedures which would be participatory but which would not themselves become oppressive? Thirdly, what are prisons for and what purpose do they serve? And finally, although the prison in various guises has survived for over 200 years and has been a dominant institution in society, shouldn't we as society become more imaginative in finding alternatives to our over-reliance on the prison in responding to phenomena as socially complex and controversial as crime and punishment?

Moreover, as the prison system has reached a crisis point illustrated by the increase in deaths in custody, incidents of self harm, and violence in prisons to name a few, the question we must ask is how best to break the cycle of crime which brings the same people back, year in, year out, to repeated terms of imprisonment—disenfranchising whole sectors of the community. For example in America, one in 75 men are in prison and one black man in nine is placed under the criminal gaze (Wacquant, 2005). In terms of placing prisons in context we need to have a critical review of what we mean and understand by imprisonment and examine the role prisons play in contemporary society. As Garland comments:

> The punishment of offenders is a peculiarly unsettling and dismaying aspect of social life. As a social policy it is a continual disappointment, seeming always to fail in its ambitions and to be undercut by crises and contradictions

of one sort or another. As a moral or political issue it provokes intemperate emotions, deeply conflicting interests, and intractable disagreements. (Garland, 1990: 1)

REVIEW QUESTIONS FOR DISCUSSION

1 Discuss the problems associated with overcrowding in prison.
2 How can the Prison Service and the Ministry of Justice address the rising numbers of offenders receiving a custodial sentence?

QUESTIONS FOR DISCUSSION

1 How might we explain the rise in the prison population over the past decade and what steps, if any are necessary to reduce it?
2 Even if it is desirable, is a significant move towards a reductionist /abolitionist stance a realistic option for contemporary societies?
3 What are the alternatives to imprisonment?
4 Does prison work?

GUIDE TO FURTHER READING

Cavadino, M. and Dignan, J. (2007) *The Penal System: An Introduction*. London: Sage.
This is the most authoritative and sophisticated textbook on the penal system of England and Wales.

Tonry, M. (ed) (2004) *The Future of Imprisonment*. Oxford: Oxford University Press.
The edited collection is a definitive guide to imprisonment policies for the future; this volume convincingly demonstrates how we can prevent crime more effectively at lower economic and human cost.

Mathews, R. (1999) *Doing Time: Introduction to the Sociology of Imprisonment*. London: Sage.
This book draws on a range of sociological theorising in order to analyse the organisation and the functioning of the prison. It examines the conditions for the expansion of the prison and explores the possibilities for limiting prison use through the development of alternatives to custody.

Ignatieff, M. (1978) *A Just Measure of Pain*. London: Macmillan.
This book provides an inspirational account of the emergence of imprisonment as the principal penalty for serious crime at the end of the eighteenth century.

WEB LINKS

http://www.alternatives2prison.ik.com
Radical Alternatives to Prison (RAP) is a voluntary campaigning group that is seeking to resist the use of mass incarceration in the United Kingdom and calls for more effective non-punitive responses to law breaking.

http://www.howardleague.org

The Howard League for Penal Reform is the oldest penal reform charity in the UK. It was established in 1866 and is named after John Howard, one of the first prison reformers. The Howard League for Penal Reform is entirely independent of government and is funded by voluntary donations.

http://www.hmprisonservice.gov.uk

The official site of HM Prison Service, offering a virtual prison tour, library of publications, PS documents, links to relevant government departments and organisations, and details of all aspects of prison life.

http://prisonreformtrust.org.uk

The Prison Reform Trust is a long-standing non-governmental organisation; the site of the Prison Reform Trust offers current news, publications, and research briefings.

http://www.prisons.org.uk

The Prisons Handbook provides a comprehensive guide to the penal system of England and Wales. It is packed with the latest information about all 139 prison establishments and provides information on the latest law, rules and regulations, independent reports regarding prisons and penal policy.

REFERENCES

Adam Smith Institute (n.d.) *Privatising America*. Washington, D.C.: Adam Smith Institute.

Bennett, J., Crewe, B., and Wahidin, A. (eds) (2007) *Understanding Prison Staff*. Cullompton: Willan Publishing.

Bianchi, H. and von Swaaningen, R. (1986) *Abolitionism towards a non-repressive approach to crime*. Proceedings of the second international conference. Amsterdam: Free University Press.

Carlen P. (1988) *Women, Crime and Poverty*. Milton Keynes: Open University Press.

Carlen, P. and Worrall A. (2004) *Analysing Women's Imprisonment*. Cullompton: Willan Publishing.

Cavadino, M. and Dignan, J. (2007) *The Penal System: An Introduction*. London: Sage.

Christie, N. (1981) *Limits to Pain*. London: Martin Robertson.

Clare, E. and Bottomley, A.K. (2001) *Evaluation of Close Supervision Centres*. Research Study 219. London: Home Office.

Cohen, S. (1985) *Visions of Social Control: Crime, Punishment and Classification*. Cambridge: Polity Press.

Corston, J., Baroness (2007) *The Corston Report: a review of women with particular vulnerabilities in the criminal justice system*. London: Home Office.

Council of Europe (2007) Annual Penal Statistics SPACE I: Enquiry 2000: Prison Population. Strasbourg: Council of Europe

Crow, I. (2001) *The Treatment and Rehabilitation of Offenders*. London: Sage.

de Haan, W. (1991) 'Abolitionism and Crime Control: a Contradiction in Terms' in K. Stenson and D. Cowell (eds) *The Politics of Crime Control*. London: Sage.

Duff, A. and Garland, D. (eds) (1994) *A Reader on Punishment*. Oxford: Oxford University Press.

Edgar, K., O'Donnell, I., and Martin, C. (2002) *Prison Violence: Conflict, Power and Victimization*. Cullompton: Willan Publishing.

Garland, D. (1990) *Punishment and Modern Society: A Study in Social Theory*. Oxford: Oxford University Press.

Hagell, A., Newburn, T., and Rowlingson, K. (1994) *Financial difficulties on release from custody*. London: Policy Studies Institute.

Hannah-Moffat, K. (2002) *Punishment in Disguise*. Toronto: University of Toronto Press.

Hansard (2007a) House of Commons written answers, 9 January. London.

Hansard (2007b) House of Commons, written answers, 25 October. London.

Hansard (2008) House of Commons written answers, 19 July. London.

Halliday Report (2000) *Making Punishment Work: Report of a review of the sentencing framework for England and Wales*. London: Home Office.

Harding, R. (1997) *Private Prisons and Public Accountability*. New Brunswick, NJ: Transaction Publishing.

Her Majesty Chief Inspector of Prisons (HMCIP) (1997) *Women in Prisons: A Thematic Review*. London: Home Office.

Home Office (1991) *Custody, Care and Justice: The Way Ahead for the Prison Service in England and Wales*. London: HMSO.

Home Office (1994) *Report of the Woodcock Enquiry* Cm 2741. London: HMSO.

Home Office (1995) *Report of the Learmont Inquiry into Prison Service Security in England and Wales*. London: Home Office.

Home Office (2005) *Population in Custody*. March 2005. London: Home Office.

Hough, M. and Mayhew, P. (1985) *Taking Account of Crime: Key Findings from the 1984 British Crime Survey*. Home Office Research Study No. 85. London: HMSO.

Howard League For Penal Reform (2006) *Prison Numbers Out of Control and Puts Public at Risk*. Press Release 29 November. London: Howard League.

Jackson, G. (1972) *Blood in my Eye*. Harmondsworth: Penguin.

King, R. and McDermott, K. (1995) *The State of Our Prisons*. Oxford: Oxford University Press.

Lilly, J. R. (1993) 'An International perspective on the privatisation of corrections'. *The Harvard Journal* 31(3): 18–27.

Mathiesien, T. (1974) *The politics of abolition*. London: Martin Robertson

Mathesien, T (1986) 'The politics of abolition' *Contemporary Crisis* 10: 81–94.

Mathiesen, T. (1990) *Prison on Trial*. London: Sage.

Mathiesen, T. (2004) *Silently Silenced: essays on the creation of acquiescence in modern society*. Winchester: Waterside Press.

McHugh, M., Heavens, J., and Baxter, K. (2008) 'Recruitment and assessment of prison staff' in J. Bennett, B. Crewe, and A. Wahidin (eds) *Understanding Prison Staff*. Cullompton: Willan Publishing.

Ministry of Justice (2007) *Population in Custody, England and Wales, October*. London: Ministry of Justice.

Ministry of Justice (2008a) *Prison Population Projections 2008–2015*. London: Ministry of Justice.

Ministry of Justice (2008b) *Gender Equality Scheme 2008–2011, March 2008*. London: Ministry of Justice.

Ministry of Justice (2008c) *Population in Custody England and Wales, March 2008*. London: Ministry of Justice.

Mountbatten Report (1966) *Report of the Inquiry into Prison Escapes and Security*. Cmnd 3175. London: HMSO.

NACRO (2000) *The Forgotten Majority*. London: NACRO.

NOMS (2008) *Monthly Bulletin* July 2008. London: Prison Service.

Omega Report on Justice Policy (1984) Adam Smith Institute (ASI Report).

Prison Reform Trust (2008) *Bromley Briefing Papers*. London: PRT.

Prison Officer's Association (1987) 'The State and Use of Prisons in England and Wales   Written Evidence to the Inquiry of the Home Affairs Select Committee of the House of Commons', unpublished study.

Prison Service, Prison Service Order, 1900, Certified Prisoner Accommodation—<http://www.hmprisonservice.gov.uk/resourcecentre/psispsos/listpsos>.

Rutherford, A. (1986) *Prisons and the Process of Justice*. Oxford: Oxford University Press.

RDS NOMS (2005) *Offender Management Caseload Statistics 2004*, Home Office Statistical Bulletin 17/05. London: Home Office.

Ryan, M. (1983) *The Politics of Penal Reform*. Harlow: Longman.

Ryan, M. and Ward, T. (1989) 'Privatisation and penal politics' in R. Matthews (ed) *Privatising Criminal Justice*. London: Sage.

Shefer, G. and Liebling, A. (2008) 'Prison privatisation: In search of a business-like atmosphere' *Criminology and Criminal Justice* 8: 261.

Singleton, N., Meltzer, H., and Gatward, R. (1998) *Psychiatric morbidity among young offenders in England and Wales*. London: Stationery Office.

Sim, J. (1994) 'The Abolitionist Approach: A British Perspective' in A. Duff S. Marshall, R. Dobash and R. Dobash (eds) *Penal Theory and Practice: Tradition and Innovation in Criminal Justice*. Manchester: Manchester University Press.

Sim, J. (2005) 'Abolitionism' in E. McLaughlin and J. Muncie (eds) *The SAGE Dictionary of Criminology*. Sage: London.

Social Exclusion Unit (2002) *Reducing Re-offending by Ex-prisoners*. London: Office of the Deputy Prime Minister.

Sparks, R. (1996) 'Penal "Austerity": The Doctrine of Less Eligibility Reborn?' in R. Matthews and P. Francis (eds) *Prisons 2000*. Basingstoke: Macmillan.

Statistics <http://www.homeoffice.gov.uk/rds/omcs.html>.

Sparks, R. (2003) 'Punishment, populism and political culture in late modernity' in S. McConville (ed) *The Use of Punishment*. Cullompton: Willan Publishing.

Stern, V. (1987) *Bricks of Shame: Britain's Prisons*. Harmondsworth: Penguin.

Thomas, J. and Boehlefeld, S. (1991) 'Re-thinking Abolitionism: "What do we do with Henry?"' *Journal of Social Justice* 18 (Fall): 239–51.

Wacquant, L. (2005) 'The great penal leap backward: incarceration in America from Nixon to Clinton' in J. Pratt, D. Brown, M. Brown, S. Hallsworth, and W. Morrison (eds) *The New Punitiveness: Trends, Theories, Perspectives*. Cullompton: Willan Publishing.

Walmsley, R. (2003) *World Prison Population List* (4th edn). Home Office Research, Development and Statistics Directorate Findings 188. London: Home Office.

Whitfield, D. (ed) (1991) *The State of the Prisons 200 years on*. Howard League, London: Routledge.

Woolf, H. and Tumim, S. (1991) *Woolf Report of the Inquiry into Prison Disturbances April 1990*. Cm 1456. London: HMSO.

Zimring, F. and Hawkins, G. (1991) *The Scale of Imprisonment*. Chicago: The University of Chicago Press.

8 Community sentences

George Mair

INTRODUCTION

The aim of this chapter is to discuss the policy and practice of community sentences as alternatives to custody. The term 'community sentences' can potentially—cover all court sentences apart from custody; all other sentences are served in the community. But while such an inclusive application of the term has its uses, it can also be confusing as community sentences are often seen as only those sentences run by the Probation Service (this chapter does not deal with the youth justice system which is covered in Chapter 13). Even this delimited use of the term, however, does not lead to clarity: in the first place, the number of disposals run by the Probation Service has changed over the years, so that community sentences would mean one thing in 1970, another in 1992, and something else again in 2009; and second, for at least 50 years, agencies and organisations other than *probation* have had a role in the provision of community sentences—the police and attendance centres being one early example, with the most recent significant case being the operation and organisation of electronic monitoring by private companies.

It is important to emphasise immediately that community sentences are more than just alternatives to custody; they are sentences in their own right. But the alternatives to custody debate has been a dominant theme in criminology and in criminal justice policy for at least 40 years and this chapter will provide an overview of the key issues.

In the next section the precise focus will be defined: some general definitional issues about what constitute community sentences for the purposes of the chapter will be explored, as will the implications of the concept of alternatives to custody—on the surface, a fairly simple idea but one which is, in fact, rather complicated. The remainder of the chapter is divided into a further four parts. The first provides a brief overview of the history of community sentences as alternatives to custody. The second examines the more significant pieces of research on this topic. The third section looks at the current situation with regard to community sentences and alternatives to custody, drawing on the most up-to-date research available; it also briefly speculates about the future and how matters might develop. In the concluding section, the key issues around the topic will be summarised.

BACKGROUND

For the purposes of this chapter, community sentences will be defined as those court disposals that are—or have been—run by the Probation Service, as well as senior attendance centres (for the most part, run by the police) and Curfew Orders (run by the private companies that have been awarded contracts). 'Disposals' has been used in the preceding sentence as, technically speaking, the Probation Order was—for most of its life—not a sentence of the court. A Probation Order was made *instead* of a sentence from its inception in 1907 until it legally became a sentence with the Criminal Justice Act 1991. All of these sentences (for the sake of simplicity, this term will be used from now on), to a greater or lesser degree, involve the direct supervision of offenders aged 17 and older. Some are more likely to be used (or to have been used) as alternatives to custody than others, and over the years they have included:

- the Probation Order (renamed the Community Rehabilitation Order under the Criminal Justice and Court Services Act 2000);
- the Money Payment Supervision Order;
- the Attendance Centre Order;
- the Community Service Order (renamed the Community Punishment Order following the 2000 Act);
- the Combination Order (renamed the Community Punishment and Rehabilitation Order under the 2000 Act);
- the Curfew Order;
- the Drug Treatment and Testing Order;
- the Community Order; and
- the *Suspended Sentence Order* (legally a custodial sentence but, if all goes well, it is served in the community).

Thus, we will not examine here such sentences as the fine or the conditional discharge. It is unlikely that either of these sentences would be used as a direct alternative to a sentence of imprisonment, although there are two points to bear in mind with such a claim. First, if a general recalibration or de-escalation of the *tariff* were to occur, then they would operate as *indirect* alternatives to custody, so that as some offenders were shifted down-tariff from custody to community sentences a similar movement would occur from community sentences to fines and discharges (see Mair, 2004). Second, while the numbers involved have decreased significantly in the past decade, failure to pay a fine can still lead to imprisonment and in 2006 there were 1,904 receptions into custody for fine default (Ministry of Justice, 2007a).

As noted earlier, the idea of a sentence acting as an alternative to custody may not sound particularly problematic, but it carries with it a number of implications that need to be borne in mind when using the concept. In the first place, referring to a sentence as an alternative to custody—defining it in relation to something more important—immediately confines that sentence to the margins. It is difficult for something to have an identity in its own right if it acts only or primarily as an alternative to something else. Closely related to this issue is the privileged place given to custody by the use of the term; if something is an alternative to custody the clear implication is that custody is more important, it is custody that really counts. Second, because of the very obvious gulf between even the most rigorous and demanding community sentence and a sentence of imprisonment, it is difficult for a government officially to declare a community sentence as an alternative to custody. This would be seen as suggesting that dangerous offenders who should be in prison can be dealt with in the community—not a good move for any government, least of all at the present time when *crime* and fear of crime are such important policy issues. Third, the likelihood of custody is increased for an offender if, having served what is considered to be an alternative to a custodial sentence, there is a further reconviction. Fourth, efforts to toughen up community sentences in order to try to make them more demanding and—by implication—more like a custodial sentence and therefore a more realistic alternative to custody, have to face several immediate problems: the alternatives may become so demanding that offenders prefer custody; they may lead to offenders failing to meet their demands and thus ending up in prison as a result of breach proceedings; and they may lead to a blurring of the boundaries between custodial and community sentences, an important phenomenon that has been developing since the end of the Second World War.

Although the term blurring the boundaries was not used then, its beginnings can be glimpsed on various occasions during the inter-war years—usually related to proposals about keeping young adult offenders out of prison—and emerged in the form of the attendance centre in the Criminal Justice Act 1948 (Mair, 1991). It can be seen in the concept of *parole* (whereby prisoners are released early and subject to probation supervision) and in the original suspended sentence, both introduced as part of the Criminal Justice Act 1967. The Younger report (Home Office, 1974) recommended the introduction of a Custody and Control Order for offenders aged between 17 and 21 which would be served partly in custody and partly in the community under the supervision of a probation officer. A Green Paper (a government consultative document) was published in 1984 examining the possibility of introducing a sentence of intermittent custody (Home Office, 1984a). And the Curfew Order—marketed partly as offering the idea of home imprisonment—was introduced by the Criminal Justice Act 1991. There is, therefore, a considerable history to a greater overlap between sentences of imprisonment and community sentences even before proposals about a *'seamless sentence'* appeared in the Halliday report (Home Office, 2001a) and the Suspended Sentence Order was introduced by the Criminal Justice Act 2003 (see below). While blurring the boundaries between custody and community could lead to offenders avoiding imprisonment, it is also likely to lead to tougher community sentences and an overall more punitive sentencing climate.

It is also important to emphasise that there are a variety of reasons for using alternatives to custody, and it is necessary to try to tease out which of these may apply in any given situation. Alternatives to custody may be used first for humanitarian reasons—prison is considered to be a cruel and degrading *punishment* and this is reason enough to use an alternative to custody whenever possible. Secondly they may be used for cost reasons—prison is an expensive commodity and the cost of a custodial sentence is considerably more than a community sentence and this may be a good enough reason to use the latter. Thirdly, alternatives to custody may be used for reasons of effectiveness—prison may be adjudged to be a less effective sentence than a community sentence. Finally, prison overcrowding may result in the use of alternatives to custody—if prisons are bursting at the seams with prisoners (as they currently are), then this may be a justification for resorting to alternatives to custody.

Given that it is difficult for a government to acknowledge openly that a policy of using alternatives to custody is under way, it may not be easy to pin down the reasons for such a policy. More often than not, more than one of the above reasons will be involved, and there may be a disjunction between the official reasons offered and more unofficial reasons. Almost 20 years ago Michael Tonry (1990) argued that Intensive Supervision Programmes (ISP) in the USA, which were intended to provide alternatives to custody, had both stated and latent goals. The former were to reduce prison overcrowding, cut costs, and reduce reoffending, while the latter were to improve the credibility of probation, to make it more publicly visible, win public acknowledgement for its professionalism, and align it more closely with the popular politics of law and order. Tonry argued that while ISP was failing to meet its stated goals, it was meeting the latent ones and these were more significant.

In general, the direction of policy (and it would be an exaggeration to refer to it as a strategy) has been to introduce more community sentences, to make them more rigorous and demanding, and to move towards central control of them—all of which are designed to make community sentences more attractive to sentencers and to encourage their use.

A brief history of alternatives to custody

Early moves towards alternatives to custody can be seen in the first half of the nineteenth century when various charitable organisations began to take an interest in crime and juvenile offenders, and to argue for the need to separate adults from young offenders in prisons. A prison for young delinquents—Parkhurst on the Isle of Wight—was opened in 1838 and closed as a failure in 1864. Reformatory Schools began in 1854 and Industrial Schools in 1857 (eventually together becoming approved schools), with the former aiming to keep young offenders out of prison. By the time of the Probation of Offenders Act 1907 there was a general feeling that young offenders should not be imprisoned (see e.g. Morrison, 1896; Russell and Rigby, 1906). Reformation had been officially acknowledged as an aim of the penal system. And it was obvious that—with the bulk of court sentences being made up of custody and fines—there was a need for a sentence that could act to keep offenders (particularly juveniles) out of prison. While a variety of reasons can be discerned to explain the emergence of probation supervision, there is little doubt that to act as an alternative to custody—particularly for juveniles—was one of these (Mair and Burke, forthcoming).

For the most part, however, probation represented help and support for those whose offending resulted from personal or social problems, and this led to the disposal having image problems from the start. It was, and still is, viewed as a 'soft option'. For the 20 years between the end of the First World War and the beginning of the Second World War, there was no pressure on prisons in terms of overcrowding; indeed, the average daily prison population for the period was just over 11,000 (Rutherford, 1984). But there was continuing pressure to restrict the use of custody for those under 21 and also to abolish whipping, as recommended by the Cadogan Committee (Home Office, 1938). As a result, the Criminal Justice bill 1938 included provision for attendance centres which were planned to provide a new mode of punishment for those who might otherwise have been imprisoned or whipped. The impending war meant that the bill had to be abandoned, but attendance centres reappeared in the Criminal Justice Act 1948, and while they rarely seem to have acted as an alternative to custody, they do represent the first of the post-war efforts to find a sentence that could act in such a way (Mair, 1991).

Probably the key driver for the development of alternatives to custody has been the number of offenders being sentenced to custody. Thus, while compared to today prisons were not bursting at the seams during the second half of the 1950s—the average daily population rose from 21,000 in 1955 to 27,000 in 1960, an increase of almost 30 per cent (Rutherford, 1984)—there was still considerable policy interest in the number being imprisoned (particularly young offenders aged between 17 and 20). This resulted in the Advisory Council on the Treatment of Offenders (ACTO) report *Alternatives to Short Terms of Imprisonment* (1957) which advocated setting up an attendance centre on an experimental basis for 17- to 20-year-olds. The first such centre opened in Manchester in December 1958. It also resulted in the First Offenders Act 1958 which extended to adults a provision in the Criminal Justice Act 1948 that restricted the use of imprisonment for young offenders.

During the 1960s the prison population began to rise from 27,000 in 1960 to 39,000 in 1970, an increase of 44 per cent (Rutherford, 1984), and it is notable that Roy Jenkins, the then *Home Secretary*, when introducing the second reading of the Criminal Justice bill 1966 to the House of Commons, stated that 'The main range of the penal provisions of the bill revolves around the single theme, that of keeping out of prison those who need not be there' (738 H.C. Deb., 5s col. 64, 12 December 1966). The Criminal Justice Act 1967 introduced two major provisions: parole (intended to get prisoners out of prison earlier); and the suspended sentence (intended to act as an alternative to custody). The Wootton Committee (ACPS, 1970), which proposed the introduction of community service for offenders, noted that it was not easy to come up with satisfactory alternatives to custody: '...sentencers who were impressed with the futility of committing any offender to prison in many cases were generally baffled by the difficulties of devising any satisfactory alternative' (ACPS, 1970: 3). The Criminal Justice Act 1972 introduced Community Service Orders, Probation and bail hostels for adults, day training centres, and deferment of sentence—all intended to act as alternatives to custody. Community service (which became community punishment in 2001 and is now the unpaid work requirement of the Community Order) has often been seen as the archetypal alternative to custody, but many commentators (e.g. Pease and McWilliams, 1980; Young, 1979) have noted a lack of clarity about its role as a sentence—a confusion that began with the Wootton Committee report itself (see Mair and Canton, 2007).

Hostels and day training centres both represent a significant development of the Probation Order: adding requirements to the basic order to toughen it up, partly—and in the case of day training centres (DTCs) wholly—to make the sentence more attractive as an alternative to custody. Only four DTCs were ever set up, but Vanstone and Raynor (1981) emphasise their importance as alternatives to custody. In the 1980s they mutated into probation day centres (see below). This rather ad hoc and pragmatic development of alternatives to custody was given a penological rationale of sorts in the mid-1970s with the publication of Martinson's controversial '*What Works*' article (1974) in the USA, and the results of two *Home Office* studies published in 1976 (Brody, 1976; Folkard *et al.*, 1976). Widely assumed to show that *rehabilitation* was not effective, these studies—along with the national availability of community service—led to a change of mission for probation and community service. Now they were seen to be offering alternatives to custody. As the prison population rose through the 1970s and 1980s this was accepted as a perfectly viable aim. One clear signal of the significance of the increasing prison population is the three-volume House of Commons Expenditure Committee report *The Reduction of Pressure on the Prison System* (House of Commons, 1978) and the Government's response to its 52 separate recommendations, many of which were accepted (Home Office, 1980).

 CASE STUDY: PROBATION DAY CENTRES

Day centres drifted on to the probation scene in a rather vague and unformed way in the second half of the 1960s. As there was little central control over what probation services did, many initiatives emerged from ideas put into practice by individual probation officers. As such, attendance at a day centre was voluntary. The introduction of Day Training Centres (DTCs) in the Criminal Justice Act 1972—which aimed to divert from custody older, petty persistent offenders with a court order—thus set up a tension with the informal day centres. Only four DTCs were ever set up, and despite being successful in terms of acting as an alternative to custody, they were expensive to run, had to compete with the introduction of community service at the same time, and slowly faded from the scene. Such fragmented, haphazard development was not uncommon in probation at this time.

The voluntary day centres flourished and in Sch. 11 s. 4(B) of the Criminal Justice Act 1982 the power was provided for a court to order an offender to attend at a day centre for up to 60 days as part of his/her Probation Order. These day centres were perceived by their supporters as providing a viable alternative to custody (just to confuse the matter, some probation services did not set up any of the new-style day centres, and voluntary centres continued to operate too). Day centres tended to have different regimes, different levels of staffing, different times of opening, and different costs. The types of offenders they accepted also differed—a wide range of offences had been committed by those attending, only around half had previously experienced a custodial sentence, and 20 per cent had two or less previous convictions (proxy measures of whether the centres were acting as alternatives to custody). Indeed, only 60 per cent of those attending centres were there as a result of a court order.

Some of the day centres were far more successful than others at attracting more high-risk offenders—and therefore more likely to act as an alternative to custody. But the drawback for these centres was that their reconviction rates were higher than for those centres where offenders had fewer previous convictions and less experience of custody. It was also evident that some centres were pressured by the courts to loosen their criteria for taking offenders, thereby weakening their role as an alternative to custody. Issues around diversity also emerged. There were relatively few female offenders who could be diverted from custody, but was it fair to order a female to attend a day centre where she could be the only woman offender amongst a group of 15 to 30 males most of whom were under the age of 30? Similar questions arose about ethnic minority offenders. The problem was that it was difficult to justify separate provision for female or ethnic minorities due to their relatively small numbers in most of England and Wales.

The lack of any central control meant that day centres drifted along with little sense of direction. Specified activity requirements grew in popularity and began to eclipse the centres. By 1990 an Intensive Probation (IP) initiative had been set up by the Home Office and the significance of day centres as an alternative to custody receded. The IP initiative, too, went nowhere as the Combination Order was introduced by the Criminal Justice Act 1991 .

This brief overview of day centres demonstrates clearly the difficulties with alternatives to custody: the lack of any clear focus and direction, inconsistent practice, difficulties in measuring success, the problems that come with success and the government's need to come up with new initiatives (see Fairhead, 1981a; Fairhead, 1981b; Mair, 1988; Mair and Nee, 1992; Raynor, 1988; Vanstone, 1985; Vass and Weston, 1990).

The Criminal Justice Act 1982 introduced two more conditions that could be added to a Probation Order; a requirement to participate or refrain from participating in specified activities and a requirement to attend a day centre (both of which were for a maximum of 60 days). Day centres in particular grew rapidly and in 1985 it was estimated that there were more than 80 in England and Wales. They quickly became seen as *the* alternative to custody and for the second half of the decade one might be forgiven for thinking that they were the only part of probation that counted given the amount of research that examined their role (see, for example, Mair, 1988; Raynor, 1988; Vass and Weston,

1990). But probation officers were not all happy with the idea of providing alternatives to custody; they did not wish to be seen as 'screws on wheels'. By this time, too, arguments about *net widening* were becoming commonplace and thus naïve ideas about community sentences as alternatives to custody began to be questioned (see the next section).

The Criminal Justice Act 1991 called a halt to the idea of alternatives to custody by introducing a *just deserts* framework for sentencing which required that community sentences be seen as sentences in their own right (and making the Probation Order a sentence rather than an alternative to a sentence symbolised this development). But the Act also introduced two new sentences that it was difficult to see as anything other than alternatives to custody: the Combination Order which—as its name suggests—combined probation supervision with community service; and the Curfew Order with electronic monitoring which could mean an offender having to stay at an address (usually his/her home) for up to 12 hours a day for up to six months. Both of these sentences could easily be seen as high-level alternatives to custody, and in addition more conditions were introduced that could be added to Probation Orders or Combination Orders thereby increasing their rigour. By this time, given the number of community sentences that were available as 'alternatives to custody', it could be claimed that the currency had been cheapened.

Figure 8.1 Key dates in the history of community sentences

1907   Probation of Offenders Act—the Probation Order

1948   Criminal Justice Act—the attendance centre

1957   Advisory Council on the Treatment of Offenders report *Alternatives to Short Terms of Imprisonment*

1967   Criminal Justice Act—suspended sentence, parole

1970   Advisory Council on the Penal System report *Non-Custodial and Semi-Custodial Penalties*

1972   Criminal Justice Act—community service

1974   Robert Martinson's article 'What Works? Questions and answers about prison reform'

1978   House of Commons Expenditure Committee report *The Reduction of Pressure on the Prison System*

1982   Criminal Justice Act—day centres, specified activities

1991   Criminal Justice Act—Combination Order, Curfew Order

1998   House of Commons Home Affairs Committee report *Alternatives to Prison Sentences*

1998   Crime and Disorder Act—Drug Treatment and Testing Order

2000   Criminal Justice and Court Services Act—the Probation, Community Service and Combination Orders renamed

2003   Criminal Justice Act—Community Order, Suspended Sentence Order

2004   Coulsfield Inquiry *Crime, Courts and Confidence: report of an independent inquiry into alternatives to prison*

Despite the arrival of Michael Howard as Home Secretary in 1993 with his claim that 'Prison Works'—indeed, to some extent because of this intervention—the continuing rise in the prison population (it grew from 45,800 in 1992 to 65,000 in 1998 (Home

Office, 2003)) meant that the search for alternatives never really stopped. Another House of Commons Committee examined *Alternatives to Prison Sentences* (House of Commons, 1998) and came up with 47 recommendations. By this time, a Labour government was in power and in the Crime and Disorder Act 1998 the Drug Treatment and Testing Order (DTTO) was introduced, partly as a response to the increasing number of drug-related crimes and partly because it was acknowledged that imprisoning offenders with drug problems was not always the most appropriate solution. It required offenders to undertake drug treatment and to submit to regular drugs tests. If they failed to comply, breach proceedings could result in custody.

In addition to introducing new sentences and toughening up those already in existence, in 1984, with the *Statement of National Objectives and Priorities* (Home Office, 1984b), government began a process that culminated in 2001 when the National Probation Service replaced the old, separate, local services. Slowly, a series of initiatives were introduced—driven for the most part by Conservative demands for economy, efficiency, and effectiveness—that aimed at reducing inconsistent practice and led to increased central control of probation. The most significant of these were: the introduction of Performance Indicators in 1988; the introduction of the first National Standards in 1989 (for community service, a full set of Standards covering probation work as a whole was introduced in 1992); the introduction of cash limits on probation funding in 1992; the introduction of a national, actuarial risk assessment scale in 1996 (OGRS—the Offender Group Reconviction Scale); the introduction of a new training scheme in 1998 after a two-year gap when the old training scheme had been scrapped; the publication of Probation Circular 35/1998 heralding the Effective Practice Initiative (Home Office, 1998); and the establishment of the Joint Prison/Probation Services Accreditation Panel (now the Correctional Services Accreditation Panel) in 1999.

All of these developments made the Probation Service generally more accountable and consistent, and thus led to community sentences becoming more rigorous. This, in turn, was likely to increase the confidence of sentencers in community sentences and, therefore, encourage their use for more serious offenders who might receive a custodial sentence. Significantly, government did not have to take the initiative on the enforcement of community sentences, an issue where probation had always been seen as weak. Following noises from the Home Office in 1999, the Association of Chief Officers of Probation (ACOP) itself commissioned several audits of enforcement in an effort to tighten up breach procedures (Hedderman and Hough, 2004). The problem is that there is little evidence to suggest that tougher enforcement leads to improved compliance with a community sentence and therefore less likelihood of reconviction; indeed, tougher enforcement may just as easily lead to increased failure to comply and a possible custodial sentence. Thus, more rigorous enforcement to encourage greater use of community sentences as alternatives to custody is quite likely to lead to increases in the use of custody (for more on the phenomenon of 'net widening' see below).

During the present century, the pace has—if anything—quickened and one can see alternatives to custody behind many official initiatives. The prison population now—June 2008—stands at 83,194 (Ministry of Justice, 2008a) and building more prisons to cope with the increase in prisoners is not the answer: it is costly, time-consuming, and exacerbates the problem. Labour's response—besides building more prisons—has been to toughen sentencing by pushing community sentences ever closer to custody, and a variety of reports have made the case for this: the consultation document *Criminal Justice: the way ahead* (Home Office, 2001b); the Halliday report *Making Punishments Work* (Home Office, 2001a) which advocated the 'seamless sentence'; the White Paper *Justice for All* (Home Office, 2002); the Carter report *Managing Offenders, Reducing Crime* (Carter, 2003); and the government response *Reducing Crime—Changing Lives* (Home Office, 2004). There has even been a major independent review of alternatives (Coulsfield, 2004) which, to its credit, took a much more balanced and holistic approach than government did.

The end result of all this activity has been the *National Offender Management Service* (NOMS), the Community Order, and the Suspended Sentence Order, each of which will be discussed in more detail below. How far all of the initiatives discussed so far have impacted upon the prison population is the question to which we now turn.

REVIEW QUESTIONS

1 How closely related are the introduction of alternatives to custody and the growth of the prison population?

2 Can any community sentence provide a realistic alternative to custody?

Research into alternatives to custody

The major difficulty in researching the effectiveness of alternatives to custody is that there is no simple way of estimating how many offenders are sentenced to a community penalty *as a direct alternative to imprisonment*. Sentencers do not generally announce when passing sentence that individuals have received sentences as an alternative to custody, and even if they did how could we know that they were being completely truthful? They could, for example, make such a claim in order to try to impress offenders with the seriousness of the case and to deter them from further offending, but have had no intention of using custody. Thus, research has to fall back on other ways of trying to estimate the effectiveness of alternatives to custody.

One could look at the use of custody over time and compare it with the use of the alternative(s). If the former decreases while the latter increases, then a case could be made for the alternative acting as an alternative to custody. But there are limitations to this approach, the most significant of which is that there may be no causal relationship whatsoever between the two variables. One might examine the characteristics of those given an alternative to custody and compare these with a group sentenced to imprisonment. But it is very difficult to take account of all the factors that might affect the sentencing decision; offence, age, *gender*, previous criminal record are relatively easy to collect, but employment status, drug use, the details surrounding the offence, mitigating and aggravating circumstances, the defendant's attitude are all much more problematic to get hold of. One might study *pre-sentence reports* that propose the alternative and examine the sentence that is passed when the proposal is not followed. This is time-consuming, would only be possible for small numbers, and would still be no guarantee that the sentence in question was being used as an alternative to custody.

The problems are demonstrated in one of the first studies of a community sentence that was aimed at providing an alternative to custody. The second Home Office study of community service (Pease *et al.*, 1977) used four different approaches to estimate how often the Community Service Order was being used in place of custody. These were: probation officer judgements about what the sentence would have been if community service had not been available; analysis of the sentencing outcomes for those who breached their Community Service Order; analysis of the sentencing outcomes of those cases where the court initiated consideration for community service but where an order was not made; and, analysis of the sentencing outcomes for those recommended for community service by probation officers but who did not receive an order.

The conclusion reached from these four methods was that between 45 and 50 per cent of those who were sentenced to community service were diverted from custody. And this proportion was found in other studies (e.g. McIvor, 1992; Mair, 1988), so that it became something of a truism that alternatives to custody only act as such for at best half of those sentenced to them.

This finding immediately raised the question of where did the other half of those who were being sentenced to alternatives come from? And the answer is clear: they are offenders who would not have been sentenced to custody and therefore had been pulled up-tariff to a more severe sentence than they would have received if the alternative had not existed. The implications of such a phenomenon are considerable, not just for the individuals who are involved in it, but for the process of justice as a whole. Perhaps the key thinker with regard to this issue and the person responsible for coining the term 'net widening' is Stan Cohen (1979; 1985), whose work has contributed significantly to illuminating arguments around the Dispersal of Discipline Thesis.

Put simply, the Dispersal of Discipline Thesis claims that forms of *social control* (both formal and informal) have been emerging and spreading insidiously. Alternatives to custody—particularly if they are not successfully diverting offenders from imprisonment—make control and surveillance more widespread. They offer covert coercion rather than the overt coercion of prison. Cohen, using his now-famous fishing net metaphor, explains how alternatives work in practice:

- nets get bigger, thus catching more offenders;
- they are cast in different parts of the sea, thus catching different offenders;
- the mesh of the net is thinned, thus retaining offenders for longer;
- the identity of the net may not be clear, leading to the blurring of boundaries so that 'it is by no means easy to know where the prison ends and the community begins or just why any deviant is to be found at any particular point' (Cohen, 1985: 57).

All of the initiatives discussed in the preceding section, therefore, may only have served to contribute to the extension of state control in general, and for particular offenders may have increased the demands of their sentence (and, if they fail to meet such demands they may end up in custody in any event). Net widening rapidly became the overriding criticism of any alternative to custody so that 'the conventional wisdom of the critical literature on community corrections is that the development of alternatives has been synonymous with a widening "net" of penal control' (McMahon, 1990). In an important article published in 1990, after 10 years or so of research into alternatives to custody, Maeve McMahon argued that the pessimism associated with net widening was misplaced and pointed to various methodological problems with the research.

Worries about net widening led directly to another key development that has now become one of the defining features of community penalties—risk. As noted earlier, probation day centres aimed to offer a credible alternative to a short custodial sentence, but how could they guarantee that the offenders who received a Probation Order with a day centre requirement were heading for custody in the first place? The clinical judgement of probation officers was based on unofficial, unarticulated, and highly personal methods of classifying offenders, and their *discretion* had come under sustained attack as a result of the '*Nothing Works*' juggernaut. A better method was needed to try to ensure that alternatives to custody were restricted as far as possible to those who were likely to receive a custodial sentence. And in the early 1980s, a scale to predict risk of custody was devised by a Cambridgeshire probation officer in order to ensure that the local day centre effectively targeted those who were *at risk* of imprisonment (see Bale, 1987; 1989):

> The scale is, therefore, used as a means of diminishing any net-widening which might occur around the Cambridge day centre; if potential day centre candidates score certain points on the risk of custody scale then it may be reasonably assumed that they are diversions from custody and not from another community-based disposal (Mair and Lloyd, 1989: 3).

Risk of custody scales developed into sentencing prediction scales but with the Criminal Justice Act 1991, when community penalties were re-labelled as sentences in their own right, predicting sentence diminished in importance and predicting risk of reconviction became significant. While a variety of reasons can be put forward to explain the development of OGRS (the Offender Group Reconviction Score) and its successor OASys (the Offender Assessment System), it is important to remember that one significant source was debates about the effectiveness of community sentences as alternatives to custody.

Even if a community sentence is acting effectively as a direct alternative to custody, there are real dangers associated with such success including the presence of high-risk offenders in the community; high reconviction rates; widening the target group; and loss of identity. If a community sentence is dealing with high risk-offenders in a community setting it is—in effect—walking a tight-rope. It may have had to engage in protracted negotiations with local residents to set up the initiative in its location—indeed, may have fudged the issue of precisely what kind of offenders will be dealt with—and one case of an offender absconding or reoffending could not only lead to a serious crime, but a threat to the existence of the initiative and questions about the abilities of the Probation Service as a whole

If a sentence is successfully diverting offenders from custody, then these offenders are likely to have committed fairly serious offences, have lengthy criminal records, and experience of custody. Unfortunately, these variables are also associated with high rates of reconviction so that success on one measure can mean failure on another. As Mair and Nee (1992: 332) argue '. . . a fairly high rate of reconviction . . . may be built into the very aims and objectives of day centres. If day centres aim to divert offenders from custody and are successful in this, then they will almost certainly be committing themselves to a high reconviction rate'.

Similarly, if a community sentence is seen to be successful at diverting offenders from custody it is quite likely that sentencers (and perhaps the local Probation Service itself) may feel that success should be celebrated and extended. Thus, pressure to expand the sentence in question in terms of numbers dealt with emerges. The target group is widened and the sentence becomes used for offenders who have little or no likelihood of a custodial sentence as well as the original group. The focus of the sentence is thereby weakened, and it becomes less effective with regard to its original aim.

While the previous two phenomena can be subjected to empirical measurement, loss of identity is more nebulous. As noted earlier, as soon as a sentence becomes perceived as an alternative to custody, it is effectively acting as such, its own identity—as a day centre, for example—becomes weakened and it becomes seen predominantly as an *alternative*. The boundaries between custody and community are thereby blurred. This, as Cohen has argued, is not something to be welcomed. And with the introduction of the National Offender Management Service (NOMS) which blurs the organisational boundaries between custody and community sentences, it is even more relevant.

Two of the key issues in criminal justice—net widening/dispersal of discipline and risk—have emerged from the alternatives to custody debate and have shaped and been shaped by it. And they remain pertinent today as the next part of the chapter will show.

REVIEW QUESTIONS

1 What are the main difficulties in measuring the effectiveness of an alternative to custody?

2 Are the problems associated with success as an alternative to custody inevitable?

Present and future

Although this chapter does not intend to discuss in detail the significance of NOMS (see Bailey *et al.*, 2007; Hough *et al.*, 2006; Morgan, 2007; Nellis and Goodman, this volume; Raynor and Vanstone, 2007), partly as it remains unclear as to precisely what shape it will take and how it will impact upon practice, it is worth briefly pointing to its implications in relation to alternatives to custody. In the first place, simply as an organisation it very clearly pulls community sentences and custody closer together, thereby blurring the boundaries even further. Second, the proposed introduction of such sentences as 'custody plus' and 'custody minus' signalled a real desire to eradicate differences between custody and community (although it should be noted that the introduction of custody plus has been deferred—possibly indefinitely). Third, a lot will depend upon how *contestability* is taken forward. And fourth, the introduction of the Community Order and the Suspended Sentence Order (SSO) following the Criminal Justice Act 2003 marks another significant development in the history of alternatives to custody.

Both orders were made available to courts on 4 April 2005 for offences committed on or after that date. Both orders are made up of one or more of 12 possible requirements. The Community Order could last for as short a time as a few hours (a very brief curfew requirement, for example) or as long as three years. The SSO is, legally, a custodial sentence and can only be used where the court proposes to pass a custodial sentence of less than 12 months but in the absence of breach is served in the community; it can last for between six months and two years. Official statements noted that the new sentences were planned to offer rigorous and demanding alternatives to short custodial sentences, with the *Sentencing Guidelines Council* making this clear in guidance for the courts:

> ...even where the threshold for a community sentence has been passed a financial penalty or discharge may still be an appropriate penalty...The top range would be for those offenders who have only just fallen short of a custodial sentence *and for those who have passed the threshold but for whom a community sentence is deemed appropriate* (Sentencing Guidelines Council, 2004: 5, 8 emphasis added).

Although the two new orders are sentences in their own right, they are also intended to act as alternatives to custody. The SSO is indeed a custodial sentence that is served in the community. And the demands of both sentences could—potentially—be heavy depending upon how many requirements are passed. Further, sentencers have less discretion with the new orders than they had previously to avoid imprisonment in cases of breach, which means that failure could add to the prison population rather than decrease it. At the end of March 2005, just as the new orders were about to be made available to the courts, the prison population was 75,000 (Home Office, 2005)—an increase of 10,000 since 1998.

Figure 8.2 Requirements for the Community Order and the Suspended Sentence Order

Unpaid work (40–300 hours).

Supervision (up to 36 months; 24 months maximum for SSO).

Accredited programme (length to be expressed as the number of sessions; must be combined with a Supervision requirement).

Drug rehabilitation (6–36 months; 24 months maximum for SSO; offender's consent is required).

Alcohol treatment (6–36 months; 24 months maximum for SSO; offender's consent is required).

Mental health treatment (up to 36 months; 24 months maximum for SSO; offender's consent is required).

Residence (up to 36 months; 24 months maximum for SSO).

Specified activity (up to 60 days).

Prohibited activity (up to 36 months; 24 months maximum for SSO).

Exclusion (up to 24 months).

Curfew (up to 6 months and for between 2–12 hours in any one day; if a stand-alone Curfew Order is made, there is no probation involvement).

Attendance centre (12–36 hours with a maximum of 3 hours per attendance).

In terms of use, both orders can be judged as successful. In the April–June 2006 quarter, a year after their introduction, 30,500 Community Orders commenced and almost 7,800 SSOs (Ministry of Justice, 2007b), making the latter twice as popular as Home Office estimates. The most recent figures, for the first quarter of 2008, show 33,000 Community Orders and 12,000 SSOs (Ministry of Justice, 2008b). The key question, however, is whether they are being used as alternatives to custody, and while a definitive answer cannot be given, the bulk of the available evidence suggests that they are not.

The availability of two orders as alternatives to custody does not double the chances of their being used to divert offenders from imprisonment; on the contrary, it decreases them. Two alternatives suggest a hedging of bets; neither is clearly delineated as the obvious answer to a short term in custody, and therefore which should be used? Trends in the use of custody do not suggest that the new orders have made any serious impact. As noted, the prison population stood at 75,000 at the end of March 2005 (Home Office, 2005); in June 2008 it was 83,194 (Ministry of Justice, 2008a), an increase of 10 per cent in three years. Is it possible that without the new orders the increase would have been even greater? Focusing more particularly on short terms of imprisonment (those of six months or less) does not offer any better news. In April 2005, the custodial population with sentences of six months or less was 5,461; in April 2006, a year after the introduction of the orders, it was 5,721 (an increase of 5 per cent); 12 months later it was 5,532 (a drop of 3 per cent); but in April 2008 it had increased again to 5,773 (+4 per cent). There is no sign of a sustained drop in the numbers sentenced to short terms of custody (the data used in this paragraph are taken from Home Office (2006) and Ministry of Justice (2008c)). The only study so far of the new orders shows that the average number of requirements for the Community Order is 1.7, while for the SSO it is 1.9 (Mair *et al.*, 2007; Mair *et al.*, 2008). The average length of a Community Order is 14 months and for the SSO 16.6 months. Essentially the Community Order looks just like its predecessors the Community Rehabilitation Order, the Community Punishment Order, and the Community Punishment and Rehabilitation Order, none of which could be said to have been acting in any serious way as alternatives to custody. Even government comments make it clear that the new orders are not achieving what they were intended to:

> The evidence so far is that the courts are not using Community Orders as fully as they might. The anticipated switch to these new community sentences from short terms of imprisonment that was envisaged has not happened but is a crucial part of the package we wish to achieve...Nor are Suspended Sentence Orders being used appropriately: 'many of those sentenced to an SSO would have previously been sentenced to a community sentence' (see Mair *et al.*, 2007: 26).

And a recent report from the House of Commons Justice Committee (2008: 42–44) has argued that not only are the orders failing to displace short custodial sentences, but that they are in fact acting as alternatives to fines.

Sentencers do not agree on how far the Community Order acts as an alternative to custody, but they do think that the SSO tends to be used in this way; although it must be added that more than two-thirds of SSOs are made in the magistrates' courts, and around 40 per cent are made in respect of summary offences (Mair *et al.*, 2008).

The government's reaction to this is to do what government has always done in response to the perceived failure of an alternative to custody: make sentences tougher. While one might argue about the details, it is possible to discern a progressively more demanding series of alternatives to custody as we have moved through the second half of the twentieth century and into the twenty-first: senior attendance centres, community service, day centres/specified activities, the Combination Order, Curfew Orders, the Community Order, and the SSO. The latest proposal is for Higher Intensity Community Orders which could take two forms:

Intensive Control Sentence demonstrators: these might include supervision, programme and activity requirements, plus other requirements as necessary.

We envisage bids will emphasise new aspects such as peer monitoring, judicial monitoring, engagement with the police and resettlement work.

Intensive Punitive Sentence demonstrators: made up of unpaid work and curfew adapted to provide a short intensive community punishment as an alternative to very short term custody (6 months and under), including a supervision requirements where appropriate. This could involve a set number of hours of physically demanding unpaid work to be served immediately following sentence and within a short space of time, combined with supervision appointments and curfew restrictions to last for 3–6 months. (Ministry of Justice, 2008d: 22)

Several pilot projects to test out these ideas began in the first half of 2008. But if the views of sentencers about them are borne out in practice, their future does not look promising:

Apart from resources, sentencers also mentioned other problems with the idea: loading offenders up with requirements was already something that could be done if they wished to; such an approach was setting people up to fail; what would be done with offenders who were employed; and it was all just yet another example of political window-dressing. For the most part, however, comments were strongly negative: 'simply nonsense', 'rubbish' and 'pointless'. (Mair *et al.*, 2008: 37)

REVIEW QUESTIONS

1 Can we conclude that the Community Order and the Suspended Sentence Order have failed as alternatives to custody?

2 Is there any difference between the Community Order and the Suspended Sentence Order?

CONCLUSION

If alternatives to custody are aimed at cutting the prison population, then their history is one of complete failure. But, as McMahon (1990) has argued, alternatives are condemned for failing when half of their cases would not have been imprisoned, but little is said about the remaining half which represent, presumably, successful diversions from custody. And it is possible to claim that the use of custody would have been even greater if alternatives did not exist. It must also be emphasised that the success of community sentences can be assessed by other measures of effectiveness. Their reconviction rates, for example, are certainly no worse (indeed, may be marginally better) than custodial sentences and they are considerably cheaper than custody. In addition, they provide help with a variety of problems that are associated with offending, e.g. substance abuse, accommodation, employment and training, anger management (see Mair (1997) for a wide-ranging discussion of the effectiveness of community sentences).

Perhaps it is more useful to think of alternatives as not having realised their full potential, although this is to view them as having only one simple goal. The problem here is that community sentences have always had other goals (e.g. rehabilitation, *retribution*, *restoration*) and it may be impossible to fulfil all of these goals equally effectively. This problem is exacerbated by the unwillingness of governments openly to define a community sentence as an alternative to custody. The outcome is that a community sentence is expected to act as an alternative in a half-hearted way, without the full-scale commitment necessary to succeed (and this is to ignore the necessity to have sentencers fully signed up to this aim). In addition, following Michael Tonry (1990) we may see community sentences—even where they are understood to be alternatives to custody—to have other latent aims that are at least as significant. Whether governments have been fully aware of it or not, there can be little doubt that one effect of what might be called the alternatives to custody industry has been to toughen up community sentences. This might have been much more difficult to achieve if government had simply set out to make community sentences more demanding and rigorous for their own sake. But by doing this with the intention of making the sentence a feasible alternative to custody—and probation traditionally has been opposed to custody—opposition has been muted. And toughening up community sentences could lead to greater public credibility and less criticism of them as soft options—although it must be said that there is scant evidence of this occurring as yet.

Other reasons for community sentences failing to act as alternatives to custody as much as they might can also be adduced. The development of alternatives to custody has never been a clearly constructed, carefully planned, and co-ordinated policy. On the contrary, it has been fragmented, haphazard, and usually a reaction to a perceived crisis in prisons. Thus, one can legitimately ask how sentencers are going to be convinced by the introduction of various community sentences—community service, day centre requirements, the Combination Order, the Curfew Order—all aimed at providing an alternative to a prison sentence. How can all of these act in such a way? Surely they would need to be categorised according to gradations of seriousness in the way that Ken Pease (1978) argued that Community Service Orders of less than 100 hours should not be used as alternatives to custody, those of between 100 and 240 hours be equivalent to custodial sentences of up to one year, and orders of 240 hours (at the time the maximum available) be equivalent to imprisonment of not less than one year.

There has also been a failure to investigate the nature of the problem that an alternative is intended to resolve. Prison crowding, for example, could be an immediate result of too many fine defaulters being imprisoned, too many remands in custody, too many offenders being imprisoned, or too many long sentences. It may result from increases in crime, increases in punitiveness on the part of sentencers, or changes in penal policy. It is unlikely that a community sentence could be designed that might tackle all of these issues effectively.

In the end, community sentences have been asked to act as alternatives to custody as short-term reactions to pressing problems, as safety valves for issues that persistently threaten to explode. And from this point of view, they have worked. But the problems of clouding the identity of practicable community sentences, of blurring the boundaries between prison and community, of inexorably ratcheting up the severity of community sentences, of net widening, have not been resolved. Although the Criminal Justice Act 1991 officially declared community penalties to be sentences in their own right, the

Community Order and the Suspended Sentence Order are widely acknowledged to be alternatives to custody. The constantly increasing prison population means that alternatives to custody will continue to be needed. NOMS and contestability could mean that probation officers do indeed become prison officers in the community. Curfew Orders are, essentially, house imprisonment, and it would be interesting to explore the perceptions of electronic monitoring staff about the nature of their job.

Community sentences must be understood as more than alternatives to custody, but their role as such has been a major issue for the last 40 years. It has contributed to important theoretical developments and been responsible for a great deal of research. Little of this seems to have informed the policy process, however, and for the foreseeable future it looks as if community sentences will remain constrained as alternatives to custody.

QUESTIONS FOR DISCUSSION

1 What are the advantages and disadvantages of developing alternatives to custody?

2 Is net widening inevitable in relation to alternatives to custody?

3 What other ways might be tried to reduce the prison population and what kind of problems might they throw up?

4 Should community sentences be used as alternatives to custody?

5 Would officially defining certain community sentences as alternatives to custody be helpful?

GUIDE TO FURTHER READING

Bottoms, A., Rex, S., and Robinson, G. (2004) *Alternatives to Prison: options for an insecure society*. Cullompton: Willan.

This is the most authoritative and up-to-date academic study of the issues surrounding community sentences and their use as alternatives to custody.

Cohen, S. (1985) *Visions of Social Control: crime, punishment and classification*. Cambridge: Polity Press.

An exceptionally well-written and readable account of the spread of social control. The ideas contained in this book have influenced countless studies and continue to do so.

Coulsfield, Lord (2004) *Crime, Courts and Confidence: report of an independent inquiry into alternatives to prison*. London: Esmee Fairbairn Foundation.

Not an official report but the closest we are likely to have for the immediate future, this is a comprehensive study of the key issues.

McMahon, M. (1990) '"Net Widening": vagaries in the use of a concept', *British Journal of Criminology* 30(2): 121–49.

An important empirical study that questions the negativity of research into the effectiveness of alternatives to custody.

Vass, A.A. (1990) *Alternatives to Prison: punishment, custody and the community*. London: Sage.

A detailed study covering theory, policy, and practice of alternatives to custody during the 1980s.

WEB LINKS

http://www.noms.homeoffice.gov.uk

The website of the National Offender Management Service has details of the structure of the organisation and how it works; it also contains various policy and strategy documents.

http://www.justice.gov.uk

This is the website of the Ministry of Justice which is responsible for probation. It provides probation and prison statistics, consultation papers, and recent research reports.

http://www.probation.homeoffice.gov.uk

The National Probation Service website describes what probation does and contains key policy documents.

http://www.homeoffice.gov.uk

The Home Office website contains an archive of all Home Office Research Studies, a number of which cover the issue of alternatives to custody.

http://www.crimeandjustice.org.uk

The Centre for Crime and Justice Studies is an independent charity that focuses upon crime and the criminal justice system. A series of studies of the Community Order and the Suspended Sentence Order are available on its website.

REFERENCES

Advisory Council on the Penal System (ACPS) (1970) *Non-Custodial and Semi-Custodial Penalties*. London: HMSO [the Wootton Committee].

Advisory Council on the Treatment of Offenders (1957) *Alternatives to Short Terms of Imprisonment*. London: HMSO.

Bailey, R., Knight, C., and Williams, B. (2007) 'The Probation Service as part of NOMS in England and Wales: fit for purpose?' in L. Gelsthorpe and R. Morgan (eds) *Handbook of Probation*. Cullompton: Willan Publishing.

Bale, D. (1987) 'Using a Risk of Custody Scale' *Probation Journal* 34(4): 127–31.

Bale, D. (1989) 'The Cambridgeshire Risk of Custody Scale' in G. Mair (ed) *Risk Prediction and Probation*. Research and Planning Unit Paper 56. London: Home Office.

Brody, S. (1976) *The Effectiveness of Sentencing: A Review of the Literature*. Home Office Research Study No. 35. London: HMSO.

Carter, P. (2003) *Managing Offenders, Reducing Crime*. London: Strategy Unit.

Cohen, S. (1979) 'The Punitive City: notes on the dispersal of social control'. *Contemporary Crises* 3: 339–69.

Cohen, S. (1985) *Visions of Social Control: crime, punishment and classification*. Oxford: Polity Press.

Coulsfield, Lord (2004) *Crime, Courts and Confidence: report of an independent inquiry into alternatives to prison*. London: Esmee Fairbairn Foundation.

Fairhead, S. (1981a) *Day Centres and Probation*. Research and Planning Unit Paper No. 4. London: Home Office.

Fairhead, S. (1981b) *Petty Persistent Offenders*. Home Office Research Study No. 66. London: HMSO.

Folkard, M.S., Smith, D.E., and Smith, D.D. (1976) *IMPACT: Volume 2 The Results of the Experiment*. Home Office Research Study No. 36. London: HMSO.

Hedderman, C. and Hough, M. (2004) 'Getting tough or being effective; what matters?' in G. Mair (ed) *What Matters in Probation*. Cullompton: Willan Publishing.

Home Office (1938) *Report of the Departmental Committee on Corporal Punishment*. London: HMSO [The Cadogan Committee].

Home Office (1974) *Young Adult Offenders: report of the Advisory Council on the Penal System*. London: HMSO [The Younger Report].

Home Office (1980) *The Reduction of Pressure on the Prison System: Observations on the Fifteenth Report from the Expenditure Committee*. London: HMSO.

Home Office (1984a) *Intermittent Custody*. London: HMSO.

Home Office (1984b) *Probation Service in England and Wales: Statement of National Objectives and Priorities*. London: Home Office.

Home Office (1998) *Effective Practice Initiative: National Implementation Plan for the Supervision of Offenders*. Probation Circular 35/1998. London: Home Office.

Home Office (2001a) *Making Punishments Work: Report of a Review of the Sentencing Framework for England and Wales*. London: Home Office [The Halliday Report].

Home Office (2001b) *Criminal Justice: the way ahead*. London: The Stationery Office.

Home Office (2002) *Justice for All*. London: The Stationery Office.

Home Office (2003) *Prison Statistics England and Wales 2002*. London: The Stationery Office.

Home Office (2004) *Reducing Crime—Changing Lives: the government's plans for transforming the management of offenders*. London: Home Office.

Home Office (2005) *Population in Custody: monthly tables March 2005 England and Wales*. Available at <http://www. homeoffice.gov.uk/rds/omcs.html>.

Home Office (2006) *Population in Custody: monthly tables April 2006 England and Wales*. Available at <http://www. homeoffice.gov.uk/rds/omcs.html>.

Hough, M., Allen, R., and Padel, U. (2006) *Reshaping Probation and Prisons: the new offender management framework*. Bristol: Policy Press.

House of Commons (1978) *Fifteenth Report from the Expenditure Committee: The Reduction of Pressure on the Prison System*. London: HMSO. 3 vols.

House of Commons (1998) *Home Affairs Committee Third Report: Alternatives to Prison Sentences*. London: The Stationery Office.

House of Commons Justice Committee (2008) *Towards Effective Sentencing: fifth report of session 2007–08. Vol. 1*. London: The Stationery Office.

Mair, G. (1988) *Probation Day Centres*. Home Office Research Study No. 100. London: HMSO.

Mair, G. (1991) *Part Time Punishment? The Origins and Development of Senior Attendance Centres*. London: HMSO.

Mair, G. (ed) (1997) *Evaluating the Effectiveness of Community Penalties*. Aldershot: Avebury.

Mair, G. (2004) 'Diversionary and non-supervisory approaches to dealing with offenders' in A. Bottoms, S. Rex, and G. Robinson (eds) *Alternatives to Prison: options for an insecure society*. Cullompton: Willan Publishing.

Mair, G. and Burke, L. (forthcoming) *A Short History of Probation*. Cullompton: Willan Publishing.

Mair, G. and Canton, R. (2007) 'Sentencing, Community Penalties and the Role of the Probation Service' in L. Gelsthorpe and R. Morgan (eds) *Handbook of Probation*. Cullompton: Willan Publishing.

Mair, G., Cross, N., and Taylor, S. (2007) *The Use of the Community Order and the Suspended Sentence Order*. London: Centre for Crime and Justice Studies.

Mair, G., Cross, N., and Taylor, S. (2008) *The Community Order and the Suspended Sentence Order: the views and attitudes of sentencers*. London: Centre for Crime and Justice Studies.

Mair, G. and Lloyd, C. (1989) 'Prediction and Probation: an introduction' in G. Mair (ed) *Risk Prediction and Probation*. Research and Planning Unit Paper 56. London: Home Office.

Mair, G. and Nee, C. (1992) 'Day centre reconviction rates'. *British Journal of Criminology* 32(3): 329–39.

Martinson, R. (1974) 'What Works? Questions and answers about prison reform'. *Public Interest* 35: 22–54.

McIvor, G. (1992) *Sentenced to Serve: the operation and impact of community service by offenders*. Aldershot: Avebury.

McMahon, M. (1990) '"Net Widening": vagaries in the use of a concept'. *British Journal of Criminology* 30(2): 121–49.

Ministry of Justice (2007a) *Statistical Bulletin: Offender Management Caseload Statistics 2006*. London: Ministry of Justice.

Ministry of Justice (2007b) *Probation Statistics Quarterly Brief: April to June 2007 England and Wales*. London: Ministry of Justice.

Ministry of Justice (2008a) *Population in Custody: monthly tables June 2008 England and Wales*. London: Ministry of Justice

Ministry of Justice (2008b) *Probation Statistics Quarterly Brief: January to March 2008 England and Wales*. London: Ministry of Justice.

Ministry of Justice (2008c) *Population in Custody: monthly tables April 2008 England and Wales*. London: Ministry of Justice.

Ministry of Justice (2008d) *Prison Policy Update: briefing paper*. London: Ministry of Justice.

Morgan, R. (2007) 'Probation, Governance and Accountability' in L. Gelsthorpe and R. Morgan (eds) *Handbook of Probation*. Cullompton: Willan Publishing.

Morrison, W.D. (1896) *Juvenile Offenders*. London: T. Fisher Unwin.

Pease, K. (1978) 'Community service and the tariff' *Criminal Law Review*: 269–75.

Pease, K., Billingham, S., and Earnshaw, I. (1977) *Community Service Assessed in 1976*. Home Office Research Study No. 39. London: HMSO.

Pease, K. and McWilliams, W. (eds) (1980) *Community Service by Order*. Edinburgh: Scottish Academic Press.

Raynor, P. (1988) *Probation as an Alternative to Custody: a case study*. Aldershot: Avebury.

Raynor, P. and Vanstone, M. (2007) 'Towards a Correctional Service' in L. Gelsthorpe and R. Morgan (eds) *Handbook of Probation*. Cullompton: Willan Publishing.

Russell, C.E.B. and Rigby, L. (1906) *The Making of the Criminal*. London: Macmillan and Co.

Rutherford, A. (1984) *Prisons and the Process of Justice*. Oxford: Oxford University Press.

Sentencing Guidelines Council (2004) *New Sentences: Criminal Justice Act 2003 Guidelines*. London: Sentencing Guidelines Council.

Tonry, M. (1990) 'Stated and latent functions of ISP' *Crime and Delinquency* 36(1): 174–91.

Vanstone, M. (1985) 'Moving away from help? Policy and practice in probation day centres'. *Howard Journal* 24: 20–8.

Vanstone, M. and Raynor, P. (1981) 'Diversion from prison—a partial success and a missed opportunity'. *Probation Journal* 28: 85–9.

Vass, A.A. and Weston, A. (1990) 'Probation day centres as an alternative to custody: a "Trojan Horse" examined'. *British Journal of Criminology* 30: 189–206.

Young, W. (1979) *Community Service Orders: the development and use of a new penal measure*. London: Heinemann.

9

Restorative justice

Gerry Johnstone

INTRODUCTION

The purpose of this chapter is to explain the core ideas of *restorative justice* and look at some ways in which they are being put into practice. Restorative justice has emerged as a significant alternative to the customary way of thinking about the purpose of criminal justice and how it should be conducted. Advocates of restorative justice are particularly critical of a set of core assumptions of contemporary criminal justice. First, that *crime* is a wrong committed against an impersonal society. Second, those who commit crimes are 'outsiders' who should be viewed with hostility. Third, the appropriate response to crime is to inflict reciprocal harm upon the offender. Fourth, that it is a task for professionals. Fifth, it should be carried out in an impersonal manner by a large-scale institution. Restorative justice is presented as a new type of justice based on fundamentally different ideas. First, that crime is principally a violation of a person. Second, those who commit crime are members of our community whose behaviour should be censured within a broader context of compassion. Third, the appropriate response to crime is to hold offenders liable to repair the harm they have caused. Fourth, victims and other members of the community affected by crime, and offenders, should participate meaningfully in the criminal justice process. Fifth, the justice process should be personalised, localised, and small-scale.

The reader must keep in mind that there are multiple and competing conceptions of restorative justice (Johnstone and van Ness, 2007), and that this chapter attempts to capture and describe the elemental ideas underlying all the major conceptions. It also subjects the fundamental ideas of restorative criminal justice to critical scrutiny.

BACKGROUND

Accounts of the rise of restorative justice often trace its origins to the 'Elmira Case' of 1974 (Peachey, 2003). In the small Canadian town of Elmira, two teenagers were convicted of causing criminal damage following an intoxicated Saturday night vandalism spree. Mark Yantzi, the probation officer assigned to prepare their *pre-sentence reports*, was a member of the Mennonite Central Committee, a pacifist faith group which had recently become interested in criminal justice reform. In a discussion of the case, it was decided to suggest a rather unorthodox approach to the judge: that the two teenagers should visit their victims, accompanied by Yantzi and a colleague, and find out how much damage they had caused. To the surprise of Yantzi, the judge agreed to this. After the teenagers had visited their victims (they simply knocked on their doors and explained who they were and why they were there) and reported back to the court, the judge placed them on *probation* with a condition that they should each pay $550 to their victims as restitution.

Encouraged by the successful outcome of this case, Yantzi and his fellow Mennonites launched the Victim/Offender Reconciliation Project (VORP) (Peachey, 2003; Zehr, 1990: 158–74). As the name indicates, an initial purpose of VORP was to promote reconciliation between victims and offenders.

To achieve this goal, mediated meetings between victims and offenders were arranged. In these, both parties were encouraged to tell their stories, ask questions of each other, and propose solutions to the conflict between them. At the end they were encouraged to come to an agreement on what should be done to repair the harm caused by the offence. This often included the offender paying financial restitution to the victim, but could also involve other forms of *reparation*, such as the offender doing work for the victim or the community, or agreeing to behave in certain ways (Zehr, 1990: 160–1).

In addition to its concern with reconciliation, the organisers of VORP soon began to highlight a number of other benefits of personal encounters between victims and offenders where the focus is upon identifying and repairing harm: offenders are encouraged to take greater responsibility for their actions; victims' stereotypes about offenders are challenged; lay people (both victim and offenders) become empowered (Peachey, 2003: 180–1).

What was meant by 'become empowered' is that participants in mediation gain a greater sense of self-respect, self-reliance, and self-confidence (Bush and Folger, 1994: 20). Other proponents of mediation pointed to its capacity to produce 'recognition': 'acknowledgement and empathy for the situations and problems of others' (Bush and Folger, 1994: 2). So, *victim-offender mediation* (VOM) became conceived and promoted as a process which could transform those who took part in it into better and stronger people. The aim was also to produce harmonious relationships between people who previously had been either indifferent or antagonistic to each other.

Throughout the 1970s and 1980s victim–offender mediation proliferated throughout north America and some projects surfaced in the United Kingdom. During this period there was considerable academic interest in the broader development of community mediation and *informal justice* as alternatives to formal legal justice (Matthews, 1988). However, the first major publication focusing specifically on restorative justice was Howard Zehr's book *Changing Lenses*, published in 1990. Zehr criticised the dominant 'retributive' model of criminal justice and proposed an alternative restorative model. Restorative justice, he claimed, would better meet the needs of victims, offenders, and crime-affected communities. It was also, he argued, more consistent with the way justice was conceived throughout most of human history.

Around the time that Zehr's book was published other important developments were taking place independently. In New Zealand, the juvenile justice system was transformed in 1989 by the adoption of Family Group Conferences (FGCs) as the standard response to offences committed by young people (Morris and Maxwell, 2003). FGCs, modelled upon traditional Maori methods of dealing with troublesome behaviour, are similar in many ways to victim–offender mediation. But there are also crucial differences. In particular, many more people take part in the 'encounter', including families of offenders, families and supporters of victims, careworkers, and police officers. Some advocates of FGCs began to describe them as examples of restorative justice.

In Australia in the early 1990s, a police officer—Terry O'Connell—adapted FGCs for use as a community policing response to juvenile offences (Moore and O'Connell, 2003). In the Wagga Wagga model of *conferencing* (named after the New South Wales city in which it was pioneered), conferences are facilitated by police officers (or others in positions of authority) using a 'facilitator's script', consisting of a series of open-ended questions which encourage people to express their feelings about what happened. The police use conferences as a way of delivering more effective police cautions. In principle, this enables them to deal with a larger proportion of cases by way of cautioning, and hence diverts offenders away from the criminal justice process at a very early stage, thereby preventing much of the harm to offenders that results from a court appearance and criminal conviction.

Conferencing soon became publicized as a highly effective way of dealing with juvenile offending. According to its proponents, it significantly reduces the chances of a young person re-offending and also provides victims and communities with a more meaningful and satisfactory response to crime than that provided by conventional criminal proceedings. In order to account for these effects, conference proponents drew upon John Braithwaite's theory of reintegrative shaming (Braithwaite, 1989; Moore, 1993). It was suggested that conferencing worked because it provided a forum for the expression of community disapproval of a young person's offending conduct, but in a supportive environment and accompanied by constructive discussion of how offenders could redeem themselves by helping repair the harm they caused. Braithwaite himself wholly endorsed this view and became one of the leading advocates of restorative justice (Braithwaite, 2003).

The Wagga Wagga model of restorative conferencing was subsequently adopted in the USA and in the Thames Valley police authority in the mid-1990s, as the basis of a restorative cautioning experiment. The latter experiment attracted significant media and political attention and was a key factor in the Government's decision to establish some elements of restorative justice as part of its strategy for tackling youth offending outlined in the Crime and Disorder Act 1998. Numerous schemes incorporating some principles of restorative justice have sprung up in the UK since the late 1990s, and the government has continued to show cautious interest in using restorative justice in the criminal justice system (Home Office, 2003). Over the same period, interest in restorative justice has grown remarkably around the world. Countless schemes, programmes, and other forms of restorative intervention are now in existence in numerous countries (Miers, 2007). Increasingly, indeed, the ideas of restorative justice are being applied in strategies for dealing with non-criminal troublesome behaviour and conflict (Strang and Braithwaite, 2001).

The ideas of restorative justice

The definition of crime

Conventionally, crime is depicted as a wrongdoing which is so serious that it harms not only its *direct victims* and their kin, but society as a whole. Accordingly, it is assumed that society has an interest in seeing that something is done about crime. A related assumption is that compensation of the victim is insufficient as redress for crime.

There are significant advantages to this idea of collective victimization. As Howard Zehr puts it, it acknowledges that the effects of some wrongs against individuals 'ripple out, touching many others' (1990: 182). Accordingly, if a victim of a crime decides for some reason not to pursue legal action, the state can still initiate action on behalf of society which has an interest in the matter. From the perspective of the victim, it means that redress is possible without having to undertake personally the burden and cost of private legal action. In addition, by defining a serious wrong against an individual as a crime against all, society appears to express solidarity with the victim (Duff, 2001). Another advantage is the efficiency that comes from having professionals handle arrest, *prosecution*, and execution of judgments (Van Ness and Strong, 2006: 186).

Yet, advocates of restorative justice are highly critical of this conventional characterisation of crime. For Zehr, it fails to capture the essence of crime: that it is 'a violation of a person by another person...a violation of the just relationship that should exist between individuals' (1990: 182). The focus is on the secondary social impact of crime rather than on the primary personal aspects. This, it is contended, has detrimental consequences for the direct victims of crime: the harm they suffer is not acknowledged in the way we define and talk about crime, and their needs and interests tend to be neglected in the social response to crime (Zehr, 1990: chap. 2; see also Dignan, 2005 and Johnstone, 2002: chap. 4).

We should note that many adherents to traditional conceptions of criminal justice now accept that the direct victim's needs and interests should be given more prominence in criminal justice. But, what restorative justice advocates call for is something much more radical: the replacement of the idea of collective victimisation with a new conception of crime as *primarily* as an offence against people and only secondarily an offence against society. This would radically alter the relative priority attached to the interests of victims and society respectively in the criminal justice process.

The appropriate attitude towards the offender

At the heart of restorative justice lies a challenge to the prevailing hostile attitude towards offenders. This attitude has been characterised as one which regards offenders as:

> some kind of external threat, as people who are different from ourselves and who do not properly belong in our society and against whom we need to raise physical defences and who ought to be contained...in prison. (Faulkner quoted in Johnstone, 2002: 10)

The attitude which restorative justice advocates prefer might be described as a more paternalistic one. Our relationship to offenders should be modelled more upon the way the head of a family (or perhaps a kindly uncle) relates to family members when they commit a wrong within the family circle (Braithwaite, 1989: 56ff.; 2003). Whilst the wrongdoing should be censured, and we should demand that the wrongdoer makes amends, this should take place against 'a background of kinship or sympathy' between those who censure and the person censured (Moberly, 1968: 97).

In the discourse of restorative justice, such an attitude is presented as prudent as well as morally preferable. Most offenders will, at some point, have to be readmitted into our community, and the way they behave towards us will be shaped by the way they have been treated. If we treat offenders as our enemies, they will act like our enemies. If we treat them as outsiders, they will join and become influenced by delinquent subcultures. We will also lose an important resource, since most offenders have the potential to contribute to community wellbeing. On the other hand, if we try to strengthen bonds between offenders and law-abiding members of the community we improve our chances of influencing them to behave better and to make a positive contribution to community well-being. If we ensure that they have more of a stake in the community, they will be less likely to behave in ways that damage it. According to restorative justice advocates, experiments based on these ideas have shown that most offenders have enormous capacity to do good. In accounts of these experiments it is suggested that, given appropriate support in constructing a positive identity, most offenders will become constructive citizens (see Cayley, 1998: part III).

The appropriate response to crime

Restorative justice challenges the conventional assumption that the appropriate response to crime is to impose reciprocal harm upon the offender. It suggests instead that we should hold offenders liable to repair the harm resulting from their wrongs. The rationale of this proposal is twofold.

One line of reasoning starts by asserting that our response to crime should be oriented as much towards the victim as the offender. Contemporary criminal justice tends to be almost exclusively offender-oriented in its response, i.e. it is almost wholly organised around the question of what should be done about the offender. It neglects to address the equally or even more important issue of what should be done for the victim. It is argued further that, if we take the need to provide victims with justice as a starting point, we will realise that imposing harm upon the offender is insufficient and perhaps even an obstacle to achieving justice. Harming the offender does little, if anything, to make things better for the victim (even if it is claimed that it is done on behalf of the victim). Victims, it is claimed, derive a richer experience of justice from an approach which results in them receiving *reparation* for the harm they have suffered.

A second line of reasoning is that holding offenders liable to repair the harm they have done is more justifiable morally and politically than inflicting harm upon them, and is more effective as a method of making them accountable for their behaviour. The justificatory argument is made by Barnett (2003: 46–9). The argument about accountability is made by Zehr. He agrees with defenders of *punishment* when they insist that offenders need to be held accountable for their behaviour (1990: 40–3). He argues, however, that punishing offenders fails to achieve this. To hold offenders truly accountable we need to encourage and allow them to see 'the real human costs of what they have done' (Zehr, 1990: 41). Enabling offenders to come face-to-face with their victims, and encouraging the latter to tell the offender first-hand how the crime has affected them, is one way of achieving this. Offenders must also be encouraged to take active responsibility for the results of their behaviour:

> Offenders must be allowed and encouraged to help decide what will happen to make things right, then to take steps to repair the damage (Zehr, 1990: 42).

Participation in the justice process

Another fundamental idea of *restorative justice* is that participation in the justice process should be opened up to lay people, and especially the offender and those directly affected by the offence. Indeed, it is proposed, these 'stakeholders' should be at the centre of deliberation and decision making, with professionals becoming facilitators rather than key decision makers. A related idea is that victims and offenders should if possible encounter each other directly rather than have their interests represented by professionals (Larson Sawin and Zehr, 2007).

According to restorative justice advocates, participation of victims and offenders and other people affected by crime in encounters whereby they decide what to do about it has a number of advantages. As we have seen, it is argued that such processes enable offenders to experience real accountability. It is also claimed that offenders are more likely to comply with measures agreed at such meetings than they are with orders imposed by a court.

For the victim, such processes have numerous benefits. Meeting the person who has harmed them enables them to divest themselves of fearful images which plague many victims. The opportunity to explain the impact of the offence on their lives to the offender, in the presence of others who are likely to validate that what happened was unacceptable, plays a crucial role in their recovery from the impact of the offence. They may receive an apology and offer of reparation. Moreover, they have an opportunity to contribute to the decision on the form reparation should take. Most importantly, by being granted an effective voice in the process by which the crime which has so devastated them is dealt with, victims can begin to recover the sense of autonomy and power which the crime robbed them of. This 'empowerment' of victims is often presented as the key to their healing and recovery (Zehr, 1990: chap. 2).

Participation of community members in 'restorative processes' is also said to be beneficial in numerous ways. In particular, community members can ensure that decisions reflect what they desire and need, rather than being based upon the conjectures of 'professional outsiders' about what is in the community's interest. Also, by taking part in the censuring of crime and the search for constructive answers, as opposed to looking to outside experts for solutions, community members gain in various ways: they obtain a greater sense of ownership of their criminal law, they acquire self-confidence, and they gain a better understanding of the effects of crime and the lives and problems of both victims and perpetrators (Christie, 2003). As more and more community members take part in such processes communities themselves become stronger. Further, since—as is widely claimed—one of the causes of crime is a weak sense of community, this in turn removes a significant cause of crime.

The scale of justice

In contemporary society it is virtually taken for granted that doing criminal justice is a task for large scale specialist institutions which should operate in an impersonal, bureaucratic manner, processing cases. Restorative justice challenges this assumption. It urges us to retrieve what was valuable in pre-modern, perhaps ancient, ways of dealing with criminal behaviour (Christie, 2003; Johnstone, 2002: chap. 3). Criminal justice should be reconfigured as a task for ordinary people. They should engage personally with those who offend and their victims and relate to them as people rather than cases. The justice process should be in tune with local concerns and needs, rather than oriented to the needs of the state or bureaucracy. The process should have the informality found in everyday social interaction. It should resemble to a large extent the manner in which trouble and conflict are handled in everyday life. Space should be provided for the expression of emotion, the telling of personal stories, the communication and acknowledgement of ambivalent and shifting thoughts and feelings. There should be space for the emergence of creative and distinctive solutions which people frequently adopt to resolve interpersonal conflict.

Restorative justice advocates recognise, of course, that in contemporary societies we will need professionally-staffed institutions to coordinate such activity, provide facilities and ensure that certain standards are maintained. However, it is suggested, the role of these institutions needs to be carefully defined and controlled. Their role is not to deliver justice but to enable ordinary people to practice justice. Also, to the largest extent possible, these agencies should be locally based and in tune with local needs. Criminal justice should be de-centralized as well as de-professionalized.

The thinking behind this proposal is complex. Partly, it echoes a more general concern to make our institutions, including our criminal justice institutions, more hospitable (Pavlich, 2005). At another level, it might be understood as an attempt to make the criminal justice process more *meaningful* for those whom it is meant to be for. Another argument for reducing criminal justice to a human scale, however, is that it seems a condition for a move away from the instrumental use of punishment as a mechanism for controlling crime and resolving conflicts (something we would do only with strangers) towards moral communication and education focused upon harm and the need for repair. These ideas permeate the work of Nils Christie (2003), a significant influence upon the restorative justice movement.

REVIEW QUESTIONS

1 In what ways does restorative justice challenge conventional thinking about crime and justice?

2 Is it possible to respond to crime in a way that benefits offenders, victims, and communities?

Restorative processes

The ideas of restorative justice have been developed in close connection with practical experimentation with 'restorative processes' as alternatives to conventional criminal justice processes. The three best known restorative processes are victim-offender mediation, conferencing, and circles. Circles of support and accountability are also worthy of consideration. In what follows, these models are described in prototypical form. In practice, programmes with these names are likely to be much more flexible, depending on the needs of the parties (see Van Ness and Strong, 2006: chap. 4)

Victim-offender mediation

Victim-offender mediation (VOM) offers victims of crime an opportunity to meet in a safe setting with the person who has harmed them. The meeting is organised and structured by one or two trained mediators. Mediators allow and encourage victims to tell offenders about how the offence affected their lives and to ask offenders questions which victims often have, such as why they were the target of an offence. Victims are also able to take part in developing a restitution or reparation plan. Offenders are given the opportunity to account for their behaviour, to tell their story, and to contribute to the construction of an action plan for repairing the harm they have caused.

VOM can occur at any stage of a criminal justice process. It is often triggered by cases being referred to it by agencies in the conventional criminal justice process as part of a diversion scheme. For instance, the police might offer victims and offenders the option of

VOM as an alternative to sending a person who has admitted involvement in an offence to court. Alternatively, it can be integrated with conventional forms of case 'disposal', e.g. a magistrate or judge might suggest that VOM occur as part of a Probation Order. Or, it can take place alongside and in addition to conventional processes, e.g. offenders serving prison sentences might take part in VOM prior to being released.

Conferencing

A second form of restorative justice practice is conferencing. This is similar in many respects to VOM. In conferencing, however, the number of participants is extended to include family members or supporters of victims, and family members and community contacts of offenders where they are interested in supporting the offender's reparative efforts. There is a greater emphasis in family group conferencing on construction of an action plan which will help the offender—quite often a young offender—not only to repair the damage caused by the crime but also change their way of life so that they have less chance of re-offending. Conferences can take place at any stage of the criminal justice process, in much the same way as VOM.

In some places, conferencing is heavily influenced by the theory of reintegrative shaming, which suggests that potent expressions of community disapproval of offending behaviour, followed by gestures of reacceptance of the offender into the community of law-abiding citizens, is a powerful and just form of *crime control* (Braithwaite, 1989). Consequently, facilitators of conferences allow participants to express strong disapproval of the offender's behaviour, but in a context of respect for the offender as a person and followed by gestures of care and love for the offender. According to Braithwaite (1989) such a process works extremely well as a form of *social control*. It puts crime off the 'menu' for most people, without subjecting them to any of the harsh, exclusive, punitive measures we currently rely upon to deter would-be offenders.

Circles

A third form of restorative justice practice is the sentencing or peacemaking circle (Cayley, 1998: chap. 16). Based upon the traditional sanctioning and healing practices of aboriginal people in North America, they were re-introduced in various aboriginal communities in the 1990s, usually at the sentencing stage of the criminal justice process. In circles, the number of participants tends to be much larger than in a family group conference, as many community residents and justice and social service personnel also take part. There is usually some way of ensuring that everybody who wishes to speak gets at least one chance to do so.

The process is often referred to as circle sentencing, since one of its functions is to enable the community to recommend a sentence to the judge. However, circles have broader functions. For instance, their role is often said to be that of teaching people—through respectful dialogue—about the right way to behave. They are also regarded as processes which promote healing, in the sense of reconnecting people with their community and hence with their true selves. As well as recommending a sentence, the circle will also come up with a broader plan of community action to tackle some problem which is perceived as debilitating the community. Circles, then, are often promoted, not simply as a better way of dealing with individual criminal cases, but as a means of rebuilding a sense of community and using the community to resolve conflicts and tackle underlying social problems.

Circles of support and accountability

A related, but less well-known form of restorative justice practice is the circle of support and accountability (Cayley, 1998: chap. 16). In these, community members form support groups around feared ex-prisoners, in particular sex offenders. The circle both supports the ex-offender in their efforts to be law-abiding and informally monitors their behaviour. The basic principle of this form of intervention is that ex-offenders should be allowed to live safely in the community, whilst the community should also be allowed to live safely with the ex-offender in their midst.

REVIEW QUESTIONS

1 What underlying ideas do different restorative processes have in common?

2 How do these processes challenge conventional thinking about crime and justice?

Implementation and values

Governments, policy-makers, and criminal justice practitioners have shown significant interest in incorporating restorative processes into the criminal justice system, using them at various stages as alternatives or supplements to conventional criminal justice processes for cases deemed appropriate. For instance, in the UK, restorative processes have been used in youth justice since the late 1990s, and in 2003 the government published a consultation paper announcing its intention to use restorative justice in the adult criminal justice system (Home Office, 2003).

Perhaps not surprisingly, most restorative justice advocates have been delighted that there is such interest in their ideas and have eagerly participated in the implementation of restorative justice. Some worry, however, that what is often happening is less a move from conventional criminal justice towards restorative justice, more the utilisation within criminal justice systems of certain techniques and processes associated with restorative justice. The concern here is that certain processes themselves come to be thought of as 'restorative justice' and that sight is lost of the wider body of ideas, principles, and values.

In an effort to check such tendencies efforts are being made to define restorative justice with more care and precision than has been the case. In particular, efforts are being made to identify and articulate the distinctive *values of restorative justice*, and to use these as a guide to how restorative a programme, process, or scheme actually is. Indeed, key restorative justice advocates suggest that values or principles are the key means of distinguishing restorative justice from other approaches to crime and wrongdoing (Pranis,

2007). The idea here is that what unifies all restorative practices, and differentiates these practices most clearly from conventional approaches to crime, is that they are informed by and seek to give expression to a radically new (although actually ancient) set of moral and social values. For example, some of the distinctive values of restorative justice appear to be: 'show respect for all persons', 'heal those harmed rather than impose recipro-cal suffering upon those who cause harm', 'the wisdom of ordinary people should be respected', and 'people should be empowered to solve their own problems' (cf. Pranis, 2007: 61–2).

REVIEW QUESTIONS

1 What underlies the concern to articulate more clearly the distinctive values of restorative justice?

2 How, precisely, do the values of restorative justice differ from those of other common ways of responding to crime?

Critical issues

As the above section indicates, the development of restorative justice has been accompa-nied by a great deal of critical reflection amongst advocates and supporters. In addition to this internal critical discourse various 'external' commentators have subjected the ideas of restorative justice to criticism. Some of these seek to defend core elements of traditional thinking about criminal justice (e.g. Ashworth, 2003). Others present a quite different argument: that for all its claim to offer a distinctive alternative, restorative jus-tice fails to question some foundational assumptions of contemporary criminal justice and hence fails to live up to its own rhetoric (Pavlich, 2005). Some contend that restora-tive justice, contrary to its own claims, is primarily designed for the benefit of offenders rather than victims. Others suggest that the whole idea of restorative justice, as so far presented, is dangerously vague and incoherent (Johnstone, 2007: 598–600). Another critic has argued that, although the idea of a 'nicer way of doing justice' is enormously seductive, restorative justice is intellectually and morally indefensible: it fails in its aspi-ration of effecting 'a practical and theoretical reconciliation between the values of love and compassion, on the one hand, and justice and accountability, on the other' (Acorn, 2004: quotes from 6 and 18).

Some of the leading critical perspective on restorative justice are explained and dis-cussed elsewhere (Johnstone, 2007). The remainder of this chapter will look briefly at just a few critical issues.

A fully restorative justice system?

According to Zehr, 'restorative justice advocates dream of a day when justice is fully restorative' (2002: 59). Most realise that the more realistic goal is to 'move as far as we can toward a process that is restorative' (Zehr, 2002: 60), recognising that in the meantime a 'traditional criminal justice model' will continue to govern much of the way we see and respond to crime.

There are important questions about the precise relationship of traditional criminal justice and restorative justice during this 'transitional' phase. An equally vital question, however, is: what would a system of justice that is 'fully restorative' look like? Restorative justice advocates have, of course, provided us with some clear indications, e.g. it would be a system in which ordinary people affected by crime are allowed and encouraged to participate, in which the central goal would be to repair the harm arising from crime, and in which efforts are made to find solutions which mutually benefit victims, offenders, and crime-affected communities. On other vital questions, however, advocates tend to be silent, vague, and occasionally incoherent, although there are important exceptions (e.g. Van Ness and Strong, 2006: chap. 9, who consider models of how restorative justice might be integrated with contemporary criminal justice; see also the *RJ City* Project, in particular, the paper summarizing phase 1 of the project at <http://www.rjcity.org>).

One fundamental question is how much of the existing criminal justice system will be retained, in more or less its current form, in a fully restorative justice system. Advocates of restorative justice often write or talk as if many central features of this system will be dismantled. Hence, restorative justice is frequently contrasted sharply with retributive justice, state justice, legal justice, adversarial justice, and coercive justice—with the implication that none of these things will form part of a system of justice that is fully restorative. Indeed, restorative justice is often contrasted with criminal justice, implying that a fully restorative system will be something other than criminal justice.

As Zehr (2002: 58–9) (who himself in his earlier writing drew a sharp contrast between retributive justice and restorative justice) has pointed out, such ways of representing restorative justice are misleading and result in restorative justice advocates failing to address important issues (see also Roche, 2007). For instance, we can presume that, in order to have a restorative response to the commission of crimes, a police force will be needed. Its role, moreover, would include exercising coercion over those who commit crime but do not respond to invitations to take part in a restorative process or who do not cooperate with such processes. This will surely be the case even if offenders are far less likely to want to avoid the justice process if it is restorative rather than punitive (since they will have much less to lose from it and even much to gain). Even allowing for this, participating in restorative justice will be burdensome and even painful for offenders, and many will seek to avoid it. So, despite frequent claims that restorative justice is a voluntary alternative to coercion and violence (cf. Van Ness and Strong, 2006: 73), it will only be possible to practice restorative justice if the coercive forces that make the practice of conventional criminal justice possible remain largely in place.

If we accept that restorative justice is inconceivable without the use of coercion, we need to think about how individuals will be protected from unjustified coercion. Police powers will presumably need to be legally defined and citizens will need legal assistance to ensure that limits are not transgressed. Then, what do we do if people accused of crime deny doing what they are charged with, or deny that their behaviour was criminal, or deny that it fits the criteria of a particular crime of which they are accused? These disputed issues would need to be resolved before we could proceed with restorative dialogue, and the resolution process will need to be governed by a sophisticated system of substantive and procedural criminal law. In short, unless restorative justice advocates indicate otherwise, it seems that a fully restorative system of justice will have to rest upon a system of legal, adversarial, coercive, state-controlled criminal justice that is pretty much like the one we have at present. Hence, the presentation of restorative justice as an alternative to legal justice, state justice, adversarial justice, etc. is very misleading.

In fact, if we look carefully at the practical proposals of restorative justice, as opposed to its rhetoric, it seems clear that what is proposed is an alternative way of proceeding in cases where somebody admits to committing a crime either at a pre-trial stage of the criminal justice process, or after they have been convicted but before they are sentenced, or after they have been sentenced. In such circumstances, it is proposed that the case be fully or partially diverted from conventional criminal justice proceedings towards restorative processes.

There are still a range of important questions to ask about the above scheme. For instance, are all such cases suitable for a fully restorative process? Or, are there some cases where conventional penal interventions are necessary and justifiable, although they may be supplemented with restorative interventions? If the latter, how does one distinguish between cases appropriate for a fully restorative process and those which are not? Is it to do with the seriousness of the offence and if so by what criteria is seriousness to be determined? Or, is it to do with other matters such as the attitude of the victim?

 CASE STUDY: A RESTORATIVE INTERVENTION

'I was a recently divorced mother of three children and we had moved into a new home. One New Year's Day I discovered all four tyres on my car were flat, I was devastated. It was snowing heavily; we were going to visit my elderly father who lived six miles away....

Over the next nine months my car was badly damaged on eleven separate occasions... I felt angry, scared and inadequate... One morning my car was broken into and the radio stolen... Collecting my daughter later that night the damaged wires left behind from the theft caused my car to catch fire. My daughter was in the back... terrified...

Three offenders were caught stealing my car... I gave a statement and presumed that was the end of the matter...

I then received a telephone call from the Police. Two of the offenders had been charged and the third was to receive a caution. I was asked if I would like to consider attending a conference where I would meet the offender and his parents and talk to him about the effects his actions had had on myself and my family... I didn't know what would happen during the conference and what the offender or his parents would be like. I went alone feeling nervous and anxious...

I was shown into the conference room and made comfortable by the facilitator, Stuart... When the offender came in with his family I could see they were nervous too which made me feel better. Stuart began by asking the offender to tell everyone what has happened. He sunk into his chair whilst he told us the events of that evening. As he spoke the questions that were in my head were beginning to be answered and I hadn't yet said a word. My imagination was replaced with reality and I began to relax.

He was uncomfortable talking but carried on anyway, he was left to take his time and gradually the whole story came out. The more honest I believed John was being the better I felt…It was a very emotional experience for everyone…

John began to look me in the eye towards the end and his mum stopped crying. I was asked what I wanted out of the conference? I had already received what I need without asking—an apology. As soon as he looked at me and said how sorry he was for what he had done I felt a hundred times better. He was not only apologising for stealing my car but also for the consequences of his actions. He was absolutely horrified when he heard what had happened to my family. He realised he had actually done far more than he ever intended.

Weeks later I saw John at my local newsagents. We stopped and spoke to one another and I asked him how things were going. It was a pleasure for me to hear how much better things were in his life. He still had problems but he was confident and determined not to re-offend. He felt much better about himself…

No one could have convinced me in words that this process would have made such a difference to how I was feeling. My faith in the police was restored. After the conference, I started sleeping again and could switch the light off at night for the first time in months…'

(Used with the permission of the Restorative Justice Consortium. This is an edited version—for the full version and other case studies go to <http://www.restorativejustice.org.uk/?Media:Case_Studies>).

Limits to reparation

Restorative justice advocates have powerful things to say about the limitations and adverse consequences of responding to crime by punishing offenders. They also have convincing things to say about the advantages of holding offenders liable to restitution or repair of the harm they have caused. However, there are fundamental limitations to reparative responses which need to be recognised.

For instance, restorative justice advocates seem to have a strong argument when they say that reparation is essential to create an experience of justice in the aftermath of crime, and that a criminal justice system which fails to encourage offenders to recognise a liability to repair the harm they have done is failing to provide a rich experience of justice. It also seems reasonable to suggest that the question of reparation should be dealt with first, before asking what punishment, if any, the offender deserves. Moreover, as Christie (2003) suggests, the question of punishment might then be transformed into the question of what burdens or suffering if any offenders should undergo *in addition* to those incurred in the process of repairing harm.

However, to the extent that some restorative justice advocates argue that reparation can completely take the place of imposing a just measure of pain upon offenders, they seem on weaker ground both morally and practically. Indeed, insistence on such an argument is probably a major factor in creating the perception that restorative justice may be appropriate for many juvenile offenders and less serious forms of criminal wrongdoing, but not for serious crime. The public are highly unlikely to accept reparation as a replacement for punishment according to *just deserts* for serious crime. Nor is this due to backward thinking that might be overcome: the moral arguments for punishing serious wrongdoers, although not foolproof, seem at least as solid as those for not punishing (Duff, 2001).

The crucial point, however, is that this need not exclude restorative justice and that a commitment to restorative justice has profound implications for the way in which we punish and the amount of punishment we impose on wrongdoers (Duff, 2001). The insistence on presenting punishment and restorative justice as stark alternatives has hampered the development of restorative justice because it has resulted in many advocates failing to think in any detail about what a response to serious offending incorporating restorative justice would look like. This is changing, however, and the issues of whether reparation can take the place of punishment, and whether punishment has a place in restorative justice, is emerging as a matter of serious debate within the restorative justice movement (cf. Duff, 2001).

Problems with lay participation

As we have seen a central theme of restorative justice is that participation in the justice process should be opened up to lay people affected by a criminal offence. This proposal is frequently condemned as dangerous and naïve by adherents to traditional conceptions of criminal justice who regard professional control as a crucial condition for an impartial, rational, and civilised system of criminal justice. To allow and encourage victims and members of the public to participate directly in the process by which it is decided what to do about a crime is tantamount, for many, to placing such decision making in the hands of people who, because of their personal interest in the matter and their lack of expertise, are in no position to reach fair and judicious decisions (Ashworth, 2003).

Equally alarming for such critics are related suggestions, such as that victims and offenders should encounter each other directly, as part of the criminal justice process and without being legally represented. It is argued that, without legal representation, vulnerable offenders and victims will often 'agree' to decisions which are by no means in their interests and which may be contrary to their rights. Further, in such encounters, there is every chance of vulnerable participants being stigmatised, hectored, humiliated, and dominated (Roche, 2003: 2).

One response to such objections is that they are based on the assumption that what is being discussed and decided in restorative encounters is the punishment to be inflicted upon offenders, whereas in fact restorative encounters are about teaching and healing. In such a context, it is suggested, the sort of professional controls and legal regulation which are quite appropriate in punitive contexts are entirely inappropriate (Moore, 1993).

The problem with this response is that, as we have seen, restorative encounters will inevitably take place within a wider coercive system of criminal justice. In such a context, even if the outcome sought is not punishment of the offender (or not described as punishment of the offender) it is still necessary to ensure that the process is subject to control and legal regulation. A more fruitful line of argument may be to follow the lead of Roche (2003) who accepts that the concerns of critics are warranted, but goes on to argue that it is possible to design new forms of accountability for these processes which are consistent with the broad principles of restorative justice. His detailed account of what such a system of accountability would look like is a model of the hard thinking which restorative justice advocates need to undertake if they are to make a convincing case for a less formal, more participatory justice process in which there can be public confidence.

REVIEW QUESTIONS

1 Precisely how would the existing system of criminal justice be reformed if the ideas of restorative justice were implemented in full?

2 Can reparation take the place of punishment for serious crime?

3 Have restorative justice advocates responded satisfactorily to concerns about their proposals for lay participation in the justice system?

CONCLUSION

Restorative justice provides a challenging new way of thinking about the purpose of criminal justice and how it should be practiced. It encourages us to reconsider taken-for-granted notions about what crime is, what we should try to achieve when responding to it, how we should relate to those who commit it, and who should take part in the justice process.

Certain processes such as victim-offender mediation and conferencing are closely associated with restorative justice. However, these processes are not themselves restorative justice. Rather, restorative justice consists of a broader pattern of thinking about what crime is, what aims and values should guide our response to it, and how these aims and values can be best pursued in practice. Leading advocates of restorative justice insist that certain processes can only be restorative if used as part of a broader approach to crime guided by *restorative values*.

Restorative justice advocates present us with a dream of a future in which justice is fully restorative. However, the image of such a justice has yet to be clearly and comprehensively articulated. In order to do this, restorative justice advocates need to revise some of their rhetoric, which although useful for getting the restorative justice movement going and arousing interest, is now misleading as a guide to what is actually proposed. What is now needed is an image of a reformed criminal justice system in which key restorative justice ideas—such as the need for reparation and stakeholder participation—have been fully integrated.

QUESTIONS FOR DISCUSSION

1 Who would gain, and in what ways, if restorative justice became the standard way of viewing and responding to crime?

2 Would anything of value be lost?

3 Overall, how desirable would such a change be?

4 Even if it is desirable, is a significant move towards restorative justice a realistic option for contemporary societies?

ACKNOWLEDGEMENT

The author is grateful to Daniel Van Ness and the late Brian Williams for their helpful comments on an earlier draft.

GUIDE TO FURTHER READING

Johnstone, G. (2002) *Restorative justice: Ideas, Values, Debates*. Cullompton: Willan.

An introduction to the most fundamental and distinctive ideas of restorative justice and to the key arguments for and against it.

Johnstone, G. (ed) (2003) *A Restorative Justice Reader: Texts, sources, context*. Cullompton: Willan.

An edited collection of key original literature on restorative justice, encompassing a range of authors and topics from a number of continents.

Johnstone G. and Van Ness, D. (eds) (2007) *Handbook of Restorative Justice*. Cullompton: Willan.

A comprehensive, authoritative, and accessible survey of the field of restorative justice.

Van Ness, D. and Strong, K. (2006) *Restoring Justice: An Introduction to Restorative Justice* (3rd edn). Cincinnati: OH: Anderson.

A highly comprehensible introduction to the theory and practice of restorative justice and to key issues in the field.

Zehr, H. (1990) *Changing Lenses: A New Focus for Crime and Justice*. Scottdale, PA: Herald Press.

Zehr, sometimes called the grandfather of restorative justice, presents his classic critique of the retributive paradigm and proposes a restorative alternative.

WEB LINKS

http://www.restorativejustice.org.uk/

Website of the British-based *Restorative Justice Consortium* which brings together a range of organisations and groups with an interest in restorative justice. Lots of useful links and resources, and advice on how to get involved in restorative justice.

http://www.restorativejustice.org/

Restorative justice online—invaluable website maintained by the Prison Fellowship International under general editorship of Daniel Van Ness (a leading US-based authority on restorative justice).

http://www.rjcity.org/

To quote its creators: 'an adventurous and perhaps audacious attempt to imagine a city of 1,000,000 responding as restoratively as possible to all crimes, all victims and all offenders'.

http://www.euforumrj.org/

The European Forum for restorative justice aims to establish and develop victim-offender mediation and other restorative justice practices throughout Europe.

http://www.homeoffice.gov.uk/crime-victims/victims/restorative-justice/

The Home Office's restorative justice website. Useful for information on government-sponsored or approved initiatives.

REFERENCES

Acorn, A. (2004) *Compulsory Compassion: A Critique of Restorative Justice*. Vancouver: UBC Press.

Ashworth, A. (2003) 'Responsibilities, Rights and Restorative Justice' in G. Johnstone (ed) *A Restorative Justice Reader*. Cullompton: Willan Publishing, 426–37.

Barnett, R. (2003) 'Restitution: A New Paradigm of Criminal Justice' in G. Johnstone (ed) *A Restorative Justice Reader*. Cullompton: Willan Publishing, 46–56.

Braithwaite, J. (1989) *Crime, Shame and Reintegration*. Cambridge: Cambridge University Press.

Braithwaite, J. (2003) 'Restorative Justice and a Better Future' in G. Johnstone (ed) *A Restorative Justice Reader*. Cullompton: Willan Publishing, 83–97.

Bush, R. and Folger, J. (1994) *The Promise of Mediation: Responding to Conflict through Empowerment and Recognition*. San Francisco: Jossey-Bass Publishers.

Cayley, D. (1998) *The Expanding Prison: The Crisis in Crime and Punishment and the Search for Alternatives*. Cleveland, OH: Pilgrim Press.

Christie, N. (2003) 'Conflicts as Property', in G. Johnstone (ed) *A Restorative Justice Reader*. Cullompton: Willan Publishing, 57–68.

Dignan, J. (2005) *Understanding Victims and Restorative Justice*. Maidenhead: Open University Press.

Duff, R. A. (2001) *Punishment, Communication, and Community*. New York: Oxford University Press.

Home Office (2003) *Restorative Justice: the Government's strategy*. London: Home Office Communication Directorate. Available at: <http://www.crimereduction.homeoffice.gov.uk/workingoffenders/workingoffenders42.htm>.

Johnstone, G. (2002) *Restorative Justice: Ideas, Values, Debates*. Cullompton: Willan Publishing.

Johnstone, G. (2007) 'Critical Perspectives on Restorative Justice' in G. Johnstone and D. Van Ness (eds) *Handbook of Restorative Justice*. Cullompton: Willan Publishing, 598–614.

Johnstone, G. and Van Ness, D. (2007) 'The Meaning of Restorative Justice' in G. Johnstone and D. Van Ness (eds) *Handbook of Restorative Justice*. Cullompton: Willan Publishing, 5–23.

Larson Sawin, J. and Zehr, H. (2007) 'The Ideas of Engagement and Empowerment' in G. Johnstone and D. Van Ness (eds) *Handbook of Restorative Justice*. Cullompton: Willan Publishing, 41–58.

Matthews, R. (ed) (1988) *Informal Justice?* London: Sage.

Miers, D. (2007) 'The International Development of Restorative Justice' in G. Johnstone and D. Van Ness (eds) *Handbook of Restorative Justice*. Cullompton: Willan Publishing, 447–67.

Moberly, W. (1968) *The Ethics of Punishment*. London: Faber and Faber.

Moore, D. (1993) 'Shame, Forgiveness and Juvenile Justice'. *Criminal Justice Ethics* 12(1): 3–25.

Moore, D. and O'Connell, T. (2003) 'Family Conferencing in Wagga Wagga: a Communitarian Model of Justice' in G. Johnstone (ed) *A Restorative Justice Reader*. Cullompton: Willan Publishing, 212–24.

Morris, A. and Maxwell, G. (2003) 'Restorative Justice in New Zealand: Family Group Conferences as a Case Study' in G. Johnstone (ed) *A Restorative Justice Reader*. Cullompton: Willan Publishing, 201–11.

Pavlich, G. (2005) *Governing Paradoxes of Restorative Justice*. London: Glasshouse Press.

Peachey, D. (2003) 'The Kitchener Experiment' in G. Johnstone (ed) *A Restorative Justice Reader*. Cullompton: Willan Publishing, 178–96.

Pranis, K. (2007) 'Restorative Values' in G. Johnstone and D. Van Ness (eds) *Handbook of Restorative Justice*. Cullompton: Willan Publishing, 59–74.

Roche, D. (2003) *Accountability in Restorative Justice*. Oxford: Oxford University Press.

Roche, D. (2007) 'Retribution and Restorative Justice' in G. Johnstone and D. Van Ness (eds) *Handbook of Restorative Justice*. Cullompton: Willan Publishing, 75–90.

Strang, H. and Braithwaite, J. (eds) (2001) *Restorative Justice and Civil Society*. Cambridge: Cambridge University Press.

Van Ness, D. and Strong, K. (2006) *Restoring Justice* (3rd edn). Cincinnati: OH: Anderson.

Zehr, H. (1990) *Changing Lenses: A New Focus for Crime and Justice*. Scottdale, PA: Herald Press.

Zehr, H. (2002) *The Little Book of Restorative Justice*. Intercourse, PA: Good Books.

10 Probation and offender management

Mike Nellis and Anthony Goodman

INTRODUCTION

This chapter is concerned with the protracted and controversial process by which the Probation Service in England and Wales was finally subsumed into a *National Offender Management Service* (NOMS). The New Labour government, building on the previous Conservative one, repeatedly portrayed these reforms as a necessary process of public sector modernisation, a means of making the sector more cost effective and efficient. Some of the earlier challenges to the Probation Service, including some that pre-dated New Labour's election victory in 1997, were arguably necessary, because the service had clung to practice ideals that had been formed a generation earlier, and were genuinely in need of renewal. In respect of the later New Labour initiatives it is, however, impossible to find any serious *criminologi-cal* or *administrative* justification for them, and it is less surprising that they were strongly resisted by the service itself. The *Home Office* (and later the *Ministry of Justice*), and indeed some academics and professionals, tend to portray the 'big probation story' in the first eight years of the twenty-first century as a move towards more effective forms of practice, underpinned by a more appropriate organizational structure. While that was part of it, conceptions of effectiveness were actually redesigned to suit new organisational forms that progressively gave central government much more control over the activities and ethos of the service, in ways which left little room for what the service itself might have thought of as good practice.

Given the breadth and depth of change that has taken place in the period variously designated 'late modernity' or (by Bauman (2007)) *'liquid times'*, some degree of modernisation (and its corollary, detradi-tionalisation) was inevitable and desirable. Governments, businesses, and citizens in the West have had to adapt to *globalisation* and to changed social and cultural circumstances—diminished security, fore-shortened time-horizons, greater individualisation, and weakened solidarities—in their own countries. The emergence of a 'culture of control' within Western criminal justice systems has been a key feature of such adaptation—and there was never an option for any Probation Service anywhere in the world to retain the *pure* social work identity upon which it was (probably) founded and to which its traditions and practices have given expression. But while 'the culture of control' has indeed been exported globally (largely emanating from the USA), it is not inexorably implanted everywhere to exactly the same extent (Newburn and Sparks, 2004, Lacey, 2008). Different countries and different institutions within countries adapt differently, depending on particular political-professional configurations and the general relation-ship between state and civil society. Different outcomes can result, confirming what philosopher John Gray (2003) has repeatedly pointed out, that there is more than one way to be modern.

The focus of this chapter will largely be on *probation* events between 2002 and 2008. It will focus on the way in which a National Offender Management Service was promoted to supersede the newly cre-ated National Probation Service before the latter had time to bed down and work effectively. While there was considerable academic and policy-relevant debate about the future of the Probation Service in this period, it has to be said that academics in traditional policy communities had very little influence on the process of change, either as researchers or reflective commentators (Chui and Nellis, 2003; Winstone and Pakes, 2005; Hough, Allen, and Padel, 2006; Morgan and Gelsthorpe, 2007). The serious challenges to NOMS were led by the Probation Boards Association (PBA) and the *National Association of Probation Officers* (Napo), who (sometimes in conjunction with academics) had a better understanding of what frontline effectiveness at local level entailed and promoted better models of professionalism and service governance. The PBA in particular had a strong orientation towards the future, but both organisations were conscious, particularly in 2007, the service's centenary year, of having a tradition to defend.

BACKGROUND

There is a difference between tradition—an imagined sense of what the past has been, which serves present interests and future ambitions—and history, a scholarly chronological record of events. While space precludes a detailed account of the latter, a rich and still expanding literature on it has emerged in late modernity (Raynor, 2002; Vanstone, 2004; Whitehead and Statham, 2006; Nellis, 2007; Vanstone and Raynor, 2007), precisely because the service's sense of tradition has been under threat, and historical evidence has been felt necessary to shore it up. The new probation history has in fact been much more sensitive to the social, cultural, and political circumstances in which probation developed in the late nineteenth and twentieth centuries, and goes beyond the merely administrative accounts (Bochel, 1976: Radzinowicz and Hood, 1986)—and McWilliam's (1983; 1985; 1986; 1987) four-part history of guiding ideas in the service—which had prevailed until then. Fine-grained administrative accounts remain important, however, because they tend to show that in any given structural and cultural configuration, within certain parameters, more than one political strategy and administrative option—marginally better or worse ways of doing reform—is possible. Political and professional struggle is always worthwhile: it may not achieve all its goals, and it may have to compromise, but with a mix of measured argument, obstinacy, and attrition it may at least prevent the worst from coming to the worst. Actual outcomes at particular moments in probation's history have been far more contingent than is often realised, dependent on the agency of particular individuals and organizations at particular times, and impinged upon by unforeseen events, rather than being inexorably determined by impersonal structural imperatives.

Thus from 1876 the Church of England Temperance Society did supply 'missionaries' (to the few urban police courts whose magistrates were willing to have them) in order to save alcohol-affected offenders and their families from the revolving door of imprisonment, but the long campaign of the Howard Association (later the Howard League for Penal Reform) and its allies to import and adapt the model of probation established in Massachusetts was arguably more important in generating the Probation of Offenders Act in 1907. This Act created the Probation Order as an 'alternative to *punishment*' and specified that its purpose was to 'advise, assist and befriend' those whom the courts placed under the supervision of a 'probation officer' (an American term). There was, however, no *sudden* infusion of humanitarianism in the penal system. The expansion of probation in England was slow, and embroiled in an increasingly bitter dispute between the Home Office and the National Association of Probation Officers (founded in 1912), on the one hand, who favoured a secular orientation to probation, and the tenacious influence of the Church of England's more theological *temperance*-oriented approach. The secularists won, but quasi-Christian ideals about the redeemability of offenders continued to influence probation even as it adopted a more scientific, treatment-oriented approach, so much so that at its half-century in 1957 it was celebrated, by government and the service alike, as a Christian—and quintessentially British—institution.

Throughout the 1960s the service grew even closer, philosophically, to other fields of social work, even while it had tasks imposed upon it by government—aftercare and the supervision of parolees—which required a more controlling, and sometimes coercive, stance which initially made many of its frontline staff uneasy. The main threat to the service in this period, however, was structural rather than ideological. The then Labour government planned to merge it into new 'generic' Social Services Departments that were coming into being as a result of drastic reforms to the provision of social work in local authorities (Hall, 1976). From the outset, the service and the local committees of magistrates to whom it was administratively accountable resisted this—but it was contingency and expedience rather than strategy that was to save the service. Had it not been for the calling of an election in 1970, and the Home Office's need to drop the more controversial aspects of the bill—like incorporating probation—in order to get the legislation onto the statute book before Parliament was adjourned, it is highly likely that the Probation Service would indeed have ceased to exist at that point, and become part of local government social services provision. This is what happened in Scotland (under equivalent legislation—see McIvor and McNeill, 2007) and whilst perceived at the time by probation officers in both countries as a regressive development, Scotland has actually proved able to sustain a welfare ethos in its approach to supervising adult offenders in the community for far longer than the Probation Service did south of the border.

In England and Wales, emboldened by its survival, chastened by its close shave, the service added a more sociological perspective on offending to its existing psychological one, and became almost as concerned with promoting *social justice* as providing alternatives to custody and rehabilitative interventions. It nonetheless questioned whether or not day training centres and Community Service Orders, introduced in the Criminal Justice Act 1972, were consistent with its social work ethos, before somewhat reluctantly accepting administrative responsibility for them. In the late 1970s Napo's leadership came under Marxist influence and promoted 'critical probation practice'—its equivalent of the 'radical social work' then developing in local authorities and on academic training courses—but a key consequence of this 'turn' was the final breaking of its once close and collaborative relationship with the Home Office. Except in pockets, frontline probation practice did not become seriously Marxist or socialist—not all field probation officers, especially the older generation, were comfortable with Napo's stance—but it is true that in the 1980s the service began to conceive of itself less as a servant of the court, and more of an independent (albeit part of a wider social work) profession. This lost them the sympathy of some magistrates, whilst the cloying purity of their claim to a social work identity—at least where this produced ambivalence towards the provision of alternatives to custody, and the elements of control required—sometimes irritated their more pragmatic allies in the penal reform network.

Simultaneously with these developments—and perhaps paradoxically—debates were being initiated among a rising cadre of younger managers in the service, aligned with some old hands, asking whether or not probation supervision did indeed need to become more controlling, given the perception that some of those under supervision, particularly those on *parole*, were more difficult, dangerous, and risky than clients had hitherto been. Critics of this cadre caricatured it as the 'sentenced to surveillance' movement and felt that it was unnecessarily repudiating social work ideals. Whilst by no means dominant in the service, this cadre had nonetheless made its presence felt *before* the Conservative government proposed changing probation into an agency of 'punishment in the community' in 1988, and announced plans for central government control over the 55 relatively autonomous local probation areas (Home Office, 1988). The service—Napo in particular, still radical, but no longer Marxist—vigorously resisted both threats to its autonomy and the taint of punishment, initially with some success, insisting that this was utterly dissonant with its 'social work traditions', and with the welfare-based training of its staff. The proud sense of tradition which it constructed to defend and explain itself in an increasingly hostile climate obscured the more desultory, contingent, and indeed controlling aspects of its history, and privileged a narrative of enduring professional altruism. There is no doubt, in fact, that in the post-World War II years the service had indeed been staffed by people who sincerely believed that tough-minded compassion had a key place in the reform of offenders, and who were deeply resentful of the political pressure to embrace punishment (Napo, 2007). Examples of tough-minded compassion in practice in the post-War era are legion (see, for example, Goodman, 2007), and although there was little formal evaluation in this period, there was much, morally speaking, to commend the service's socially inclusive stance towards offenders. In the course of the 1990s the service recognised that it needed to discover more effective, evidence-based methods of rehabilitative practice—to prove '*what works*'—in order to defend itself politically and publicly against the retributive ethos that was being imposed upon it. On the basis of largely Canadian evidence (Ross and Fabiano, 1990) it took up the idea of short, intensive groupwork programmes using cognitive behavioural principles which were designed to change offenders' attitudes and behaviour, e.g. the Mid-Glamorgan 'Straight Thinking on Probation' project (Raynor and Vanstone, 1993). On the basis of such initiatives, spearheaded by the Probation Inspectorate, the service looked hopefully towards the prospect of a Labour government in May 1997, only to find that their views were not significantly different from the Conservatives who had first attacked it.

Probation reform under New Labour: the early years

Whilst in opposition, Tony Blair had wrested 'law and order' from its traditional place as a bastion of Conservative Party ideology, and his New Labour government embarked on a root and branch reform of the criminal justice system, initiating both short-term and (ostensibly) long-term changes. To the chagrin of some in the Probation Service one of the Government's first steps was the setting up of a Prisons-Probation Review (Home Office, 1998) which had the clear intention of merging prisons and probation into a single organisation. Such was the opposition to this—from both dominant voices in the Probation and Prison Services, and among sentencers—that the idea of merger was dropped. This move also reflected a residual sense of deference towards the Probation Service, a belief in government that it had to be a willing partner in any change process. The Probation Service had, in any case, its own ideas about its future, borne of reflection on the intense criticism of its alleged ineffectiveness in reducing *crime* and protecting the public to which the previous Conservative government had subjected it. The service, whose intellectual leadership resided in the Probation Inspectorate at this point, con-cluded that the way forward was to deliver high quality effective practice programmes carefully targeted on offenders according to clear criteria of risk and need. There were officials in the Home Office who agreed with this, and indeed the Home Office took it upon itself to accredit the new programmes, thereby becoming the arbiter, for the first time in the service's history, of good and bad probation practice (Goodman, 2003; Mair, 2004). Thus, the compromise position after the failure of the Prisons Probation Review to deliver the merged structure that key Home Office officials had wanted was the *centrali-sation* of the Probation Service—the reconfiguring of (the once relatively autonomous) local Probation Service areas from 54 to 42 (to make them coterminous with Police Service and Crown Prosecution areas) and the establishment of the National Probation Directorate (NPD) to lead it, with (for the first time) its own Director-General, on a par with the already existing Director-General of the Prison Service. The purpose of the new service would be to deliver effective practice to agreed national standards. The National Probation Service (NPS) and the creation of local Probation Boards in each of the 42 areas was legislated for in the Criminal Justice and Court Services Act 2000 and established operationally in 2002.

Centralisation and a commitment to the more or less standardised delivery of new forms of effective practice represented a dramatic change in the structure and culture of the service. Some of the smaller local services had to merge, and all services now had to orient themselves towards NPD edicts in a way which, whilst not without precedent, required greater attentiveness (and time) than ever before. Managerial energies inevitably flowed upwards, towards the NPD, away from frontline practice—precisely at a time when the introduction of new forms of practice required considerable managerial flair and professional judgement. The newly appointed members of Probation Boards—often local business people hitherto unfamiliar with Service, rather than, as in the past, magistrates who were familiar with it—needed time to learn the strengths and weaknesses of their local services and to evolve a role for themselves. The NPD encouraged them to think of themselves as endorsers and enforcers of centrally made decisions, whereas the newly formed Probation Board's Association (PBA) (which represented them nationally) encouraged them to be responsive champions of distinct local needs and approaches. The National Association of Probation Officers (Napo), which had functioned for decades as both a professional association and a trade union, had supported the centralisation of the service and the prestigious post of Director-General, but remained concerned that the new body did not become too centrally driven, or merely target-driven, or too single-minded in its pursuit of the new effective practice programmes when tried and tested older probation methods still had much to offer. While the leadership role of the Probation Inspectorate changed once the NPD was established, it remained a significant voice in respect of the development and direction of the service. All of this meant that the years after 2002 would inevitably become times of tension and uncertainty as the NPD became integrated into the Home Office planning structures and the National Probation Service became a coherent operational reality. There was nonetheless a belief—and a hope—in the service, even among those who had been sceptical of it, that if it were allowed to consolidate itself the National Probation Service would eventually deliver viable forms of offender supervision in the community.

It was not immediately obvious that New Labour's 'permanent revolution' in respect of criminal justice (McLaughlin, Muncie, and Hughes, 2001) would have deeply unsettling consequences for the NPS, not least because—to people *within* the service—jeopardising the potential of such a fledgling body by further organisational upheaval seemed unthinkable. The Criminal Justice Act 2003, whose provisions, derived via the White Paper *Justice for All* (Home Office, 2002) from the Halliday review of sentencing (Home Office, 2001), the Auld review of court structure (Lord Chancellors Department, 2001), and the Social Exclusion Unit's (2002) review of resettlement, would clearly pose implementation challenges to the NPS without any accompanying organisational change. Following Halliday in particular, the 2003 Act proposed a radical restructuring of sentencing, particularly as it affected the supervision of offenders in the community. Among other things, Halliday had proposed the idea of a *'seamless sentence'*—a mix of prison and post-release supervision—as a significant way forward if the ever rising prison population was to be effectively managed. This was a quintessentially detraditionalising/modernising idea, because it blurred a time-honoured distinction in British penal thought between community and custodial penalties. It signalled that the unthinkable had become thinkable. At the time too few people realised that civil servant Halliday had in mind a seamless service to deliver seamless sentences, but this was how the idea of merging prisons and probation into a single organisation, dropped in 1998, regained prominence on internal Home Office agendas. *Justice for All's* recommendation that a review of correctional services be undertaken to assess the implications of Halliday's sentencing proposals was to have very fateful consequences for the NPS. Lord Patrick Carter, a welfare entrepreneur who had already produced a favourable review of contracting-out prisons for the government, was appointed to head the review team.

REVIEW QUESTIONS

1 What does it mean to call probation a social work service in the years prior to 1997?

2 What sort of organization did New Labour want the Probation Service to become?

The advent of National Offender Management Services (NOMS)

The Carter report was published in December 2003. It painted an accurate and disturbing picture of the prevailing penal crisis, derived from the findings and arguments of earlier reports, much of which was already being addressed (or was potentially addressable) by existing strategies, within existing structures. Drawing on Halliday, and on language already in use among Home Office planners, it sought to redefine key elements of the penal vocabulary, affirming the use of 'correctional services' and introducing *'offender management'* and 'end-to-end management of offenders' as slightly more precise analogues of the term 'seamless sentence'. It saw the Social Exclusion Unit's (2002) key finding that the period immediately after release from prison was high risk in terms of re-offending as illustrative of the poor quality of coordination between prison and probation services *at national level*, although the real problem was coordination between particular prisons and particular services *at local level*, and not all practice on this interface was in fact bad, as Fox *et al.* (2005) confirmed later.

At the Carter report's core were twin recommendations for the creation of a National Offender Management Service (NOMS). Its aim was firstly to break down the silo-like mentalities of the prison and probation services and to facilitate joint planning, and secondly to introduce the idea of *contestability*, a strategy for increasing the contracting-out of hitherto public services to the private and voluntary sectors (in respect of both prisons and probation). The potential strain between these two recommendations—one pointing to *unification* of management, the other towards *fragmentation* of service delivery—was obscured by carefully crafted language, and in general the report was long on aspiration and short on operational detail. Despite later Home Office claims to the contrary, it did not amount to a business plan, and nor—given all the change that had gone before—did it make a compelling case for further change. In any case, as penologist Carol Hedderman (2006) later noted, the report's

> underlying assumption that a lack of co-ordination [between prisons and probation] was due to being separate organisations, was questionable. That may be part of the reason but over-stretched resources caused by increased caseloads, staff turnover, poor information technology, and even data protection legislation played their part. Overloading both services with new demands to prioritise without ever saying what they should stop doing has also created cynicism and resistance to new ideas (even the good ones!) (Hedderman, 2006: 43).

The Correctional Services Review was not in any real sense, independent, despite the presence of Lord Carter. It was originally set up within the Home Office, was quickly transplanted into the Prime Minister's Strategy Unit—but was still nonetheless prepared in close alignment with Home Office planners, confirming the direction that some of them already wanted to go in. The *utopian managerialism* exhibited by the report—its willingness to impose the once unthinkable on already overstretched stakeholders—derived significantly from the Strategy Unit, from which blue sky thinking on the modernisation of the public sector routinely emanated. Consultation with those stakeholders during the course of the review had been so minimal as to be meaningless; consultation on its proposals after publication was—astonishingly, given their scope and ambition—even less. The Home Office (2004) itself endorsed the Carter report within a matter of weeks, signalling its intention to proceed along the path outlined. The Carter report was in essence a victory for those cadres in the Home Office who had not got what they wanted from the earlier Prisons-Probation Review and for whom the creation of the NPD, despite hopes to the contrary in the service itself, had been only a stop-gap, a temporary anchorage on the voyage to complete centralisation and unification of correctional services. The Carter review signified the moment when the Probation Service finally ceased to be a partner in change, and became an object of change, to be done to rather than consulted with.

There are other aspects to the Carter report which ought to be examined. The figure of 80,000, at which the daily prison population would be capped, was largely plucked from thin air, partially appeasing hardliners by allowing prisoner numbers to rise beyond their at-the-time level of 67,000, and partially appeasing liberals by placing a clear, down-the-line limit on prison expansion. If the figure was grounded in anything it lay in the—undoubtedly commendable—refusal of the Treasury under Chancellor Gordon Brown to allocate more money for prison building. This was, undeniably, a powerful incentive to make community penalties work more effectively but it still represented a significant failure on Carter's part to be truly bold, and to argue for a phased reduction in prisoner numbers, rather than a controlled rise. The report's utopianism, conceived in terms of a decisively imposed managerial strategy which would bring about large and quantifiable reductions in crime, did not encompass the long-standing and still cogent view of penal reform organisations that England and Wales both could and should seek to reduce its imprisonment levels to something closer to that of more liberal European countries. In the event, however, as we shall see, Carter's figure of 80,000 turned out itself to be an instance of over-the-rainbow optimism.

Carter took for granted that the forthcoming sentencing changes in the Criminal Justice Act 2003 would improve the efficiency and effectiveness of community supervision, but, beyond that, he had a particular and distinct enthusiasm for both existing and new forms of electronic monitoring. His report not only commended the expansion of existing electronically monitored curfews, but also greenlighted the establishment of GPS satellite tracking pilots—something the Home Office had been intending to do since 2000—with the clear implication that the pilots would quickly be mainstreamed. The Home Office's (2004) Strategic Plan, published shortly after the Carter report, fleshed this out, projecting an increase in the use of electronic monitoring from the present day levels of 9,000 per day to 18,000 by 2008. Part of this would be satellite tracking. Both the Carter report and the Strategic Plan were clearly enamoured of the innovative potential of new technologies in offender supervision, which derived from a deep-seated but often unnoticed New Labour belief that the private sector was much better at implementing technological innovation than the public or (by implication) voluntary sectors, and that that was a further reason for cultivating it (Nellis, 2006).

Contestability was, in fact, Carter's big idea. It was arguably—more so than the perceived need to merge services—the rationale of NOMS, the one thing that might not have been politically achievable under the earlier compromise arrangements signified by the NPS. The term 'contestability' had been in use within the Treasury, but only came to wider public prominence in the Carter-inspired debates about the future of the penal system. It meant, in essence, opening up service provision (in a controlled way) to market forces, but beyond that the Government's precise intentions were not particularly clear. At its most minimal, contestability meant no more than 'market testing', comparing and benchmarking the cost-effectiveness of services delivered by the public, private, and voluntary sectors with a view to making the public sector become progressively more efficient and competitive. In its stronger form, contestability seemed to signal an intention to deliberately create a mixed economy of provision, on the grounds that it is only when the public sector actually has real, up-and-running competition, that it becomes truly efficient and competitive. The Home Office officials may well have been divided among themselves as to how far to pursue contestability, but, unsurprisingly, their vagueness led probation service interest groups to worry that drastic intentions were being camouflaged by superficially emollient language.

The National Offender Management Model (NOMM) (Home Office, 2005a; 2005b), issued for consultation in October 2005, fuelled these anxieties. This proposed the winding up of the 42 local Probation Boards, which had merely been tasked with improving the performance of the Probation Service, and their replacement with Probation Trusts which would then compete with voluntary and private organisations to sell probation services to the regional offender managers. To this end trusts would be more business-like, more commercially oriented than boards. This undeniably suggested that the government was committed to the second, strong version of contestability; but once again the kind of detail one might have expected, given the drastic nature of the changes being proposed, was not forthcoming. It was not clear which aspects of probation might be put out to tender—the management of entire local service areas, or just particular services within them—hostels, community punishment, *pre-sentence reports*. It was clear that Probation Trusts could finish up as both commissioners of services and as service deliverers to a commissioning agency above them, raising questions as to which side of the divide probation staff might in future be deployed on. This raised the prospect of very different patterns of provision being established in each of the ten regions—some with more public provision, some with more private or more voluntary provision, with all three relating to the prisons in their area. This mosaic seemingly contradicted the intention to create a more seamless service, undermining NOMS's much vaunted ideal of 'end to end offender management' (Raynor and Maguire, 2006).

Whilst not made explicit by the Home Office, the proposed arrangements would have finally destroyed the Probation Service as a distinct national organisation. For most of its century-long existence the service had been a loosely federated organisation which had progressively been subject to more and more central control, especially after 1984. Talk of replacing it with another organisation had figured in Home Office rhetoric in the late 1980s, deployed then as a way of compelling the Service's compliance with the 'punishment in the community' strategy. In reality there was no other organisation that could, in practice, have replaced the service, and in the event it complied anyway. The creation of the NPD did begin the process of destroying what little remained of local service autonomy, but did not comprehensively jeopardise the existence of the organization and its associated identity. NOMS did both. It sought to create an offender management service made up of multiple service providers in which probation would at best have had only a residual and marginal identity. Any sense of it as a unified profession, with distinct values and forms of practice would finally disappear, subsumed under a dubious rubric that without being precise seemingly encompassed more than *mere* probation—'offender management'.

The second consultation paper (Home Office, 2005b) further galvanised the already strong opposition to NOMS. The absence of an evidence-base to justify the changes was reiterated, especially in respect of contestability. The point was made again that the Probation Service needed local roots and local ties, and to be integrated with other local services, if it was to be effective in *crime reduction*. The service had been far from perfect in this respect in the past, but had made some progress, and in other areas of public policy government seemed to favour localism. In respect of offender management, however, commissioning from ten remote regional headquarters, augmented by commissioning from central government, both threatened the service's progress, and seemingly disregarded the very principle of localism.

Reconfiguring offender supervision: the Criminal Justice Act 2003

The Criminal Justice Act 2003 represented the legislative revolution of which NOMS was notionally the organisational equivalent, the means by which an array of new (or altered) community penalties were to be delivered. By reframing existing community sentences (and adding some new ones) it sought to address two long-perceived problems: how to create credible community sentences which reduce the use of short and wasteful custodial sentences; and how to reduce the incidence of *up-tariffing*. Despite concerns that a single community sentence might confuse rather than clarify judicial decision making for both sentencers and offenders alike, the Probation Service did not oppose its general principles. They were sceptical of the seamless sentences, questioned its workload implications, and saw the simultaneous introduction of legislative and organisational change as singularly inauspicious.

Most of the key changes in the Criminal Justice Act 2003 related to the kind of supervisory penalties for which the Probation Service had traditionally had responsibility, and to the creation of a *Sentencing Guidelines Council* which would advise sentencers on their use (see Chapter 5). The more nominal penalties (various sorts of discharge) and fines were left untouched (despite the Carter report having tried to resurrect the *unit fine system*, which fined offenders in terms of 'units' of daily income, so that rich and poor alike could, notionally, be fined in proportionate ways). In respect of supervisory penalties the key shift was from an array of separate measures which had originated at different points in time, and had different purposes, into a single generic Community Order containing a menu of 12 'requirements' from which sentencers could draw on a pick-and-mix basis.

The Act also legislated for three semi-custodial sentences, which gave expression to the Halliday report's (2001) conception of 'seamlessness' and to the symbolic dissolution of the once hallowed distinction between community and custodial penalties which underpinned the arguments for the creation of NOMS. Suspended sentences (called 'custody minus' in the Halliday report) had existed before as a means of symbolically imposing a custodial sentence without actually sending someone to prison, unless they breached it: henceforth they were to be combinable with any of the requirements available in a community sentence, giving the Probation Service a new role in such sentences. Intermittent custody—entwining elements of custody with elements of community supervision—had been considered several times in the past and always rejected as administratively unwieldy. Even Halliday was sceptical, but the 2003 Act introduced it. After an unsuccessful pilot, it was jettisoned in November 2006. Custody Plus was arguably the 2003 Act's 'flagship order', because it sought ostensibly directly to address the problem of the short custodial sentences, albeit by using even shorter periods of custody (of between two and 23 weeks) backed by a period of community supervision. Critics warned that far from solving the problem it would exacerbate it, by inviting sentencers to up-tariff, and the strategy was abandoned, untried, in July 2006, officially because of insufficient resources.

The Criminal Justice Act 2003 significantly altered processes of *early release* as well as introducing extended periods of imprisonment for dangerous offenders, which were to have significant impact on probation workloads. Most commentators on the 2003 Act believed that, despite its supposed 'fit' with the NOMS strategy, it would increase prison numbers rather than facilitate their capping at 80,000 (Prison Reform Trust, 2005). One aspect of this increase would be the further intensification of already increasing recalls to prison, occasioned firstly by the larger pool of people out on licence, and secondly by the greater pressure on the Probation Service to enforce compliance with licences more rigorously and mechanistically than hitherto. The Act not only required probation officers to breach any second failure to comply, but also required courts to increase the severity of the penalty for breach (which, in the past, they had not always been required to do). Recalls were running at 9,000 per year in 2006—'the equivalent of nine large prisons', as an ex-prisoner-turned-journalist acidly put it (Allison, 2007).

A full discussion of the impact of the new community penalties, implemented from April 2005, is to be found in Mair (this volume), Mair, Cross, and Taylor (2007), and Stanley (2007). Seamlessness has to date not become a reality and the new orders failed to divert offenders from custody or to reduce up-tariffing. Indeed, in respect of the unexpectedly popular suspended sentences, they appeared to compound it. The Home Office's own review of the 2003 Act's operation concluded:

> The evidence so far is that the courts are not using Community Orders as fully as they might. The anticipated switch to these community sentences from short terms of imprisonment that was envisaged has not happened but is a crucial part of the sentencing reform that we wish to achieve. (Home Office, 2006b: 6–7)

It had also became clear, from 2003 onwards, that the effective practice initiative, on which so much emphasis had been placed to secure the Probation Service's future, was proving much less successful than its champions had hoped. Official targets for numbers of offenders going through the programmes had always been too high, and many offenders appear to have been inappropriately placed on them. Both completion rates and recidivism rates (although there was variety in this respect) were lower than expected, and the quality of evaluations varied. Raynor (2004) characterised what had happened as 'finding the path and losing the way', insisting that the programmes were mostly well conceived and that the failure was largely one of implementation, not least too rapid a national roll out of programmes and inadequate case management skills in the service itself. At root he blamed the convulsive changes which the Home Office put the Probation Service through, fuelled by a marked political preference for looking tough rather than smart, and an excessive confidence in grand managerialist strategies. The architects of NOMS had never had as much confidence in the effective practice initiative as the original NPS leadership, and while it never was a perfect strategy, NOMS failed to deliver anything that was genuinely better. It was never clear what 'offender management' might mean in practice.

REVIEW QUESTIONS

1 In what ways were NOMS and the Criminal Justice Act 2003 meant to fit with each other?
2 What were the main elements of the Criminal Justice Act 2003?

The expansion of NOMS

NOMS formally came into being in Spring 2004, administrative work having begun on it from the moment Carter announced it. It never properly became operational, other than as a headquarters organisation, and in a very real sense it began to fail from the moment it was launched. David Blunkett, an ardent moderniser who had nurtured the Carter proposals to fruition, had become *Home Secretary* in 2001, but lost his post, through private folly, in the very year NOMS was first constituted. He had been unimpressed by the (in his view) unmodernised structures left behind by his predecessor Jack Straw, and gave momentum and energy to the new reforms (Pollard, 2005: 271). Because they were still being championed by the Prime Minister's Strategy Unit, Blunkett's successor, Charles Clarke, could not easily have repudiated them, but he seems not to have been as keen, and in any case he became preoccupied with devising new responses to a perceived terrorist threat. He did not relate as well as Blunkett to the NOMS Chief Executive Martin Narey, and in 2005 Narey—a very significant thinker in respect of NOMS—left to become Chief Executive of a children's charity. Helen Edwards, a quietly efficient administrator without his messianic zeal for NOMS, replaced him. Clarke's *Five Year Strategy for Protecting the Public and Reducing Offending* (Home Office, 2006a) in February 2006 reaffirmed both the importance of restricting prison to dangerous, violent, and persistent offenders, endorsed Custody Plus, argued for the reintroduction of community prisons (near to where offenders live, as recommended by the Woolf report (Woolf and Tumim, 1991)), and suggested the rebranding of 'unpaid work' as 'community payback'. The NOMS goal of stabilising the prison population at 80,000 was, however, being threatened by inauspicious sentencing trends, and by September 2005 Clarke had abandoned it. In October 2005 the prison population surpassed 80,000 for the first time, and continued to rise.

In May 2006 Clarke lost his job after media revelations that foreign prisoners designated for deportation after sentence remained at large in the community, because of a failure of communication between the immigration and prison services. His successor as Home Secretary, John Reid, inherited a department reeling from criticism on several fronts and inevitably promised significant changes. No further word was heard on community prisons, but in July 2006 it was announced that Custody Plus was being abandoned and that a further 8,000 prison places would be created, albeit by 2012, well after current capacity had been reached. The perception of failure and inadequacy in the Home Office drew scorn from the Conservative opposition and the conservative press, and to regain the initiative Prime Minister and Home Secretary resorted to talking tough, declaring that the criminal justice system was still in need of 'rebalancing' in the interests of victims and away from the interests of criminals (as if, after years of progressively harsher policies, a kind of offender-friendly libertarianism still prevailed!) (Home Office, 2006c). The various proposals that went with this—including the tough-sounding Violent Offender Orders, Parental Compensation Orders, and even swifter returns to custody for those who breach licences—would inevitably increase the prison population; but without the constraint of a policy commitment to cap the prison population at 80,000, punitive rhetoric ruled.

Probation Inspectorate reports into the murders of John Monkton and Naomi Bryant in London and Winchester respectively (HM Inspectorate of Probation, 2006a; 2006b) by released prisoners under supervision cast the service in a bad light in respect of high-risk offenders. The Home Office used the reports to legitimate the 'improvements' they were making, while the Opposition claimed that those very changes were damaging—or at least not improving practice. The report on Bryant claimed that the service had attended excessively to the human rights of the parolee who killed her, and inevitably played into existing Conservative animus towards human rights legislation. Further revelations about the torture and murder of a 16-year-old girl by five men under probation supervision in Reading left no doubt about the riskiness of some offenders on probation caseloads. While the PBA (2007: 3) rightly said of all three cases that they were 'isolated examples of failure which were seized upon to denigrate the service as a whole' and expose the very real inadequacies in front line practice, the question of what it might take to actually improve practice—as opposed to endlessly redesigning service delivery structures—was not adequately explored.

Meanwhile, the prison population continued rising, and apart from exhortations to sentencers to use the Criminal Justice Act 2003 as intended, early release was the only safety valve that Reid had. His first attempt to use this in August 2006 (releasing 30,000 prisoners ten days early on a hastily invented 'transitional home leave' scheme, freeing up 500 prison places) was, however, blocked by the Prime Minister's Office, who feared an adverse media reaction. In October he resurrected a legal power to use police station cells to alleviate prison overcrowding, and by January 2007 was using court cells as well. In June 2007 the government finally bowed to the inevitable and used the safety valve—1,000 prisoners serving under four year sentences were released 18 days early, reducing the daily prison population by 1,200 (Fletcher, 2007a). Nothing illustrated better than these developments the abject failure of the core NOMS strategy. Not only had prison numbers not been capped, thereby soaking up resources that had been intended for non-custodial measures, but the sudden early releases, for which many local probation services did not have the supervisory resources to cope, meant that reducing reoffending in the initial phase of resettlement, one of the key problems that NOMS had aspired to address remained a mere pipedream (except in the pre-existing pockets of good practice). The reality of short-term imprisonment and post-release work in 2007 was less the 'end-to-end management' that NOMS had promised, and more endless 'end-to-end *crisis* management'.

 CASE STUDY: PRIVATE SECTOR INVOLVEMENT IN CRIMINAL JUSTICE

The private sector became a small but significant presence in penal provision in England and Wales with the advent of 'contracted-out prisons' and the provision of electronic monitoring. It has always been unclear how much lobbying of government by individual companies goes on behind the scenes, and while there is no doubt that, once contracted, companies are subject to detailed regulatory regimes, it is not unreasonable, now, to think of the private sector more generally as an active force in penal politics, and not merely as a service provider. In the course of the twenty-first century the business community's most influential pressure group, the Confederation of British Industries (CBI) became a significant public voice for increased private sector involvement in penal provision. Its accumulated thinking is distilled in a report, *Getting back on the Straight and Narrow: a better criminal justice system for all* (CBI, 2008). It portrays commercial organizations as more innovative than public sector ones, implies that it has espoused more decent values in the treatment of prisoners, takes pride in having challenged the vested interests of trade unions, and claims to have saved taxpayers money. It makes its own case for contestability, commissioning, and transformational change, arguing that within current political and administrative structures the private sector is simply not able to make as strong a contribution to penal affairs as it is capable of doing, to the detriment of the nation as a whole. Some of its proposals, such as increasing the employability of offenders, are undoubtedly worthwhile, but are hardly original. Its claim that the 11 privately-run prisons in England and Wales are indisputably cheaper to run than public ones, and that their success in meeting various key performance indicators is underappreciated by government, is more suspect. Most worryingly it simply accepts that the prison estate needs to expand its capacity, at least to allow for an estimated daily prison population of 96,000 by 2012. The above report and the activities of the private sector in the penal market more generally would repay further study.

The survival of NOMS

Despite early evidence that the NOMS strategy was not working, and that its critics had been right, Reid had still pressed on with legislation to introduce contestability into service provision, in what seemed like a desperate bid to salvage the one last remnant of policy from the Carter report. The Offender Management bill, published in November 2006, became the terrain on which the 'last battle' to secure the future of the Probation Service was fought. The cogency of Napo's and the PBA's case against it remained. They acknowledged that while many of the bill's crime reduction and public protection aims were laudable, it was seeking to create mechanisms which would seriously reduce the likelihood of their achievement. They found or mobilised allies across the political spectrum. The Archbishop of Canterbury, in a Prison Reform Trust lecture, worried about 'the constant drift to tendering, competition and privatisation' (Williams, 2007). The House of Lords inflicted several defeats on specific provisions, and although mechanisms for engineering contestability—slightly weakened—got through, the final Act, which received the Royal Assent in July 2007, 'bore little resemblance to the original' (Fletcher, 2007b). The groundwork for a very different model of probation practice had nonetheless been laid, and it is significant that in the course of the bill's passage through Parliament the National Probation Directorate was quietly dissolved and its functions dispersed into NOMS's internal structures. The post of Director-General, once used by the Home Office to signal the esteem in which it held probation, and to legitimate the centralisation process, was removed.

Yet, even as the Offender Management bill was going through Parliament, an equally far-reaching change was taking place in the Home Office itself, namely the hiving off of responsibility for prisons, probation, and constitutional affairs (including courts) into a separate Ministry of Justice. This emerged as a result of ongoing discussions within New Labour about the role of the erstwhile Lord Chancellor's Department, but was precipitated by Reid's attack on the Home Office's apparent unfitness for purpose. Over the decades there had in fact been principled arguments for just such an organisational split (Allen, 2007), but in this instance it was done with absurd haste, without adequate public consultation or parliamentary scrutiny. The intention was announced in March 2007; the split was effected in May 2007. Huge and likely-to-be troublesome constitutional questions are raised by the split, not least about the continuing independence of the judiciary (Pannick, 2007), but one wholly positive consequence was that the future of NOMS, as it had been envisaged to date, immediately became problematic. This was possibly because its elaborate headquarters infrastructure was too large for a smaller ministry; possibly because, as a government insider put it, 'the brand is too damaged to continue' (quoted in Fletcher, 2007b: 3), or possibly because the new Minister of Justice, Jack Straw (whose own work as Home Secretary establishing the NPS had been torn down by his successor David Blunkett and displaced by NOMS) was unsympathetic to it. Straw commissioned a review of the new Ministry's potential structures from the Office of Criminal Justice Reform, whose resulting report in October 2007 seemingly has no place for NOMS, *at least on the grand scale that had once been envisaged*. NOMS's running costs had grown to £900 million per year; it had produced endless blueprints on different aspects of policy, some useful, some not; its computer system (C-NOMIS) had been abandoned as too expensive; and still the cost-driven stabilisation of the prison population had not been achieved, reducing the availability of resources for more and better forms of community supervision.

In the event, the outcome of Straw's review, announced in February 2008 with zero consultation, was a much slimmed-down organization, but which was still called NOMS, presumably to give the impression of sense and continuity to a process that had been embarrassingly chaotic. The new structure was no longer as grand as Blunkett had envisaged but was more akin to what Straw had wanted from New Labour's Prisons-Probation Review in 1998, insofar as the Probation Service now became, in governance terms, a subsidiary of the Prison Service. However, as Judy McKnight (2008), General Secretary of Napo throughout the period covered in this chapter, has said, very little about the internal structure of the new NOMS was clear. It was firmly under the control of the former Director-General of the Prison Service, Phil Wheatley. A less senior post called Director of Probation survived, but would cease to exist once all Probation Boards had been phased into Trusts. Exactly as before, however, the language in which the new structure was announced emphasised managerial improvements in quality control and value for money, but of a clear practice-philosophy to underpin the supervision of offenders there was still no sign.

The fact that a grander version of NOMS was never realized was mostly a consequence of splitting the Home Office's responsibilities and creating the Ministry of Justice. It reflected the influence of its many critics only because of the delays that engagement with them entailed, preventing grander structures from being set in place any earlier. The Home Office never formally accepted the intellectual cogency of their critics' warnings, and despite effective attrition by probation's allies as it passed through Parliament, the Offender Management Act, which received Royal Assent in July 2007, retained the principle of contestability, giving the new Probation Trusts greater powers to commission services from the private and voluntary sectors. £40 million was allocated to support this legislation, but as an independent Napo-commissioned report was soon to show, despite significant increases in resource since 2001, the Probation Service was no longer able to cope with the range of legislative tasks now imposed on them (Oldfield and Grimshaw, 2008), and was suffering from a severe shortage of experienced staff.

That NOMS as Blunkett and Narey had once envisaged it was now passé was indicated not only by Straw opting for a more modest version, but also by a second report from Lord Carter. This had been commissioned by the Ministry of Justice in the very first month of its existence, in recognition of the fact that, given prevailing sentencing trends, the daily prison population would not at some point in the near future be held steady at 80,000, as had been piously hoped in 2004. Carter (2007) reported in December 2007 and simply accepted that on top of existing expansion plans, a further 6,500 prison places would be needed by 2012, the majority in three new *'Titan' prisons*. Carter's observation on the future governance of the penal estate envisaged opportunities 'to reduce...corporate overheads' (Carter, 2007: para. 4.38) and may also have played its part in the shrinking of the original NOMS model. The report's immense significance as a final departure from any pretence of penal reductionism in government policy was not officially remarked upon, but it signalled a shift in the penal climate towards custody which will inevitably have both ideological and resource repercussions for those supervising offenders in the community, by whatever name they might in future be known, probation officers or offender managers.

REVIEW QUESTIONS

1 Are there any criteria on which NOMS might be judged a success?

2 How did the advent of the Ministry of Justice affect NOMS?

CONCLUSION

Given the social and political conditions prevailing at the end of the twentieth century, and in the years thereafter, the Probation Service could not have avoided modernisation in some shape or form, if it was to be equal to the crime challenges posed by economic deregulation and the shrinking of welfare states. Within the criminological and public policy communities in academia, and eventually within probation interest groups themselves, there was ample knowledge, both empirical and normative, which might have guided the nature, pace, and direction of change, as well as open channels of communication. It was precisely these knowledge bases, however, from which New Labour distanced itself, opting instead for a hypermanagerialist approach and attending instead to experts outside traditional policy communities. This approach, which had little regard for democratic protocols and properly consultative practices, presumes that organisational structures are infinitely malleable, that the sensibilities of people working within them are easily reconstituted to suit new, politically-driven needs and aspirations, and that various sorts of information technology make it possible both to accelerate and micromanage the change process. The first Carter report and the politicians, officials, and advisers who set out to implement NOMS epitomise this approach.

In retrospect, it can be seen that the champions of the Probation Service did not initially realise that they were up against people in government who regarded the traditional probation knowledge and value bases as obsolete and anachronistic, and who had a messianic faith in the capacity of merely managerialist knowledge to transform large organizations in a relatively short period of time (see Haggerty, 2004 for some broader insights into this development). It will remain a matter for the virtual historians whether life under the earlier, more modest NPS initiative would actually have been better if the advent of NOMS had not interrupted its trajectory; governance structures would probably have been consolidated more quickly, uncertainty reduced, and more time and energy devoted to improving practice, but some of the issues faced, generated by internal conflicts within and external pressures on, the government, would have been the same. Crucially, however, the NPS was never envisaged as a commissioning body on the scale that NOMS was (indeed is), and it is through contestability creating a fragmented mosaic of statutory, private, and voluntary organizations delivering services to offenders that the Probation Service as a single entity, and the professional identity associated with it, may finally be broken up.

What Zygmunt Bauman (2007: 3) sees as the character of 'liquid society' in general—'the collapse of long term thinking, planning and acting, and the disappearance or weakening of social structures in which thinking, planning and acting could be inscribed for a long time to come' is reflected in miniature in NOMS itself and illustrates why the Probation Service found it so difficult to defend itself and its tradition:

> Past successes do not necessarily increase the probability of future victories, let alone guarantee them; while means successfully tested in the past need to be constantly inspected and revised since they may prove useless or downright counterproductive once circumstances change. A swift and thorough forgetting of outdated information and fast ageing habits can be more important for the next success than the memorisation of past moves and the building of strategies on a foundation laid by previous learning (Bauman, 2007: 3).

The architects of NOMS might, of course, claim that theirs was a necessary and legitimate way to modernize, reflecting changes in the wider world, but its utopian confidence in what transformative managerialism might achieve was deeply misplaced, and it patently did more harm than good. There was simply no justification for initiating a new wave of change when the previous wave exemplifed by the NPS had been given insufficient time to prove itself. Even if the Criminal Justice Act 2003 had delivered seamless sentences in the way intended, the NPS structure could probably have delivered them. The attempt at transformative government which NOMS represented constantly deflected professional energies upwards towards managing unwanted organizational change, rather than allowing them to settle and focus downwards and outwards on much needed improvements to frontline practice in the service. Above all, NOMS failed dismally to achieve what it had ostensibly aimed for—stabilizing the prison population, which stood at an unprecedented 83,181 in June 2008. From the outset, NOMS's critics all knew better, but such was the Government's determination to transform offender supervision that all they were able to do was fend off the worst and limit the damage. The turbulence caused by the initiative has left the Probation Service in late 2008 in a worse place than it might otherwise have been, under resourced, demoralised, uncertain of its role and future. The very survival of the term 'probation', and with what referent, in a structure that may be 'liquefied' by contestability, is moot; whatever loyalties it still inspires in the service's present staff, and despite the convivial meaning it retains internationally (van Kalmthout and Derks, 2000; van Kalmthout, Roberts, and Vinding, 2003) it has few champions in government. Progressive penal ideals—humanistic rather than managerial—are being revitalised among concerned academics (Robinson, 2005; McNeil, 2006; Ward and Maruna, 2007), but the prospect of sustaining them in work with offenders in the community will be difficult enough even if a coherent public sector organization survives; in a post-contestability mosaic of 'commissioned' organizations it will surely be formidable. Napo, the Probation Association (as the PBA has been renamed), and the newly formed Association of Chief Officers and Chief Executives of Probation may well uphold such ideals, but infusing them into the hearts, minds, and actions of staff employed by a variety of different local agencies, subject every few years to renewals of contract, will pose challenges that have never been faced before.

QUESTIONS FOR DISCUSSION

1 What is meant by the Probation Service's tradition?

2 What would it have meant to modernise the Probation Service on its own terms?

3 What are the advantages and disadvantages of contestability?

4 Can the professional identity 'probation officer' survive within the new NOMS structure?

GUIDE TO FURTHER READING

Canton, R. and Hancock, D. (eds) (2007) *Dictionary of Probation and Offender Management*. Cullompton: Willan.

An indispensable guide to key concepts, old and new.

Bauman, Z. (2007) *Liquid Times: living in the age of uncertainty*. Cambridge: Polity Press.

A short and readable account of how Bauman sees late modernity, explaining how organizational forms become looser, more transient, more liquid under conditions of global deregulation.

Gelsthorpe, L. and Morgan, R. (eds) (2007) *Handbook of Probation*. Cullompton: Willan.

An edited collection which draws together a wide range of material in relation to probation and offender management.

Mair, G. (2004) *What Matters in Probation?* Cullompton: Willan.

A collection of articles which explore the interaction of policy and practice in the Probation Service and point towards a different and better vision of what probation might have become.

Oldfield, M. (2002) *From Welfare to Risk: discourse, power and politics in the Probation Service*. ICCJ Monograph No. 1. London: Napo.

A sophisticated theoretical account of changes in the governance of probation in the late 20th century.

Tonry, M. (2004) *Punishment and Politics: evidence and emulation in the making of English crime control policy*. Cullompton: Willan.

A very severe critique of New Labour's approach to criminal justice, all the more telling because it comes from an ideologically moderate penologist.

Burke, L. (2005) *From Probation to NOMS: issues of contestability, culture and community involvement*. ICCJ Monograph No. 6. London: Napo.

A more detailed and wide-ranging account of the early stages of planning for NOMS than is offered here, with a deep sense of what risked being lost.

REFERENCES

Allen, R. (2007) 'This New Ministry Will Allow a Rethink of Penal Policy'. *The Guardian* May 2007.

Allison, E. (2007) 'Many Unhappy Returns to Prison'. *The Guardian (Society)* 30 June 2007.

Bochel, D. (1976) *Probation and Aftercare: its development in England and Wales*. Edinburgh: Edinburgh University Press.

Bauman, Z. (2007) *Liquid Times: living in an age of uncertainty*. Cambridge: Polity Press.

Carter, P. (2003) *Managing Offenders, Reducing Crime*. London: Prime Minster's Strategy Unit (the Carter report).

Carter, P. (2007) *Securing the Future: proposals for the efficient and sustainable use of custody in England and Wales*. London: Ministry of Justice.

Chui, W.H. and Nellis, M. (2003) *Moving Probation Forward, theory policy and practice*. London: Longman.

Confederation of British Industry (CBI) (2008) *Getting Back on the Straight and Narrow: a better criminal justice system for all*. London: Confederation of British Industry.

Fletcher, H. (2007a) 'Early Release Confirmed' *NAPO News* July/August 2007: 1

Fletcher, H. (2007b) 'The End of NOMS' *Napo News* October 2007, 3.

Fox, A., Khan, L., Briggs, D., Rees-Jones, N., Thompson, Z., and Owens, J. (2005) *Throughcare and Aftercare: approaches and promising practice in service delivery for clients released from prison or leaving residential rehabilitation*. Online report 01/05 London: Home Office.

Garland, D. (2001) *The Culture of Control*. Oxford: Oxford University Press.

Goodman, A. (2003) 'Probation into the Millennium: The Punishing Service?' in R. Matthews and J. Young (eds) *The New Politics of Crime and Punishment*. Cullompton: Willan Publishing.

Goodman, A. (2007) '289 Borough High Street: the aftercare and resettlement unit (ACU) in the Inner London Probation Service 1965–1990' *British Journal of Community Justice* 5(2): 9–28.

Gray, J. (2003) *Al Qaeda and What it Means to Be Modern*. London: Faber.

Hall, P. (1976) *Reforming the Welfare*. London: Heinemann.

Haggerty, K. (2004) 'Displaced Expertise: three constraints on the policy relevance of criminological thought' *Theoretical Criminology* 8(4): 449–197.

Hedderman, C. (2006) 'Keeping the Lid on the Prison Population—Will it Work?' in M. Hough, R. Allen, and U. Padel (eds) *Reshaping Probation and Prisons: the new offender management framework*. Bristol: Policy Press.

HM Inspectorate of Probation (2006a) *An Independent Review of a Serious Further Offence Case: Damian Hanson and Elliot White*. London: HM Inspectorate of Probation.

HM Inspectorate of Probation (2006b) *An Independent Review of a Serious Further Offence Case: Anthony Rice*. London: HM Inspectorate of Probation.

Home Office (1988) *Punishment, Custody and the Community* Cmnd 424. London: Home Office.

Home Office (1998) *Joining Forces: The Prisons Probation Review*. London: Home Office.

Home Office (2001) *Making Punishments Work: report of a review of the sentencing framework for England and Wales*. London: Home Office (the Halliday report).

Home Office (2002) *Justice for All* Cm 5563. London: The Stationery Office.

Home Office (2004) *Reducing Crime—Changing Lives: the government's plans for transforming the management of offenders*. London: Home Office.

Home Office (2005a) *The National Offender Management Model*. London: Home Office.

Home Office (2005b) *Restructuring Probation to Reducing Offending*. London: Home Office.

Home Office (2006a) *Five Year Strategy for Protecting the Public and Reducing Offending*. London: Home Office.

Home Office (2006b) *Making Sentences Clearer*. London: Home Office.

Home Office (2006c) *Rebalancing The Criminal Justice System in Favour of the Law Abiding Majority: cutting crime, reducing offending and protecting the public*. London: Home Office.

Hough, M., Allen, R., and Padel, U. (eds) *Reshaping Probation and Prisons: the new offender management framework*. Bristol: Policy Press.

Lacey, N. (2008) *The Prisoner's Dilemma: political economy and punishment in contemporary democracies*. Cambridge: Cambridge University Press.

Lord Chancellor's Department (2001) *Review of the Criminal Courts in England and Wales*. London: Lord Chancellor's Department (the Auld report).

Mair, G. (2004) 'The Origins of What Works in England and Wales: a house built on sand?' in G. Mair (ed) *What Matters in Probation*. Cullompton: Willan.

Mair, G., Cross, N., and Taylor, S. (2007) *The Use and Impact of the Community Order and the Suspended Sentence Order*. London: Centre for Crime and Justice Studies.

McIvor, G. and McNeil, F. (2007) 'Probation in Scotland: past, present and future' in L. Gelsthorpe and R. Morgan (eds) *Handbook of Probation*. Cullompton: Willan Publishing.

McKnight, J. (2008) *Speaking up for Probation*. Paper delivered as the Eleventh Bill McWilliams Memorial Lecture Institute of Criminology, University of Cambridge 25 June 2008.

McLaughlin, E., Muncie, J., and Hughes, G. (2001) 'The Permanent Revolution: New Labour, new public management and the modernisation of criminal justice'. *Criminal Justice* 1(3): 301–18.

McNeil, F. (2006) 'A Desistance Paradigm for Offender Management'. *Criminology and Criminal Justice* 6(1): 39–62.

McWilliams, W. (1983) 'The Mission to the English Police Courts 1876–1936'. *Howard Journal* 22: 129–47.

McWilliams, W. (1985) 'The Mission Transformed: professionalisation of probation between the wars'. *Howard Journal* 24: 257–74.

McWilliams, W. (1986) 'The English Probation System and the Diagnostic Ideal'. *Howard Journal* 25: 41–60.

McWilliams, W. (1987) 'Probation, Pragmatism and Policy'. *Howard Journal* 26: 97–121.

Morgan, R. and Gelsthorpe, L. (2007) *The Handbook of Probation*. Cullompton: Willan Publishing.

Napo (1987) *Changing Lives: an oral history of Probation*. London. Napo.

Nellis, M. (2006) 'NOMS, Contestability and the Process of Technocorrectional Innovation' in M. Hough, R. Allen, and U. Padel (eds) *Reshaping Probation and Prisons: the new offender management framework*. Bristol: Policy Press.

Nellis, M. (2007) 'Humanizing Justice: the English Probation Service up to 1972' in L. Gelsthorpe and R. Morgan (eds) *Handbook of Probation*. Cullompton: Willan.

Newburn, T. and Sparks, R. (eds) (2004) *Criminal Justice and Political Cultures*. Cullompton: Willan Publishing.

Oldfield, M. and Grimshaw, R. (2008) *Probation Resources: Staffing and Workloads 2001–2008*. London: Centre for Crime and Justice Studies.

Pannick, D. (2007) 'Preventing the Ministry of Justice Causing Injustice'. *The Times* 8 May 2007.

Pollard, S. (2005) *David Blunkett*. London: Hodder and Stoughton.

Prison Reform Trust (2005) *Recycling Offenders Through Prison. Briefing Paper*. London: Prison Reform Trust.

Prison Reform Trust (2007) *Titan Prisons: a gigantic mistake. Briefing Paper*. London: Prison Reform Trust.

Probation Board's Association (PBA) (2007) *Annual Report*. London: Probation Board's Association.

Radzinowicz, L. and Hood, R. (1986) *The Emergence of Penal Policy in Victorian and Edwardian England*. Oxford: Oxford University Press.

Raynor, P. (2002) 'Community Penalties: probation, punishment and "what works"'. in M. Maguire, R. Morgan, and R. Reiner (eds) *The Oxford Handbook of Criminology* (3rd ed). Oxford: Oxford University Press.

Raynor, P. (2004) 'Finding the Path and Losing the Way'. *Criminal Justice* 4(3): 302–25.

Raynor, P. and Maguire, M. (2006) 'End-to End Or End in Tears? Prospects for the effectiveness of the Offender Management Model' in M. Hough, R. Allen, and U. Padel (eds) *Reshaping Probation and Prisons: the new offender management framework*. Bristol: Policy Press.

Raynor, P. and Vanstone, M. (1993) *STOP (Straight Thinking On Probation): Third interim evaluation report*. Bridgend: Mid-Glamorgan Probation Service.

Robinson, G. (2005) 'What Works in Offender Management?'. *Howard Journal* 44: 307–418.

Ross, R. and Fabiano, E.A. (1990) *Reasoning and Rehabilitation: Instructor's Manual*. Ottawa: Cognitive Station.

Sentencing Guidelines Council (2004) *New Sentences: Criminal Justice Act 2003*. London: Home Office.

Social Exclusion Unit (2002) *Reducing Re-offending by Ex-Prisoners*. London: Social Exclusion Unit.

Stanley, S. (2007) *The Use of the Community Order and the Suspended Sentence Order for Young Adult Offenders*. London: Centre for Crime and Justice Studies.

van Kalmthout, A.M. and Derks, J.T.M. (eds) (2000) *Probation and Probation Services: a European perspective*. Nijmegen, Netherlands: Wolf Legal Publishers.

van Kalmthout, A.M., Roberts, J., and Vinding, S. (2003) *Probation and Probation Services in the EU Accession Countries*. Nijmegen, Netherlands: Wolf Legal Publishers.

Vanstone, M. (2004) *Supervising Offenders in the Community: a history of probation theory and practice*. Aldershot: Ashgate.

Vanstone, M. and Raynor, P. (2007) 'Towards a Correctional Service' in L. Gelsthorpe and R. Morgan (eds) *Handbook of Probation*. Cullompton: Willan Publishing.

Ward, T. and Maruna, S. (2007) *Rehabilitation: beyond the risk paradigm*. London: Routledge.

Williams, R. (2007) *Criminal Justice—Building Responsibility.* Prison Reform Trust Annual Lecture 1 February 2007. London: Prison Reform Trust.

Whitehead, P. and Statham, R. (2006) *The History of Probation: politics, power and cultural change 1876–2005.* Crayford, Kent: Shaw and Sons.

Winstone, J. and Pakes, P. (2005) *Community Justice: issues for probation and criminal justice.* Cullompton: Willan Publishing.

Woolf, H. and Tumim, S. (1991) *Prison Disturbances April 1990* Cm 1456, London: HMSO.

11 Gender and the criminal justice system

Sandra Walklate

INTRODUCTION

The aim of this chapter is to explore the extent to which questions relating to *gender* permeate the work of the criminal justice system. Gender refers to all those qualities that human beings are expected to possess on the basis of being male or female. Being male or female is a biological category that is assigned to us at birth most frequently on the basis of observable sex organs (though it has to be noted that this is not possible in every instance—go to the UK Intersex Association at <http://www.ukia.co.uk/>). Being masculine or feminine is a socially ascribed process; we learn about our gender in the light of our biological categorisation. This distinction between sex and gender is crucial to understanding the issues with which this chapter is concerned and it is a distinction that is frequently conflated and or confused. To be clear, this chapter is concerned to outline how the socially ascribed characteristics of *masculinity* and *femininity* permeate people's experiences of the criminal justice system as an offender, a victim, and as a professional working within that system. So, it should be noted that the characteristics of masculinity and/or femininity do not necessarily attach themselves consistently to being either male or female, and it is frequently that which is considered to be anomalous, the violent female offender, or the male victim of *rape* for example, that tells us the most about how the criminal justice system operates with the gender question.

BACKGROUND

The gender question in criminal justice

There has been a long tradition within criminology of addressing the sex differential of criminal behaviour. As Braithwaite (1989) observed, the disproportionate offending behaviour of males as compared with females is a 'fact' that every criminological theory should be able to address, and as Wootton (1959: 32) stated, 'Yet if men behaved like women the courts would be idle and the prisons empty'. However, criminologists did not really begin to think seriously about the way in which gendered assumptions might help make sense of the 'facts' until the 1970s, when feminists writing about *crime* began to talk about 'women and crime' as opposed to 'sex and crime'. Notably the work of Smart (1977) and Heidensohn (1985) reflected a desire to enhance the criminological awareness of the maleness of crime. The successes of these incursions into the criminological agenda notwithstanding, a focus on just the 'women and crime' question was never going to be sufficient in addressing the '*gender* and crime' question. This is because work focused in this way failed to escape the trap of essentialism, that is, that there are essential, immutable, unchangeable differences between men and women. In other words it takes us little further forward than just talking about sex differences. Focusing just on women leaves out men, and, as was stated above, gender means thinking about men and women. However without the pioneering work of feminist criminologists, the question of the maleness of crime, that is, of thinking about the extent to which the social expectations associated with being male, would never have been placed on the criminological agenda.

The maleness of crime, and indeed the maleness of the criminal justice system as a workplace, came to the fore in criminological thinking during the early 1990s. Writers such as Connell (1987) and Messerschmidt (1993) amongst others have done much to encourage a deeper exploration of the way in which 'doing crime' might also be a way of 'doing gender'. In other words, how might gendered expressions of being male or female contribute to making sense of criminal behaviour. In addition that same thinking has also been applied to how victimisation is experienced and responded to (see for example Newburn and Stanko, 1994) and to how the criminal justice system does its work (see for example Naffine, 1990). It should be noted, however, from the outset that gender is only one of the variables that contributes to the patterning of crime, criminal victimisation, and the criminal justice system. Other structural variables, like social class, ethnicity, age, and sexuality, also have their part to play in how the criminal justice system does its work. The way in which these variables interact with each other is complex and need not concern us here. The key question for this chapter is: when is gender the salient variable? In other words, how and under what circumstances does gender matter?

In order to explore this question this chapter will offer an overview of the ways in which gender impacts upon offenders (defendants), victims (complainants), and the people working within the criminal justice system. In the final part of this chapter we shall spend a little time considering the ways in which gender might also permeate the law itself, but first of all a brief statistical overview of the patterning of crime, criminal victimisation, and the professions in the criminal justice system.

The gendered patterning of crime and the criminal justice system: a snapshot

According to the Office of National Statistics, in 2004 there were four times as many male offenders as female offenders. In addition men outnumbered women across all the major crime categories. So for burglary, robbery, drug offences, criminal damage, or violence against the person, between 83 per cent and 94 per cent of the offenders were male (National Statistics, 2006). The offence that was most commonly committed by men and women was theft (70 per cent of theft-related offences were committed by men). Yet when this offence is examined in relation to how these offenders are dealt with by the court, 55 per cent of the female offenders were found guilty or cautioned for theft or handling stolen goods as compared with only 32 per cent of the male offenders. These figures are thus suggestive of the possibility of gendered assumptions being in play in the criminal justice system as well as the possibility that the pattern of male and female behaviour in relation to particular crimes is different. If we consider the final point of disposition of the criminal justice system, imprisonment, of a prison population standing at around 84,139 prisoners in July 2008, 4,449 or just over 5 per cent of these were women (Ministry of Justice, 2008a), and over a third of female adult prisoners had no previous convictions (double the figure for men) and 64 per cent of female offenders served six months or less (RDS NOMS, 2006), the majority are held for non-violent offences with a third being held for drug offences (Ministry of Justice, 2008b), making the experience of prison a predominantly male one.

If, on the other hand, we consider the patterning of criminal victimisation, the recurrent finding of the *British Crime Surveys* indicates that it is young males who are most likely to be the victims of violent (street) crime with the 2005/06 British Crime Survey reporting that men are three times more likely than women to be the victim of a violent crime committed by a stranger. In contrast that same survey reports that women are three times more likely than men to be victims of *domestic violence*, that is violence committed by someone that they know. Walby and Allen (2004: v) state:

> Inter-personal violence is both widely dispersed and it is concentrated. It is widely dispersed in that some experience of domestic violence (abuse, threats or force), sexual victimisation or stalking is reported by over one third (36 per cent) of people. It is concentrated in that a minority, largely women, suffer multiple attacks, severe injuries, experience more than one form of inter-personal violence and serious disruption to their lives.

For the Fawcett Society (2004) this concentration of interpersonal criminal victimisation contributes to the willingness, or otherwise, of women to report their experiences to the police: a process that can be heightened by the way in which their case might be handled after it has been reported. Linking the problem of criminal victimisation with how a case might be handled is particularly difficult for the victims of sex crimes, whether male or female. How either victim may or may not be treated by the police, the Crown Prosecution Service, and in the courtroom, is still subject to much concern and scrutiny (see for example HMIC/CPSI (2007)), and takes its toll on both men and women as victims in similar ways. Some would argue that part of these problematic experiences lie with the gendered nature of the criminal justice professions.

The Fawcett Society (2004) reports that 19 per cent of all police officers are female, most of whom are concentrated in the lower ranks. One in five constables are female, whereas fewer than one in ten Chief Officers are female. Sixty-seven per cent of workers in the Crown Prosecution Service are female, though again these workers are concentrated in the lower grades of the service, only occupying about one in three of senior positions (Ministry of Justice, 2008c). Table 11.1, compiled from <http://www.judiciary.gov.uk>, illustrates the number of women in the judiciary and compares data from 2001 with 2007.

These figures stand somewhat in contrast with the number of female law graduates (around 59 per cent), the number of female solicitors (40 per cent), and the number of female barristers (30 per cent) (Fawcett Society, 2004). According to *Ministry of Justice*

Table 11.1 Number of Women in the Judiciary 2001 and 2007

Position held	2001	2007
Lord Justices of Appeal	6.1% (two)	8.3% (three)
High Court Judges	8.1% (eight)	9.3% (nine)
Circuit Judge	7.9% (four)	10.8% (59)
Recorder	12.3% (168)	13.7% (172)

figures for 2005/06, 52 per cent of people working for the *Youth Justice Board* are male (48 per cent female), again with the male presence becoming stronger the further up the organisation one goes (Ministry of Justice, 2008c). That same report indicates that 64 per cent of the Prison Service is male. The figures for the various voluntary agencies who work within and without the criminal justice system are available but are less reliable, given a high percentage of volunteer workers who choose not to return such data.

From a point of view this data illustrates that the criminal justice system reflects the patterning of male/female employment found elsewhere in the workforce. It is both vertically segregated insofar as the higher one moves up the criminal justice system as an employee the more likely it is that your work environment will be male dominated; and it is also horizontally segregated, that is certain tasks are seem to be female tasks and others male tasks. This is still evident in many areas of police work, for example, where it is assumed that women workers are more suited to working on cases of domestic violence, rape, and child abuse (though as research has shown this presumption is hugely problematic: see below). However, whilst the gendered nature of work is problematic across the board, it is arguably particularly problematic in the criminal justice system, given the power that these presumptions have over not only the workers in the system itself but also the defendants and complainants that come before the system.

The question of gender in the criminal justice system workforce became particularly focused on 6 April 2007 when the gender equality duty came into force. This duty is found in Part 4 s. 84 of the Equality Act 2006. This Act states that:

A public authority shall in carrying out its functions have due regard to the need to;

a) eliminate unlawful discrimination and harassment and
b) to promote equality of opportunity between men and women.

As a public authority the criminal justice system is certainly not exempt from this duty and this chapter will by implication raise some questions about this legal requirement for the workings of this system. In order to do this it will be necessary to establish the ways in which questions of gender pervade the working of the criminal justice system at all levels. Obviously in a chapter of this length it is impossible to do justice to the wealth of literature now available on this issue, the reader is therefore advised to use the further reading and the references assiduously.

Offenders, gender, and the criminal justice system

From some of the statistics above it is possible to infer that male and female offenders are not necessarily dealt with in the same way by the criminal justice system. In some respects this different treatment is a reflection of their different pattern of offending behaviour and consequently their different exposure to the agencies of the criminal justice process. This comment holds despite recent rising concern about young women's supposed increasing propensity to resort to violence. As Burman (2003) argues, such increases as have been reported are on very small base numbers and are for the most part in the less serious offence categories. However, concern about the violent female offender reflects deep-seated assumptions not only about the kind of offending that is 'acceptably female' (like, for example, prostitution or shoplifting) but also wider cultural assumptions about behaviour that is 'acceptably feminine'. Thus the violent female offender is an anomaly: a contradiction in terms, and the rising concern with female violence tells us much about how gendered assumptions impact on female offenders not only in popular media coverage but also the disposition they are likely to receive from the court (see below). As Burman (2003) states, the most striking fact about violent crime is that it is disproportionately committed by men, not women. However its maleness is rarely made explicit, thus reflecting a further gendered assumption that violence is merely an extension of 'acceptably male behaviour'.

Despite the complex ways in which gender impacts upon the criminal justice system that is illustrated by the violent female offender, there has been an enduring assumption that women are treated more leniently than men by the criminal justice system as a result of chivalry. To a certain extent a cursory glance at the official statistics would support this hypothesis, since women are much less likely to be stopped and searched and/or arrested than men; important experiences on the ladder to further involvement in the criminal justice process. Such a hypothesis is in reality difficult to either prove or disprove; however, it is clear that even when men and women have committed the same offences they are likely to be handled differently by the criminal justice system.

In an early study on the workings of the magistrates' court by Eaton (1986) she found that when men and women appeared before the court in similar circumstances charged with similar offences they received similar treatment. This was because the court drew equally upon their family background, except for men the concern of the court was with a man's employment record (that is whether or not he met the needs of his family in accordance with commonly understood conceptualisations of masculinity) and for women it was whether or not she complied with commonly understood conceptualisations of good child care and housewifery. This finding is echoed in the work of Worrall (1990) in which 'the compassion trap', as she calls it, fails to separate women offenders from the presumptions of femininity that expect them to be nurturing and domestic. The 'nondescript' women of her study were those who resisted this categorisation by the criminal justice system and as a result posed significant problems for the criminal justice system. Hedderman and Gelsthorpe (1997) reached similar conclusions in their comparative study of the disposition of male and female defendants from the magistrates' court. Their study added another ingredient to the way in which magistrates considered the appropriateness of *punishment* for female offenders: the extent to which the magistrates thought that the female offender was 'troubled' or 'troublesome'. 'Troubled' offenders were in need of help: 'troublesome' ones, that is, those that resisted the 'compassion trap' or the '*gender* contract' (Carlen, 1988) like the violent female offender, were more likely to receive a custodial sentence than those merely 'troubled'.

Thus gendered assumptions permeate how not only women are treated by the criminal justice process but also by implication men. This is illustrated by the way in which the court might be impressed by a male defendant being a 'good husband' or 'the breadwinner' (images that buy into the more comfortable aspects of masculinity), or at the other extreme the way a man on trial for murder might be created as a 'monster', these latter processes tapping into the more uncontrollable and threatening urges associated with other aspects of masculinity. The way in which the offender is socially constructed is triply damning for the female murderer of children, an act that transgresses all the bounded understandings of femininity: Myra Hindley being the archetypical case in point.

If we trace the treatment of male and female offenders through to the ultimate disposition of the court, imprisonment, it is possible to see, as Eaton (1993: 16) has stated, 'the disciplined subject is also a gendered subject'. It is the case, as Carlen (1994) has observed, that prison 'grinds' people down whether male or female, but it does this in particularly gendered ways. Women in prison are subjected to processes of normalisation that are designed to reconstruct them as individuals in the image of acceptable versions of femininity. In a similar fashion, surviving the prison experience for men entails that they be 'tougher than the rest' (Sim, 1994) despite the loss of autonomy that is so central to their status as men (Newton, 1994). When both of these processes are taken together they contribute to the nature and extent of violence in prison by both prisoners and to the experiences of prison officers (see Bennett, Crewe, and Wahidin, 2006). In essence, the prison system is run for men and by men in the absence of any real understanding of masculinity and all that might entail. Moreover, research does suggest that the experience of imprisonment has a differential impact on women insofar as the regime they experience neither matches their needs as offenders nor matches their needs as women but endeavours to reshape them into stereotypical roles.

The processes that *gender* male and female offenders in the ways outlined above need to be understood in the context of the criminal law that frames these experiences. The criminal law seeks to establish not only that an 'actus reus' has occurred (i.e. a wrong act) but also that it has been committed by a 'mens rea' (i.e. a guilty mind). In connecting the act with the state of mind of the offender the criminal justice process engages in decision making that can either assign or deny the defendant a sense of agency, that is, that they intended to commit the act of which they are accused. Moreover, even within this process it is possible to delineate the readiness with which men are given the autonomy to act and make choices (even when they are considered mad), and the readiness with which women are denied this capability and thus are deemed as being either not really criminal or not really women. This question of the state of mind of the offender and the gendered assumptions that are contained within it has implications that are also felt by those who present themselves as complainants (victims) in the criminal justice system, and it is to those considerations that we shall now turn.

REVIEW QUESTIONS

1 Discuss the different ways in which the distinction between 'troubled' offenders and 'troublesome' offenders might impact upon men as well as women.

2 Do you think that men and women offend for the same or different reasons, and in respect of what kinds of crimes?

3 Examine the different ways in which you think that prison grinds men and women down. Is this what the prison system is for?

Victims, gender, and the criminal justice system

If it is the violent female offender that transgresses all the gendered assumptions of the criminal justice system's understanding and constructions of the offender, it is the male victim of rape that transgresses its gendered assumptions of the victim. Given this challenge posed by this particular example, this section will focus on the relative experiences of the male and female rape complainant in the criminal justice system.

Charting the nature and extent of sexual violence and developing appropriate policy responses to this problem is fraught with difficulties. Nevertheless, it is the case that much effort over the last 20 years has been focused on improving the response of all the criminal justice agencies to the rape victim. These improvements have ranged from the development of specialised police units designed to respond to rape complainants, to the establishment of specialised Domestic Violence Courts, to changes in the law. Nevertheless, as Kelly *et al.*, (2005) report, the conviction rate for rape cases in England and Wales remains low at 5.6 per cent. A HMIC/CPSI Thematic Report published in 2007 entitled 'Without Consent' and cited earlier attempted to offer some understanding of why this conviction rate remains so low despite the evidence that the reporting of complaints of rape has increased. This report examined what happened once a complaint of rape has been recorded as a crime. Its findings reveal that, of 573 recorded complaints of rape (and it must be noted that all these cases involved female complainants), in 491 (85.7 per cent) the suspect and the victim knew each other, in 102 of these cases (20.8 per cent) the victim withdrew the charges, leaving 398 cases. Of these the suspect was charged in 160 cases; the main reason for not charging was because of insufficient evidence (229 cases). Of 160 cases in which the suspect was charged, 75 case files were examined further that revealed that out of these 75 cases there were 39 convictions, 20 as a result of a guilty plea and 19 on the basis of a jury decision.

This snapshot of what happens to cases is illustrative of not only the problem of attrition but the points at which cases of rape pose problems for the criminal justice system, and these data point to at least three of these: the point at which the incident is reported (this involves the police); the point at which a case for charging a suspect is being made (this involves the Crown Prosecution Service); and the point of conviction (this involves the court and the jury). As this thematic report indicates, much work remains to be done in supporting complainants of rape through the criminal justice process, though arguably this is not the only arena in which complaints of rape face a challenge. An Amnesty International sponsored opinion poll published in 2005 revealed that 26 per cent of those asked thought that a woman was partially or totally responsible for being raped if she was wearing sexy or revealing clothing, and more than one in five held the same view of a woman who had had many sexual partners, with 30 per cent 'blaming the woman' if she was drunk. These findings echo a range of problems that are exploited in the *criminal court* during the course of a trial. However, it is important also to notice the absence of the male complainant in this discussion so far, an absence that we shall return to.

Whilst much still remains to be done to ensure that complainants of rape are handled sensitively by the criminal justice process, much of the focus of complaint around this issue still lies with the experience of the criminal court. Women's experiences of the rape trial arguably are still governed by what Adler (1987) called 'the importance of being perfect'. This observation delineates a process of cross-examination in the witness box that is designed to render a woman's evidence less than believable on the grounds of her womanhood rather than the quality of her evidence. Such questioning can not only go beyond the incident in question, but can also touch upon very private aspects of a woman's body. The issue of penetration, i.e. where the penis went and by how far, still remains crucial to rape trials notwithstanding the Sexual Offences Act 2003. This focus on the penis results in what Smart (1989) has called the celebration of phallocentrism in the legal system. This tells us much that is implicit in the law with respect to gender and why the rape trial proceeds in the way that it does.

This celebration of the penis privileges a male-centred view of both female and male sexuality. Women do not know what they want; they have to be persuaded. So a woman whose dress or behaviour challenges this assumption is problematic. Men cannot be blamed for acting on deep-seated sexual needs: in the face of temptation these are uncontrollable. As a result the few who are convicted must be the psychologically deranged 'other men' in whose name men, as a group, dare not speak. Moreover, it is the question of this manhood that proves equally problematic for the male complainant of rape. It is the case that the majority of men who rape other men are heterosexual and, as Lees (1997: 106) states:

> One of the most damaging insults to be thrown at a man is to call him a woman, a bitch or a ****. The act of coercive buggery can be seen as a means of taking away manhood, of emasculating other men and thereby enhancing one's own power.

Moreover Allen's (2002) typology of men's reactions to having been the victim of rape clearly indicates the necessity of understanding these through the lens of what it is to be a man. These presumptions surrounding appropriate manhood (masculinity) render the male complainant of rape hugely problematic for the criminal justice system in general and the *criminal trial* in particular, given the implicit celebration of (heterosexual) phallocentrism commented on above.

Consequently, not only are women denied their experiences and sometimes the knowledge of their own bodies, we also fail to see men as they really are. The privileging of the male world-view over the female in the law thus becomes the means whereby highly gendered views of sexuality take their toll on male and female complainants of rape. They also take their toll on male defendants who become the subject of their uncontrollable urges and as a consequence they are also denied a sense of agency. Though for some, of course (those 'other' men) this denial results in conviction rather than acquittal. As Naffine (1997: 119) suggests:

> It is not only women who suffer from the culture of the strong man, though it is women who are consistently dispossessed by it...There are a range of other masculinities which are simultaneously implied and then cast out. They are by implication, rendered unnatural and undesirable. Thus are the men who depart from the masculine ideal rendered silent.

This observation is not only pertinent to the courtroom it is also an apt comment on those who work in the criminal justice system.

REVIEW QUESTIONS

1 Why do you think the *attrition rate* for cases of rape is the way it is? Why do you think this is important if at all?

2 How and under what circumstances might men be victims?

3 How might gendered assumptions feature in other areas of criminal victimisation?

The criminal justice system as a gendered place of work

As the figures cited earlier suggest, whilst the proportion of males and females in employment in the different branches of the criminal justice system varies, two factors remain constant: it is an arena of work that is for the most part dominated by men; the higher up the system you are the more likely it is that you will find men in charge. Moreover, whilst much of the empirical work that has considered the occupations within the criminal justice has focused on police women and the problems and possibilities that they face in the workplace, there is evidence to suggest that women working in other branches of the criminal justice system face similar problems. Put simply these difficulties amount to how best to meet the demands of the job; do you do what the men do, that is become one of them, or do you retain your sense of womanhood and do your job in the light of the different qualities you might bring to it as a result of being female? It is, of course, a moot point whether or not women working in the criminal justice system meet any more difficulties than women working in other professions, but it is also important to note that this debate raises a more fundamental question: are there 'essential' differences between men and women? This question cannot be covered here but it is nevertheless an important one to think about. However, it is the case that the higher up an organisation a woman moves the more likely it is that she will be considered an anomaly.

As Smith (1990) observed, anomalies have the powerful effect of throwing into relief those things that appear to be socially acceptable and those that do not. This was particularly the case for Alison Halford who, in the early 1990s, endeavoured on several occasions to gain promotion to Chief Constable. Her case is interesting and we shall discuss it further as a Case Study. She was a powerful woman, indeed already a high ranking female police officer in a male-dominated organisation, but her application to be placed in control of such an organisation with the added access to the use and deployment of legitimate force (like, for example, authorising the use of firearms), raised all kinds of (implicit) uncomfortable questions about women, power, and control. The first female Chief Constable was appointed in 1995 and in the intervening years considerable efforts have been put into policing in particular to deal with the problems of sexual harassment and presumptions concerning the appropriate deployment of female officers. However as Westmarland's (2001) and Silvestri's (2003) work illustrates, sexism and the problems associated with it still remain.

The Fawcett Society's 2004 Report stands as testimony as to the nature and extent of the difficulties faced by women working across the criminal justice system. Yet, as the beginning of this chapter suggested, understanding gender requires that we understand how gendered assumptions impact upon men and women. Whilst as the Fawcett Society's own document in relation to the impact of the Equality Act 2006, 'Understanding Your Duty', illustrates the importance of taking account of women at every point in the work of the criminal justice system, in order to achieve the kind of gendered outcome that such practice might wish for, requires working with and taking account of men too. For example, it requires encouraging policemen to think again about what kind of work they might be valued for, like being domestic violence officers, and developing their skills appropriately, just as much as it might be about encouraging policewomen to become police motorcyclists. At this juncture it will be useful to return to the case of Alison Halford.

 CASE STUDY: ALISON HALFORD

Alison Halford was born in 1940 and after three years in the Women's Royal Air Force she joined the Metropolitan Police in 1962 at the age of 22. In 1966 after a spell in the C.I.D. she was accepted at the (then) Bramshill Police Staff College for the accelerated promotion course that saw her promoted to Inspector in 1967 at the age of 27. In 1975 she was the first female police officer to take operational command of a police station. In 1978 she was promoted to Superintendent and then to Chief Superintendent, Scotland Yard in 1981. She was appointed as Assistant Chief Constable, Merseyside Police, in 1983 at the age of 43. She was then the highest ranking female police officer in England and Wales. Between April 1987 and April 1990 she was rejected nine times for promotion to Deputy Chief Constable in a range of different police forces in England and Wales. In May 1990 the Equal Opportunities Commission agreed to take her case to an Equality Tribunal. After a long-drawn-out case in which Alison was the subject of a discipline enquiry within Merseyside Police Force and suspended from duty, an out-of-court settlement in July 1992 brought the tribunal case to a close and Alison retired from the police. In 1995, Pauline Clare, who had been appointed as an Assistant Chief Constable on Merseyside in the post once occupied by Alison Halford, was made Chief Constable of Lancashire, the first female officer to reach that rank.

Alison Halford's pursuit of her case through an Equality Tribunal was a very public and rather messy affair. During the course of it much information was leaked to the press including the 'swimming pool incident' in which it was alleged that she had stripped to her underwear and taken a swim with a (male) sergeant at the home of a local businessman whilst being on duty. In addition her sexuality was the subject of much discussion as accusations of her lesbianism fuelled further concerns about how this might impact upon questions of discipline. Moreover, during the tribunal hearing there was much press coverage of the hard-drinking macho culture of the Merseyside Police in which it was suggested that Alison herself had participated. Nevertheless the Equal Opportunities Commission have suggested that her case had a major impact in raising the profile of the kinds of problems faced by women in reaching the higher echelons of their chosen career, that in contemporary terms might be referred to as the 'glass ceiling'. Alison Halford wrote her own account of her experiences that was published in 1993 and titled: 'No Way Up the Greasy Pole'.

What is the relevance of this case today?

The reader might like to reflect upon the statistics on the sex patterning of workers in the criminal justice system and consider what has changed and what has remained the same in the period since the appointment of Pauline Clare to Chief Constable in 1995. There are clearly more women in higher ranking positions contemporarily, but what has remained the same? The reader might like to access the Annual Report from their own police force and examine:

1 How many male and female officers are employed in their local force?

2 What rank are they?

3 What tasks are they involved in?

4 Do the answers to these questions reveal anything about gender?

5 Do you think that the Equality Act 2006 and the associated code of practice will have an impact on the patterns you have observed?

6 So what has changed and what has remained the same since the case of Alison Halford made the headlines?

7 Is the prospect of a female Chief Constable still rather anomalous and what does that reveal, if anything, about gender in the contemporary criminal justice system?

Of course, Alison Halford's experiences were and are very similar to women's experiences in other work settings, not just those within the criminal justice process. They are experiences, however, that operate within a system that is framed by particular gendered assumptions that are found within the law itself and it is to a consideration of these issues that we shall now turn.

Gender and the law

This chapter has focused on the way in which anomalies reveal how gendered assumptions make their presence felt within the criminal justice system. However, there are two problems with this focus. The first returns us to the question of when is gender the salient variable. In other words when is it that gendered assumptions are the explanatory variable for the patterns and processes that are being observed and when might it be a question of age, ethnicity, class, or sexuality? The second question lies with the focus on the law, and changing the law as epitomised by the Equality Act 2006. Kendall (1991: 80) expresses this dilemma in this way:

> The question feminists face is whether justice for women is best achieved through legal recognition of sexual difference (special treatment) or by regarding sexual difference as largely irrelevant (equal treatment).

Her question poses a problem for those committed to using the law as an instrument of change, whether that be in regard to sexual offences legislation or equality legislation. Can the law be a vehicle for such change for women *as a group* as distinct from the value of the law in producing change for individual women? Recourse to the law as a vehicle of change accepts the view that the law is abstract, objective, and rational and thereby a site through which social change might be achieved. But is the law like this, or to put this question in another rather more critical way, whose interests are served by the law?

Naffine (1990) suggests that it is important to consider who is the 'man of law'. In her analysis the images of masculinity that underpin the liberal philosophy of legal thinking is the competitive entrepreneur, the successful market individual who has an 'eye for the main chance'. These images conjure a particular masculinity. It is the masculinity of the intellect, of the middle classes, not the masculinity of brute force. So the man of law is the middle class, entrepreneurial, rational man. This idealised version of masculinity that informs the framework and practice of the law impacts upon all those, men and women, who do not fit with this image. Thus the working class, black unemployed youth is problematic for the law not just as a lawbreaker but also as a man. This understanding facilitates an appreciation of the way in which professionals work in the court, for example, in constructing images of their clients that tap into these dominant assumptions and thus render their clients more acceptable to the court. The implication of this view of the law is that changing the law, in and of itself, will not necessarily change the gendered framework in which the law and the criminal justice system operate. The more meaningful question to think about might be, given that sex, as a biological or a cultural imperative cannot be avoided (we are all constructed in relation to the category 'sex' in some form or another), how do we make gender less relevant?

REVIEW QUESTIONS

1 Do you think that men and women should receive the same treatment or different treatment under the criminal law? What are the implications of your answer?

2 Explore the ways in which you think Naffine's characterisation of the 'man of law' manifests itself in the criminal justice system.

3 How might it be possible to make gender less relevant to the criminal justice system?

CONCLUSION

This chapter has endeavoured to paint a picture of the ways in which the social expectations associated with being male and female, masculinity and femininity permeate the work of the criminal justice system. These expectations colour the way in which offenders are handled by the system, to the way in which victims are responded to, through to the way in which it is expected that the various professionals working within the system engage with their work. It has been suggested that these gendered assumptions are unlikely to alter much whilst the imperative that underpins the work of the system, the criminal law, remains as the middle class, intellectual, entrepreneurial, man of law. It is clear that the question of gender, and how it permeates the workings of the criminal justice system in relation to the women who work in and are subject to that system now has a much higher profile than it did when Alison Halford was struggling to achieve promotion in the early 1990s. This is clearly evidenced by the codes of practice that will necessarily come into play as a consequence of the Equality Act 2006. However, the extent to which this means that the question of gender in relation to men might be addressed is a moot point. There are strong arguments both for and against about how to best manage the promotion of women's interests towards greater equality. As was intimated above, one of the key issues is whether or not you move for different treatment, that is treat women as a special case, or move for the same treatment, that is treat men and women equally. At the present moment in time the direction seems to be towards the former rather than the latter. Yet, if we are to take gender seriously this also means understanding and responding to the way in which social expectations of masculinity act as a constraint on men in a similar way to which the social expectations of femininity act as a constraint on women. Thus making progress through legislation alone runs the risk of not only failing both because of the powerful imperative of the man of law, it also runs the risk of subjecting those groups who are privileged by the legislation being subjected to a backlash scenario that does little to help either party.

QUESTIONS FOR DISCUSSION

1 What do you understand by masculinity and femininity? Make a list of the key characteristics you would expect a police officer, a probation officer, a prison officer, a judge to possess. Are these lists gendered in any way?

2 Do you think women are treated leniently by the criminal justice system? To what extent is their treatment the same or different than men's?

3 To what extent do you think that the criminal justice system is composed of gendered institutions? How does this manifest itself?

4 What do you think is the role of legislation in relation to gender? What further policy changes do you think are required to make questions of gender matter less?

GUIDE TO FURTHER READING

Heidensohn, F. (1996) *Women and Crime* (2nd edn). Basingstoke: Macmillan.

This book offers a critical exploration of theoretical and empirical issues that pertain to women's experiences of the criminal justice system as offenders, victims, and workers.

Kennedy, H. (1992) *Eve was Framed*. London: Chatto and Windus.

A very readable and accessible account of a leading QC's encounters with the question of gender and the legal system.

Newburn, T. and Stanko, E. (eds) (1994) *Just Boys Doing Business: Men, Masculinities and Crime*. London: Routledge.

This is a collection of readings that take the concept of masculinity as being central to understanding men's experiences of crime.

For those interested in first hand accounts of imprisonment it would be good to compare and contrast the account of Peckham, A. (1985) *A Woman in Custody*. London: Fontana with that of Boyle, J. (1977) *A Sense of Freedom*. Edinburgh: Canongate.

Walklate, S. (2004) Gender, *Crime and Criminal Justice* (2nd edn). Cullompton: Willan.

This book explores the theory, practice, and policy implications of taking the gender question seriously in the context of criminal justice.

WEB LINKS

http://www.fawcettsociety.org.uk

A valuable resource for documentation on women in the criminal justice system and those interested should also take a look at their report 'Understanding Your Duty' in reference to the Equality Act 2006.

http://www.justice.gov.uk

An essential source of information on men and women in relation to offending, victimisation, and working in the criminal justice system.

http://www.crimeinfo.org.uk

Run by the Centre for Crime and Justice Studies at King's College, London, it provides a useful database on all aspects of crime and responses to it.

http://www.womeninprison.org.uk

The base for the campaign work of Women in Prison, offers a wealth of interesting material, and raises issues of women's experiences of imprisonment that could usefully be compared and contrasted with men's.

http://www.bawp.org

The website for the British Association of Women Police where you can find their Gender Agenda for Policing.

REFERENCES

Adler, Z. (1987) *Rape on Trial*. London: Routledge, Kegan and Paul.

Allen, S. (2002) 'Male victims of rape: responses to a perceived threat to masculinity' in C. Hoyle and R. Young (eds) *New Visions of Crime Victims*. Oxford: Hart Publishing.

Braithwaite, J. (1989) *Crime, Shame and Reintegration*. Cambridge: Cambridge University Press.

Bennett, J., Crewe, B., and Wahidin, A. (eds) (2006) *Understanding Prison Staff*. Cullompton: Willan Publishing.

Burman, M. (2003) 'Girls behaving violently?'. *Criminal Justice Matters* 53: 20.

Carlen, P. (1988) *Women, Crime and Poverty*. Milton Keynes: Open University Press.

Carlen, P. (1994) 'Why study women's imprisonment or anyone else's?'. *British Journal of Criminology* 34: 131–40.

Connell, G.W. (1987) *Gender and Power*. Oxford: Polity Press.

Eaton, M. (1986) *Justice for Women? Family, Court and Social Control*. Milton Keynes: Open University Press.

Eaton, M. (1993) *Women After Prison*. Buckingham: Open University Press.

Fawcett Society (2004) *Women and the Criminal Justice System*. London: The Fawcett Society.

Hedderman, C. and Gelsthorpe, L. (1997) *The Sentencing of Women*. Home Office Research Study 170. London: Home Office.

Heidensohn, F. (1985) *Women and Crime* (1st edn). London: Macmillan.

HMIC/CPSI (2007) *Without Consent* <http://www.inspectorates.homeoffice.gov.uk/hmic>.

Kelly, L., Lovatt, J., and Regan, L. (2005) *A gap or a chasm? Attrition in reported rape cases*. Home Office Research Study 293. London: Home Office.

Kendall, K. (1991) 'The politics of premenstrual syndrome: implications for feminist justice'. *Journal of Human Justice* 2(2) Spring.

Lees, S. (1997) *Ruling Passions*. London: Sage.

Messerschmidt, J. (1993) *Masculinities and Crime*. Maryland: Rowman and Littlefield.

Ministry of Justice (2008a) *Population in custody England and Wales, monthly tables July 2008*. London: Ministry of Justice.

Ministry of Justice (2008b) *Offender Management Caseload Statistics 2006*. London: Ministry of Justice.

Ministry of Justice (2008c) *Statistics on Women and the Criminal Justice System 2005/06*. London: Ministry of Justice.

Naffine, N. (1987) *Female Crime*. Sydney: Allen and Unwin.

Naffine, N. (1990) *Law and the Sexes*. London: Allen and Unwin.

Naffine, N. (1997) *Feminism and Criminology*. Cambridge: Polity Press.

National Statistics (2006) *Focus on Gender* <http://www.statistics.gov.uk>.

Newburn, T. and Stanko, E.A. (1994) *Just Boys Doing Business*. London: Routledge.

Newton, C. (1994) 'Gender theory and prison sociology: using theories of masculinities to interpret the sociology of prisons for men'. *Howard Journal of Criminal Justice* 33(3): 193–202.

RDS NOMS (2006) *Offender Management Caseload Statistics 2005*. London: Home Office.

Silvestri, M. (2003) *Women in Charge: Policing, Gender and Leadership*. Cullompton: Willan Publishing.

Sim, J. (1994) 'Tougher than the rest' in T. Newburn and E.A. Stanko (eds) *Just Boys Doing Business*. London: Routledge.

Smart, C. (1977) *Women, Crime and Criminology*. London: Routledge, Kegan and Paul.

Smart, C. (1989) *Feminism and the Power of Law*. London: Routledge.

Smith, D. (1990) *The Everyday World as Problematic*. Milton Keynes: Open University Press.

Walby, S. and Allen, J. (2004) *Domestic violence, sexual assault and stalking: findings from the British Crime Survey*. Home Office Research Study 276. London: Home Office.

Westmarland, L. (2001) *Gender and Policing: Sex, Power and Police Culture*. Cullompton: Willan Publishing.

Wootton, B. (1959) *Social Science and Social Pathology*. London: George, Allen and Unwin.

Worrall, A. (1990) *Offending Women*. London: Routledge.

12 Minority groups and the criminal justice system

Basia Spalek

INTRODUCTION

Recent years have witnessed the emergence of a *'minority perspective'* within criminology as well as the criminal justice sector, whereby the experiences of specific communities, their specific histories and identities, have been increasingly focused upon and taken into account, by both researchers and policy makers (Phillips and Bowling, 2002; Garland, Spalek, and Chakraborti, 2006). These developments reflect the emergence of new social movements, consisting of politicised identities based on 'race'/ethnicity, *gender*, faith, sexual orientation, disability, and age, whose activities include demands for a recognition, or greater recognition, of their identities within the public sector. At the same time, increasing institutional reflexivity (Lash, 1994), as associated with conditions of late modernity, has led agencies of the criminal justice system to acknowledge, monitor, engage with, and minimise harms in relation to a wide range of minority groups, where harms are to be understood in relation to the prejudice and discrimination experienced by minority groups through their interaction with agencies of the criminal justice system and in relation to *hate crimes* perpetrated against them.

The following chapter aims to highlight some of the key issues when exploring *crime*, victimisation, and criminal justice in relation to minorities. Minorities are defined as consisting of those groups who constitute the 'Other', the devalued, within oppositional binaries that straddle contemporary Western society. An overriding framework to the issues raised in this chapter is that whilst social groupings in relation to 'race'/ethnicity and gender (see the chapter by Walklate in this volume) have generated substantial research and policy attention within a criminal justice context, increasingly, a broader range of minority groups are being focused upon in research, policy and practice arenas, including faith minorities, lesbian, gay, bisexual, and *transgender* (LGBT) minorities, individuals with physical or learning disabilities, and older people. At the same time, there is growing awareness of the diversity of experiences that such broad social groupings contain; therefore, researchers and policy makers are increasingly concerned with documenting and acknowledging the specific experiences and needs of individuals belonging to a wide range of minority groups. It is important to stress that the subject of minorities in relation to the criminal justice system is a very broad and complex area. As a result, this chapter constitutes only a snapshot of some of the important debates and key findings.

Defining minority groups

A way of conceptualising and defining minority status is to draw upon those taken-for-granted assumptions about the world that researchers have highlighted as underpinning Western cultures and discourses: constituting minorities as those individuals and groups as Other (see Hooks, 1990). Drawing upon the work of Hooks (1990), the Other might be viewed as those groups whose experiences lie outside of dominant social norms. For example, in relation to Black women, even when difference is viewed positively, White women's lives and the norms that govern those lives occupy a central position against which Black women's experiences are compared and analysed (Hooks, 1990). Thus, according to Collins (1998), Western scientific discourse has created the illusion of binary oppositions, so that human differences have been viewed simplistically in opposition to each other. Oppositional binaries like male/female, straight/gay, or normal/deviant underpin Western culture, constructing taken-for-granted assumptions and norms about the world. Taylor (2004) argues that components of language find their meaning through the presence of an Other, an opposite that is devalued, so that differences are stressed between these antagonistic opposites, and those considered to constitute the Other are often perceived as being inferior and so excluded and prevented from entering the borders of the dominant category making up the particular dichotomy.

It can be suggested that minority groups constitute those individuals and communities that lie outside of dominant, yet largely invisible norms. Regimes of power in relation to whiteness, *patriarchy*, secularism, *heterosexism*, disablism, ageism, and sedentarism (according to James (2006), sedentarism is a norm that underpins mainstream society, serving to construct traveller communities as deviant) cast Black and minority ethnic groups, women, faith identities, LGBT communities, people with disabilities, older people, and travellers and gypsies as minorities, as lying outside of dominant/mainstream norms, thereby occupying a marginalised and often deviant status. Moreover, it is also important to highlight that minorities exist within minorities because there are 'hidden' minorities, consisting of populations that have traditionally been neglected or excluded from research and/or policy agenda. For example, individuals of dual heritage have often been overlooked in research that has focused upon 'race'/ethnicity (Garland *et al.*, 2006). Similarly, within the umbrella term 'transgender' lie groupings in relation to the following categories: the cross-dresser, drag queen, drag king, transgender male, transgender female, intersexed, stone butch, and nellie queen, who may have specific experiences of violence that law enforcement agencies and victim services need to take into account (Moran and Sharpe, 2004). Indeed, in relation to the gender category, women with disabilities have particular issues that need to be addressed by agencies of the criminal justice system, yet they are often marginalised. Therefore, although the nomenclature used in relation to 'race'/ethnicity, gender, faith, sexual orientation, disability, and age is suggestive of in-group homogeneity, it is important to highlight that there is considerable and significant diversity within such groupings.

A further point to note is that different minority groupings have attracted different levels of research and policy attention, this being the product of a complex combination of social, political, and legislative factors (see Spalek, 2008). It is perhaps fair to argue that minorities in relation to the groupings of 'race'/ethnicity and gender have traditionally attracted the most research and policy focus within the criminal justice arena. This can be evidenced by the amount of information about race/ethnicity and gender that is routinely assembled by agencies of the criminal justice system, as part of a wider strategy of ensuring that policies and practices are not disadvantaging minority ethnic communities or women (see, for example, Ministry of Justice, 2008a and b). No similar statistics are collated in relation to other social groupings in terms of faith, disability, or sexual orientation.

A definition of minority status has been provided in the above sections. The sections which follow focus upon specific minority groupings, addressing key areas of concern within a criminal justice context.

Black and minority ethnic groups

Since the *Home Office* began monitoring for 'race'/ethnicity, statistics have consistently shown that Black, particularly African Caribbean, men and women are overrepresented in the prison population (Shute, Hood, and Seemungal, 2005). For example, on 30 June 2007, the prison population stood at 79,700 with 26 per cent of prisoners identifying themselves as belonging to Black and minority ethnic (BME) groups (Ministry of Justice, 2008b). Just over a quarter of the male population described themselves as from BME groups. Of these, 15 per cent were Black, 7 per cent were Asian, 3 per cent Mixed and 1 per cent Chinese and other. A larger proportion of the female population comprises women from BME groups (29 per cent), of which 19 per cent were Black, 2 per cent were Asian, 5 per cent were Mixed, and 2 per cent Chinese and other (Ministry of Justice, 2008b). Foreign nationals also make up a significant proportion of the prison population. In June 2007, foreign nationals accounted for 39 per cent of the BME prison population (Ministry of Justice, 2008b). Women are more disproportionately represented than men (25 per cent of female BME prisoners are foreign nationals compared with 14 per cent of males). This comprises a substantial proportion of the BME prison population and suggests that foreign nationals charged or sentenced for importing drugs significantly influence the disproportionate number of BME prisoners. According to Kalunta-Crompton (2004), this is particularly the case for female prisoners. Thus, in June 1997, Black foreign nationals made up 80 per cent of the UK female foreign nationals serving a prison sentence for drug offences (Kalunta-Crompton: 2004: 13).

The issue of crime rates within Black communities has generated much research interest. According to researchers adopting a critical position, linking crime to the 'race'/ethnicity of offenders propagates racist stereotypes. For example, writing about criminal offences taking place within Black communities can lead to crime being associated with being Black, thereby stigmatising entire communities (Bridges and Gilroy, 1982). Lea and Young (1993) argued that crime rates within Black communities are intra-class and intra-racial and thus crime has a very real impact upon Black communities. For example, gun crime traumatises not only victims and their families but whole communities (see the Metropolitan Police Authority website for more details <http://www.mpa.gov.uk/issues/gun-crime/default.htm>). However, 'race'/ethnicity may not be *the* significant factor which explains the link between 'race' ethnicity and crime because higher levels of offending are associated with poverty, low educational attainment, unemployment, as well as a young demographic age profile, all of which are more prevalent in BME communities.

Turning to the issue of victimisation, Phillips and Bowling (2003: 583) argue that the recording of racist incidents by the police has risen by 523 per cent between 1988 and

1998/9. This may be due to improved recording practices, greater confidence to report crimes to the police, as well as the introduction of a victim-defined approach to racist crime. It is important to note that although there has been a significant increase in the number of racist incidents that are recorded by the police, recorded crime levels under-represent the actual extent of victimisation. National crime surveys are considered to constitute a more accurate reflection of the extent of victimisation because they directly target households, allowing individuals to reveal experiences of crime that they have not necessarily reported to the police. National crime surveys indicate that people belonging to minority ethnic groups experience high levels of victimisation. For example, the *British Crime Survey* shows that Pakistanis and Bangladeshis are significantly more likely than White people to be the victims of household crime. They are also significantly more likely to be the victims of racially motivated attacks than Indians, Blacks, or Whites (Clancy, Hough, Aust, and Kershaw: 2001: 2). According to the British Crime Survey more than one-third of assaults directed against Asians and Blacks are considered by respondents to be racially motivated (Phillips and Bowling, 2003). Perhaps the high levels of risk of victimisation account for individuals' high crime anxiety levels. The British Crime Survey 2001/02 and 2002/03 indicates that people from BME backgrounds were more likely to have high levels of worry about burglary, car crime, and violence than White people (Salisbury and Upson: 2004: 1). The impact of racist crime is particularly severe. For example, victims' reactions may include anger, feeling shocked, and being fearful. Victims might move house; avoid certain places (for example, football matches, the pub), or invest in crime *prevention* techniques such as shatterproof glass and fireproof mailboxes (Bowling, 1999). The British Crime Survey (2000) shows that a much larger proportion of victims of racial incidents said that they had been very much affected by the incident (42 per cent) than victims of other types of incident (19 per cent) (Clancy *et al.*, 2001: 37).

A particularly shocking racist incident occurred on 22 April 1993, when 18-year-old Stephen Lawrence was murdered in Eltham, South London. This incident stimulated fresh political and social concern over racism within the police service as well as within wider society. A public inquiry, led by Sir William Macpherson, found the police to be institutionally racist, which was defined as:

> The collective failure of an organisation to provide an appropriate and professional service to people because of their colour, culture or ethnic origin. It can be seen or detected in processes, attitudes and behaviour which amount to discrimination through unwitting prejudice, ignorance, thoughtlessness and racist stereotyping which disadvantages minority ethnic people. (Macpherson: 1999: 6.34)

Rowe (2004) argues that the Macpherson report (1999) is significant because it provided the political impetus to develop a wide range of policies and initiatives: improving minority ethnic communities' trust and confidence in the police service; reducing racism within the police service; establishing a greater representation of minority ethnic police officers; addressing retention and promotion issues of minority ethnic staff; and improving race relations training for officers.

REVIEW QUESTIONS

1 What is meant by minorities in the context of the criminal justice system?

2 In what ways do BME groups' experiences of the criminal justice process differ from those of White people?

Faith minorities

According to Lerner (2000: 5–6), 'religions are the various historical attempts to organise a set of doctrines, rituals and specific behaviours that are supposed to be the right way to live'. The major world religious traditions consist of Judaism, Christianity, Buddhism, Hinduism, Sikhism, and Islam, although within these groupings there can be a large variety of sub-groupings. For example, Christianity includes: Anglican, Catholic, and Protestant groups as well as other sects. Islam is diverse with many different religious strands, including Sunni and Shi'a. Within these religious strands there are many different schools of Islamic thought. For example, within the Sunni tradition, there are a number of different movements, including Barelwis, Deobandis, Tablighi Jamat, and Jama'at-I-Islami. Amongst Hindus and Sikhs there is also much diversity. For instance, within the Hindu faith there are caste or jati groupings which are significant in how these communities are organised. A jati is the hereditary group that people identify with and is associated with one of the four varnas making up the 'ideal' structure of Hindu society. Varnas consist of the intelligentsia and priests, the administrators and the military, the agriculturalists and the merchants, and the labourers and servants. These groups are often referred to in English as castes (Beckford, Gale, Owen, Peach, and Weller, 2006: 8). Over 2,000 New Religious Movements (NRMs) also exist, which include groups like the Children of God, Krishna Consciousness, and Scientology.

Only limited criminal justice information is available in relation to faith communities, although more information is likely to be made available in the future. Most of the monitoring procedures used by agencies of the criminal justice system to record suspects', offenders', victims', and employees' identities only use racial and/or ethnic and not faith categories. Only the Prison Service systematically records offenders' religious identities. Thus, for example, statistics in relation to the police use of stop and search under counter-terrorism legislation use ethnic rather than religious categories. This means that although statistics may suggest an increase in the number of Asians being stopped and searched, it is not possible to gauge the faith of the individuals stopped (Garland *et al.*, 2006). The British Crime Survey includes race/ethnic monitoring but does not generally include religious monitoring. Consequently, it is not possible to measure accurately victimisation levels within and between faith communities. However, data relating to the faith identities of respondents has been recorded since 2005/06 so data will become more easily available. The Home Office Citizenship Survey documents faith identities and looks at perceptions and experiences of prejudice and discrimination (although not actual experiences of criminal victimisation). It reveals that Hindus, Muslims, and Sikhs are substantially more likely to report that they are very worried about being attacked due to their skin colour, ethnic origin, or religion than Christians, those of other religions, and those of no religion (Department of Communities and Local Government, 2006: 28).

The focus upon ethnicity, rather than on religion, as an identity marker has meant that the significance of religious identity to the policies and practices of criminal justice agencies has traditionally been largely omitted. Whilst direct and *institutional racism* by the police, the courts, and the penal system has been extensively documented (Phillips and Bowling, 2002; Shute, Hood, and Seemungal, 2005), and policies have been implemented to tackle these issues, discrimination on the grounds of religion has rarely been addressed. The emphasis upon 'race'/ethnicity rather than religion has no doubt been due partly to the historical separation of modern institutions from their religious roots (Beckford, 1996). In the past, religious convictions have been a motivating factor for those individuals who have volunteered their services towards rehabilitating offenders and reducing crime. Thus, the historical roots of the Probation Service lie in the police court missionaries in England in the late eighteenth and early nineteenth centuries, many of whom had religious convictions. The Probation of Offenders Act 1907 put this work onto a statutory footing which means that courts could now appoint and pay probation officers, thereby absorbing the original court missionaries into these new services. The 1920s was the period when probation work moved away from religious, missionary ideals to become a professional based service (Whitfield, 1998).

One particular strand within criminological research that has focused upon religiosity is in relation to youth offending, exploring the question of whether participation in religious activities, as well as having religious beliefs, has any effect on delinquency. The findings are mixed, with some researchers rejecting the relevance of religiosity on delinquency, whilst other researchers argue that the relationship between religiosity and delinquency varies according to different contexts and different types of offence. More recently, Johnson *et al.*, (2001: 37–8) have claimed that their study provides empirical evidence that the 'effects of religiosity are neither spurious nor completely indirect via secular (non-religious) models of *social control*'. Rather, Johnson *et al.*, (2001) argue that religiosity is linked to reduced delinquency and this may be due, in part, to the finding that an adolescent's disapproval of delinquent acts increases with increasing religious involvement.

Religion may be used by individuals as a cultural resource in order to justify committing crime. For instance, in a study exploring *domestic violence* experienced by Black women, it was found that some men might invoke 'tradition' or 'religion' to justify their violent actions (Mama, 2000). It has also been claimed that within some Muslim youth subcultures, religion may be used to justify and/or absolve deviant or criminal acts. Justifications may include claims that the victims are not Muslim or that they belong to a different religious community, and individuals may pay some of the proceeds from crime to Islamic causes or centres as a way of absolving themselves from guilt (Pargeter, 2006).

The true extent of faith-related hate crimes is unknown because most victims do not report their experiences to the police and the number that are prosecuted is nominal.

However, there are several sources of data. The Anti-Terrorism, Crime and Security Act 2001 introduced legislation relating to religiously aggravated offending. It brought in higher penalties for offenders who are motivated by religious hatred. So far, there have been relatively few religiously aggravated *prosecutions*. The majority of victims involved are Muslim. Between 2004 and 2005, out of total of 34 cases of religiously aggravated offences, 23 incidents involved Muslims victims, four involved Christian victims, and two involved Hindu victims. Community groups, often working in partnership with local police services, play an important role in monitoring and documenting instances of hate crime. For example, the Community Security Trust (CST), which represents the Jewish community on matters of anti-Semitism in the UK, recorded 455 anti-semitic incidents in 2005, this being the second-highest annual total since the CST started recording incidents in 1984 (CST, 2006: 4). The Forum Against Islamophobia and Racism (FAIR), the Islamic Human Rights Organisation (IHRO), and the Muslim Council of Britain are three community groups that monitor hate crimes committed against Muslim communities. According to the IHRC, there is a rise in the number of anti-Muslim attacks during the holy month of Ramadan. This serves to illustrate how the incidence of faith hate crimes can be influenced by particular national, international, and cultural/religious events. Indeed, in the aftermath of the London bombings on 7 July 2005, the Metropolitan Police Service recorded a sharp increase in faith-related hate crimes, including verbal and physical assaults (European Monitoring Centre on Racism and Xenophobia, 2005).

Within *victimology*, researchers are increasingly acknowledging the role that religion and spirituality may play. Critical Black feminists have introduced the notion of 'spirit injury' as constituting an important aspect of the process of victimisation. According to Kennedy *et al.*, (1998) some research has documented the role that spirituality plays in individuals' reactions to stressful, non-criminal events, such as bereavement. Nonetheless, research has not generally examined the role of spirituality in relation to individuals' responses to crime. However, Spalek (2002) has highlighted how some Muslim women who experience victimisation may turn to prayer, meditation, and their local Imam (a religious leader or teacher in Islam) as a way of helping them cope with the aftermath of crime. Kennedy *et al.*, (1998: 322) studied spirituality in relation to female victims of sexual assault. They found that the majority of the female victims (60 per cent) revealed an increased sense of the spiritual in the aftermath of the crimes. Furthermore, those victims with increased spirituality appeared to cope better than those victims whose spirituality did not rise. Indeed, according to Shorter-Gooden (2004), participation in a congregation or spiritual community may be part of a technique that some African-American women draw upon to help them cope with racism and sexism.

REVIEW QUESTIONS

1 Why have faith identities traditionally been marginalised within a criminal justice context?

2 How, and in what ways, might religion be a significant factor in how individuals experience crime and the criminal justice process?

Other minority groups within the criminal justice system

There are a range of other minority groups which the criminal justice system has traditionally ignored including lesbian, gay, bisexual, and transgender communities, the disabled, and older people. The experiences of these groups will be discussed in this section.

Lesbian, gay, bisexual, transgender communities

The experiences of lesbian, gay, bisexual, and transgender (LGBT) communities in relation to crime, criminal justice, and victimisation have traditionally been marginalised by policy makers and researchers. Surveys carried out with LGBT minority groups illustrate that the level of hate crimes is significant. According to Mason (2002), surveys carried out in the US, Canada, Great Britain, Australia, and New Zealand suggest that 70 to 80 per cent of lesbians and gay men report experiencing verbal abuse in public on the basis of their sexuality; 30 to 40 per cent report threats of violence; 20 per cent of gay men report physical violence; and 10 to 12 per cent of lesbians report physical violence. Incidents included being: chased, sexually assaulted, pelted with objects, spat at, and having property vandalised (Mason, 2002). Although random attacks by strangers appear to be common, Mason (2002) argues that lesbians may experience a significant higher level of abuse at home or at work, involving ongoing campaigns of abuse perpetrated by a person known to the victims. This may also be the case in relation to the experiences that gay men have of abuse. Mason (2002) interviewed 75 lesbians and found that almost every woman had experienced a verbally, physically, or sexually abusive reaction to her sexuality at least once in her life. Words commonly used to insult lesbians include 'dirty' and 'butch'. Mason (2002) argues that in order to understand violence committed against lesbians it is important to look at the regime of heterosexuality, as well as patriarchy, as the binary Hetero-Homo sexuality can serve to produce and perpetuate prejudices that underpin violence against lesbians.

Hate crimes against LGBT minorities affect all individuals, not only those who have directly experienced violence, as violence against LGBT groups serves to influence how individuals negotiate their personal safety both in public and private spaces. Felsenthal (2004) argues that due to the transphobic violence and abuse experienced by transgender people, individuals may limit their use of public space, remaining behind closed doors. Indeed, some individuals may pretend to be heterosexual due to the fear of possible violence (Mason, 2002).

Over the last two decades or so the police and prosecution authorities have striven to engage with LGBT communities, and male homosexuality has been partially decriminalised with the passing of the Sexual Offences Act 1967. However, distrust of the police amongst LGBT communities remains significant, so that only a small proportion of crimes committed against LGBT groups are reported; even serious crimes such as *rape* or blackmail often remain unreported. Indeed the Association of Chief Police Officers (2001 in McGhee, 2002: 359) acknowledged that many LGBT individuals believe that homophobia is widespread within the police service. Other reasons for the under-reporting of hate crimes is the belief that an incident will not be taken seriously by the authorities or that an incident is not serious enough to report (McGhee, 2002: 359).

It is also important to note that there are significant differences between and within LGBT communities. These variations have implications not only for research but also for policy and practice-related issues. Moran and Sharpe (2004) argue that there are significant differences between transgender males and females in how they experience violence and that these differences should be taken into account by law enforcement and victim services. For example, the police may view transgender women as being engaged in overtly risky behaviour, and therefore may judge them as being illegitimate victims, thereby responding inappropriately to their experiences. Transgender men may have a significant fear of rape which is not likely to be taken seriously by law enforcement agencies. Transgender men may also be less likely to report crimes to the police than transgender women. This may be because the perceptions that transgender men have of violence are likely to be informed by their previous experiences as women. Moreover, victim services that help women who have experienced gender violence are not likely to cater for the needs of cross dressers or transgender women (Moran and Sharpe, 2004). Older people within LGBT minority groups are also likely to have specific issues that agencies of the criminal justice system, as well as victim services, need to address (Pugh, 2002).

Community consultation raises a number of issues. It appears that although considerable advances have been made with respect to consultation with gay men, lesbians' needs have tended to be overlooked because of a lack of political organisation and power.

The disabled

Disabled people who experience crime have been labelled 'invisible victims' because crimes committed against these individuals are often hidden and not reported to agencies of the criminal justice system. At the same time, little research has been generated regarding the incidence of crimes against people with disabilities, and crimes that may take place in institutional care are not included in the British Crime Survey (Williams, 1995). A number of surveys have been carried out with disabled respondents, and these show that hate crimes are a significant issue for people with disabilities. For example, in a survey of disabled people and their carers carried out in Scotland by the Disability Rights Commission (2004), out of 158 completed questionnaires it was found that approximately half the disabled people who responded experienced hate crime because of their disability. It was also found that 31 per cent of disabled people surveyed who were the victims of hate crime experienced the attacks at least once a month. Hate crimes leave people feeling scared, embarrassed, humiliated, and stressed. Moreover, individuals are likely to avoid specific places and change their usual routines and many may also move home as a result of being victimised.

Interestingly, developments since the 1990s suggest that equality legislation is increasingly taking into account individuals with disabilities and this is likely to impact upon the policies and practices of agencies of the criminal justice system. For example, the Disability Discrimination Act 1995 provided legal rights for disabled people, covering employment, access to services, education, transport and housing. This Act was amended by the Disability Discrimination Act 2005 which places a duty on all public sector authorities to promote disability equality. This means that all public sector bodies, including criminal justice agencies, have a duty to promote equality of opportunity for disabled people through preparing and publishing disability equality schemes.

Older people

According to Wahidin and Cain (2006), although age constitutes a key variable in the study of criminality, the tendency has been for researchers to focus upon young offenders. As a result the 'unyoung', defined as those individuals 'deemed beyond the pale of the human because of their perceived frailties, dependence, failure to be contributing members of society' have traditionally been overlooked (Wahidin and Cain: 2006: 4). Nonetheless, over the last decade or so, researchers and policy makers have increasingly turned their attention towards older people, as both the victims and perpetrators of crime. It has to be stressed, however, that there is considerable debate over the definition of 'old'. Some studies have used 60+ or 70 whereas others have used 50+ (see Phillips, 2006 for further discussion).

Turning to the issue of older people as the victims of crime, elder abuse is a key research and policy area. There is an expanding literature on this issue, and the work carried out by groups campaigning for equal rights for older people, like Help the Aged and Age Concern, now includes a focus upon elder abuse. Action on Elder Abuse (AEA) was established in 1993 and is a national organisation which aims to prevent the abuse of older people. A helpline was set up in 1997, offering a free and confidential service. According to the AEA, elder abuse is 'a single or repeated act or lack of appropriate action occurring within any relationship where there is an expectation of trust which causes harm or distress to an older person'. This may involve physical, psychological, financial, sexual abuse, and/or neglect. An analysis of the calls received by the AEA telephone helpline reveals that between 1997 and 1999, most calls were about abuse in people's own homes, although a quarter referred to abuse in hospitals, nursing and residential homes; two-fifths of the calls reported psychological abuse, one-fifth physical, and one-fifth financial abuse; over a quarter of calls identified workers as the abuser (Jenkins, Asif, and Bennett, 2005). According to Fitzgerald (2006), the prevalence of elder abuse in the UK is difficult to estimate because there has been only one study on the community prevalence of elder abuse and no research into abuse within institutions catering to the welfare and social needs of older people. According to a survey carried out by the Office of Population Census and Surveys in 1992, which included 593 individuals aged over 60, 5 per cent of this sample of 593 reported having been orally abused, 2 per cent reported experiencing physical abuse, and 2 per cent reported experiencing financial abuse (in Fitzgerald, 2006: 96). Older people can also be the victims of a wide range of other crimes, including burglary or physical assault. Indeed, older people can be the victims of corporate crime, this being a particularly under-researched area (Spalek, 1999; Powell and Wahidin, 2004).

Turning to the issue of older people as the perpetrators of crime, the proportion of older prisoners has been rising over the last two decades. According to Phillips (2006: 56) the proportion of older prisoners between 1990 and 2000 almost trebled, constituting 1 per cent of prisoners in 1990 and rising to 2.3 per cent by 2000. Many older prisoners have been convicted of sexual or violent offences. Most of them are men, although the proportion of older female prisoners has also significantly risen since 1992 (Phillips, 2006: 56). Older prisoners present particular challenges for the Prison Service. It is also important to acknowledge significant diversity within the population of older prisoners. Some prisoners may, for example, be career criminals whose experiences may be very different from lifers who have aged in prison (Phillips, 2006).

REVIEW QUESTIONS

1 To what extent are the experiences of LGBT, the disabled, and older people considered by the criminal justice system?

2 Why might the impact of hate crime upon people from LGBT, people with disabilities, and older people be particularly severe?

CONCLUSION

The subject of minorities in relation to the criminal justice system raises many issues. This chapter illustrates how the phrase *'equality and specificity within diversity'* might be used to capture contemporary developments within the criminal justice system. Traditionally, there has been a hierarchy between different groupings in terms of the levels of protection and research afforded them, with 'race'/ ethnicity and gender generating most attention. However, recent trends suggest that this hierarchy is levelling out, so that minority groupings in relation to faith, sexuality, disability, and age are attracting more research and policy attention. At the same time, there is a growing awareness that the distinct voices and experiences of certain specific groups of individuals are obscured within such broad-based approaches, and so, increasingly, more nuanced methods are being adopted, whereby the needs of specific communities are increasingly being taken into account. These developments mirror wider processes taking place in late modern society, consisting of the interaction of two contradictory yet interrelated mechanisms: the 'imperative of order' (Lash, 1994) arising out of, and being located within, the framework of modernity, whereby group collectivities are formed around politicised identities in relation to 'race'/ethnicity, gender, faith, sexuality, disability, and age, these being underpinned by a belief in emancipation from oppression. At the same time, standing in contradiction to, but also interacting with this imperative is rising individualisation, the growing fragmentation of identity attachments (where identities might be viewed as being socially constructed, being influenced by micro and macro factors in relation to historical, geographical, cultural, institutional, biological, and psychological processes), and increasing institutional reflexivity. These processes are integral to understanding the broader context to the subject of minorities and criminal justice.

 CASE STUDY: HOMOPHOBIC VIOLENCE

In October 2005, 24-year-old Jody Dobrowski was murdered on Clapham Common as he crossed a gay cruising area. Walker and Pickford, Dobrowski's murderers were motivated by homophobia and inflicted serious head, neck, and body wounds. One of the attackers said, 'We don't like poofters here, and that's why we can kill him if we want'. In court, the judge told the attackers: 'It was a pre-meditated attack on a gay man. As it continued and increased in ferocity, there was an intention to kill. He suffered considerably before his death.' Outside the court, the victim's mother, Sheri, said: 'It was a political act. It was an act of terrorism. Jody was not the first man to be killed, or terrorised, or beaten or humiliated for being homosexual, or for being perceived to be homosexual. Tragically, he will not be the last man to suffer the consequences of homophobia which is endemic in this society. This is unacceptable. We cannot accept this. No intelligent, healthy or reasonable society could.' The Old Bailey judge sentenced both Pickford and Walker to a minimum of 28 years imprisonment, this constituting the first instance in Britain where a judge has been able to use motivation based on sexual orientation as an aggravating feature when sentencing for murder. (Source: James Sturke, 16 June 2006, 'Barman Killer had been Released Early' Guardian Unlimited at <http://politics.guardian.co.uk/homeaffairs/story/0,,1799521,00.html> accessed 27 March 2007)

QUESTIONS FOR DISCUSSION

1   What does the development of a 'minority perspective' within criminal justice involve?

2   To what extent can the criminal justice system be viewed as 'institutionally racist'?

3   How can the criminal justice system's treatment of hate crime be improved?

4   In what ways do minority groups' experiences of the criminal justice system differ?

GUIDE TO FURTHER READING

Bowling, B. and Phillips, C. (2002) *Racism, Crime and Justice*. Harlow: Longman.

This text focuses on 'race' issues in relation to criminal justice, highlighting many key areas of research and policy.

Garland, J., Spalek, B., and Chakraborti, N. (2006) 'Hearing Lost Voices: Issues in Researching Hidden Minority Ethnic Communities' *The British Journal of Criminology* Vol. 46: 423–437.

This article highlights some of the key issues and tensions that a focus upon the development of a minority perspective poses within Criminology.

Spalek, B. (2008) *Communities, Identities and Crime*. Bristol: Policy Press.

This book examines the implications that the emergence of a 'minority perspective' has upon criminological knowledge production.

Wahidin, A. and Cain, M. (2006) (eds) *Ageing, Crime and Society*. Devon: Willan.

This provides an excellent source of material around ageing issues in relation to crime and the criminal justice system, focusing on areas such as elder abuse, older prisoners, and older people and fear of crime.

Walklate, S. (2001) *Gender, Crime and Criminal Justice*. Cullompton: Willan.

This text focuses on key issues and debates in relation to gender and crime, including Criminology, victimology and feminism, sexual violence, and police work.

WEB LINKS

Stonewall

http://www.stonewall.org.uk/

The website of the professional lobbying organisation dedicated to addressing the needs of LGBT minorities in the wider community which includes information about their current and past campaigns, and a useful information bank covering a range of topics.

Community Safety Trust

http://www.thecst.org.uk/

An excellent source of information in relation to Jewish communities, what is being done to protect them from hate crimes, and the history of anti-Semitism in the UK.

Forum Against Islamophobia and Racism

http://www.fairuk.org

An excellent source of information about Muslim minorities, crime, and criminal justice issues which includes a useful collation of factsheets, reports on Islamophobia, media monitoring, and legal and policy documents.

Equality and Human Rights Commission

http://www.equalityhumanrights.com/en/Pages/default.aspx

This is the website of this new organisation that in 2007 amalgamated the Equal Opportunities Commission, the Commission for Racial Equality, and the Disability Rights Commission. It includes information on current policy and research, publications and resources, and news and comment.

Action on Elder Abuse

http://www.elderabuse.org.uk/

A helpful source of information about elder abuse which includes downloadable pamphlets, reports, and a useful reference guide.

REFERENCES

Beckford, J. (1996) 'Postmodernity, High Modernity and New Modernity: three concepts in search of religion' in K. Flanagan and P. Jupp (eds) *Postmodernity, Sociology and Religion*: 30–47.

Beckford, J., Gale, R., Owen, D., Peach, C., and Weller, P. (2006) *Review of the Evidence Base on Faith Communities*. London: Office of the Deputy Prime Minister.

Bridges, L. and Gilroy, P. (1982) 'Striking Back' *Marxism Today*: 34–5.

Bowling, B. (1999) *Violent Racism: victimisation, policing and social context* (revised edn). Oxford: Oxford University Press.

Clancy, A., Hough, M., Aust, R., and Kershaw, C. (2001) 'Crime, Policing and Justice: the experiences of ethnic minorities. Findings from the 2000 British Crime Survey'. *Home Office Research and Statistics* 223. London: Home Office.

Collins, P. (1998) *Fighting Words*. Minneapolis: University of Minnesota Press.

Community Security Trust (CST) (2006) Anti-Semitic Incidents Report 2005. The Community Security Trust <http://www.thecst.org.uk>.

Department of Communities and Local Government (2006) 2005 Citizenship Survey race and faith topic report. London: DCLG.

Disability Rights Commission (2004) 'Research reveals impact of hate crime on disabled Scots' available at <http://www.drc-gb.org/about.us/drc_scotland/news/research_reveals_impact_of_hat.aspx>.

European Monitoring Centre on Racism and Xenophobia (2005) *The Impact of 7 July 2005 London Bomb Attacks on Muslim Communities in the EU*. Vienna: EUMC.

Felsenthal, K. (2004) 'Socio-Spatial Experiences of Transgender Individuals' in Jean Lau Chin (ed) (2004) *The Psychology of Prejudice and Discrimination: bias based on gender and sexual orientation* Vol. 3. London: Praeger Publishers, 201–25.

Fitzgerald, G. (2006) 'The realities of elder abuse' in A. Wahidin and M. Cain (2006) (eds) *Ageing, Crime and Society*. Devon: Willan Publishing, 90–106.

Garland, J., Spalek, B., and Chakraborti, N. (2006) 'Hearing Lost Voices: Issues in Researching Hidden Minority Ethnic Communities'. *The British Journal of Criminology* Vol. 46: 423–37.

Home Office (2007) Hate Crime <http://www.homeoffice.gov.uk/crime-victims/reducing-crime/ hate-crime/?version=3> accessed 1 March 2007.

Hooks, B. (1990) *Yearning race, gender and cultural politics*. Boston: South End Press.

James, Z. (2006) 'Policing Space: managing New Travellers in England'. *British Journal of Criminology* 46(3): 470–85.

Jenkins, G., Asif, Z., and Bennett, G. (2005) *Listening is not Enough*. London: Acton on Elder Abuse.

Johnson, B., Jang, S., Larson, D., and De Li, S. (2001) 'Does Adolescent Religious Commitment Matter? A re-examination of the effects of religiosity on delinquency'. *Journal of Research in Crime and Delinquency* 38(1): 22–43.

Kalunta-Crompton, A. (2004) 'Criminology and orientalism' in A. Kalunta-Crompton and B. Agozino (eds) *Pan-African Issues in Crime and Justice*. Aldershot: Ashgate, 5–22.

Kennedy, J., Davis, R., and Taylor, B. (1998) 'Changes in Spirituality and Well-Being Among Victims of Sexual Assault'. *Journal of the Scientific Study of Religion* 37(2): 322–8.

Lash, S. (1994) 'Reflexivity and its Doubles: structure, aesthetics, community' in U. Beck, A. Giddens, and S. Lash *Reflexive Modernization: politics, tradition and aesthetics in the modern social order*. Cambridge: Polity Press, 110–73.

Lea, J. and Young, J. (1993) *What is To Be Done About Law and Order? Crisis in the Nineties*. London: Pluton Press.

Lerner, M. (2000) *Spirit Matters*. Charlottesville: Hampton Roads Publishing Company.

Macpherson, W. (1999) *The Stephen Lawrence Inquiry*. London: HMSO.

Mama, A. (2000) 'Woman Abuse in London's Black Communities' in K. Owusu (ed) *Black British Culture and Society*. London: Routledge, 89–110.

Mason, G. (2002) *The Spectacle of Violence homophobia, gender and knowledge*. London: Routledge.

McGhee, D. (2002) 'Joined-Up Government, Community Safety and Lesbian, Gay, Bisexual and Transgender Active Citizens'. *Critical Social Policy* 23(3): 345–374.

Ministry of Justice (2008a) *Statistics on Women and the Criminal Justice System 2005/6*. London: Ministry of Justice.

Ministry of Justice (2008b) *Statistics on Race and the Criminal Justice System 2006/7*. London: Ministry of Justice.

Moran, L. and Sharpe, A. (2004) 'Violence, Identity and Policing: the case of violence against transgender people'. *Criminal Justice* 4(4): 395–417.

Pargeter, A. (2006) 'North African Immigrants in Europe and Political Violence'. *Studies in Conflict and Terrorism* 29(8): 731–47.

Phillips, C. and Bowling, B. (2002) 'Racism, Ethnicity, Crime, and Criminal Justice' in M. Maguire, R. Morgan, and R. Reiner (eds) *The Oxford Handbook of Criminology* (3rd edn), 579–620.

Phillips, C. and Bowling, B. (2003) 'Racism, Ethnicity and Criminology: Developing Minority Perspectives'. *British Journal of Criminology* 43(2): 269–90.

Phillips, J. (2006) 'Crime and Older People: the research agenda' in A.Wahidin and M. Cain (2006) (eds) *Ageing, Crime and Society*. Cullompton: Willan Publishing, 53–70.

Powell, J.L. and Wahidin A. (2004) 'Corporate Crime, Aging and Pensions in Great Britain'. *Journal of Societal and Social Policy* 3(1): 37–50.

Pugh, S. (2002) 'The Forgotten—a community without a generation—older lesbians and gay men' in D. Richardson and S. Seaman (eds) *Handbook of Lesbian and Gay Studies*. London: Sage.

Rowe, M. (2004) *Policing Race and Racism*. Cullompton: Willan Publishing.

Salisbury, H. and Upson, A. (2004) 'Ethnicity, victimization and worry about crime: findings from the 2001/02 and 2002/03 British Crime Surveys'. *Home Office Research Findings* 237: 1–6.

Shorter-Gooden, K. (2004) 'Multiple Resistance Strategies: how African American women cope with racism and sexism'. *Journal of Black Psychology* 30(3): 406–25.

Shute, S., Hood, R., and Seemungal, F. (2005) *A Fair Hearing? Ethnic minorities in the criminal courts*. Cullompton: Willan Publishing.

Spalek, B. (1999) 'Exploring Victimisation: a study looking at the impact of the Maxwell scandal upon the Maxwell pensioners'. *International Review of Victimology* 6: 213–230.

Spalek, B. (2002) 'Muslim Women's Safety Talk and their Experiences of Victimisation: a study exploring specificity and difference' in B. Spalek (ed) *Islam, Crime and Criminal Justice*. Cullompton: Willan Publishing, 50–71.

Spalek, B. (2008) *Communities, Identities and Crime*. Bristol: Policy Press.

Taylor, M. (2004) 'Socio-historial constructions of race and language: impacting biracial identity' in Jean Lau Chin (ed) *The Psychology of Prejudice and Discrimination: ethnicity and multiracial identity, volume 2*. London: Praeger, 87–108.

Wahidin, A. and Cain, M. (2006) 'Ageing, Crime and Society: an invitation to a criminology' in A. Wahidin and M. Cain (2006) (eds) *Ageing, Crime and Society*. Cullompton: Willan Publishing, 1–16.

Whitfield, D. (1998) *Introduction to the Probation Service* (2nd edn). Winchester: Waterside Press.

Williams, C. (1995) *Invisible Victims: crime and abuse against people with learning difficulties*. London: Jessica Kingsley.

13

Youth justice

Barry Goldson and John Muncie

INTRODUCTION

Since the election of the first New Labour administration in 1997, the youth justice system in England and Wales has been radically restructured. Both the pace and the scope of reform have been extraordinary. Few areas of criminal justice law, policy, and practice have been as energetic as youth justice. This chapter subjects these developments to descriptive and critical appraisal. It has five key objectives. First, to establish the complex and contested nature of youth justice in England and Wales and to signal some of the continuities and changes that have characterised its history. Secondly, to review key developments in youth justice law, policy, and practice that have been introduced since 1997. Thirdly, to consider the structure of the contemporary youth justice system, by focusing upon the courts and sentencing and the organisational apparatus at both central and local government level. Fourthly, to critically examine the impact of reform and the various modes of intervention that target children and young people in trouble—from pre-emptive responses to custodial disposals. Fifthly, to analyse some of the more contested, unsettled, and controversial aspects of contemporary youth justice.

BACKGROUND

Youth justice 'old' and 'new'

The evolution of youth justice in England and Wales comprises a particularly complex, even contradictory, state of affairs (Goldson, 2002; Muncie and Hughes, 2002; Muncie, 2006). At one and the same time, the youth justice system aims to promote crime prevention *and* impose *retribution*. Interventions aspire to have regard for the *welfare* of 'children in trouble' whilst also *punishing* the 'young offender'. The system makes claims for *restoration* and reintegration, yet adopts some of the most punitive measures of surveillance, intervention, and penal confinement in any Western society (Goldson, 2008a). It is not just concerned with controlling *crime*, but it has a much broader remit of *pre-emptive intervention* towards all manner of behaviours deemed nuisance, anti-social, and disorderly. Accordingly, it targets children and young people (including those below the age of criminal responsibility) thought to be *'at risk'* of offending alongside those arrested for, and convicted of, criminal transgressions (Smith, R., 2006; Kemshall, 2008). To add to such complexity, youth justice is delivered by a disparate and yet ostensibly 'joined up' range of agencies, concerned with education, health, housing management, and social care as well as more orthodox criminal justice services.

Above all, contemporary youth justice is characterised by fluid patterns of continuity *and* change; the incremental accretion of myriad initiatives that have emerged, developed, and consolidated over two centuries. Despite 200 years of reforming zeal however, the 'old' has never been fully supplanted by the 'new'. In the twenty-first century divergent discourses co-exist—diversion *and* intervention; child protection *and* public protection; care *and* control; welfare *and* justice; restoration *and* exclusion; rights *and* responsibilities; rehabilitation *and* retribution; treatment *and* punishment—forming a series of complex antagonistic relations. Indeed, from the early nineteenth century when troubled and troublesome children and young people were first thought to require a different response to that afforded adults, to the present time, the history of youth justice has been riddled with ambiguity and inherent tension (Goldson, 2002; Hendrick, 2006; Muncie, 2009).

On coming to power in 1997 the first New Labour government placed youth justice towards the top of its reforming agenda. New Labour pledged that there would be 'no more excuses' (Home Office, 1997) and it reformulated the fundamental purpose of youth justice in England and Wales by defining its statutory aim as the *prevention* of offending.

New Labour's criminal justice reforms

To fully understand contemporary developments in youth justice we must first place them in a context of broader criminal justice and social policy reform. Since the election of the first New Labour government a wide range of legislative, policy, and practice initiatives have precipitated industrial-scale growth in the criminal justice system in England and Wales. In just under a decade, for example, successive administrations legislated on more than 50 occasions in the criminal justice sphere, creating more than 3,000 new offences (Morris, 2006). Within government itself the *Home Office* central staff doubled in size, not least to oversee major system expansion including significant growth in police forces and the appointment of over 6,000 *'Community Support Officers'*. Prison places have expanded by 19,000 since 1997 and, expressed as a rate per 100,000 of the national population, the general prison population is the highest among countries of the European Union (Walmsley, 2003). More specifically, greater use of penal custody for children is made in England and Wales than in most other industrialised democratic countries in the world.

Indeed, within the wider context of criminal justice reform and system growth young people have been especially targeted. Many of the new developments in legislation, policy and practice have been driven by a systematic demonisation of children, creating a problematic climate of fear and mistrust of youth (Hancock, 2004). As stated, policy reform is tainted by a series of tensions and contradictions that defy straightforward interpretation and explanation. Nonetheless, as we discuss later in the chapter, core aspects of reform have combined to comprise a youth justice system increasingly underpinned by interventionist, correctional, and, ultimately, punitive imperatives.

REVIEW QUESTIONS

1 Why do you think there has been so much concern expressed about the behaviour of children and young people over the past decade or so?

2 Is the youth justice system the most appropriate place for responding to 'troubled' and 'troublesome' children and young people? Can you imagine any possible alternatives?

The new youth justice system

Key developments in legislation and policy have served to fundamentally re-structure the youth justice system in England and Wales. For our purposes here three core dimensions are particularly important: courts and sentencing; the *Youth Justice Board*; and Youth Offending Teams (YOTs).

Courts and sentencing

In England and Wales the overwhelming majority of 'young offenders' (aged 10 to 17 years inclusive) are sentenced in Youth Courts, whereas a minority (usually those charged with, or convicted of, the most serious offences) are processed in the Crown Court. Youth Courts are normally presided over by up to three magistrates (also known as Justices of the Peace, JPs) who together comprise the 'bench'. Less commonly, legally qualified District Judges (previously known as Stipendiary magistrates) 'sit' in the Youth Court, either alone or with one or two magistrates. The Crown Court is presided over by a judge, a High Court Judge in the most serious cases but, more often, a Circuit Judge or a Recorder. Magistrates who serve in the Youth Court are recruited from the local community and although they receive some special training from the Judicial Studies Board, they are not required to be qualified legal professionals. Judges, on the other hand, are fully qualified, and prior to their appointment they normally have substantial experience as solicitors and/or barristers. Children and young people appearing in the Youth Court are usually represented by a solicitor, whereas those attending the Crown Court are normally represented by a barrister.

The court structure that prevails within the contemporary youth justice system in England and Wales actually pre-dates the election of the first New Labour government in 1997. Indeed, the modern Youth Courts derive from the Juvenile Courts that were first established in England and Wales by the Children Act 1908. At that time, and until the implementation of the Children Act 1989, both civil (welfare) and criminal (justice) proceedings where heard in Juvenile Courts. The Children Act 1989 provided for the removal of civil cases from the Juvenile Courts, however, and the Criminal Justice Act 1991 renamed them Youth Courts, with jurisdiction in criminal cases involving children and young people aged 10 to 17 years inclusive. The Crown Court was established by the Courts Act 1971.

A three-tiered 'sentencing framework' determines the nature of disposal imposed upon children and young people in the *criminal courts* (Monaghan, 2008). Lower-level disposals are used when the offence/s before the court are not considered serious enough to meet the community or custodial sentence *threshold*. Such disposals include discharges, fines, and compensation orders. *Community sentences* (or punishment in the community) apply in cases where restriction of liberty within the community is deemed to be necessary. Finally, *custodial sentences* are ostensibly reserved as a last resort for the most serious offenders.

The Youth Justice Board

The Crime and Disorder Act 1998—by far the most important piece of legislation for contemporary youth justice in England and Wales—established the Youth Justice Board (YJB). The YJB is an executive non-departmental public body comprising 12 members appointed by the Secretary of State for Justice. It is statutorily responsible for overseeing the youth justice system and its principal functions include:

- providing advice to the Secretary of State for Justice on the operation of, and standards for, the youth justice system;

- monitoring the performance of the youth justice system in general and YOTs (see below) in particular. Regionally-based YJB officers use a nationally applicable 'Performance Framework' to monitor the practice of YOTs in accordance with specified plans (Youth Justice Board, 2008a; 2008b). Levels of compliance with 'National Standards for Youth Justice Services' (Youth Justice Board, 2004a) and progress in reaching 'key performance indicators' (Youth Justice Board, 2008c; 2008d) are employed as primary measures of success or failure;

- setting standards for, and monitoring the performance of, each of the custodial establishments within the 'Juvenile Secure Estate'. In monitoring penal establishments the YJB uses its 'Effective Regimes Monitoring Framework'. The Board is also responsible for purchasing 'placements' and allocating children to such establishments when they are remanded or sentenced to custody by the courts (Youth Justice Board, 2004b; 2007). The YJB spends in excess of 70 per cent of its overall budget on custodial institutions (Youth Justice Board, 2008e);

- identifying and promoting 'effective practice'. The YJB has defined 'Key Elements of Effective Practice' and in order to ensure that they are implemented a 'Quality Assurance Framework' is used (Baker, 2008).

Youth Offending Teams

If the YJB is responsible for policy and practice at the *national* level, Youth Offending Teams (YOTS) implement it at the *local* level. The Crime and Disorder Act 1998 requires local authorities to prepare an annual youth justice plan and to provide and coordinate services to 'tackle' youth offending in their area. Equally, the Police, the Probation Service, and the Regional Health Authorities are statutorily obliged to contribute to, and cooperate with, such arrangements. Since April 2000, therefore, locally-based plans for 'tackling' youth crime have been implemented primarily by YOTs in 157 areas of England and Wales. Each YOT comprises a *'partnership'* of staff drawn from social services, police, *probation*, education, health, and housing authorities.

Some matters of concern

Although the organisation, structure, and functioning of the new youth justice system in England and Wales might appear straightforward enough, it is actually open to question on a range of fronts. For example, why have the former youth *justice* teams (designed to limit the criminalisation of children and young people by diverting them from court and custody) been replaced by Youth *Offending* Teams (driven by the logic of early intervention and *net widening*, and encompassing all aspects of 'at risk', 'anti-social', and 'disorderly'—in addition to criminal—behaviour) (Goldson and Muncie, 2006)? To what extent has professional autonomy and expert discretion been negated by centrally imposed performance targets, standardised monitoring, assessments, and audits (Eadie and Canton, 2002)? How can the system respond appropriately to the specificities of individual cases at a time when managerialised and mechanistic processes are increasingly geared towards the delivery of cost-effective and economic 'products' (Muncie, 2009)? If the system is designed to uphold and deliver justice, how is it that distinctively gendered processes endure (Gelsthorpe and Sharpe, 2006) and young black people are negatively discriminated against at every stage of the youth justice process (Webster, 2006)? How do we account for the fact that the number of children and young people remanded and sentenced by the courts to penal custody has almost doubled during a time when the incidence and gravity of youth crime has remained stable (Bateman, 2006)? Critical inquiry of this nature exposes a range of concerns and suggests that a 'new correctionalism' has come to characterise contemporary youth justice reform (Muncie and Goldson, 2006).

REVIEW QUESTIONS

1 What have been the main changes in the organization and delivery of youth justice over the past decade?

2 The reforms have been designed to construct a 'joined-up' system of complementary national and local objectives. What obstacles do you think might lie in the way of delivering a nationally uniform and standardized system?

The new correctionalism

Although youth justice continues to be shaped and structured around the competing discourses and dynamic tensions that we identified at the beginning of this chapter, it is equally true that contemporary developments in law, policy, and practice have tilted the system towards a set of correctional and punitive imperatives.

Pre-emptive intervention

In England and Wales children are held to be fully responsible for criminal transgressions from the age of ten. This is known as the age of criminal responsibility. It effectively means that, once a child reaches their tenth birthday, the criminal law, the courts, and the wider youth justice system regard them as being as culpable as any adult. Full criminal responsibility is legally activated at a very young age in England and Wales when compared to other European jurisdictions (see Table 13.1).

Table 13.1 Ages of criminal responsibility in selected European countries (as of 2008)

Country	Age of criminal responsibility (years)
Scotland	8
England and Wales	10
Northern Ireland	10
Greece	12
Ireland	12
Netherlands	12
Turkey	12
France	13
Austria	14
Germany	14
Italy	14
Spain	14
Denmark	15
Finland	15
Norway	15
Sweden	15
Portugal	16
Belgium	18
Luxembourg	18

The conspicuously low age of criminal responsibility in England and Wales (and other countries in the UK) has attracted critical attention from international human rights agencies, most particularly the United Nations Committee on the Rights of the Child (1995 and 2002). Successive New Labour governments have not only resisted calls for the age of criminal responsibility to be increased, however, they have also introduced a range of civil powers and statutory orders targeted at children *below* the age of ten. Furthermore, such interventions are pre-emptive in nature and can be applied without either the *prosecution* or, indeed, even the commission of a criminal offence.

Child Safety Orders (Crime and Disorder Act 1998, ss. 11–13) can be imposed by a Family Proceedings Court on any child below the age of criminal responsibility who is considered to be 'at risk'. Justified as a 'protective' measure, the order places the child under the supervision of a social services authority or a YOT, and the court is empowered to specify certain requirements and restrictive conditions, such as attending identifiable programmes or avoiding particular places and people. 'Failure to comply' may result in the substitution of a full care order as provided by the Children Act 1989 for no more than a perceived 'risk of becoming involved in crime' (Home Office, 1998: 7).

Perhaps the most controversial form of pre-emptive intervention is the *Anti-social Behaviour Order* (ASBO), provided by the Crime and Disorder Act 1998 and the Anti-social Behaviour Act 2003 (Squires, 2008). The ASBO is a civil order that can be imposed on any child over the age of ten whose behaviour is *thought likely* to cause nuisance, alarm, distress, or harassment. In many respects the identification of 'anti-social behaviour' is the organising principle for coordinating any number of issues surrounding family policy, education, housing, health, and employment (Muncie, 2009). The criminalisation of the 'non-criminal' has been subject to a barrage of criticism. However, it is argued that ASBOs serve to merge civil and criminal law; negate *due process*; allow hearsay 'evidence'; criminalise incivility; and impose social exclusion (Burney, 2005; Squires and Stephen, 2005; Hughes and Follett, 2006; Squires, 2006). Furthermore, since their implementation there is increasing evidence that ASBOs are primarily targeted at children and young people, and almost 50 per cent of all orders made have applied to under 18-year-olds (Jamieson, 2006).

The Anti-social Behaviour Act 2003 also made the parents of children regarded as 'disorderly', 'anti-social', or 'criminally inclined', eligible targets for formal statutory orders. Moreover, the same Act provided the police with additional powers of 'dispersal', to remove under 16-year-olds from public places if they 'believe' that a member of the public 'might be' 'intimidated, harassed, alarmed or distressed'. If two or more young people, together in a public place, fail to disperse under the instruction of a police officer they commit a criminal offence and face the prospect of custodial detention (Walsh, 2003; Crawford and Lister, 2007). In 2004, 'dispersal zones' were established in over 800 areas. The conversion of 'civil transgression' (that might lead to the imposition of an ASBO) to 'imprisonable offence' (for breaching the Order) is particularly problematic. Indeed, approximately 42 per cent of ASBOs imposed on children and young people are breached and 46 per cent of such breaches result in custodial sentences. As a consequence, some 50 children a month are being imprisoned under anti-social behaviour legislation (Statewatch, 2008). Furthermore, the Serious Organised Crime and Police Act 2005 removed legal safeguards protecting the anonymity of children who breach the terms of an ASBO, thus allowing for them to be publicly 'named and shamed'.

The diminution of welfare and the erosion of protective safeguards

Having regard for the welfare of children and young people in trouble has long been a key function of the courts. The Children and Young Persons Act 1933 (s. 44) established that all courts should 'have regard to the welfare of the child' and this was bolstered by the Children Act 1989 (s. 1), which provides that: 'the child's welfare shall be the court's paramount consideration'. Similarly, the United Nations Convention on the Rights of the Child (formally adopted in England and Wales in 1991) requires that the 'best interests' of the child shall prevail in all legal proceedings. Furthermore, two major policy programmes—*Every Child Matters: Change for Children* (Department for Education and Skills, 2003) and *Youth Matters* (Department for Education and Skills, 2005)—emphasise the importance of safeguarding the welfare of children and young people and these have since been extended through the Government's *Children's Plan* (Department for Children, Schools and Families, 2007).

Such welfare protection is particularly important given the inherent and structural vulnerabilities of children and young people in the youth justice system, the substantial majority of whom are drawn from particularly disadvantaged families, neighbourhoods, and communities. Recent developments in youth justice policy and practice itself, however, have served to diminish welfare imperatives and erode protective safeguards by exposing even the youngest children to the full weight of the criminal law. In addition to the low age of criminal responsibility in England and Wales and the new emphasis towards pre-emptive intervention, key provisions of the Crime and Disorder Act 1998 further compound such 'responsibilising' tendencies.

Hitherto, the principle of *doli incapax* provided legal safeguards to the youngest children processed within the youth justice system. Under this principle, children between the ages of 10 and 13 were presumed to be incapable of criminal intent. This presumption had to be 'rebutted' before they could be convicted and, in order to do this, the prosecution had to show 'beyond reasonable doubt' that the child appreciated that what they did was 'seriously wrong', as opposed to merely naughty or mischievous. Thus the doctrine of *doli incapax*—a long-established part of the law dating back to the time of Edward III—was an important legal safeguard for 10- to 13-year-old children who would be below the age of criminal responsibility in most other European countries. The Crime and Disorder Act 1998 (s. 34) provided for the abolition of the rebuttable presumption that a child is *doli incapax*, however, thus removing an important legal safeguard in respect of the youngest children in the justice system. Furthermore, the Act gives no specific direction to either the courts or the YOTs that child welfare should be a primary consideration. Taken together, this is 'symbolic of the state's limited vision in understanding children, the nature of childhood or the true meaning of an appropriate criminal law response' (Bandalli, 2000: 94).

Intensified early intervention

The issuing of informal warnings and cautions, as distinct from formal prosecution, is a long-established response to children and young people in trouble. Indeed, two particularly important Home Office Circulars—14/1985 and 59/1990—actively promoted the use of such *diversionary* measures (Home Office, 1985; 1990) and there is a robust body of evidence confirming their relative effectiveness (Goldson, 2000). In accordance with correctional priorities, however, the Crime and Disorder Act 1998 (ss. 65 and 66) put an end to cautioning and established instead, on a statutory basis, the system of Reprimands and Final Warnings. The Reprimand is reserved for children who 'have not previously been convicted of an offence' (s. 65(1)(d)) whilst the Final Warning normally applies to 'second-time' offenders. When a Final Warning is administered the police officer is required to refer the child to the local YOT for a *rehabilitation* programme' assessment (s. 66(1)). Thus diversion is effectively supplanted by early intervention and formal criminalisation.

Furthermore, the Crime and Disorder Act 1998 (s. 66(4)) stipulates that where a child commits an offence within two years of receiving a Final Warning, the sentencing court 'shall not make an order' for conditional discharge unless it is of the opinion that there are 'exceptional circumstances relating to the offence or the offender which justify its doing so'. Instead, such children are normally made the subjects of Referral Orders under the provisions of the Youth Justice and Criminal Evidence Act 1999 (Part 1), and are referred by the court to a Youth Offender Panel (made up of local volunteers and YOT members—victims and family members may also be included). This has produced a very substantial 'push-in' effect, whereby children appearing in court for the first time— many of whom would have otherwise been conditionally discharged—are exposed to potentially quite intensive modes of correctional intervention.

Some commentators have lauded the more positive lines of communication—between offenders, parents, victims, and communities—that Referral Order schemes have potentially opened up (Earle and Newburn, 2001; Earle, Newburn, and Crawford, 2002). Others have lamented the coercive nature of intervention; problems of low victim participation; blurred lines of accountability; and a general failure to provide children and young people with the socio-economic resources necessary for them to develop a 'stakehold' in community life (Wonnacott, 1999; Goldson, 2000; Crawford and Newburn, 2003; Gray, 2005). More broadly, early intervention per se has been subjected to criticism on the basis of its counter-productive, criminalising, and discriminatory tendencies (Smith, R., 2006; Goldson, 2008b).

Punishment in the community

Since the implementation of the Crime and Disorder Act 1998 a range of statutory orders have been available to the courts for sentencing *all* children and young people (aged 10 to 17) including: 'Action Plan Orders'; 'Attendance Centre Orders', 'Curfew Orders'; 'Exclusion Orders'; 'Supervision Orders'; and 'Intensive Supervision and Surveillance Programmes' (not orders in their own right, but measures that can be attached to court bail, a Curfew Order, a Supervision Order and—in the case of 16- to 17-year-olds—a Community Rehabilitation Order). Additional community-based court orders that are specifically reserved for those young people aged 16 to 17 include: 'Community Rehabilitation Orders'; 'Community Punishment Orders'; 'Community Punishment and Rehabilitation Orders'; and 'Drug Treatment and Testing Orders' (for accounts of each separate order see Goldson, 2008c). The Criminal Justice and Immigration Act 2008— which received Royal Assent on 8 May 2008—promises to introduce further sweeping reforms. However, at the time of writing the implementation schedule for the new legislation is unclear but, when fully implemented, it will radically change the youth justice sentencing framework (Monaghan, 2008).

A new generic sentence, the 'Youth Rehabilitation Order' (YRO), will be the standard community-based disposal for the majority of children and young people, replacing all of the orders referred to above. This move follows a similar development in community sentences for adults with the introduction of the community order in the Criminal Justice Act 2003. The YRO represents a more individualised 'risk'-based approach to community sentencing, enabling greater choice from a 'menu' of available requirements including:

- Activity Requirement;
- Attendance Centre Requirement;
- Curfew Requirement;
- Drug Testing Requirement (for children aged 14 or over);
- Drug Treatment Requirement;
- Education Requirement;
- Electronic Monitoring Requirement;
- Exclusion Requirement;
- Extended Activity Requirement—either Intensive Supervision and Surveillance and/or Intensive Fostering (for persistent or serious offenders who are over the custody threshold);
- Local Authority Residence Requirement;
- Mental Health Treatment Requirement;
- Programme Requirement;
- Prohibited Activity Requirement;
- Residence Requirement (for young people aged 16 to 17);
- Supervision Requirement;
- Unpaid Work Requirement (for young people aged 16 to 17).

The Criminal Justice and Immigration Act 2008 places no restrictions on the number of times a child/young person can be sentenced to a YRO. Indeed, courts are expected to use the YRO on multiple occasions, adapting the 'menu' of requirements as appropriate.

Expanding incarceration

Children serving custodial sentences are detained in one of three institutions within the 'juvenile secure estate': *secure children's homes*; *secure training centres*; and/or *young offender institutions*. The nature of 'placement' is determined by the age, *gender*, and/or level of perceived 'vulnerability' of the child. Children aged between 10 and 12 are normally detained in secure children's homes (SCHs), most of which are managed by local authorities under the auspices of the Department for Education and Skills and the Department of Health. Children aged between 12 and 14 are usually held in SCHs or secure training centres (STCs). STCs are private jails owned and managed by global

Table 13.2 Comparison of under-18 populations in custodial facilities (at 31 May) since 2000

Year	Number of children and young people (aged 10–17) in penal custody in England and Wales
2000	2,804
2001	2,792
2002	3,071
2003	2,838
2004	2,809
2005	2,740
2006	2,868
2007	2,879
2008	3,006

Source: Youth Justice Board (2008f)

security corporations. Girls aged between 15 and 17 are given priority for 'places' in SCHs and STCs, whereas boys of the same age are normally sent to young offender institutions (YOIs), prisons managed by the Prison Service under the auspices of the Home Office. Most child prisoners are held in YOIs. On 31 May 2008, for example, from an overall total of 3,006 young prisoners in England and Wales (see Table 13.2), 2,550 were detained in YOIs, 239 were held in STCs, and the remaining 217 were in SCHs (Youth Justice Board, 2008f).

Between 1993 and 2000 the number of children and young people detained in penal custody almost doubled and, with only minor fluctuations, this punitive trend has remained since.

Prisons for children are stark environments as can be seen from the photograph in Figure 13.1. Indeed, a range of concerns have been raised about child imprisonment including. the disproportionately high numbers of child prisoners in England and Wales when compared to other jurisdictions in Europe; the ineffectiveness of custodial disposals to prevent future offending (reconviction rates are as high as 90 per cent); the enormous costs incurred in sustaining high rates of imprisonment; the inappropriate treatment and conditions endured by child prisoners and the harm and damage routinely visited upon them. Perhaps most controversial of all is the fact that between July 1990 and November 2007, 30 children and young people died in penal custody (Goldson, 2006; 2008a; Goldson and Coles 2008).

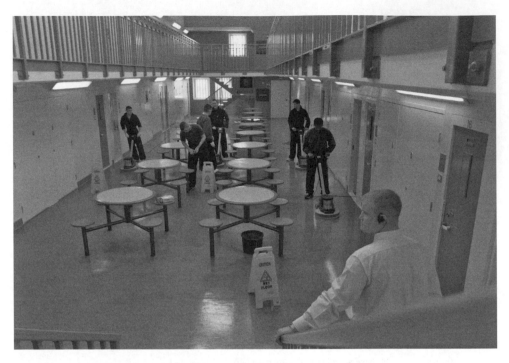

Figure 13.1 Young offenders in custody

Source: © www.TopFoto.co.uk

 CASE STUDY: JOSEPH SCHOLES

Joseph was born in 1986. He had an unsettled childhood and became increasingly distressed through adolescence. Late in 2001 he was received into the care of the Local Authority and placed in a Children's Home. The Residential Social Work staff described Joseph as well-mannered and polite. On 6 December 2001, however, just a week after his arrival, Joseph went out with four other children from the home, two boys and two girls. After a spontaneous bout of drinking strong alcohol the children came across another group of youngsters and demanded their money and mobile telephones. Joseph, along with his companions, was subsequently arrested. Joseph was no seasoned young offender and such behaviour was completely out of character, yet in the eyes of the law he faced the serious charge of street robbery.

As Joseph's court appearance drew closer he became increasingly anxious and agitated. On one occasion, in the privacy of his bedroom at the Children's Home, he took a knife to his face and inflicted more than 30 slash wounds. On 26 February 2002 Joseph entered a guilty plea to Manchester Crown Court. It was accepted that, although present, and by definition culpable, Joseph's role in the offence was largely peripheral. Even the prosecutor in the case stated in open court that: 'Joseph Scholes offered no physical violence to any person on December 6, 2001' (cited in Goldson and Coles, 2005: 62). The judge requested reports and adjourned the case until 15 March 2002.

When Joseph reappeared in court for sentence the Judge stated that: 'it is an unhappy fact that these serious offences of street robbery are against a background of anxiety and fear the length and breadth of this country and only in the last couple of weeks, the Lord Chief Justice has said what has always been the policy in my court, that is that people . . . committing street robberies, receive immediate custodial sentences' (cited in Goldson and Coles, 2005: 63). He sentenced Joseph to two years' detention, fully exploiting the maximum and most severe sentencing powers available to him in the circumstances.

On 15 March 2002 Joseph was taken to Her Majesty's Young Offender Institution Stoke Heath in Shropshire. On the afternoon of Sunday 24 March 2002, on the ninth day of his two-year custodial sentence, Joseph placed a noose, made from a bed-sheet, around his neck and hung himself from the bars of his cell. His body was discovered by a maintenance worker who had been called to the Health Care Centre to attend to blocked toilets. Joseph Scholes left a message: 'I love you mum and dad. I'm sorry I just can't cope. Don't be sad. It's no one's fault. I just can't go on. None of it was any of your fault, sorry. Love you and family, Joe'. His very final words are haunting: 'I tried telling them and they just don't fucking listen'. Joseph died alone in a dirty and barren prison cell. He was just 16 years old.

REVIEW QUESTIONS

1 What are the constituent elements of the 'new correctionalism'?

2 What are the practical implications of introducing notions of 'risk' into systems of youth justice?

3 Why has the criminalisation and incarceration of children in England and Wales attracted so much national and international criticism?

New sites of contestation and controversy

In the same way that the *history of youth justice*—its continuities and changes and its intrinsic tensions and contradictions—has encapsulated a range of competing discourses, *modern youth justice* also comprises key sites of contestation and controversy. Indeed, critical engagement with the nature and direction of contemporary law, policy, and practice raises some pressing questions.

'In need' or 'at risk'?

On coming to power in 1997, the first New Labour government made various pledges to secure *social justice* for children in general, and on 'tackling' child poverty in particular. Premised upon a construction of children '*in need*', therefore, a wide-ranging sequence of cross-government initiatives, policy developments, and 'modernising' service re-configurations have been introduced which, it is claimed, will make the UK 'the best place in the world for our children and young people to grow up' (Department for Children, Schools and Families, 2007: 3).

Such approaches are not beyond criticism, however. Despite the multitude of new initiatives, child poverty continues to prevail and when account is taken of key measures of 'well-being'—including material well-being, health and safety, education, peer and family relationships—children in the UK are more disadvantaged than those in any of the 21 OECD (Organisation for Economic Co-operation and Development) countries surveyed by Unicef (2007). Such initiatives have not only imposed limited positive effect, but their underpinning rationales are problematic in themselves. Many government programmes are formulated on the basis of correcting individual 'deficits', as distinct from addressing social polarisation, poverty, and structural inequality by way of redistributive economic strategies. Furthermore, whilst the rhetorical claim is that 'every child matters', it is also plain to see that some children appear to 'matter' more than others, and the policy trajectory within contemporary youth justice serves to distance 'child offenders'—both symbolically and institutionally—from the inclusionary thrust (Goldson and Muncie, 2006).

The 'child in need' construct, which is central to the 'Every Child Matters' agenda, is substituted by a conceptualisation of 'risk' within youth justice discourse. Accordingly, benign expressions of welfare are displaced by the imperatives of control and correction, and notions of family support and relief are reframed as questions of parental (ir)responsibility and family failure. The very fact that troubled and troublesome children are invariably one and the same is seemingly disregarded. The entire body of research evidence and practice experience—confirming that child 'offenders' are almost exclusively drawn from the most disadvantaged, neglected, and damaged families, neighbourhoods, and communities—is dismissed as an 'excusing' distraction within a context in which there can be 'no more excuses' (Home Office, 1997). New Labour's political calculations are such that being 'tough on crime', and hard on the children who commit it, is crucial, despite all of the manifest contradictions. This produces a conceptual complex within which policy rationales move across and between two quite different discursive registers, and children are conceived *either* as 'in need' of welfare support *or* 'at risk' of offending. The former implies care and protection, whereas the latter invokes control and *punishment*.

Restoration or responsibilisation?

Much has been made of the principles of *restorative justice*—restoration, reintegration, as well as responsibility—that are said to inform key elements of contemporary youth justice reform. Within restorative justice the emphasis tends to rest with informal offender/victim participation and harm minimisation as distinct from formal *crime control*. Much of this draws upon cultural practices in Maori, Aboriginal, and Native American indigenous populations. Further, it has come to find practical expression in various forms of *'conferencing'* in Australasia, in 'healing circles' in Canada, and in the processes that underpin the work of the 'Truth and Reconciliation Commission' in South Africa. Both the United Nations and the Council of Europe have given their firm backing to restorative justice and its potential to reduce punitive modes of intervention. Perhaps the key point of reference is 'Family Group Conferences' (FGCs) pioneered in New Zealand in the late 1980s and based upon traditional systems of conflict resolution within Maori culture. The defining element of progressive restorative practice is that the offender (at least in theory) is not marginalised, but rather accepted as a key contributor to decision making (Haines and O'Mahony, 2006). Restorative approaches hold the *potential* for the fundamental redirection of youth justice policy and practice, by replacing legal definitions of crime and formal adversarial procedures (particularly involving courts) with processes of reconciliation, conflict resolution, harm minimisation, and healing (Muncie, 2005).

Within contemporary youth justice in England and Wales, restorative principles ostensibly underpin referral orders, reparation processes, final warning interventions, and action plan orders. In reality, however, their impact appears rather more partial and circumspect. Gelsthorpe and Morris (2002) contend that restorative practices are additions to, rather than core defining components of, a system that remains built around, and continues to act upon, notions of *just deserts*, retribution, and punishment. Rather than providing alternatives to classic correctional modes of intervention, restorative processes primarily apply to a new population of children deemed 'at risk', and/or 'low level' young offenders drawn into the system at an increasingly early age as a consequence of pre-emptive and/or early intervention. Thus restorative justice might serve as a means of net widening on the one hand, and as a mechanism for separating the 'high risk' from the 'low risk' on the other (Cunneen, 2003). Furthermore, situated within the politicised context of 'no more excuses' and burgeoning *responsibilisation*, the danger always remains that any form of compulsory restoration may degenerate into a ceremony of public shaming and degradation. Within restorative programmes in England and Wales, therefore, the transformative emphasis tends to remain with children and young people atoning for, or changing, their behaviour, rather than on the agencies of the state recognizing their responsibilities for improving the social circumstances of their young 'clients'. In other words, notions of individual responsibility rather than community empowerment, social inclusion, and 'restorative *social* justice' tend to proliferate (White, 2003). All of this exposes the limitations of the claims made for restoration and its future potential to resolve the injustices of retribution and punishment.

Evidenced-based policy, managerial pragmatism, or vindictive punitiveness?

Successive New Labour administrations have claimed that 'modernisation' is being applied across all policy domains. The principal contention is that 'modernised' government (and governance) provides for greater coherence, operationalised and delivered through 'joined-up' approaches under an overarching commitment to 'evidence-based' policy formation within a general rubric of '*what works*' (Smith, D., 2006). This is presented as a progressive and rational shift from 'opinion-based' to 'evidence-based' policy; from ideological conviction and/or pure speculation to 'scientific realism' and the 'pragmatic solution' (Goldson, 2001; Muncie, 2002).

The *rhetoric* of 'evidenced-based' policy and 'what works' rationales has claimed significant purchase within contemporary youth justice. On one level it is difficult to quarrel with any tendency that claims to apply evidence—drawn from research and evaluation findings and/or reflexive praxis—to the processes of policy formation and practice development. At its simplest, it is a mechanistic formulation whereby youth justice policy is no longer 'hampered' by any adherence to competing philosophical principles. Policy-makers are liberated from having to wrestle with the thematic complexities that we considered earlier—welfare, justice, restoration, restitution, rights, responsibilities, rehabilitation, retribution, treatment, and punishment—rather, they simply need to translate 'hard evidence' into policy by means of technical scientific transfer.

The *reality*, however, is that both the social world and the processes of youth justice policy formation are far more complex. The supposition that intervention 'programmes', in and of themselves, might produce certain readily measurable results or 'outcomes' or, to put it another way, that such results and outcomes can be directly attributed, in the short-term, to particular forms of intervention, is, at best, tenuous. Indeed, this is a 'way of seeing' more akin to public sector *managerialism* than it is to serious criminological reasoning. Within the managerialist project, rationalised inputs and outputs are conceptualised in scientific and technical terms, and evaluations are dominated by notions of productivity, task remits, and quantifiable outcomes whereby evaluation comes to rest solely on indicators of internal system performance. The unpredictability, variability, and intrinsic complexity of the social and the political, however, militates against such crude generality and supposed uniformity. The search for the consistently efficient (and cost-effective) practice tends to mean that the dynamics of (unpredictable) personal biographies and local contingencies are overlooked (Webster, McDonald, and Simpson, 2006). 'What works' in some contexts (spatial and temporal) may not 'work' in others. The lives of children and young people involved in youth justice processes are complex, and reliance on a generalised 'risk factor paradigm' obscures those complexities. Whilst it is possible to view some modes of intervention with a guarded optimism, it is unlikely that any can be readily transferred from one jurisdiction to another, or indeed from one locality to the next, in a way that might deliver the same 'results' (Goldson and Muncie, 2006).

There are multiple problems and controversies associated with 'evidenced-based' policy and 'what works' rationales as they are currently formulated within contemporary youth justice. Particularly noteworthy are the processes of selective filtering whereby some 'evidence' is privileged and emphasised, whilst other 'evidence' is 'forgotten' and 'buried'. Such subjective and conditional (as distinct from objective and scientific) processes are seemingly contingent upon the extent to which 'evidence' is politically convenient, rather than methodologically rigorous and/or criminologically significant (Goldson, 2001). There is, then, a conspicuous discordance between key messages from research and practice experience (the evidence) on the one hand, and core aspects of 'modern' youth justice policy on the other. The contemporary politicisation of youth crime and justice is, as stated, accompanied by extraordinarily energetic and consistently 'tough' reform, within which any genuine notion of rational 'evidenced-based' policy formation is all but subverted by political and electoral imperatives (Goldson and Muncie, 2006). Such 'tough' approaches are pursued in the explicit knowledge that they not only fail to deliver—in terms of crime prevention, *community safety*, or reducing rates of re-offending—but they impose substantial costs in terms of social harm.

Within this contested context, therefore, tensions centre around evidence-based policy and managerial pragmatism on the one hand, and politicised 'get tough' imperatives—often expressed as crude vindictive punitiveness—on the other. Moreover, rationality is frequently eclipsed by populist ideology. Thus, it doesn't seem to matter that numerous self-report and other studies indicate that offending is a relatively 'normal' part of growing-up for most young people, the majority of whom 'grow out of crime' (Rutherford, 1992). Nor does it count that children and young people are responsible for a relatively small amount of recorded and detected crimes or, perhaps more significantly, that the incidence of youth crime appears to have remained stable, with some commentators even arguing that it is in decline when measured over the last decade or so (Bateman, 2006). Equally irrelevant, it would seem, is the fact that most offences committed by children and young people are directed against property not people, and that those offences generally regarded as the least serious comprise almost half of all offences for which children and young people are responsible (Bateman, 2006). Within the politics of youth justice policy all of this becomes secondary to appeasing public concern and securing electoral gain, and this gives vent to vindictive punitiveness: the ultimate expression of which is penal expansion and diversifying forms of child incarceration.

REVIEW QUESTIONS

1 How do the conceptualisations of 'in need' and 'at risk' impact on responses to children and young people in trouble?

2 How far do you consider that restorative approaches challenge or complement other youth justice interventions?

3 How would you explain the persistence of the juvenile prison in a context of managerial demands for effectiveness and 'value for money'?

CONCLUSION

The 'Offending, Crime and Justice Survey' (OCJS), based upon interviews with 5,000 children and young people, offers a 'unique picture of the extent and nature of offending, anti-social behaviour and drug use among young people in the general household population' (Budd *et al.*, 2005: i). The survey reveals that 64 per cent of children and young people interviewed had neither committed an offence—or a defined act of anti-social behaviour—in the 12 months prior to interview and, amongst the minority 'who did admit to a delinquent act the picture was dominated by the less serious behaviours' (Budd *et al.*, 2005: i). Furthermore, many 'incidents' officially recorded as 'violent' are, in actual fact, 'non-injury incidents often committed on the "spur of the moment" against someone the perpetrator knew and involving relatively low levels of force…attributed to being annoyed or upset with someone'. Indeed, 68 per cent of the 'violent incidents' reported by 10- to 17-year-olds are actually 'non-injury assaults…a grab or a push [or] a punch, slap or hit' (Budd *et al.*, 2005, ii). Similarly, the majority of 'property offences' reported by children are low-level, involving 'miscellaneous thefts from school of items of relatively low value' (Budd *et al.*, 2005, ii).

Whilst it is always necessary to exercise some care in reading, analysing, and interpreting official crime statistics, such figures certainly appear to challenge populist constructions of burgeoning child lawlessness, widespread moral breakdown, and rampant 'yob culture'. In the final analysis, whilst recognising that youth crime and the socio-economic contexts within which it is invariably situated might well be matters of legitimate concern, and, at the extremes, a small minority of children are occasionally prone to behave in ways that place themselves and/or others at risk of serious harm, the statistical evidence fails to sustain the caricatured notion of spiralling behavioural decline and an ever-more victimised citizenry.

It is against this backdrop that, in recent years, child deviance in general has been 'defined-up', and youth crime in particular has been 'amplified'. This, as we have seen, has given rise to a substantial volume of new legislative activity and policy development. Moreover, it has both precipitated significant *system growth* and considerably extended *system reach*.

Whilst the contemporary youth justice system continues to accommodate multiple discourses and conceptual tensions, a new correctionalism has consolidated. Concepts of 'need' are increasingly overshadowed by constructions of 'risk'. The 'restorative' potential of youth justice is severely hampered and harnessed by the 'responsibilising' impulse. The appeal of 'evidence-based policy' has, at best, served to usher in modes of managerial pragmatism whilst, at worst, it has been fundamentally eclipsed by a 'new punitivism'. Ultimately, contemporary youth justice in England and Wales is itself the victim of a crude and populist politics of crime control.

QUESTIONS FOR DISCUSSION

1 Make a list, with notes, of the numerous new initiatives and interventions that have been applied to youth justice over the past decade. Do these suggest coherence or contradiction in the Government's strategy?

2 Is youth justice becoming more effective in crime prevention or simply more inclined to punish?

3 Consider the proposition that risk management has radically transformed the purpose and practice of youth justice.

4 To what extent is the 'new youth justice' informed by research evidence and how far does it act upon it?

5 What in your view should youth justice be for? From your reading of this chapter does the present system come anywhere near meeting these objectives? If not, what alternative reforms would you suggest need implementing?

GUIDE TO FURTHER READING

Barry Goldson's (2000) edited volume *The New Youth Justice* (Dorset: Russell House) provides a range of essays engaging with key aspects of New Labour's youth justice programme. The third edition of John Muncie's (2009) *Youth and Crime* (London: Sage) and the second edition of Roger Smith's (2006) *Youth Justice: Ideas, Policy, Practice* (Cullompton: Willan) provide the best single-authored analyses available in the UK. Goldson's (2008) *Dictionary of Youth Justice* (Cullompton: Willan) offers the most comprehensive introduction to youth justice theory, law, policy, and practice, whereas the companion volumes *Youth Crime and Justice: Critical issues* and *Comparative Youth Justice: Critical issues* (London: Sage) edited by Goldson and Muncie (2006), comprise the most authoritative *critical* accounts with contributions from some of the world's leading youth justice scholars and policy analysts. *Youth Justice: An international journal*

(London: Sage) is the leading peer-reviewed journal in the field in the UK, providing articles, youth justice news, and legal analysis.

WEB LINKS

The National Association for Youth Justice
http://www.nayj.org.uk/website/

An excellent free-to-register site providing up-to-date news and comment and a distinctive children's human rights emphasis.

The Howard League for Penal Reform
http://www.howardleague.org/

The house-site of the UK's leading penal reform agency with a long history of pioneering work in the youth justice field. The weekly 'prison watch', providing regularly updated penal statistics, is particularly useful.

Office of the United Nations High Commissioner for Human Rights
http://www2.ohchr.org/english/bodies/crc/index.htm

A mine of information on the human rights of all children—including those in conflict with the law.

Nacro: the crime reduction charity
http://www.nacro.org.uk/

Nacro's youth crime section provides some of the most accessible, yet authoritative, guidance and analysis on youth justice law, policy and practice.

Youth Justice Board
http://www.yjb.gov.uk/en-gb/

The official government site providing useful material regarding the structure of the youth justice system in England and Wales.

REFERENCES

Baker, K. (2008) 'Key Elements of Effective Practice (KEEPS)' in B. Goldson (ed) *Youth Justice Dictionary*. Cullompton: Willan.

Bandalli, S. (2000) 'Children, Responsibility and the New Youth Justice' in B. Goldson (ed) *The New Youth Justice*. Lyme Regis: Russell House Publishing.

Bateman, T. (2006) 'Youth Crime and Justice: Statistical "Evidence", Recent Trends and Responses' in B. Goldson and J. Muncie (eds) *Youth Crime and Justice: Critical Issues*. London: Sage.

Budd, T., Sharp, C., Weir, G., Wilson, D., and Owen, N. (2005) 'Young People and Crime: Findings from the 2004 Offending, Crime and Justice Survey'. Home Office Statistical Bulletin 20/05. London: Home Office.

Burney, E. (2005) *Making People Behave: Anti-social behaviour, politics and policy*. Cullompton: Willan Publishing.

Crawford, A. and Lister, S. (2007) *The Use and impact of Dispersal Orders: Sticking Plasters and Wake-Up Calls*. Bristol: The Policy Press.

Crawford, A. and Newburn, T. (2003) *Youth Offending and Restorative Justice*. Cullompton: Willan Publishing.

Cunneen, C. (2003) 'Thinking critically about restorative justice' in J. McLaughlin, R. Fergusson, G. Hughes, and L. Westmarland (eds). *Restorative Justice: Critical Issues*. London: Sage.

Department for Children, Schools and Families (2007) *The Children's Plan: Building brighter futures*. London: DCSFs.

Department for Education and Skills (2003) *Every Child Matters*. London: DFES.

Department for Education and Skills (2005) *Youth Matters*. London: DFES.

Eadie, T. and Canton, R. (2002) 'Practising in a Context of Ambivalence: The Challenge for Youth Justice Workers'. *Youth Justice* 2(1): 14–26.

Earle, R. and Newburn, T. (2001) 'Creative Tensions? Young Offenders, Restorative Justice and the Introduction of Referral Orders'. *Youth Justice* 1(3): 3–13.

Earle, R., Newburn, T., and Crawford, A. (2002) 'Referral Orders: Some Reflections on Policy Transfer and "What Works"'. *Youth Justice* 2(3): 141–50.

Gelsthorpe, L. and Morris, A. (2002) 'Restorative youth justice: the last vestiges of welfare?' in J. Muncie, G. Hughes, and E. McLaughlin, (eds) *Youth Justice: Critical Readings*. London: Sage.

Gelsthorpe, L. and Sharpe, G. (2006) 'Gender, Youth Crime and Justice' in B. Goldson and J. Muncie (eds) *Youth Crime and Justice: Critical issues*. London: Sage.

Goldson, B. (2000) 'Wither Diversion? Interventionism and the New Youth Justice' in B. Goldson (ed) *The New Youth Justice*. Dorset: Russell House.

Goldson, B. (2001) 'A Rational Youth Justice? Some critical reflections on the research, policy and practice relation'. *Probation Journal* 48(2): 76–85.

Goldson, B. (2002) 'Children, Crime and the State', in B. Goldson, M. Lavalette, and J. McKechnie (eds) *Children, Welfare and the State*. London: Sage.

Goldson, B. (2006) 'Damage, harm and death in child prisons in England and Wales'. *Howard Journal* 45(5): 449–67.

Goldson, B. (2008a) 'Child Incarceration: Institutional Abuse, the Violent State and the Politics of Impunity' in P. Scraton and J. McCulloch (eds) *The Violence of Incarceration*. London: Routledge.

Goldson, B. (2008b) 'Early Intervention in The Youth Justice Sphere: A Knowledge-Based Critique' in M. Blyth and E. Solomon (eds) *Prevention and Youth Crime*. Bristol: The Policy Press.

Goldson, B. (ed) (2008c) *Dictionary of Youth Justice*. Cullompton: Willan.

Goldson, B. and Coles, D. (2005) *In the Care of the State? Child Deaths in Penal Custody in England and Wales*. London: Inquest.

Goldson, B. and Coles, D. (2008) 'Child Deaths in the Juvenile Secure Estate' in M. Blyth, C. Wright, and R. Newman (eds) *Children and Young People in Custody*. Bristol: The Policy Press.

Goldson, B. and Muncie, J. (2006) 'Critical Anatomy: Towards a Principled Youth Justice' in B. Goldson and J. Muncie (eds) *Youth Crime and Justice: Critical* issues. London: Sage.

Gray, P. (2005) 'The Politics of Risk and Young Offenders' Experiences of Social Exclusion and Restorative Justice'. *British Journal of Criminology* 45(6): 938–57.

Haines, K. and O'Mahony, D. (2006) 'Restorative Approaches, Young People and Youth Justice' in B. Goldson and J. Muncie (eds) *Youth Crime and Justice: Critical issues*. London: Sage.

Hancock, L. (2004) 'Criminal Justice, Public Opinion, Fear and Popular Politics' in J. Muncie and D. Wilson (eds) *Student Handbook of Criminal Justice and Criminology*. London: Cavendish Publishing.

Hendrick, H. (2006) 'Histories of Youth Crime and Justice' in B. Goldson and J. Muncie (eds) *Youth Crime and Justice: Critical issues*. London: Sage.

Home Office (1985) *The Cautioning of Offenders, Circular 14/1985*. London: Home Office.

Home Office (1990) *The Cautioning of Offenders, Circular 59/90*. London: Home Office.

Home Office (1997) *No More Excuses—A New Approach to Tackling Youth Crime in England and Wales*. London: Home Office.

Home Office (1998) *Crime and Disorder Act 1998: Introductory Guide*. London: Home Office.

Hughes, G. and Follett, M. (2006) 'Community Safety, Youth and the "Anti-Social"' in B. Goldson and J. Muncie (eds) *Youth Crime and Justice: Critical issues*. London: Sage.

Jamieson, J. (2006) 'New Labour, Youth Justice and the Question of "Respect"'. *Youth Justice* 5(3) 180–93.

Kemshall, H. (2008) 'Risks, Rights and Justice: Understanding and Responding to Youth Risk'. *Youth Justice* 8(1): 21–37.

Monaghan, G. (2008) 'Sentencing Framework' in B. Goldson (ed.) *Youth Justice Dictionary*. Cullompton: Willan.

Morris, N. (2006) 'Blair's "frenzied law making": a new offence for every day spent in office'. *The Independent* 16 August.

Muncie, J. (2002) 'A new deal for youth?: early intervention and correctionalism' in G. Hughes, E. McLaughlin, and J. Muncie (eds) *Crime Prevention and Community Safety: New Directions*. London: Sage.

Muncie, J. (2005) 'The globalization of crime control—the case of youth and juvenile justice: Neo-liberalism, policy convergence and international conventions'. *Theoretical Criminology* 9(1): 35–64.

Muncie, J. (2006) 'Governing Young People: Coherence and Contradiction in Contemporary Youth Justice'. *Critical Social Policy* 26(4): 770–93.

Muncie, J. (2009) *Youth and Crime* (3rd edn). London: Sage.

Muncie, J. and Goldson, B. (2006) 'England and Wales: The New Correctionalism' in J. Muncie and B. Goldson (eds) *Comparative Youth Justice: Critical issues*. London: Sage.

Muncie, J. and Hughes, G. (2002) 'Modes of youth governance: political rationalities, criminalization and resistance' in J. Muncie, G. Hughes, and E. McLaughlin (eds) *Youth Justice: Critical Readings*. London: Sage.

Rutherford, A. (1992) *Growing Out of Crime: The New Era*. Winchester: Waterside Press.

Smith, D. (2006) 'Youth Crime and Justice: Research, Evaluation and "Evidence" ' in B. Goldson and J. Muncie (eds) *Youth Crime and Justice: Critical issues*. London: Sage.

Smith, R. (2006) 'Actuarialism and Early Intervention in Contemporary Youth Justice' in B. Goldson and J. Muncie (eds) *Youth Crime and Justice: Critical issues*. London: Sage.

Squires, P. (2006) 'New Labour and the politics of anti-social behaviour' *Critical Social Policy* 26(1): 144–68.

Squires, P. (ed) (2008) *ASBO nation: The criminalisation of nuisance*. Bristol: The Policy Press.

Squires, P. and Stephen, D. (2005) 'Rethinking ASBOs'. *Critical Social Policy* 25(4): 517–28.

Statewatch (2008) <http://www.statewatch.org/asbo/ASBOwatch.html>.

Unicef (2007) *Child poverty in perspective: An overview of child well-being in rich countries*. Florence: Unicef.

United Nations Committee on the Rights of the Child (1995) *Eighth Session. Consideration of Reports Submitted by States Parties Under Article 44 of the Convention*. Geneva: Office of the United Nations High Commissioner for Human Rights.

United Nations Committee on the Rights of the Child (2002) *Concluding Observations of the Committee on the Rights of the Child: United Kingdom of Great Britain and Northern Ireland*. Geneva: United Nations.

Walmsley, R. (2003) *World Prison Population List* (5th edn). Findings 234. London: Home Office.

Walsh, C. (2003) 'Dispersal of Rights: A Critical Comment on Specified Provisions of the Anti-Social Behaviour Bill'. *Youth Justice* 3(2): 104–11.

Webster, C. (2006) ' "Race", Youth Crime and Justice' in B. Goldson and J. Muncie (eds) *Youth Crime and Justice: Critical issues*. London: Sage.

Webster, C., MacDonald, R., and Simpson, M. (2006) 'Predicting criminality? Risk factors, neighbourhood influence and desistance'. *Youth Justice* 6(1): 7–22.

White, R. (2003) 'Communities, conferences and restorative social justice'. *Criminal Justice* 3(2): 139–60.

Wonnacott, C. (1999) 'New Legislation: The counterfeit contract–reform, pretence and muddled principles in the new referral order'. *Child and Family Law Quarterly* 11(3): 271–87.

Youth Justice Board (2004a) *National Standards for Youth Justice Services*. London: Youth Justice Board.

Youth Justice Board (2004b) *Strategy for the Secure Estate for Juveniles: Building on the foundations*. London: Youth Justice Board.

Youth Justice Board (2007) *Update on the Strategy for the Secure Estate for Children and Young People*. London: Youth Justice Board.

Youth Justice Board (2008a) *Youth Justice Planning Framework 2008/09: Guidance for YOT managers and management boards in England*. London: Youth Justice Board.

Youth Justice Board (2008b) *Youth Justice Plan Cymru 2008/09: Guidance for YOI managers and management boards in Wales*. London: Youth Justice Board.

Youth Justice Board (2008c) *Youth Justice Planning Tool 2008/09—England*. London: Youth Justice Board.

Youth Justice Board (2008d) *Youth Justice Plan Cymru 2008/09—England*. London: Youth Justice Board.

Youth Justice Board (2008e) *Annual Report and Accounts 2007/08*. London: The Stationery Office.

Youth Justice Board (2008f) *Youth Justice System Custody Figures* at <http://www.yjb.gov.uk/en-gb/yjs/Custody/CustodyFigures/>.

14 Victims in the criminal justice process

Brian Williams and Matthew Hall

INTRODUCTION

In this chapter we will examine the position of victims of *crime* within the criminal justice system. Beginning with a discussion of the development of the victim's movement in the 1970s, the chapter goes on to consider key issues such as: the scope of 'victimhood'; victim rights; the needs and expectations of victims within the criminal justice process; and the policy response to such issues. The chapter will conclude by posing critical questions of the present reform agenda and the extent to which it has led to real benefits for victims.

BACKGROUND

Victims and *victimology*, once on the periphery of criminological research, have, since the late 1970s, taken a central role in academic research and policy (Doerner and Lab, 2002). These developments represent a true sea change in attitudes and political priorities by which debate concerning victims' needs and rights within the criminal justice system have taken centre stage to challenge entrenched notions of retributive *punishment* (Crawford and Newburn, 2003). Indeed, the magnitude of this ideological shift in the established norms of penological thought has prompted many to describe such developments as a *victims' movement*. Certainly this label conveys accurately the significance of the ideological shift which has seen victims go from the 'forgotten people' of the criminal justice system (Shapland *et al.*, 1985: 1) to the subject of extensive policies with the stated purpose of putting them 'at the heart' of that system (Home Office, 2004: 28); although, as Williams (1999) has argued, this label is problematic as it suggests a consistency and unity of purpose which was largely absent amongst many of those involved. Goodey (2005) highlights three distinct components to this 'movement': rising crime levels and the loss of faith in the rehabilitative ideal; the emergence of centre-right politics in Britain and North America, encapsulating a tough-on-crime approach; and the growth of the feminist movement. Pointing and Maguire (1988) discuss how the 'victims' movement' in the US was driven by a host of 'strange bedfellows' concerned with different aspects of victimisation, ranging from mental health practitioners to survivors of Nazi concentration camps (Young, 2000).

By the end of the 1970s, a common view was developing amongst most victimologists that victims of crime were being neglected by the criminal justice system (Maguire, 1991). In a seminal contribution, Nils Christie (1977) argued that the conflicts between victims and offenders had been monopolised by the state. By the early twenty-first century, the victims' role within the criminal justice system, along with their perceptions and experiences of it, had become a key feature of victimology and criminal justice policy-making (Joutsen, 1989, 1991; Home Office, 2002; JUSTICE, 1998; Crawford and Goodey, 2000; Zedner, 2002).

Victims in criminal justice

Most commentators now agree that victims are marginalised within the criminal justice system (Zedner, 2002). Many go further to argue that the lack of information, support, and courteous treatment afforded to victims at every stage of the process contributes significantly to their feelings of intimidation and bewilderment. One of the goals of this chapter will be to explore the extent to which such negative experiences amount to *secondary victimisation* at the hands of the system and the state itself (Pointing and Maguire, 1988).

The other theme informing this chapter is what might be called the social construction of victimisation. This is the notion that society ascribes the term 'victim' in a discriminatory manner, such that only some of those falling foul of criminal activity are widely accepted as 'worthy victims'. Characteristics attributed by Christie (1986) to the so-called *ideal victim* include being weak, carrying out a 'respectable project', being free of blame, and being a stranger to a 'big and bad' offender. Ideal victims also 'make their case known' to the authorities and cooperate with the criminal justice system. As 'genuine victims', this group are deemed worthy of society's sympathy, and with it support from public funds to provide information, facilities, and compensation from the state (see below). Others, however, are portrayed as 'unworthy victims' to whom such facilities—and even basic courteous treatment—are denied and secondary victimisation is disproportionately rife. These include victims with criminal convictions, victims who may have contributed to their own victimisation, or victims who come from socially excluded groups such as the homeless, those living in 'problem estates', or immigrants without appropriate papers (Davies *et al.*, 2007). Commentators have increasingly recognised that the former, stereotypical image of what it means to be a 'victim of crime' is often the exception rather than the norm, meaning that groups like those noted above which receive the least support may well be those who suffer crime most regularly. This issue is picked up in the next section.

Who are the 'victims'?

'Ideal' victims?

In contrast to socially prevailing notions of the 'ideal victim', it has become increasingly clear that the categories of victim and offender overlap, and that a large proportion of crime victims have previous criminal convictions or 'character, past conduct, or actions [which] can be considered undesirable' (Goodey, 2005: 124). Goodey draws on the example of women who stray beyond traditionally acceptable notions of female *gender* roles. This includes prostitutes, who are often met with a dismissive attitude from the police when they complain of sexual assault or *rape* (Jordan, 2008). Indeed, research indicates that victims of sexual assault or domestic violence have traditionally been labelled as liars or exaggerators by the police unless they react in the visibly distressed manner typical of the ideal victim (Jordan, 2004), despite the fact that it is actually very common for victims of rape to withdraw into a dazed state for several hours after the incident (Lees, 2002). This poor treatment (engendered by a lack of understanding of the impact of crime) of course amounts to secondary victimisation in that it leads to a denial of services, support, and information whilst intimidating the victim in an already very traumatic situation. Such secondary victimisation may continue in the court process where, despite statutory attempts to limit the practice (in s. 34 of the Youth Justice and Criminal Evidence Act 1999), such victims can still be questioned at length about their past sexual activities, and defence lawyers may apply to adduce the 'bad character' of any victim, including previous convictions (see s. 100 of the Criminal Justice Act 2003).

In some instances, the poor treatment of non-ideal victims by the criminal justice process has proved to be truly systemic. Francis (2007) draws on the well-known example of Stephen Lawrence, a black teenager murdered in Eltham, South London, in April 1993. Following multiple failings in the investigation and two failed *prosecution* attempts against the group of white youths suspected of the crime, the report by Lord Macpherson into the case concluded that the Metropolitan Police were *institutionally racist*. This led to officers wrongly treating the case as a gang or drug-related incident rather than a racist attack, resulting in the appalling treatment of the Lawrence family and community and of Stephen's friend who had witnessed part of the incident. In the police's view, black teenagers meant gang violence which meant 'unworthy' victims, and thus any semblance of support and understanding was denied.

Another area in which the state—if not the criminal justice system *per se*—discriminates against 'non-ideal' victims is with regard to the state compensation scheme. The scheme compensates for physical injuries and very limited psychological injury resulting from violent crime. The system is restrictive from the outset in that it generally excludes all but the most seriously injured. More significantly for present purposes, however, is the manner in which the scheme judges the victim as carefully as it judges the injuries (see CICA, 2001: para. 13). The scheme will not compensate victims of 'bad character' evidenced by criminal convictions or by other 'evidence available to the claims officer'. The scheme also denies compensation to victims who fail to report the crime or do not cooperate with the police. This raises particular issues in relation to *domestic violence* and other such offences with very low reporting rates, and where victims often withdraw support for prosecutions. Indeed the scheme also excludes applicants who live with their assailant, which again may pose problems for some domestic violence sufferers. As the vast majority of domestic violence victims are women, feminists would argue that this puts a whole gender at a disadvantage (see Walklate, 2007). Certainly a number of studies have demonstrated the persistence of problems such as the aggressive questioning of rape victims by police and lawyers (Temkin, 1999, 2002) and the failure to take violence against women seriously (Dobash and Dobash, 1998). Such findings again reflect entrenched notions that only 'worthy' victims should receive the highest standards of support and investment.

Expanding the scope of 'victimhood'

Aside from the 'worthiness' of most *direct victims* of criminal activity, there has been a growing understanding that 'victimisation' stretches beyond such individuals (Dignan, 2005). So, whilst the direct victim of burglary suffers the immediate harm (loss and damage to property, anger, inconvenience, fear) so-called *indirect victims*, including the friends, family, and wider community of the primary victim, may be affected too; say by increasing their fear of crime, or practically through increased insurance premiums (Rock, 1998). We saw this in the case of Stephen Lawrence, where the murder of a young man in the local area had a significant impact on the local community, as well as Stephen's family and the witness to the crime (Reiner, 2000). Recent comparisons can be drawn with high-profile cases such as the murder of schoolgirls Holly Wells and Jessica Chapman, and the effect this had on their home community of Soham (see Case Study).

This body of work and policy responses is also characterised by its sensitivity to newly-identified and emerging problems. Many examples can be drawn of these 'new' victims, including the 'discovery' of child victims in the 1980s (see Case Study) and the recognition of racially aggravated victimisation in the 1990s, which led to increased penalties being introduced under the Crime and Disorder Act 1998. Such protection was subsequently extended to the victims of crime motivated by homophobia and bigotry based on disability and religion. We have already noted that domestic violence was traditionally ignored at many stages of the criminal process. In addition, the Protection from Harassment Act 1997 made it an offence to pursue a 'course of conduct' (on at least two occasions) which the reasonable person with the same information would consider 'harassment' against a victim, even when the individual incidents do not amount to any other crimes. More recent examples include the increased attention being paid to international people trafficking (Kelly and Regan, 2000; Goodey, 2004) and violence against Muslims ('Islamaphobia') (Spalek, 2002).

 CASE STUDY: CHILD VICTIMS

The recognition of child victims and child sexual abuse provides an example of how the criminal justice system has adapted to meet particular problems, especially in relation to 'worthy' victims with popular appeal. The recognition of this particular social harm was greatly assisted by feminist campaigning and research (for example Dominelli, 1986; T., 1988). Nevertheless, although it is generally agreed that child victims need specialist support—both in relation to the impacts of crime outside the criminal justice system and their increased susceptibility to intimidation (a form of secondary victimisation) within it—the victimisation of children remains under-researched. It is clear, however, that the child victim of sexual abuse represents the archetypal 'ideal victim', conjuring images of vulnerability and lost innocence versus the 'demonic' offender (Francis, 2007). Greer (2007) comments on the mediatisation of such incidents, which focuses on completely innocent children abused by adults in positions of authority—such as teachers, priests, or youth leaders—despite the fact that most child sexual abuse occurs within the home.

A combination of academic discussion and the increased attention being drawn to the problem by the media throughout the 1980s and 1990s prompted the criminal justice system to react by affording child victims increased protection whilst giving evidence in court. This included allowing them to give evidence through live video-link or behind screens—when such equipment was available. This was being done on an *ad hoc* basis, long before such provisions were rolled out to adult victims of crime in the Youth Justice and Criminal Evidence Act 1999. Since the Act, children under 17 are automatically deemed 'vulnerable witnesses' eligible to give evidence though video-link or via pre-recorded examination in chief. Such *special measures* are principally designed to allow children to articulate their evidence without the intimidation of the courtroom environment or seeing their assailant. The advent of pre-recorded examination is a significant step forward, whereby children answer questions in specially designed police suites prior to coming to court, and the tape is then played for the jury. This is all intended to reduce the stress on the victims and, with it, the impact of secondary victimisation.

Overall, the advent of special measures has been received positively by vulnerable and intimidated witnesses as a whole. Nevertheless, criticisms have been made concerning the lack of real choice afforded to children when it comes to deciding whether to give evidence in this way (Hall, 2007). Arguably, the system also relies on technology to cure the problems faced by children in court without a more fundamental examination of the cultural practices of lawyers. Birch (2000: 223) labels the 1999 Act 'a somewhat hurried piece of work, enacted to fulfil election promises' and that its impact will be minimal whilst practitioners remain sceptical of the measures.

There is almost no modern research on lawyers' questioning strategies or the reaction of judges and magistrates to child witnesses. The two exceptions are a report from Plotnikoff and Woolfson (2005) and Applegate (2006), who both saw evidence of judges stepping in to guard children against 'over-rigorous' cross-examination, to ensure the language used is suitable to the child's age, and that the child has the opportunity to answer questions. These findings suggest that special measures must be backed with an accompanying change in the practices of questioning advocates and others involved in the process.

Plotnikoff and Woolfson (2005) were commissioned by the National Society for the Prevention of Cruelty to Children to examine the use of video-linked evidence for children. The authors concluded that 'the essentially compulsory use of TV links for young witnesses in cases of sex or violence' (p. 11) restricts the options available to children. This may go against Article 12 of the 1990 UN Convention on the Rights of the Child, which requires children to be involved in the decision-making process on matters relevant to their lives. The report suggests that—given a genuine choice—some children might choose to forgo the TV-link in favour of being screened off from the defendant and gallery in the courtroom. Burton *et al.*, (2006) were also critical of the lack of real explanation given to children over the implications of giving evidence via special measures. One of us (Hall, 2007) has highlighted the confusing aspects of giving evidence in this manner from the child's point of view, including problems with static over the equipment and the confusing aspects of children seeing lawyers on video screens—out of context—rather than live in court. Hence, whilst the policy reaction to this particular group of 'ideal' victims has certainly brought benefit to many, lingering doubts remain as to whether, by forcing child victims down a particular path, the system once again is responsible for the secondary victimisation of some of the most vulnerable victims.

Hence, the range of victims to be catered for by the criminal justice system is always expanding, with much work still to be done. For example, with a few exceptions (Walklate, 1989; Levi and Pithouse, 1992; Spalek, 1999; 2001), corporate crime victims have been neglected by research. This is no doubt partly because of the hidden nature of much crime of this kind: victims may see themselves as suffering misfortune or accidents rather than the consequences of a deliberate act. Alternatively, it may be very difficult to seek redress against a remote and powerful offender. Furthermore, Tombs (2005) suggests that, in our society at present ' "conventional criminals" tend to be represented as a burden upon society in a way that corporations will not be' (p. 272). If victims of corporate crime are to be taken more seriously, a cultural change in which the crimes themselves are seen as such—and are regarded as serious—will be required. On the other side of this equation, Croall (2007) has recently highlighted that the victims of such crimes often find themselves labelled within the 'unworthy' camp.

Victims' views of the criminal justice system

Quantitative study of victims, victim services, and victim-related policies has blossomed since the late 1970s, and much more is now known about the effects of victimisation and the perceived effectiveness of the criminal justice system as a result (see Spalek, 2006: chap. 5). Of particular significance has been the emergence of *victimisation surveys* in the US in the late 1960s, and the first *British Crime Survey* (BCS) conducted in 1982. These are wide-scale, household surveys which question respondents about their experiences of, and concerns about, crime. As such, the BCS has revealed a lot about the so-called 'dark figure' of crime which goes unreported to the police. More recently, the BCS has included questions concerning victims' feelings about the criminal justice system. The 2006/2007 BCS survey (Nicholas *et al.*, 2007) reveals that 79 per cent of respondents were confident that the criminal justice system respects the rights of defendants and 67 per cent believed the system treats witnesses well. Confidence was lower, however, in how the system deals with young offenders (25 per cent), its effectiveness in bringing offenders to justice (41 per cent), and its overall efficiency (40 per cent). Only 33 per cent of respondents were confident that the criminal justice system met the needs of victims of crime. Amongst respondents who had been victimised in the last 12 months and where the case had involved the police, 58 per cent were satisfied with the police's handling of their case.

The BCS paints a rather more complex picture of how views of the criminal justice system are affected by socio-demographic grouping. Generally speaking, young people seem to have greater confidence in the system than older people, whilst the differences between men and women in this respect were less obvious (Kershaw *et al.*, 2008). In terms of ethnicity, people from Asian, Black, Chinese, or Other ethnic groups generally had more overall confidence in the criminal justice system compared to White groups or people with mixed ethnic origins. That said, people from Black ethnic backgrounds were less likely to believe that the criminal justice system respected the rights of defendants compared to all other racial groups, which may reflect the fact that they are often perceived as offenders by that system rather than victims (Jansson *et al.*, 2007).

Significantly, the 2006/2007 BCS also indicates that being a victim of crime in the last 12 months has a negative impact on respondents' views of all aspects of the criminal justice process. Findings such as this have led policy makers to focus increased attention on the role of criminal justice agencies in contributing to secondary victimisation (see Williams, 2005, chap. 4). The main victim assistance charity—*Victim Support*—have commissioned their own research to demonstrate the need for new services and to draw attention to problems arising from the ways in which existing ones are delivered (see, for example, Paterson *et al.*, 2006). Two other key sources of information are the Witness Satisfaction Surveys (WSS) (Whitehead, 2001; Angle *et al.*, 2003) and the Vulnerable and Intimidated Witness Surveys (Hamlyn *et al.*, 2004a, 2004b). The 2000 and 2002 WSS revealed high levels of satisfaction with the police amongst witnesses, with 88 per cent of those questioned being 'very' or 'fairly' satisfied with their treatment in 2000 and 89 per cent in 2002. Nevertheless, both surveys failed to produce much data on the differing experiences of different social-demographic groups. One exception was the finding that witnesses (including victims) from ethnic minority groups were less likely to have contact with Victim Support. This is a worrying finding given that the BCS has consistently shown that people from minority ethnic communities—and especially those with mixed-race backgrounds—are more likely to fall victim to many crimes compared to White groups (Nicholas *et al.*, 2007). The implication is once again that the support offered to victims benefits some groups disproportionately compared to others, with people from the groups most frequently victimised often receiving poorer service provision.

It is clear that policy makers are now very concerned about how the criminal justice system is perceived by victims of crime and the criminal justice system in general, and that this has been a factor driving policy. Most recently, a Cabinet Office report by Casey (2008) has emphasised how many of the reforms and policy responses we have seen to date are direct attempts to address the widespread perception that the criminal justice system deals with victims poorly. In particular, Casey emphasises the BCS finding that only 33 per cent of respondents feel the criminal justice system meets the needs of victims, whereas 79 per cent agreed that the system respected defendants' rights. We will examine some of these policy responses in more detail in the next section.

REVIEW QUESTIONS

1 How wide is the scope of 'victimisation'? Could it be argued that the true impact of some crimes goes far beyond the immediate, direct victims, and even beyond their friends, families, and communities?

2 How would you describe a 'stereotypical' victim of crime? What kinds of people are more likely to be labelled this way? Do we view all potential 'victims' equally?

Victims in the criminal justice system: problems and policy responses

There is insufficient space here to discuss the full range of issues identified by vicitimologists and addressed by policy makers which have made the criminal justice system a daunting and unsupportive process for victims of crime from different parts of society (see JUSTICE, 1998). The following section will therefore identify the key difficulties faced by victims whilst introducing the academic responses and the reforms designed to address them.

Lack of information and explanation

A general concern voiced by many commentators has been that victims' lack of party-status within the adversarial justice system means they often do not receive basic information about the progress of their case, amendment of charges, or the date of the trial. Victims also have little information to explain and prepare them for the criminal justice process itself, including practical information like the location of the court, how to get there, or what to bring. Even less explanation was traditionally given about how the process would operate and what was expected of victims. After giving evidence, no system was in place to inform victims about the outcome of the case or the disposition or *parole* arrangements of the offender.

The need to address such problems initially led to a flurry of publications for victims and witnesses, including information leaflets, explanatory DVDs, and online 'virtual walkthroughs' to explain different aspects of the criminal justice system. Although these were a positive step forward, it is questionable what use they were to the large number of victims from low socio-economic groups, who may not have access to the internet, sufficient literary skills, or a postal address to which the information could be sent. In an effort to coordinate the provision of such information, the government sought to make the police the 'One Stop Shop' where victims and witnesses could get their questions answered. Problems persisted, however, with the pilots of these schemes when it became clear that police did not have all relevant information, and could not *explain* the decisions reached by the Crown Prosecution Service (CPS) in adequate detail (Hoyle *et al.*, 1999). Following the failure of the One Stop Shop pilots, the view developed that criminal justice agencies must work together to ensure the victim is kept up to date and prepared before, during, and after formal criminal proceedings (see Young, 2000). This has led to the provision of more timely and fuller information to victims by all the actors within the process, including the Probation Service (see Williams, 2005: 11–12 and 105–10), the Police (Williams and Goodman, 2007), courts, and prosecutors (Dignan, 2005: 71–3), guaranteed by a national Code of Practice (Home Office, 2005b) with legal force from 2006 (under the Domestic Violence, Crime and Victims Act 2004).

The successors to the One Stop Shop pilots have been Witness Care Units (WCUs), which have now been set up in all local criminal justice areas. These are joint ventures run collaboratively by the police force and the CPS. The role of the WCU is to keep witnesses (including victims) informed of the progress of a case and to establish whether they require special facilities at court. In addition, the WCU will send a letter (again, assuming the victim/witness has an address) informing witnesses about the outcome of the case they had been involved with, and may refer victims on to organisations that could provide further help and support.

Treatment, facilities, and services

The grievances of victims in the criminal justice system have been grounded not just in the lack of information they receive, but also a lack of basic courteous treatment from lawyers and the absence of basic facilities (including seating and toilets) and services to assist them within court buildings and beyond (Shapland *et al.*, 1985). Rock (1993) has commented on the position of witnesses (including victims' witnesses) attending to give evidence at a typical English Crown Court. His conclusions show that witnesses are kept at the margins of the court's social community and receive little support, because the criminal justice professionals are afraid of being professionally compromised. Traditionally, this has led to a situation where no one at court has been responsible for ensuring victims and other witnesses are supported throughout the process.

One of the most significant developments in this area has been the inception of the *Witness Service*, providing support to defence and prosecution witnesses at court. This is run by Victim Support and has grown since 1989 from a small action-research project to a national service operating in all courts, following significant government subsidies. Witness Services are generally staffed by volunteers who, as well as meeting and greeting victims and other witnesses, provide separate waiting areas for prosecution witnesses and pre-court familiarisation visits. They also provide a vital link with the courtroom, collecting information on progress and relaying it back to waiting victims.

Vulnerability and intimidation

A courtroom is an unfamiliar environment for most people and can be frightening and intimidating (Hamlyn *et al.*, 2004a). As victimology focused attention on victims of crime, commentators began to recognise that some witnesses—and especially some forms of victim—were particularly susceptible to intimidation (secondary victimisation) by this system. Public attention was drawn to these issues in Britain in the mid-1990s following the case of Julia Mason, a rape victim who became the subject of a brutal onslaught of repetitive cross-examination from her rapist, Ralston Edwards, after he elected to represent himself. Edwards questioned Mason for six days in the same clothes he had worn during the rape (Cretney and Davis, 1997).

The government's response was to commission a report on the treatment of *vulnerable and intimidated witnesses* (Interdepartmental Working Group, 1998). The resulting *Speaking up for Justice* report discussed the difficulties inherent in defining *vulnerable and intimidated witnesses*. Based on distinctions drawn from Healey (1995) a 'combined' approach was advocated for such definitions. Witnesses could be 'vulnerable' by reason of personal characteristics (age, disability, mental and physical disorders) but also for wider circumstantial reasons (being related to or involved with the defendant).

The statutory grounding of so-called special measures came the following year in Part II of the Youth Justice and Criminal Evidence Act 1999. These are a list of facilities available to assist vulnerable and intimidated victims and other witnesses give evidence in court. Sections 23 to 30 of the Act list the measures available to 'vulnerable or intimidated' witnesses as defined under ss. 16 and 17 in accordance with *Speaking up for Justice*. Evidence from the Vulnerable and Intimidated Witness surveys and the general Witness Satisfaction Surveys suggests these measures are having a beneficial impact for a great number of victims (Hamlyn *et al.*, 2004b; Hall, 2007).

Nevertheless, the 1999 reforms remain controversial. Ellison (2001) states that the reforms did not go far enough and reflected an 'accommodation approach' preserving the traditional adversarial model. This raises the complex question of whether a more European-style inquisitorial system would serve victims better (see Brienen and Hoegen, 2000, Jackson, 2003). Special measures also appear to be afforded largely to stereotypical ideal victims, deemed 'worthy' of them (Hall, 2007).

Lack of participation

One of the most controversial issues to face victimologists and reformers has been the question of whether victims should be afforded some degree of *participation* in the criminal justice process. In particular, these debates have centred on the extent to which victims should be able to make or influence decisions traditionally left to criminal justice practitioners. These include decisions on issues such as charging, *plea-bargaining*, and sentencing.

Generally speaking, policy makers seem to have leaned towards slowly expanding the range of decisions for which victims are afforded consultative participation. As such, the statutory *Victims' Code of Practice* requires victims to be consulted, and their opinions taken into account, on matters such as dropping charges, bail, and parole. Significantly, however, victims are not given decision-making roles. According to the JUSTICE committee (1998) this is the better position, as giving victims decision-making powers can burden them with unnecessary pressure, and amounts to a refusal by the state to enforce the law, which is one of its responsibilities.

One of the key grounds of debate has been the influence of victims on sentencing decisions. Edna Erez argues in favour of so-called *victim impact statements* (VIS) as a means of affording victims participation rights in criminal justice (Erez, 1999, 2000). VIS statements developed in the US for victims to communicate information to the court about the effects of crime. These were adopted in Britain (nationally in October 2001) as 'victim personal statements' (VPS), although the British system excludes judicial consideration of comments made by the victim on sentencing. The argument against victims' involvement in sentencing has been most strongly put by Ashworth (2000), who argues that victim personal statements will lead to the inconsistent application of justice for different offenders. The concern of Ashworth and others is that the sentence an offender receives for a given offence will differ depending on factors such as how articulate the victim is at describing the impact of the crime. In this way, justice becomes unpredictable and inconsistent.

Nevertheless, there may be alternative ways for victims to participate in the disposal of cases. In recent years there have been increased opportunities for victims to participate in *restorative justice* initiatives, mainly where the offender is under 18 (Williams, 2005: chap. 3). Group work with perpetrators of family violence has flourished, and in some areas victims can be directly involved if they so wish: this is a response to research which found that victims generally did not want perpetrators imprisoned; rather, they wanted them to change, which may help counteract the concern that victims are excessively punitive and should therefore be excluded from the sentencing process (Doak, 2007). As a response to such findings, the government included within the Crime and Disorder Act 1998 provisions to allow courts to order young offenders to make *repar ations* to victims or offenders. Furthermore, under the scheme of Youth Offending Panels set up by the Youth Justice and Criminal Evidence Act 1999, victims can participate in a process by which a 'contract' of good behaviour is agreed with young offenders with the principle aim of preventing them from reoffending (Crawford and Newburn, 2003).

Victims' rights

Underlying many of these debates has been the wider question of whether victims should have *rights* in the criminal justice system. The acceptance of victims' rights has been a key issue for much of the victims' movement and from an early stage in its developments, empathised in particular though the more aggressive, politicised strategies favoured by its proponents in the United States (Maguire and Shapland, 1997). This reflected a general growth in 'human rights' discourse internationally, which blossomed in Europe following the introduction of the European Convention on Human Rights, enshrined into British law by the Human Rights Act 1998.

A common distinction drawn in these debates is that between 'service rights' and 'procedural rights'. For Ashworth and Redmayne (2005) 'service rights' include respectful and sympathetic treatment, support, information, court facilities, and compensation from the offender or state. Ashworth (2000) argues that such rights should not stray beyond this, into areas of 'public interest'. In particular, Ashworth is very much against affording 'procedural' rights to victims: which is taken to mean rights of participation either through being allowed to speak in court, having their situation and opinions considered, or, at the most extreme, giving them influence over decision making in matters such as bail or sentencing.

In some countries, mostly richer ones, the law has been changed to give crime victims statutory rights. In England and Wales, the 1990 Victim's Charter, which was recognised as a failure remarkably soon after its introduction (Fenwick, 1995), was eventually replaced by a statutory Code of Practice which responds to real needs (Home Office, 2005b). For example, it sets deadlines for the statutory criminal justice agencies to keep victims informed of important decisions such as releasing accused individuals on bail and dropping charges, and requires them to give reasons in certain circumstances for such decisions. It remains to be seen how consistently these changes will be implemented. There is also a lingering question of enforceability as the Code is not law, and cannot lead to prosecution, but is rather enforced by complaining to a Parliamentary Commissioner with few compulsive powers. Nevertheless, the Code certainly represents a step forward in the British system.

REVIEW QUESTIONS

1 Should victims be allowed a degree of participation in the criminal process? What would be the advantages and the disadvantages of such a system?

2 What other kinds of victims might find it particularly difficult to give evidence in court? How can the court address such problems?

CONCLUSION

The above discussion reflects a substantial programme of policy activity relating to crime victims, mainly since 1997. While this activity has undoubtedly improved matters for some victims in a variety of ways, it is interesting to note that not all the changes were evidence-based. Strange as it may seem, some of these provisions were not the result of demand from victims' organisations or of research findings showing that they were required. Indeed, the much heralded state compensation system to provide money to victims of violent crime was implemented with no consultation from victims at all (Rock, 1990).

Policy-making in relation to victims of crime has largely been based upon politics rather than evidence in the UK over recent decades. With the increasing politicisation of victim issues (Elias, 1983; Williams, 1999, chap. 4), there has been a trend towards gesture politics in the criminal justice field. Huge amounts of legislation have been passed, creating hundreds of new criminal offences and ostensibly aimed at placing the victim 'at the heart' of the criminal justice system (Home Office, 2004: 28).

Nevertheless, it is often difficult to discern any real benefits for victims, especially non-ideal victims, and some elaborate and expensive arrangements have been introduced in the name of improving matters for them, without necessarily doing so. Recent examples include victim personal statements and state victim compensation arrangements, which, as we have seen, effectively exclude 'unworthy' victims who happen to have serious criminal records themselves (Williams, 2005). In other cases, legislation appears to be passed for presentational reasons, and not enforced: examples include the requirement that courts give reasons if they do not order offenders to pay compensation to victims in relevant cases, and the law which restricts discussion in court of complainants' previous sexual history in rape cases. Victims have been used 'in the service of severity' (Ashworth, 2000; see also Williams, 2005) to justify increasingly harsh sentencing policies; the notion of 'rebalancing' justice has been part of the argument for introducing targets aimed at increasing the number of prosecutions which result in convictions (or 'narrowing the justice gap'—a concept which seems tailor-made to increase the likelihood of *miscarriages of justice*). This kind of rhetoric does little if anything to improve victims' actual position, and particularly those not fortunate enough to be deemed 'worthy' of society's sympathy.

QUESTIONS FOR DISCUSSION

1 Will the reforms ostensibly aimed at improving the lot of victims and witnesses in reality lead to increased prosecutions?

2 How can reformers balance the needs of victims with the right of defendants to be tried fairly in court?

3 What benefits do reforms intended to assist victims and witnesses in court bring for the criminal justice system itself?

4 Is the Government's policy of victim assistance and reform an example of rhetoric over reality?

GUIDE TO FURTHER READING

A number of recent books provide further information on the issues discussed in this chapter: James Dignan's *Understanding Victims and Restorative Justice* (Open University Press, 2005) is particularly good on legal issues; Jo Goodey's *Victims and Victimology* (Longman, 2005) is strong on gender and international issues; and Brian Williams' *Victims of Crime and Community Justice* (Jessica Kingsley, 2005) considers community and restorative justice from the point of view of what is good for victims of crime. Pamela Davies and colleagues tackle some wider issues such as social exclusion and the news media relating to victims (Davies *et al.*, 2007). A more difficult, but very rewarding, read is Sandra Walklate's *Imagining the Victim of Crime* (McGraw Hill, 2007) which looks at victim policy from a sociological perspective. It is particularly strong on gender issues and the impact of globalisation.

WEB LINKS

http://www.victimology.nl

There are several useful websites dealing with issues relating to victims of crime. Probably the most informative is this Dutch-hosted International Victimology website. This provides access to a vast library of material and links to all the relevant academic journals.

http://www.vaonline.org

This is an American site with worldwide links to service providers; this site also hosts a number of specialist services including *Victimology Research*.

http://www.victimsupport.org

The UK agency Victim Support has a helpful site, which focuses on providing leaflets and other information to victims, but also has press releases, policy documents, research reports, and links to other organisations.

http://www.homeoffice.gov.uk/crime-victims/

This UK government website provides basic information to victims, with links to research and other organisations. It is part of a vast and complex website with a search facility which is not very user-friendly, but it is good for what it does.

http://www.cjsonline.gov.uk/victim/walkthrough/index.html

The online Victim Walkthrough also has some key information about victims in the criminal justice process and is a useful example of the output of policy making in this area.

REFERENCES

Angle, H., Malam, S., and Carey, C. (2003) *Witness Satisfaction: Findings from the Witness Satisfaction Survey 2002*. Home Office Online Report 19/03. London: Home Office.

Applegate, R. (2006) 'Taking child witnesses out of the Crown Court: a live link initiative'. *International Review of Victimology* 13: 179–200.

Ashworth, A. (2000) 'Victims' Rights, Defendants' Rights and Criminal Procedure' in A. Crawford and J. Goodey (eds) *Integrating a Victim Perspective Within Criminal Justice: international debates*. Aldershot: Ashgate Dartmouth, 185–204.

Ashworth, A. and Redmayne (2005) *The Criminal Process* (3rd edn). Oxford: Oxford University Press.

Birch, D. (2000) 'A Better Deal for Vulnerable Witnesses'. *Criminal Law Review* Apr: 233–49.

Brienen, M. and Hoegen, H. (2000) *Victims of Crime in 22 European Criminal Justice Systems: The Implementation of Recommendation (85) 11 of the Council of Europe on the Position of the Victim in the Framework of Criminal Law and Procedure*. Niemegen: Wolf Legal Productions.

Burton, M., Evans, R., and Sanders, A. (2006) *An evaluation of the use of special measures for vulnerable and intimidated witnesses*. Home Office Research Findings 270. London: Home Office.

Casey, L. (2008) *Engaging Communities in Fighting Crime*. London: Cabinet Office.

Christie, N. (1977) 'Conflicts as Property'. *British Journal of Criminology* 17: 1–15.

Christie, N. (1986) 'The Ideal Victim' in E. Fattah (ed) *From Crime Policy to Victim Policy*. Basingstoke: Macmillan, 17–30.

Crawford, A. and Goodey, J. (eds) (2000) *Integrating a Victim Perspective within Criminal Justice: international debates*. Aldershot: Ashgate Dartmouth.

Crawford, A. and Newburn, T. (2003) *Youth Offending and Restorative Justice: Implementing reform in youth justice*. Cullompton: Willan Publishing.

Cretney, A. and Davis, G. (1997) 'Prosecuting Domestic Assault: Victims Failing Courts or Courts Failing Victims?'. *Howard Journal of Criminal Justice* 36: 146–57.

Criminal Injuries Compensation Authority (CICA) (2001) *Compensation for Victims of Violent Crime*. CICA: London.

Croall, H. (2007) 'Victims of White-Collar and Corporate Crime' in P. Davies, P. Francis, and C. Greer (eds) *Victims, Crime and Society*. London: Sage.

Davies, P., Francis, P., and Greer, C. (2007) 'Victims, Crime and Society' in P. Davies, P. Francis, and C. Greer (eds) *Victims, Crime and Society*. London: Sage.

Dignan, J. (2005) *Understanding Victims and Restorative Justice*. Maidenhead: Open University Press.

Doak, J. (2007) *Victims' Rights, Human Rights and Criminal Justice: Reconceiving the Role of the Third Parties*. Oxford: Hart.

Dobash, R.P. and Dobash, R. (eds) (1998) *Rethinking Violence against Women*. London: Sage.

Doerner, W.G. and Lab, S.P. (2002) *Victimology* (3rd edn). Cincinnati, OK: Anderson.

Dominelli, L. (1986) 'Father-daughter incest: patriarchy's shameful secret'. *Critical Social Policy* 16: 8–22.

Elias, R. (1983) *Victims of the system: crime victims and compensation in American politics and criminal justice*. New Brunswick: Transaction.

Ellison, L. (2001) *The Adversarial Process and the Vulnerable Witness*. Oxford: Oxford University Press.

Erez, E. (1999) 'Who's Afraid of the Big Bad Victim? Victim Impact Statements as Victim Empowerment and Enforcement of Justice'. *Criminal Law Review* Jul: 545–56.

Erez, E. (2000) 'Integrating a Victim Perspective in Criminal Justice Through Victim Impact Statements' in A. Crawford and J. Goodey (eds) *Integrating a Victim Perspective Within Criminal Justice: international debates*. Aldershot: Ashgate Dartmouth, 165–84.

Fenwick, H. (1995) 'Rights of victims in the criminal justice system: rhetoric or reality?'. *Criminal Law Review* Nov: 843–53.

Francis, P. (2007) '"Race", Ethnicity, Victims and Crime' in P. Davies, P. Francis, and C. Greer (eds) *Victims, Crime and Society*. London: Sage.

Goodey, J. (2004) 'Promoting good practice in sex trafficking cases'. *International Review of Victimology* 11(1): 89–110.

Goodey, J. (2005) *Victims and Victimology: Research, policy and practice*. Harlow: Pearson Education.

Greer, C. (2007) 'News Media, Victims and Crime' in P. Davies, P. Francis, and C. Greer (eds) *Victims, Crime and Society*. London: Sage.

Hall, M. (2007) 'The Use and Abuse of Special Measures: Giving Victims the Choice?' *Journal of Scandinavian Studies in Criminology and Crime Prevention* 8(1): 33–53.

Hamlyn, B., Phelps, A., and Sattar, G. (2004a) *Key Findings from the Surveys of Vulnerable and Intimidated Witnesses 2000/01 and 2003*. Home Office Research Findings 240. London: Home Office.

Hamlyn, B., Phelps, A., Turtle, J., and Sattar, G. (2004b) *Are Special Measures Working? Evidence from Surveys of Vulnerable and Intimidated Witnesses*. Home Office Research Study 283. London: Home Office.

Healey, D. (1995) *Victim and Witness Intimidation: New Developments and Emerging Responses*. Washington: US Department of Justice.

Home Office (2002) *Justice for all* Cm 5563. London: The Stationery Office.

Home Office (2004) *Compensation and Support for Victims of Crime: A consultation paper on proposals to amend the Criminal Injuries Compensation Scheme and provide a wide range of support for victims*. London: Home Office.

Home Office (2005a) *Domestic Violence: A National Report*. London: Home Office.

Home Office (2005b) *The Code of Practice for Victims of Crime*. London: Home Office.

Hoyle, C., Cape, E., Morgan, R., and Sanders, A. (1999) *Evaluation of the 'One Stop Shop' and Victim Statement Pilot Projects*. London: Home Office.

Interdepartmental Working Group on the Treatment of Vulnerable or Intimidated Witnesses in the Criminal Justice System (1998) *Speaking up for Justice*. London: HMSO.

Jackson, J. (2003) 'Justice for All: Putting Victims at the Heart of Criminal Justice?' *Journal of Law and Society*. 30: 309–26.

Jansson, K., Budd, S., Lovbakke, J., Moley, S., Thorpe, K. (2007) Attitudes, perceptions and risks of crime: Supplementary Volume 1 to Crime in England and Wales 2006/07 (2nd edn). London: Home Office.

Jordan, J. (2004) 'Beyond Belief? Police, Rape and Women's Credibility'. *Criminal Justice* 4: 29–59.

Jordan, J. (2008) *Serial Survivors: Women's narratives of surviving rape*. Sydney: Federation Press.

Joutsen, M. (1989) 'Foreword' in HEUNI (ed) *The Role of the Victim of Crime in European Criminal Justice System*. Helsinki: HEUNI.

Joutsen, M. (1991) 'Changing victim policy: International dimensions' in G. Kaiser, H. Kury, and H. Albrecht (eds) *Victims and criminal justice*. Freiburg: Max Planck Institute, 765–98.

JUSTICE (1998) *Victims in Criminal Justice, Report of the JUSTICE Committee on the Role of Victims in Criminal Justice*. London: JUSTICE.

Kelly, L. and Regan, L. (2000) *Stopping Traffic: Exploring the extent of, and responses to, trafficking in women for sexual exploitation in the UK*. Police Research Series No. 125. London: Home Office.

Kershaw, C., Nicholas, S., and Walker, A. (2008) Crime in England and Wales 2007/08: Findings from the British Crime Survey and police recorded crime. London: Home Office.

Lees, S. (2002) *Carnal Knowledge: Rape on trial*. London: Women's Press.

Levi, M. and Pithouse, A. (1992) 'The victims of fraud' in D. Downes (ed) *Unravelling Criminal Justice*. London: Macmillan.

Macpherson, W. (1999) *The Stephen Lawrence Enquiry*. London: Stationery Office.

Maguire, M. (1991) 'The Needs and Rights of Victims of Crime' in M. Tonry (ed) *Crime and Justice: A Review of Research* 14. Chicago: Chicago University Press, 363–433.

Maguire, M. and Shapland, J. (1997) 'Provision for Victims in an International Context' in R. Davis, A. Lurigio, and W. Skogan (eds) *Victims of Crime* (2nd edn). Thousand Oaks: Sage Publications, 211–30.

McLaughlin, E. and Muncie, J. (2006) *The Sage Dictionary of Criminology*. London: Sage.

Nicholas, S., Kershaw, C., and Walker, A. (2007) *Crime in England and Wales 2006/07*. London: Home Office.

Paterson, A., Dunn, P., Chaston, K., and Malone, L. (2006) *In the Aftermath: The support needs of people bereaved by homicide, a research report*. London: Victim Support.

Plotnikoff, J. and Woolfson, R. (2005) *In their own words: the experiences of 50 young witnesses in criminal proceedings*. London: NSPCC.

Pointing, J. and Maguire, M. (1988) 'Introduction: the rediscovery of the crime victim' in M. Maguire and J. Pointing (eds) *Victims of Crime: A New Deal?* Milton Keynes: Open University Press, 1–13.

Reiner, R. (2000) *The Politics of the Police* (3rd edn). Oxford: Oxford University Press.

Rock, P. (1998) *After Homicide: Practical and Political responses to Bereavement*. Oxford: Clarendon Press.

Rock, P. (1993) *The Social World of an English Crown Court: witnesses and professionals in the Crown Court Centre at Wood Green*. Oxford: Clarendon Press.

Rock, P. (1990) *Helping Victims of Crime: The Home Office and the Rise of Victim Support in England and Wales*. Oxford: Oxford University Press.

Shapland, J., Willmore, J., and Duff, P. (1985) *Victims and the Criminal Justice System*. Aldershot: Gower.

Spalek, B. (1999) 'Exploring the impact of financial crime: a study looking into the effects of the Maxwell scandal upon the Maxwell pensioners'. *International Review of Victimology* 6: 213–30.

Spalek, B. (2001) 'White collar crime and secondary victimisation, an analysis of the effects of the closure of BCCI'. *Howard Journal of Criminal Justice* 40(2): 166–79.

Spalek, B. (ed) (2002) *Islam, Crime and Criminal Justice*. Cullompton: Willan.

Spalek, B. (2006) *Crime Victims: Theory, policy and practice*. Basingstoke: Palgrave Macmillan.

T., Anna (1988) 'Feminist responses to sexual abuse: the work of the Birmingham Rape Crisis Centre' in M. Maguire and J. Pointing (eds) *Victims of Crime: A new deal*. Milton Keynes: Open University Press, 60–5.

Temkin, J. (1999), 'Reporting Rape in London: A Qualitative Study'. *Howard Journal of Criminal Justice* 38: 17–41.

Temkin, J. (2002) *Rape and the Legal Process* (2nd edn). Oxford: Oxford University Press.

Titus, R.M., Heinzelmann, F., and Boyle, J.M. (1995) 'Victimisation of persons by fraud'. *Crime and Delinquency* 41(1): 54–72.

Tombs, S. (2005) 'Corporate crime' in C. Hale, K. Hayward, A. Wahidin, and E. Wincup (eds) *Criminology*. Oxford: Oxford University Press, 267–87.

Walklate, S. (1989) *Victimology: The victim and the criminal justice process*. London: Unwin Hyman.

Walklate, S. (2007) *Imagining the Victim of Crime*. Maidenhead: Open University Press.

Whitehead, E. (2001) *Witness Satisfaction: findings from the Witness Satisfaction Survey 2000*. Home Office Research Study 230. London: Home Office.

Williams, B. (1999) *Working with Victims of Crime: Policies, politics and practice*. London: Jessica Kingsley.

Williams, B. (2005) *Victims of Crime and Community Justice*. London: Jessica Kingsley.

Williams, B. and Goodman, H. (2007) 'Victims' in S. Green, E. Lancaster, and S. Feasey (eds) *Addressing Offending Behaviour*. Cullompton: Willan Publishing.

Young, R. (2000) 'Integrating a Multi-Victim Perspective into Criminal Justice Through Restorative Justice Conferences' in A. Crawford and J. Goodey (eds) *Integrating a Victim Perspective Within Criminal Justice: international debates*. Aldershot: Ashgate Dartmouth, 227–52.

Zedner, L. (2002) 'Victims' in M. Maguire, R. Morgan, and R. Reiner (eds) *The Oxford Handbook of Criminology* (3rd edn). Oxford: Oxford University Press.

15 The criminal justice system in Scotland

Anne Wilson

INTRODUCTION

This chapter provides an introduction to the Scottish criminal justice system, raising awareness of 'different' responses to *crime* and different processes that are embedded in Scottish political, economic, cultural, and socio-historical practices. It examines the key defining characteristics and principles of the system, but does not examine the sources of Scots law and the civil justice system in Scotland. The aim of this chapter is, first, to assess how the creation of the Scottish Parliament (Holyrood) has impacted upon the Scottish legal system and the impact of European Union legislation on the Scottish criminal justice system; and, secondly, to describe the legal personnel in Scotland, the Scottish *criminal courts*, and the criminal justice process. This chapter will also examine how these defining characteristics affect what happens when people break the criminal law in Scotland.

The criminal justice system deals with the problem of crime through prosecuting and punishing offenders for behaviour that is considered to be unacceptable, and in their response to that behaviour nation states impose specific processes on individuals from the moment of arrest to whatever may comprise the *ultimate sanction* for offending behaviour in that society. In the United Kingdom there are three distinct criminal justice systems across three jurisdictions: Scotland; Northern Ireland; and England and Wales, with the ultimate sanction being life imprisonment.

The structure and organisation of a criminal justice system is complex and comprises a range of institutions that respond to crime in widely differing ways. The key institutions are: the police; the prosecution service/authorities; the courts; and the penal system whose roles are determined by *legislation*, and each nation has different sanctions and penalties associated with particular offences. The Scottish criminal justice system is concerned with offences committed in Scotland, although complications may arise when crimes committed in Scotland have effects beyond its borders, or are committed abroad but have an impact in Scotland.

BACKGROUND

Scotland possesses an independent legal system which is accountable to the Scottish government. It has 'its own distinctive character' (Busby *et al.*, 2000: 1) embedded in the idea of a Scottish nation, although there are some who believe that the Scottish legal tradition is threatened by apathy and a tendency to accept English law, 'English books and judgements...[and] English legal training as of value in Scotland...' (Walker, 2001: 197). Under the Scotland Act 1998, Scottish legislative power was *devolved* from the UK Parliament in Westminster, but is still subordinate to it. However, whilst the UK Parliament legislates for both England and Wales and Scotland (unless otherwise stated), the Scottish Parliament has an exclusive right to legislate for Scotland in all Scottish matters, with some 'reserved areas' (identified below).

The Scottish criminal justice system has a long, complex, and troubled history. As with any other legal system, the current system has developed and evolved through numerous historical changes to the system that exists today. Scottish legal history has been shaped by many factors that have contributed to and helped to establish the traditional principles of Scots law. The most significant include: Feudal law; Canon law; Roman law; Christianity; The law Merchant (mercantile law); maritime law; English law; and European law. These factors have all played a role in the development of the law in Scotland, but it is in tandem with the development of English law and its domination through Westminster that the Scottish legal system has matured. Nevertheless, the influence of European law is also important, as Member States are collectively bound by it and cannot alter European law which is regarded as superior to British law 'as long as Britain remains a member of the European Union' (Wylie and Crossan, 2004: 22). English law, however, remains the most powerful factor in determining some principles of Scots law, although there is resistance to this 'borrowing from England'. As Walker (2001: 196) explains, English law is sometimes 'applied by mistake, in ignorance... frequently without appreciation of the subtle differences between the two systems of law, and by subordination to a single parliament often ignorant and careless of Scottish conditions, traditions and sentiment, composed of men [sic] sometimes more concerned with party than with country...'.

The section which follows provides an overview of how criminal justice in Scotland 'works', highlighting some of the ways in which the system differs from the administration of criminal justice in the rest of the United Kingdom.

Criminal justice in Scotland

Criminal justice systems aim to punish people who have acted in a manner contrary to criminal law. In Scotland, the *District Court* deals with minor offences, the *Sheriff Court* with more serious cases, and the most serious crimes are dealt with in the *High Court*. Scotland also has courts of special jurisdiction such as 'Children's Hearings' (see Case Study) which deal with those under age 16 who may come into contact with the law.

The criminal law in any society technically reflects the will of the people notwithstanding the range and diversity of theoretical debates that examine these matters from a critical perspective suggesting that the law may serve only to protect the interests of the powerful. The protection of people and communities from harm and crime, however, is regarded as the guiding principle of Scots law. However, crime and harms are relative to time, place, and society; definitions of 'criminal behaviour', 'crimes', and even 'the criminal' change and so therefore does the law; for example, the classification, de-classification, and re-classification of certain drugs changes over time. The fact remains, however, that those activities deemed to break the law can result in individuals gaining a criminal record and a range of sanctions being imposed from fines to prison sentences. In Scotland there are specific stages which accused people encounter as they 'progress' through the Scottish criminal justice system. In summary form, these are:

- detention, arrest, and search;
- preliminary inquiries by the Procurator Fiscal;
- prosecutor's duties at the end of preliminary inquiries;

- plea adjustment (not 'plea bargaining');
- bringing an accused before the court;
- bail;
- solemn and summary procedure;
- pre-trial solemn and summary procedure;
- trial;
- sentence;
- appeal.

In the Scottish criminal courts, the person on trial is known as the accused and may receive one of three possible *verdicts*: guilty; not guilty; or not proven. 'Not guilty' and 'not proven' are acquittal verdicts resulting in the accused being freed. The criminal justice process in Scotland differs from the rest of the UK in that its 'not proven' verdict is unique and an alternative to the 'not guilty' verdict. However, this verdict is not without criticism, affecting both the status and reputation of the accused, and because it fails to meet the expectations of victims and their families. As Wylie and Crossan (2004: 51) point out: '. . . it is a mechanism whereby a judge or a jury can make a statement that they are not completely satisfied about the accused person's innocence, but at the same time it is condemnation of the *prosecution's* failure to present a sufficiently strong case that will secure a conviction'.

In common with all UK courts, the accused is innocent until proven guilty. State prosecutors are charged with the task of proving defendants' guilt. Should they be unable to persuade the court of someone's guilt, then acquittal must follow. Prosecutors in Scotland and elsewhere in the UK must also prove guilt for crime 'beyond reasonable doubt', also known as a 'nagging doubt'. If a person has a reasonable doubt that leads them to conclude that a guilty verdict is unsafe and unjust then acquittal must follow. This is described as a 'very strict burden' because prosecutors in *criminal trials* have to corroborate evidence against the accused. This means, for example, that evidence has to be proved by witness testimony and the use of forensic evidence.

In Scotland, it is the Lord Advocate (see below) who has responsibility for the *prosecution* of a crime and for the system of public prosecution. The Lord Advocate is generally located at the Crown Office in Edinburgh. At local levels in Scotland, the representative of the Lord Advocate who has responsibility for the prosecution of a crime is known as the *Procurator Fiscal* (see below). In theory, the police in Scotland follow the Fiscal's instructions in a criminal investigation, although they are often left to pursue and conduct their own lines of enquiry. The police do not determine whether a criminal trial goes ahead in Scotland, the decision is made by independent state prosecutors.

Anyone who stands accused of serious crime must undergo trial within 110 days once a Procurator Fiscal decides on trial. This period of time is to be extended due to new rules in the Criminal Procedure (Amendment) (Scotland) Act 2004. Further points of procedural interest relating to criminal justice in Scotland are as follows: individual members of the public do not have the right to insist that someone face a criminal trial in Scotland; private prosecutions are rare in Scotland; and criminal law cannot be used to further private interests in disputes with other citizens (Wylie and Crossan, 2004: 52).

The following sections of the chapter examine the Scottish criminal justice system in detail, commencing with a brief overview of the impact of the creation of the Scottish Parliament on the Scottish legal system following *devolution*.

REVIEW QUESTIONS

1 In what ways does the Scottish criminal justice system differ from the rest of the UK?

2 What are the possible verdicts or decisions that can be given in a criminal court in Scotland?

The creation of the Scottish Parliament

The Scottish Parliament at Holyrood in Edinburgh was created following a referendum held in Scotland in 1997 to see whether the people of Scotland wanted a parliament and, following a vote in favour, the Scotland Act 1998 saw its creation. Nevertheless, it is not a sovereign parliament. It is subordinate to the Westminster Parliament which has *devolved* or handed down certain powers to Holyrood, and it can make certain laws, 'within its field of competence'. It makes laws that Scottish people have to abide by, and those laws have a direct impact upon Scottish society. Nevertheless, Westminster still makes laws that affect Scotland. As Walker (2001: 192) states: '...Westminster still has full power to legislate even in an area, e.g. criminal law, devolved to Holyrood and can at any time legislate if it chooses to do so or if Holyrood failed to do so, or overrule anything in Holyrood legislation, or repeal anything Holyrood did. Westminster moreover retains power to extend or restrict the powers of Holyrood or even abolish it.' More specifically, Westminster can make laws that affect Scotland in 'reserved matters', and Scottish legislation is felt to be secondary, possessing, therefore, 'an inferior status to primary legislation which Westminster deals with' (Wylie and Crossan, 2004: 4). Reserved matters include: constitutional matters; data protection; employment law; energy; equal opportunities; foreign policy, defence, and national security; immigration and nationality; social security; taxation; economic; and monetary matters; and transport. The Scottish Parliament cannot pass laws that are related to defence matters—an issue frequently of concern to those Scottish people who would like to see the closure, for example, of nuclear submarine bases in Scotland. If an Act was passed relating to this matter, there would be no legal challenge. Consequently, there is the potential for conflict between Holyrood and Westminster in some areas of the law. Immigration is another 'reserved matter', but there are very grey areas and blurred edges, not to mention controversies that highlight the complexities of a devolved government and its impact upon the law.

The Westminster Parliament is still the supreme law-making authority in the United Kingdom, and one of the consequences of this remains the fact that the Scottish Parliament cannot legislate completely for Scotland—if it did, it would be seen as a challenge before the courts. As Wylie and Crossan (2004: 7) point out: '...Holyrood...is an inferior and a subordinate body to Westminster and this will remain the case if and when the people of Scotland ever decide to vote for Scottish independence.'

Understanding of the Scottish criminal justice system has to be undertaken with some appreciation of the creation of the Scottish Parliament. There are those who believe that the creation of the Parliament has not really strengthened the Scottish legal tradition which is in danger of being swallowed up by both Westminster and the growing importance of European law. In the following section we will consider the role of European Union legislation on the Scottish criminal justice system.

REVIEW QUESTIONS

1 What are 'reserved matters' in Scots law?

2 Why is the Scottish Parliament unable to legislate on defence matters?

3 What are some of the consequences for Scotland caused by Westminster being the supreme law-making authority in the UK?

The impact of European Union legislation on the Scottish criminal justice system

The creation of the European Union (EU) impacted upon the legal systems of each of the Member States. When Britain joined the European Union in 1973, many key laws were already in place and these laws can be used by Member States, private individuals, and organisations in any of the national courts. The EU Parliament (one of five main European Union institutions) cannot pass laws in its own right, but the European Union Council, which is the most powerful of the five European Union institutions, can with the cooperation and consent of the European Union Parliament. The Human Rights Act 1998, which came into force in October 2000, implements the European Convention on Human Rights into UK law (Wylie and Crossan, 2004: 23), the aim being to 'protect basic human and democratic rights'. In Scotland, the Act was incorporated into Scots law as a result of the Scotland Act 1998. The European Court of Human Rights at Strasbourg also has a significant role to play as the United Kingdom is bound by the court's jurisdiction. The European Convention on Human Rights is now directly enforceable in British courts and the European Articles incorporated under the Scotland Acts cover Articles 2 to 16.

Articles of the European Convention on Human Rights

Article 2—The right to life.
Article 3—Prohibition of torture and cruel and degrading treatment.
Article 4—Prohibition of slavery and forced labour.
Article 5—The right to liberty and security.
Article 6—The right to a fair trial/hearing.
Article 7—The general prohibition of the enactment of retrospective criminal offences.
Article 8—The right to respect for private and family life.

Article 9—Freedom of thought, conscience and religion.

Article 10—Freedom of expression.

Article 11—Freedom of assembly and association.

Article 12—The right to marry.

Article 14—Prohibition of discrimination.

Article 16—No restrictions on the political activity of aliens (i.e. those who are not British or European Union citizens).

Source: <http://www.echr.coe.int/NR/rdonlyres/D5CC24A7-DC13-4318-B457-5C9014916D7A/0/EnglishAnglais.pdf>

The European Convention on Human Rights is important for understanding the way in which the Scottish criminal justice works because it can lead to changes being made within the Scottish legal system. All UK legislation has to be interpreted in order to protect human rights and democratic freedoms. Furthermore, any Acts of the Westminster Parliament that are not 'human rights friendly' can now be challenged in the Scottish courts through the issuing, by judges, of a 'declaration of incompatibility'. In Scotland, the Court of Session, the High Court of Justiciary, the Privy Council, and the House of Lords (see below for detail on Scotland's courts) have the power to issue such a declaration. This declaration 'signifies that the legislation in question breaches human rights in a particular way and it is now up to the Westminster Parliament to take the appropriate steps to bring the law into line with the European Convention' (Wylie and Crossan, 2004: 24).

A final point worth noting with regards to the impact of European legislation is that the Scottish courts can directly enforce the European Convention on Human Rights without the necessity of taking the case to the European Court of Human Rights. In addition, judges in Scotland can 'strike down' legislation of the Scottish Parliament (which is seen as secondary legislation) if it breaches human rights or democratic freedoms. Cases have occurred in Scotland as a result of the introduction of the European Convention into Scots law, and its significance cannot be underestimated. Most of the cases brought to the European Court of Justice so far have been civil cases, but if decisions made in criminal courts infringe European law, then the European Court of Justice may be asked for clarification.

The next section of the chapter considers the roles of the legal personnel in Scotland who could potentially be involved in taking such decisions.

REVIEW QUESTIONS

1 To what extent has European legislation influenced Scots criminal law?

2 To what extent has the Human Rights Act 1998 influenced Scots criminal law?

3 In what way can the Scottish courts challenge the Westminster Parliament?

The legal personnel in Scotland

This section describes the groups of people involved in the Scottish criminal justice system who, in some instances have names and titles that are quite different from those used in the English system. The names, titles, and functions of the legal personnel in Scotland have their origins in history and there are two branches of the legal profession, i.e. two groups of lawyers known as *solicitors* and *advocates*. Overall, however, the legal profession in Scotland can be divided into the following groups: judges; public prosecutors—including the *Procurators Fiscal* who prosecute in the Sheriff and District Courts and who are independent of the judiciary; lawyers; and witnesses, jurors, messengers-at-arms, and sheriff officers.

Solicitors and *Solicitor-Advocates* who are all members of the Law Society of Scotland appear before both criminal and civil courts. The Law Society regulates and disciplines solicitors who receive their training within existing firms of solicitors and have to pass Law Society or university examinations as well as a further Diploma in Legal Practice at a relevant Scottish university. They then have to undertake a further period of training for two years after which they can apply to the Law Society of Scotland for a full practising certificate. *Advocates* are specialist lawyers who are involved in the prosecution and presentation of cases. They are self-employed and not members of a law firm. They are represented by the Faculty of Advocates in Edinburgh, a self-regulating body that determines who becomes an advocate. Some are experts in particular fields of law providing opinions on complex legal questions (Wylie and Crossan, 2004). They are organised into units called 'stables' and they have clerks who are responsible for administration. Advocates are referred to as Junior Counsel or Senior Counsel (known as Queen's Counsel or QC after ten years). The training is intensive and advocates can appear in all Scottish courts, instructed by solicitors to appear in a case. Solicitors do most of the work in preparing cases; advocates do not deal directly with the public but most usually with a client's solicitor. Advocates have a distinctive appearance in court wearing a wig and gown, whereas solicitors wear only a black gown. In court a QC will be assisted by a Junior Counsel.

Procurators Fiscal are responsible for the investigation and prosecution of a crime at local level—a Fiscal is a civil servant employed by the Scottish government. Within the legal profession in Scotland there are also clerks and paralegals. Clerks are involved in legal work such as conveyancing, executries, and trusts, whilst paralegals have some background in law, for example, professional or vocational qualifications in legal services. The final category of legal personnel in Scotland is the *Law Officers of the Crown* consisting (since the Scotland Act 1998) of: Lord Advocate; Solicitor-General for Scotland; and Advocate-General for Scotland. These are political appointments, with the First Minister for Scotland appointing both the Lord Advocate and the Solicitor-General, and the Prime Minister of Britain appointing the Advocate-General who, at the time of writing, sits on the Labour benches of the House of Lords. Any changes in the Scottish government or British government will be reflected in changes in these posts.

As the most senior Scottish law officer, the *Lord Advocate* has a number of functions, which may or may not impact upon the experiences of those within the criminal justice system. The Lord Advocate is the principal state prosecutor responsible for the Scottish public prosecution system; appears as prosecutor in major criminal trials, e.g. Lockerbie, before the High Court of Justiciary; is Head of the Crown Office and Procurator Fiscal Service, which is the Scottish government department with responsibility for all crimes in Scotland; is legal adviser to the Scottish government; and represents the Scottish Executive in the Scottish Courts, the European Court of Justice, and the European Court of Human Rights.

The *Solicitor-General* is the Lord Advocate's assistant and is entitled to use the initials QC, acting as counsel to the Crown. Both law officers are assisted by *Advocate Deputes* (collectively referred to as Crown Counsel) who are experienced and practising members of the faculty of Advocates. They are generally in post for three years and appear before criminal courts in jury trials as prosecutors. The *Advocate-General* for Scotland (also known as Crown Counsel) has a number of key functions and is a member of the United Kingdom government—see Figure 15.1.

The appointment of judges and sheriffs (judicial appointments) in Scotland is made through recommendation to the First Minister for Scotland who is in turn advised by the independent Judicial Appointments Board consisting of five lay and five legal members. Scotland's most senior judge is known as the *Lord President of the Court of Session* and is also involved in recommending judicial appointments.

Sheriffs are usually lawyers, solicitors, or advocates who have been practising for ten years, and after five years experience as Sheriffs can be appointed to the High Court or Court of Session. The title sheriff derives from 'shire-reeve' and dates back to before

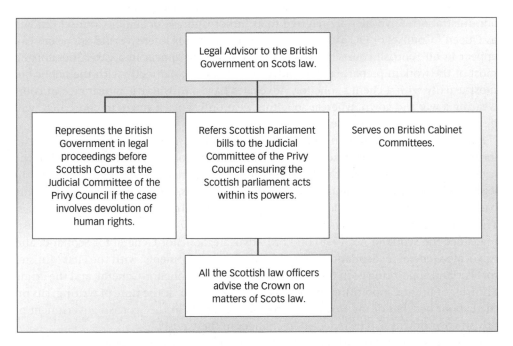

Figure 15.1 The Advocate-General for Scotland

the eleventh century when parts of Scotland (and England) were divided into shires for administrative purposes. The sheriff's duties consisted of holding a sheriff or shire-reeve court which had civil and criminal jurisdiction and, historically, the Scottish sheriff had a wide range of duties including military, financial, and administrative matters—as there was no other form of local government and sheriffs were required to keep the King's Peace (Sheehan and Dickson, 2003: 4–5). Judges are not appointed to the House of Lords by the Scottish Parliament, although there will be consultation between the Prime Minister, the Lord Chancellor, the First Minister for Scotland, and the Lord President of the Court of Session to appoint Scottish Law Lords.

A final point relating to the legal personnel in Scotland is that judges and sheriffs of the High Court and the Court of Session are completely independent of the Scottish government other than in the investigation of complaints about the handling of cases via appeals to superior courts, and the following section examines the types of courts people may encounter within the Scottish criminal justice system.

REVIEW QUESTIONS

1 What are the names of the legal personnel in Scotland?

2 What is the role of the procurators fiscal?

3 What are the origins of the title 'sheriff'?

The Scottish criminal courts

'...the Scottish Courts are ranked in order of importance from the highest in the land to the lowest'. (Wylie and Crossan, 2004: 14)

The criminal justice system in Scotland is 'uncodified', meaning that the criminal law is not brought together in one single Act of Parliament. Many crimes are based on the common law of custom, 'embodied in the decisions of the criminal courts' (McCall Smith and Sheldon, 1997: 25). Accordingly, this is felt to be one of the strong points of Scots criminal law, with courts being more 'flexible' and 'responsive', and not always having to amend legislation (see Reuss, 2004: 286).

Today the Scottish courts which accused persons come into contact with are divided into superior courts, namely: the House of Lords; the Court of Session (a Supreme Court which hears civil cases); and the High Court of Justiciary. These courts have jurisdiction over the whole of Scotland. The inferior courts are the Sheriff Court and the District Court. These courts hear cases at local level. There is an Executive Agency, the Scottish Court Service (SCS), which ensures effective administration of the Supreme and Sheriff Courts and which is responsible for administrative staff working in the courts—with the exception of the District Courts. Judges can sit either in civil or criminal courts and a key characteristic of the judicial function is that it is contentious rather than inquisitorial. The judge's function is therefore to preside over or supervise 'the contending parties and to arrive at a decision on the facts submitted to him [sic], not to engage himself [sic] in the search for evidence of information' (Walker, 2001: 287).

The three main courts in the criminal justice system in Scotland are therefore the District Court, the Sheriff Court, and the High Court of Justiciary. All appeals are heard in the High Court; proceedings in the District Court are heard under 'summary procedure'; and in the Sheriff Court under summary or 'solemn procedure' (see below). *The High Court of Justiciary* is a trial court and also hears appeals. In matters of human rights or devolution, appeals can be heard by the Privy Council in London.

The following section examines the workings of these three courts in criminal justice matters.

The District Court

The District Court is a local court, having responsibility for crimes committed in a local authority area; it is the most junior criminal court in Scotland. Local authorities run District Courts, not the Scottish Court Service. Examples of the kinds of offences that the District Court deals with are: vehicle excise; theft (not housebreaking); breach of the peace; assault (not wounding); vandalism. There is no jury in District Court trials, the judge (a Justice of the Peace (JP) or a Stipendiary Magistrate) sits alone (summary procedure) and decides whether the accused is guilty—if so, an appropriate sentence is passed. JPs cannot act as solicitors or advocates, they are lay justices and not legally qualified although they are trained. They arrive at verdicts independently and are advised by legally qualified clerks of the court. They can impose a maximum 60-day prison sentence and a maximum fine of £2,500 (at the time of writing). Stipendiary Magistrates are legally qualified and are practising lawyers (solicitors or advocates). They also sit alone and do not have legally qualified clerks. They can impose prison sentences up to a maximum of six months depending upon the nature of the crime and previous convictions, and they have the same powers as a Sheriff under summary procedure in the Sheriff Court. A solicitor will represent someone who is on trial in the District Court; the prosecutor will be from the Procurator-fiscal Service. An accused person receives a document known as a 'complaint' that details the charges. Any appeals go to the High Court of Justiciary.

The Sheriff Court

In Scotland, the Sheriff Court is the busiest criminal court; it also hears civil cases and is organised according to geographical areas known as *Sheriffdoms*, of which there are six (Glasgow and Strathkelvin; North Strathclyde; South Strathclyde, Dumfries and Galloway; Tayside, Central and Fife; Lothian and Borders; and Grampian, Highland and Islands). The Sheriffdoms are further divided into 49 districts known as Sheriff Court Districts, with the 'central belt' of Scotland (between the Forth and Clyde rivers) being the busiest, as it is the most densely populated area of Scotland. Each Sheriff Court district has one or more *Sheriffs*. They are judges and administer justice in disputes brought before the courts. They will have been practising lawyers for ten years. All offences committed in a specific Sheriffdom will be heard before the Sheriff Court with the exception of those offences deemed to be most serious. Such crimes are heard in the High Court of Justiciary, which is the supreme criminal court in Scotland. The most serious crimes heard include: murder; *rape*; treason; incest; piracy; drug trafficking; and armed robbery.

There are two types of criminal procedure in the Sheriff Courts: an accused person's trial is heard under *summary procedure* with the Sheriff sitting alone to decide whether the accused is guilty or innocent. According to Wylie and Crossan (2004) the Sheriff has to be 'master of the facts' and will decide on an appropriate punishment if the prosecution proves guilt beyond reasonable doubt. Summary procedure is used for less serious crimes, and, as in the District Courts, the accused receives a 'complaint document' detailing the charges. The sentencing powers of a Sheriff can be affected by Acts of Parliament which may determine a sentence or punishment. Any appeals are, again, heard in the High Court of Justiciary.

The second type of procedure is *solemn procedure* and is used for more serious crimes. It involves trials with a Sheriff and a jury of 15 men and women. Here the jury is 'master of the facts' and it decides on the guilt or innocence of the accused, but the Sheriff imposes appropriate punishment. Under solemn procedure a Sheriff can impose a maximum five-year prison sentence and/or an unlimited fine. A Sheriff can also send an accused to the High Court of Justiciary if his/her powers are not sufficiently adequate to deal with the case, as the High Court has unlimited sentencing powers. Under solemn procedure, a solicitor or advocate represents the accused in the Sheriff Court. The Procurator Fiscal conducts the prosecution, or an Advocate Depute, with appeals going to the High Court of Justiciary.

The High Court of Justiciary

The supreme criminal court in Scotland is the High Court of Justiciary, founded in 1672, and it has jurisdiction over the whole of Scotland. It can sit as a trial court, known as a court of 'first instance' in larger towns and cities in Scotland to which it travels. This is known as 'going on circuit'. This court deals with serious crimes (see <http://www.scotcourts.gov.uk/justiciary/index.asp>). A single judge and a jury of 15 men and women are involved in cases dealt with in the High Court which always start with a preliminary hearing.

The judge at this hearing has to be satisfied that the case is sufficiently prepared 'to appoint the case to a trial diet'. This is a new procedure which should cut down the number of cases that have to be adjourned because they are not ready to proceed at the trial diet stage. This is one example of new and far-reaching reform for the High Court in Scotland.

At the appeals stage, at least three judges will hear appeals against convictions, with two judges hearing appeals against sentence, unless the case is really important or difficult. The Scottish Criminal Cases Review Commission can refer cases to the High Court also for appeal, as can District and Sheriff Courts. The High Court can also give directions setting out the law for similar cases in the future where the Lord Advocate has referred a point of law to the High Court for an opinion. It has to be noted that the High Court of Justiciary differs altogether from the English High Court. It comprises the Lord Justice General, who is the president, and his deputy Lord Justice Clerk, plus 30 judges of the Court of Session, known as Lords Commissioners of Justiciary. The High Court judges are predominantly male.

The permanent base and headquarters of the High Court is in Edinburgh except when the court is 'going on circuit'. It has jurisdiction over all crimes committed in Scotland, and always sits under solemn procedure, i.e. one Lord Commissioner of Justiciary and a jury of 15. Prosecution in the High Court is made by Advocates or Solicitor-advocates (*Advocate Deputes*). They are chosen to represent the Lord Advocate where all prosecutions are brought in the public interest. Defence is also conducted by an Advocate or Solicitor-Advocate.

Appeals

Miscarriages of justice in Scotland are considered by the Scottish Criminal Cases Review Commission. This Commission was established as a result of the Criminal Procedure (Scotland) Act 1995 and its role is to investigate potential miscarriages of justice. It is answerable to the Scottish Parliament and is based in Glasgow. Where the Commission believes a criminal conviction decision is unsafe, it can refer to the High Court of Justiciary and can also investigate any sentences from the courts if someone requests such an investigation. The Commission only investigates the circumstances of a conviction and then makes recommendations to the High Court; therefore it is only appropriate to contact the Commission after an appeal has been heard in the High Court.

The Lockerbie bombing of January 2001 provides an example of how a referral to the Commission would take place. Abdelbaset Ali Mohed Megrahi unsuccessfully appealed against his conviction of the murder of 270 people. Subsequently his solicitors requested that the Commission review the case in September 2003.

A further court is the Judicial Committee of the Privy Council. Under the Scotland Act 1998 and the Human Rights Act 1998 this court can challenge decisions taken in the High Court of Justiciary if matters under both these Acts, i.e. devolution and human rights, are breached.

REVIEW QUESTIONS

1 What are the Scottish courts called?

2 What is a Sheriffdom? How many are there in Scotland and can you name them?

3 Name the three Scottish Criminal Courts.

Courts of special jurisdiction

These courts operate outside the Scottish traditional legal system and they hear particular kinds of civil and criminal disputes, involving such diverse matters as employment, land, and the use of ancient titles. The most significant for the purposes of gaining a deeper understanding of Scottish criminal justice are the *Children's Hearings* or *Panels* which are widely admired by other jurisdictions, and, following a brief introduction, the Case Study below details the special procedures that characterise these hearings.

In Scotland the age of criminal responsibility is eight and thus a child under age eight cannot be found guilty of a criminal offence and therefore cannot be prosecuted. However, a child under 16 can only be prosecuted in a criminal court if the Lord Advocate grants permission: 'Children will only appear in the Sheriff Court and the High Court of Justiciary if they are accused of murder, assault which endangers life or driving offences which are punishable by disqualification' (Wylie and Crossan, 2004: 61).

Children's Hearing Panels are unique in the UK and were set up in 1971 following original recommendations made by the Kilbrandon Committee 1964 (Hughes, 2001: 269 in McLaughlin and Muncie, 2001). The Panels deal with children under the age of 16 in need of care and protection, and also deal with children who offend and who are in need of control and discipline. A panel will decide on the appropriate disposal, i.e. the measures to be taken for each child who may be referred to them from the courts. The Panels are based on welfare principles according to the Social Work (Scotland) Act 1968, which states that distinctions between children who offend and children needing care and protection are 'irrelevant'. The circumstances of each case are assessed and interventions are based on the need for protection or the need for control and discipline. There is perhaps an assumption that 'normal' processes of socialisation will have been inadequate in both instances. The panels function as tribunals and consist of male and female lay people drawn from the local authority in which a child resides, with every local authority in Scotland having its own Children's Panel. When the Panel sits, the chairperson and two other members must be present and they make their decisions based on 'needs' not 'deeds'. The Scottish courts become involved only under certain circumstances, for example, if facts are in dispute, if there is an appeal, or if a serious offence has been committed.

Only a Sheriff can decide on questions of law or fact prior to a disposal being made by a panel and according to Busby *et al.*, (2000), the Children's Hearing system works in the best interests of the child—as a community-based intervention. (Reuss, 2004: 285). The aim of this Children's Hearing is to divert young people away from the Scottish criminal justice system and the Case Study illustrates the different stages of the process of the hearing.

CASE STUDY: CHILDREN'S HEARINGS IN SCOTLAND

This case study highlights the process of the Children's Hearings in Scotland, drawing attention to the debate on whether justice or welfare are the appropriate 'means' of dealing with young children who may find themselves in trouble in Scotland.

Scotland does not have juvenile courts and children under the age of 16 when prosecuted are dealt with in the Sheriff Court or the High Court of Justiciary, with the District Court having no jurisdiction. Child offenders are dealt with by the Principal Reporter to the Children's Hearing and children are rarely prosecuted. The remit of the Children's Hearing is to deal with children as victims of offences, children as offenders, and/or children in need of 'compulsory measures of supervision'.

When or if a Procurator Fiscal receives a report in respect of a child, the case is then discussed with the Principal Reporter. A decision is then made whether prosecution in the public interest is the best option. Under Scots law a child under the age of eight cannot be guilty of any offence. The term 'child' is defined in criminal proceedings as not yet 16, or over 16 and under 18 subject to a supervision requirement imposed by a Children's Hearing.

Reference to Children's Hearings are made where a child pleads guilty to, or is found guilty of an offence, other than in cases where the sentence is fixed by law, as in murder. If a court remits the case to a Children's Hearing to be dealt with entirely, this brings the court proceedings to an end unless the court makes a request that the Children's Hearing advises the court as to how a child shall be treated. The court may then refer the case back to the Principal Reporter to the Children's Hearing for disposal or the child may be brought back to court for sentence.

The juvenile system in Scotland is certainly 'radical and unique'. There are general guidelines regarding children and criminal justice in Scotland, for example, children under the age of 16 cannot be prosecuted other than on the instructions of the Lord Advocate, who has also directed: '...that no child under 13 is to be prosecuted without his prior express authority'. Procurators fiscal have also been given guidelines and instructions by the Lord Advocate on which cases proceedings may be instituted and against which categories of offences—if committed by a child aged between 13 and 16.

There is a Youth Court at Hamilton Sheriff Court which deals with Young Offenders between the ages of 16 and 18, resident in North and South Lanarkshire. The young offenders who appear before this court generally 'have a history of three separate incidents of offending resulting in criminal charges within a six-month period or are currently undergoing youth court proceedings' (Sheehan and Dickson, 2003: 237).

Notification of the prosecution of children in Scotland has to be given to the local authority in whose area (the Sheriffdom) the court sits and also to the parent or guardian of the child. The Local Authority has to make certain investigations and provide a report about the child's home background, educational and health records, and character in order to assist the court dealing with the case. The parent or guardian, if they reside near the court, must attend throughout all proceedings unless deemed unreasonable.

A parent or guardian can also assist in defence of a child except where a solicitor or counsel represents the child, as can any other responsible person. The proceedings take place on different days from normal court proceedings and most notably, precautions are taken so that children do not mix with adult offenders or other children, except when a child is charged alongside an adult. If a child is detained by the police, there is no contact with any adults charged with an offence.

Within the court, simple language is used before a child and the court must have regard to the child's welfare and remove a child from undesirable surroundings. The child's parent or guardian has an opportunity to make a statement, but the words 'conviction' and 'sentence' cannot be used in dealing with children under summary procedure (see above). The phrase 'a finding of guilt' is preferred. The media cannot release or reveal a child's name, address, or school nor use pictures to identify a child, whether accused or a witness. Only those who have direct interest in a case can be present in court. Finally, some of the provisions may be dismissed in the case of public interest if a court feels the case merits this.

The system is not without its critics, due to the tensions which can arise in achieving a balance between child welfare, justice, children's rights, and parents' rights (McGhee,

Waterhouse and Whyte, 2002: 228); and important questions arise regarding whether the system can adequately deal with persistent young offenders and/or those in need of care, particularly in a climate of punitive sanctions.

Having examined the Scottish Children's Hearing system the final section will provide an overview on sentencing decisions and contemporary sanctions used in Scotland. The chapter will then conclude highlighting the significance of understanding that within the United Kingdom there are different legal systems with their own essential characteristics, but which are nonetheless subject to change, and that those changes must be understood through examining the context of whose interests are best served according to the implementation of specific criminal laws.

REVIEW QUESTIONS

1 Why are the Scottish Children's Hearings considered to be 'radical and unique'?

2 Are children who offend in need of welfare or justice?

3 Should young offenders be isolated in order to protect the community?

Sentencing decisions and contemporary sanctions in Scotland

The range of penalties and punishments given to those who have committed crimes under Scottish jurisdiction has changed throughout history. The principle of *deterrence* played a key role in that punishment was meant to be carried out in such a way as to be off-putting to others who may commit crimes. Until the Criminal Procedure (Consequential Provisions) (Scotland) Act 1995, indictment contained the following words should an accused person be convicted: '...he[sic] "ought to be punished with the pains of law to deter others from committing the like crimes in all times coming"...' (Sheehan and Dickson, 2003. 42). The ideals of reformation and *rehabilitation* were not really considered in Scotland—as elsewhere in the UK—until the nineteenth century.

Courts have wide *discretion* in Scotland in relation to the type of sentence given to an individual, apart from murder which has a fixed penalty of life imprisonment. Custodial sentences are the most severe form of sanction in Scotland today.

Adult males in Scotland can be sentenced to one of 14 prisons: Aberdeen, Barlinnie (Glasgow), Dumfries, Glenochil, Greenock, Inverness, Kilmarnock, Low Moss, Perth, Peterhead, Saughton (Edinburgh), Shotts, Castle Huntly (open prison), Noranside (open prison). Young male offenders are sentenced to Polmont and all female offenders to Cornton Vale. Debates surrounding the use of imprisonment as a means of 'effective' punishment are wide-ranging in contemporary academic discourse and beyond the remit of this chapter, but the ever-increasing 'crisis' (Cavadino and Dignan, 2007) within the UK penal system relating to over-crowding transcends borders, and the use of non-custodial penalties such as *probation*, fines, Community Service Orders, Restriction of Liberty Orders, Drug Treatment and Testing Orders, etc., are all characteristic of sentencing decisions. Evaluations of the effectiveness of these sanctions continue to characterise the relationship between academic discourse in a number of disciplines, such as criminology, sociology, forensic science, psychology, and the policy-makers who work within the field of Scottish criminal justice.

CONCLUSION

This chapter has examined some of the key features of the Scottish criminal justice system. It is by placing the discussion within a framework of the wider social and cultural settings that characterise this nation that the reader can understand the context of the criminal justice system in Scotland.

Justice is not timeless and unchanging, it is not absolute, and the very fact that bias would seem to exist within criminal justice systems across the world shows that criminal justice may not be fair or just at all. Pressure groups, the general public, the media, academic researchers, theorists, practitioners, and policy-makers all lend their voices to the debates on crime and what to do about it. In some instances, those voices justify and can be used to justify legislation at any one moment in history. The criminal laws of a nation are but one example of how various attempts are made to try and 'solve the problem of crime'. A nation's laws can also play a significant role in criminalizing sections of communities; they can 'confirm deviant or criminal identities' (Croall, 1998).

New laws, new reforms in criminal justice, and new policies, including approaches to *offender management* in Scotland, inform us about how criminal justice operates in Scotland today (see <http://www.scotland.gov.uk>), but there are likely to be further changes taking place within the Scottish criminal justice system as the Scottish National Party take the reins within the Scottish Parliament. The Management of Offenders (Scotland) Act 2005 saw the establishment of eight Community Justice Authorities (CJAs) with area plans to be rolled out during 2007/08. The CJAs will be bringing together a number of agencies involved in criminal justice with the aim of creating '... a more coherent and flexible system of offender management, which builds services round the offender' (<http://www.scotland.gov.uk>). The overall objective is to synthesise the work of the Scottish Prison Service, local authorities, and criminal justice social work services in order to provide 'joined up delivery' with a national strategy aimed at reducing reoffending and serious harm within the community. The strategy echoes those within other UK jurisdictions of 'managing risk' in ways that covers all those who come into contact with the criminal justice system.

A further characteristic of what is a radical reform of the Scottish criminal justice system is *partnership* working with the voluntary sector, police, Crown Office, sentencers, courts, legal professionals, Risk Management Authorities, Accreditation Panels, and the Parole Board. Furthermore, agencies involved with housing, education, health, benefits, training, and employment will also be central in playing a role in integrating offenders into the community.

This chapter has examined only one aspect of offender management—covering the processes and people encountered within the criminal justice system. However, it remains to be seen how effective the new CJAs will be and whether the 'targets' will be met.

QUESTIONS FOR DISCUSSION

1 Should a 'united' kingdom have only one system of law '... careless of Scottish conditions, traditions and sentiment...' (Walker, 2001: 196)?

2 To what extent has the creation of the Scottish Parliament strengthened the Scottish legal tradition?

3 Examine the possible consequences of Scottish independence for the Scottish criminal justice system.

4 To what extent can a philosophy based on the 'needs not deeds' of children 'work' within the Scottish criminal justice system?

GUIDE TO FURTHER READING

The most comprehensive account of the Scottish criminal justice process and agencies is Peter Duff and Neil Hutton's (eds) *Criminal Justice in Scotland* (1999). For a comprehensive account of criminal procedure in Scotland see A. Sheehan and D. Dickson, *Criminal Procedure* (2003). This text provides a wealth of detail on both historical and recent developments in this area of law. Similarly, Wylie and Crossan's *Introductory Scots Law* (2004) provides an accessible text on the theory and practice of Scots law and the Scottish legal system. D.M. Walker's *Scottish Legal System* (2001) is a classic text that covers every aspect of Scots law, both contemporary and historical.

WEB LINKS

http://www.sccjr.ac.uk/index.php

This site provides excellent information on The Scottish Centre for Criminal Justice Research and links to all areas of the criminal justice system in Scotland, recent and current research and consultancy.

http://www.scotland.gov.uk/Topics/Justice/criminal

These two sites provide very valuable and informative links to criminal justice policy and practice in Scotland. There are links to criminal justice research in all areas of policy-making.

http://www.scotcourts.gov.uk

http://www.bbc.co.uk/crime/fighters/scottishcourtservice.shtml

http://www.scotland.gov.uk

These sites are excellent for information on the administration of criminal justice law and the operation of the Scottish courts. The above sites also contain links to the Ministry of Justice and Court Service, police forces, and the Prison Service in Scotland, as well as containing statistics and more general information on the criminal justice system.

http://www.scottishlaw.org.uk

This is a comprehensive independent web portal with links to a wide range of resources on all aspects of Scots law.

http://www.journalonline.co.uk

http://www.news.bbc.co.uk

These sites are generally very useful for media information on specific cases such as Lockerbie.

http://news.bbc.co.uk/onthisday/hi/dates/stories/december/21/newsid_2539000/2539447.stm

This site provides a description of the Lockerbie Air disaster on 21 December 1988.

http://www.scotcourts.gov.uk/justiciary/index.asp

A site that provides a very good introduction to the Scottish courts and how they work and which also provides detailed information on legal personnel.

REFERENCES

Busby, N., Clark, B., Mays, R., Paisley, R., and Spink, P. (2000) *Scots Law.* Edinburgh: Butterworths.

Cavadino, M., Dignan, J. (2007) *The Penal System* (4th edn). London: Sage.

Croall, H. (1998) *Crime and Society in Britain.* Harlow: Pearson Longman.

Duff, P. and Hutton, N. (eds) (1999) *Criminal Justice in Scotland.* Aldershot: Ashgate.

Hughes, G. (2001) 'The Competing Logics of Community Sanctions: Welfare, Rehabilitation and Restorative Justice' in E. McLaughlin and J. Muncie, (2001) *Controlling Crime* (2nd edn). London: Sage.

McCall Smith, R.A.A. and Sheldon, D. (1997) *Scots Criminal Law.* Edinburgh: Butterworths.

McGhee, J., Waterhouse, L., and Whyte, B. (2002) 'Children's Hearings and Children in Trouble' in J. Muncie, G. Hughes, and E. McLaughlin (2002) *Youth Justice: Critical Readings.* London: Sage.

McLaughlin, E. and Muncie, J. (2001) *Controlling Crime* (2nd edn). London: Sage.

Reuss, A. (now Wilson) (2004) 'Criminal Justice in Scotland' in J. Muncie and D. Wilson (eds) (2004) *Student Handbook of Criminal Justice and Criminology.* London: Cavendish Publishing.

Sheehan, A. and Dickson, D. (2003) *Criminal Procedure Scottish Law and Practice Series.* Edinburgh: Lexis Nexis Butterworths.

Walker, D.M. (2001) *The Scottish Legal System; An Introduction to The Study of Scots Law* (8th edn). Edinburgh: Sweet and Maxwell.

Wilson, A. (2005) 'Counterblast: Penal reform in Scotland'. *Howard Journal of Criminal Justice* 44(5) December 2005.

Wylie, A. and Crossan, S. (2004) *Scots Law: Theory and Practice.* Paisley: Hodder Gibson.

16 Crime and criminal justice in Northern Ireland

Graham Ellison and Aogán Mulcahy

INTRODUCTION

In Northern Ireland the operation of criminal justice has been intimately connected to the dynamics of conflict, and the impact of 'the Troubles' (as the conflict was often described colloquially) was fully evident across the criminal justice system as a whole, particularly through emergency legislation and other 'extraordinary' measures that were designed to 'defeat' terrorism. In many respects, a dual system of criminal justice operated in Northern Ireland: one system to deal with 'ordinary' criminality, the other to deal with those offences that were defined as 'terrorist' by the State, but which nevertheless were perceived to have a political motivation by a large section of the Catholic/Nationalist community in Northern Ireland. However, the implementation of a range of controversial measures to deal with the issue of *political violence* added further volatility to Northern Ireland's political landscape. As the peace process developed from the mid-1990s onwards, and with the signing of the 1998 *Belfast/Good Friday Agreement* in particular, reform of the criminal justice system formed a key component of this political agreement. While Northern Ireland may (at last) be on the road to a lasting peace, many of the tactics and strategies that were devised to deal with the issue of political violence there are now advocated to counter the threat from fundamentalist extremism elsewhere in the United Kingdom, and can be seen in the controversial move to grant the police extended powers to detain suspects for up to 42 days without charge. It is here that Northern Ireland provides salutary lessons, and a useful vantage point from which to survey such developments.

While we should be aware of the historical backdrop of the conflict in having a determining role in shaping criminal justice policy and practice in Northern Ireland, any discussion of contemporary trends needs to be seen in the context of three inter-connected dynamics. First, in administrative terms we need to consider Northern Ireland's regional status within the United Kingdom and the recent political developments that have occurred there. Following the peace negotiations that led to the signing of the Belfast/Good Friday Agreement in 1998, Northern Ireland once again became a region of devolved administration within the United Kingdom with powers transferred to the Northern Ireland Assembly (although it should be noted that the Assembly has been suspended at several junctures in the intervening years). Like the Scottish Parliament, but unlike the Welsh Assembly, the Northern Ireland Assembly has what is referred to as primary legislative powers. This means that as long as any proposed legislation complies with the provisions of s. 6 of the Northern Ireland Act 1998, the Assembly can create its own laws in respect of a number of key areas, such as health and social services, education, criminal justice, and policing. The Welsh Assembly, by contrast, has secondary legislative powers and may vary Westminster legislation only slightly. However, illustrating the contested terrain that criminal justice and policing have traditionally occupied in Northern Ireland, the proposed *devolution* of criminal justice and policing powers to the Assembly has proved to be an incredibly fractious issue for local politicians to agree on.

Second, debates about criminal justice policy in Northern Ireland are increasingly embedded in the broader conceptual and theoretical framework of *transitional justice*. This locates criminal justice policy within a conflict-resolution process, whereby the criminal justice system as a whole is rendered democratic, accountable, and reflective of a normative commitment to human rights. The aim here is to transform the institutions of criminal justice and thereby build public trust in them, particularly among those groups most alienated from them in the past.

Third, in rather more prosaic terms, recent reforms have also attempted to enhance the operational efficiency of the criminal justice process in Northern Ireland since in resource terms it is significantly more expensive to administer than other regions of the United Kingdom. On a *per capita* basis, Northern Ireland has a higher proportion of people employed *directly* by the state in the criminal justice and security sector than other regions of the United Kingdom, and in fact this sector continues to provide a major source of employment in Northern Ireland (Equality Commission for Northern Ireland, 2005). In the latest spending round Northern Ireland was allocated £1.2 billion per annum for criminal justice and policing services, with policing costs alone accounting for over £700 million of this (Northern Ireland Office, 2007). By way of comparison, the Greater Manchester Police budget for 2007/08 was just over £524 million for a population almost twice that of Northern Ireland. For a small jurisdiction these costs are unsustainable in the longer term and will lead to some difficult choices being made in the future in respect of the prioritization of resources and spending plans.

In what follows we provide an overview of *crime* and criminal justice in Northern Ireland. Our discussion is divided into four main sections, and considers in turn: crime and victimisation; policing and police reform, prisons, and *punishment*; the courts, sentencing and disposal. In addition to outlining the historical context of these issues, we also consider significant recent developments arising from the peace process and the 1998 Belfast/Good Friday Agreement that has placed Northern Ireland at the forefront of international debates about the transformation of criminal justice.

Crime and victimisation

As was the case for most other western European nations, levels of recorded crime in Northern Ireland increased considerably in the decades after the Second World War, albeit from a very low base figure. A total of 5,709 indictable offences were recorded in 1945, rising to 6,049 in 1955 and 12,846 in 1965 (Brewer *et al.*, 1997). Prior to the outbreak of widespread disturbances and sustained political violence from the late 1960s onwards, levels of violent crime were strikingly low. In only three years between 1945 and 1968 were more than three murders recorded in Northern Ireland, and in six separate years not a single murder was recorded (Brewer *et al.*, 1997). From the late 1960s onwards, as civil unrest escalated, levels of violence increased dramatically, and in 1972 a total of 479 deaths were recorded, the highest figure in Northern Ireland's history (Brewer *et al.*, 1997: 37).

However, while levels of conventional crime remained low, the scale of victimisation arising from the political situation was profound for a society of 1.7 million people. During the course of the conflict, over 3,000 people lost their lives, while tens of thousands were seriously injured. A corresponding scale of violence in Britain and the United States would have yielded over 100,000 and 500,000 deaths respectively.

Table 16.1 The scale of political violence in Northern Ireland 1969–1998

	Estimate by population		
	N.Ireland	Britain	United States
Deaths	3,289	111,000	526,000
Injuries	41,837	1,406,000	6,673,000
Shooting incidents	35,669	1,188,000	5,161,000
Bomb explosions	15,246	503,000	2,388,000
Persons charged with terrorist offences	18,258	589,000	2,797,000

Source: S. Elliott and W.D. Flackes, *Northern Ireland: A Political Directory* (Blackstaff Press, 1999) In Hayes & McAllister (2001). Reprinted by kind permission of Blackstaff Press.

Figure 16.1 Belfast's own 'Berlin Wall': A 'Peace Line' through an interface area of the city
Source: Martin Melaugh, CAIN (cain.ulst.ac.uk)

Although Northern Ireland was routinely presented as a low-crime society in governmental and official documentation, this tends to ignore or overlook the complex dynamics of victimization in Northern Ireland. For instance, patterns of inter-communal violence were often highly localised and concentrated in urban working-class areas of Belfast and Derry/Londonderry with West and North Belfast intersected by several miles of euphemistically named 'peace lines' (see Figure 16.1). The high volume

Table 16.2 Crime Levels in Northern Ireland 1998–2007

	Number of offences	Clearance rate (%)
1998/99	109,053	29.0
1999/00	119,111	30.2
2000/01	119,912	27.1
2001/02	139,786	20.1
2002/03	142,496	23.0
2003/04	127,953	27.4
2004/05	118,124	28.2
2005/06	123,194	30.6
2006/07	121,144	23.6

Source: Lyness *et al.*, (2005: 16), and Nicholas *et al.*, (2007: 42).

of sectarian incidents such as assaults and harassment impacted disproportionately on communities in *interface areas*, and no amount of reassurance about the low level of crime in general terms could ease the resulting fear of victimisation. Consequently, for many deprived communities—both *loyalist* and *republican*—the issue of crime and anti-social activity became a source of enormous debate and controversy and led to a system of *informal justice* in parts of Belfast and Derry/Londonderry (see Case Study; Ellison and Shirlow, 2008).

Recent trends

Following national *Home Office* guidelines, changes to the counting rules by which crimes are recorded by the police were introduced to Northern Ireland in 1998, with the consequence that crime levels before and after this date are not directly comparable. Implementation of the new rules led to a significant increase in levels of recorded crime in 1998/99, from 76,644 offences under the old rules, to 109,053 under the new ones—an increase of 42 per cent. In subsequent years, the level of recorded crime increased further, reaching a peak of 142,496 offences in 2002/03, before dropping by approximately 15 per cent since then. As the crime level increased, the clearance rate decreased significantly, falling to 20 per cent in 2001/02 (Table 16.2). This occurred against a backdrop of significant changes in policing structures and the loss of many experienced police officers who were availed of the severance package proposed in 1999 following the Report of the Independent Commission on Policing (ICP). The clearance rate climbed back to

Table 16.3 Crime Rates in Northern Ireland and England and Wales per 100,000 population

	Northern Ireland	England and Wales
1998/99	6,457	9,785
1999/00	7,040	10,111
2000/01	7,062	9,814
2001/02	8,199	10,436
2002/03	8,399	11,323
2003/04	7,542	11,308
2004/05	6,938	10,531
2005/06	7,203	10,328
2006/07	6,954	10,024

Source: Lyness *et al.*, (2005: 16), and Nicholas *et al.*, (2007. 42).

30.6 per cent in 2005/06, although it fell to 23.6 per cent in 2006/07 (largely due to a change in the classification of cases in which no *prosecutions* resulted).

The overall crime rate in Northern Ireland has generally been lower than that of England and Wales. In 1995, for instance (under the old counting rules), Northern Ireland recorded a rate of 4,158 offences per 100,000 population, compared to a rate of 9,719 in England and Wales. More recently, the crime rate in Northern Ireland has edged closer to that in England and Wales, but still remains lower overall.

Recent victimization studies have found that the risk of being a victim of crime still remains lower in Northern Ireland than in England and Wales. A comparison of data from the Northern Ireland Crime survey (NICS) and the *British Crime Survey* (BCS) for 2006/07 reveals that 2.9 per cent of adults in Northern Ireland were the victim of violent crime, compared to 3.7 per cent in England and Wales. For household crimes, the figures were 10.5 and 18.9 per cent respectively; and for all personal crime, 4.3 and 6.6 per cent respectively. Overall, the risk of victimisation for all crimes surveyed was 14.2 per cent in Northern Ireland, and 24.4 per cent in England and Wales (Freel and French, 2008: 26).

As the level of political violence receded, other issues have gained greater prominence in recent years, and much public debate has focused on the emergence of such issues as '*hate crime*' and organised crime; the latter because of an unguarded land border with the Republic of Ireland (Northern Ireland Affairs Committee, 2005, 2006). The formal ending of the conflict also witnessed a huge upsurge of debate surrounding victimisation and policy measures (including 'truth commissions' and other proposals) that might help address the human and social costs of the conflict.

Policing and police reform

Northern Ireland has always been a separate policing jurisdiction within the United Kingdom, and was policed by the *Royal Ulster Constabulary* (RUC) from 1922 to 2000 until its replacement by the Police Service of Northern Ireland (PSNI) in 2001. Historically, policing in Northern Ireland—at least up until the reforms in the aftermath of the Independent Commission on Policing (discussed below)—displayed many of the characteristics of a *divided society* model of policing, which in several fundamental respects can be distinguished from that found in more socially integrated societies (Brewer, 1991).

The Divided Society model of policing

- Police recruited almost exclusively from dominant social / ethnic groups.
- Usually military or quasi-military in orientation.
- Widespread reliance on emergency legislation and special powers.
- Maintaining internal order is the core mandate of the police.
- Little attention paid to crime prevention /detection.
- Accountability structures generally weak or non-existent.
- Close operating links between the police and political elites.

Compiled from Brewer (1991).

In part, this divided society model reflected the disputed constitutional status of Northern Ireland since its formation, with the RUC—clearly aligned with both Protestantism and unionism—responsible for upholding and maintaining a 'contested order' (Weitzer, 1995). Expressed simply, the very *legitimacy* of public policing was contested in Northern Ireland. Broader ethno-national tensions were mirrored in tensions or over policing: for many Catholics and *Nationalists* the RUC represented 'symbols of oppression', while for many Protestants and *Unionists* they were the 'custodians of nationhood' (Independent Commission on Policing, 1999: 2).

The RUC in Northern Ireland performed a dual role. As well as having a responsibility for dealing with 'ordinary' crime, it performed a counter-insurgency role in relation to political violence which became part of its core practice (Ellison and Smyth, 2000). From

Figure 16.2 RUC Officers in riot gear. Note the Federal Riot Gun which deploys plastic baton rounds that some officers are carrying

Source: © Pacemaker Press International Ltd

the mid 1970s onwards policing in Northern Ireland became highly militarised, with the RUC having access to the latest technologies of control, while there was a heavy reliance on covert operations and the establishment of specialised tactical units.

One of the key issues surrounding policing during the conflict was the lack of accountability, a situation that was exacerbated when the RUC's counter-insurgency role was taken into consideration. From the mid 1970s onwards the force was embroiled in a number of controversial incidents. For example, special undercover units of the RUC were involved in the fatal shootings of a number of suspected *republicans*—all in highly disputed circumstances—leading to claims that the force was operating a 'shoot-to-kill' policy (see Ellison and Smyth, 2000, chap. 7). Persistent allegations also were made that the RUC's Special Branch and other sections of the security forces colluded with loyalist paramilitaries and allowed them to conduct their operations unhindered. Indeed, collusion continues to be a significant legacy issue from the past and has recently been the subject of a highly critical report from the Police Ombudsman's Office which outlined the role played by the RUC's Special Branch in the deaths of a number of (mainly) Catholic civilians (Office of the Police Ombudsman for Northern Ireland, 2007) (see Figure 16.2).

In dealing with these issues, accountability and oversight structures were generally found to be weak and ineffectual. The Police Authority of Northern Ireland (PANI), for instance, had even fewer powers than its counterparts in England and Wales, with its membership being entirely appointed by government. The operation of the police complaints machinery in Northern Ireland was also problematic since the investigations were not independent of the RUC. Substantiation rates were often less than 1 per cent of the many thousands made annually, while they were effectively zero for those arrested under emergency legislation (Mulcahy, 2006). This was at variance with the huge payments in civil damages made to complainants every year by the RUC.

Catholic/Nationalist participation in the RUC was further limited by the fact that in terms of its ethos, culture, and symbolism the RUC was a visibly Unionist and Protestant organization. Catholics comprised only 8 per cent of the RUC, even though they comprised more than 40 per cent of the population of Northern Ireland (Ellison, 2007).

As the Northern Ireland peace process unfolded, it became clear that any lasting political settlement, and in particular the laying down of arms by the various armed factions—the IRA most notably—was to be contingent upon fundamental reform of the RUC.

The peace process and the Independent Commission on Policing

Under the terms of the 1998 Belfast Agreement, the Independent Commission on Policing (ICP) was established to 'bring forward proposals for the future organization of policing structures and arrangements in Northern Ireland' (ICP, 1999: 123). The ICP reported in September 1999 and made 175 recommendations for the reform of the RUC across 19 thematic areas, including major changes to accountability and oversight mechanisms; independent structures for dealing with complaints against the police; an emphasis on human rights as the core value of modern police-work; changes to police training and education, recruitment, and cultural ethos; and finally, changes to anti-terror policing. The majority of ICP reforms were given a statutory implementation in the Police [Northern Ireland] Acts of 2000 and 2003 and in two implementation plans drawn up by the *Northern Ireland Office* in 2000 and 2001.

At an institutional level, accountability and oversight mechanisms were enhanced by the creation of the Policing Board and District Policing Partnerships (DPPs). The former performs a similar function to Police Authorities in England and Wales, but unlike its counterparts elsewhere, has greatly enhanced statutory powers and can hold inquiries into police actions. DPPs monitor the performance of the police at local level and raise issues of concern with local police commanders. Both the Policing Board and DPPs comprise elected political representatives as well as independent members.

One of the most significant elements in enhancing the legitimacy of the new policing structures in Northern Ireland has been the creation of the Office of the Police Ombudsman for Northern Ireland (OPONI). Unlike the system for dealing with police complaints elsewhere in the United Kingdom, the model adopted in Northern Ireland is based around a model of civilian control that is fully independent of the police and which possesses wide statutory and investigative powers. The OPONI can also investigate past police actions and in this sense has performed something of a surrogate 'truth recovery' role in Northern Ireland.

Other changes included a substantial reduction in the number of police personnel in Northern Ireland to bring the region more into line with the recommended Home Office ratio for England and Wales. Currently there are 9,081 officers in the PSNI, comprised of 7,542 in the regular force and 1,539 in the full and part-time Reserve (Northern Ireland Policing Board, 2008). To increase the number of Catholic recruits to the PSNI, a controversial 50: 50 recruitment strategy was introduced whereby equal numbers of Catholics and non-Catholics are recruited from a pool of qualified applicants. As a result, Catholics currently comprise 24 per cent of police officers, up from 8 per cent in 2001. Efforts have also been made to address the gender imbalance in the police, with the percentage of female officers now standing at 20 per cent (Northern Ireland Policing Board, 2008). It should be noted, however, that female officers in the PSNI are disproportionately concentrated not only in the lower ranks of the organization, but are also under-represented in certain specialisms such as detective branch, which have historically been regarded as male bastions. In October 2004 the PSNI established a Gender Action Plan in an effort to address these issues (Ellison, 2007).

Current trends

The changes brought about by the ICP reforms have addressed many of the fundamental deficiencies that have existed in relation to policing in Northern Ireland historically. Arguably, Northern Ireland now has the most robust structures for police accountability and oversight that currently exist anywhere in Ireland or Britain, particularly in relation to police complaints. However, in spite of the progress to date some of the reforms are not working as well as they might, while others have been hampered by a lack of movement in the political arena (Ellison, 2007) For example, it was only in January 2007 that *Sinn Féin*—currently Northern Ireland's largest political party—agreed to take its seats on the Policing Board and the DPPs. Other problems are evident at the level of the organization itself and concern the steep learning curve in 'doing' democratic policing, but also a degree of institutional resistance on the part of some PSNI officers (O'Rawe, 2007).

REVIEW QUESTIONS

1 What are the main features of policing in divided societies?

2 What were the key concerns raised in connection with policing during the conflict?

3 What are the main recommendations of the ICP? What impact has their implementation had on policing in Northern Ireland?

Prisons and punishment

History and context

Like other elements of the criminal justice system, the conflict had an enormous impact on the nature of Northern Ireland's prison system. In terms of the scale of imprisonment, the prison population changed dramatically during the course of the conflict, increasing from approximately 600 inmates in 1969 to a peak of approximately 3,000 by 1979. By the early 1990s it had declined and stabilised at between 1,600 and 1,900 prisoners. During the height of the conflict paramilitary prisoners comprised between a half and two-thirds of the entire prison population in Northern Ireland (all figures from McEvoy, 2001: 16).

Like policing, the issue of prisons and punishment cannot be separated from the dynamics of conflict in Northern Ireland. One of the most striking aspects of the prison system in Northern Ireland is the ways that specific prison regimes were purposely adapted to deal with and 'manage' political violence (for a detailed analysis of this issue see McEvoy, 2001; Shirlow and McEvoy, 2008). To this end a number of strategies were attempted.

In August 1971 the British government introduced *internment*, consisting of the indefinite detention without trial of those suspected of engaging in paramilitary activities. Initially internees were detained in a prison ship, HMS Maidstone, docked in Belfast Lough, but by 1972 internees were housed in compounds at Long Kesh, a former military airfield outside Belfast. Internees were granted the right to wear their own clothes, not to do prison work, and to be housed on the basis of paramilitary affiliation.

Once convicted of an offence, however, a prisoner was stripped of all these privileges and treated in the same way as any other prisoner. Convicted republican prisoners were strenuously opposed to this and in 1972 embarked on a hunger strike, demanding the same conditions and 'political' status accorded to internees. As Billy McKee, the leader of the strike, neared death, the Secretary of State for Northern Ireland granted prisoners convicted of *'scheduled' offences*—which referred to the list or 'schedule' of offences associated with paramilitary activity—'special category status', the features of which were noteworthy by any standards. Prisoners were segregated according to paramilitary allegiance; they paraded in military formation with mock weapons; and held lectures on revolutionary ideology and guerrilla warfare. To the outside world, the parallels with 'prisoner of war' status were unmistakeable. The legitimacy this conferred on paramilitary prisoners was a source of ongoing concern for the British government, and in 1975 the Gardiner Report sharply criticised the introduction of 'special category status' specifically on this point.

In 1976, as part of the larger shift in security strategy, the policy of criminalisation was introduced. This entailed relying on the 'ordinary' criminal justice system rather than the emergency measures on which the British government's conflict management strategy hitherto had depended. As such, special category status was no longer provided to prisoners convicted of *scheduled offences* (although it continued to be available to prisoners to whom they had previously been accorded). In terms of day-to-day issues, criminalisation meant that all paramilitary prisoners would henceforth be housed in a maximum security prison—male prisoners in Her Majesty's Prison Maze, known colloquially as the 'H Blocks' (see Figure 16.3) due to the distinctive shape of the buildings; and female prisoners in Armagh prison. Prisoners would be treated as 'ordinary' prisoners, and required to wear a prison uniform—in symbolic terms, it was an overt attempt to deny paramilitary prisoners any vestige of legitimacy. This struggle over legitimacy was a crucial element of the respective strategies of the British government and paramilitary organisations, and ensured that the prison regime played a hugely prominent role in following years. This was manifest not just in terms of day-to-day prison management, but also in terms of the intensity of violence outside the prison walls. Although most analyses of paramilitary imprisonment in Northern Ireland have focused on the experiences of male prisoners, it is important to note that over 1,000 women were imprisoned between 1972 and 1998 for a variety of offences directly related to the conflict (Corcoran, 2006).

Republican prisoners vehemently opposed this change in status. Initial protests involved prisoners refusing to wear prison uniforms, and draping themselves instead in

Figure 16.3 Aerial view of the Maze Prison compound illustrating the distinctive shape of the 'H blocks'

Source: © Pacemaker Press International Ltd

their prison blankets (the 'blanket protest'). When they were refused permission to leave their prison cells dressed in that manner, they smeared the cell walls with their excreta (the 'dirty protest'). These protests culminated in hunger strikes in 1980 and 1981 in which prisoners made various demands in pursuit of political recognition. Several of the prisoners contested elections while on hunger strike, giving the protest enormous international media coverage. One prisoner—Bobby Sands—was even elected as an MP to the Westminster Parliament before his death. Overall, 10 republican prisoners starved themselves to death during the 1981 hunger strike. In the face of a resolute British government, the strike collapsed in late 1981 as prisoners' relatives intervened when prisoners lost consciousness. Subsequently, however, in terms of day-to-day prison management, the prisoners' demands were largely met.

The shift from 'special category status' to the criminalisation regime may have seemed like the normalisation of imprisonment in Northern Ireland, but the concentrated imprisonment of so many individuals convicted of scheduled offences posed enormous challenges for the prison system. It necessitated the segregation of prisoners on the basis of paramilitary affiliation, and security concerns dominated all aspects of day-to-day prison management. Some 29 prison staff were murdered during the conflict, and violence within prison was common. Escape attempts by prisoners remained a constant possibility (albeit overwhelmingly by republicans), and in one instance, 38 republicans escaped in September 1983. Even after the 1994 paramilitary ceasefires, a number of escape attempts were made.

The 1998 Belfast Agreement included provisions for the release of paramilitary prisoners as part of the conflict resolution process. Specifically, prisoners who were affiliated with organisations that maintained a ceasefire were eligible for release on licence after they had completed two years of their sentence. Under the Northern Ireland (Sentences) Act 1998 introduced in July 1998, prisoners could apply to the Independent Sentence Review Commissioners for *early release*. The first prisoners were released under this scheme on 11 September 1998, and all those eligible were released by 28 July 2000. In total, 450 prisoners were released under this scheme, comprising 196 loyalists, 242 republicans, and 12 non-aligned prisoners. Of these, 20 prisoners have had their licences revoked (10 for alleged involvement in paramilitary activity, and 10 for alleged involvement in ordinary criminal activity). A relatively small number of paramilitary prisoners remain in custody—31 republican and 34 loyalist prisoners housed in segregated conditions (Northern Ireland Affairs Committee, 2007: 32). The Maze Prison was closed down in September 2000 and currently is the subject of on-going debate over whether it should be redeveloped as a sports stadium and complex, or designated a heritage memorial park in light of its prominent role in the Northern Ireland conflict (Crumlin Road Gaol in Belfast, which during the conflict was the main remand prison, has also been turned into a museum).

Structure of the prison system

Currently the prison system in Northern Ireland comprises three operational establishments: Maghaberry; Magilligan; and Hydebank Wood. Maghaberry prison opened in 1987 and is a high-security establishment. It houses long-term and remand prisoners for those charged or convicted of the most serious offences, including those charged or sentenced under anti-terrorism legislation. Magilligan is a medium-security prison, housing shorter-term prisoners, and some low-security prisoners approaching the end of their sentence. Hydebank Wood is a medium-to-low security prison housing male young offenders aged between 17 and 21 years on conviction, serving a period of 4 years or less in custody. Since June 2004 female prisoners are also held at Hydebank Wood, and currently there is no separate facility for female inmates in Northern Ireland. A new juvenile justice centre for young offenders was opened at Woodlands outside Bangor in November 2007. This state-of-the-art facility is operated and managed by the Youth Justice Agency for Northern Ireland (rather than the Northern Ireland Prison Service) and accommodates up to 48 boys and girls aged between 10 and 17 who have been given a custodial sentence by the courts. The Northern Ireland prison system has a staff of approximately 1,650, and the total prison population as of March 2008 was 1,484, which includes 477 on remand, and five immigration detainees (see Table 16.4).

The peace process led to significant changes in the prison population, dropping from 1,740 inmates in 1995 to 877 by 2001 (an imprisonment rate of 52 prisoners per 100,000 population). As the number of prisoners declined following the early release scheme, the number of prison officers was also reduced. An early retirement/severance scheme was introduced for prison officers, and by March 2001 approximately 1,100 officers (40 per cent of the total) had availed themselves of this scheme. Since 2001 the prison population in Northern Ireland has been on a gradual upward trend. Nevertheless, the overall rate is still considerably lower than that of a number of other European jurisdictions and considerably lower than the rate for England and Wales and Scotland (see Table 16.5).

Table 16.4 Northern Ireland Prison Population (March 2008)

Establishments	Sentenced	Remand	Immigration detainees	Total
Maghaberry	476	367	5	848
Magilligan	422	0	0	422
Hydebank Wood (female)	15	17	0	32
Hydebank Wood (male)	89	93	0	182
Total	1002	477	5	

Source: Northern Ireland Prison Service (figures are updated weekly from <http://www.niprisonservice.gov.uk/>)

Table 16.5 Prisoners per 100,000 population for selected European jurisdictions

England & Wales	148
Spain	145
Scotland	139
Netherlands	128
Italy	104
Germany	96
Greece	90
France	85
Northern Ireland	84
Denmark	77
Republic of Ireland	72
Norway	66

Source: Walmsley (2007: 5)

In addition to lower levels of imprisonment, the nature of the prison population in Northern Ireland differs from that in England and Wales in a number of other ways. First, remand prisoners comprise a far higher proportion of Northern Ireland's prison population—34 per cent, compared to 15 per cent in England and Wales (Northern Ireland Affairs Committee, 2007: 17). Government officials attribute this largely to the fact that the criminal justice process in Northern Ireland is considerably lengthier than in England and Wales (discussed further below). Second, in Northern Ireland, fine

Table 16.6 Percentage Female Prison population 1994–2003 (UK and Republic of Ireland)

	1994 %	1995 %	1996 %	1997 %	1998 %	1999 %	2000 %	2001 %	2002 %	2003 %
Northern Ireland	2.16	1.99	1.77	1.84	1.79	1.69	2.15	1.76	2.34	1.90
Republic of Ireland	1.77	1.84	2.19	2.60	2.72	2.93	2.44	3.15	3.29	3.05
Scotland	3.17	3.11	3.23	3.02	3.21	3.52	3.46	4.06	4.33	4.55
England & Wales	3.69	3.91	4.17	4.35	4.78	4.97	5.15	5.59	6.17	6.24

Source: Amelin and O'Loan, 2005: 7. Reproduced with the kind permission of the Northern Ireland Office.

defaulters have traditionally comprised a significant proportion of sentenced prisoners—59 per cent of prison receptions in Northern Ireland compared to 2.2 per cent in England and Wales—a disparity that 'astounded' the British Parliamentary, Northern Ireland Affairs Committee (Northern Ireland Affairs Committee, 2007: 3). However, recent legislative changes in the Criminal Justice (Northern Ireland) Order 2008 have attempted to address this issue by proposing non-custodial, community-based sentences for fine default. It remains to be seen, however, whether magistrates will use these new powers in preference to custodial sentences.

For offences that were unrelated to the political conflict, Northern Ireland has traditionally had a lower rate of female imprisonment than any other region of the United Kingdom and the Republic of Ireland (see Table 16.6). However, it is not at all clear that the prison establishment has been sufficiently geared to provide an adequate standard of care to female prisoners. Following the deaths in custody of a number of female prisoners, the Northern Ireland Human Rights Commission (NIHRC) commissioned a report into the conditions experienced by women in prison (Scraton and Moore, 2007). The report noted that the Northern Ireland Prison Service was failing in its 'duty of care' to female prisoners, with some women locked in their cells for periods of up to 17 hours per day and denied basic exercise and education facilities. Oppressive staffing levels, the lack of a gender-specific prison regime, and the absence of psychiatric beds for those women deemed to pose a suicide or self-harm risk were also particular causes of concern (Scraton and Moore, 2007).

REVIEW QUESTIONS

1 How has the Northern Ireland conflict impacted on the nature and scale of imprisonment in Northern Ireland?

2 Why was the attainment of 'political' status so important for paramilitary inmates, particularly those representing republican organizations?

3 What are some of the likely challenges currently facing the Northern Ireland prison system?

The courts, sentencing, and disposal

The court system in Northern Ireland is similar in structure to that of England and Wales, albeit historically set against a backdrop of political conflict that has affected its operation in significant ways. Magistrates' courts deal with all minor criminal matters, and hold preliminary hearings for more serious cases. The Crown Court hears all serious criminal cases, as well as 'either-way' cases (which may be heard in either the magistrates' or Crown Court) which are committed for trial in the Crown Court. Appeals may be made to the Court of Criminal Appeal, the highest criminal appeal court within Northern Ireland, and ultimately to the House of Lords, the highest court of appeal within the UK.

The outbreak of the conflict changed the character of the court system markedly, through the heightened security levels required in court proceedings, and particularly through the introduction of the Diplock court system. The 1972 Diplock Commission was established to consider ways in which the government could respond to political violence and paramilitary activity other than through internment. It noted that the court system in Northern Ireland faced special difficulties, particularly through the risk of witness and juror intimidation, and of 'perverse acquittals' by partisan jurors. It proposed that defendants charged with scheduled offences should be tried in single-judge non-jury courts. Although the Commission's evidence of juror intimidation and perverse acquittals was weak, the government nevertheless proceeded to enact its recommendation in the Northern Ireland (Emergency Provisions) Act 1973 (which was amended by the Prevention of Terrorism (Temporary Provisions) Act 1994 and other subsequent emergency legislation; see Walker, 1992).

The suspension of jury trials in Northern Ireland proved controversial in itself, but Diplock courts were further criticized for appearing to constitute simply one further component of the government's wider security policy. Suspects could now be detained for up to seven days, and allegations routinely surfaced that detainees were beaten during interrogation (resulting in a highly critical Amnesty International report in 1978 and a government-appointed inquiry chaired by Lord Bennett in 1979; see Taylor, 1980). Analyses of the operation of Diplock courts revealed high conviction rates, particularly through reliance on confession evidence, and Diplock judges were criticised for their willingness to accept such evidence, and for becoming 'case-hardened' and increasingly attuned to the needs of the government's security policy rather than to the integrity of the criminal justice system (Boyle, Hadden, and Hillyard 1975; 1980; Greer and White, 1986; Jackson and Doran, 1995).

Within this context, while the courts functioned as legal arenas for the determination of guilt and the imposition of sanctions, they also became hugely symbolic venues wherein competing legitimacy claims were dramatically enacted. On the one hand, the fact that these were 'criminal' courts was central to wider state strategies of conflict management, that the conflict was at heart a breakdown in law and order, and paramilitary organizations were essentially criminal in nature and action. On the other, court appearances gave republican paramilitary defendants an opportunity to challenge the very legitimacy of the state on whose behalf they were being prosecuted. Republican strategies of withholding legitimacy from the criminal justice system by 'refusing to recognize the court' gradually gave way to a more strategic engagement with the court process by contesting the charges brought against defendants (see McEvoy, 2001: chap. 6).

The number of cases heard before Diplock courts gradually declined as the dynamics of the conflict changed, falling from 329 cases in 1986 to approximately 60 cases per annum by the mid-2000s (Northern Ireland Office, 2006: 4). The Diplock court system was largely abolished in 2007 (although 'exceptional cases' may still be heard in Diplock courts) in light of the changed security environment arising from the peace process.

Sentencing

During the years of conflict the sentencing framework applied by the courts had to respond to, on the one hand, ordinary criminality, and on the other, the exigencies of politically motivated violence. Consequently, the overall picture of sentencing policy in Northern Ireland is distorted by the relatively high numbers of people given custodial sentences for the commission of a scheduled offence prior to the signing of the Belfast Agreement in 1998.

However, the years since 1998, and in particular the reforms to the criminal justice system brought about by the *Criminal Justice Review* (CJR) in 2000, have gone some way to normalise the operation of criminal justice in Northern Ireland and to bring a number of aspects, such as prisons, the structure of the courts, the public prosecution service, and the Probation Service broadly into line with the standards applicable in England and Wales. However, the sentencing framework applied in Northern Ireland was not scrutinised in any great detail by the CJR with the consequence that some aspects of sentencing—particularly around public protection sentences and post-release supervision—lagged some way behind that adopted in England and Wales, while the sentencing provisions of the Criminal Justice Act 2003 did not apply to Northern Ireland.

In March 2005 the Northern Ireland Office duly embarked on a public consultation exercise to review the sentencing framework in Northern Ireland. This was given a powerful impetus by the public and political outcry following the brutal *rape* and murder of Attracta Harron in 2003 by Trevor Hamilton. Hamilton, a prolific and violent sex offender, had just been released from a young offenders centre, having served a prior sentence for rape and serious sexual assault. The details that emerged from the Harron case highlighted the lack of effective public protection sentences and deficiencies in the mechanisms and structures for post-release supervision in Northern Ireland. In 2008 a new sentencing framework was proposed in the Criminal Justice (Northern Ireland) Order which brought the sentencing framework broadly into line with that adopted in England and Wales. In particular, the legislation introduced two new types of disposal in Northern Ireland: *indeterminate custodial sentences*, and *extended custodial sentences* for those individuals deemed to pose a significant risk or threat to public safety.

Disposal trends

As is the case in England and Wales, magistrates' courts in Northern Ireland deal with the majority of offences. Again, as is the case elsewhere, the majority of offenders sentenced in magistrates' courts are overwhelmingly male with the fine being the most common means of disposal (Figure 16.4). Motoring offences comprise the single largest

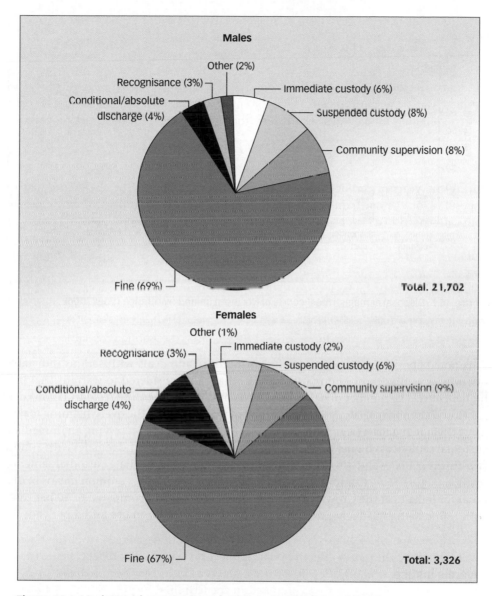

Figure 16.4 Magistrates' courts sentencing by gender and disposal (2006)

Source: Northern Ireland Office, 2008: 81. Reproduced with the kind permission of the Northern Ireland Office.

category of offences at magistrates' courts, followed by summary and indictable offences (Figure 16.5). Males and females are just as likely to receive Community Supervision Orders, while females are slightly more likely to be given a conditional or absolute discharge compared to males (10 per cent compared to 4 per cent). Relatively few cases that are brought before a magistrates' court result in an immediate custodial sentence, although when this does occur males are three times more likely to receive a custodial sentence than females (Figure 16.4).

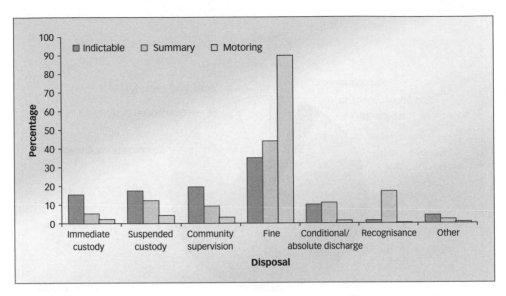

Figure 16.5 Disposal at magistrates' courts in Northern Ireland by offence type (2006)

Source: Northern Ireland Office, 2008: 81. Reproduced with the kind permission of the Northern Ireland Office.

As noted above, the Crown Court in Northern Ireland deals with serious indictable offences as well as those summary offences which are considered to warrant trial in a higher court. The number of defendants who come before the Crown Court is considerably lower than in magistrates' courts: a total of 1,335 in 2006, the overwhelming majority of them being male (Figure 16.5). However, the likelihood of receiving an immediate custodial sentence is higher in the Crown Court for both males and females with almost two-thirds of males and one-third of females receiving an immediate custodial sentence in 2006 (Figure 16.6). Community supervision orders are a more common means of disposal for females at the Crown Court than males (20 per cent compared to 10 per cent) with a fine being relatively rare in both cases (4 per cent for males and 5 per cent for females).

Juvenile justice

Perhaps the most fundamental difference between Northern Ireland and the rest of the United Kingdom in terms of the sentencing framework concerns the existence of a statutory system for restorative and reparative youth cautioning in relation to juvenile offenders—laid down by the Justice (Northern Ireland) Act 2002. Indeed, in the field of youth *conferencing* there has been considerable international and national interest in the pioneering work been done in this area (O'Mahony and Campbell, 2006). The age of criminal responsibility in Northern Ireland is 10, so all young offenders aged 10 to 17 inclusive are referred—with few exceptions—to the Youth Conference Service to engage in a process of restorative conferencing. There are two kinds of conference in operation in Northern Ireland: *Diversionary Conferences* which are recommended by the

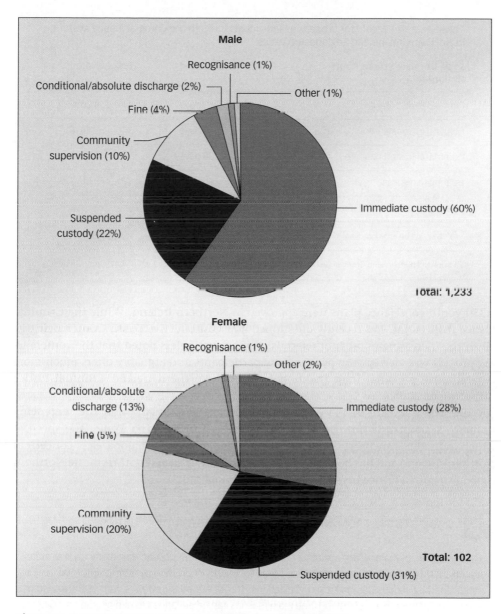

Figure 16.6 Crown Court sentencing by gender and disposal (2006)

Source: Northern Ireland Office, 2008: 83. Reproduced with the kind permission of the Northern Ireland Office.

Public Prosecution Service as an alternative to prosecution; and *Court Ordered Conferences* which are used whenever a particular young person has been brought to trial and are used as an alternative to a custodial sentence by the court. The scheme was piloted in Belfast in late 2003, and since December 2006 has been used by all of the youth courts across Northern Ireland for the vast majority of young offenders. In 2007/08 a total of

Table 16.7 Timescale for processing individuals through the criminal justice system in Northern Ireland and England and Wales

Type of Case: Crown Court defendants	N. Ireland	Eng & Wales
Remand to disposal	360 days	214 days
Remand to committal	170 days	52 days
Committal to start hearing	130 days	114 days
Hearing to disposal	60 days	48 days
Charge / Summons to disposal	113 days	61 days
Charge / summons to disposal	134 days	55 days

Source: Northern Ireland Criminal Justice Inspectorate (2006: 11)

1,350 youth conference plans were approved in Northern Ireland. While the Criminal Justice Inspectorate has recently questioned how cost-effective Youth Conferencing is, given the increasing number of referrals, it was nevertheless noted that the conferencing process was viewed very positively by participants and arguably offers much more rehabilitative potential than traditional custody (Northern Ireland Criminal Justice Inspectorate, 2008a).

While the structure of the court system in Northern Ireland and the sentencing framework adopted is now broadly comparable to England and Wales, the speed at which individuals are processed through the system remains a major area of concern in Northern Ireland and has been the subject of a highly critical report from the Northern Ireland Criminal Justice Inspectorate (2006) (see Table 16.7).

 CASE STUDY: FROM INFORMAL JUSTICE TO RESTORATIVE JUSTICE

The difficulties of maintaining a routine police presence in all republican and many loyalist areas meant that a 'policing vacuum' developed that was partly filled by a system of informal justice established by various paramilitary organizations. This operated *outside* the formal state system and was largely independent of it. Three main reasons can be advanced to explain the emergence of informal justice in Northern Ireland. First, the development of informal justice is a common feature in those societies where the legitimacy of the state, the police, and the broader criminal justice system is contested. Organizations such as the **Irish Republican Army** (IRA) and **Ulster Volunteer Force** (UVF) used informal justice to establish legitimacy for themselves and to mark out their respective territories. Second, Belfast, in common with many UK cities, experienced phenomenally high levels of unemployment and urban deprivation from the mid 1970s onwards with knock-on effects in terms of anti-social activity and low-level crime in urban working-class communities (Ellison and Shirlow, 2008). In addition, the aftermath of the first paramilitary ceasefires (from 1994) saw massive increases in the use of Class A drugs in some areas (Ellison and Shirlow, 2008). Third, there were numerous problems with the nature of public policing. There was widespread concern that active criminals and drug dealers were offered immunity by the RUC in return for serving as informants. Perhaps most fundamentally, the RUC's primary counter-terrorism role meant that it became disconnected from, and in many respects disinterested in, the problems of crime that afflicted urban working-class communities, and was to play only the most limited role in terms of crime *prevention* and detection.

In the absence of an adequate public policing response many community residents called on paramilitary organizations to take responsibility for controlling crime and anti-social activity in their respective areas. The operation of informal justice is complex, and contrary to popular opinion there was some attempt at adhering to a rudimentary process. For instance, mirroring in some respects aspects of the formal criminal justice system, the IRA established a 'civil administration unit' which investigated complaints, gathered evidence, collected witness statements, passed a sentence, and carried out a designated punishment. A graduated tariff system operated which meant that in theory the punishment was supposed to be proportional to the offence. In practice, however, particularly for repeat offenders, the punishments were extremely brutal and involved beatings with iron bars, baseball bats, or hurling sticks (similar to a hockey stick), while in other cases individuals were shot in the thighs, kneecaps, elbows, or ankles with low-velocity handguns. The specialist orthopaedic unit at Belfast's Royal Victoria Hospital was to garner unrivalled experience in treating such injuries over the years. Sometimes 'banishment' was the preferred tactic, with transgressors given 24 hours to leave Northern Ireland and seek sanctuary in Britain or elsewhere. The alternative was death or at the very least a violent physical punishment.

In the context of the developing peace process it became clear that such punishments were indefensible in human rights terms and here Northern Ireland has provided international lessons in *restorative justice* and non-violent means of dispute resolution. Both republican and loyalist paramilitary organizations such as the IRA and the UVF have been closely involved in establishing restorative justice schemes in a number of areas across Northern Ireland through organizations such as *Community Restorative Justice Ireland* (for republicans) and *Northern Ireland Alternatives* (for loyalists). These have been broadly successful in preventing punishment attacks against individuals accused of criminality and anti-social activity, but also appear to have been effective in reducing more concentrated patterns of offending. Restorative justice programmes in republican areas have tended to operate independently from the formal criminal justice system (particularly the PSNI) *except* where cases involving *domestic violence*, serious sexual assault, or child abuse are involved. These are referred either directly or indirectly to the appropriate statutory agency. Restorative justice schemes have been subject to a broadly positive evaluation by the Criminal Justice Inspectorate (Northern Ireland Criminal Justice Inspectorate, 2008b) who noted that in terms of local community *crime reduction* strategies they were just as effective, and in some cases more so, than the statutory agencies in dealing with low-level criminality and in providing help and assistance to victims of crime.

CONCLUSION

Attempting to summarise the operation of the entire criminal justice system in Northern Ireland into one chapter of this length is a daunting task, and inevitably some issues of significance and nuances of context have not received the attention they warrant. Nevertheless, in this brief review, we have sought to highlight three specific points that we feel are essential to a full understanding of crime and criminal justice in Northern Ireland. First, we have tried to highlight the specific impact that decades of political conflict had on the landscape of criminal justice in Northern Ireland, particularly in the form of emergency legislation, modes of policing, the operation of the courts, and regimes of imprisonment. Second, notwithstanding the extent to which emergency measures became normalised across the institutions of criminal justice as a whole, we have also sought where possible to disentangle issues directly related to the conflict from other more mundane concerns, including the nature and extent of 'ordinary' crime. In that respect, we have been concerned to demonstrate that many concerns relating to crime and the efficiency of criminal justice in Northern Ireland are also evident in other jurisdictions. Third, in light of the enormous changes heralded by the peace process, we have attempted to outline the nature of these institutional shifts, and the contribution that they can make to the conflict resolution process in Northern Ireland. Only time will tell if the reforms to the criminal justice system undertaken over the course of the past decade in Northern Ireland are enough to bring a fully-fledged 'peace' to Northern Ireland. What is not in doubt, however, is that in the context of the violence of the past 30 years, they have provided an important first step.

QUESTIONS FOR DISCUSSION

1 What challenges does political violence pose for the criminal justice system of any society, and what principles should underpin how a society responds to these?

2 What was the relationship between 'ordinary' crime and political violence in Northern Ireland?

3 Are the recommendations of the Independent Commission on Policing a suitable model for other societies to follow?

GUIDE TO FURTHER READING

Brewer, J.D., Lockhart, B., and Rodgers, P. (1997) *Crime in Ireland 1945–95*. Oxford: Oxford University Press.

A thorough, if now somewhat dated, account of crime levels and trends in both parts of Ireland. It includes a detailed ethnographic analysis of crime and its management in different Belfast communities.

Corcoran, M. (2006) *Out of Order: The Political Imprisonment of Women in Northern Ireland 1972–1998*. Cullompton: Willan.

The most thorough account available of female paramilitary imprisonment in Northern Ireland.

Ellison, G. (2007) 'A Blueprint for Democratic Policing Anywhere in the World? Police Reform, Political Transition and Conflict Resolution in Northern Ireland' *Police Quarterly* 10(3): 243–69.

A recent appraisal of the police reform process in Northern Ireland considering the progress of change to date and outlining remaining obstacles.

Independent Commission on Policing (1999) *A New Beginning: Report of the Independent Commission on Policing*. Belfast: Stationery Office.

A highly readable and very influential report outlining measures to develop new policing arrangements in Northern Ireland.

Shirlow, P. and McEvoy, K. (2008) *'Beyond the Wire'. Former Prisoners and Conflict Transformation in Northern Ireland*. Pluto: London.

A detailed discussion of the dynamics of paramilitary imprisonment including the tensions between resistance and management strategies.

Mulcahy, A. (2006) *Policing Northern Ireland: Conflict, Legitimacy and Reform*. Cullompton: Willan.

A sustained analysis of policing in Northern Ireland during the Troubles and of the changes ushered in by the ICP report.

WEB LINKS

http://www.bbc.co.uk/northernireland/learning/history/stateapart/

An excellent resource from the BBC's Education Department providing an interactive chronicle covering the 30 years of the conflict in Northern Ireland. Sections outline the background to the conflict as well as dealing with more contemporary issues such as policing and prison reform.

http://www.cain.ulst.ac.uk

The Conflict Archive on the Internet website provides a wealth of information about different aspects of the Northern Ireland conflict.

http://www.caj.org.uk

The Committee on the Administration of Justice is an independent and highly-regarded civil liberties association.

http://www.nio.gov.uk

The website of the Northern Ireland Office provides information about different aspects of the Northern Ireland criminal justice system, including policy statements and empirical research findings.

http://www.nipolicingboard.org.uk

The website provides useful information about the Policing Board and District Policing Partnerships, including a variety of surveys on different aspects of policing and *community safety*.

http://www.policeombudsman.org

The Police Ombudsman's website.

http://www.psni.police.uk

The website of the PSNI.

REFERENCES

Amelin, K. and O'Loan, C. (2005) *Northern Ireland Projections 2005–2009,* Research & Statistical Bulletin 12/2005. Statistics and Research Branch, Belfast: Northern Ireland Office.

Boyle, K., Hadden, T., and Hillyard, P. (1980) *Ten Years On: The Legal Control of Political Violence in Northern Ireland*. London: Cobden Trust.

Brewer, J.D. (1991) 'Policing in divided societies: theorising a type of policing'. *Policing and Society* 1: 179–91.

Brewer, J.D., Lockhart, B., and Rodgers, P. (1997) *Crime in Ireland 1945–95*. Oxford: Oxford University Press.

Corcoran, M. (2006) *Out of Order: The Political Imprisonment of Women in Northern Ireland 1972–1998*. Cullompton: Willan Publishing.

Diplock Commission (1972) *Report of the Commission to Consider Legal Procedures to Deal with Terrorist Activities in Northern Ireland* Cmnd. 5185. Belfast: Stationery Office.

Ellison, G. (2007) 'A Blueprint for Democratic Policing Anywhere in the World? Police Reform, Political Transition and Conflict Resolution in Northern Ireland'. *Police Quarterly* 10(3): 243–69.

Ellison, G. and Shirlow, P. (2008) 'From War to Peace: Informalism, Restorative Justice and Conflict Transformation in Northern Ireland' in H. Miller-Ventura (ed) *Restorative Justice: From Theory to Practice.* Elsevier series in Sociology of Crime, Law and Deviance, Vol.11: 31–57.

Ellison, G. and Smyth, J. (2000) *The Crowned Harp: Policing Northern Ireland.* London: Pluto.

Equality Commission for Northern Ireland (2005) *Fair Employment Monitoring Report No. 15 (Part 1)* 'A Summary of the Northern Ireland Workforce: Summary of Monitoring Returns 2004'. Belfast: Equality Commission for Northern Ireland.

Freel, R. and French, B. (2008) *Experience of Crime: Findings from the 2006/7 Northern Ireland Crime Survey. Research and Statistical Bulletin 1/2008.* Belfast: Stationery Office.

Greer, C. and White, A. (1986) *Abolishing the Diplock Courts: The Case for Restoring Jury Trial to Northern Ireland.* London: Cobden Trust.

Hayes, B. and McAllister, I. (2001) 'Sowing Dragons Teeth: Public Support for Political Violence and Paramilitarism in Northern Ireland'. *Political Studies* 49(5): 901–22.

Independent Commission on Policing (ICP) (1999) *A New Beginning for Policing in Northern Ireland.* Belfast: Northern Ireland Office.

Jackson, J. and Doran, S. (1995) *Judge Without Jury: Diplock Courts in the Adversarial System.* Oxford: Oxford University Press.

Lyness, D. Campbell, P., and Jamison, C. (2005) *A Commentary on Northern Ireland Crime Statistics 2004.* Belfast: Northern Ireland Office.

McEvoy, K. (2001) *Paramilitary Imprisonment in Northern Ireland.* Oxford: Oxford University Press.

Mulcahy, A. (2006) *Policing Northern Ireland: Conflict, Legitimacy and Reform.* Cullompton: Willan Publishing.

Nicholas, S., Kershaw, C., and Walker, A. (2007) *Crime in England and Wales 2006/07, 4th Edition (Statistical Bulletin).* London: Stationery Office.

Northern Ireland Affairs Committee (2005) *The Challenge of Diversity: Hate Crime in Northern Ireland (HC 548-I).* London: Stationery Office.

Northern Ireland Affairs Committee (2006) *Organised Crime in Northern Ireland (HC 886-II).* London: Stationery Office.

Northern Ireland Affairs Committee (2007) *The Northern Irish Prison Service: Volume 1 (HC 118).* London: HMSO.

Northern Ireland Criminal Justice Inspectorate (2006) *Avoidable Delay: A Thematic Inspection of the Delay in Processing Criminal Cases in Northern Ireland.* Northern Ireland Criminal Justice Inspectorate: Belfast.

Northern Ireland Criminal Justice Inspectorate (2008a) *Youth Conference Service: Inspection of the Youth Conference Service in Northern Ireland.* Northern Ireland Criminal Justice Inspectorate: Belfast.

Northern Ireland Criminal Justice Inspectorate (2008b) *Community Restorative Justice Ireland Inspection Report,* Northern Ireland Criminal Justice Inspectorate: Belfast.

Northern Ireland Office (2006) *Replacement Arrangements for the Diplock Court System: A Consultation Paper.* Belfast: HMSO.

Northern Ireland Office (2007) Criminal Justice Directorate *Annual Report.* Belfast: Northern Ireland Office.

Northern Ireland Office (2008) *Digest of Information on the Northern Ireland Criminal Justice System,* 6. Statistics and Research Branch, Belfast: Northern Ireland Office.

Northern Ireland Policing Board (2008) *Annual Report & Accounts 2007.* Belfast Northern Ireland Prison Service, <http://www.niprisonservice.gov.uk/>.

O'Mahony, D. and Campbell, C. (2006) 'Mainstreaming Restorative Justice for Young Offenders through Youth Conferencing: The Experience of Northern Ireland', in J. Junger-Tas and S.H. Decker (eds) *International Handbook of Juvenile Justice.* Springer: Netherlands.

O'Rawe, M. (2007) 'Human Rights, Transitional Socieities, and Police Training: Legitimating Strategies and Delegitimating Legacies' *St John's Journal of Legal Commentary* 22(1): 199–259.

Office of the Police Ombudsman for Northern Ireland (OPONI) (2007) *Statement by the Police Ombudsman for Northern Ireland on her investigation into the circumstances surrounding the death of Raymond McCord Junior and related matters.* Belfast: Office of the Police Ombudsman for Northern Ireland.

Scraton, P. and Moore, L. (2007) *The Prison Within.* Belfast: Human Rights Commission.

Shirlow P. and McEvoy, K. (2008) *'Beyond the Wire'. Former Prisoners and Conflict Transformation in Northern Ireland.* Pluto: London.

Taylor, P. (1980) *Beating the Terrorists? Interrogation in Omagh, Gough and Castlereagh.* Harmondsworth: Penguin.

Walker, C. (1992) *The Prevention of Terrorism in British Law* (2nd edn). Manchester: Manchester University Press.

Walmsley, R. (2007) *World Prison Population List* (7th edn). London: International Centre for Prison Studies.

Weitzer, R. (1995) *Policing Under Fire: Ethnic Conflict and Police-Community Relations in Northern Ireland.* Albany: State University of New York Press.

17 The future of criminal justice

Michael Cavadino and James Dignan

Judge Dredd

2000 AD Comics feature Judge Dredd – a law enforcement officer of the future equipped with deadly technology, empowered to mete out extreme and summary sanctions on the street. Is criminal justice moving in this direction?

Figure 17.1

INTRODUCTION

Criminal justice can currently be said to be in a state of crisis. Why is this, and what sort of crisis is it? And where do we go from here? How might criminal justice alter and develop in future in response to the current crisis? And will these changes actually solve the crisis, or only make things worse, possibly much, much worse?

This chapter addresses these questions. First we sketch out some of the characteristics of the current crisis, emphasizing that it has two main aspects, being both a 'crisis of resources' and a 'crisis of legitimacy'. We then proceed to speculate about some different ways in which criminal justice might develop in the foreseeable future, and the effects that these possible future developments would be likely to have on these twin crises.

BACKGROUND

Futurology is a hazardous enterprise. We do not just mean the obvious fact that it is easy to get the future wrong: remember all those people who blithely predicted that telephones would never catch on, or that we would all be flying around with our personal jetpacks by 1990? We must also bear in mind that, however clever or well informed we are, there may in reality be no such thing as a foreseeable criminal justice future. Budding futurologists should beware, as the following examples illustrate, of making predictions that may look perfectly reasonable at the time—indeed, may actually be perfectly reasonable—but that turn out to be horribly wrong. In 1983, Tony Bottoms (1983) suggested that criminal justice might be moving away from a 'carceral' system in which imprisonment is central, towards a 'juridical' system which imposes on offenders standard and limited penalties (such as fines and compensation orders)

---

1. Judge Dredd © & ® Rebellion.

which largely do not involve imprisonment or supervision of offenders. This suggestion was based on an exemplary and insightful analysis of penal trends up to that point—but subsequent events (at least so far) have largely served to falsify it. Since Bottoms wrote, both imprisonment and *probation* caseloads have increased (Morgan, 2003; Robinson, 2005), with the development of an increasing array of more intensive supervision and surveillance techniques (such as Intensive Supervision and Surveillance Programmes for young offenders, first introduced in 2001).

Again, in 1992 an unfortunate conference participant gave a paper commenting on '*law and order ideology*' (also known as '*populist punitiveness*')—the popular notion that what is required in criminal justice is the harshest dose of punishment we can manage to mete out to offenders. His paper misleadingly claimed that 'the influence of law and order ideology seems to have passed its peak' (Cavadino, 1994: 50)—although, to be fair, at the time it did so seem, and he was not the only criminologist who failed to spot the looming advent of a government-led, harshly punitive 'law and order' revival which occurred within a matter of months and whose effects are still being felt today (Cavadino and Dignan, 2007a: Introduction and chap. 11).

Perhaps mindful of such pitfalls, criminologists are often wary of making too many predictions. They have often, however, analysed recent and current trends in criminal justice, sometimes in a manner suggesting that these trends are likely to continue into the indefinite future. They have developed concepts such as 'managerialism', '*the new penology*', '*the new punitiveness*', 'postmodern penality', and 'the culture of control', which we shall be explaining shortly. They have also at times, without being too presumptuous about what might actually happen, sketched out various possible *alternative* futures for criminal justice—different roads which *could* be taken leading from the current situation, the possible beginnings of which may be traced in the here and now. This is what we shall be attempting in this chapter.

Our starting point, then, is the current situation in criminal justice. How should we describe this current situation? Although some query the use of the term (see Cavadino and Dignan, 2007a: chap. 1; Cavadino and Dignan, 2007b) it may well be appropriate to talk about a '*crisis*' in criminal justice (see also Bottoms and Preston, 1980, and especially Bottoms, 1980.) This crisis (if we choose to call it such) is multifaceted, but it is possible with some simplification to allude to two main aspects: a *crisis of resources*, and a *crisis of legitimacy*. 'Crisis of resources' refers to the ways in which the criminal justice system, or parts of it, often seem to be desperately short of the material resources (money, staff, buildings, equipment) they need to do the job—not only dealing with *crimes*, criminals, and suspected criminals, but also (hopefully) helping to control crime. 'Crisis of legitimacy' refers to the system's unpopularity and apparent moral unacceptability: criminal justice is constantly being attacked for being in a variety of ways unfair, unjust, and poor at doing its job.

In considering the possible futures of criminal justice, we shall be taking into account the extent to which different kinds of development might contribute towards either solving or exacerbating these twin crises. Always bearing in mind the perils of prediction, this might cast some light on the question of whether they are likely to come to pass, since people may be wise enough to choose courses which are more likely to bring success. Or then again it might not cast much light on this, since human beings and their societies are capable of some enduring follies, as criminal justice policy has often borne witness. Examples include extended and *indeterminate sentences* of imprisonment for large numbers of persistent and allegedly dangerous offenders, and in general the perennial naive belief—against all the evidence—that harsh *punishments* are an obvious and effective solution to the problem of crime (see Cavadino *et al.*, 1999: 37–40).

The current crisis in criminal justice

It might not seem unduly alarming to hear that the prison system in England and Wales is close to its useable operational capacity. Until, that is, you realize that this means that prisons are not merely grossly overcrowded, but that the numbers of prisoners are perilously close to what is informally called the 'bust limit', or the number that the system can supposedly hold safely (more precisely and officially, the number that the prison estate can hold 'taking into account control, security and the proper operation' of prison regimes (H.M. Prison Service, 2008). In 2006 and 2007 this limit (which had already once been briefly exceeded in April 2004) was neared repeatedly. From October 2006 the practice of holding hundreds of prisoners in police cells was revived (under the reassuring title of 'Operation Safeguard'), with prisoners also being kept in cells in courthouses and ministers considering housing them three to a cell in prisons. In January 2007 the *Home Secretary* and *Lord Chancellor* urgently called on judges and magistrates to send fewer offenders to prison; in June, with prison numbers at a record 81,040, emergency measures were introduced to release around 1,000 prisoners per month up to 18 days early. This brought about an instant cut in prisoner numbers by almost 1,500, but by September they had crept back up to a new record of 81,133. In February 2008 the 'bust limit' was finally busted as prison numbers reached another all-time high of 82,180 on 29 February, 156 over the limit (H.M. Prison Service, 2007 and 2008).

A prison system in a state of crisis, then (or, for those who object to the c-word, in a very bad way). But in our view the crisis is not simply a matter of sheer numbers of prisoners, overwhelming and urgent though the 'numbers crisis' is. This is partly because excessive numbers of prisoners inevitably bring other problems in their wake, most obviously overcrowding and squalid physical conditions, with the overstretching of resources such as staff time leading to a general impoverishment of conditions, facilities, and regimes for both prison staff and inmates. These may lead in turn to dissatisfaction and unrest among staff and prisoners, potentially culminating in disorder and violence from the latter, and/or industrial action by the former—such as the lightning national strike by the Prison Officers' Association in August 2007. However, these consequential adverse effects of the prison numbers crisis are still not the whole story. If they were, one way of solving the crisis might simply be to ensure that, however expensive it might be, sufficient resources were provided to house and contain all the people sent to prison by the courts, with a certain amount of tweaking as required by releasing some prisoners earlier. But this strategy would be unlikely to work, because the problems run deeper.

The crisis in criminal justice is not just composed of material factors such as numbers of prisoners and the resources needed to cater for them. Nor is it confined to the prison system, since the malaise pervades the whole criminal justice system from the police through to the courts and Probation Service, as the foregoing chapters have borne witness. To simplify somewhat, it can be said that there are two interacting aspects to the crisis. On the one hand there is a material 'crisis of resources' and on the other an ideological 'crisis of legitimacy'. Both these crises affect not only prisons but the entire criminal justice enterprise. The crisis of resources can also be seen, for example, in a Probation Service struggling to handle excessive caseloads, or in agencies such as the police, the Crown Prosecution Service (CPS), and courts system. Similarly with legitimacy. The crisis of legitimacy relates to the 'sense of injustice' which the Woolf report of 1991 (Woolf and Tumim, 1991) found to be of crucial importance in explaining the riots at Strangeways and other prisons in 1990. It is not only prisoners who feel a sense of injustice. Other subjects of criminal justice—those at the receiving end of the system as suspects, defendants, and as convicted offenders dealt with by penalties other than imprisonment—victims of crime, criminal justice practitioners of all kinds, the general public, and the 'chattering classes' whose views find themselves voiced by politicians and the media, can and do all feel that the criminal justice system is lacking in the very justice its title proclaims. Scarcely a day goes by without producing some media image of an apparently lenient court decision, a victim of crime let down, a defendant wrongly convicted, or an abominable prison regime. Nor is the system merely seen as unjust; it is also commonly perceived to be defective in other ways as well—ineffective, grotesquely expensive, incompetent, poorly managed, and trying to do the wrong thing much of the time.

This ideological crisis of legitimacy is not simple, straightforward, or all one way. For not only does the criminal justice system have a number of different audiences to satisfy, with varying interests and standpoints, but there are competing and often contradictory diagnoses of what is wrong. Most obviously, there is the split between those who take what might be characterized as a traditional liberal view—that criminal justice is unjust because it is excessively harsh to convicted offenders and provides insufficient *due process* safeguards to suspects and defendants—and those who take the opposite view that it is leniency and excessively scrupulous concern for due process that is the problem. To some extent cutting across these opposed viewpoints are different concerns, such as that the system is unfair to particular sections of the population (see, for example, the chapters by Walklate and Spalek in this volume) or insufficiently victim-friendly (see chapters by Williams and Hall and Johnstone in this volume).

This complex ideological context of the criminal justice crisis does not just make solving it difficult (if only for the obvious reason that it is impossible to satisfy all the different constituencies who want contradictory things), but can also generate false solutions to some aspects of the crisis which have the effect of making other aspects, and the crisis as a whole, worse than ever. Thus, for example, the New Labour government which has been in power since 1997 has sought to assuage the crisis of legitimacy (and court electoral popularity) with policies intended to reassure the public that (in the words of Tony Blair's classic soundbite) the government is 'tough on crime and tough on the causes of crime'. The 'toughness' of both the rhetoric and many of the criminal justice policies of New Labour has contributed to a public atmosphere of 'law and order ideology' (or 'populist punitiveness') which has most crucially encouraged sentencers to imprison even greater numbers of offenders—predictably, but against the actual interests and wishes of a government that needs to manage the crisis of resources. This has—again predictably—not even improved the legitimacy of the system with those who might welcome such increased harshness, as their perceptions of unwarranted softness have remained by and large undented. Indeed, these perceptions have even been exacerbated by some of the more pragmatic measures which the government has found necessary to deal with the crisis, notably new forms of *early release* from prison such as home detention curfew (early release with electronic tagging).

So where might criminal justice go from here, and what effect might there be on the crises of resources and legitimacy? We start by considering a few current and recent trends, before trying to project where they might lead us.

REVIEW QUESTIONS

1 Is it reasonable to talk of a current 'crisis' in criminal justice, or is such talk alarmist and melodramatic?

2 Explain what is meant by 'the crisis of resources' and 'the crisis of legitimacy'.

New penology, new punitiveness, or new humanism?

Two particular trends in criminal justice in recent years have been christened 'the new penology' and the 'new punitiveness'. Similar sounding names, but very different phenomena. Probably the most obvious trend has been the new punitiveness: a general increase in the harshness of punishment, noticeable in a wide variety of countries in the last few decades (Pratt *et al.*, 2005; Cavadino and Dignan, 2006). In recent years nearly three quarters of all the countries in the world have seen increases in their rates of imprisonment (Walmsley, 2007). In many respects, this new harshness has been led by the United States, whose prison population and imprisonment rates are the highest in the world with over two million prisoners and an imprisonment rate of 738 per 100,000 in 2005 (compared with 148 in England and Wales (Walmsley, 2007)), and where numbers of prisoners have quintupled since the early 1970s. (The US has also effectively reintroduced and massively expanded its use of capital punishment since 1977, despite having carried out no executions between 1967 and 1977.) The United Kingdom, along with many other nations, has followed the lead of the US towards this 'new punitiveness', albeit without going anywhere like as far.

Associated with these harsher penal practices has been the 'law and order ideology' (or 'populist punitiveness') we mentioned earlier, as public and media discourse about crime has increasingly taken the form of urging tougher punishment as the appropriate response to crime. Populist policies and slogans, such as 'three strikes and you're out' sentences or 'zero tolerance', are manifestations of the new punitiveness. The result has been a very real and measurable increase in the amount of punishment meted out to offenders. The numbers of those going to prison have rocketed despite a significant *decrease* in crime (however measured) since the mid-1990s and no great increases in the numbers of offenders coming before the courts (Cavadino and Dignan, 2007a: 101). Non-custodial penalties have also become tougher, in what they entail, how they are enforced, and in the people they are imposed upon. Offenders who a decade ago might have received a fine are now likely to receive a more onerous 'community sentence'; those who might have received a community sentence are now more likely to be imprisoned; and those imprisoned face longer prison terms. The entire relationship between offences and sentences has been '*ratcheted up*' a gear (Morgan, 2003).

The 'new penology' on the other hand (Feeley and Simon, 1992: 452) is a rather different concept from the 'new punitiveness'. The 'new penology' is *managerial* in nature. This means that its main objective is efficient and effective management, of the crime problem on the one hand and of the criminal justice system on the other. Unlike the new punitiveness, it is not overly concerned about being harsh to offenders. On the other hand, nor is it concerned about being lenient or humanitarian, whether to offenders, suspects, or victims of crime. It seeks to manage the problems of crime and criminal justice in particular kinds of ways, which contrast with some older strategies. Rather than trying to reform and treat offenders so that their characters improve and they do not re-offend, the new penology 'is concerned with techniques to identify, classify, and manage groupings sorted by *dangerousness*' (Feeley and Simon, 1992: 452). Such techniques include statistical methods of carrying out 'risk assessments' of offenders, and applying new tools of *offender management* (for example, electronic surveillance and monitoring) based on the outcome of such assessments. There is a lot of bureaucracy associated with the new penology.

These trends (along with some other parallel developments) have been notably analysed and explained by David Garland (2001; see also Cavadino and Dignan, 2006: 46–8) as an emerging punitive 'culture of control', related to long-term changes in society including a rise in crime leading to an alteration in attitudes towards offenders. Others have claimed that we are witnessing a transition out of the 'modern age' (including importantly the 'modernist' project of reforming offenders) towards a 'postmodern penality' with rather different concerns (for example Pratt, 2000).

But as well as this mixture (whatever we choose to call it) of increased punitiveness and an increasing interest in applying managerial techniques to criminal justice, there have been other developments which seem different again. The most notable of these developments has been the rise of interest in *restorative justice* (see the chapter by Johnstone in this volume). True, some practitioners and politicians have expressed interest in restorative justice in an almost managerial way, viewing it as no more than one effective method of controlling crime and running criminal justice. But the ethos of the restorative justice movement and of most of its enthusiasts is built around a concern about the interests and rights of human citizens, their relationships with each other, and the communities they live in together. This concern outshines other considerations: human rights and interests are prioritized over the minimization of crime and of costs. Moreover, the restorative ethos flatly contradicts both the new punitiveness and the new penology in important respects. Restorative justice is seen as an *alternative* to punitiveness—far from being more punitive towards offenders, we should seek reconciliation and forgiveness. And far from bureaucratically managing offenders as the new penology does—treating them as objects to be administered in a neutral manner—restorative justice insists that we should engage with them as human subjects, forging and restoring our human relationships with them. Thus, restorative justice can be seen as an aspect of a third kind of recent and current development, a *new humanism*. (Others who take a humanistic and humanitarian approach take a rather different track, preferring to attempt the *rehabilitation* of offenders rather than *restoration*.) The new humanism may be a weaker trend than the new punitiveness and the new penology, but the counter-current is there.

Judge Dredd: A punitive dystopia?

As we have seen, one path that we have been treading lately is the path of increasing punitiveness. Perhaps we will simply carry on further down that road? It is not unimaginable, and the prospect would be attractive to many. Certainly there is much in the realm of politics which encourages policy-makers in the direction of a crowd-pleasing 'toughness' which appeals to common sense and populist sentiment. To take just one example—chosen purely because it was published as this chapter was being written—a 2007 'mini-manifesto' on crime from the Conservative Opposition called for 'zero tolerance' of low-level disorder, the end of some early release schemes for prisoners and a substantial prison building programme (Conservative Party, 2007). This followed a decade in which the New Labour government had itself built more prisons and planned even more, while also pursuing 'zero tolerance' of minor public disorder in the shape of its 'Respect Agenda' (Home Office, 2006)

Such a scenario projected sufficiently far into the future might see imprisonment rates in Britain rivalling or surpassing those currently found in the United States (which would mean at least quadrupling the present prison population). Sentencing would be further ratcheted up, with more and more offenders going to prison for longer and longer. More offenders would spend the rest of their lives in prisons, while an increasing number of the rest would be subject to surveillance in the community on their release and the possibility of being recalled to prison at any time on the slightest pretence as a justification. Non-custodial penalties would also become even more controlling and punitive. And what about the logical extreme of reintroducing capital punishment? Admittedly this would require withdrawal from (or amendment of) the European Convention on Human Rights, which under current arrangements would in turn require leaving the European Union, but it is a logical possibility.

A further ratcheting up of punitiveness would doubtless avail itself of new technological opportunities to make penalties more tightly controlling, for example developing increasingly intrusive and perhaps even increasingly effective surveillance of offenders in the community, whether as a penalty in itself or following release from custody (for the diminishing number of prisoners who eventually made it back out).

How would the ultra-punitive society operate with those who have not yet been found guilty of a crime? The authoritarian mindset of 'law and order ideology' would get tougher with suspects and defendants as well, with traditional notions of 'due process' taking a poor second place (if that) to the perceived needs of *crime control*. Without even looking into the future it is already possible to see due process suffering a death by a thousand cuts, whether we consider the police powers to stop and search citizens introduced in the Police and Criminal Evidence Act 1984 and progressively extended thereafter, or ever-longer powers to detain suspected terrorists. The presumption of innocence, which places the burden on the state to prove the guilt of the individual, is already coming into question and being eroded (see chapter by Hucklesby in this volume). Examples are to be found in New Labour's 'Respect Agenda', mostly concerned with repressing petty anti-social behaviour. Launching a 'Respect Action Plan' in 2006, then Prime Minister Tony Blair admitted, or rather boasted, that his proposals to extend the powers of the police to issue summary fixed penalty notices (or 'on the spot fines') and to seize the suspected proceeds of drug dealing in the street would *'bluntly, reverse the burden of proof'*—because he regarded the traditional criminal process as being *'simply too cumbersome, too remote from reality, to be effective'* in dealing with the problems of modern crime. Nor was this approach to be confined to low-level anti-social behaviour, as Mr Blair made clear that it would soon be applied also in creating new powers to deal with serious and organized crime (Blair, 2006).

Indeed, even those who are not (yet) suspected of any crime will be subjected to ever more intrusive control and surveillance in this particular emerging dystopia. Individuals may already be stopped and searched despite there being no grounds for suspicion, under laws aimed at terrorism and the carrying of weapons (Terrorism Act 2000, s. 44 and the Criminal Justice and Public Order Act 1994, s. 60). Information about the lives and behaviour of citizens generally is, at least potentially, becoming progressively available to the state by means such as CCTV, biometric identification, and computerized data-bases (for example the national DNA database), with the government currently planning to introduce compulsory identity cards for all. All of this is again legitimized by law and order ideology: although many observers doubt how useful such intrusion really is in controlling crime let alone whether it is worth it, advocates again prioritize the alleged crime control benefits of such measures above everything. Indeed, the downsides—in terms of loss of privacy, potential for abuse, and even the misery likely to be caused to individuals by the simple malfunctioning of such systems leading to false information being used against them—are often not even acknowledged, or brushed aside with the simplistic assertion that the innocent have nothing to fear. Increasingly, according to many observers (most notably Simon, 2007), we are being *'governed through crime'*, with governments exploiting fear of crime (and especially terrorism) to increase the might of the state and erode traditional civil liberties.

Taking this scenario to its ultimate might involve compulsory continuous surveil-lance of everyone at all times by means such as CCTV and electronic tags. Indeed, we could all be compulsorily fitted with microchips which would allow all our movements to be constantly monitored; the chips could even be programmed to allow or deny us access to the buildings or locations deemed appropriate by the authorities (Ramesh, 1997). Naturally, everyone's DNA would be permanently on file. The powers that the police have over ordinary citizens would also be massively increased, as would the equip-ment (including weaponry) routinely available to them. (Since the police have already evolved from being largely composed of foot-patrolling bobbies just armed with whistle, notebook, and truncheon to a motorized force bristling with radios, sophisticated computers and communications equipment, tasers, body armour, and often firearms, further moves in this direction are only to be expected.)

The kind of society which would ensue could variously be described as a police state, or 'Orwellian'. Or perhaps an equally good model can be found in the comic strip character Judge Dredd—a law enforcement officer of the future equipped with deadly technology, empowered to mete out extreme and summary sanctions on the street without so much as a 'You do not have to say anything...' (although as we recall, a battle cry of 'I Am The Law!' was regarded as good etiquette). This scenario has much in common with the 'Dispersal of Discipline' theory put forward by Stanley Cohen (1979), that *social control* is increasingly being 'dispersed' outwards from the prison (see Mair in this volume). Whereas in the past, formal social control by the state was concentrated on criminals being held inside prisons, it is now being increasingly 'dispersed' outwards throughout society. Once it was just prisoners who were subject to surveillance and had their movements and behaviour constantly observed and regulated, but no longer: soon we will all be prisoners, whether or not we are physically behind bars.

How likely are we to reach this extreme? We have already mentioned some recent and current moves in this direction, and some of the forces encouraging those moves. In particular, introducing such measures can seem a good idea, not only as likely to assist in controlling crime, but also as a promising response to the crisis of legitimacy affecting criminal justice currently. As we have seen, one important aspect of this crisis is the widespread feeling that criminal justice is ineffective exactly because it is too liberal, too concerned with the rights of criminals and of people who are quite likely to be criminals (defendants, suspects, people the police would like to search in the street, and so on). Authoritarian toughness carries the promise of crime reduction for the populace and popularity for politicians.

There are, however, reasons to believe that such a strategy would be unlikely to meet with total success. Firstly, how would it affect the crisis of legitimacy? Yes, many people would approve of a greater punitiveness, at least in theory, but the harsher the system became the greater would be the likelihood of it appearing excessive to a greater number of people. It should be borne in mind that surveys indicate that public opinion is by no means as punitive as politicians normally seem to imagine (Cavadino and Dignan, 2007a: 388; Roberts and Hough, 2005; see also the ICM poll reported in *The Guardian*, 28 August 2007). Thus accelerating punitiveness would risk creating a public opinion backlash which would exacerbate rather than alleviate the legitimacy crisis. Even those who remained of the opinion that more harshness is called for would be unlikely to be pacified, however tough the system got: there would still be complaints about its ineffectiveness, which some would continue to put down to excessive leniency. Populist punitiveness is a ravenous beast which is never satisfied however much red meat it is thrown: it always demands more. 'Just don't feed it at all' might be the wisest advice.

If such might be the effect on the system's legitimacy with the general public, even worse would be the effect on the minds and hearts on the increasing number of citizens who would find themselves in receipt of harsh treatment from the criminal justice system and whose sense of injustice would be exacerbated as a result, as would that of many of the practitioners on whose work the system depends. All in all, this scenario's promise on the legitimacy front is starting to look highly dubious.

But probably even more catastrophic would be the effects on the crisis of resources. Almost all the extra punishment inflicted under this scenario would come at a huge extra cost, which would not only put pressure on the exchequer but also place additional intolerable strain on the resources and operation of the criminal justice system itself. We could predict extreme delays, overloads, and horrendous errors and failures in the system, probably leading to prison riots, escapes, and disastrous lapses in security, supervision, and surveillance. And, incidentally, such a massive overkill of punishment would do little to control crime (see for example Cavadino *et al.*, 1999: 37–40; Cavadino and Dignan, 2007a: 37–43, 382–3). There are already some signs that many American states are beginning to draw back from their current harsh sentencing policies, a development partly driven by the inevitable budgetary problems which these policies cause (King, 2007). This is not to say that this scenario could not come to pass, but a wise society and its policy-makers would hopefully draw back from the brink.

REVIEW QUESTIONS

1 What are the main features of the 'Judge Dredd' scenario?

2 How plausible do you find this scenario? Why?

Technocop: a brave new world of rational crime control?

A different route into the future might be suggested by 'the new penology' we discussed earlier. Perhaps criminal justice will become more efficient and effective because rational managerial techniques and technological innovations will be applied systematically, on the basis of scientific research about what works to control crime. Thus, where it has been found that, for example, CCTV or biometric ID methods are effective (and cost-effective) in cutting crime, such methods will be applied. Similarly, methods to treat and train offenders into law-abiding ways, or to quantify the risks of individuals or groups of people committing crimes and to exercise effective control over those most *at risk* will be researched and evaluated, and then applied (or discarded) accordingly. As time goes on, the effectiveness of the criminal justice system should progressively improve. The crisis of resources could in theory be solved by this approach, because only cost-effective measures would be deployed. For example, scientific developments such as electronic monitoring could mean that offenders were subject to effective surveillance without the use of expensive prisons—*technological decarceration*. At the same time, crime would be well controlled, thus reducing the workload of the criminal justice system. And the system could be made legitimate, because it would be clear how well and efficiently it protected the public from crime.

Sounds good, so where's the catch? Indeed, since criminal justice practitioners and policy-makers have been seeking to improve the system's effectiveness and efficiency over many decades, nay centuries, why has it not already happened? Why have we not already seen criminal justice make huge strides in efficiency and effectiveness, rather than becoming increasingly and hugely expensive, and seemingly incapable of controlling crime? There are two main reasons, both of which would suggest that this brave new managerial world will continue to be unattainable. The first is that science is never that good. The second is that people are awkward.

Firstly, science is never that good. Despite decades of research, it is still not possible to predict with sufficient accuracy who will commit crimes (especially serious crimes) or to provide treatment or surveillance that will prevent them from doing so. A recent example illustrates one of these failings, the limitations of technology. Continuous electronic tracking of the whereabouts of offenders has long been canvassed as a method of providing 'prison without bars' for offenders (technological decarceration), including particularly persistent and even particularly dangerous criminals. Pilot schemes found, impressively, that the equipment on trial could pinpoint offenders' locations to within 2 to 10 metres—except, often, when they were inside, or there were tall buildings in the way of the signal. Moreover, it was always possible for offenders simply to remove their tracking devices. Even when the equipment worked, the scheme was often ineffective, as 58 per cent of the tracked offenders were recalled to prison or had their community penalty with the tracking requirement revoked (Shute, 2007). So technology can always (and often does) go wrong, or prove inadequate to the task, or it can have unforeseen adverse consequences, bringing in its wake ruinous expense and failure. But there are other, distinct reasons why science is not good enough to provide this brave new world; reasons which connect to the second problem, that people are awkward. All technology requires people to operate it, and, awkwardly, people can always make mistakes, or indeed deliberately misuse or misapply the technology. The people the technology is used upon are also awkward, in the sense of being often unpredictable and of limited malleability, so crimes cannot—probably can never—be adequately predicted or prevented by scientific means. Science will consequently not be able to deliver on its promises of cheap and popular crime control.

People are awkward in yet another relevant way: they will insist on having moral reactions and on being largely ruled by their moral instincts. The scientific approach is always likely to fall foul of this apparently incorrigible aspect of human nature. For one thing, this scenario depends on crime control measures being applied according to how well (science says) they *work*, which may bear no relation to what human moral instincts suggest about how we should react towards an offender or potential offender. Suppose, for example, that efficient crime control measures included giving murderers some rather pleasant therapy on the one hand, while subjecting some poor unfortunate who has not yet committed a crime (but who is predicted to be a future offender) to some serious deprivation of liberty combined with painful treatment. The deep-seated feeling that the punishment should bear some relation to the crime that has been committed means that such a system will struggle to achieve legitimacy, whether with the general public or with those who are more intimately affected by specific measures. Then again, the managerial approach would seek to streamline pre-trial and trial processes according to what was cheap, speedy, and efficient, which would be likely not only to erode or eliminate some traditional civil liberties (such as trial by jury) which many people are attached to, but also to give victims of crime short shrift. The fact that *managerialism* treats human beings as objects to be administered in a neutral, bureaucratic manner rather than as moral agents and people with feelings will always be a stumbling block. So the scientific approach will never be able to solve the crises of criminal justice—certainly not on its own—due to the imperfections of science and its lack of connection with the real emotions of human beings.

REVIEW QUESTIONS

1 What are the main features of the 'Technocop' scenario? How plausible do you find this scenario? Why?

2 What is 'technological decarceration'? Is it likely to happen?

Restoring the future?

What of the third strand of developments in criminal justice we noted earlier, towards a 'new humanism' exemplified by restorative justice? Could this presage a third type of future for criminal justice?

Again, it is perfectly possible to imagine such a future. Indeed, we can envisage a future criminal justice system which made maximum use of restorative measures and minimal use of punitive ones such as imprisonment—and which even made little use of courts (see Cavadino and Dignan, 2007a: 387–8). Most offences, certainly in cases where the offender admits some wrongdoing, could be dealt with by a local mediation service—often perhaps without even needing to involve the police, let alone the courts. A suitable 'restorative package' could be agreed between the offender and the victim and arranged by the local mediation service. Cases could still go to court if no suitable agreement was reached, if mediation was inappropriate, if either party refused mediation, or if the alleged offender denied that they were responsible. The most serious crimes would normally still go to court in any event. But even in these cases, the usual outcome could still be that the offender would be ordered to make *reparation* either to the victim or to the community generally, whether in the form of financial compensation, unpaid work, or anything else appropriate. People might stop automatically thinking in terms of punitive measures like imprisonment as the right sort of response to crimes, and instead might come to assume that some restorative solution would normally be found. Incarceration would still be a possibility, but would only be used where this was necessary to prevent genuinely danger-ous offenders from committing serious offences. Even then, the custodial regime should be geared towards respecting the prisoner's rights, giving them as much freedom as pos-sible, encouraging them to make reparation to their victims and to society, facilitating their voluntary rehabilitation, and securing their earliest possible release back into the community. It would look very different from the prison of today.

In terms of policing and criminal procedure the approach would again be one of respecting the rights of every individual to privacy and due process. Moves in the direc-tion of Judge Dredd-style policing would be resisted and maybe even reversed, with an emphasis on 'community policing', *partnership* between the police and community (with the community exercising democratic control over the police), and the strengthening of civil liberties. The old tradition of 'policing by consent' (rather than by coercion) would be revived. Technological advances in policing and criminal procedure (for example in the shape of improved forensic science techniques such as DNA testing) would not necessarily be opposed; indeed if they were likely to be effective in solving crimes and protecting innocent citizens from *miscarriages of justice* they would be welcomed. So might new technical devices which, for example, gave individuals access to view the records (such as CCTV images) which concern themselves. Similarly, managerial techniques which promised to improve the efficiency of criminal justice and assist in its democratization would also be welcomed, but all innovations would be vigilantly scrutinized to ensure that they were not abused to infringe civil liberties or incriminate the innocent. Managerialism and technology could therefore be employed to empower the citizenry rather than to objectify or enslave it.

How would such developments affect the crises of resources and legitimacy? Taking resources first, they would be highly economical. Most obviously, the prison population could be reduced to an absolute minimum, literally saving hundreds of millions of pounds per annum (at least). The use of mediation rather than police and courts would also be likely to bring about huge net financial savings. What of legitimacy? Here, it all depends. Restorative justice measures are known to be popular with victims and offenders, who tend to view them as fair responses to crime (Dignan, 2005: chap. 5; Sherman and Strang, 2007: 62). If the population at large could become equally convinced of the desirability and efficacy of such an approach to crime it could be highly successful in re-legitimizing the system. But this would mean that the public mindset would need to alter radically from its current 'love affair with custody' (Travis, 2003)—a massive cultural shift in society. How likely is this to occur?

How likely any of these possible futures turn out to be will not just depend on criminal justice, viewed in isolation from the rest of society (although that is how we have been looking at it so far). In our conclusion we will consider where society, as well as criminal justice, is going—for the two are intimately connected.

REVIEW QUESTIONS

1 What are the main features of the restorative/humanistic scenario? How plausible do you find this scenario? Why?

2 Could public opinion ever accept a criminal justice system which is significantly less punitive than that of the present day?

CONCLUSION

If we were being judgmental, we could say that societies get the crime and the criminal justice they deserve. At any rate, the crime and criminal justice they get is certainly related to the kind of societies they are. For example, as all societies develop, 'progress', and become more 'modern', they have a general tendency to become more regulated, more bureaucratic, more *managed*—a tendency famously noted by Max Weber (1968: chaps 3 and 11) long ago. It should not surprise us, then, that criminal justice systems have also tended to take on a more managerialist flavour over time: something like the 'new penology' could have been foreseen, and we can expect an even greater level of managerialism in the future in some form or another. But, as we have seen, this is unlikely to be able to progress to an extent that provides a technical fix for the problems of criminal justice, whether resource problems or legitimacy problems.

The growth of managerialism is a development that has been occurring across a wide range of societies. But in terms of their crime problems and of how punitive societies are—how much they lean in the direction of our punitive dystopia or our restorative future—it is possible to divide modern societies into certain useful categories. Many present-day countries can be usefully categorized as being *neo-liberal*, *corporatist*, or *social democratic* in their political economies, with more or less punitive criminal justice systems accordingly. '*Neo-liberalism*' refers to the free-market capitalism exemplified by the United States (and to a lesser extent Britain since the 1980s). Such countries have a generally *individualistic* culture in which people are expected to fail and succeed by their own unaided efforts; they have high levels of inequality and a relatively ungenerous welfare state. '*Corporatist*' countries (such as Germany and other nations in continental western Europe) have a *communitarian* culture in which the community is expected to look after all its citizens: there is less inequality and a more generous welfare state. '*Social democratic*' countries (such as Sweden and the other Nordic countries) combine this communitarianism with a greater degree of *egalitarianism*; here there is the least material inequality and the most generous welfare state. We also find that criminal justice has a different flavour in these different types of country, with (for example) the neo-liberal countries having the highest rates of imprisonment and the social democratic countries the lowest (Cavadino and Dignan, 2006). (The more unequal countries also tend to have the worst crime problems: see for example Ormerod, 1997; Wilkinson, 2005.)

This suggests that the future of criminal justice might largely depend on how society as a whole develops in terms of its political economy and culture. If we continue to move (as Britain has been doing) down the neo-liberal road, we might find ourselves getting closer to the world of Judge Dredd. Key factors here are *inequality* and the extent to which society seeks to *include* or *exclude* those (such as poor people and offenders) who find themselves outside its mainstream. In the Judge Dredd comics, the city of the future ('Mega-City One') was sharply, physically divided between the 'haves' and the 'have-nots', the latter comprising a literal '*underclass*' relegated to a super-ghetto area—impoverished, violent, and policed with an iron fist—located *underneath* the main city, with transit between the two sectors being very limited. Similarly, there has been a tendency in those societies which have been becoming increasingly neo-liberal for those with money and social status to physically segregate themselves as far as possible from the less fortunate; 'gated communities' are an obvious manifestation of this (see further Davis, 1994; Blandy, 2007). Corporatist societies do not generate the same degree of material inequality, while their communitarian culture militates against this sort of exclusion of large sections of the population. Social democracies are even less unequal, while their cultures are not only communitarian but also value the civil liberties of individuals highly—so they will have the least tendency to go down the Judge Dredd road, and are likely to be most open to the restorative, humanistic approach to criminal justice.

It is also quite possible—indeed, quite likely—that the future will not simply follow a single one of these three scenarios. Perhaps we will get a mixture of the three, as the state tries a bit of everything to manage the problems of crime and criminal justice. Maybe, for example, there will be an increased amount of new technology and managerialism combined with a more informal, restorative approach for minor offending and juveniles, but alongside a tougher and more punitive regime for adult offenders. The future remains open, but it is ours to make. And it depends, crucially, on what sort of society we want to live in, and on how we choose to treat our fellow human beings.

QUESTIONS FOR DISCUSSION

1 Which, if any, of the three possible futures put forward for criminal justice in this chapter do you prefer? Which do you like least? Why?

2 Does this chapter provide a fair analysis of the different options for criminal justice in the future? Does it leave out any important possibilities?

3 Might criminal justice in the future hold a mixed picture, with some elements of two or all three of these scenarios? If so, what might it look like? Would this be a good option to pursue?

4 Why might the shape of criminal justice be related to the general political economy and culture of society?

5 'The onward march of neo-liberal economics is unstoppable. Equally unstoppable, therefore, is a continued rise in punitiveness.' Discuss.

6 If a country wished to change the direction of its criminal justice policies, does it follow from what we have said that it would first need to change the nature of its culture and political economy?

GUIDE TO FURTHER READING

Criminologists are not usually so rash as to try to predict the future of criminal justice. One classic and splendid exception is Stan Cohen's 'The Punitive City: Notes on the Dispersal of Social Control' (1979, *Contemporary Crises*, 3: 339–63), which puts forward his 'dispersal of discipline' theory, mentioned above in the 'Judge Dredd' section. (The paper is still, however, more about current trends than about predicting the future.) Mike Davis's much-cited *Beyond Blade Runner: Urban Control—The Ecology of Fear* (1994, Open Magazine Pamphlet Series, Pamphlet 23, New York: The New Press) paints a picture of how fear of crime might reshape the city of the future, but with relatively little reference to criminal justice as such.

Now it's time to plug our own products. M. Cavadino and J. Dignan's *The Penal System: An Introduction* (4th edn, 2007, London: Sage, chaps 1 and 11) discusses the current 'penal crisis' and how it has been and could be tackled, while our *Penal Systems: A Comparative Approach* (2006, London: Sage) shows by comparing 12 different countries how criminal justice is related to a society's culture and political economy.

For discussions of the 'new punitiveness', the 'new penology' and the 'culture of control' respectively, see J. Pratt, D. Brown, S. Hallsworth, M. Brown, and W. Morrison (eds) *The New Punitiveness: Trends, Theories, Perspectives* (2005, Cullompton: Willan); M. Feeley and J. Simon, 'The New Penology' (1992, *Criminology*, 39: 449–740); and D. Garland's *The Culture of Control: Crime and Social Order in Contemporary Society* (2001, Oxford: Oxford University Press). See also on the 'culture of control' Jonathan Simon's *Governing through Crime: How the War on Crime Transformed American Democracy and Created a Culture of Fear* (2007, Oxford: Oxford University Press).

And if you ever come across any Judge Dredd comics, read them too. Then send them to us.

WEB LINKS

As yet we do not know of many good web links to the future. However, the following sites may be of interest, albeit mostly in providing information about the present day:

CrimLinks

http://www.crimlinks.com/

A general portal which provides access to a wide range of key online source materials and sites.

Centre for Criminal Justice Studies at King's College London

http://www.crimeandjustice.org.uk/

Rethinking Crime and Punishment

http://www.rethinking.org.uk

Restorative Justice Online

http://www.restorativejustice.org/

A useful first port of call on restorative justice matters.

RJ City

http://www.rjcity.org/

A quasi-futuristic website dedicated to imagining how a community would operate if it adopted a fully restorative approach to offending.

REFERENCES

Blair, T. (2006) *The Respect Action Plan 2006*, Speech 10 January 2006.

Blandy, S. (2007) 'Gated Communities in England as a Response to Crime and Disorder: Context, Effectiveness and Implications'. *People, Places and Policy Online* 1/2: 47–54. Available online at: <http://extra.shu.ac.uk/ppp-online/issue_2_100907/documents/gated_communities_england_crime_disorder.pdf>.

Bottoms, A.E. (1980) 'An Introduction to "The Coming Crisis"' in A.E. Bottoms and R.H. Preston (eds) *The Coming Penal Crisis: A Criminological and Theological Exploration*. Edinburgh: Scottish Academic Press, 1–24.

Bottoms, A.E. (1983) 'Neglected Features of Contemporary Penal Systems' in D. Garland and P. Young (eds) *The Power to Punish: Contemporary Penality and Social Analysis*. London: Heinemann, 166–202.

Bottoms, A.E. and Preston, R.H. (eds) (1980), *The Coming Penal Crisis: A Criminological and Theological Exploration*. Edinburgh: Scottish Academic Press.

Cavadino, M. (1994) 'The UK Penal Crisis: Where Next?' in A. Duff, S. Marshall, R.E. Dobash, and R.P. Dobash (eds) *Penal Theory and Penal Practice: Tradition and Innovation in Criminal Justice*. Manchester: Manchester University Press, 42–56.

Cavadino, M. and Dignan, J. (with others) (2006) *Penal Systems: A Comparative Approach*. London: Sage.

Cavadino, M., Crow, I., and Dignan, J. (1999) *Criminal Justice 2000*. Winchester: Waterside Press.

Cavadino, M. and Dignan, J. (2007a) *The Penal System: An Introduction* (4th edn). London: Sage.

Cavadino, M. and Dignan, J. (2007b) 'The Penal Crisis' in Y. Jewkes and J. Bennett (eds) *Dictionary of Prisons and Punishment*. Cullompton: Willan Publishing, 200–2.

Cohen, S. (1979) 'The Punitive City: Notes on the Dispersal of Social Control'. *Contemporary Crises* 3: 339–63.

Conservative Party (2007) *It's Time to Fight Back: How a Conservative Government Will Tackle Britain's Crime Crisis*. London: Conservative Party.

Davis, M. (1994) *Beyond Blade Runner: Urban Control—The Ecology of Fear*. Open Magazine Pamphlet Series, Pamphlet 23. New York: The New Press.

Dignan, J. (2005) *Understanding Victims and Restorative Justice*. Maidenhead: Open University Press.

Feeley, M. and Simon, J. (1992) 'The New Penology'. *Criminology* 39: 449–74.

Garland, D. (2001) *The Culture of Control: Crime and Social Order in Contemporary Society*. Oxford: Oxford University Press.

H.M. Prison Service (2007) *Population Bulletins—Monthly June and September 2007.* Available online at: <http://www.hmprisonservice.gov.uk/resourcecentre/publicationsdocuments/index.asp?cat=85>.

H.M. Prison Service (2008), *Population Bulletin—Weekly 29 February 2008*. Available online at: <http://www.hmprisonservice.gov.uk/resourcecentre/publicationsdocuments/index.asp?cat=85>.

Home Office (2006) *Respect Action Plan*. London: Home Office. Available online at: <http://www.respect.gov.uk/>.

King, R.S. (2007) 'Changing Direction: State Sentencing Reforms 2004–2006'. Available online from the Sentencing Project at: <http://www.sentencingproject.org/PublicationDetails.aspx?PublicationID=579>.

Morgan, R. (2003) 'Thinking about the Demand for Probation Services'. *Probation Journal* 50: 7.

Ormerod, P. (1997) 'Stopping Crime Spreading'. *New Economy* 4: 83–8.

Pratt, J. (2000) 'The Return of the Wheelbarrow Men: or, The Arrival of Postmodern Penality'. *British Journal of Criminology* 40: 127–45.

Pratt, J., Brown, D., Hallsworth, S., Brown, M., and Morrison, W. (eds) (2005) *The New Punitiveness: Trends, Theories, Perspectives*. Cullompton: Willan Publishing.

Ramesh, E.M. (1997) 'Time Enough? Consequences of Human Microchip Implantation' *Risk* 8: 373. Available online at: <http://www.fplc.edu/risk/vol8/fall/ramesh.htm>.

Roberts, J.V. and Hough, M. (2005) *Understanding Public Attitudes to Criminal Justice*. Maidenhead: Open University Press.

Robinson, G. (2005) 'What Works in Offender Management?' *Howard Journal of Criminal Justice* 44: 307–18.

Sherman, L.W. and Strang, H. (2007) *Restorative Justice: The Evidence*. London: The Smith Institute.

Shute, S. (2007) *Satellite Tracking of Offenders: A Study of the Pilots in England and Wales*. Research Summary 4. London: Ministry of Justice. Available online at: http://www.justice.gov.uk/publications/research020807a.htm.

Simon, J. (2007) *Governing through Crime: How the War on Crime Transformed American Democracy and Created a Culture of Fear*. Oxford: Oxford University Press.

Travis, A. (2003) 'Courts Send Record Numbers to Prison'. *Guardian*, 29 December 2003.

Walmsley, R. (2007) *World Prison Population List* (7th edn). London: International Centre for Prison Studies, King's College London. Available online at: <http://www.kcl.ac.uk/depsta/law/research/icps/downloads.php?search.title=world+prison&type=0&month=0&year=0&lang=0&author=&search=search>.

Weber, M. (1968) *Economy and Society*. New York: Bedminster Press.

Wilkinson, R. (2005) *The Impact of Inequality: How to Make Sick Societies Healthier*. London: Routledge.

Woolf, H. and Tumim, S. (1991) *Prison Disturbances April 1990* Cm 1456. London: HMSO.

Abolitionism is a theoretical and political perspective which holds that the penal system creates social problems rather than providing solutions. Abolitionists call for new understandings of social harms and radically alternative social policies.

Aggravation an aggravating factor is one which makes the offence more serious than usual and which usually leads to a more severe sentence being imposed. An example would be where the victim was particularly vulnerable.

Antecedents are previous convictions or cautions.

'At risk' are assumptions made about particular sections of the population based on the statistical probability of their becoming offenders and/or victims in the future.

Attorney-General is the Chief Legal Advisor to the Crown in England and Wales. The Attorney-General has the right to challenge unduly lenient sentences in certain circumstances.

Attrition rate refers to the proportion of cases which do not end in a conviction or caution because they drop out of the criminal justice process at various points. For example, when the Crown Prosecution Service decide that there is no case to answer. The attrition rate is high and results in between two and three per cent of offences ending up with a conviction.

Belfast/Good Friday Agreement was the constitutional settlement signed by the majority of Northern Ireland's political parties in 1998. It established the basis for a return to devolved government in Northern Ireland.

Bridewell was a type of prison that emerged in England in the sixteenth century. The first Bridewell was the adapted Bridewell palace, hence the name. These prisons were used as places for short periods of detention, often for petty offenders, and were also known as houses of correction.

The British Crime Survey is a national crime survey that is carried out in England and Wales every year by the Home Office. The British Crime Survey explores levels of crime reporting to the police, why people do not always report incidents and what types of incidents tend not to be reported. The British Crime Survey also focuses upon attitudes to the police, the criminal justice system and sentencing and individuals' fear of crime.

Capitalist state is the institutional and relational means through which political, economic, and coercive power is exercised and consent is secured in capitalist societies.

Community safety is a politically progressive variant of crime prevention. Community safety offers a holistic approach to preventing crime that combines social and situational approaches. Its object of concern—safety—is also potentially broader than crime, encompassing a range of hazards (e.g. discrimination, pollution, social exclusion) that may threaten safety and security, more broadly conceived. In practice, particularly because community safety partnerships are heavily funded by criminal justice-related bodies such as the Home Office, it is crime that tends to dominate their agendas.

Conferencing is an informal process in which a third person helps the people affected directly by crime—victims, offenders, and close contacts of both—to have constructive dialogue about what happened and reach a mutually acceptable plan for repairing harm.

Contestability is a term that first appeared in the Carter Report (2003) and which is synonymous with competition. Carter argued that the private, voluntary and public sectors—or mixed consortia involving more than one sector—should compete to provide services for offenders. Contestability is expected to lead to innovation, better integration of services and cost savings.

Consequentialism is a philosophical approach where current actions and policies are justified through their [positive] future consequences.

Convict prisons were operated by the government and held prisoners who were sentenced to longer periods of imprisonment (then known as penal servitude). The convict system was set up after the decline and then end of transportation of offenders to the colonies.

Crime refers to any action which breaks the laws laid down by a political authority, although crimes can also be committed by those authorities. Every crime is deviant, but not every deviant act is criminal.

Crime and Disorder Reduction Partnerships are a statutory requirement of the Crime and Disorder Act 1998 that bring together a range of local agencies (e.g. police, local authority, fire service, health) to promote a coordinated and holistic response to community safety.

Crime Control is a model of criminal justice which prioritises convicting the guilty over protecting the innocent in which criminal justice professionals are trusted to ensure that the correct individuals are convicted. Suspects' and defendants' rights are seen as barriers to ensuring that the guilty are convicted.

Crime facilitators is a concept used by proponents of situational crime prevention. Put simply, it is more likely that a crime will be committed if there are external facilitators available to the potential offender, such as physical items (e.g. glass bottles in nightclubs) or chemical substances (e.g. alcohol). Where possible, proponents of situational crime prevention seek the removal or control of crime facilitators.

Crime reduction is a variant of crime prevention that valorises demonstrable performance. Crime prevention is difficult to measure because the phenomenon of a prevented crime is a non-event. By contrast, crime reduction uses crime data, particularly police crime statistics, to seek demonstrable reductions in crime figures in specific places, or indeed nationally. Perhaps paradoxically, crime reduction can be achieved by measures not normally considered as measures of crime prevention, including traditional criminal justice responses, such as arrest and conviction.

Criminal Courts are places where criminal cases are heard. They include the magistrates' court, Crown Court, and Courts of Appeal.

Criminal Justice Review was the Northern Ireland Criminal Justice Review which was established by the Belfast/Good Friday Agreement in 1998 to examine the operation of criminal justice in Northern Ireland and to make recommendations for reform.

Criminal Trial is any hearing in a criminal court whose purpose is to determine the guilt or innocence of an accused person.

Crisis of Legitimacy is the crisis in criminal justice caused by the widespread feeling that the system lacks legitimacy, i.e. moral acceptability.

Crisis of Resources is the crisis in criminal justice caused by the scarcity of material resources for running the system, including staff, money, buildings, and equipment.

Dangerousness is a social and historical construction used to refer to a number of different groups of defendants and offenders who may pose a risk to the public including those with mental health problems.

Defensible space is a concept associated with the work of Oscar Newman, whose empirical research showed a correlation between certain design characteristics, such as high-rise buildings, and crime rates. Having identified design characteristics that were positively correlated with high crime levels, Newman developed his theory of defensible space to show that crime could be 'designed out' by following a set of principles—such as the privatisation of 'unowned' public spaces—that in their application would either remove these criminogenic design characteristics, or mitigate their effects.

Deterrence is the philosophical justification of punishment that aims to prevent future law breaking through efficient and effective penal sanctions. Deterrence may be directed at individual offenders (specific deterrence) or others (general deterrence).

Devolution is the process by which a national body delegates or distributes powers to a local or regional body.

Direct victims are usually the most immediate and clear victims of a criminal offence, often suffering the most appreciable impacts. Direct victims include, for example, the owner of stolen property or someone suffering injuries or trauma as a result of a violent attack.

Discretion is the latitude which criminal justice professionals have to use their judgement to decide what action to take or decision to make in any given situation.

Divided Society is the term used in the literature to refer to a society like Northern Ireland that is fractured to a dysfunctional extent along a particular cleavage or cleavages. All societies are, however, divided to some extent along the lines of social class, race/ethnicity, gender, and so on.

Domestic violence is officially 'an incident of threatening behaviour, violence or abuse (psychological, sexual, financial or emotional) between adults who are or have been intimate partners or family members, regardless of gender or sexuality' (Home Office, 2005a). The scope of 'domestic violence' is greatly debated.

Due Process is a model of criminal justice which ensures that suspects' and defendants' are protected from the power of the state and that individuals are convicted only if the investigation and prosecution conforms to legal rules and procedures. Due process safeguards include the right to a fair trial and the presumption of innocence.

Early Release is the practice of prisoners leaving prison early—i.e. before the formal end of the custodial sentence which the court had imposed. It has a long history in penal policy. Initially, in the nineteenth century, it was introduced as a means of improving prison discipline—the prospect of early release was held out to prisoners as an incentive to good behavior while they were incarcerated. This rationale can still apply, but increasingly, from the latter part of the twentieth century onwards, early release has been used as a 'safety valve' to reduce pressure on overcrowded prisons (and on hard-pressed prison staff). Most forms of early release entail supervision in the community in the immediate post-release period, but remain controversial because it can appear that 'the executive' (prison managers and government) are undermining the traditional role of 'the judiciary' to set sentence length. Various mechanisms have been used to facilitate early release, including parole and, more recently, the use of electronic monitoring.

Extended Policing Family refers to the range of public and private agencies, including police, municipal authorities, and commercial policing, that undertake policing and security-related activities in local communities.

Femininity are the socio-cultural values expected of women.

Fortress society is a dystopian concept that describes a society where situational crime prevention measures of surveillance and target hardening are taken too far, evidenced by a proliferation of CCTV cameras, impenetrable walls and fences, razor wire and so forth. In such a society, there is a generalised suspicion and mistrust that militates against social cohesion. Thus, fortress societies are also divided societies, where 'us' (typically those who can afford to protect themselves) are protected from 'them' (typically the urban poor who are regarded as a threat to safety) by various means of physical exclusion.

Futurology is the enterprise of trying to predict the future by scientific or quasi-scientific means.

Gaols are prisons with a long history which held prisoners until trial, sentence or punishment was carried out.

Gender is socially ascribed qualities associated with being male or female.

Globalisation is a general term that summarises important social changes in the late-twentieth century. In particular it has an economic component that draws attention to the increasingly transnational nature of capitalist enterprise, as multinational corporations are able to move their businesses around the globe to places where the costs of production, particularly wages, are most favourable. This has hastened economic decline in many developed countries as old industries have collapsed, and has prompted nation states to reduce taxes and public spending in order to remain 'competitive' in the global economy. Culturally, developments in transport and communications have effectively shrunken the world, encouraging population movements that have radically altered the ethnic profile of urban areas, and facilitating cultural influences that bypass more traditional local structures such as family and community. One overall effect of this is taken to be an insecurity that may be translated into the fear of crime, and

the 'othering' of particular identity groups, such as youths or ethnic minorities.

Hard labour, hard board, hard fare was a deterrent philosophy of punishment used in prisons from 1865 until the beginning of twentieth century. The regime denotes harsh living conditions, minimal food, and long hours of hard labour.

Hate Crime is any criminal offence committed against a person or property that is motivated by an offender's hatred of someone because of their 'race', ethnic origin, religion, gender, sexual orientation and disability' (Home Office, 2007). In Britain, the Crime and Disorder Act 1998 and provisions made under the Anti-Terrorism Crime and Security Act 2001 and the Criminal Justice Act 2003 can be considered to be 'hate crime' legislation.

Heterosexism is the normalisation of heterosexuality, through institutional practices, serving to delegitimise other expressions and forms of sexuality.

Home Office is the government department responsible for the police, crime, anti-social behaviour, drugs policy, anti-terrorism and immigration. Prior to the creation of the Ministry of Justice in May 2007 it was also responsible for prisons, probation and criminal justice policy generally.

Home Secretary is the Secretary of State (i.e. the senior minister) in charge of the Home Office.

Hotspots are geographic areas where crime is concentrated. The identification of crime hotspots has been greatly assisted by technological advances, particularly in geographic information systems that allow the precise electronic plotting of crimes and their temporal analysis. Rather than being applied generally, much crime prevention practice concentrates on tackling crime hotspots, because such hotspots show where the risk of crime is greatest, and it is against such hotspots that the greatest impact on crime can be made (and measured).

House of correction is another term for bridewell.

Ideal victim was coined by Dutch victimologist Nils Christie (1986) to describe the characteristics attributed by society to 'worthy' victims of crime. Generally such victims are entirely blameless, vulnerable, and have impeccable characters. The concept has been drawn on by many commentators arguing that policies ostensibly aimed at all victims often seem to benefit ideal victims, especially as the research increasingly reveals that a large proportion of victims do not meet such criteria (Dignan, 2005).

'In need' are assumptions made about (typically child) offending which stress vulnerability and limited capacity and thereby the necessity of responding to offending through welfare and support, rather than punishment.

Incapacitation A philosophical justification of punishment that calls for the removal of offenders' physical capacity to offend.

The Independent Police Complaints Commission is a non-departmental public body which has responsibility for overseeing the system of police complaints that covers the 43 police forces of England and Wales, and other 'non-territorial' police forces (e.g. British Transport Police, the Ministry of Defence Police, and the Serious and Organised Crime Agency).

Indeterminate sentence is a custodial sentence where the judge does not set a fixed term. The usual example is a life sentence but there is also a sentence of imprisonment for public protection designed for certain dangerous offenders. Instead of setting a fixed term the judge sets a period when offenders are eligible to be considered for release, although in some cases offenders will never be eligible for release.

Indirect victims are individuals who, whilst not enduring the immediate impacts of crime as with direct victims, nevertheless suffer other impacts which can be social, financial, psychological or physical. This group can include the friends and family of direct victims and local communities for example if their fear of crime is increased by the initial victimisation.

Informal Justice is a common aspect of conflict states which refers to a system of 'justice' that takes place in opposition to the formal state structures.

Institutional racism was defined by Macpherson (1999: para. 6.34) as 'the collective failure of an organisation to provide an appropriate and professional service to people because of their colour, culture, or ethnic origin. It can be seen or detected in processes, attitudes and behaviour which amount to discrimination through unwitting prejudice, ignorance, thoughtlessness and racist stereotyping which disadvantage minority ethnic people'.

Interface areas is a term used in Northern Ireland to refer to areas that contain a highly volatile population balance in ethno-national terms. For example, in North Belfast there are a number of nationalist/republican enclaves located within a much larger predominantly unionist/loyalist area.

Internment is the practice whereby individuals are arrested and held indefinitely—sometimes for years—without charge.

Irish Republican Army (IRA) is the largest nationalist paramilitary organization in Northern Ireland and a strong advocate of the use of violence to bring about a British

withdrawal. While the IRA targeted police and military personnel it was nevertheless responsible for the largest number of civilian deaths during the conflict. The IRA called a ceasefire in 1994 which temporarily broke down between 1995 and 1997. The ceasefire was reinstated in 1997, with the organization formally ending its 'military' campaign in 2005.

Jurisdiction is the legal power as constituted and practiced within a particular nation.

Just deserts An approach to sentencing that is tied to the philosophical justification of retribution. Offenders receive the punishment they deserve by receiving a sentence that is proportionate to the seriousness of the offence(s) committed. The Criminal Justice Act 1991 introduced a just deserts sentencing framework in England and Wales that remains at the heart of sentencing today.

Justice by Geography is the term used to describe variations in decisions made by criminal justice agencies and institutions according to geographic area.

Labelling Theory is a sociological perspective that refers to the social processes by which an individual becomes categorised as 'deviant'; in a self-fulfilling way, however, this process tends to reinforce the very behaviour that initially led to the application of the label 'deviant'.

Law and Order Ideology is a set of attitudes including the beliefs that people must be strictly disciplined by restrictive rules, and that they should be harshly punished if they break the rules.

Legislation is the body of laws that comprise the legal system of a nation.

Legitimacy is the normative and political justifications and acceptability for the exercise of power and authority. It relates to perceptions of justness and fairness.

Less eligibility is the principle originating in the nineteenth century that argues that conditions in prison should be materially worse than the worst conditions for free honest poor people in the community, for example, prisoners should have less food and more limited access to medical care.

Liquid times or liquid modernity is Zygmunt Bauman's distinctive term for the socio-cultural configuration in which contemporary people live. The metaphor of 'liquidity' denotes a situation of constant organizational change, transient cultural reference points, and uncertain moral norms, in which there are few stable and reliable structures by which people can orient their lives for a sustained period of time.

Local prison has been used since the Prison Act 1865 as a collective name for gaols, houses of correction and bridewells to distinguish them from convict prisons. Until 1877 local prisons were run by local authorities but they were then taken over by the government. Local prisons held offenders sentenced to periods of imprisonment that were two years or less.

The Lord Chancellor is the government minister who has responsibility for the administration of justice and is also the Secretary of State for Justice (in charge of the Ministry of Justice).

Loyalist/s wish to maintain the constitutional link with Great Britain, but many advocate the use of violence to achieve this goal. They are associated with the activities of paramilitary organizations such as the Ulster Volunteer Force (UVF).

Managerialism is the application of private sector practices to the public sector which involves attempts to increase 'economy, efficiency and effectiveness'.

Mandatory sentence is a punishment for a particular offence which is fixed by law. The most famous example is life imprisonment for murder. There has been a trend since the Crime (Sentences) Act 1997 to introduce more mandatory sentences for persistent offenders but, in the context of that Act, the judge does not have to impose the penalty if it would be unjust to do so.

Masculinity are socio-cultural values expected of men.

Ministry of Justice is the government department responsible for the courts and much of the criminal justice system. It was created in May 2007, replacing the Department for Constitutional Affairs and assuming many responsibilities previously belonging to the Home Office.

Minority perspective is often applied to Black and minority ethnic groups, however, recent developments suggest that a more inclusive approach is being taken whereby groups in relation to gender, faith, sexual orientation, disability, and age are taken into consideration by researchers and policy makers. The development of a minority perspective might be defined as 'the inclusion, and focus upon, the lived experiences of minority groups' (Phillips and Bowling, 2003).

Miscarriages of Justice are cases in which individuals have been wrongly convicted of offences.

Mitigation makes the offence less serious than usual. It usually leads to a reduction in the sentence imposed. It is usually brought to the court's attention when the offender's lawyer submits a 'plea in mitigation'. An example of a mitigating factor would be that the offender surrendered to the police shortly after the offence.

Moral education is a non-punitive strategy that aims to provide a guide to right and wrong through exposing people to moral stories, media campaigns, and public education.

National Association of Probation Officers is a professional association which was formed in 1912, with the support of the Home Office, by the first generation of probation officers. It aimed to promote the interests of probation, especially among local committees of magistrates who were reluctant to appoint them. It subsequently became a trade union as well, and, historically, it was a major force in probation's development, only becoming a serious critic of Home Office policy in the 1970s.

National Policing Improvement Agency is a national policing body set up to enhance the performance of 43 police forces of England and Wales through the dissemination of good practice, sharing of expert knowledge and other mechanisms of strategic support.

National Offender Management Service (NOMS) was created in 2004 following a review of correctional services (Carter, 2003; Home Office, 2004). It brings together the work of the Prison and Probation Services as a new single service to oversee the management of offenders. The arguments in favour of closer working relationships between the two services are difficult to counter, but the politics of crime control and lack of resources mean that four years on (2008) the potential of NOMS remains unfulfilled.

Nationalist/s are generally, but not exclusively, associated with the Catholic community in Northern Ireland. It refers to those individuals who want Northern Ireland to become part of an all-Ireland Republic at some point in the future via democratic and constitutional means.

Neighbourhood policing is a style of policing that emphasises officers being dedicated to highly localised areas, thereby enabling them to engage the community and stakeholder agencies in the co-production of neighbourhood security.

Net widening is a term first used by Cohen (1985) to describe processes whereby attempts to prevent crime (for example targeting those considered a 'risk') act to expand the remit of justice agencies and draw more people into the reach of formal criminal justice intervention. For example, non-custodial sentences which aim to divert offenders from custody are used for offenders who would have received a less severe sentence. Instead of reducing the number of offenders being imprisoned, more offenders end up in custody. The net of the criminal justice system has, therefore, been widened.

New Penology A managerial approach to crime control and the punishment which is 'concerned with techniques to identify, classify, and manage groupings sorted by dangerousness' (Feeley and Simon, 1992), including 'risk assessments' of offenders.

New Punitiveness is an international trend, on the rise since the 1970s, for increased harshness of punishment, associated with 'populist punitiveness' and law and order ideology.

Northern Ireland Office is the nerve-centre of British government administration in Northern Ireland. Until recently, it was responsible for the running of all government departments in Northern Ireland.

Nothing works is a phrase widely used to summarise the state of criminological knowledge, especially in the 1970s, on the effectiveness of criminal justice measures. Criminological research showed, for example, that police patrolling did not do much to deter potential criminals, or that most offenders who went to prison were reconvicted within two years of their release. The idea that 'nothing works' was misleading, because the research findings were not that negative, but the phrase was used politically as a stick, particularly to beat certain parts of the criminal justice system, such as the Probation Service.

Occupational culture is a shared set of understandings, values and beliefs that is common to criminal justice professions. It has been most widely applied to the police, particularly the lower ranks.

Offender Management is the Ministry of Justice's preferred term for both the overarching structure of service provision for offenders, encompassing both prisons and community penalties—and the generic term for the panoply of measures used in face-to-face work with offenders. In some contexts it means little more than the 'case management' of individuals.

Panopticon was a prison design by Jeremy Bentham which allowed prisoners to be observed at all times without them being aware of being watched. It has since been used to explore concepts of power, discipline, and surveillance.

Parole is a system of early release from prison on licence involving supervision in the community and possibly other conditions. It is granted at the discretion of the Parole Board.

Parsimony is the presumption that the minimum restrictions possible should be used in response to wrongdoing and that the case must be made for the continued legitimacy of the deployment of state intrusion upon individuals.

Partnership is an approach to policy and practice that requires the collaboration of more than one agency to provide more effective service delivery, often combining agencies not only within the public sector, but also across sectors, such as the private and voluntary sectors. Partnerships have emerged in several areas of criminal justice, such as crime prevention, especially in the last two or three decades. Their existence heralds the emergence of a new approach to governing problems such as crime, and implicitly critiques older approaches that were based on the excessively narrow specialisms or competencies of single agencies such as the police service.

Patriarchy might be viewed as consisting of male economic and social power, underpinned by the use of, or threat of, violence (Radford, 1992).

Plea bargaining takes place when the prosecution and the defendant agree that a guilty plea will be accepted to a less serious offence than the original offence charged.

Police community support officers are uniformed, civilian employees of the police authority, who are directed and controlled by their respective Chief Officer and possess a range of limited and discretionary police powers.

Political violence is the term used in preference to 'terrorism' in the social science literature since it recognises that what counts as a terrorist act is highly subjective and generally the result of definition as such by the State or other powerful actors.

Populist punitiveness is a near-synonym for 'law and order ideology' coined by Bottoms (1995).

Positivism is the theoretical assumption that scientific methodologies can be neutrally applied to the study of human societies.

Pre-emptive intervention is 'nipping crime in the bud' by intervening in the lives of those who have not committed any criminal offence but who are thought likely to become offenders in the future.

Pre-sentence reports are prepared by probation officers at the request of the court to provide sentencers with information about offenders, an assessment of their risk of harm and further offending, and proposals regarding sentence (previously known as social inquiry reports).

Prevention is interventions designed to stop crime before it occurs.

Privatisation is the incidence or process of transferring ownership of business from the public sector (government) to the private sector (business). In a broader sense, privatization refers to transfer of any government function to the private sector including governmental functions like revenue collection and law enforcement.

Probation is the supervision of offenders in the community, classically by members of the Probation Service under the terms of Probation Orders. In England and Wales this now occurs under supervision requirements in Community Orders

Problem Analysis Triangle (PAT) is a conceptual device used by those with a responsibility for crime prevention or crime reduction to address specific crime problems. The PAT breaks down a specific crime problem into three constituent elements, the offender, the target or victim, and the place. An examination of each individual element will lead to the identification of measures to prevent or reduce the problem, and the PAT therefore provides, in theory, a systematic approach to crime problem solving.

Prosecution is the bringing of a criminal charge in court or a group of people involved in prosecuting someone in court.

Prosecution process is the process which individuals accused of criminal offences go through in order to be convicted.

Punishment is the deliberate infliction of pain.

Punitive rationale is the logic of punishment as understood as an appropriate response to moral conflicts and problematic behaviours.

Rape as defined in law by the Sexual Offences Act 2003 states that a person (A) commits the offence of rape against B if:

1) he intentionally penetrates the vagina, anus, or mouth of another person (B) with his penis;
2) B does not consent to that penetration;
3) A does not reasonably believe that B consents.

Rehabilitation is a philosophical justification of punishment which claims that punishments can be used to readjust and reform offenders' behaviour and re-integrate them into society as a law abiding citizen.

Reparation is making amends for harmful behaviour.

Republican/s seek to bring about a British withdrawal from Northern Ireland using violent means. It is associated with the activities of paramilitary organizations such as the Irish Republican Army (IRA).

Responsibilisation is a political strategy based on making individuals accountable for their own behaviour and encouraging families and communities to take a more active role in preventing and controlling crime.

Restoration is a group of interventions based on principles of resolving conflict and healing damaged relationships.

Restorative justice is a distinctive way of thinking about how we should view and respond to crime and analogous conduct, revolving around the ideas that crime is in essence a violation of a person, that justice requires that the harm caused be repaired, and that offenders, victims, and others directly affected should participate meaningfully in the justice process.

Restorative values are those values (moral principles and beliefs of a person or group) which—according to some advocates of restorative justice—distinguish genuine restorative justice from other approaches to crime. Precisely what those values are is a matter of ongoing discussion.

Retribution is a philosophical justification of punishment which claims that people deserve to be punished for their crimes.

Royal Ulster Constabulary was the police force of Northern Ireland between 1922 and 2001. It was replaced by the Police Service of Northern Ireland (PSNI).

Scheduled Offence is an offence specifically listed in a schedule to the Northern Ireland (Emergency Provisions) Act [1973]. Scheduled offences were assumed to have a 'terrorist' motivation and were committed by members of proscribed organizations, such as the UVF and IRA. All scheduled offences were tried by a single judge sitting alone under the Diplock system. The Emergency Provisions Act was amended several times since 1973 and repealed in 2000 when Northern Ireland was brought within the remit of the Terrorism Act (2000).

Seamless Sentence was coined by civil servant John Halliday in his review of the sentencing framework (Home Office 2001) to denote penalties which combined elements of both custodial and community supervision, thereby breaking with a century long tradition of keeping such measures conceptually and practically separate. The model for seamless sentences was essentially prison-followed-by-parole, but Halliday's version allowed for a number of permutations, including intermittent custody, in which periods of imprisonment alternated with periods of community supervision. The idea of 'seamless sentences' was important to the NOMS story because it implied that a seamless organization—prisons and probation combined, engaging in 'end to end offender management'—would be needed to deliver them once they were made available to courts.

Secondary victimisation is a phrase which has come to mean the re-victimisation of crime victims at the hands of the criminal justice system itself. Secondary victimisation can result from a lack of information, support or facilities or any other actions or omissions which make the justice process more difficult and intimidating for the victim.

Sentencing Advisory Panel is the body created by the Crime and Disorder Act 1998 whose task is to provide the Court of Appeal with detailed information and suggestions on the sentencing of particular offences. The Panel's reports are now considered by the Sentencing Guidelines Council before they issue definitive guidelines.

Sentencing circles are a variety of forums in which victims, offenders, interested community members, justice officials and others meet to have constructive dialogue about the impact of a crime upon a community and what should be done about it. Circles hold offenders accountable to the community, discuss what should be done to reintegrate the offender into the community, and address underlying community problems that contribute to and arise from offending behaviour. Some recommend a 'sentence' to the judge.

Sentencing Guidelines Council The Council was introduced in the Criminal Justice Act 2003. Its function is to provide courts with definitive guidelines on sentencing particular offences or for dealing with certain sentencing issues such as the appropriate discount for a guilty plea. The Council's membership comprises of judges and those with experience of policing, prosecution, defending criminals and working with victims of crime. All courts have to have regard to the definitive guidelines before passing sentence.

The separate system is a prison regime under which prisoners are kept separate from each other at all times. Prisoners would undergo long periods of separation in which they would eat, sleep and work in their cells, only leaving the cells to attend chapel or for exercise.

Serious and Organised Crime Agency is a non-departmental public body funded by the Home Office and dedicated to combating serious and organised crime through law enforcement and crime disruption strategies.

The silent system is a prison regime under which prisoners were kept silent at all times. Although prisoners would work in large workshops with other prisoners communication was prevented at all times and prisoners punished for breaking such regulations.

Sinn Féin is a political party in Northern Ireland that historically has been closely associated with the IRA. Mr Gerry Adams MP is currently President of the party. The party has polled extremely well in recent years, particularly among younger voters.

Social control is the formal and informal mechanisms deployed to ensure people conform to social expectations.

Social justice is the equitable redistribution of wealth and power allowing individuals to meet their necessary needs.

Socio-legal research is a type of legal scholarship which seeks to analyse the law in a broader social context than traditional legal scholarship which concentrates on the law itself. Socio-legal research is often 'inter-disciplinary' in that it draws upon the subject matter or methodological approaches of other disciplines such as sociology or social policy.

Special constables are volunteer, uniformed police officers who possess the full powers of constable and work a minimum of four hours per week.

Special measures are a set of facilities regulated under the Youth Justice and Criminal Evidence Act 1999 designed to assist 'vulnerable and intimidated witnesses' give evidence in court'. The special measures are: the giving of live evidence through video-links; the removal of the traditional wigs and gowns worn by judges and barristers; screens to block the witness' view of the defendants and/or public gallery; giving evidence via pre-recorded examination in chief or cross-examination; clearing the public gallery and the use of registered intermediaries and aids to communication to assist those with communication difficulties.

Suspects' and defendants' rights are the rights given to individuals who are accused of criminal offences in order to ensure that they are treated fairly and justly and that the powers and resources of the state and the accused are matched to some extent.

Suspended Sentence Order is a sentence of imprisonment of between 28 and 51 weeks' which is suspended. This means that offenders are not actually imprisoned unless they either fail to comply with the requirements of the order, for example by breaching curfew requirements, or they commit a further offence during the period of the order.

Tariff has two separate meanings in sentencing. First, it refers to the idea that the punishments available to the court form a scale depending upon their relative seriousness. A court should impose a sentence whose gravity is proportionate to the seriousness of the offence. This idea is based on retributivism and was most evident in the Criminal Justice Act 1991. The second meaning is the period of time that a person serving an indeterminate sentence such as life imprisonment must serve before he can be considered for parole. This period is determined by the judge. It should be noted that some individuals sentenced to life imprisonment are never eligible for parole and that, even if offenders are eligible for parole, it will not automatically be granted. Offenders who are granted parole are released on licence and are liable to be recalled to prison if the terms of the licence are breached.

Temperance is the promotion of abstinence from alcoholic drinks, usually as an aspect of Christian evangelism, in which drinking is seen as sinful, and manifestly responsible for exacerbating the social problems faced by the urban poor.

'Titan' prisons are the large, American-style prisons which are to be built in England and Wales. In Greek mythology, the Titans—human-looking deities whom Zeus perceived to be 'super-criminals'—were imprisoned in Tartatus, a deep, escape-proof place within the underworld. Lord Carter (2007) chose this somewhat chilling image to name the large, American-style prisons, which, he believes, will be necessary to take account of inexorable increases in the use of custody in England and Wales. The government is committed to building three—the first by 2012—each holding 2,500 prisoners, at a cost of £450m each. The Prison Reform Trust (2008) has pointed out that available evidence does not support the concept of large prisons, that smaller ones, (no larger than 700 places) have better records on a number of indices, including prisoner safety and resettlement. Only 17 of the 51 organisations consulted by Carter were asked about Titans—9 of these were private sector organizations who may have an interest in building them, 6 were government departments

Transgender is an umbrella term that emerged in the 1990s to capture the multiplicity of gender experiences that lie between the medically constructed categories of transvestite and transsexual (Moran and Sharpe, 2004).

Transitional Justice is a developing field of law and criminology that refers to criminal justice reform in post-conflict, and as the term implies, transitional states. The emphasis is on making the structures of criminal justice democratic and compliant with human rights principles.

Ulster Volunteer Force (UVF) is the largest loyalist paramilitary organization in Northern Ireland. Historically it has perceived its role as maintaining the link with Great Britain through the use of violence, although in practice this involved the routine targeting of Catholic civilians. The UVF has been on intermittent ceasefire since 1994, but formally renounced violence and an end to its 'military' campaign in May 2007.

Ultimate sanction is the most serious action that can be taken against a person (or country) who has broken a law or rule.

Underclass is a concept regarded by many liberals as offensive when used to describe the disposition of a social grouping that is perceived to be particularly crime-prone. The underclass is thought to be culturally disposed to crime, and is recognised by its place of residence (usually run-down deprived urban areas), by its social characteristics (high rates of unemployment, single parent households, welfare benefit dependency), and by its behaviour (high impulsivity, hedonism, instant gratification, violence, machismo, etc.). The idea of an underclass is peddled especially by right wing commentators, who argue that the cultural disposition is transmitted inter-generationally, and thus so entrenched that it cannot be reformed, but rather requires physical containment through firm policing and punitive incapacitation in prison, for those convicted of offences.

Unionist/s are generally, but not exclusively, associated with the Protestant community in Northern Ireland. Unionists want to maintain Northern Ireland's current constitutional status and the link with Britain.

The Unit Fines system was modelled on the Scandinavian day fine system. It is ostensibly a way of making financial penalties fairer to rich and poor offenders alike, by fining them each according to their income rather than imposing a fixed sum which is notionally proportionate to the offence. A fixed sum imposed on each may have a far more deleterious impact on a poor person (and therefore be more punitive) than it would on a wealthier person. In a unit fines system the wealthy always pay more than the poor, but in terms of units of lost income the proportion taken by the court from each of them is comparable.

Uptariffing relates to the 'tariff' which is the full scale of sentences available to courts, ranging from the least to the most severe. Uptariffing is a feature of sentencing practice in which offenders are given more severe sentences than they might otherwise have received, because sentencers perceive that they have already, on a previous occasion, received a sentence which did not prevent them from offending. For example, an offender who has already served a Community Order may be more likely to be given a custodial sentence. If the Community Order was more severe than the original offence warranted i.e. if net-widening had occurred, the offender would be closer to a future custodial sentence than they would otherwise have been. Net-widening is the logical precondition of uptariffing, but whether it actually occurs depends on the judgement which sentencers make about the initial, net-widening sentence—they may choose not to go higher up the 'tariff' but simply to impose a penalty of similar severity to the earlier one, in which case uptariffing cannot be said to have occurred.

Utilitarianism is a philosophical credo rooted in the principle of the greatest happiness of the greatest number and where morality is shaped by considerations of utility.

Utopian managerialism is the ideological and practical expression of the New Public Management, a theoretical approach which developed in the 1980s to assist in the reform of public sector organizations, in effect to make them function with the presumed efficiency levels of private sector organizations, without actually privatising them (although that can come later). It subordinates all other values to narrowly conceived notions of economy, efficiency and effectiveness and imposes a regime of meticulous regulation, geared to incessant change, on hitherto more autonomous, stable-yet-flexible ways of working. It becomes utopian because the claims it makes for itself, and the ease with which it imagines its goals can be accomplished are invariably unrealistic, taking no account of the personal social realities on which it seeks to impose transformation.

Verdict is the decision made by a jury in Crown Court or magistrates or District Judges in magistrates' courts at the end of a trial on whether the accused is guilty or not guilty (or 'not proven' in Scotland).

Victim–offender mediation is an informal process in which a third person helps the victim and offender to have constructive dialogue about what happened and reach a mutually acceptable plan for repairing harm.

Victimisation surveys 'are concerned with crime measurement and reasons for the under-reporting of crime; the correlates of victimization; the risk of victimization; the fear of crime and its relationship to the probability of victimization; the experience of crime from the viewpoint of victims; and the treatment of victims in the criminal justice system' (Jupp, in McLaughlin and Muncie, 2006: 449).

Victims code of practice are the basic standards of service and support for victims within the criminal justice system through a statutory Code of Practice which was laid down by the Domestic Violence, Crime and Victims Act 2004. The Code's basis in statute is significant, although its provisions are not law and failure to comply with the Code does not leave anyone liable to legal proceedings. The enforceability of the Code therefore remains with the complaints procedures of individual criminal justice agencies. If dissatisfied with the outcome of such procedures, members of the public can report the matter to their MP who can refer it to the Parliamentary Commissioner for Administration for investigation. The new Victims and Witnesses Commissioner created under the Act is charged with monitoring the operation of the Code, although it has not been said that discontented victims can complain directly to him/her.

The victims' movement is a term used loosely to describe the development of academic, political and activist interest in victims of crime (and, indeed, victims of other hardship like natural disasters and war) in the late 1960s to early 1970s.

Victimology is 'a field of study focusing on the victims of crime, the consequences [of crime] for victims and the way they and others respond to it' (Dignan, 2005: p.200).

Victim Support is the largest organisation providing services to victims and campaigning on their behalf. The charity largely kept out of politics from its inception in the early 1970s. In terms of government funding and in terms of influence upon policy, this undeniably paid off—98 per cent of its funding comes from a government grant—although Victim Support has increasingly taken up political stances on particular issues since the mid-1990s.

Vulnerable and intimidated witnesses are defined in ss. 16 and 17 of the Youth Justice and Criminal Evidence Act 1999 as including witnesses who are under 17 years of age or suffer from a mental or physical disability and/or witnesses whose quality of evidence is likely to be diminished by reason of fear or distress.

What Works is an approach to rehabilitation rooted in the psychological theory known as cognitive behaviourism. The rise to ascendancy of the 'what works' agenda in the last two decades is closely tied to forms of governmental sovereignty shaped by concerns around risk control and the responsibilisation of the powerless.

The witness service is a court-based organisation run by Victim Support and staffed by volunteers. There is now a Witness Service in every court in England and Wales, charged with supporting witnesses and ensuring they are kept up to date with case progression.

Youth Justice Board is an executive non-departmental government body aimed at preventing offending by children and young people.

NAME INDEX

SUBJECT INDEX